Items should be returned on or before th
shown below. Items not already request
borrowers may be renewed in person, in
telephone. To renew, please quote the nu....... on the
barcode label. To renew online a PIN is required.
This can be requested at your local library.
Renew online @ **www.dublincitypubliclibraries.ie**
Fines charged for overdue items will include postage
incurred in recovery. Damage to or loss of items will
be charged to the borrower.

Leabharlanna Poiblí Chathair Bhaile Átha Cliath
Dublin City Public Libraries

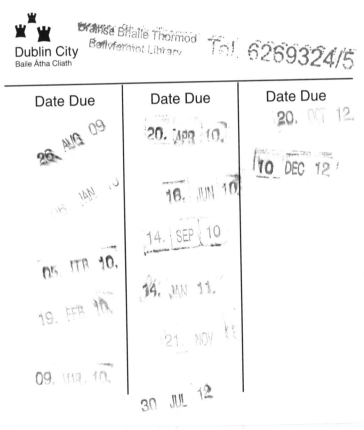

Dublin City
Baile Átha Cliath

Brainse Bhaile Thormod
Ballyfermot Library

Tel. 6269324/5

Date Due	Date Due	Date Due
26. AUG 09	20. APR 10.	20. OCT 12.
16. JAN 10	16. JUN 10	10 DEC 12
05. MAR 10.	14. SEP 10	
19. FEB 10.	14. JAN 11.	
09. MAR 10.	21. NOV 11	
	30 JUL 12	

THE
WORLD
AT WAR

THE LANDMARK ORAL HISTORY
FROM THE PREVIOUSLY UNPUBLISHED ARCHIVES

RICHARD HOLMES

EBURY
PRESS

3 5 7 9 10 8 6 4 2

Published in 2007 by Ebury Press, an imprint of Ebury Publishing
A Random House Group Company
This edition published 2008

Text copyright © Richard Holmes 2007

The World at War is a trademark of FremantleMedia Limited
Licensed by FremantleMedia Enterprises

The Random House Group Limited Reg. No. 954009

Addresses for companies within the Random House Group can be found at
www.randomhouse.co.uk

A CIP catalogue record for this book is available from the British Library

The Random House Group Limited supports The Forest Stewardship Council
(FSC), the leading international forest certification organisation. All our titles that
are printed on Greenpeace approved FSC certified paper carry the FSC logo. Our
paper procurement policy can be found at www.rbooks.co.uk/environment

Mixed Sources
Product group from well-managed
forests and other controlled sources
www.fsc.org Cert no. TT-COC-2139
© 1996 Forest Stewardship Council

Printed and bound in Great Britain by Clays Ltd, St Ives plc

ISBN 9780091917524

To buy books by your favourite authors and register for offers visit
www.rbooks.co.uk

CONTENTS

FOREWORD

BY SIR JEREMY ISAACS

All film-makers shoot more footage than they use; *The World at War* was
no exception. We always knew we had more good stuff than could
conceivably be crammed into twenty-six hours of commercial television –
each 'hour' only fifty-two minutes, thirty seconds long, to be precise. We
never kept a strict tally, but I'd guess the ratio of newsreel printed to that
used was about fifteen to one; for interviews it was higher still, well over
twenty to one. The first assemblies of strong, relevant material ran at over
three hours; hard choices always had to be made to get each episode down
to transmittable length.

We shot, from the outset, for the series and for the record. What was
omitted was left, not on the cutting-room floor, but in the Imperial War
Museum (IWM). Thames Television, at its all-round best the finest of the
ITV franchise holders, sturdily footed the bill.

In a way, the money Thames spent was public money. The ITV
companies, fifteen of them, enjoyed near monopolies, in their own areas,
of television advertising revenue. In February 1971, after years of pressure, the government agreed to change the basis of the special levy on ITV
franchises – the price they paid for their monopoly – from a tax on revenue
to a tax on profit; their income would no longer be taxed at source. The
condition was that the companies spend, and be seen to spend, more on
programmes. I went at once to my bosses at Thames and suggested we
make a history of the Second World War. A few weeks later, on April

Fool's Day 1971, we started work. Our principal collaborator was the IWM; its director, Noble Frankland, our historical adviser. It was a condition of the contract that all the original footage we shot be deposited in the IWM's archive. There it has lain to this day.

The World at War's key ingredients were the image and the word, newsreel and eye-witness interview. Music and narration held all together. Some programmes went short of pictures; there is little visual record of war at sea, or acts of resistance, or of genocidal gas-chambers. Those episodes relied on interviews. One episode, on Stalingrad, used no witnesses; no Red Army veterans would face the camera in 1972–73, at the height of the Cold War. But those were the exceptions. For the most part we reckoned to use newsreel and interviews, split fifty-fifty; so only about thirteen hours of interview made it to the screen.

Some voices are heard only for a moment. An American paratrooper, who dropped in France before the D-Day landing, tells us: 'I was afraid. I was nineteen, and I was afraid.' I hear him still.

Others, particularly the leaders, talked at greater length. What interviewer, researcher or producer, facing a Supreme Commander, a presidential aide, the Foreign Secretary, an SS General, could resist seeking an overview, a *tour d'horizon*? It might serve in several programmes, after all. As you read these pages, remember *The World at War*'s interviewers; they did a fine job.

The World at War took fifty of us three years to make: we talked to hundreds of survivors and printed a million feet of film. When it was finished – the final episode screened in May, 1974 – we made three lengthy specials from the ample surplus to hand. Then, the team broke up; each moved on to other things. Making *The World at War* took over our lives, but we never thought of transferring what we'd done to other media. Now, triumphantly, the voices we recorded speak again on the printed page. Rereading the transcripts today, I am impressed by how successfully, in skilled hands, they transfer to print; vivid, articulate, revelatory.

Television history is narrative history. Several interpretations of a strategic decision may be worth considering, but the film-maker must choose one, and stay with it. On the page, there is time and freedom to

review the options. On complex issues, a wealth of opinion is easily
displayed, and differing experiences related. In commissioning this oral
history, Ebury Press has taken a visionary initiative. Richard Holmes has
done a superb job of selection, and of organising the mass of material. On
many topics he presents a broader and more nuanced account than did
TV's linear narrative. His book deserves a vast readership. I salute him.

Jeremy Isaacs describes the making of The World at War *in* Look Me in the
Eye: A Life in Television, *published by Little Brown 2006.*

INTRODUCTION

I always rather dislike being called a television historian, preferring to see myself as an historian who enjoys talking about his subject: in that sense, at least, television, books and lectures are simply different parts of the same process. Yet there is no doubt that I am exactly of an age to have been profoundly influenced by television history. The BBC series *The Great War* appeared in my last year at school, and I can well remember watching some of its episodes on a tiny television in the worn and fusty setting of a house-room at my boarding school. It introduced the real complexities of its subject to an audience that either knew nothing about the war or had accepted at face value some of the more egregious comments that then passed for fact. Despite the best endeavours of Dr Noble Frankland, then Director of the Imperial War Museum (whose generosity in reducing the charges that the museum might otherwise have charged for copyright material had made the series possible in the first place), it took some extraordinary liberties with its use of visual images, blurring the boundaries between reconstructed and actuality sequences. It nevertheless deserves the much overused description 'landmark', and, as Dr Frankland has written, 'it launched the idea of history on screen'.

In 1973, almost a decade later, when I was in the early stages of my career as a military historian, pecking away at my doctoral thesis with the one-finger typing that kept the makers of Tipp-Ex in profits, the Thames Television series *The World at War* appeared. I was captivated at once. The poignant rise and fall of Carl Davis's music; the montage of extraordinary facial photographs in the pre-title sequence, each successively burned away to reveal another, like pages of an album seared by heat, and the mellifluous enunciation of Laurence Olivier, all had me enthralled even before I had properly watched a single episode. Once I began to watch, I was hooked. The breadth of the 26-episode series, shaped and sustained by the directing brain of Jeremy Isaacs, the series producer, was simply breathtaking. This was no narrowly Eurocentric story, but just what its name implied, the Second World War from background to legacy, and from the freezing waters of the North Atlantic through the sands of the Western Desert to the jungles of Burma. What struck me then was the remarkable quality of the eyewitnesses who had been interviewed, and the way in which the words of the men and women who had 'fought, worked or watched' were put at the very centre of the television treatment. For instance, I shall never forget hearing Christabel Bielenberg, a British woman married to a German lawyer, describing the rise of Hitler: suddenly the events of 1933–36 were not something that had happened long ago and far away, but a personal story being told by a familiar voice. She was to call her book *The Past is Myself*, and reading the transcripts of her interview I see how apt that phrase is, and just what an impact personal accounts like this have had on my own development as a historian.

Looking at the series when it was first screened I was struck by its success in gaining access to so many men and women who had seen the wider picture, and having now had access to the full range of interviews, I am even more impressed. To select a few names, almost at random, there are the words of John Colville, Churchill's urbane and perceptive Private Secretary; Hasso-Eccard Freiherr von Manteuffel, one of the most successful practitioners of armoured warfare; Vera Lynn, 'The Forces' Sweetheart', whose songs caught the mood of Britain at war; 'Manny' Shinwell, veteran Labour politician; Francis de Guingand, Montgomery's Chief of Staff; Albert Speer, Hitler's architect turned Armaments Minister, with his insider's view of power politics in the Third Reich, and two of the apostles of air power, Arthur Harris of the RAF's Bomber Command and Curtis LeMay of what was then still the United States Army Air Force.

But of course this was not a series that concentrated on 'captains and the kings'. There were many ordinary men and women too – American,

British, Canadian, German, Japanese – telling us about the extraordinary times they lived through, and who, but for their necessarily brief appearances, might otherwise have left no mark on history. A mother describes the death of her children in an air-raid shelter, a rescue worker tells of holding a teenage girl's hand as she choked to death, and a Merchant Navy officer catalogues the deaths of his crew in an open boat in the Atlantic. There are moments of quite extraordinary and sometimes shocking intimacy. One interviewee reflected on Neville Chamberlain's 'deadly decency'; another remembered how Stalin looked like 'a most cunning and cruel peasant' when seen across the table, and a Singapore veteran saw the first Japanese soldiers, 'extremely tired men, grim-visaged', enter the city.

When I was invited to edit the archive of interview transcripts compiled when the series was made, I first saw the material, on a blazing hot afternoon in the early summer of 2006, in the Imperial War Museum's quiet annexe in Austral Street, behind the main museum. It was contained in twenty-nine files housed in the sort of brown metal filing cabinet that I remember, from my first job as a lecturer at the Royal Military Academy Sandhurst, as standard civil-service issue. Because of complex copyright issues the material had previously been inaccessible to researchers, and I knew that it had taken a small army of lawyers and publishers to reach the agreement that made this book possible. Although, at this stage in my life, I am not easily impressed, there was a real sense of excitement and discovery as the door to the cabinet grunted open. It was immediately clear, as I flicked through the files on that first afternoon, that there was far, far more material than was ever aired. I knew from my own experience as a television presenter that an extraordinary amount of interviews (usually including my own favourite pieces to camera) finishes up on the cutting-room floor, and this series was certainly no exception. There were all sorts of reasons for his. Often an individual producer simply had too much material to fit into his programme; several interviewees might say much the same thing and only the most cogent would be used, and reflective grunts or long pauses defeated even the sharpest editorial scissors. Many transcripts included the questions, and it was intriguing to see how some interviewers obtained (or at times, despite their best efforts, failed to obtain) the answers they sought. I have used extracts from 280 of 368 transcripts, both using a wider selection of material from individuals who did indeed feature in the finished series, and rescuing some interviewees from total obscurity.

The transcripts were made as guides to producers and directors, and naturally lack the polish of something always designed for publication: this was a nuisance at times, but it was also part of the immediacy of the accounts and the project's excitement. Numerous ums and errs were faithfully reproduced in typescript, but personal and place names sometimes defeated the transcribers. In addition to tidying up the transcripts, for instance by the deletion of repetitions and murmurs, I have added or corrected names that had been omitted from, or been distorted in, the originals, and remedied some of the more obvious translation errors to make the transcripts more accessible. I have enjoyed the advantage of being able to insert occasional explanatory footnotes, so as to use material disqualified from the programmes because it was not adequately self-explanatory. I am delighted to have the opportunity of filling in some of the blanks and of developing some areas that the makers of the series could not address. In this sense my task was far easier than theirs, for I could manoeuvre the material within a framework of my own design, and was under no obligation to make all my chapters the same length. They did not have the same luxury with their episodes.

It is important to remember that oral history has both strengths and weaknesses. In my previous work I have found that even interviews conducted soon after an event reveal memories rapidly conforming to a narrative conditioned by what interviewees have heard from others, like witnesses chattering before a court case. Sometimes there is a deliberate desire to bend or even break the truth. To take an extreme example, we now know that Alger Hiss (not definitively exposed as a Russian agent when the series was made) was certainly not speaking the whole truth when interviewed for this series. Sometimes an interviewee makes an honest error. General Gamelin did not, as Edwards Spears suggests, travel to England to tell Winston Churchill that there was no strategic reserve in 1940: Churchill actually received this disquieting information from French premier Edouard Daladier. Sometimes two well-informed interviewees differ on points of significant detail: one Japanese naval officer tells us that the British experience of torpedo-bombing in shallow water at Taranto influenced the Japanese plan for Pearl Harbor, while another assures us, no less categorically, that it did not. Historians often strive to strike a balance, and those who lived through history often feel no need to equivocate, but have firm views which they are happy to express. An RAF bomber pilot regretted the end of the war only because some Germans were still alive, and a senior Staff Officer described Churchill's decision to send troops to Greece in 1941 bluntly as 'military nonsense'. Noble Frankland was interviewed both in his capacity as a veteran of Bomber Command and as a distinguished historian. He wisely points out that the words of interviewees are indeed primary evidence, not just about the war itself, 'but how it appeared to these people in 1971–3' as well.

There are moments when first-hand evidence confirms the truth of what is sometimes written off as myth, or establishes an intriguing and counter-intuitive line of argument. In the deadly chaos of Pearl Harbor one interviewee did indeed hear a chaplain say, 'Praise God and pass the ammunition', although a popular song soon had it as 'Praise the Lord and pass the ammunition'. The SS maintained a legal department throughout the war, and once of its officials, following the trail of dental gold removed from concentration-camp victims, successfully prosecuted an SS colonel for corruption: the officer was executed by the Germans shortly before the war ended.

As the work progressed I realised that the great virtue of the material lay not in its narrative detail but in its impressionistic quality, and that I could deal with the chronology by using a short commentary at the beginning of each chapter. In a sense the whole anthology, not just the last chapter, is about the experience of war. I have included some purely factual excerpts that add significantly to the written record, but overall I have followed the flow of the material and selected for vividness and human interest.

These recordings were made at a point almost exactly midway between the Second World War and our own times, and I quickly became aware that the interviews reflected an assumption of common knowledge about the events that they described. This assumption was probably rather tenuous even when the interviews were conducted and now has no basis whatever. Britain is, for better or for worse, a demilitarised society, and most of my own countrymen are unlikely to grasp the difference between a brigadier and a bombardier. We are de-historicised too. This is not the place to embark upon a tirade against the teaching of history in British schools, part of the 'commodification of education' that has betrayed so many children. Suffice it to say that there has not been a time since 1945 that school-leavers have had a poorer understanding of even the recent past. I have always believed that failure to study history properly means that the events of the past tend blithely to be forgotten or perversely misinterpreted, sadly, by politicians just as much as by school-leavers. Just as a individual's loss of memory is one of the most tragic disabling consequences of some cruel diseases, so our own loss of the collective memory furnished by history is scarcely less damaging for society as a whole.

The World at War was first shown at the height of the Cold War in 1973–74 and the decisions made by some of the writers and producers reflected the fact that their own political views, and the prevailing attitudes on the era in which they worked, sometimes coloured their work. That is a risk with any process that involves editorial selection, and I make no claim to be immune from it myself. It is easy to deconstruct their handi-work today, for we have the opportunity to watch it repeatedly on DVD, and certainly the occasional bias was less obvious when the series was first broadcast. Research was never a simple task for producers and directors working in the early 1970s. The fact that the Cold War was at its most chilly made it difficult for the series to dig deeply in Russia, and the researchers working on those episodes dealing with the Eastern Front were unable to conduct the interviews that would have told the true and heroic story of the Russian war effort. The first-hand material that makes Catherine Merridale's book *Ivan's War* (2005) such a triumphant success was just not available to them but some Stalanist propaganda footage did indeed make the final cut.

Ideological bias aside – and in justice it really is confined to a few episodes in an otherwise commendably even-handed series – I still found it difficult to balance this anthology. There was a bare minimum of interviews for some topics, most notably the Eastern Front, but the wildest embarrassment of riches for others, notably the Battle of the Atlantic, D-Day in Normandy, the Pacific War and the Holocaust. The Atlantic and the Pacific wars break down quite tidily into three and two periods respectively, but the D-Day and Holocaust chapters involved me in painful editorial choices because I had to select so little from so much. Even so the Holocaust chapter is much the longest, and would have been even longer still were it not for the dreadful sameness in the details of what happens when society tips over the rim of the crater into hell. I have placed it at the half-way point of the book, immediately after the chapter on the development of area bombing. This is not to suggest any moral equivalence, for one, terrible though it was, was an act of war and the other had no conceivable military justification, but to emphasise that the signature feature of the Second World War was the literally unimaginable civilian death-toll. Our minds may not shrink from it, but they are simply unable to encompass it.

I hope that this book will move some literally irreplaceable oral history into the written record, and so a word on methodology is appropriate. This book is based on the transcripts of interviews made for *The World at War*. A very pertinent lecture on visual history, given on 7 September 2003 at the Cambridge History Festival, observed that transcripts do not always conform accurately to the original tapes. The sheer physical labour and concomitant expense (the same talk estimated the cost of 'cleaning up' the transcripts of Sir Jeremy Isaacs's *Cold War* series to be £250,000) meant that I worked from the written record, using taped interviews only when there was an unresolved problem with sense. I have tried to behave responsibly with the evidence, and have not conflated different interviews by the same subject into the same piece of text. Maryam Philpott, whose skills as a researcher have been honed on some of my previous projects, had the onerous task of converting some of the typescript to computer disc, so that the material could be more easily edited. My old friend Hugh Bicheno widened the assault, and he and I then carved up the project between us. I could not have hoped to succeed without his industry, eye for detail and great good sense. There are only a few occasions when I exercised what I might call a casting vote, and the responsibility for the finished product is mine alone.

Interviewees are given a brief description, generally on the first occasion on which they appear in a given chapter. In a few cases the original transcripts give precious little detail, omitting first names or accurate unit designations, and there is often nothing I have been able to do to remedy the deficiency. In many others, individuals were steadily promoted during and sometimes after the war. Anthony Eden was first knighted and later created Earl of Avon, while that little tiger of a general, John Harding, began the war as a lieutenant colonel and ended it as a lieutenant general, becoming a field marshal and a peer after it. I include a list of dramatis personae that will help readers trace the careers of the most significant interviewees, and throughout I have tried (not, I fear, with complete success) to give individuals the rank or appointment they held at the time to which the quotation refers. I have translated foreign ranks, where possible, into the nearest British equivalent. Purists will rightly object to 'SS Colonel' rather than 'SS-Standartenführer', and will observe that a German *Leutnant* often enjoyed responsibilities denied to a British second lieutenant, but it is the stories that these individuals tell that matter to us, not the braid that they wore. It is a sad reflection that I know least about those interviewees who often felt the sharpest edge of war – like those Americans who landed on Omaha Beach on D-Day.

My abiding memory of a project that has claimed the best part of a year of my working life is of the sheer scale of *The World at War* and its triumphant and enduring success. I doubt if we shall ever see something of this epic dimension carried off with such panache again. In my lifetime television may have gained much in terms of technology, but it has lost at least as much in terms of scale, vision and courage. In a small way this series changed the way that I personally looked at history, and in a broader sense it changed television's relationship with the past. These transcripts, lying in the dusty darkness for half my lifetime, have something fresh to say about this war that shaped the world in which I grew up, and whose long shadow is, even now, only beginning to recede.

INTERVIEWEES

Aitken, Sir John 'Max' (1910–85), wartime RAF fighter ace, son and heir of Lord Beaverbrook, proprietor of the *Daily Express*. He became a Conservative MP, and disclaimed his father's barony as soon as he inherited it.

Alex, Private George, 101st US Airborne Division, Normandy.

Ambrose, Professor Stephen (1936–2002), influential and prolific American historian, author, among other works, of *Band of Brothers*.

Antonov, General Alexei (1896–1962), wartime Soviet Staff Officer, Red Army Chief of Staff 1945–46, Chief of Staff to Warsaw Pact Forces 1955–62.

Aviel, Avraham, survived the Radun ghetto massacre in Poland, witness at the trial of Adolf Eichmann in 1961.

Axtell, Marine C S, marine at Iwo Jima.

Ball, George (1909–94), wartime lawyer for the Lend-Lease programme and Director of the US Strategic Bombing Survey. Under-Secretary of State for Economic Affairs and UN ambassador under presidents Kennedy and Johnson, he left office in opposition to the Vietnam war.

Beatson-Hird, Lieutenant Denis, 51st Highland Division, Rhine crossing 1945.

Beaufre, General André (1902–75), captain on the French General Staff in 1940, post-war strategic theorist, exponent of the French independent nuclear deterrent, author, among other books, of *The Fall of France* and *Deterrence and Strategy*.

Beckett, Sergeant Bill, Sherwood Foresters group interview, Nottingham.

Beese, Hertha, Berlin housewife and Social Democrat.

Behrendt, Captain Hans-Otto, Rommel's intelligence staff, author of *Rommel's Intelligence in the Desert Campaign*.

Belchem, Major General Ronald (1911–81), 7th Armoured Division in North Africa, 21st Army Group Staff for the Normandy landings.

Bernhard of Lippe-Biesterfeld, Prince (1911–2004), German consort to Queen Juliana of the Netherlands who fought against the Nazi occupation and became a rallying figure for the Dutch Resistance.

Bielenberg, Christabel (1909–2003), Englishwoman married to an anti-Nazi German lawyer, author of *The Past is Myself*.

'Bill', coal-mine striker, Betteshanger, Kent

Boas-Koupmann, Rita, Dutch–Jewish teenage survivor of Auschwitz.

Bock, SS Lance Corporal Richard, guard at Auschwitz-Birkenau.

Bohlen, Charles (1904–74), US diplomat and Soviet expert.

Bokiewicz, Z T, Polish Home Army, Warsaw uprising.

Boller, Major W S, Ordnance Corps, Burma.

Bolzano, Private, Italian Army, North Africa.

Bonhoeffer, Emmy, sister-in-law of German Resistance martyr Pastor Dietrich Bonhoeffer.

Boothby, Robert Lord (1900–86), British Conservative politician, confidant of Churchill and RAF officer. Ennobled in 1958. His colourful private life led Queen Elizabeth the Queen Mother to describe him as 'a bounder but not a cad'.

Bosnik, Private Anton, Russian defender of Stalingrad.

Bottomley, Arthur Lord (1907–95), British trade-union leader, Mayor of Walthamstow, Labour MP, held ministerial posts 1945–50 and 1964–67, ennobled in 1984.

Broher, Thérèse, French civilian in Normandy.

Broth, Private Henry, US serviceman in the Battle of the Bulge, 1944.

Brown, Guardsman, Scots Guards, Glasgow-pub group interview.

Brown, Private Leonard, The Queen's Own Royal West Kent Regiment, Burma.

Buckthorpe, Private, Fourteenth Army, Burma.

Bundy, McGeorge (1919–96), US wartime official in the Facts and Figures Department, later National Security Adviser to presidents Kennedy and Johnson during the Vietnam War, later Professor of History at New York University.

Bunt, Gwen, Plymouth housewife, whose children were killed in the Blitz.

Bush, Lewis, pre-war English teacher in Tokyo, later prisoner of war.

Bush, Professor Vannevar (1890–1974), Chairman of the US National Defense Research Committee 1940, Director of the Office of Scientific Research and Development 1941–46.

Butler, Mr, London air-raid warden during the Blitz.

Butler, Seaman Edward, Royal Navy escort-ship crewman.

Butler, Lord Richard (known as 'Rab' from his initials) (1902–82), British Conservative politician, leading pre-war appeaser, author of the Education Act, 1944, Chancellor of the Exchequer 1951–55, Home Secretary 1957–63, Foreign Secretary 1963–64, ennobled in 1965.

Calvert, Brigadier Mike (1913–98), British irregular-warfare expert who led a column in the first Chindit operation in Burma and a brigade in the second. Commander of the Special Air Service Brigade until it was disbanded in 1945. Dismissed from the Army after a questionable court martial for homosexuality in 1951.

Chandos, see Lyttelton.

Chantrain, Frau, Cologne Red Cross.

Chistyakov, General-Colonel Ivan (1900–79), Soviet anti-tank specialist (158th Guards Artillery) at the Battle of Kursk 1943, Commander-in-Chief Manchurian Front 1945–47.

Christiani, Eddi, orchestra leader in occupied Holland.

Clark, General Mark (1896–1984), Deputy Commander Operation Torch, Commander US Fifth Army, Allied Forces in Italy, UN Forces in Korea.

Clark, William, merchant seaman.

Cochrane, Air Gunner John, Eighth Air Force, USAAF.

Colacicchi, Lieutenant Paolo, Italian Tenth Army, author of *L'ultimo fronte d'Africa*.

Coleman, Marine Richard, marine at Iwo Jima.

Collins, Major-General J Lawton (1896–1987), US Army Divisional Commander on Guadalcanal, Corps Commander in Normandy and across Europe. US Army Chief of Staff during the Korean War.

Colville, Sir John (1915–87), British official, Assistant Private Secretary to Chamberlain 1939–40, Churchill 1940–41 and Attlee 1945. Pilot in the RAF Volunteer Reserve 1941–44.

Combs, Gunner's Mate Tom, on board USS *New Orleans* at Pearl Harbor.

Cooke, Sergeant Wilson, US marine at Iwo Jima.

Corwin, Norman (b. 1910), American broadcaster and radio playwright: his radio series *An American in England* is especially noteworthy.

Cotton, Marine Lenly, marine at battle for Okinawa.

Cremer, Lieutenant Commander Peter-Erich 'Ali' (1911–92), commander of *U-333* and latterly *U-2519*.

Cruickshank, Private William, British Army, Japanese prisoner of war.

Daniel, Lieutenant Hugh, Eighth Army dispatch rider.

Doi, Staff Officer Akio, Japanese Army General Staff.

Dönitz, Grand Admiral Karl (1891–1980), German Navy, U-boat officer in First World War, Commander U-boats 1939–43, Commander-in-Chief of German Navy 1943–45, Head of State 1945, tried as a war criminal, imprisoned 1946–56.

Donnell, Lieutenant Patrick, British Royal Marine Commando at Gold Beach, Normandy.

Doolittle, General Jimmy (1896–1993), American aviation pioneer who led the first raid on Tokyo and commanded the Fifteenth and Eighth air forces in the Mediterranean and England.

Driberg, Tom Lord (1905–76), Member of Parliament 1942–74, Chairman of the Labour Party, promiscuous homosexual and Soviet spy, ennobled 1976.

Duffin, Guardsman, Scots Guards, Glasgow-pub group interview

Durrell, Lawrence (1912–90), British author (of the 'Alexandria Quartet' among other works), wartime press officer, Cairo. Brother of the naturalist and writer Gerald Durrell.

Eaker, General Ira C (1896–1987), first Commander of Eighth Air Force, USAAF, then of the Mediterranean Allied Air Forces 1943–45, one of the dominant influences in the founding of the USAF, retired as Chief of the Air Staff in 1948.

Easton, Marine Lieutenant Clayton, marine at Iwo Jima.

Eden, Sir Anthony, Earl of Avon (1897–1977), the youngest brigade major in the British Army during the First World War. Conservative politician, Foreign Secretary 1935–38, 1940–45, 1951–55, Prime Minister 1955–57 (responsible for, and broken by, the Suez operation), ennobled in 1961.

Eldering, Petronella (1909–1989), member of the Dutch Resistance.

Elliott, Private George (1917–2003), radar operator on the day of the Pearl Harbor attack.

Eyton-Jones, Captain William, Merchant Navy, skipper of SS *Ben Vrachie*, sunk 1941.

Faithfull, Lucy, English child-evacuee organiser.

Feldheim, Willy, member of Hitler Youth, defence of Berlin.

Finch, Captain Thomas D, Merchant Navy, skipper of SS *San Emiliano*, sunk 8 August 1942.

Finke, Colonel John, Company Commander, 1st Division, at Omaha Beach, Normandy.

Fiske, Marine Richard, on USS *West Virginia* at Pearl Harbor.

Fitzpatrick, Private Tom, 9th Australian Division, Eighth Army, North Africa.

Foot, Sir Dingle (1905–78), Liberal MP and wartime Parliamentary Secretary to the Ministry of Economic Warfare. Lost his seat in the 1945 election and subsequently joined the Labour Party: Solicitor-General 1964–67. Brother of Michael Foot.

Foot, Michael (b. 1913), left-wing journalist (*Tribune, Daily Herald*), anti-appeaser in 1940, Labour Party leader 1980–83.

Frankland, Dr Noble, Bomber Command navigator, co-author of the excellent but controversial 1961 *The Strategic Air Offensive against Germany 1939–1945*. Director of the Imperial War Museum 1964–82, Chief Historical Adviser to *The World at War* series.

Fry, Private Ronald, British Army, Japanese POW on the Death Railway, Burma.

Fuchida, Captain Mitsuo (1902–76), Japanese naval airman who led the attack on Pearl Harbor and became an Evangelical Christian post-war.

Galbraith, Professor John Kenneth (1908–2006), Canadian–American, influential Keynesian economist and official under presidents Roosevelt, Truman, Kennedy and Johnson.

Galland, General Adolf (1912–96), German fighter ace with 104 air-to-air victories, Commander of JG-26 by the end of 1940, Commander of Germany's fighter force 1941–45.

Gardiner, Private Noel, 2nd New Zealand Division, Eighth Army, North Africa.

Gariepy, Sergeant Leo, Canadian tank commander, Juno Beach, Normandy. A Sherman tank recovered from the sea in 1970 and displayed on the sea front of Courseulles-sur-Mer bears a plaque dedicated to him.

Gary, Commander Donald (1901–77), won the Medal of Honor during the near sinking of the aircraft carrier USS *Franklin* on 19 March 1945.

Gawalewicz, Dr Adolf, Polish–Jewish lawyer and Auschwitz survivor.

Genda, Major General Minoru (1904–89), Japanese naval airman who planned the Pearl Harbor attack and played a prominent role in the post-war Japanese Self Defence Force.

Good, Chief Steward Bertie, Channel ferry *Royal Daffodil* at Dunkirk.

Gray, Dr J Glenn (1913–77), US Army, served in Italy, France and Germany, author of *The Warriors: Reflections on Men in Battle*.

Gray, Ursula, wartime resident of Dresden, later wife of Dr Gray.

Greene, Sir Hugh Carleton (1910–87), *Daily Telegraph* correspondent in Berlin in the 1930s, head of German Service, BBC, 1940, Director-General of the BBC 1960–68.

Greenfield, Lieutenant George, British Army Officer at Tehran Conference.

Greet, Marine John, marine at Iwo Jima.

Gretton, Vice-Admiral Sir Peter (1912–92), wartime Escort Group Commander and author of *Convoy Escort Commander* and *Former Naval Person: Churchill and the Navy*.

Gudgeon, Private Denis, British Army, captured by the Japanese during the first Chindit operation.

Guingand, Major General Sir Francis de (1900–79), Chief of Staff to Field Marshal Montgomery 1942–45.

Hammersley, Private Joe, Fourteenth Army, Burma.

Harding, Field Marshal John Lord (1896–1989), commanded 7th Armoured Division in North Africa, Chief of Staff to Field Marshal Alexander, Chief of the Imperial General Staff 1952–55, ennobled 1953, governor of Cyprus 1955–57.

Harriman, Ambassador W Averell (1891–1986), US diplomat and politician, Special Envoy to Europe 1940, Ambassador to Moscow 1943–46, Secretary of Commerce 1946–48, Governor of New York 1954–58, chief US negotiator at Paris peace talks with North Vietnam 1968–69.

Harris, Air Chief Marshal Sir Arthur (1892–1984), joined the Royal Flying Corps in 1915, Commander-in-Chief of Bomber Command 1942–45, retired 1945.

Hart, Captain Raymond (1913–99), Escort Group Commander.

Herget, Major Wilhelm, German fighter ace with 58 night kills.

Hiejenk, Commissioner, Amsterdam police officer.

Hilse, Willi, German railwayman at Auschwitz.

Hinrichs, General Hans, German engineer officer in France, Russia and North Africa.

Hiss, Alger (1904–96), senior US diplomat and foreign-policy adviser to President Roosevelt at Yalta, convicted of perjury in 1950 in relation to his activities as a Soviet spy.

Hodgkinson, George (1893–1986), Labour Party agent and Coventry town councillor.

Hoffman, Private Wilhelm, diarist, German Sixth Army, Stalingrad.

Hogan, Captain Neville, Burma Rifles, Indian Army, survived the retreat from Burma and took part in the Chindit expeditions in February 1943 and March 1944.

Holmes, Flight Lieutenant Ray (1914–2005), RAF fighter pilot who rammed a German bomber over London on 15 September 1940.

Honda, Lieutenant Ukikuro, Japanese Army in Burma.

Horrocks, Lieutenant General Sir Brian (1895–1985), Middlesex Regiment in WW1, commanded XIII Corps in North Africa and XXX Corps in Western Europe. Often wounded, he was invalided out of the British Army in 1949. An extraordinarily successful presenter of military history on television.

Hoshino, Naoki, Japanese Fascist ideologist.

Höttl, Dr Wilhelm (1915–99), SS official who worked with Adolf Eichmann in the Reich Security Main Office (RSHA) and was the original source for the figure of six million Jewish Holocaust victims.

Howard, Private John, Fourteenth Army, Burma.

Hruska, Marine Joe, 2nd Marine Division, Tarawa.

Iwanska, Professor Alicja, participant in the Warsaw uprising who emigrated to the USA, author of *Polish Intelligentsia in Nazi Concentration Camps and American Exile: A Study of Values in Crisis Situations.*

James, Brigadier William (1895–?), 100th Indian Brigade, Burma.

John, Dr Otto (1909–97), member of the German Resistance involved in the prosecution of war criminals at Nuremberg, later Head of the West German Security Service (BfV) who defected to East Germany in 1954 then returned to be imprisoned for treason 1955–58.

Johnson, General Leon (1904–97), won the Medal of Honor leading 44th Bomb Group USAAF in the bombing attack on the Ploesti Romanian oilfields in August 1943.

Jong, Dr Louis de, announcer on Radio Orange.

Junge, Gertrud 'Traudl' (1920–2002), married to an SS officer killed in 1944, member of Hitler's stenographer pool who typed his last testament shortly before his suicide.

Kase, Ambassador Toshikazu (1903–2004), Principal Secretary to two wartime Japanese foreign ministers, present at the surrender ceremony on USS *Missouri*, later Japan's first Ambassador to the United Nations.

Kehrl, Hans (1900–84), Nazi industrialist, Chief of Planning Office in the Armaments Ministry. Sentenced to fifteen years' imprisonment in 1949, released in 1951.

Kempner, Dr Robert (1899–1993), Chief Legal Adviser to the Prussian police until fired following the Nazi takeover in 1933. Expelled from Germany he returned as part of the US prosecution team at Nuremberg.

Kido, Marquis Koichi (1889–1977), Japanese Lord Keeper of the Privy Seal 1940–45, sentenced to life imprisonment 1946, released 1953 for health reasons.

Kii, Tsuyako, Tokyo housewife.

King, Cecil (Harmsworth) (1901–87), hugely influential left-wing British newspaper proprietor, who in 1926 joined the *Daily Mirror*, at time of interview the biggest-selling newspaper in the world. As chairman (1963–68) of the post-war International Publishing Corporation he headed what was then the world's largest publishing group.

Kleist-Schmenzin, Lieutenant Ewald-Heinrich von (b. 1922), German officer, July 1944 bomb-plot conspirator; his father Count Ewald was hanged.

Koch, Private Robert, US 29th Division, Omaha Beach, Normandy.

Kochavi, Avraham, survivor of Lodz ghetto and Auschwitz concentration camp.

Kodama, Yoshio (1911–84), Japanese Nationalist politician, drug-smuggling millionaire and post-war power broker.

Kretschmer, Rear Admiral Otto (1912–98), U-boat ace (*U-99*) who sank 46 ships. Joined the Bundesmarine in 1955, retiring as a rear-admiral in 1970.

LeMay, General Curtis (1906–90), developed the defensive 'box' used by USAAF bombers over Europe and the strategic-bombing campaign against Japan. Post-war he directed the Berlin Airlift, built up the Strategic Air Command and was an aggressive Air Force Chief of Staff.

Levi, Primo (1919–87), Italian-Jewish chemist sent to Auschwitz in February 1944. First published *Se questo è un uomo* in 1947, which became a best-seller in translation as *If This Is A Man* in the UK and *Survival in Auschwitz* in the US. Overcome by survivor guilt, he took his own life.

Levin, Private Arnold, US 1st Division, Omaha Beach, Normandy.

Lindsay, Lieutenant Colonel Sir Martin (1905–1981), regular British Army Officer turned Arctic explorer. Took part in the 1940 Norwegian Expedition, wrote *So Few Got Through,* an atmospheric account of 2nd Gordon Highlanders in 1944–45. Post-war Conservative MP, baronet 1962.

Lomov, General Nikolai (1899–1990), Deputy Head of Red Army Operations 1944–46, then head of the Soviet General Staff's Far East Department who coordinated the invasion of South Korea by Kim Il Sung in 1950. Later in charge of the Chief Operative Directorate and for many years Head of the Department of Strategy at the General Staff's Military Academy.

Looks, Lieutenant Commander Hartwig (b. 1917), commander of *U-264,* 1942–44.

Loveless, Private John, US serviceman in the Battle of the Bulge, 1944.

Luft, Friedrich, Berlin civilian.

Lynn, Dame Vera (b. 1917), sang with the Ambrose Orchestra 1937–40, had her own radio show 1941–7. Famous for such wartime songs as 'We'll Meet Again', 'White Cliffs of Dover' and 'It's a Lovely Day Tomorrow'. Known as 'The Forces' Sweetheart' because she travelled as far as Burma to sing for troops in the field.

Lyttelton, Oliver, Viscount Chandos (1893–1972), Conservative MP, President of the Board of Trade 1940–41 and 1945, Minister for the

Middle East 1941–42, of Production 1942–45, for the Colonies 1951–54, ennobled 1954.

McBeath, Lieutenant Commander John (1907–82), captain of HMS *Venomous* at Dunkirk.

McCloy, John (1895–1989), US corporate lawyer, Assistant Secretary of War 1941–45.

McGee, Private John, Infantry, Eighth Army.

Mahaddie, Group Captain Thomas Gilbert 'Hamish' (1911–97), flew many bombing missions until rested as an instructor in July 1940. He returned as a Pathfinder from August 1942 until March 1943. Post-war he was the aviation consultant on the films *633 Squadron* and *The Battle of Britain*.

Manson, Captain Frank (1920–2005), crewman on USS *Laffey*, hit by five kamikazes on 16 April 1945.

Manteuffel, General Hasso-Eccard Freiherr von (1897–1978), German Army, served in France, Eastern Front and North Africa, commander of Fifth Panzer Army in the Ardennes offensive and latterly Third Panzer Army in the East. Free Democrat representative in the Bundestag 1953–57.

Marshall, David, Malayan member of the Straits Settlement Volunteer Corps.

Mash, Sapper Bob, British combat engineer, Eighth Army.

Matsukawa, Kishi, Hiroshima housewife.

Mauldin, Bill (1921–2003), American cartoonist who created the archetypical GIs 'Willie and Joe' for *Stars and Stripes*, the Forces' newspaper, wounded at Anzio, later won two Pulitzer prizes as an editorial cartoonist.

Maurer, Dr Ekkehard (1918–2002), German infantry captain on the Eastern Front, later a leading West German industrialist.

Meyer, Major General John (1919–75), 352nd Fighter Group USAAF, who flew 200 combat missions with 24 confirmed kills. Eighth Air Force's top-scoring ace, three times awarded the Distinguished Service Cross.

Middleton, Drew (1913–90), American journalist, foreign correspondent and military correspondent for the *New York Times*.

Miller, Harry, British civilian in Singapore.

Miner, Vernon, merchant seaman.

Minogue, Joe (1923–96), Royal Engineer who landed at Gold Beach, Normandy, on D-Day, later Foreign Editor of the *Guardian* newspaper.

Mitchell, Harry, stretcher-bearer, 50th Division, Eighth Army, North Africa.

Morgen, Dr Konrad (1910–76), German lawyer and SS investigating magistrate 1943–44, dealt with 800 cases of corruption and murder, resulting in 200 sentences, many of the so-called 'camp aristocracy'.

Mountbatten, Admiral of the Fleet Lord Louis, Earl Mountbatten of Burma (1900–79), British Chief of Combined Operations 1941–43, Supreme Allied Commander South-East Asia 1943–46, Viceroy of India 1946–47. Murdered by the IRA along with his 14-year-old grandson, a local teenager and his eldest daughter's mother-in-law.

Murray, Lieutenant Ken, staff officer, US Pacific Fleet.

Mutsu, Ian (1907–2002), Japanese–English journalist.

Nakajima, Captain Tadashi, Commander Mabalacat air base, the Philippines, organiser of first Special Attack Unit (kamikaze), co-author of *The Divine Wind*.

Nakamoto, Michiko, Hiroshima schoolgirl.

Nance, Lieutenant Ray, US 29th Division, Omaha Beach, Normandy.

Nehring, General Walter (1892–1983), commanded 18th Panzer Division in 1940, the Afrika Korps in 1942 and Panzer Armies on the Eastern Front in 1943 and 1945.

New, Private Wally, Fourteenth Army, Burma.

Noguchi, Isamu (1904–88), Japanese–American artist and landscape architect.

Oakley, Private H R, British POW on the death railway, Burma

O'Connor, General Sir Richard (1889–1981), Commander Western Desert Force 1940–41, captured, later commanded VIII Corps in North Europe: subsequently served in India and on the Army Board, resigning on a point of principle.

Okada, Lieutenant Teruo, Intelligence Officer, Japanese Army in Burma.

Osterholz, SS Colonel Wilhelm, battalion commander, Sixth SS Panzer Army 1944–45.

Oulton, Air Vice Marshal Wilfrid (1911–97), RAF Coastal Command pilot and post-war air-traffic control pioneer.

Overlander, Mr, Canning Town resident during the Blitz.

Owen, Corporal Eddy, 2nd Marine Division, Tarawa.

Owens, Lieutenant J K, staff officer, Fourteenth Army, Burma.

Paerl, Jetje, singer on Radio Orange.

Paisikowic, Dov, Russian–Jewish survivor of Auschwitz.

Pederson, Marine, 2nd Marine Division, Tarawa.

Pene, Private Ruhi, Maori member of the 2nd New Zealand Division in North Africa.

Pheffer, Herman, disabled US serviceman.

Piers, Lieutenant Desmond 'Debbie', Canadian commander of anti-submarine sloop HMCS *Restigouche*.

Priestley, J B (1894–1984), served in the infantry in First World War, prolific English novelist, playwright and wartime broadcaster.

Pullini, Lieutenant Emilio, Italian Folgore (Lightning) Parachute Division, North Africa.

Pusch, Werner, pre-war German Social Democrat who joined the SS.

Putterman, Lieutenant Felix, Jewish–American US Army Civilian Affairs officer.

Rabeck, Marine Corpsman Herman, marine at Iwo Jima.

Reed, Private Robert, 2nd New Zealand Division, Eighth Army, North Africa.

Rees, Major Goronwy (1909–79), Marxist intellectual, British Combined Operations Staff Officer in the Planning Staff for D-Day, journalist, author and briefly a Soviet spy.

Reeves, Private Bert, Anglo-Indian Fourteenth Army, Burma.

Reid, Flight Lieutenant William (1921–2001), RAF Bomber Command pilot who won the VC on his eighth mission in November 1943, later flew with 617 Squadron until his aircraft was hit by a falling bomb in July 1944, from which he barely escaped to end the war as a POW.

Reiner, Lieutenant, Fourth Panzer Army at Stalingrad.

Remer, Heipke, member of the League of German Maidens.

Remer, Major General Otto-Ernst (1912–97), commanded Guard Regiment in Berlin during 20 July bomb plot and instrumental in crushing the revolt.

Rheinheimer, Heinz, German civilian living in Darmstadt.

Roberts, Captain Gilbert, Director, Western Approaches Tactical Unit, Liverpool, developed anti-submarine techniques. His characteristic phrase 'the cruel sea' became the title of a book by Nicholas Monsarrat, a wartime naval officer.

Robertson, Second Lieutenant William, US Army, met Russians at Torgau.

Rogan, Air Navigator John, Eighth Air Force, USAAF.

Ronke, Christa, Berlin schoolgirl.

Russell, Sir John, British Minister in Moscow 1940–41.

Rybakova, Olga, Leningrad housewife.

Sakai, Lieutenant Saburo (1916–2000), Japanese Navy fighter ace.

Sakomizu, Hisatsune (1902–77), Chief Cabinet Secretary to Prime Minister Kantari Suzuki, 1945.

Samuelson, Dr Paul (b. 1915), member of the US War Production Board, Nobel Prize-winning Professor of Economics at MIT.

Sanematsu, Commander Yuzuru, Naval Attaché at Japanese Embassy in Washington 1941.

Schimpf, Private Albrecht, German Army on the Eastern Front.

Schmidt-Schmiedebach, Lieutenant Heinrich, German artillery officer, Eastern Front.

Schroer, Major Werner (1918–85), German fighter pilot who shot down 117 Allied aircraft, 59 over North Africa, 22 over Italy and the rest over Germany.

Schulze-Kossens, SS Lieutenant Colonel Richard (1914–88), Adjutant to Hitler in the 1930s.

Schwerin-Krosigk, Lieutenant General Gerhard Graf von, capable divisional commander who tried to yield Aachen to the Allies in 1944 and was only relieved of command, although his cousin Ulrich von Schwerin-Schwanenfeld had been hanged for treason only a month before. Had a major influence on the post-war Bundeswehr.

Senator, André, Mayor of Asnelles, Normandy, 1944.

Seney, Private John, US paratrooper, northern Europe.

Shawcross, Hartley Lord (1902–2003), Labour MP, Chief British Prosecutor at Nuremberg, Chief British Delegate to the UN and Attorney-General, ennobled 1959.

Shearer, Guardsman, Scots Guards, Glasgow pub-group interview.

Sherrod, Robert, American war correspondent who reported on the battles for Tarawa and Iwo Jima.

Sherwood, Lieutenant Robert, commanded anti-submarine corvette HMS *Bluebell* and frigate HMS *Tay*.

Shinwell, Emanuel 'Manny' Lord (1884–1986), left-wing British trade unionist and Labour politician, refused to serve in the wartime government, held several post-war ministerial posts, ennobled 1970.

Shkavravski, Dr Faust, Soviet pathologist who performed the autopsy on Hitler's body.

Shoup, General David (1904–83), Commanding Officer of 2nd Marine Regiment at Tarawa, where he won the Medal of Honor, later Commandant of the Marine Corps.

Sijes, B J, member of the Dutch Resistance.

Silberstein, Yaacov, Jewish teenager at Buchenwald and Auschwitz.

Sink, Colonel James, US 29th Division, Omaha Beach, Normandy.

Slattery, Marine George, marine at Iwo Jima.

Slot, Dr Bruins, member of the Dutch–Christian Resistance.

Smith, Seaman George, flight-deck crewman on USS *White Plains*, Battle of Leyte Gulf.

Smyth, Brigadier Sir John (1893–1983), Indian Army, won the VC in France 1915, the MC in Waziristan 1919, and commanded 17th Indian Division in Burma 1941–42. Relieved of his command after the Sittang battle, baronet 1955.

Solarczyk, Stefan, Polish resident in the town of Auschwitz.

Spears, Major General Sir Edward (1886–1974), distinguished First World War career as a liaison officer with the French (his book *Liaison 1914* is important and atmospheric), Conservative MP and Winston Churchill's representative in France in 1940 and later with General Charles de Gaulle, baronet 1953.

Speer, Albert (1905–81), Hitler's chief architect, coming to his attention through the 1932 design for a Nazi Party headquarters in Berlin; Minister of Armaments 1942–45. When tried at Nuremberg was the only defendant to admit complicity in Nazi crimes and to express contrition, imprisoned 1946–66.

Stagg, Group Captain James (1900–75), Chief Meteorological Officer to General Eisenhower, gave crucial advice prior to D-Day.

Stearn, Marine Jack, marine at Iwo Jima.

Stewart, Brigadier General James M 'Jimmy' (1908–97), pre- and post-war Hollywood star who volunteered for the Air Force and flew twenty combat missions in B-24s, rising to the rank of colonel and Chief of Staff of the Second Bombardment Wing of the Eighth Air Force. Became a post-war USAF reserve brigadier general.

Stone, Captain Rodney, Merchant Navy, skipper of SS *Gharinda* sunk 5 May 1943.

Strong, Major General Sir Kenneth (1900–82), Chief Intelligence Officer to General Eisenhower. His 1969 book *Intelligence at the Top* characteristically made no mention of *Ultra*, the breaking of German cyphers that was the most significant Allied intelligence success of the war, which remained Top Secret until 1974.

Sugita, General Ichii, Japanese Army, present at fall of Singapore.

Suzuki, General Teichi (1899–1999), Japanese Army Minister condemned to life imprisonment for war crimes 1948, released and pardoned 1955.

Sweeney, Brigadier General Charles (1919–2004), pilot of the instru-mentation-support aircraft for the atom bombing of Hiroshima and of the aircraft that dropped the bomb on Nagasaki.

Tanimoto, Reverend Kiyoshi, Christian Hiroshima resident.

Thomas, Emily, Plymouth housewife, whose children were killed in the Blitz.

Thomas, Jimmy, merchant seaman.

Tibbets, Brigadier General Paul (b. 1915), commander of the 509th Composite Bomb Group and pilot of the *Enola Gay* – named after his mother – for the atom bombing of Hiroshima.

Tokaty, Dr Grigori (1909–2003), Ossetian aeronautical engineer, defected to Britain 1947, Professor of Aeronautical and Space Technology at City University, London, 1967–75.

Tokugawa, Yoshihiro (1906–96), Chamberlain to Emperor Hirohito from 1936, saved the recording of the Emperor's surrender broadcast from rebel army officers.

Tregaskis, Richard (1916–73), war correspondent who covered the Doolittle raid on Japan, went ashore with the marines at Guadalcanal and stayed for six weeks. His *Guadalcanal Diary* is regarded as a classic of war reporting.

Uno, Edison, teenage Japanese–American internee and Nisei civil-rights activist.

Ushiba, Tomohiko, Private Secretary to pre-war Japanese Prime Minister, Prince Konoye.

Valavielle, Michel de, French farmer, Normandy 1944.

Van der Boogard, Mr, Dutch factory worker.

Van der Veen, Mr, member of Dutch–Christian Resistance.

Van Hall, Mr, Dutch banker who ran an illegal welfare organisation to help victims of the Occupation.

Vaughan-Thomas, Wynford (1908–87), BBC radio journalist, reported on a bombing mission to Berlin, the invasion of southern France and Belsen extermination camp. Had a distinguished post-war broadcasting career, published an eyewitness account of Anzio in 1968.

Voris, Captain Roy 'Butch' (1919–2005), US Navy fighter ace in the Pacific War, later founder of the Blue Angels precision-flying team.

Vrba, Rudolf (1924–2006), Jewish Slovak who was one of only five men to escape from Auschwitz-Birkenau and whose testimony cracked the carapace of disbelief among the Western Allies about the full extent of the Nazi 'Final Solution'.

Wagenaar, Gerbern, member of Dutch–Communist Resistance.

Warlimont, General Walther (1894–1976), artillery officer 1914, Wehrmacht (OKW) Deputy Chief of Operations under Alfred Jodl 1939–44, prison 1945–57, his book *Inside Hitler's Headquarters* was published in 1964.

Waterfield, Gordon (1903–87), British journalist and broadcaster.

Wedermeyer, General Albert (1897–1989), the first US officer to study at the Kriegsakademie since the First World War, author of the US Army's 'Germany First' strategic plan, later Chief of Staff to Mountbatten and then Commander-in-Chief of the Chinese portion of Stillwell's former command.

Weltlinger, Sigmund, member of the Berlin Jewish Council set up by the Nazis.

Westphal, General Siegfried (1902–82), German Operations Officer to Rommel in North Africa, then Chief of Staff in Italy and northern Europe.

Whitmore, Private, Sherwood Foresters pub-group interview, Nottingham.

Witter, Ben, Hamburg journalist.

Witzendorff, Lieutenant Commander Ernst von (b. 1916), commander of *U-121*, *U-46*, *U-101*, *U-650*, *U-267*, *U-2524* and *U-1007*, 1942–45.

Wolff, Waffen-SS Colonel General Karl (1900–84), Chief of Staff to Himmler, Governor of North Italy 1943–45, helped arrange German surrender in Italy and was a prosecution witness at Nuremberg. After publishing his memoirs in 1961 was tried and imprisoned by a German court for the mass deportation of Jews to Treblinka concentration camp.

Woudenberg, Dick, teenage son of a prominent Dutch Nazi.

Wozenski, Brigadier General Edward (1915–88), US Company Commander on Omaha Beach, Normandy.

Wright, Wing Commander Robert, Personal Assistant to Air Chief Marshal Dowding during the Battle of Britain and later his biographer.

Yonaha, Momoko, Okinawan girl conscripted into medical service with the Japanese Army.

Yoselevska, Rivka, Polish–Jewish survivor of the Hansovic ghetto massacre in Poland, witness at the trial of Adolf Eichmann in 1961.

Yoshikawa, Takeo (1914–93), Japanese naval officer and spy at Pearl Harbor in 1941.

CHAPTER 1

GERMANY'S HITLER

The 1914–18 war was often known in Britain as 'the Kaiser's War' and, with far more justice, its continuation in 1939–45 deserves to be known as Hitler's War. Its long-term causes may be traced back at least as far as the Franco-Prussian War of 1870–71, and both Germany's defeat in 1918 and post-war economic collapse helped set its preconditions. It came about because a political party built around blind obedience to a psychopath took control of one of the world's most powerful states, and it was to take an alliance of most other world powers to defeat him. The World at War *interviews explored the character of only one man – Hitler. Many reasons have been advanced for his meteoric rise, but the ugly fact remains that a party whose uniformed followers chanted, 'Blood must flow, let's smash it up, that godamned Jewish republic', made sound progress through the democratic process. The Nazis received eighteen per cent of the popular vote in the Reichstag elections of September 1930 and thirty-seven per cent in July 1932. Perhaps even more significant was that in the Presidential election of 1932, with the slogan 'Hitler over Germany' emphasised by his much publicised use of air transport, Hitler received thirty per cent of the votes in the first round and thirty-six per cent in the run-off against the incumbent, the elderly war hero and nationalist icon Field Marshal Paul von Hindenburg. Hitler was appointed Chancellor on 30 January 1933 and a month later a fire set by a Dutch Communist in the Reichstag building was used to justify an emergency decree banning the German Communist Party and suspending many civil liberties. Surfing a wave of anti-Communist hysteria the Nazi Party won forty-four per cent of the vote in the national elections of March 1933 and the first act of the new Reichstag was to pass the Enabling Act that reduced its functions to simply rubber-stamping the initiatives of the Chancellor. President Hindenburg died on 2 August 1934 and instead of holding new elections Hitler was invested with the powers of Head of State and Supreme Commander of the armed forces, who swore an oath of loyalty to him. This constitutional coup was approved in a plebiscite by eighty-five per cent of the electorate.*

KARL WOLFF

Founding member of the SS in 1931

Hitler's conception regarded Christianity as a sort of sickness in the natural Germanic nature. He considered it his duty to renew and improve the Germanic race as far as possible where it was still to be found, despite the terribly unfortunate mingling with other influences, but also to renew and improve religion and lead them back, step by step, to a new sort of recognition of God and new forms of worship that broke away from the supranational Christian emasculation, which was opposed to inner Germanic interests. Since there was no example for this, no textbook from which one could learn, paths were followed, some of which were fine and good, and others that were regarded as very controversial and even ridiculous.

ALBERT SPEER

Hitler's Chief Architect and later Armaments Minister

When I was a young man and was joining the Party I missed everything, which was really seriously searching the possibilities of other parties or the programme of this Party. I was just convinced by Hitler's attitude in a speech he made, and in such a comparatively small decision as just joining a Party was already the step to everything which happened afterwards to me. I lost those twenty years of my life when I was quite superficially joining this Party in 1931.

CHRISTABEL BIELENBERG

Englishwoman married to an anti-Nazi German lawyer

I came to Germany in 1932 and that was a period of time I think you can say that the Weimar Republic was dying. They had changed the government – they changed the government in Germany practically every three months – and the government was already ruling by emergency decree. I think the atmosphere of Germany was one of great poverty, there's no doubt about it, it was very distinguishable when one even came from England, which wasn't in a very good way either. There were six and a half million unemployed, every weekend there were political marches taking place between the Nazis on one side, the Communists on the other. Every political party had its military wing, which of course was quite different to England, and they marched around and practically every weekend there were deaths through shootings and so forth. I think the ordinary burgher was absolutely tired of this situation and was on the lookout for someone who could come along to clean up the place. The emergency laws of course were there. They had [to be], they were on the statute book simply because no government – there were forty-eight political parties altogether I believe – and no government had been able to govern, to get a majority in parliament. That's why those emergency laws were there, and they were on the statute book ready to be used by anybody who wanted to.

HUGH GREENE

Daily Telegraph *correspondent in Berlin*
I think that the great bulk of Germans did feel that Versailles had been a wicked thing and that they had been hardly done by. It had been drummed into them by Nationalist professors in the universities and Nationalist teachers in schools.*

DR ROBERT KEMPNER

Chief Legal Adviser to the Prussian police until dismissed in 1933
I happened to know that these so-called self-defence units, mostly posted near the Polish borders, worked unofficially under the German Ministry of Defence. It was illegal, but illegal things are often done even by democratic governments. At that time a number of these self-defence people were quitting their jobs; they just didn't like what they saw was going on

---

* By the Treaty of Versailles in 1919 the Germans accepted war guilt and the obligation to pay reparations.

because it was not just self-defence, it was the nucleus of a kind of radical right-wing movement. Now if these fellows left or tried to leave the secret organisations they were tried by their own superiors, sentenced to death and murdered without any real legal procedure. These murder cases of course came to the knowledge of the police and to the knowledge of the Prussian legal authorities. As Legal Counsellor of the Ministry of the Interior I had to think how could I cause the prosecution of murders if these murderers are the members of an official organisation of the legal German Reich, even if they work undercover. In Prussia at the time there was a democratic coalition government between the Social Democrats and the Catholic Party and also another democratic party. The government and my minister, my department chief, decided that we should go ahead with the prosecution. Their defence, of course, was that they did it as officials of a legal organisation of the German Reich. There were big murderers and smaller ones, and one who participated in these murders was a person, Martin Bormann; another was a certain Rudolf Höss, who later became the infamous commandant of the Auschwitz concentration camp. All these men including Höss and especially Bormann were sentenced for murder or accessory.*

KONRAD MORGEN
Law student compelled to join the SS
My family was a bit critical towards National Socialism at least certainly my father was. My father was an engine driver and a very calm and silent, modest man without any sort of ambition. He said, 'I'm an official, I serve the state and I do my duty and who tells me what I have to do,' and all this 'carry-on' as he put it, he didn't understand it at all. My mother had a more sanguine nature and she let herself get carried away a bit with all the flags and speeches and the singing and marching columns, and she believed, and hoped that the great turning point had now come with Hitler. This scepticism I spoke of was not a definite opposition to National

---

* Martin Bormann (1900–45) became the powerful head of the Party Chancellery and Private Secretary to Hitler.

Socialism, it was in fact true that National Socialism had a programme which one could agree with and support.

SIGMUND WELTLINGER
Member of the Berlin Jewish Council set up by the Nazis
When Hitler came I regarded him as just one of the many political idiots which were springing up all over the place as far back as I could remember in recent times and I did not take him seriously. With time, however, I gradually changed my mind – but very gradually. At the beginning I did not believe such mad ideas could find any echo in Germany.

WERNER PUSCH
Pre-war Social Democrat who joined the SS
I think it was shortly after the 30th of January 1933 there was still great opposition to Nazism particularly among the workers, and I think they were ready at that time to fight and to go on strike, but they weren't called to do that. The reason is that there was a big gap between the two parties. The Communists just had their period of strong anti-social-democratic propaganda with their formula of 'Social Fascism', and the Social Democrats were very suspicious about the Communists. They never knew if the Communists wouldn't try to carry on every measure against Nazism to bring about the Communist revolution. So they couldn't come together.

KONRAD MORGEN
After the change in 1933 the SA [Sturm Abteilung – the 'Brownshirts'] and SS leaders appeared on the sports field and then we got a new sports instructor and then we heard that this instructor was a former officer in civilian clothes. Then these sports and exercises got more and more like pre-military physical practice, then we had formation exercises as well. And they said, by the bye, it would be quite nice if you could wear a brown shirt, then a brown tie and then boots and so on. And so gradually a uniform grew up, a bit makeshift, but it already looked somewhat military and then we often had to march routes and parade ourselves and then one day there was an inspection. After the inspection they said, on the

basis of height, that lot over to the right and those over to the left, and then we heard, in the future those will belong to the SS and others to the SA. And so I came to the SS.

HEINZ RHEINHEIMER
Darmstadt civilian
I was a child in 1933, you must remember that. My principal impression was that there was something rotten, that is to say there was very little work. The factories had little work, they were working short time and my father often spoke of hard times when we were having our meals, of the difficulties there were in getting work. I remember very clearly the Labour Exchange was at the bottom of our street and the workers, that is the unemployed – there wasn't any work – would go to the Exchange and get their unemployment pay. That was a sad, grey, unhappy – you could almost call it an army – that used to go there every day.

HANS KEHRL
Nazi industrialist
Well, really, it was the only party that promised to get us out of the hole and the idea was principally that it would only be possible if we developed as a nation a team spirit and solidarity, pulling all on the same rope instead of quarrelling about petty differences of opinion, foreign politics, social politics and so on and so forth. That was the first point and that seemed pretty logical. And they promised to do away with unemployment and to reorganise and build up agricultural life again and they thought they could do that in the course of about five to six years, and as this was much better than anything else that was brought forward and as there was such a hopelessness I thought it was a real chance to follow them and their advice.

KONRAD MORGEN
What did he promise? Work and bread for the millions of unemployed and hungry masses. Nowadays in our prosperous society work and bread doesn't mean anything any more, but then it was a basic need of life, and this

promise sounded like a promise of paradise. Many parties promised work and bread but National Socialism, with its leader Adolf Hitler, said, 'We shall prove that we can do it,' and he did actually manage to do it, which nobody had thought possible. And in a relatively short time too. And all these people who had just really been vegetating without any future were now visibly shown there is some point to your life and you have a duty – you can feed and support your family again by working and not charity. And your children will have a trade. They were of course delighted. Now there were many who had reservations because of the military tone. They muttered, 'Hitler, it'll mean war,' but he behaved like a pacifist and it sounded so convincing that one really couldn't argue with it. He said, 'I have been a front-line soldier; for five long years, I was a courier alone on the battlefield, I was wounded, blinded and I saw so many of my comrades fall in the fighting. I know what war means and we *Frontsoldaten* have only one desire: to stop any continuation of war.* But Germany has disarmed now and the others promised to disarm so that at last we can have peace in the world.' Then the older generation, they welcomed the somewhat military attitudes and said, 'The youth is unruly, they lack military training, it was so much better before when they had a military training, it was so much better and they learned to be a man.'

HEIPKE REMER
Member of the League of German Maidens
People were enthusiastic and accepted the events because they had got work and food again. Even we children were able to meet and be friends in Hitler Youth when we previously had not been able to understand each other, been against one another because our parents held different political views. In the Hitler Youth we sang together, went for long walks, made things, for the kindergarteners and old people, for Christmas. All the negative aspects had vanished and we became a real community.

---

* *Frontsoldaten*, front-line soldiers: veterans of the First World War, also name adopted by several organisations formed to combat Communist revolutionaries immediately after the war.

ALBERT SPEER

I was sometimes shocked but in the same way I was enthused about the possibilities he saw in the field of new buildings and it was a mania in any case and, as I see nowadays, it was an expression of the whole system of his schemes. But in the time when I was working for him I thought those buildings are just matching the political era which was coming with Hitler, with his successes in which were still to be due.

HUGH GREENE

Showmanship was very important to the Nazis. I think that Hitler quite consciously wanted to keep the German people, or the mass of them, in a state of constant intoxication. The annual event at Nuremberg was of particular importance but there would be constant other occasions for demonstrations following various successes Hitler had achieved. I remember Propaganda Minister Josef Goebbels issued an announcement that 'spontaneous demonstrations will take place throughout Germany at noon tomorrow'.

WERNER PUSCH

In the Great Hall at Breslau I had to go behind the big curtain with the eagle on it that was hung before the organ, and before that curtain was the rostrum. Hitler of course was late, he was always late, that was part of his technique in a big assembly, he wrote about it even in his book *Mein Kampf*, so he was late and people were waiting and military bands were playing. Then he turned up and for the first ten minutes he wasn't a good speaker, he just began warming up and finding the words. But then he turned out to be a terribly good speaker, you know he just worked his public and the whole atmosphere grew more and more hysterical. He was interrupted nearly after every phrase by the big applause and women began screaming. It was like a mass religious ceremony and my feelings were rather queer in that moment. Hitler wasn't very far from me, about ten metres I think, and for a while I thought, well, that would be an occasion to shoot him. I'm in the dark and I would have the time and if I had a machine gun or something like that but of course I had none and of course if I did I should have lost my life afterwards, that was quite clear.

Well, I listened to his speech and felt that more and more excited atmosphere in the hall and for some seconds again and again I had a feeling what a pity that I can't share the belief of all these thousands of people, that I am alone, that I am contrary to all of that. It was very funny – I thought, well, he's talking all the nonsense I know, the nonsense he always talked, but still I felt it must be wonderful to jump into that pot, yes, and be a member of all who are believers, who were very happy at that moment.

SS LIEUTENANT RICHARD SCHULZE-KOSSENS
Personal Adjutant to Hitler
He was often talking about all the problems, religion, art and music, and about his plans for the future. He talked about these things but we could discuss them too. He could hold a speech that meat is not very healthy because he was vegetarian, but you could listen to him and say, 'Ah, my Führer, I like very much this meat, I like it more than vegetable or fruit.' You could say this.

ALBERT SPEER
Hitler was, I would say, in some ways fundamentally an aggressive type. He was always towards aggression; when there was some offensive means, he tried to employ them. He could never grasp the meaning of a proper defence, and so it was always the same with him, that you shall see it doesn't work to defend, it's better we'll start some strong retaliation.

DR FAUST SHKAVRAVSKI
Soviet pathologist who performed the autopsy on Hitler's body in 1945
One of his testicles definitely was missing. Although this was a find that had no relevance at all to the essence of the examination, this is a very rare occurrence. Usually we find the testicle in the inguinal canal or in a duct but it was not there either. The testicle could have been in the abdominal cavity but we did not find it there so we drew the conclusion that he did not have one. There is such a Philistine attitude that the absence of a testicle is regarded as a vice, as a disgrace. None of Hitler's people would have admitted to his being in such a position.

HUGH GREENE

The key thing was the Enabling Law, which passed with a majority of two-thirds – which it had to be under the German Constitution – towards the end of 1933. Only the Socialist Party had the courage to vote against it – the Catholic Centre Party voted with Hitler, otherwise he would not have got his two-thirds majority. But the Enabling Law made it possible for the civil service and other elements, respectable elements in the state, to think that Hitler's dictatorship was basically legal and constitutional. Even his elimination of other parties, including his allies the Nationalists, could be argued to be legal under the Enabling Law, so that was a very important event in Hitler's career.

KONRAD MORGEN

Reichspresident Hindenburg died and the Reichpresident was elected by the people. Now the Party had put up Hitler as the only candidate and this went against my whole legal conviction. Because in this case, the highest offices of state, that of the Reichspresident and the Reichschancellor, would be put into one person's hands. According to the principle of the division of power in which I as a student of law had been brought up, these offices must be filled by different people. It went so radically against my conviction that I could not vote for Hitler, but I could not say this openly because I don't know what would have happened to me, but something pretty terrible. I didn't want to commit suicide so I said to myself, if I don't vote then you don't need to act against your convictions, but on the other hand nobody will notice so it won't turn out too badly. So I didn't vote. In less than a fortnight the Party in Frankfurt wrote to me, 'Please inform us where you exercised your duty to vote.'

SIGMUND WELTLINGER

I did not recognise the danger from one day to the next but all the same, on the day of the Nuremberg Race Laws, that was 15th September 1935 as far as I can remember, then I said it was getting very serious. And I fully realised the danger when I was taken off to the concentration camp after the

Kristallnacht.* Then of course I saw that it was a great danger but I was still convinced that the words of the late Reichspresident Hindenburg were valid, that Front Soldiers would be protected, and I was a Front Soldier.

KONRAD MORGEN

The anti-Semitic programme and the attitude of the Party itself was only too obvious, and it was in fact one of the points in the programme which was generally found repellent and against which, to a greater or lesser extent, one put up some opposition. But, one said, there hasn't been a party which came to power and then carried out their programme one hundred per cent. In other words, lots of otherwise iron principles get filed down and smoothed out and everything isn't eaten as hot as it's cooked. The National Socialists were also very clever and understood how to play down their earlier slogans. I can remember that in *Simplicissimus* – that was one of their great satirical magazines, like *Punch* in England – they published a cartoon with a caption 'Heads will roll!' and there was a long train and lots of fat, well-fed Jews were looking out of it. And they were travelling towards Switzerland, they were rolling off to Switzerland very happily. Those who were making them roll were the National Socialists but not with the guillotine, they were making sure that they went somewhere else with their money. And then, of course, nobody had anything against that if it was all going on so peaceably.

EMMY BONHOEFFER

Sister-in-law of German Resistance martyr Pastor Dietrich Bonhoeffer
I remember that the husband of my sister Lena, when he went in the morning after the day of the Kristallnacht, he went by train to his office downtown and he saw that the synagogue was burning and he murmured, 'That is an insult for cultured people, an insult to culture.' Well, right away a gentleman in front of him turned and showed his Party badge and took out his papers. He was a man of the Gestapo and my brother-in-law had to show

---

* The Night of the Broken Glass, a pogrom against Jewish shops and homes on the anniversary of the birthday of Martin Luther, 10 November 1938.

his papers, to give his address and he was ordered to come to the Party office next morning at nine o'clock. When my brother-in-law came home in the evening he told my sister what had happened and she said, 'Couldn't you keep your mouth? What will happen now? They will take you in a concentration camp.' I don't know how he talked himself out of it but his punishment was that he had to arrange and to distribute the ration cards for the area each beginning of each month for years, until the end of the war.

HUGH GREENE

I was in Berlin at that time and saw some pretty revolting sights – the destruction of Jewish shops, Jews being arrested and led away, the police standing by while the gangs destroyed the shops and even groups of well-dressed women cheering. Maybe those women had a hangover next morning, as they were intoxicated all right when this was taking place. I found it, you know, really utterly revolting. In fact to a German journalist who saw me on that day and asked me what I was doing there, I remember I just said very coldly, 'I'm studying German culture.'

J B PRIESTLEY

English author and broadcaster

There was this period before the war when I think a great many ordinary people in England thought all of this was very unreal. You know – burning books and baiting Jews and so on – that this was some eccentricity that would pass away.

EMMY BONHOEFFER

Standing in the line for vegetables or something like that I told my neighbours standing next to me that now they start to kill Jews in the concentration camps and they even make soap out of them. And they said, 'Frau Bonhoeffer, if you don't stop telling such horror stories you will end up in a concentration camp too and nobody of us can help you. It's not true what you're telling, you shouldn't believe these things, you have them from the foreign broadcasts and they tell those things to make enemies for us.' Going home I told that to my husband and he was not at all applauding to me and the very contrary he said, 'My dear, sorry to say but you are absolutely idiotic what you are doing. Please understand the dictatorship is like a snake. If you put a foot on its tail, as you do, it will bite you. You have to strike the head and you can't do that, neither you nor I can do that. The only and single way is to convince the military who have the arms to do it, to convince them that they have to act, that they have to make a coup d'état'.

SIGMUND WELTLINGER

I did not leave because in my life I have seldom gone out of my way to avoid danger, because I was deeply rooted in Germany – I had grown up in the sphere of German culture and found no obstacles, I had friendships with all and did not believe that there was any threat to me personally for my body and life. And I thought, I shall get through this – I did not run away from it.

ALBERT SPEER

It shouldn't be forgotten that to be in the middle of a powerful group, a very powerful man admired by people, is so tempting that it's very difficult to get away. Thinking back to my time when I was at the height of planning those huge buildings, of course it was a chance to be one of the well known, even in the history of arts, and this was a chance no young man would willingly destroy. And afterwards when I was a minister, the sweetness of power also was tasting very good to me. Certainly all power corrupts and certainly in Hitler's circle the power was [of an] extraordinary scale, so the corruption was much larger than [it] is normally.

SS LIEUTENANT SCHULZE-KOSSENS

Very often when we were sitting in the so-called table talks he told us we will hear some music, but he liked very much serious or classic music and sometimes opera. He was an Austrian but he didn't like dancing music or the popular music we like as young people. One day I was sitting in my little office when I was Adjutant on duty, I was sitting in my room and was just writing something and hearing on the radio popular music and the door was opened and someone entered the room. I thought it was a servant of Hitler or somebody else and I was writing and tapping with my foot to the rhythm and suddenly I hear his voice behind me say, 'What terrible music, Adjutant.' And he laughed about me and so I closed the music and we talked together.

ALBERT SPEER

Hitler was warlord in many directions. What for others would have been discussions for weeks and weeks, for him was a decision of just a fraction of a minute. I tried to counteract this by bringing Hitler a lot of experts, sometimes we were ten or fifteen experts because I knew from my time as an architect he is respecting the opinion of experts, and for a while we succeeded quite well. He listened to them and his decisions were more or less reasonable concerning the technical parts. But of course there was a change too, one can't ever say that a man is always the same person and Hitler changed a lot from 1942 to 1943.

ADMIRAL KARL DÖNITZ

Commander U-boat arm, later C-in-C Kriegsmarine

Hitler was a soldier of the Army and his thoughts were influenced by continental experience and continental thinking. It was difficult for him to see the chances of sea power and see the ways in which a sea power could go and clear the way.

MAJOR GENERAL WALTHER WARLIMONT

Deputy Chief of Wehrmacht Operations

Hitler's leadership was always distrusted by me until nothing was left any more of the belief in Hitler as a soldier, or as a man. As to his character I have made very bad experiences already in the first days, weeks and months of the war. The first was when he, at the end of August 1939, was informed that Mussolini would go to war at the same time as Germany and he almost broke down and postponed the beginning of war against Poland for a few days. The second time was on the 3rd of September 1939 when the Western Powers declared war on Germany. Hitler didn't want to take back troops but he thought of halting on the lines that had been reached up to that time. And worst of all his manner when the British landed at the north of Norway when I just came to Reichschancellery and saw him sunk in a chair and entirely despairing about the future of this country. So his character did not come up to the demands of military leadership.

ALBERT SPEER

Of course thinking back Hitler is still to me a human being, he's not an object for historians which don't see blood and life with him and his humanity was one of my main objects in spite of everything he did, the crimes he committed and the consequences he brought about for our world. But it's necessary to know that he was a human being, that he could be charming, that he could treat those around him nicely and so on, because if there is one day somebody else showing up who is dangerous for the world and you have this picture of Hitler who is just a lifeless monster, then everybody would say, well, this new man is not Hitler, he is charming with children, he has good manners.

HUGH GREENE

Hitler's great strength was instinct and insight. Although he had never been outside Germany except in the trenches in France in the First World War, and later a visit to Italy, he seemed to have an instinctive understanding of the weakness of the French and British governments of that time. He knew much better than his generals or his civil servants that in spite of all appearance of strength they were weak. And he had patience, he had cunning, he had coolness. In spite of all the ranting, behind the ranting was a cool, calculating brain. I think Hitler at his best or worst, however you prefer to look at it, was one of the great men of history in his thoroughly evil way.

LIEUTENANT OTTO-ERNST REMER
Nazi and Army officer
I believe that the revolution of 1933 was really a genuine revolution. The truth was that it meant the continuation of the French Revolution, except that the French Revolution led to unrestrained liberalism and class differences. To overcome those was Adolf Hitler's aim, that is why he said,

'Common interest before self interest'. The 'I' became a genuine 'we'. I believe that the true causes of the last war were that Hitler has said, 'Work is capital' and 'Gold is nothing to me, gold is dirt.' A world, however, which clings to gold cannot tolerate such a state of affairs and must oppose such a revolutionary element, just as the world took sides against the French Revolution, against Napoleon. Napoleon, just as Hitler, won everywhere in the world, but the world in the end proves stronger than the revolutionary, and it follows that after such revolutions wars are always lost. I am nevertheless of the opinion that the good of this National Socialist Revolution will eventually come in the following centuries, just as the ideas of the French Revolution survived.

ALBERT SPEER

Dr Theodor Morell tried to bridge those gaps of overwork by stimulation, stimulating medical drugs and vitamins and sugar and so on and so on. And he used them in an odd scale and he used things which were obviously not already tried out in sufficient way, in hospitals or so, and the other doctors were quite afraid of this system. I think it affected Hitler but it wasn't the main cause, because the main cause was the life Hitler was leading. A man with such a load and such responsibility he needs sometimes he rests, he can't go on for ever and ever, and for every day and night. A few of the former followers of Hitler would like to say that for many things which happened in the last period of the war were to a mistreatment by Morell. I am not of this opinion – I think Hitler stayed generally what he always was.*

---

* Theodor Morell (1886–1948), Hitler's private physician, injected him with a cocktail of drugs including some known to cause euphoria, personality changes and psychosis.

CHAPTER 2

JAPAN'S MILITARISM

Following successful wars against China (1894–95) and Russia (1904–05), Japan had annexed Korea and exerted de facto hegemony over Manchuria, and her participation in the First World War on the Allied side brought her a string of Pacific islands that had once been part of the German Empire. The Japanese judged that Western racism had caused them to receive less than their due from the treaties following these wars and that a double standard was applied to their imperialism. In the China of the late 1920s a national-ist reaction against warlordism, led by Generalissimo Chiang Kai-shek, threatened Japan's privileged trading status with its huge neighbour, which, combined with the effects of the Great Depression led the Japanese Army to provoke the 'Manchurian Incident' in September 1931.

The ensuing, undeclared war led to Japan's condemnation by, and with-drawal from, the League of Nations in 1933. Japanese politics became domi-nated by assassinations carried out by nationalist societies and the field armies increasingly ignored not only the civilian government but also their own High Command. The 'Manchurian Incident' became a formal war in July 1937 and led to an undeclared border war with the Soviet Union, which ended with the crushing defeat of the Japanese at Khalkhyn Gol on the eve of the outbreak of war in Europe in 1939. Faced with an expensive stalemate in China, Japan was also hit by a series of economic sanctions imposed by the USA, joined by the British and the Dutch government in exile whose hopes for victory in Europe now depended entirely on US support. The government of Prince Fumimaro Konoye was unable to negotiate a compromise acceptable to the Japanese mili-tary and in October 1941 General Hideki Tojo was appointed Prime Minister, principally to restore respect for hierarchy in the armed forces. In November an ultimatum delivered by US Secretary of State Cordell Hull demanded with-drawal from China on pain of the total embargo of the oil (from the Dutch East Indies) and steel without which the Japanese war economy would collapse.

TOSHIKAZU KASE
Japanese diplomat

We have an excellent book in Tokyo, by one who happened to be one of my very good friends, called *Government by Assassination* – assassination followed one after the other since the outbreak of the Manchurian Incident in the autumn of 1931. This had the effect of intimidating the government leaders and they lost gradually the courage to speak up in the face of a military operation. A rather mysterious devotion was growing between the Army and the 'Young Turks' who were growing as an influ-ence in the Army at home and together they tried to reform or reconstruct Japanese society. Most people were not told the truth of the situation because the large papers and periodicals, most of them, followed the lead of the reactionaries and military elements, and to the effect they did, public opinion ceased to function.

IAN MUTSU
Japanese–English journalist

There was always a sort of censorship, from cradle to grave you might say, because there were certain things you couldn't say. This intensified, start-ing about the time of the Manchurian Incident. The bans of censorship as applied to the radio and the press came in those days from the Home Ministry. As often as several times a week editors would receive notices of what could and could not be mentioned, such as any references to the Imperial household. But they came to assume more and more of a mili-tary nature as the Japanese war on the continent progressed.

STAFF OFFICER AKIO DOI
Japanese Army General Staff

Politically, Japan wanted to join with China to check the attempt of the European powers to divide up China, and to prevent the advance of the

Soviet Union into Manchuria and North Korea. But the Nationalist government of China thought it better to get the support of the United States and Britain than to join with Japan and so continued an anti-Japanese policy. Japan wanted to secure Manchuria and Korea and for this they had to use force.

LEWIS BUSH

English teacher in Japan

The Japanese Army had been in disrepute from about 1922 when Japan was in Siberia with the British and the Americans after World War One, but the Japanese were the last to go and there were various scandals connected with Army corruption. And it remained in disrepute for several years, I should say until about the beginning of the 1930s, and then they came back through the so-called Patriotic Societies, many of them no more than gangsters who would commit any misdeed in the name of patriotism. There were several assassinations of Prime Ministers and leaders in those days just because they had liberal views or because they favoured better relations with the United States, Britain or other democratically minded nations.

YOSHIO KODAMA

Nationalist politician

We, the Japanese people, were told that the situation with the United States had reached such a stage that they wanted Japan to get out of not only China, but also Taiwan. They wanted Japan to withdraw completely from all parts of Asia and we were told that only if we do so, if we were to withdraw from all these various places, then the United States would lift its economic blockade of Japan for the first time. Of course we wanted the economic blockade lifted but the hardest part of this condition was the demand that we get out of Manchuria. After all, Manchuria had been the prize that we had gained after two wars, the Sino-Japanese and the Russo-Japanese, in which hundreds of thousands of soldiers had been sacrificed. We, the Japanese people, felt that if Japan were forced to withdraw from Manchuria it would immediately fall prey to the Russians. And so it was felt that unless Manchuria was defended by Japan it would be completely dominated by Russia and that all the past precious lives that were sacrificed to make Manchuria safe would have been a complete waste.

TOSHIKAZU KASE

I had some sympathy with the idealism of the young officers, partly because of the depression, which was pretty bad, and the young officers in the Army and also in the Navy were reacting to a hostile policy adopted by the democratic powers of America and Britain.

LIEUTENANT TERUO OKADA

Intelligence Officer, Japanese Army

We have this belly-band, which is the girls stand on the corner in the streets of, say, Tokyo and ask each passer-by woman to make a stitch and she must collect a thousand stitches. This is given to a soldier – I got one – and you wrap it round your belly. It's supposed to keep your stomach warm so that you don't catch cold or this or that, but also to ward off bullets. I used to think – I don't know whether I should say this – but I felt it was very unfair, especially when I got the order to go overseas, that the Japanese girls were giving me these thousand stitches. I'm going to die and I have not experienced a woman – why cannot they give me their body for me to enjoy and let me live, however short my life is, to enjoy the fullness of it. Because sleeping with me is not going to kill the girl, you know, maybe she likes it, I don't know. But I am going to die and all I get is a thousand stitches, which is a charm and it's very nice of her to give it to me, but after all it's just a piece of cloth with a thousand stitches.

TOMOHIKO USHIBA

Private Secretary to pre-war Prime Minister Konoye

There were so many causes in Japan those days – party politics very important and great division between the rich and the poor. In general public life was very hard and most young military officers came from low-class agricultural families, and agriculture was very, very hard position in those days.

LEWIS BUSH

The military came back to power because of the plight of the farmer classes, who did have a difficult time in the early Thirties, and you must remember that the military obtained its recruits mainly from the agricultural class, which before the war represented possibly seventy-five per cent of the Japanese working class.

STAFF OFFICER DOI

It was very bad, there were farmers' riots and many small and medium enterprises, and some big enterprises went bankrupt. Prime Minister Osachi Hamaguchi and others were assassinated too. The cause of all this was the economic situation. In mainland China there was an anti-Japanese movement; in the United States there was discrimination against Japanese immigrants; Japan was being opposed all over the world. And because of that Japan found itself in a very difficult economic situation.

EDISON UNO

Japanese–American teenager

As a child I remember going to school and having to fight my way home and having to argue and to justify my Americanism, my loyalty, to my classmates and my friends. My brothers and sisters all had trouble going to school and coming home from school, to the point where we pretty much felt we were no longer wanted in society and therefore we sort of kept to ourselves.

LEWIS BUSH

I remember my former wife, it must have been about 1938, coming from the hairdresser where she had her hair waved and being stopped by a policeman who told her this was a sign of Western decadence; even Western music, except classical music, which was mostly German, Beethoven and that sort of thing, was frowned upon and gradually all any kind of pleasure introduced from the West the military did their best to prohibit and rub it out altogether.

MARQUIS KOICHI KIDO
Lord Keeper of the Privy Seal

1930 was around the time Japan began to enter what might be called a convulsive period. The Army did not have such a strong power in 1930, but the growing influence of the ultra-nationalists and the 15th May young officers' insurrection and other incidents that occurred around this time placed Japan step by step under the influence of the Army.* The thing that helped the Army most was the fact that in selecting the War Minister it was necessary to have the agreement of the Chief of Staff and the Army Inspector General, and that the War Minister must be an active officer. This system gave the Army a chance to manipulate the Cabinet as it pleased.

HISATSUNE SAKOMIZU
Chief Cabinet Secretary

The constitution at the time, prerogative of the Emperor to use the Army and Navy, it belonged to Emperor himself, so the government could not control them. The Manchuria Army abused this Emperor's prerogative.

LEWIS BUSH

When I left Japan in early 1940 to join the Royal Navy there was rationing, prices were high, students of high school and the universities were doing military training practically every day. You had Army officers attached to every school to supervise such training. And so it was a nation preparing for war. By that time you must remember they'd already been in an undeclared war with China since the time of the so-called Manchurian Incident in 1931 and practically every day if you went near any railway station you'd see a crowd of people dressed in black – mothers, fathers, grandfathers, receiving the white boxes of ashes of their sons, which had been returned from the battle front in China.

---

* On 15 May 1932 a group of young officers assassinated Prime Minister Tsuyoshi Inukai and attacked the home of Marquis Kido's predecessor.

LIEUTENANT OKADA

When I left for war I had to clip my nails and hair and write a last will and testament because from that moment our lives were in the Emperor's hands. In other words my family will put that in the urn in case my body is not recovered. Our training is to die for the Emperor, beat the enemy and die for the Emperor so that death was nothing to be afraid of and in any attack we never even thought of dying. We only thought of this when perhaps we had a rearguard action and you are being shot from behind, that to die when shot in the back would be a shame.

TOSHIKAZU KASE

Japan wanted to pursue peace if possible, and that is why the government undertook the difficult negotiations with the United States. But on one hand the temper of the nation grew each day more militaristic, on the other because of the growing frictions with the democratic powers, which made it practically impossible to continue the negotiations.

LEWIS BUSH

Just before the war broke out Prime Minister Konoye tried very, very hard to settle affairs in China, but it didn't seem the military were very interested in ending the war: they wanted to go south, they were preaching the 'Greater East Asia Co-Prosperity Sphere' – the whole of Asia under the umbrella of Japan.

YOSHIO KODAMA

We knew it was impossible to stop Prince Konoye from going by ordinary means but we knew that in order for him to go to the United States he would have to take the train from Tokyo to Yokosuka, and then he would take a warship from Yokosuka to the United States. We knew of his route on the other side of the bay from Yokosuka beforehand so our plan was to blow up a bridge half-way between Tokyo and Kamagawa. Our plan was to blow up the train together with the bridge with the help of Colonel Masanobu Tsuji, later Chief of Staff to General Tomoyuki Yamashita in the lightning conquest of Malaya of the Japanese Army.

TOSHIKAZU KASE

The Soviet Union had always been thought a threat to Japanese security and the Army was itching for a showdown with the Soviet Union, if and when the latter suffered defeat in the European theatre, and the Army wanted to take the advantage of the Russian weakness. But in order to move north the climatic conditions come into play. After October the military operations against the north became rather more difficult, technically speaking. The Navy, on the other hand, wanted to advance further south because the resources our country lacked were largely in South Seas. And so Japan was pointing apart between the Army ambition and Naval design. But when the time for an attack against the north passed, the Army naturally joined the Navy.

MARQUIS KIDO

In 1941 there was still no proposal that Japan should advance southwards because Japan's hypothetical enemy was still Russia. I think the southward idea came somewhat later.

DR NOBLE FRANKLAND

Historian and post-war Director of the Imperial War Museum

The Japanese war was really a separate war to that against Hitler. The struggle between Hitler and the Western Alliance gave the Japanese the opportunity to secure what they believed was their right – an overseas empire which was based upon the view that they must have natural resources, as Japan is not a self-supporting country rather like Britain, and they sought an empire which would give them access to oil, rubber and all the commodities which great industrial nations need. And the Germany/Britain/America struggle gave the Japanese the opportunity; it was the Japanese who projected the Americans into the war against Germany. But the opportunity was created for Japan by Hitler.

LEWIS BUSH

They were building up to the Rome – Tokyo – Berlin Axis and so quite naturally they did their best to sell their people on the merits of Hitler and

Mussolini as opposed to the America of Roosevelt and the Britain of Chamberlain, two decadent, weak nations.*

IAN MUTSU

Even before Pearl Harbor, during the time of the Triple Alliance with Germany and Italy, you were asked to refer in certain ways to the Axis Powers. I noticed that the Japanese press was quite willing to cooperate with this, to be unfree, to convert themselves into printing shops for what came down to them from the High Command.

COMMANDER YUZURU SANEMATSU

Naval Attaché at Japanese Embassy in Washington

The Army took Prussia, later Germany, as its teacher and the Navy learnt from Great Britain and the United States. So there was naturally a great gap of thinking between the Army and the Navy. This was the biggest cause of the clash of interests. As a result of this the Navy wanted to maintain friendship as much as possible with Great Britain and the United States, while on the other hand the Army wanted to maintain friendship with Germany. This, then, was the biggest difference between the two.

ANTHONY EDEN

British Foreign Secretary 1935–38

Cadogan and I had been working with the Foreign Office for two years trying to improve our relations with the United States, particularly in respect to the Far East, and we had made some progress.** Rather remarkably when we opened the new dock at Singapore the United States offered to send two cruisers to attend the ceremony, which was quite an unusual gesture for those days, and then later Roosevelt offered to send a senior naval officer across to London to discuss how we would coordinate our naval policies in the Far East.

---

* The Tripartite Pact also known as the Axis Pact was signed on 27 September 1940.
** Sir Alexander Cadogan, Permanent Under-Secretary at the Foreign Office, 1938–46.

LEWIS BUSH

In Hong Kong in 1940 when I went there in the Royal Navy there were certain people like myself who knew full well the potentialities of the Japanese as fighting men. There were others, however, who were completely with their heads in the sand, completely ignorant, who even expressed the opinion that the Japanese hadn't a hope of taking Hong Kong, or hadn't a hope of fighting a European power let alone achieving a victory over them. I remember on one occasion, I think it must have been about the beginning of 1939, when a British national newspaper ran a story in which the opinion was expressed that the Japanese could never be good fliers because they had no sense of balance through being carried on the backs of their mothers as children. And people used to argue with me or other people who had been in Japan and quite frankly it became rather ridiculous. If any one of us just pointed out the power of the Japanese fighting ships or what they were doing in the air, the aircraft they were designing, we were either laughed at or looked upon as being traitors.

TOSHIKAZU KASE

In the Navy, to cope with the combined strength of British and American navies without being an act of suicide, any intelligent naval officer would have chosen to limit hostilities to either one of them, not take on two great navies at the same time. I know that some of the officers thought that it would be possible to separate the two but it proved that this was impossible, that they are one and the same. Particularly we in the Foreign Office thought that hostility with Britain would automatically involve America and vice versa. The Navy simply had to accept this judgement that to fight only with America or only with Britain was impossible, so it had to take on the two powerful navies, like it or not.

STAFF OFFICER DOI

Germany informed Japan that it was going to invade the Soviet Union about twenty days before they took action. There were two views in the Japanese General Headquarters, one said that Japan should take considered action with Germany, the other said that Japan should wait and see. This view was that Germany's war against the Soviet Union might not go as well as Germany thought; moreover it was thought that there was no definite cause for going to war against the Soviet Union. The decision of the General Headquarters was to wait for a while and see how the situation would develop.

HISATSUNE SAKOMIZU

The Japanese similar to German people, especially military people, believed that Germany Army will destroy Russia within a very short period.

TOSHIKAZU KASE

Sorge I knew not very well, but those who knew him did not suspect that he was a spy, a master spy.* He infiltrated the inner circle of Prince Konoye, the Prime Minister. Prince Konoye had with him intelligent people like Ozaki Hotsumi, and Ozaki was frequented and consulted by Konoye on the count of our policy of China. That Sorge was employed by the Russians was not known to us but he had many tentacles and penetrated into the secrets of our government. Also because of his connection to the German Ambassador, he had full access to the German archives and he also had his own sources of information. Sorge was sent abroad to find out the intention of the Japanese High Command as regard the Soviet Union: are they attack Soviet Union or not? And Sorge concentrated on finding out this question, which was vital to the security of the Soviet Union, and shortly before the German attack, when Sorge was arrested, he confided to the Military Police that about a month beforehand he had come to a definite conclusion that Japan was not moving against the Soviet Union. The fact that the Soviet Union had easy access to our government and High Command naturally militated against our interests.

---

* Richard Sorge (1895–1944), German agent of the Comintern who joined the Nazi Party and worked under cover as a *Frankfurter Zeitung* journalist in Japan from 1933.

TAKEO YOSHIKAWA

Japanese spy at Hawaii

I went to Hawaii in 1940, 7th March I think it was, and I worked ten months in Hawaii until the bombing attack over Honolulu and Hawaii. Sometimes I went to a geisha house early in the morning, at dawn, so I get up early and I saw the moving of the fleet go through the narrow strait. I go round by taxi or by bus around the Pearl Harbor Road and took the names of the ships. There are many names but there are sisters, you know sister ships, so it is very difficult to find out the name of one.

GENERAL TEICHI SUZUKI

Army Cabinet Minister

Ever since the First World War, or rather ever since the Russo-Japanese War, the United States had followed a policy of checking Japan's expansion. Therefore in the negotiations of 1940–41 the United States was not prepared to listen to what Japan said – the American idea was to check Japan completely before listening to what Japan had to say. It was because of this mounting pressure that Japan decided to go into Indochina, and it was very clear that if Japan did make the advance the economic embargo against Japan would be tightened further, therefore Japan was prepared for it.*

YOSHIO KODAMA

Japan, at that time, was not able to purchase anything abroad because of the economic blockade and so the Navy gave specific orders to me to set up a secret mission to obtain as much material for the Navy Air Arm as possible. This Kodama Mission was not known to the public, it was a completely secret organisation. But for three and a half years we purchased material abroad and in secret, and we got everything for the Navy Air Arm from China, from Singapore and Thailand. We collected all this material, and I can say the truth is that it was thanks to our efforts that for three and a half years of war the Navy Air Arm was able to continue in existence.

---

* The Japanese occupied French Indochina in July 1941.

COMMANDER SANEMATSU

It was the Army that was most surprised. This was because the Army did not know the United States. For example this is shown by the fact that the Army did not think that even though they went into Indochina it would call for such a strong retaliation from the United States as an embargo on the exports of oil to Japan.

TOSHIKAZU KASE

As to the action in choosing General Tojo, I myself asked Konoye and he said that nobody except Tojo would offer enough to control the Army, which 'was running our morgue'. This was heard by many other people. Also Tojo was deeply devoted to the Empire and if His Majesty made Tojo Prime Minister, Tojo would faithfully abide by his wish.

GENERAL SUZUKI

It was in 1941 that I became a Cabinet Minister. Japan was in very poor economic straits as a result of the incident with China. Japan's economy was already on a war footing but the planning of the war economy was not going so well.

DINGLE FOOT

British Liberal MP and Wartime Parliamentary Secretary to the Ministry of Economic Warfare

We were responsible for keeping track of all neutral shipping because we had to exercise contraband control. We might bring neutral ships into Gibraltar or the West Indies in order to search them for any goods that might be reaching the enemy. On some day, I don't remember the exact date, in October 1941 when Japan was still neutral, I was summoned to the blockade committee which met each day. Our shipping experts presented a very interesting report: they said apart from one whaler lost in the Antarctic every Japanese ship in their mercantile marine is heading for home as quickly as it possibly can. There were no outbound Japanese merchant ships, they said, we therefore reckon that by the 1st of December every single ship in the Japanese mercantile marine will be back in home waters. Well, you couldn't have had a clearer intimation than that. We reported to our own government and to the American government because although the United States were technically neutral we had an American observer on the committee, so they must have been fully informed as to our conclusions.

MARQUIS KIDO

Of course Japan tried to reach a diplomatic solution but Secretary of State Cordell Hull's attitude was very firm. That made negotiations very difficult and finally when the Hull Note was delivered, Japan was place in a position where she had no alternative but to fight.

GENERAL SUZUKI

It was not only Tojo but the entire nation which became determined to fight when Japan was presented with the Hull Note.

TOSHIKAZU KASE

When General Tojo was called upon to organise the new Cabinet before the outbreak of war, the Emperor conveyed his wish to the effect that the time limit attached to the negotiations with America, previously adopted by the liaison conference of government and High Command, should be disregarded. The Emperor tried to shape a fresh course in conducting our negotiations with America, but, unfortunately, events then overtook us. Even General Tojo tried at one time, at least during the first fortnight, to make the divisions but that was physically impossible because the situation was that American and British troops and fleet were at a strategic point in the South Seas and there was the mass circulation of the papers and periodicals inflaming the war question. This made it very difficult for General Tojo and the horse ran away from the stable.

HISATSUNE SAKOMIZU

The Emperor was very strict idea that he must obey the constitution, so if the Cabinet decide by the Cabinet Meeting then best way for the Emperor not to deny them, always say yes.

GENERAL SUZUKI

Tojo had no intention to go into war in the first place – it was the momentum of the situation that caused him to go to war. He understood well that Japan's economy lacked the strength to conduct a long-term war against the United States.

STAFF OFFICER DOI

The General Headquarters knew that Japan's oil supply, combining those of the Army and the Navy, was sufficient for only half a year or a year of fighting. So the plan was to get oil from Sumatra and continue the defensive war.

TOSHIKAZU KASE

Tojo was an honest man, he was deeply devoted to the Emperor, but he was, I do not think, suitable to be Prime Minister. He was very studious; he was rather famous as a Commander of Military Police in Manchuria. As Prime Minister he would assemble details after details: he always carried the famous black notebook; into it he entered surprising amount of details, not only of military affairs but also diplomatic matters. For instance, Privy Council met and Foreign Minister was there to present diplomatic case for approval. Tojo would incessantly intervene asking the Foreign Minister for a minute or two, during which time he would explain the why and how of a situation.

MARQUIS KIDO

The Emperor did not think the raid would be conducted before a declaration of war. We told him that Pearl Harbor would be raided but that it would only be as soon as possible after war had been declared.

TOSHIKAZU KASE

Some people say that Pearl Harbor was a sneak attack. It was a surprise attack but it was meant to be not quiet, because I was in charge of the American desk and took personal charge of the negotiations with America, and together with the Foreign Minister Mr Togo tried very hard to notify the breakdown of the negotiations before the active attack took place.*

IAN MUTSU

On the eve of Pearl Harbor, Japan had already been at war for many years, rather hopelessly bogged down in China for years, and things were getting scarce and the military were everywhere. All you could read about was the war, so the declaration of war against the rest of the world was just a development rather than a sudden plunging into war.

MARQUIS KIDO

When the war began, Japan's Army and Navy were at the height of their power, Japan could not step back when it was presented with the Hull Note, which was tantamount to an ultimatum. The Emperor was unable to prevent a war by himself. When the decision to stop fighting was made Japan was already completely defeated, Japan had nothing left. I think it was all a matter of how the world situation stood at each stage.

---

* Shigenori Togo (1882–1950), Foreign Minister 1941–42 and 1945.

CHAPTER 3

APPEASEMENT
AND PHONEY WAR

Thanks partly to a successful effort by some journalists and historians to portray appeasement as a sin to be visited solely on the British Conservative government, remarkably little attention has been given to the fact that European Communist and Socialist parties alike were adamantly opposed to rearmament until late 1936, while Communist parties continued to denounce the war and to sabotage the war effort until Hitler attacked the Soviet Union in 1941. The result has been an over-emphasis on the efforts of Prime Minister Neville Chamberlain to avoid war at almost any price in 1937–39, with far too little importance attached to the isolationism of the USA and the fact that, without active Soviet connivance, Germany could never have rearmed. Britain and France certainly failed to show the united opposition that might have deterred Hitler and damaged him domestically while, crucially, at Munich in September 1938, they refused to support Czechoslovakia against German aggression, persuading Hitler that they were morally bankrupt and would be unlikely to resist an attack on Poland. Chamberlain may indeed deserve obloquy for proclaiming that a meaning-less document signed at Munich guaranteed 'peace in our time', but in essence he was making the best of a bad job; his supporters argue that the fiasco did at least buy time for rearmament. Britain and France ultimately honoured their obligations when Hitler invaded Poland in 1939, though there was nothing practical they could do to help the Poles. Thanks to its own agreement with Germany, the Soviet Union took the opportunity to seize a third of all Polish territory and later to massacre thousands of captured Polish officers. France was locked into a defensive strategy behind the Maginot Line and Britain's principal military effort was invested in the Royal Navy and in what proved to be the false deterrent of the RAF's long-range bomber force. The Phoney War was a holding action to give time for an Allied blockade and economic warfare, including the failed intervention in Norway that brought Chamberlain down, to collapse the German economy while the Allied war effort reached full pitch. It was not an inherently foolish strategy, but it required time to reach fruition and Hitler had already shown that he was not a man for inaction.

DR GRIGORI TOKATY

Ossetian lecturer in Aeronautical Engineering at the Zhukovsky Academy of the Soviet Air Force

From about 1929 to 1933 the Soviet Union carried out two tragic campaigns. One was the liquidation of, the collapse of, our small-holder peasants; parallel to this and on the basis of this liquidation a forced collec- tivisation was carried out. I was a witness and a contemporary of both campaigns and I say that they created a tragic situation, famine, and the economy paralysed. And as the armed forces were fed from agriculture, and soldiers used to come from mainly peasantry, the moral and psycho- logical effect of these tragedies demoralised in a degree the armed forces. Secondly in 1933–1934 there were Party purges aimed at one thing, to eliminate those who had some kind of critical, independent mind, who questioned the wisdom of the collectivisation and liquidation of the peas- ants. In 1939 the country was weakened; the economy grew but the growth was despite, not because of, the tragedies. It is also exceptionally important to remember that all the places freed by those purged were taken up by second- and third-raters, by yes-men, by inexperienced men.

DR PAUL SAMUELSON

American economist

You know, when Franklin Roosevelt took office in 1933 he said there's nothing to fear except fear itself and his brave words did help a lot. But you can't just lift an economy out of a depression by its bootstraps just by singing slogans. You've got to spend money, and it wasn't until 1938, five years after the bottom of the Great Depression, that we really had the determination and the knowledge to have large deficit spending.

ANTHONY EDEN
British Foreign Secretary 1935–38
I think that fundamentally the differences between Chamberlain and myself lay in our respective assessments of the amount of confidence we could place in the men we were dealing with. Chamberlain put that very well himself at one of our meetings when he said that I hadn't the same confidence as he had in Mussolini's entering the conversation with a serious intention of carrying out any agreement. Chamberlain himself was more and more sure that his view was correct. I couldn't share that confidence because I had had some negotiations with Mussolini already: I made an agreement with him after the Abyssinian War was over, about the Mediterranean; that was in 1936. We agreed to respect each other's rights, to take no steps which might injure each other's interests or spoil our relations. Mussolini called it a 'gentleman's agreement'. A few weeks later he broke it: he interfered with the Spanish Civil War, which he knew perfectly well must affect our relations, and the agreement didn't count.

JOHN COLVILLE
Assistant Private Secretary to the Prime Minister 1939–41
Neville Chamberlain was deeply devoted to the idea of peace, to him war was the ultimate horror, he'd seen his contemporaries die in Flanders in 1914–1918 and he felt that his life's work was to prevent a repetition of the appalling massacres of the First World War. He gave everything he had to that end, perhaps more than was justified in the circumstances.

ANTHONY EDEN
The one success we were able to register between the two wars was at Nyon, a conference [held in] September 1937 in a small town in Switzerland, which the French and we mounted because merchant ships of all countries were being torpedoed in the Mediterranean by submarines of unknown

nationality. We knew they weren't Spanish submarines because we knew how many they had, and there was only one possible source: they were Italians, Mussolini's submarines. We decided this must be stopped so we called a conference, which we invited him to join, and we decided to patrol the Mediterranean with our joint destroyers, we and the French had produced over sixty destroyers to do it. We were going to give him a bit of sea. Yugoslavia, Greece and Turkey all played their part in the Adriatic and Russia also from the Black Sea area, so it was complete. We offered Mussolini a share, which didn't matter very much but was very large on the map, and invited him in. He wouldn't come to the conference. From that moment we patrolled the Mediterranean and the submarine sinkings stopped.

DR TOKATY

In 1937, in June, Marshal Mikhail Tukhachevsky's plot was uncovered. He was really the true backbone of the Soviet Armed Forces's reorganisation and reconstruction and he was shot as a German spy.* Every single assistant subordinate of Tukhachevsky was eliminated. Every single commander of a military district, every commander of an army division, every commander of a regiment, with some exceptions here, was eliminated. The Army was beheaded. The Army not yet equipped properly, the reorganisation was incomplete, the reconstruction technology was incomplete. We found ourselves in a state of complete weakness, a very dangerous weakness although the propaganda drums continued beating that we are united, we are good Russians, et cetera.

RAB BUTLER

British Under-Secretary of State for Foreign Affairs 1938–40
There was no doubt that our defences were not as strong as they became a year later but, if I think, if you want to get the record straight the real reason for not standing up in 1938 was the absolute saturation of the country in peace propaganda. There'd been all this League of Nations

---

* Marshal of the Soviet Union Mikhail Tukhachevsky (1883–1937) was the victim of Nazi disinformation that fed into Stalin's fear that the military might overthrow him.

business and Baldwin had never stood up as he should have done or rearmed in time. Baldwin told me Hitler would never do anything until 1942 and the defence hadn't been re-started and the public was pacifist-minded and the Commonwealth was divided, which it wasn't in 1939, and American opinion was not with us at the time of Munich.*

PILOT OFFICER WILFRID OULTON
RAF Coastal Command

The real fault was that the nation as a whole had not faced up to the inevitability of war and prepared for it.

AMBASSADOR W AVERELL HARRIMAN
US diplomat and President Roosevelt's Special Envoy to Europe

After World War One there was a lot of isolationism, a feeling we had no reason to become involved in world war and had made a mistake. There were lots of debts owed by European countries and we had an embargo against the sale of arms abroad called the Neutrality Act. Some people claimed we got involved in the war because we'd been selling arms and there was also the talk of the businessmen, the munitions manufacturers, who brought us into war. In addition to which there was no attack on the United States, remember, and much of that period, the Phoney War, didn't become a crisis until the attack in the Low Countries in the spring of 1940.

CHARLES BOHLEN
US diplomat in Moscow

I think that the history of isolationism is very simple. When the colonies were first united into the United States of America they were very weak militarily, economically and politically throughout the country. It was a time when the Napoleonic wars were going on and George Washington in his farewell address admonished the people of this country not to get drawn into quarrels that were not their own, not to form political alliances

---

* Stanley Baldwin (1867–1947), British Prime Minister 1923–24, 1924–29, 1935–37.

with countries in Europe but to try and deal with trade and matters of that kind equally with other countries. I think that, in the circumstances, made a good deal of sense. In addition, the United States government started with a strip of colonies along the east coast and then they found they had an entire continent to play with and they saw no particular reason for getting involved in quarrels in which they didn't feel their interests were directly involved. The United States was extremely fortunately located geographically with two wide oceans protecting either side and I think this just became a habit, an instinctive habit, on the part of American public opinion. When World War One came and we finally got into it in 1917, we fought that like a boxing match. We went into the ring, we helped to defeat the enemy, came back, hung up our gloves and went back to what we thought was the main task of developing this continent.

ANTHONY EDEN

In January 1938 President Roosevelt sent Chamberlain as Prime Minister a private message saying how disturbed he was with the state of the world and increasing disrespect for engagements and treaties, piling up of armament and so on. He wanted to make a great effort to try and stop this and he suggested that he should call together the diplomatic corps in Washington one day and they would try to produce a few suggestions for our various differences and difficulties and these were then to be discussed if they were thought reasonable by the larger, more important powers. Our ambassador in Washington was Lindsay, a very experienced diplomatist who'd been head of the Foreign Office and also our ambassador in Berlin before he went to Washington. He sent this message across endorsing it strongly and urging a quick and cordial response. Without consulting me or any of the Cabinet, Chamberlain returned a reply of cold water. The Foreign Office was much disturbed at this development and cabled me in the south of France to return. I was deeply disturbed because Lindsay, in one of his telegrams, had warned us that if we argue against this too much we might undo all the good work we'd done in the last two years, and to me the Anglo-American relations were capital. Just the one chance, I thought, that we can get closer together stage by stage, that we might avert the war. I telephoned to Lindsay and told him I was going to see the Prime Minister at Chequers, which I did the next day and then we had our first serious difference. He was more optimistic than I could be of the outcome of the present discussions with Hitler and Mussolini, and he felt the American proposals were woolly and that they would get in the way of his negotiations. I felt on the contrary that Roosevelt was trying to get into the business to try to help in the only way he could – with his strong isolationist lobby he couldn't do it any other way. I thought any American presence in Europe would be quite invaluable in that very difficult time so I couldn't agree. There's no doubt that Cadogan and I would have resigned had we been able to do so on that issue in January 1938, but we couldn't, obviously, without putting Roosevelt in the most embarrassing position, as it would have made public what he was trying to do. So after that it really was a question of waiting for the next issue because we knew it couldn't last.

RAB BUTLER

Our Chiefs of Staff, particularly General Ironside, expressed themselves in no uncertain terms about the paucity of our own armaments. There were not enough anti-aircraft guns and the radar, which a year later covered the whole country from Scotland to the south, was not really in existence.*

ROBERT BOOTHBY
British Conservative MP

I think the final verdict lies with Churchill: he said there could have been no air Battle of Britain in 1938. We might have suffered some grievous casualties from being bombed for which we were lamentably unprepared, but those Germans would have had to fly from German bases with airfighter protection which was quite inadequate and couldn't cover them all the way to these shores, and nothing like the Battle of Britain could have taken place until they'd occupied the coasts of Holland, Belgium

---

* Field Marshal Sir Edmund Ironside (1880–1959), Chief of the Imperial General Staff 1939–40.

and France. Munich was one of the greatest disasters in British and French history. We could have called his bluff and we could almost certainly have got rid of him and in my firm conviction if Beneš had stood firm and said, 'I'm going to fight, and you're going to support me,' we could either have beaten them in a matter of weeks or else there would have been no war and the German generals' plot would have been carried into execution.*

The 'Peace in Our Time' document signed by Hitler and Chamberlain on 30 September 1938

We, the German Führer and Chancellor and the British Prime Minister, have had a further meeting today and are agreed in recognising that the question of Anglo-German relations is of the first importance for the two countries and for Europe.

We regard the agreement signed last night and the Anglo-German Naval agreement as symbolic of the desire of our two peoples never to go to war with one another again.

We are resolved that the method of consultation shall be the method adopted to deal with any other questions that may concern our two countries, and we are determined to continue our efforts to remove possible sources of difference and thus to contribute to assure the peace of Europe.

ANTHONY EDEN

To put it bluntly, how much better it would have been if the Czech crisis had arisen a year later, at the time when [the] Polish crisis arose and we had to go to war. A much better military position from every other point of view. Therefore, whatever case can be made technically on the delay ground, what seems to me to be utterly wrong was the failure to gather the nation together for a supreme effort of rearmament after Munich to create a national government. Because the truth was, until we got Labour into the government, you cannot really do a full-out rearmament programme.

---

* Edvard Beneš (1884–1948), President of Czechoslovakia 1935–38, in exile 1940–45, 1945–48.

ROBERT BOOTHBY

There's absolutely no doubt that Germany gained enormously from the year's delay in the outbreak of war as a result of Munich and we have it on irrefutable authority from all the German generals and from various historical sources. The Czechs had the strongest fortified line in Europe on their northern frontier and they had thirty well-trained, well-armed divisions. Against which Germany could only put thirty-three or thirty-four. Two of the senior German generals said that the line was almost impregnable. On the west they had eight reserve divisions and five regular divisions against ninety French divisions, and a 'West Wall', which another German general described as purely a construction site. All the German generals were convinced that if war broke out over Czechoslovakia in September 1938 they would have been defeated in about three weeks and I think that has been borne out. They had intended to arrest Hitler and proclaim a military government and they were prevented from doing so by the sudden announcement of Neville Chamberlain's flight to see Hitler – and that's what stopped them, to wait and see what happened. And then events flowed and Munich was in fact the biggest bluff ever known in history. The German General Staff stood abashed because they knew they must be defeated if we'd gone to war then.

DR TOKATY

From about 1933 the vast Soviet propaganda machine advocated an idea, quite rightly, that the greatest danger to our country was growing Nazism. Parallel to this, especially from the mid-Thirties, the Soviet propaganda developed one idea, with which I agreed entirely, that Hitlerism represented the most barbaric form of social organisation of our times.

ALBERT SPEER
Hitler's Chief Architect 1934–42
The same day when we got the news that a pact was signed in Moscow between Germany and Russia, the armed forces showed to Hitler the

movie of the last parade before the Kremlin in Moscow.* Hitler was very impressed and that this is a very strong army and was glad that since the signing of the pact this army was no more on the other side. Then after we had entered Poland and our troops met the Russian troops at their borderlines the officers came to Hitler and reported to him, said those Russian troops are very badly equipped and in poor condition; he first didn't believe it properly but then when the Russians started their attack against the Finns and they hadn't had any success Hitler remembered those facts which were told him from his officers, and he said obviously those reports were true – I had in this time the impression that Hitler was convinced that he has to deal with a weak army concerning Russia.

DR TOKATY

Here we are, we call ourselves a socialist country – we were told twenty-four hours a day without interruption that Nazism was the most barbaric social and political system and then suddenly we're declared to be progressive allies. We were told that Hitler, Mussolini and Japanese militarism represented nothing more than the vanguard of general capitalist front against the USSR. And then suddenly they become our ally, we were brothers. I found this more than my heart could swallow; I generally never hate anything but this is the one thing which I think really for the first time [I] use the word 'hate'. I couldn't accommodate myself any more with Stalin's system.

DINGLE FOOT

You must remember that in the early stages of the war, before the Nazis attacked Russia, the *Daily Worker* was thoroughly against the war effort, denounced it as an imperialist war. Their tune changed after 22nd June 1941.**

---

* The pact signed by foreign ministers Molotov and Ribbentrop on 23 August 1939 had secret provisions for 'territorial rearrangements' at the expense of Estonia, Finland, Latvia, Lithuania, Poland and Romania.
** The *Daily Worker* was the organ of the British Communist Party, which under Harry Pollitt (1890–1960) was the most Moscow-servile of all the European Communist parties.

RAB BUTLER

The Polish, as well as the Romanian and Greek undertakings, emerged from the rape of Czechoslovakia in March 1939 and the Foreign Office were absolutely determined to see that there would be a stop to Hitler at some point. I've often heard the Polish guarantee criticised because physically we really couldn't do anything about it and though it was a military guarantee, it was in essence political – it was really to show Hitler that if he decided to go on seizing one country after another we would have to come in. I know that [Foreign Secretary Lord] Halifax thought this would make war inevitable and he wasn't surprised when we got to 3rd September 1939.

COLONEL SIEGFRIED WESTPHAL
German Staff Officer

This was an absolute bluff. I cannot remember exactly the number of divisions, I think from Emden to Switzerland we had about seven or eight active divisions, and all other were jumbled up. We had no armoured cars; all other active divisions did fight in Poland. The whole Air Force was in Poland. If the French attacked during the September we had not been able to stem them longer than one or two weeks, and the war on the Western Front had been decided before the German division for Poland were able to help us. I think Hitler was very strengthened by this situation.

JOHN COLVILLE

When war broke out Chamberlain was a strong patriot. He realised that he'd done everything he could and nobody could say that he had not done the utmost to prevent the holocaust and he threw himself into the preparations for war. Deep down he still hoped that the major clash of armies could be avoided: he thought, misled by intelligence reports and reports from foreigners who had been in Germany, that Germany was on the brink of starvation or would be brought to starvation by economic warfare. He also thought the German people didn't support Hitler, that this was a clique, and if we did our propaganda properly there would be a revolt of the generals or somebody against Hitler. Dropping propaganda leaflets by Bomber Command of the RAF rather than bombs was a good way of conducting the war.

ROBERT BOOTHBY

The opening phase of the war was [one] of the most extraordinary periods through which I've lived. For a long time there was quite a lot of unemployment, while the Germans were manufacturing arms at full stretch, particularly in the Skoda works in Czechoslovakia where half the tanks that subsequently defeated France featured. All this time the Germans were a beehive of activity, we were doing absolutely nothing. We'd gone to war for the defence of Poland, we'd given a unilateral guarantee to Poland and in the event we did nothing to help Poland at all. For the first three months of the war the greatest number of casualties were in the blackout and we confined our war effort to dropping leaflets on the German people, telling them that it was a bad idea to go to war and that it was a pity that they had done it, and perhaps we might make peace. It affected even Churchill, who was First Lord of the Admiralty at the time. At lunch one day he said to me, 'I have the impression that Hitler's Germany is more brittle than the Kaiser's Germany, and that it will collapse more quickly.' And all the government were with the idea that we could fight this war without fighting it. And that's what happened – it was called the Phoney War and the Phoney War it was. All the time the Germans were building up their armaments. The whole object of the Munich agreement was to get the Russians out of Europe and give us time to build up our armaments and instead we gave the Germans time – we gave them nearly two years and by that time they were in a position to strike.

GEORGE HODGKINSON
Coventry town councillor

The members of our War Emergency Committee here felt that not enough attention had been given to the situation that would be created if a town was hit by saturation bombing. The suggestion to plaster up the windows with tape, for instance, in our view was futile and nonsensical. Impractical and it was useless. There was not enough appreciation that this was a total war and all our resources both locally and nationally, even politically, ought to have been organised in order to defeat Hitler completely and handsomely.

RAB BUTLER

Fundamentally, like the younger Pitt, Chamberlain was a man of peace and a good Chancellor of the Exchequer, and especially a good Health Minister. He wasn't used to the idea of war at all. He did have a go at foreign policy, it wasn't very easy for him, but he wasn't a great War Minister. I remember when the outbreak of war came and we were in the Cabinet Room at the moment the ultimatum expired and we were just beginning to congratulate the Prime Minister on his broadcast, when we heard a terrible wailing which was the first air-raid siren, and we all began to laugh. But Churchill and Chamberlain took it very seriously and his wife then appeared with an enormous basket full of things for the night and Thermos flasks, so we all went to the shelters. I went, after some delay, to the Foreign Office. The whole of Horse Guards was completely empty of people and I, when I got there, there was no furniture so I had to sit on the floor, and an air-raid warden said there would be no gas attack. But of course there wasn't really any war for some time, quite apart from there being no petrol.

JOHN COLVILLE

In the late winter of 1939 and the early part of 1940 the situation was a curious one. The great powers had declared war and absolutely nothing was happening, everybody was sitting biting their fingernails and expecting the bombs to fall. In this period storms brewed in teacups, storms which would certainly never have occurred at all if there'd been fighting taking place. And one of them was very much connected with the Secretary of State for War, Leslie Hore-Belisha, a remarkable man, extremely intelligent, ambitious, but unfortunately he had several defects. He was very publicity conscious and in those days that was looked upon with some suspicion by a great many people. His genuine desire was to make the Army a popular force; he wanted to get recruits and he thought by improving conditions of the ordinary soldiers, building new barracks, improving the food and by being photographed a lot with the troops he could help to improve the image of the Army. Secondly he had such a quick mind that he found it hard to tolerate those whose minds were moved slowly; he had a way of being brisk and sometimes bad-mannered with senior officers and civil servants. It was well known he was relying almost entirely for all his decisions on the advice of military theorist Captain Basil Liddell Hart. Captain Liddell Hart was a very remarkable and praiseworthy character – but he was the military correspondent of *The Times* newspaper and the generals found it hard to tolerate that a newspaper correspondent was running the War Office.

DR SAMUELSON

The US economy was converting to wartime before Pearl Harbor. Just as in World War One, when the belligerents in Europe sent us orders and that activated our economy, that was already happening from 1939. In the United States this happened through ordinary commercial channels but we were also sympathetic to the Allied side and were already beginning to give aid.

JOHN COLVILLE

The campaigns in Norway, British mining of Norwegian waters followed immediately by German invasion in April and Allied counter-attacks in May 1940, were acceptable to Chamberlain because it kept the war distant. It meant it would be localised and perhaps a miracle would happen, perhaps Hitler would die or be assassinated and the whole thing would end with the minimum of bloodshed.

RAB BUTLER

The idea was to save the iron deposits from the Germans and make an expedition to Norway which would also distract Germany from the over-running of France. But the danger of it was first Norwegian neutrality and secondly we weren't fully prepared for it, and it was in fact a complete failure. It was a providential thing that Churchill, although having had a great part in it, was not blamed for it in the House of Commons. Chamberlain got the blame – and he was Prime Minister and he had approved the policy

– but it meant that Churchill was then free in 1940, in May, to take over and become the great war leader that he was.

MAJOR MARTIN LINDSAY
Norway Expeditionary Force
I'm not suggesting it altered the course of history but I went straight up to see Labour leader Clement Attlee on the morning of the first day of the debate and I gave him a memorandum about the appalling improvisation and deficiencies in Norway because I was quite convinced that we should lose the war if we went on like that. He gave it to deputy Labour leader Herbert Morrison to help him open for the Opposition that afternoon.

ROBERT BOOTHBY
The Norway debate 7th–8th May 1940 was the only decisive debate I ever attended during my thirty-four years as a member of the House of Commons, because it was the only division which brought about the fall of the government. Gradually the temperature began to rise and when Herbert Morrison announced they were going to divide at the end of the debate against the government, there was an action group, of which Liberal Party leader Clement Davies was chairman and I was secretary, committed to pressing for more decisive action during the war. It was an enormously attended meeting, there were a great many Conservative Members of Parliament there and I felt something was happening. The meeting was passionate, and I felt that a great many Conservative members were not only prepared to abstain in the division but even to vote against the government.

MAJOR LINDSAY
At that particular time there were three main strands in political parties. First of all the large mass of Conservative supporters who were still mesmerised by Chamberlain's deadly decency. There were more than two dozen active Conservative opponents who included some of the greatest names in contemporary history and who were outright against the government and led mainly the service MPs into the Lobby against the

government, because to Tory MPs in the Services it was quite obvious that we couldn't go on as we had been doing at that time. The third, of course, were the Labour and Liberal members, who right up to the outbreak of the war had opposed rearmament, most of them, and even complained that the existing effort was too great.

RAB BUTLER

There was a very passionate atmosphere because there had been all this bitterness piling up before the opening of the war, first against Munich and then against the delay after Munich. So for nearly a year before the debate there had been anguish in the breasts of people who wanted Britain to go all out and win the war against Hitler and so the debate was a fierce one. Not only the Labour opposition, who afterwards came in to support Churchill, but also Conservative. I remember Chamberlain going to his room afterwards and saying he wondered whether this could go on. It wasn't until the next day that he really realised that his number was up. On that day the Whips tried to explain to him that it might have been worse but those of us who were with him could see the writing on the wall by that time.

ROBERT BOOTHBY

Meanwhile Churchill had been putting up a great defence of the government and it was ironical again because the debate was about Norway and Norway had been a series of disasters which I think were avoidable. He was directly responsible as First Lord of the Admiralty. [Liberal MD Leo] Amery made a famous speech in which he quoted Cromwell's words: 'You have been here long enough for any good you have done – in the name of God go.' Lloyd George came down and made the most devastating speech, in which he concluded by saying to Chamberlain, 'You have asked the nation for sacrifices but there is the sacrifice of your own office,' and I saw Chamberlain blush when he said that. It was the last effective speech Lloyd George made in the House of Commons.* Meanwhile Churchill

---

* David Lloyd George (1863–1945), a reformist pre-1914 Chancellor of the Exchequer, was Prime Minister 1916–22 of the most corrupt administration in modern British history.

was looking more and more uncomfortable because hostility was concentrated on him, oddly enough, as well on the government as a whole. The Conservative majority fell to eighty and that meant the fall of the government. Chamberlain asked for friendship from those who were his friends and he hadn't got it and he walked out of the chamber a solitary figure and I felt very sorry for him at that moment – he knew he was done, and he was determined to resign.

RAB BUTLER
Halifax had led the country away from the appeasement policy during the summer at the beginning of the war, and he had proven himself, and indeed was in India as a Viceroy, a very able Minister. But being in the House of Lords he wasn't really very well known. I never thought that the National Government with Labour idea would work with Halifax and the Labour leaders came to realise in their own ways that Churchill would be better. I had a frank talk with Halifax and I came to the conclusion that he simply didn't want to do it, and under the circumstances, with crisis looming and virtually being in the war alone, it's no good to have a man as Prime Minister who doesn't want to do it. And if you've got somebody straining at the leash, you'll probably get a better deal from him. So I really agreed with Halifax's decision.*

JOHN COLVILLE
Churchill was viewed with grave misgivings by the Establishment. Everybody at 10 Downing Street and Whitehall, the Cabinet Officers, among soldiers, sailors and airmen and in very large sectors of the Conservative Party and to some extent the Labour Party were frightened of Churchill, they thought he was an adventurer. They did not want to see the fortunes of the country at a most critical moment in its whole history handed over to somebody who might do the most extraordinary things and undertake the most astonishing adventures. They all realised that

---

* Edward Wood, Viscount Halifax (1881–1959), Foreign Secretary 1938–40, strongly urged seeking terms from Germany following the Fall of France.

Norway, this fiasco from which we had just been saved in the nick of time, was largely the inspiration of Churchill. It was a very fine idea but it didn't work. Halifax was safe, he was clever, a fellow of All Souls College, Oxford, a man of indisputable charm and absolute integrity, and it was hoped that he would perhaps be sent for by the King. Churchill would be a gamble and when you're in it, at a very serious moment of your lives, a gamble is not the thing to undertake.

ROBERT BOOTHBY

The Germans attacked the West on the 10th May 1940 as many of us had foreseen they would. I had spent a year and a half before in a little town in Switzerland watching their preparations across the Swiss frontier while we were doing nothing at all. I had received private warnings from friends in Belgium and Holland where I had been invited by Churchill to go and try and get some arms. I had no doubt that a German attack on a great scale was impending. And then Chamberlain thought in these circumstances, although he had made up his mind to resign, he ought to carry on. Political henchmen in the House of Commons told him that this was such an emergency that only a National Government could met the occasion and he said he must resign. He sent for Churchill and Halifax who were the only possible alternatives. The Labour Party made it quite clear through Party leader Clement Attlee and [Deputy Leader] Arthur Greenwood that they would never serve in any government under Neville Chamberlain, but they would under Halifax or Churchill. Halifax refused on the ground that he was in the House of Lords and couldn't conduct a war as Prime Minister unless he was a member of the House of Commons – which he couldn't be in those days. And therefore the mantle fell upon Churchill. Despite the Norwegian fiasco and the debate in which he defended the government, he became Prime Minister and formed the National Government which steered us to victory.

RAB BUTLER

The decision was largely taken by Halifax who told me he had a pain in his stomach an hour or two before the meeting and did not really want to be Prime Minister; whereas the man who really did want to be Prime Minister was quite determined on it. Chamberlain was rather hesitant because he favoured Halifax: after the India controversy of the years before, Churchill was regarded as being unsound and a rogue element. It was only when he took over with his marvellous broadcasts and all that he gradually began to get control of the nation. The people saw what an absolutely perfect Prime Minister he was for these occasions.

JOHN COLVILLE

I remember Churchill telling us that the critical moment came when Chamberlain asked Halifax and the three of them were there. Chamberlain suddenly turned to Churchill and said, 'Tell me, Winston, do you see any reason why in the twentieth century a Prime Minister should not be in the House of Lords?' and Churchill thought that this was a trap because if he said no, he thought Chamberlain would turn up to Halifax and say, 'If the King were to ask my advice I could perhaps suggest you.' On the other hand it was very difficult for him to say yes because there could be no alternative but himself, and so he turned round and stood staring over Horse Guards Parade and did not reply to the question.

CHRISTABEL BIELENBERG
Englishwoman married to an anti-Nazi German lawyer
The German opposition always felt that they would have to have the bulk of the German people with them if they didn't want to turn Hitler into a martyr, but that would change if he proved himself to have led the Germans to destruction. And they certainly pinned their hopes on the fact that if he did declare war on the West – this was after the Polish war – if he did make an active war, if what was called in Germany the Phoney War ever became no longer phoney, then he would have to attack the Maginot line, and it was the opinion of the generality in Germany that it would cost the German Army five hundred thousand men at least, and the opposition felt that would be the moment to strike. Well, as one knows very well, the Maginot line was circumvented and that did not happen.

CHAPTER 4

BATTLE OF THE ATLANTIC 1939–40

The Battle of the Atlantic, so fundamental to eventual Allied success, rolled on continuously from 1939 to 1945 but, for convenience, is divided here into three periods. The first, during the Phoney War, was characterised by failed strategies and mishaps on both sides. The Allies counted on a naval blockade to exercise the suffocating effect it had in 1914–18, although with the Soviet Union now supplying Nazi Germany with everything it needed, blockade could not be effective. The Germans calculated that the surface raiders that had put to sea before the outbreak of war would cause disproportionate disruption to British trade, but they were rapidly eliminated. U-boats scored early successes but the swift introduction of convoys limited the damage and the bulk of German anti-shipping activity was devoted to mine-laying off British ports by surface ships, submarines and aircraft. A counter to the magnetic mine (degaussing) was soon developed and Allied shipping also suffered less than it might because of a design flaw in the magnetic pistols on German torpedoes. Losses during the first four months were still significant: 323 ships, nearly a million tons. The Admiralty under Winston Churchill, meanwhile, used submarine hunting groups formed around aircraft carriers to search for U-boat needles in the immense haystack of the Atlantic instead of providing close escort for the convoys. The folly of such tactics was promptly underlined by the loss on 17 September of the aircraft carrier HMS Courageous *to* U-29. *On 14 October, Günther Prien in* U-46 *penetrated the Royal Navy's principal base at Scapa Flow and sank the battleship HMS* Royal Oak. *Following a lull during the extremely cold winter of 1940–41, when many U-boats were frozen into their Baltic bases, the entire Kriegsmarine was committed to the invasion of Norway and suffered devastating losses. However, the capture of the French Atlantic ports a month later freed the U-boat arm from the shackles imposed by Britain's geographical position across its lines of access to the Atlantic, and more than doubled its effective fighting power.*

ADMIRAL KARL DÖNITZ
Commander U-boats 1939–43

In October 1918 I was captain of a submarine and in the Mediterranean, near Malta, in a dark night I met a British convoy with schooners and destroyers and I attacked and sank a ship. But after this I had to dive and then by a fault in the construction my boat was sinking and the depth of the water, the water was three or four thousand metres deep. I made it possible to come to the surface again, but then I had to go out of the boat with the whole crew. A British destroyer stopped and we came on board. I had the impression that there was a difference in our treatment because I thought that the captain of the destroyer had the feeling 'They are warriors and they had their orders like we too'. When I came home it was clear to me that it was only by chance in that light to find this British convoy, but the chance would have been very much greater if they would not have been only one submarine but a lot of submarines – and there were a lot of ships. And that is why I developed the idea to wolf-pack, to put the submarines together in all the years from 1918 until in 1935 we had the first submarines again.

COMMANDER PETER GRETTON
Royal Navy, Escort Group Commander 1942–43

The British Army is always accused of fighting a new war with the lessons of the past. Well, no one can accuse the Royal Navy of doing this. In 1919 we promptly forgot all the lessons of the last war, particularly the most unpleasant ones, and as a result the crisis of the spring of 1917, when the German U-boat attack was sinking hundreds and thousands of tons of Allied shipping every month, was completely forgotten. As a result very few preparations were made for protection of shipping in a new war. Some were made: the sonar-projection set Asdic was making considerable progress, but unfortunately far too optimistic claims were made for it and as a result we did not build nearly enough escort ships, and the Air Force didn't get enough anti-submarine aircraft for the job needed.

VERNON MINER

Merchant seaman

We'd come through a long period of depression and the ships were old; they hadn't been replaced even though there were tramp-ship subsidies in the Thirties. The wages of the seamen had depreciated since the end of the First World War and the conditions would take a long time to alter, to raise up any standard at all. The men that were sailing were basically seamen and this was their career from which they'd started out, and having come through this period of depression where they were so long unemployed that they never dared leave their ship. They were only too glad of the permanency of employment, the fact that all ships of whatever type were going to be running.

COMMANDER GRETTON

Despite the fact that the lessons had shown that air cover had a magical effect on convoy protection, and stopped attacks altogether, Coastal Command started the war with far too few aircraft and its main role was looking for surface ships instead of the anti-submarine role. What's more, cooperation between the Navy and Air Force was then very bad indeed, mainly due to stupid quarrels among senior officers in Whitehall.

VERNON MINER

If anybody decided they wouldn't sail then they were subject to the Merchant Shipping Act, which has now been changed – in 1971 – and could have been sentenced to a term of imprisonment not exceeding three months. I never thought we were paid commensurate with the risks we ran. The normal comparison that seamen made during the war of their wage for the hours they worked was with the ammunition workers who, we heard at the time, were making a fabulous amount of money for no more risk than a housewife left at home.

SEAMAN EDWARD BUTLER
Escort-ship crewman

We used to read in the papers about bombing Germany and coming back and often the lads would say, 'Well, I wouldn't mind just going over there for a couple of hours and coming back for a good night's kip.' When you're tossing your guts out on the deck for nearly three weeks at a time, there and back three weeks, a total of six weeks, it's a pretty tough life.

ADMIRAL DÖNITZ

Britain's sea trade across the Atlantic was of vital importance to her: British sea power must be able to control the trading routes and most of her food and raw materials and her armaments comes across the Atlantic. The most important strategic object of an enemy of England is to attack these routes, that is why in a war Germany had to send her warships into the Atlantic, and they had to be able to stay for a large enough time in the Atlantic in order to fight against the ships on the British sea routes.

VERNON MINER

One ship I sailed on broke down and we went to Cardiff for repairs, and leaving Cardiff she broke down and was repaired at Milford Haven. Eventually left in convoy, broke down off Anglesey and went to Birkenhead for repairs, left Birkenhead, anchored in the Mersey, broke down there – couldn't raise the anchor. Left with a convoy, too slow to maintain a convoy speed of seven knots. The steering gear bust in a gale, the chain steering gear, the spring buffers parted, it was a common occurrence with that kind of steering gear. I think everything that could have gone wrong with that ship went wrong, until a couple of U-boats sunk it for us.

ADMIRAL DÖNITZ

If from the point of view of the geographical situation of Germany is considered, then it is easy to see how unfavourable it was for the German surface warships to perform this task – they had to go on the surface from the distant German base, the long way through the North Sea until they could go north of [the] Shetland Islands, westward into the Atlantic Ocean.

CAPTAIN GILBERT ROBERTS
Director, Tactical Unit, Western Approaches, Liverpool
History books will tell you that at the end of the first war aircraft did operate alongside of, or with, the convoys and that from that moment on there was a very significant drop in the sinking of merchant ships. But this wasn't done in the first part of the second war and aircraft seemed to be going out into the Atlantic with their own plans and told to work by themselves.

EDWARD BUTLER
We always seemed to get the 'Rear End Charlie' of a convoy, the rear position, and we were always turning round to go and investigate why a ship was falling behind and this again entailed turning around in heavy seas, and the amount of crockery that was broken and the gear that swirled around, tables overturning if they weren't secured properly. There was always something that went wrong if you turned around. They tried to warn you, probably said, 'We're turning 180 degrees in five minutes' time', then the turn, and you'd get a full wave and everything would go over – pots, pans and all your cutlery would be smashed – and next morning you'd be fighting for a cup to have a cup of tea.

PILOT OFFICER WILFRID OULTON
Coastal Command
Throughout the Twenties and Thirties the techniques of over-water flying and navigation, and all the necessary techniques for Coastal Command were certainly being practised. But only in very, very small numbers and generally speaking they were steered towards cooperation with the Navy and not in the anti-submarine field, which was not part of the requirement laid on Coastal Command. You cannot switch from one role to another at five minutes' notice: it needs the development of equipment, the development of training methods, the development of tactics and it takes time to

do all these things. So at the beginning of the war Coastal Command had a small number of very, very competent people and an enormous dilution of only partially trained people. So naturally the overall result to begin with was not what one could hope for.

VERNON MINER

I've no idea what the government paid for the tramp steamers. I should imagine they probably would have paid any price because we needed the ships, but I would suggest that they paid a lot more than the actual scrap value of the ships. I've no doubt that some of the ship owners were unscrupulous. Freight rates rose very rapidly because of the possibility of loss, but I'm afraid the increase in freights did not come the way of the seamen in the way of benefits and better accommodation. There's many millionaires who are around today who made their money through shipping in either one or both the world wars through the very high insurance on the ships because of the freight rates being raised and because of the possible loss of the ship, and through not paying sufficient attention to the upkeep of the ships, to the maintenance.

ADMIRAL DÖNITZ

Firstly, in these years before 1939 the U-boat was very less suited for the underwater torpedo attack. We also knew that the British had an invention, the Asdic, with which they could hear underwater submarine already by a distance of some thousand metres in every case. It was true that this instrument picked up all the other noises, for instance the sea waves and the noise of their own ships. This made it difficult to find the noises of German submarines so the British Asdic had its advantage but did not make an underwater attack by a U-boat impossible in every case. Secondly, the German U-boats in 1939 had a higher surface speed than they had in the First World War; that is why they were on the surface more manoeuvrable than before, and that is why they were very appropriate for surface torpedo attack at night. The U-boat had only a small silhouette consisting only of the conning-tower and that is why the submarine could only be seen with difficulty during a night attack. Gradual development in communications meant the submarines were no longer obliged to fight alone, but they could attack together. This enabled us to develop the wolf-pack tactics which became very useful against the British convoys.

COMMANDER GRETTON

After a tremendous amount of discussion between the wars it was eventually agreed that convoys would be the system used for trade protection. But unfortunately the ships set aside for trade-protection duties, instead of being used to escort the convoys, were organised into hunting groups and during the first few months of the war they spent a lot of useless time steaming many miles searching for U-boats without any success whatever.

VERNON MINER

The first time I was under attack I was on the wheel, I was steering the ship when the lookout reported that there was a U-boat on the starboard beam. The Chief Officer who was in charge of the watch ordered me to alter course to bring the U-boat astern of us. My feeling was one of excitement. This is it, I'm going to come home covered with glory – decorated – I'll strangle these submarines with my bare hands. Then the firing started and the first shell that hit the ship, the ship shuddered. There was a loud crack from it rather than a bang. There's a feeling that God is on your side but he certainly wasn't, and this is the period when it's frightening, the moment of truth. The order to abandon ship eventually comes and you look down on that grey North Atlantic, which doesn't look all that bad from the deck of a ship about twenty feet above the water but down at lifeboat level it looks rather ominous, and that's frightening also.

WILLIAM CLARK
Merchant seaman
When I saw all the other ships of the convoy going past and leaving us I did have a sickening feeling that this was going to be for a long time, because it was what I had done with other ships, like known they were torpedoed and we'd gone on, and I hadn't heard whether they'd been picked up. They always did say that there was a sort of straggler in the

convoy that was picking these chaps up so I did hope that this was going to happen to us. But I didn't feel so good when I saw them all passing. Anyway, after a few hours HMS *Sunflower* arrived on the scene and picked us up. It was quite exciting then getting on board and they made us as comfortable as they could because it was very crowded with other survivors and immediately you went into action. You was on deck at the time and before you could say very much you sighted this U-boat and attempted to ram it. Everybody thought we'd cut it in half. I was very surprised years later to find that it had survived. There was so much action during the few days I was on the *Sunflower*, depth-charges would make it ring like a bell, you know, and it was such a fragile ship it just seemed it couldn't take all that punishment. I had a really good view from the funnel where I took up my living space because I didn't want to be shut down below when the action started and I took to living by the funnel – warm, and you could move around and see what action was going on.

CAPTAIN THOMAS D FINCH

Merchant Navy, SS San Emiliano*

I had plenty of water, plenty of food so I wasn't worried on that score, but I had in the boat some injured people and no medical supplies. After a short while, to my horror, the first one to die was the young First Steward – he was only seventeen. He hadn't complained at all during the night of pain or anything. I went to him, took the blanket from him and his whole stomach had been ripped away, his intestines were hanging out. We had to bury him so we wrapped him in the blanket and slid him over the side and continued on our way. It was a terrible thing to have to do that. The next one to go was not long afterwards – he was in a terrible state, I've never seen anything like it as far as injuries. We buried him and carried on a wee bit and about ten o'clock we heard some sounds of an aircraft and sure enough one appeared very low and flew over us two or three times and opened the bomb doors and was trying to signal to us but we couldn't

---

* The *San Emiliano* was in fact sunk in 1942; this vivid extract is included here as a generic description of what merchant seamen faced, and knew they faced, every time they put to sea.

make out what he meant. I tried to signal back to him that I wanted medical supplies, pointing to the other injured people that were lying in the boat wrapped up, I wanted help for them, and he waved his hand and seemed to understand and came back later and dropped a wooden cask of water and as soon as it hit the sea it burst so we signalled to him that was no use and off he went again. We did use the parachute: we cut strips up because most of us were naked, we just had wisps of clothing left on, and we used the parachute cloth to soak in the sea water and bind these burns up to keep them cool and moist, and to make a shelter over the wounded just to keep the sun from them. Just about dusk he appeared again and this time he dropped what seemed to us a milk can and this had some food and some cigarettes but no medical supplies. But there was a message to say help was coming so we thought let's hope it does. We continued on our way and shortly after the Second Officer died, this must have been about eleven o'clock and we put him over the side the same as the others. By this time it was a boat-load of misery, pain and death. The young Senior Apprentice was terribly burned and he was singing away but I think this was more or less in an unconscious sort of way. He was singing with the hope of raising the morale of the people but he died about midday.

LIEUTENANT RAYMOND HART
Commanding destroyer HMS Vidette

The ship I was commanding was designed for the North Sea and for short World War One sorties by the Grand Fleet. She was certainly not designed for the Atlantic weather. One had to handle her very carefully in bad weather – it was extremely worrying with very heavy seas and I've known occasions where one literally had not been able to turn the ship around when she had very little fuel, with a very small metacentric height. On one occasion I found myself five miles from the convoy in the morning as I didn't dare risk turning round at night for fear of literally broaching to. The other anxiety in a ship that age was the metal fatigue we suffered. Frequently the plates used to split a little – it wasn't particularly danger-ous but on one occasion I had only forty tons of usable fuel because salt water got into the fuel tanks.

SEAMAN BUTLER

One particular instance I remember when we went over during the winter and the spray and the seas were coming over and it was freezing – the ice was freezing on everything on the upper deck and the captain had to turn all hands to chip it off because it was fast becoming over top weight and there was a very severe danger of the ship capsizing. So we had to work during the night, in complete darkness as well, to get the ice off.

COMMANDER GRETTON

Convoy defence is not a very glamorous affair and between the wars, I think rather naturally, the Navy were inclined to concentrate on more glamorous activities like great mass torpedo attacks and that sort of thing. All the information about the lessons of World War One were available and for those who bothered to read them the lessons were there. But I'm afraid no one bothered and as a result trade defence as a whole was very badly neglected. It's easy to say this now, but I was as bad as anyone else at the time and I speak entirely in the light of hindsight.

ADMIRAL DÖNITZ

As the war against England had come contrary to the wishes of our political leaders, now we had to do everything to create our missing naval armament for a sea war against England. When the war began we only had twenty-six submarines which were able to go far into the Atlantic Ocean, of these boats only one-third on average would be operating in the Atlantic, because the other boats would be sailing to or from port or at home being repaired. With this small number any decisive success was not possible. That's why it was necessary for the building of submarines to get first place in the German armament plan. But this was not done in spite of all the requests made by Admiral Raeder, Chief of the German Navy. So in February 1941 we still only had twenty-two submarines which could go in to the Atlantic Ocean because our construction of new U-boats had not even replaced the losses we suffered in the war so far.

PILOT OFFICER OULTON

Coastal Command stations were sited on the outer edges of the land – in Cornwall, in Iceland, on little islands off Scotland, in Northern Ireland – and they were all in remote cow pastures with a village alongside, a little cluster of Nissen huts, a runway which was often not adequate and not very good support facilities. So the crews were living under poorish conditions despite the efforts of the administrative staff and operating without the aids which today you would expect aviation to have. So the problems of simply getting to the patrol area and back again, never mind any interference with the enemy, were daunting and really a triumph every time a sortie was accomplished. And particularly for young and inexperienced aircrew this was really a very severe task indeed. As time went on they became more skilful and better equipment was brought in. Navigation aids were introduced – the introduction of radar helped a great deal – and with improved training it took about three years to reach a reasonable standard of performance.

LIEUTENANT HART

I think that if the weather was reasonably good one didn't have very much on one's mind except to ensure that the crew were as well looked after as possible. We exercised action stations and our communications were good, and the next anxiety was when one had to refuel at sea. This was an art we hadn't developed very seriously before the war. I think it was something we neglected and it was quite an operation and quite an evolution. This certainly worried me very considerably: if one hadn't got fuel one would just have got stuck in the Atlantic and have to be towed home, so this was an operation we began to worry about twenty-four hours before it happened.

COMMANDER GRETTON

It took nearly two years before we had anything like the right sort of cooperation between ships and aircraft, which was inexcusable. It was a disgrace and a tragedy that so many ships were sunk and so many lives were lost unnecessarily during those first few years.

CAPTAIN WILLIAM EYTON-JONES

Merchant Navy, SS Ben Vrachie

I don't think the Merchant Navy's role was recognised – it's a silent service. We lost one out of every three men and without them this nation wouldn't have survived more than three or four months. They did a wonderful job of work and I can't praise them highly enough, wonderful people. Sometime after, on another ship I was rejoined by the old boatswain and other men from the lifeboat and I asked, 'How was it you all came back with me, you men from the lifeboat?' He said, 'Captain, if you hadn't done right we wouldn't be here.' It shows you how these men relied on you and trusted you; it was a great thing to think about.

CHAPTER 5

FALL OF FRANCE AND DUNKIRK

The Phoney War ended on 10 May 1940 when the Germans launched the latest version of the much amended invasion plan 'Case Yellow'. In its final form (informally termed 'sickle-cut' or 'Sickle Stroke') this was intended to achieve a decision in the West by attacking out of the difficult terrain of the Ardennes to cut in between the Franco-British forces that the Germans knew would advance into Belgium once active hostilities began and the static French forces in the Maginot line. What has become known as blitzkrieg (though no such unified doctrine actually existed in the German forces at this time) sliced through the French positions covering the River Meuse and by 24 May the British Expeditionary Force (BEF) and the northern French forces were trapped against the Channel, principally concentrated around Dunkirk and Lille. A hastily prepared evacuation plan, known as Operation Dynamo, was devised by Vice Admiral Bertram Ramsay in Dover. It included an appeal for all civilian vessels that were able to cross the Channel to help to ferry the troops from the beaches to larger ships offshore, or to evacuate them completely.

Ramsay's most optimistic forecast was that he might be able to evacuate 45,000 men, but in the event Hitler halted the advance of his armies and the Channel enjoyed unusual calm between 26 May and 4 June, during which 220,000 British and 120,000 French troops were evacuated to England. Nine Allied destroyers and perhaps 200 civilian vessels were lost, and the RAF suffered severe casualties covering the evacuation, unseen and unappreciated by the troops on the beaches. Starting on 5 June, the Germans swung south and French resistance collapsed, though not without some heavy fighting. The Italians opportunistically declared war on 10 June; Paris fell four days later while the French government fled to Bordeaux and formally capitulated on 25 June.

Despite the popular assumption that Dunkirk was Britain's last act on the continent for the time being, 51st Highland Division – in the Maginot line when the fighting started – was later forced to surrender at St Valéry on the coast, and during the final evacuation of British troops from St Nazaire on the Atlantic coast the troopship Lancastria *was sunk with the loss of over 3,000 lives. Unwilling to take the risk that the French Navy would finish up in German hands and perhaps transform the war at sea, Churchill ordered the Royal Navy to present French warships at Mers el-Kebir in North Africa with an ultimatum to sail to Britain or to a neutral port for internment and, when this was rejected on 3 July 1940, the French fleet was bombarded with the loss of 1,600 lives. This did much to assure America of the strength of British purpose, but both it and the evacuation from Dunkirk cast a long shadow over Franco-British relations.*

LAWRENCE DURRELL
Francophile British novelist

I was only twenty-five and my France was the literary France, but it was always pretty hopeless. They're anti-militarists to a man; they despise uniforms and so on and so forth, and they have been continuously invaded by the Germans but have shown no sign of wanting a piece of German territory – Alsace is a language question rather than a land question – and so they feel much put upon and really not disposed to fight for anyone else. They had this belief that really all wars were contrived by idiots who didn't know how to live, and I wonder – how wrong were they? Particularly the sort of pumpkin-eating Protestant nations like the British and the Germans, who were always worried about territorial problems, and the French just wanted to stay home and eat well and go to bed with their girlfriends.

GORDON WATERFIELD
British journalist in France

I don't think the French people themselves were defeatist. I think the defeatism and the fifth column – if you can use that term – came at the top, among the politicians. There was a very strong peace movement among certain politicians; some of them were even pro-German and wanted jobs with the Germans. When things went badly this group got larger and became more dominant and got rid of people like Prime Minister Paul Reynaud who was trying to fight. The main trouble was that in the past there had been great animosity against Jewish Prime Minister Léon Blum's government, the 1936–37 Socialist government, and there was a great division in French society. They were frightened that if they called on the people to hold back the Germans, I mean a popular uprising as they had done before in 1871, there would be Communism and revolution. They wanted to keep the civilians out of the war and they made no effort to bring them in, with the result that the civilians had nothing to do and eventually became frightened and joined the refugees.

CAPTAIN ANDRÉ BEAUFRE
French General Staff
It was a period of decay, of very deep decay, probably caused by the excess of the effort during World War One. I think generally speaking we suffered from an illness, which is not peculiar to the French, that of having been victorious and believing that we were right and very clever.

MAJOR GENERAL SIR EDWARD SPEARS
Conservative MP and Churchill's personal representative in France
The whole of the French upper and middle classes –- the right, if you like – preferred the idea of the Germans to their own Communists and I think you can call that a very powerful fifth column, and it was worked to death by the Germans.

LAWRENCE DURRELL
You didn't have to walk round these streets and see '*Pourquoi? Pourquoi?*' written on the walls, or the hammer and sickle, to realise that nobody was going to lift a finger, you know, and the German propaganda was jolly good. It had to be a bit unimaginative of the British not to be taken in by it – the Parisians were thoroughly taken in and so we kissed Paris goodbye.

MAJOR GENERAL WALTHER WARLIMONT

Deputy Chief of Wehrmacht Operations

The origins of the Sickle Stroke plan has to be attributed to General Erich von Manstein who in autumn 1939 was Chief of Staff of Field Marshal Gerd von Rundstedt, Army Group A. He was utterly opposed to the earlier plan, which was Hitler's own and which copied the strategy, the World War One Schlieffen plan, by assembling the bulk of the forces on the northern wing with the intention to conduct the main thrust through Belgium. This was the plan, with few alterations, was held up all through the dark winter of 1939–40, when the start was postponed by Hitler's orders from one week to another, altogether thirteen times because of unfavourable weather. When I returned from a visit to the Western Front and to the headquarters of Army Group A, there General Manstein interviewed me his ideas. My report on my return to Berlin, to the Chief of the Armoured Force Operations Staff and the Chief Military Adviser of Hitler, made a slight impression on him. On the next day, he informed Hitler of these plans. Hitler grasped the value of Manstein's ideas and on 17th February 1940 received the General in Berlin where he listened most attentively. Hitler's fear that the earlier plans had been made known to the enemy gave the impulse to overthrow them and prepare the way for the Sickle Stroke plan. Hitler said, 'Manstein is the only General who understands my own ideas,' already marks the beginning of his later claim that he himself had initiated the plan. Hitler for some time had insisted upon supporting the main thrust in the northern wing by an armoured group of two or three armoured divisions, which was to advance on a narrow strip of open country through Luxemburg on both sides of the Ardennes forest in the direction of Sedan. Manstein's advice had become an entirely new strategy, shifting the centre of gravity from the northern to the southern wing. By reversing these actual facts Hitler and his propaganda took care that the overwhelming success of the campaign was attributed to him as a greatest strategist of all times – this was the slogan of the German propaganda after the French campaign.

CAPTAIN BEAUFRE

The French stuck to the foremost lessons of the First World War, the belief in the defensive, the quality of the trenches against tanks. We had tanks in the First World War and we knew all the difficulties of the game while the Germans, who didn't have them, had the feeling of those who were attacked by tanks and had a sort of, let's say, fashion for tanks. And while we considered that the tanks were a little awkward and difficult to use and so on, the Germans were like *nouveaux riches*, you know, when they jumped to the new weapons with the appetite of the starving. That was very normal from both sides: we, having been victorious, were sure of our message; the Germans, having been defeated, copied what they had thought was useful in our methods, which we didn't really feel ourselves.

MAJOR GENERAL WARLIMONT

We were conscious of the French inclination of the Maginot line thinking, particularly that the French General Staff had not yet adopted military means against a new strategy advocated by British military thinker Basil Liddell Hart, which was founded on mobility and strength of offensive operations, motorised troops strongly supported by special units of the Air Force.

GORDON WATERFIELD

The Phoney War did a lot of harm to the French soldiers, the Maginot line did a lot of harm, the whole idea that this was an impregnable fortress and that all we had to do was just sit there and wait for the Germans to come and shoot them down. I visited the Maginot line and was really rather horrified by the effect it must have had on the soldiers. I visited near Strasburg and the Germans were busy the other side constructing defences on the other side of the Rhine. I said to a colonel – the colonel was very proud of his defences – I said, 'Magnificent concrete this, very good concrete', and I asked, 'Have they got such good concrete on the other side?' 'Oh, no, certainly not.' 'Do you ever think of attacking the other side and destroying their concrete?' 'No, no, that would not be a very good idea.' And then I stayed at an observation post on the Rhine watching the Germans washing and playing football, and I said to the sentry, 'Why don't you shoot them, why don't you shoot at them?' 'No', he said, 'they're behaving perfectly all right – they don't shoot at us, why should we shoot at them?' This was all very well, probably if I'd been a sentry I wouldn't have wanted to stir up trouble. But the generals should have made their men raid to keep up their morale and to test the strength of the Germans, the strength of the fortifications. But this didn't happen.

CAPTAIN BEAUFRE

The whole story was that the war wouldn't be a war of movement. It would be attrition and the result of the war would be like in the First World War, won by indirect operations on the borders, and that is how it mushroomed, all these funny ideas of action against Russia, supposed to be the weak ally, which was entirely foolish. We had a plan to attack Russia through Norway, which led to the landing at Narvik. And we had the plan to raise the Balkans with us by landing at Salonika and join the Yugoslavs, and so on. But all this was dreams and simply foolish.

COLONEL HASSO-ECCARD FREIHERR VON MANTEUFFEL

Panzer troop consultant, German General Staff

We knew that the French High Command had dispersed his tanks. The French had more, better, heavier tanks than we have but we managed our Panzer Group, as its commander General Paul von Kleist said, 'Don't tap them – strike as a whole and don't disperse.' And so we went with our bulk, we had no care of our flanks and so it was possible, with the work of the Panzer Group, to go to the Channel.

MAJOR GENERAL SPEARS

The French High Command were beneath contempt and this was due to a fundamental dispute between generals Gamelin and Georges. The dispute between those two men was fatal to the whole of the French defence. I knew Gamelin in 1914; he was a very dapper, teasing little man, very sure of himself, and everybody thought he had a great career before him. What ruined him was politics, a desire to get on with one type of politician rather than another. That was fatal as far as he was concerned. Georges was an exceptionally fine soldier but he'd been severely damaged at the time of the 1934 assassination of King Peter of Yugoslavia in Marseilles. He was very badly hurt – the French Foreign Minister was killed and it had affected Georges very profoundly, physically. I was very fond of him but it was very painful to me to see this fall in capacity really due to that most unfortunate incident.

CAPTAIN BEAUFRE

Gamelin's choice of headquarters near Paris reveals what the man was. The enemy were not the Germans; it was the French government with which he had to deal all the time to be protected against manoeuvres to replace him and so on. This was very typical of what he, how he, understood his job. Instead of a fighting general he was a political general.

COLONEL MANTEUFFEL

I think that the French generals have very good training on paper but they have no connection with their troops. Our Air Force had destroyed all telephone cables and so it was impossible to have connection with their troops. But now in this age with motorcycles and cars it is essential to have connection with field commanders.

GORDON WATERFIELD

Well, we did get to some French HQs with only one phone, but the reason for this was that they had not expected a war of movement. They had expected to be able to sit behind the Maginot line and fight the Germans there – they were not ready with a second line of defence. So when they had to retreat to these chateaux there was no organisation of phones and they were cut off from other units and groups, and this happened almost everywhere.

MAJOR GENERAL SPEARS

When Gamelin came to England he was asked by Churchill where were his reserves and he said, 'I have none' – it was unbelievable. Churchill was absolutely appalled and began to look for means of going on with the war in North Africa, then in Brittany. Anything, you see, to carry on, not to give way. But the French very soon accepted the idea of defeat, really, and surrender. To them it was rather a conception of the old days of royalty when you just exchanged a couple of provinces, paid a certain number of millions and then called it a day, and started off next time hoping you would be more lucky.

MAJOR GENERAL WARLIMONT

The Ardennes and Sedan came to be chosen as the main points of the armoured thrust as it was possible to circumvent the Maginot line and because this way opened up a whole route towards the section of the French positions which was defended by minor forces only. So certainly there were very great difficulties of conducting the armoured troops through the Ardennes forest. They would come by the most careful preparations of the Army General Staff, which justified its claim to have played an important part in the whole plan.

LAWRENCE DURRELL

The French temperament is much more mercurial, much more given to despondency and so on than the rather phlegmatic British, and also another thing is they happen to live without the Channel between them. It's that damned Channel that's saved us over and over again. We haven't been invaded two or three times; so naturally they'd had a dose of this and didn't like it at all. Then of course the right wing had a sneaking feeling that the Germans might do it better, because the left wing was clearly going to be ruled by the Russians. All that contributed to an indecision, an enormous weakening of potential, so I suppose in the final analysis the morale of the French Army dropped entirely through indecision.

COLONEL MANTEUFFEL

The French fought in the beginning of the war, for some days, diffidently. I think this is caused by moral disarmament. The French soldiers were captured most without a struggle, and in addition to this I learned from prisoners of war that the French soldiers in the majority believed that they would have no more war on the end of the first week of this campaign.

CAPTAIN BEAUFRE

I must confess that the morale of the French High Command was very quickly broken. In fact the night when we happened to know that the front had been broken through at Sedan, at that time the feeling was that everything was lost, and as I have written in my memoirs I saw General Georges, who was commanding the north-eastern front, I saw him sobbing and saying, 'There have been some deficiencies.' You always have deficiencies like that and that's nothing new, so we made a plan to restore the situation. Then on the Somme in the beginning of June, where we had a certain superiority over the Germans because we were covering their left flank while they were attacking Dunkirk, we had given orders to attack and we achieved nothing. So that was for me the proof that the training and the mentality of the High Command was unable at that time to make an offensive which would restore the situation. From that time on I thought it was lost.

COLONEL MANTEUFFEL

The first crisis was on May 22nd when the spearhead of the Panzer Army was attacked by strong British tank units and we suffered heavy casualties. The second crisis was the halt of the German panzer troops around Dunkirk. Hitler feared his experience in First World War; the panzers needed rest and maintenance, then they will go to the second phase of the Battle of France, so Hitler stopped his advances around Dunkirk.

MAJOR GENERAL WARLIMONT

Nobody had and could have foreseen a success of such a totality, and that in a short time of hardly more than a month. There was a significant difference between the attitude of the military leaders on one side, in particular General Franz Halder, the Chief of Staff of the Army, and on the other side, Hitler, who joins the French campaign for the first time as Commander-in-Chief of the Armed Forces. Halder, after the success of the initial operation, was entirely sure of himself and of the further course of the campaign.

SQUADRON LEADER THE HON MAX AITKEN
601 Squadron RAF, Tangmere

One interesting trip we made was to escort Winston Churchill to Paris. He went to Paris to ask the French to go with him – I think it was when he proposed that France and Britain should set up joint citizenship and that the government should move to North Africa. Our great hope was that he wasn't going to come back that night so we could have a last night in Paris – which materialised, and we weren't very fit next morning.

ANTHONY EDEN
British Secretary of State for War

On the 12th of May Winston published his first list of ministers on the formation of his government. That was Whit Sunday and that afternoon I repaired to the War Office to take over my responsibilities there. Although the Battle of France had only started two days before, it was already evident that there was some grim times ahead. And, in fact, the next four weeks were a tale of continuing defeat and disaster. Almost exactly one month later, Winston asked me to fly with him to meet the French government. We took Sir John Dill, the Chief of the Imperial General Staff, with us and I can see the scene now at the table in the chateau where we met them. On the one side Winston and I and Dill; on the other side Prime Minister Paul Reynaud and General Maxime Weygand, who was the new French Commander-in-Chief, and Pétain. We discussed for three hours without really making much progress because it was soon evident that there was nothing more that the French were in a position to do.*

---

* Marshal Philippe Pétain (1856–1951), First World War hero for his defence of Verdun who became the head of the collaborationist Vichy regime 1940–44.

MAJOR GENERAL SPEARS

Whether Reynaud's mistress was paid by the Germans or not I don't know – she couldn't have been more anti-British if she had been. She was completely sold on the idea that the Germans were far better than the French Communists and she did absolutely everything to thwart any little sparks of resistance that blossomed in her lover's mind. When she heard a proposal had been made to amalgamate the two countries – France and England – she dashed off on to the phone straight away to call all the people of her way of thinking in the Cabinet.

ANTHONY EDEN

The moment came for Winston to declare that whatever happened we should go on with the war, if necessary alone, and then Reynaud was quite inscrutable, Weygand was polite, perhaps slightly doubting, and Pétain was openly 'all my eye and Betty Martin'. So we knew from that moment pretty well what must await us and I say it now we've no right to reproach the French for this. None in my opinion, because our own contribution on land had been a very diminutive one, relatively. Quite true that the Air Force had been superb and relatively numerous, but even so we could hardly be called equal partners in the Battle of France.

MAJOR GENERAL SPEARS

Some years later in Cairo I asked Churchill what was the narrowest escape we'd had in the war so far and he said undoubtedly the fact that the French might have accepted our offer of unity. When you think of it, it couldn't have worked, it would have created a mess, it would have impeded us in our methods completely – we couldn't have done that.

JOHN COLVILLE
Assistant Private Secretary to the Prime Minister 1939–43
On 19th May Lord Gort, the Commander-in-Chief of the British Expeditionary Force, concluded that if the French armies had collapsed beyond repair then there was not the slightest chance that they were going to recover in order sufficiently to continue or maintain the existing front.

He therefore instructed his people at home that they must prepare for the possibility of the evacuation of the BEF. It was not until 25th May that Lord Gort, against the orders of the French High Command and contrary to the wishes of the British War Cabinet, finally decided that the proposed attack by the BEF to the south was not feasible and that a withdrawal to the sea was the only possibility. In making this decision he saved the BEF because there can be no doubt that had he obeyed instructions and marched southwards, the entire fighting force of more than a quarter of a million men would otherwise have been killed or captured. It must be doubted whether this country could have continued to fight, Battle of Britain or no Battle of Britain, if all our trained officers and NCOs had been lost. By this single decision Gort changed the course of history.

CAPTAIN BEAUFRE

The recriminations started with the British Army whose orders were to attack near us and without warning we happened to learn the British were withdrawing. We have not the right to criticise this too much because after all we were the bosses and we lost the battle, and that is a good excuse for the British to be selfish. But anyway they were, very selfish. Let's say that also the British Army hadn't been really attacked during the battle – the French had the brunt of the German attack – so it was still in order, and they took advantage of the situation to do what they wanted and to re-embark at Dunkirk without being of any help to the French to begin with, which produced not a good feeling. At a higher level of command than where I was the discussion came from the use of the RAF, that we knew was a number of squadrons you had in Britain and we thought that you didn't support the battle as you could have supported it. I heard Churchill himself answer this question. Churchill said very clearly that he couldn't do more because he had to think of the future and save what was left to protect Britain. But we had the feeling that you were playing your game.

MAJOR GENERAL SPEARS

There was complete hatred of the English, wanting to blame them for their defeat, saying we hadn't sent over enough troops, that we kept our planes in England rather than engaging them in the last struggle of France for her life. We represented 'Perfidious Albion' in all its horror. They really disliked us, more than I can find an expression for even today.

SQUADRON LEADER AITKEN

We had been operating over France before that, gradually covering the retreat of the British Army towards Dunkirk. And it was very unattractive because none of the British troops knew whether you were German or whether you were British and everyone fired at you. But gradually it formalised as the Army came towards Dunkirk and our duty was much clearer to us. Our duty clearly was to stop the troops on the beach from being bombed or shot, so most of Fighter Command in the south was destined to protect the troops on the beach.

COLONEL ADOLF GALLAND
Luftwaffe Jagdgruppe 26
It is known that Hitler himself stopped the Army and the armoured division from taking Dunkirk. Göring offered that the Luftwaffe would fight the British Army in Dunkirk but it had been impossible to avoid the escape of the people. The material was kept and was destroyed, but for the first time the Luftwaffe was confronted with the whole of the British fighter planes and fighters were good, same quality and experience as we had, and technically also equal. And especially during the night time the Luftwaffe was not able to avoid the escape.

MAJOR GENERAL WARLIMONT
Hitler's fear to take any risk and his lack of knowledge or at least acknowledge the main Sickle Stroke principles. He was mistrusting of his generals, thus at Dunkirk he delayed the main aim of the whole campaign, which was reaching and closing the Channel coast before any other considerations. This time he was frightened that the clay plains of Flanders with its many streams and channels, which according to his own memories of World War One would endanger and possibly inflict heavy losses on the panzer divisions. Hitler failed to follow up the overwhelming success of

the first part of the campaign, and instead initiated the steps for the second part before the first had been accomplished. This was a great mistake in view of the German military principle to follow up success to the last gasp of men and horses. I do not believe that he allowed the British Expeditionary Force to escape for political reasons and by this chivalrous attitude would obtain a chance of coming earlier to terms with Britain. Such an assumption, apart from everything else, is in full contrast to Hitler's concentrating the whole power of the German Air Force on the coastline after the British retreat.

BERTIE GOOD
Chief Steward on the ferry 'Royal Daffodil'

We arrived off Gravelines and were attacked by German aircraft. They just shot a few bullets at us but they really went for the hospital ship and tried to sink her. We went on into Dunkirk and the *St Helier* went in; he was there for about a quarter of an hour and came out and shouted to George Johnson, our captain, 'There's nobody there. I don't know what they've bloody well sent us here for, I'm going back to Southampton.' Well, George Johnson took us in and we tied up alongside and the troops came up out of the ground, like a lot of rats, and they just ran to the ship. We took seventeen hundred men on board and just when we were picking the gangway up about thirty or forty ambulances came down the pier. The ambulance drivers came up the gangway and the First Mate said, 'Anybody in those ambulances?' They said, 'Yes, there's six stretcher cases in each one of 'em. We've been chased from Boulogne to here.' So the ship's crew went ashore and brought every man out of the ambulances and put them in the after dining room. None of these chaps had had their wounds dressed, they were in a hell of a state. All the officers in the ship who had first-aid kits started to dress their wounds.

LIEUTENANT COMMANDER JOHN McBEATH
Royal Navy, commanding destroyer HMS Venomous

As soon as it was obvious the German Army had broken through and that the British forces, and of course a lot of French forces, were going to be pushed back on the coast and would possibly need evacuating, the powers-that-be back in the UK got this small-boat flotilla organisation going. It started in a rather haphazard way because all sorts of boats varying from little tiny family motorboats to much larger club boats and in fact almost everything that could steam across to the other side were operating it at first, rather on their own. Some of them never made it and a lot of them went to the wrong places, but eventually they got it channelled and then one came across lots of these little boats going to and fro, may of them with a dozen or so soldiers on board heading back to England resolutely. One quite often offered to take their crews of soldiers off them so that they could go back for another load but they said, 'No fear! We've got our twelve pongos and we're going back to England with them. You go and get your own!'

SQUADRON LEADER AITKEN

Dunkirk was a shambles: there was a huge pall of smoke which came from burning ships and burning oil installations, and aircraft were flying in this smoke and it was pretty hard to tell what sort they were. They'd come out, they'd see you and they'd go back in again, and equally if we saw a large formation of German fighters coming at two or three of us we'd dodge in and out of the smoke. We'd have occasional dogfights but it was very confusing. The weather was absolutely glorious – you could see for miles except for the smoke and the smoke was fantastic. We did not try to protect the troops over the beaches; that wasn't our job. Our job was to stop any aircraft getting to those troops because, believe me, if enemy aircraft had got superiority of the air at Dunkirk they would have massacred those fellows on that beach. Nothing could have been done – they had no guns, they had no anti-aircraft, and German bombers and German dive-bombers, the Stukas, would have just murdered them and we couldn't have got those troops off.

BERTIE GOOD

On the thirteenth trip we was off Gravelines when five German aircraft came down and had a practice. These planes came down and attacked us and dropped their bombs everywhere. We missed every one bar one that went right through three decks and we passed over it and it exploded astern. I organised the chaps to get all the bedding off the beds and we filled the bomb hole with all these fibre mattresses, but she was taking water and the port engine was out. The Ship's Writer was on the stern with a Lewis gun and it jammed. Well, he ran and as he did Jerry caught him. He'd pulled the smoke-room door back when Jerry practically cut him in half. There was five of my chaps all got wounded, one chap got seven bullets in his back and today he's still a cripple.

MAJOR GENERAL WARLIMONT

I started from headquarters in a small plane on 14th June 1940; I only knew that our troops were about to come close to the French capital. Only when arriving at the air space over Paris I observed that the large columns of German infantry were already entering the inner districts of the town. Remembering then the vain efforts to reach this highest goal during the First World War, my feelings of joy and exaltation became as strong that leaning forward I tapped the pilot on his shoulder and asked whether it would be possible to perform a landing on the place de la Concorde. After circling around a while and observing that there was no traffic at all in the centre of Paris we soon came down at the base of the Champs-Elysées.

GORDON WATERFIELD

The French government went to Bordeaux. There was terrible confusion because all the refugees landed up there eventually. There was a tremendous battle going on within the government and eventually of course Pétain came to the top and agreed to accept the German terms. It was a terribly depressing time and my French journalist friends were bitter against us for leaving. They said we ought to stay and see what happens and to report it. But we felt, well, there will be another battle, from England, and we'd better get back and join up or do whatever we can do.

LIEUTENANT COMMANDER McBEATH

I had on my ship everything from the highest to the lowest. On the second to last trip, the night of 2nd to 3rd of June, we had on board

General Harold Alexander and General Arthur Percival, who subsequently gained much more fame in North Africa and Malaya respectively. But quite a lot of colonels and people less than that would come up on to the bridge and they said, 'Do you mind me being up here? I'd like to see what's going on.' And you'd say no and when you spoke to them you got the impression that although they were naturally dejected at having been kicked out of Europe, there was no sort of idea that they'd been beaten. It was just, 'Well, we'll get them next time' sort of business.

J B PRIESTLEY
English novelist and broadcaster
It was just after Dunkirk so I took the theme, the idea of victory coming from defeat, which is a very English thing, I believe. We're great improvisers, we English. I'm not sure about the British but the English are, and that was important. Then, the feeling was very strong that now everything had happened we could really start, if you know what I mean, we're by ourselves now and really we can get on with this war, which was very strong after Dunkirk. And incidentally, which I didn't mention in the broadcast but I knew about, the way in which working people in the factories and so on worked till they dropped, after Dunkirk.

CHRISTABEL BIELENBERG
Englishwoman married to an anti-Nazi German lawyer
I think one could say that the actual defeat of France in six weeks came as a complete surprise to the generality of the German people. I found that there was a difference between my attitude to this defeat of France, and England being left alone. I didn't really ever feel that England was going to lose the war, even in those days when it looked as if it was absolutely certain that a landing would take place and they would be defeated. I couldn't believe that and realised afterwards that it was because I had been brought up in a feeling of victory after the First World War. I'd been brought up in the atmosphere of victory; all the Germans of my age had been brought up in the atmosphere of defeat. They were all therefore immensely surprised that they had, that victory was theirs. They were

immensely surprised about the victory over France and equally worried about what was going to happen with England – could they win, couldn't they win – it was quite a different atmosphere.

LIEUTENANT PAOLO COLACICCHI
Italian Tenth Army in Africa

The Italian Air Force, even more than the Army, certainly felt that its equipment was bad and we were certainly not ready to go to war in 1940. It was a purely political movement by Mussolini who felt that Hitler was winning too much, too quickly and that if he didn't make some sort of gesture, take some sort of initiative, he would not be able to sit at the conference table. There was a rumour going round that he said, 'I want one thousand Italian dead to sit at the conference table,' and of course it cost many more than that.

MAJOR GENERAL SPEARS

The matter of the French fleet is a very, very big question, the French Navy being violently anti-British anyhow. Admiral Jean-François Darlan said, 'We'll never allow our ships to fall into German hands' – sounds very well and they probably believed it. But when I got back to London I said to Churchill that the one thing that's absolutely essential is to get the French fleet out of the hands of the French government because the day the Germans get hold of the fleet we've lost the war; we can't control the seas. On the day the Germans want the French fleet they'll say to the French government, 'We demand that the French fleet should be in such and such a harbour on such and such a day, if not we'll burn Marseilles on Monday, Lyons on Tuesday and so on, and we burn Paris on Saturday.' And who would resist that?

ANTHONY EDEN

So then we had to rebuild the Army at home, at least that was the responsibility of the War Office and of the munitions factories. And looking back it's quite extraordinary to register the attitude of the country at the time, and not least of the Army. I had, as Secretary of War, to go down and see the troops back from Dunkirk and I was expecting that there would certainly be some criticisms of the equipment, which was wanting, and the tanks, which had been very much wanting, and a rather general lack of preparedness in many respects. There was nothing of the kind, and even in the brigades which had been badly knocked about morale was extraordinarily high, and I think this applied to the whole country. So far as the Army was concerned I would think that this was really due to the fact that the soldiers felt that they'd measured the enemy, and all things being equal, in the form of equipment and so forth, and training, they were sure that they could defeat him. I don't suppose they'd put it into so many words, but that was the instinct I felt was there at the time.

J B PRIESTLEY

It was actually a feeling of relief, rather like – now you hadn't got to mess about with foreigners, you were on your own and this would really be much better. This goes back a long time in English history and I happened to be writing a book about the English at the time. In 1940 we felt – I think partly as a reaction from the Phoney War – everybody was miserable; I was intensely miserable, because nothing was happening and yet you knew something was happening behind the scenes, and it came at the time as a relief that it was all out in the open. Now we know what's going on and we had a lot of foreigners here because a lot of governments were here and good luck to them – but we're on our own. This gave people ... there was almost a point of gaiety in it that was missing in, say, 1941 and 1942. I think the determination went right to the end of the war but a certain almost mad gaiety which you had in the spring of 1940 disappeared.

CHAPTER 6

WINSTON CHURCHILL

*In his obituary for the man with whom his own life was so closely intertwined
– almost unbelievably, as children they had the same nanny – Labour Party
leader Clement Attlee wrote: 'He was, of course, above all a supremely fortunate mortal. Whether he deserved his great fate or not, whether he won it or
had it dropped in his lap, history set him the job that he was the ideal man to
do. I cannot think of anybody in this country who has been as favoured in this
way so much, and, into the bargain, at the most dramatic moment in his
country's history. In this, Winston was superbly lucky. And perhaps the most
warming thing about him was that he never ceased to say so.' Many of Attlee's
political persuasion have not been as generous in their estimation, and even
among Conservatives there have been many who have sniped at Churchill's
memory. The interviews confirm that one way or another Britain faced ruin
in the summer of 1940 and any objective analysis must conclude that the most
likely outcome with Churchill removed from the equation would have been a
capitulation. Fighting on made financial bankruptcy inevitable, but it
salvaged popular faith in Britain as a worthwhile enterprise. It may indeed
have been the Channel that spared Britain the trauma suffered by France,
where the deep divisions in society were pitilessly revealed by defeat and occupation, but it took a duke's grandson with decidedly pre-modern views on
honour, courage and leadership to kick the somnolent bureaucracy into
action, to bridge political divides in Parliament and to rally an uncertain
populace. He was distrusted by his own party and by the King, had been
demonised by the Labour movement, and was regarded (not without good*

*reason) as a loose cannon by the Civil Service, but when the moment came he
was unquestionably the man of the hour, and rose to its formidable challenge
as if, one might say, to the manner born.*

RAB BUTLER

British Under-Secretary of State for Foreign Affairs 1938–40

It was completely different training between Chamberlain and Churchill.
Churchill, probably alone in our history, had more apprenticeship in war
himself and in the study of war than any other living man. On the American
Civil War alone Churchill was one of the greatest experts, studying its strategy. The whole of Chamberlain's background has been specific in dealing
with internal policy and therefore he hadn't got an immediate idea as to
what should be our course of action.

ROBERT BOOTHBY

Conservative MP

The great crisis was when Churchill reached his greatest heights, but he
wasn't very popular even after he became Prime Minister. The first time
he and Chamberlain appeared in the House of Commons, Chamberlain
got a bigger cheer from the Conservative Party. Churchill took some time
to settle down and to become the hero that he was very soon to become.
But when the real crisis came, the Fall of France and the crack of Europe,
and we were left absolutely alone in the world, facing the Germans, it was
Churchill's voice which said we will fight on the hills, the seas, on the
beaches and everywhere else at the time of the Battle of Britain; he became
almost overnight a national hero. This was undoubtedly his greatest hour
of his life. There were many disasters to follow and his strategic direction
of the war was not always wise; he made grave mistakes and suffered many
disasters. But 1940 was supreme because he voiced the determination of
this nation not to submit. He once said to me, 'I had to consult the
Cabinet as to whether I should come to some kind of terms with this evil
man Hitler. And I looked up and I said, "Gentlemen, what do you think?"
And they all rose to their feet and said, "Never!" and the tears came to my
eyes.' He rallied the nation, he rallied public opinion, people listened to

him on the radio, in the pubs, everywhere. He revived their confidence, their optimism, their hope when everything seemed hopeless and whole world thought we were defeated.

ANONYMOUS MALE EAST ENDER

Pub interview in Canning Town, east London

When he visited, east Londoners, they couldn't have cared tuppence for Winston Churchill as a man or a politician. But the man who filled Chamberlain's place, he was a leader, there's no doubt about it, he was a leader, and I think every time he opened his mouth he inspired confidence into the people. Whether or not they accepted him as a Conservative it was there, he was for 'em and he was against the common enemy. Now he'd only have to open his mouth and say black was white and they would have believed him, such was their faith in him and such was the way in which he inspired confidence. You only had to listen to his broadcasts about fighting them in the fields and you could imagine people rolling up their sleeves.

JOHN COLVILLE

Assistant Private Secretary to the Prime Minister 1939–43

Immediately Churchill became Prime Minister the pace in Whitehall changed: people started to think faster and to act fast. Distinguished civil servants could be seen running down the passages, Churchill's ministers went out in all directions with his label 'Action this day' on them and the tempo became such that life was almost intolerable. There were no holidays, no weekends, no hours off. Churchill himself worked up to eighteen, nineteen hours a day with a little sleep in the afternoon, which less fortunate mortals were unable to do. And he also was physically very energetic, although he was working either in bed or at the Cabinet table most of the day, he would suddenly make the most extraordinary and energetic sorties. He would inspect troops marching at great speed down the ranks and outpacing the young men who were following him. I remember one evening he said he must go and inspect some new works that were taking place in the basement of one of his government departments where they were shored up against air raids. And the next evening he did the same thing, and the third, he'd got to know this pretty well and he was advising workmen about how to build traverses and so on. And although he was sixty-five years old he vaulted over a brick wall, a traverse which had been built at his instruction, and landed feet first in a pool of liquid cement and with impertinence, in retrospect, I said to him, 'Well, I think you've met your Waterloo,' because he was stuck in the cement. And he turned to me and said, 'How dare you! Anyhow, try Blenheim' – his energy was indeed remarkable at this time.

RAB BUTLER

Brendan Bracken was always running somewhere to another and if you wanted to consult him, it meant that you were really consulting Churchill; so it was very convenient. He was a genius: he never did very much in a ministerial way except become Minister of Information, his genius was running around, especially in Churchill's earlier days, to help him and in everything he sat in with him. He had bright red hair, he educated himself, he went up to a school and offered them the money which he pulled out of his chest, which he brought from Australia where he was a young man – most independent and extraordinary man.*

AMBASSADOR W AVERELL HARRIMAN

President Roosevelt's Special Envoy to Europe

I saw a great deal of him and when I told him my instructions he said, 'We'll find out what we need, then you see what you can do.' So I spent a number of weekends with him, saw him once or twice a week, and he had an office at the Admiralty but he used to take me with him to the different cities that were bombed. He thought it helped morale for him to go about and he thought of bringing me along as an American, Mr Harriman. I had no particular title but everyone knew that I was there to

---

* Brendan Bracken (1901–58) was widely and falsely believed to be Churchill's illegitimate son. He was Minister of Information 1941–45 and was ennobled in 1952.

Interviewee SS Colonel Karl Wolff (*right*) with Reichsführer SS Heinrich Himmler.

Adolf Galland, interviewee, during the Battle of Britain.

Interviewee Lieutenant General Mark Clark (*right*) and Montgomery after their landings in southern Italy.

Major General J Lawton 'Lightning Joe' Collins, interviewee, decorated by Montgomery in Normandy.

All in his name: the Emperor Hirohito.

Japanese bombing of the undefended Chungking in February 1938.

Appeasement at Munich, September 1938.

During the Phoney War, men of 51st Highland Division entering the Maginot line, 1940.

Troops awaiting evacuation from a beach near Dunkirk.

Destroyers were the workhorses of the Dunkirk evacuation: this 'V' class vessel is crowded with troops.

Iconic triumph:
Hitler and interviewee
Albert Speer in Paris.

Adolf Hitler and Benito
Mussolini, June 1940.

Heinkel 111 over London's East End: the
strategic blunder that saved Fighter Command.

Eastcheap ablaze: the London blitz.

Churchill and the heavily
bombed London dockers.
Most of them disliked his
politics, but they dipped their
cranes in salute when his body
made its last journey up
London's river in 1965.

Churchill in the bomb-ravaged
shell of Coventry Cathedral.

The only visit by Hitler
to a bombed city.

Interviewee U-boat ace
Otto Kretschmer in 1940.

Interviewee, then Squadron
Leader, Oulton's successful
attack on U-440, in the Bay of
Biscay, 31 May 1943.

(*above*) Crew of the carrier *Akagi* cheer the first strike at Pearl Harbor.

(*left*) The destroyer USS *Shaw* blows up.

be of assistance. And when we went to Bristol it was a very heavy night attack, everyone felt that he arrived because of the attack. He had an enormous welcome everywhere they walked through the streets. Churchill had the idea that he was entirely safe as long as he did things without any advanced notice. An assassin had to plan to take action against him so he walked very openly in the port areas and the dockers and so forth. The devotion of the people was very touching. I happened to be alone with him as [we] were in a railroad carriage leaving Bristol and, having waved to all of the people from the windows, we came to the country and he picked up a newspaper and tears were in his eyes and he said, 'They have such confidence – it is a grave responsibility.' He had a great feeling that it was his responsibility to protect the British people, to get them to put forward the greatest of effort in their own welfare, but he had to make the decisions in their interests. It was a very touching remark.

JOHN COLVILLE

What made the public impact at that time was not Churchill's remarkable energy in the machinery of government and the way in which he speeded up operations in Cabinet and of the Chiefs of Staff and of the government departments, but his speeches in the House of Commons and on the wireless. Those speeches were not like anything he prepared later, carefully over days, they flowed out of his natural feelings, the way we were all keyed up. He represented what the country was feeling, the sense of resistance at all costs and I remember one of his speeches was due to be broadcast at nine o'clock, and he didn't start preparing it until six and this was one of the great speeches of 1940. This was very much in contrast to Churchill's normal, very slow gestation of speeches in Parliament. I remember too the impact those speeches had on the Commons. Right from the beginning of his government, the very first speech he made, you could hear the silence in the House as he spoke and I walked out that day with Sir Alan Lascelles, who was the King's Private Secretary, and he turned to me and said, 'Time will show how Churchill turns out as a statesman, but of one thing I am quite sure, after listening today, he will go to history as a poet.'

LAWRENCE DURRELL

British novelist and press officer in Cairo

When he arrived he gave us a pep talk and told us what a lot of twerps we were. He looked frightfully tired and he had flown out in that kind of hay box he had invented for himself, and I was very touched because he was wearing a siren suit, smoking an immense cigar, but he had on those old-fashioned dancing pumps that you used to wear in those days with a dinner jacket, with a 'W' on one foot and a 'C' on the other. He gave us a very good pep talk and it was galvanising because at that time we were completely cut off from England, so you never felt in touch with what was going on at home although you heard it on the radio. And the presence of your Prime Minister suddenly let you have a bite at it, so's to speak. It was a very tonic thing and he played up to it, being a great showman – he did his job.

RAB BUTLER

The Burma Road, according to Churchill, had to be closed and this was regarded as an appeasement of the Japanese. So, very wisely, Churchill decided to have a secret session, so we had no press and all the galleries were cleared, and Halifax was in the Lords and said, 'Now we'll put young Butler over the sticks,' so I had to defend it. I was able to use telegrams and read them and show the reasons why the Americans had agreed with us over this, and Cranbourne, now Lord Salisbury, passed me a note of congratulations afterwards, and said it was I who helped Churchill over one of his leading acts of appeasement and he was very grateful for it.

EMANUEL SHINWELL

Left-wing trade unionist and Labour MP who refused to serve in the wartime government

I think where Churchill failed was at the beginning of the war in association with the shipping position. When Churchill was First Lord of the Admiralty under the Chamberlain government I took a delegation of seamen and navigation officers and our purpose was to persuade him to arm merchant ships in order to deal with the U-boats. At first he refused but eventually he agreed that some of them should be armed – but we hadn't the weapons and there was a bit of trouble over that. Then when he became Prime Minister I pressed him over and over again to abolish the convoy system, which was ineffective, because to group a large number of ships together with speed that didn't match the U-boats would be disastrous, and indeed it became disastrous. I suggested to start off by building ships not of nine knots but of fifteen knots or sixteen knots; the answer was, it's too expensive.

MICHAEL FOOT
Left-wing journalist

Churchill was very stupid about the newspapers and resented criticism. If anyone could see his wartime speeches, he often referred to the 'crustaceans' in the press, people who were trying to 'crab' his war efforts. He used to think we should all bow down and worship him. Well, the people weren't going to have that and I think it was in fact a great assistance that he had *Daily Express* proprietor Lord Beaverbrook in the Cabinet and of course Beaverbrook had a vested interest in ensuring that newspapers were not suppressed and were not interfered with by ministers. But certainly Churchill resented the criticism most bitterly and I remember for example the articles which we published in *Tribune* which was written by Frank Owen under the pseudonym of Thomas Rainborough, which were the first articles published in the British press which criticised the whole of Churchill's conduct of strategy. The whole of the worship of Churchill in 1940 was changing into this criticism following the invasion of Russia in June 1941 and it was first voiced in these articles written when Frank Owen was serving in the Forces. These were pretty well the first criticisms of Churchill that had been put in the press because in 1940 pretty well everybody in the country – and I think rightly – regarded the part that Churchill had played then as absolutely magnificent and beyond criticism. But as the war was going from bad to worse, as it appeared, and as we suffered during 1941 and 1942 these heavy setbacks, criticism started. Those articles in *Tribune* were the first that asked, 'Now what about Churchill's strategy, what about Churchill as Defence Minister?' Those articles were bitterly resented by Churchill and I'm sure he would have suppressed *Tribune* if he had been allowed to do so by his fellow Cabinet Ministers.

ARTHUR BOTTOMLEY
Trade-union leader and Walthamstow borough councillor
The recognition that Attlee was Deputy Prime Minister and that Ernest Bevin was in the government, this was an assurance to the mass of the people that fairness would prevail. I think it's only right to say that when history's written up Attlee will be one of the greatest men in history, because quietly and diligently he made all the preparations for helping to win this war. Although nobody can take away from Churchill his great leadership, his inspiration, I don't think Churchill would have been the same man without having as deputy Clement Attlee, and it's for this reason, in my opinion, the coalition was so successful.

CECIL HARMSWORTH KING
Proprietor of the Daily Mirror
I don't think he was a great Commander-in-Chief. He was no Marlborough: the Duke of Marlborough was one of Churchill's ancestors but he was the best available, acceptable to the armed forces and experienced in war. He was at his best, I think, in 1940 when he did a terrific job in expressing within suitable words the feelings of the British people, of defiance after the evacuation of Dunkirk. I don't think he was a great Prime Minister, I don't think he really understood much about politics but he was a great personality, a very attractive personality, very self-centred but very attractive, warm and with an immense command of the English language, written and spoken.

RAB BUTLER
Churchill didn't really have a great many intimate friends: some of us were too young to be intimate with him and he missed his early days in the Asquith Cabinet where he was among the towering giants, and his old friend [Liberal statesman John] Morley and others had died. But he had two friends, F E Smith, Lord Birkenhead, and a little later Max Beaverbrook.

Then F E Smith died and it left him for rapier work chiefly to Max Beaverbrook, because he liked to have somebody who would stick something into him and then he would reply and call them the most frightful names and say he wasn't going to speak to them again.

AMBASSADOR HARRIMAN

I don't think he was a man that worried. At that time he did what has to be done. I wasn't in Britain very long before he made it very plain to me that all Britain could do was to hold out, and he wanted to be sure that Britain held out. He wanted to hold the Middle East, Singapore. Then there was the fear in the summer of 1940, the battle for Britain in the air, of possible invasion; then there was a fear when I was there in March or April that there might be an attempt to cross the Channel and that disappeared when intelligence came through that Hitler was going to attack Russia. The interesting thing was that both Roosevelt and Churchill on their own informed Stalin of their intelligence information, and Stalin thought that was a trick on our part to get him to mobilise and to provoke Hitler to attack. Stalin was very conscious that in World War One it was the Tsar's mobilisation that caused the German Kaiser to attack Russia, and he wasn't going to have any part of it.

REAR ADMIRAL LORD LOUIS MOUNTBATTEN
Chief of Combined Operations
In October 1941 I was recalled from Pearl Harbor, where I was working with the American Fleet temporarily, to take up the job in charge of Combined Operations by Mr Winston Churchill. The very first day I reported to him he said, 'You are to prepare for the invasion of Europe for unless we can fight Hitler and beat his forces on land, we shall never win this war. You must devise and design the appliances, the landing craft, the techniques to enable us to effect a landing against opposition and to maintain ourselves there. You must take the most brilliant officers from the Navy, Army and Air Force to help, as our planners, to plan this great operation. You must take bases to use as training establishments where you can train the Navy, Army and Air Force to work as a single entity. The whole

of the south coast of England is a bastion of defence against the invasion of Hitler – you've got to turn it into the springboard for our attack.' This was October 1941, when the whole of our allies in Europe had been over-run and conquered, the Russians looked like being defeated and the Americans weren't in the war – what a hell of a decision to make, to prepare for the invasion then.

MICHAEL FOOT

Aneurin Bevan, of course, was the strongest and fiercest critic and was the one most resented by Churchill – but he was extremely well informed. Because there were in the conduct of the war and the nature of the weapons many defects and faults that had to be exposed and as Bevan was raising these matters in the House of Commons, more and more informa-tion would come to him from sources which proved to be correct. For example the whole way in which tanks were designed: Bevan and Ipswich MP Dick Stokes, who had a great knowledge of the production of weapons, constituted a most formidable criticism in the House of Commons. Again, Churchill didn't like it – Churchill wanted to go to the House of Commons and have statements made with nobody commenting on the statements. Aneurin Bevan said that this was quite contrary to parliamentary procedure and he would insist that when Churchill made these statements the matter should be opened to debate. There were some others on both sides of the House who joined with him in these criticisms but I don't think anybody would doubt that Bevan's criticism was the most formidable and the most sustained, and of course it was carried wider than any of the others. Most of the others were concentrating on individ-ual questions, whereas Bevan broadened his attack to cover the strategy of the government as a whole.

RAB BUTLER

The main opposition to Churchill during his magnificent ten years of office was over the Second Front. But long before that there were murmurings, chiefly over Tobruk, and all this led up to a vote of censure. The real trouble was having a coalition government: the trouble from the people attacking Churchill was that there were very few people of ability outside it to attack him; they were not strong enough to make an impression on the House. He called Aneurin Bevan a great hulking bully because he feared that by attacking him he might upset the government. This was only part of the characteristic of Churchill, which was that in politics he was nothing like so much a warrior as he was in dealing with warlike preparations. Churchill was always very cautious in politics: he'd had a rough time in his youth, he'd had all the Dardanelles trouble and he didn't like opposition, so he showed a certain amount of anxiety and caution, which those of us who were supporting him felt was quite unnecessary because he had this enormous majority.

ROBERT BOOTHBY

Churchill was most politically anxious in 1942 when Tobruk fell and there was a censure motion moved against his government in the House of Commons. I have never seen him so troubled as he was then. And people were talking quite freely of a possible fall of the government. I was in the Air Force at the time and came up as a Member of Parliament and I met him in the dining room of the House of Commons and he said, 'Are you in favour of the government?' So I said, 'There's no alternative,' and he said, 'Are you in favour of me?' and I said, 'Yes.' And he seized my arm and took me to the Speaker of the House of Commons and said, 'I want Mr Boothby to be called early in the debate, fifth if possible.' And I made one of my most successful speeches. It was made a little easier that Sir Roger Keyes, who had moved the vote of censure, had suggested that the Duke of Gloucester should replace Churchill as Commander-in-Chief. The Duke had been to school with me and I didn't think that it was altogether a very constructive suggestion and I was able to make fun of this and put the House in a lighter mood and make them laugh because it was a moment of great tension. Churchill listened to my speech and he took me to the smoking room and stood me a whisky and drank a toast to what he called, 'the Pegasus wings of my oratory'. I was naturally very pleased, but then he didn't bother to speak to me again, because I'd done my job, until the end of the war when he had another job to do in connection with

Europe and appointed me as one of the original members of the Council of Europe. But that was characteristic of Churchill as a man – he used men when he had a particular job, when they'd done the job he dropped them. If they had another job to do, he'd pick them up again. He was pretty ruthless in his dealings with individuals and this idea of tremendous loyalty to old friends is to a large extent fiction. He used men as relentlessly as I think Lloyd George used them in the First World War. And as I think Napoleon used them and probably any great War Minister has to do.

JOHN McCLOY
US Assistant Secretary of War
I think he certainly expressed himself and he did have an influence. He did cause us to postpone some of our major programmes but on the other hand he knew where the strength lay, he knew that the decisive factor was the American intervention and he was supposed to go along. His relations with Mr Roosevelt were very good but he had closer control over the British military thinking. Mr Roosevelt rather allowed General Marshall to dictate the course of the war, and did not participate to the extent that Mr Churchill did in the depths of strategy. Mr Churchill enjoyed this, he liked to get involved, he'd been a solider, he exerted a strong influence, he was a strong personality and highly articulate. It wasn't entirely determinative – he couldn't compel us to everything that he would prefer – but he certainly made his points clear and you knew you'd be in a contest before you prevailed. The chief issue seemed to be about the opening of the Second Front. Mr Roosevelt was very anxious to get started and have American troops to go ashore and the military people did think we had the capacity. Mr Churchill was very much impressed by the casualties that Britain had suffered in World War One and he didn't want to go through that experience again. One night I was in London before we went ashore on the continent and he asked me to have dinner with him. We went off in a car and he took me up to the Houses of Parliament, this was about one o'clock; he sat down in what was then the House of Lords – the Commons had been destroyed – had the lights turned on and he talked about the loss of an entire British generation. He said, 'I'm only an acci-

dent, I'm a sport. All my colleagues are dead – they're buried at Somme or Passchendaele – and we can't endure the loss of another British generation. And I want you to realise that this is something that has to be avoided for everybody's sake.' And suddenly I realised why he had kept me so long. I was only Assistant Secretary of War, but it was because my chief was keen on going ashore promptly and straight across the Channel, and he knew that I was rather close to my chief, Mr Stimson, and he was trying to point out to me what really was his preoccupation.

PROFESSOR VANNEVAR BUSH
Chairman of the US National Defense Research Committee 1940
I don't think anybody ever dominated Roosevelt, not even his wife. But I think Churchill had a great influence on Roosevelt, and quite properly so.

MAJOR GENERAL KENNETH STRONG
Chief of Intelligence to General Eisenhower
Mr Churchill tried to persuade General Eisenhower not to draw on the forces in Italy to help his campaign in France but to leave them in Italy and to get on with the forces he had available. And I remember Eisenhower saying to me, 'You know he's a very cunning old man. When I went to see him and he talked about this, the tears rolled down his cheeks and he said, "You must leave me with these divisions, you can't take them away." I said, "Mr Prime Minister, if indeed you have a political object in keeping the troops there, well, that is all right. You let our bosses in Washington know what it is. But if you are making this suggestion to me on military grounds I must disagree with you – I want to draw on troops from Italy to help my campaign in Europe."' And so in the end Churchill gave way and, like in all these things once he'd given way, he supported Eisenhower right to the end.

MAJOR GENERAL JOHN HARDING
Chief of Staff to Field Marshal Alexander
Churchill and Alexander were very close and very personal, and I think this was probably due to the fact that Alexander epitomised everything

that Churchill himself would have liked to have been. He was debonair, he was handsome and alert and lively, amusing and good company, and at the same time he had been a highly successful military commander. On one occasion when Winston was on a visit to Italy in September 1944, he came and had lunch in Alexander's mess and he brought with him a new photograph of himself for Alexander, which he autographed, and after lunch he presented it to Alexander who said, 'Thank you very much indeed, sir, I will take it at once and put it in my caravan,' and he went off, an erect, alert figure in a smart uniform. Winston looked after him with tears in his eyes and said, 'Ah, what a man.' I think there was admiration and affection on both sides.

MICHAEL FOOT

I think Churchill hated Aneurin Bevan during the war, and recognised him as a most serious opponent. Particularly, of course, Aneurin Bevan was out to secure the most successful prosecution of the war – he wasn't opposed to the war at all. But the idea that Churchill and Bevan fought each other with courtesy during the war, that's not the case. Both of them were concerned about the whole future of the world and Aneurin Bevan thought in those later years that Churchill was leading the country in the wrong direction and was failing to exploit the opportunities. For example when Mussolini was overthrown he thought that the way the British government reacted to it added to the whole length of the war. So there was no love lost between them and indeed after 1945 Churchill tried to have his revenge by trying to destroy Aneurin Bevan's reputation. I'm glad to say he failed. It may be that in later years there was some reconciliation because they'd known each other in the Thirties and had been common critics of the Chamberlain govern-ment at the time, but during the war years and post-war years they fought with real weapons – it was no fake fight between them.

DR STEPHEN AMBROSE
American historian
The biggest single criticism I would make of Churchill during the war was that he overstrained the British economy for victory, that he did more than

had to be done. Britain was the most mobilised nation in the war. The rail system was worn out, the industrial plant was worn out, the transport system was worn out. In addition the Americans drove a very hard bargain. The Lend-Lease Act [1941], which Churchill called 'the least sordid act in all human history', may well have been that, but there was much about it that wasn't pretty. The Americans insisted that the British sell their overseas assets; this meant that at the end of the war the income that the British counted on and depended on for so long from her overseas investments was no longer there. They had been sold at American insistence. Beyond that, the Americans had also forced the British to break up the sterling bloc to open it up to American investment and the United States had all kinds of excess capital available for overseas investment when the war ended. The Americans then moved into the areas that had previously been British colonies, whether simple or economic colonies. So Britain was in a much weaker position at the end of the war than she had been at the beginning and was not in a position to recover. Added to that was the sentiment around the world that had been built up by Allied propaganda that this was a war for human freedom, liberty, freedom from hunger, freedom from fear, from exploitation, so that you had a universal sentiment to end European colonialism, which was in the large part British colonisation.

CHAPTER 7

BATTLE OF BRITAIN
AND THE BLITZ

The Battle of Britain and the Blitz were the first major military campaigns fought entirely in the air. The battle for daylight air supremacy over southern Britain was fought from early August to the end of October 1940, and the attempt to break British resolve by night bombing ran through the following winter and spring until Hitler redeployed the Luftwaffe against the Soviet Union in May 1941. During the Battle of Britain the Royal Air Force (RAF) enjoyed the decisive advantage of defending against attacks launched from widely separated airfields (thus profiting from what strategists call 'interior lines'), optimised by Britain's system of radar tracking and guidance, with the added comfort of fighting over friendly territory so that pilots who crash-landed or parachuted out of their aircraft could return to battle. The Luftwaffe had been built around the concept of close air support for ground forces (which had worked so well in France) and was singularly ill-suited for the task Hitler and Göring called upon it to perform over England. There was no outstanding difference in the technical characteristics of the fighter aircraft employed by the two sides, and the tactical advantage that the German fighters had developed in earlier conflicts was negated once they were ordered to provide close escort to the bomber formations, which had expensively discovered they were unable to defend themselves. Even so, had the Luftwaffe persisted in attacking British airfields it is likely a transient air superiority would have been won, but once the German bombers were turned against London the RAF quickly recovered and established daylight air supremacy. It was Britain's very great good fortune that the Luftwaffe had never subscribed to the concept of strategic

*bombing, because anti-aircraft and civil-defence preparations were entirely
inadequate and if the German bombers, which roamed the night skies almost
at will, had been capable of carrying more significant payloads the results
might have been as devastating as they were to be for Germany when the boot
was on the other foot. During the Blitz more German bombers were lost to flying
accidents than to British anti-aircraft guns or night-fighters.*

ANTHONY EDEN
British Secretary of State for War

Winston rightly called it our finest hour and it was true, but it was also our
grimmest hour, without question. And there must have been moments for
all of us – there certainly was in my mind – when I didn't see how we are
going to find a way through, just couldn't see it. There were moments
when I thought the only thing that might be left for us to do would be to
take a German with us into another world.

FLIGHT LIEUTENANT ROBERT WRIGHT
*Personal Assistant to Air Chief Marshal Sir Hugh Dowding, C-in-C RAF
Fighter Command*

Dowding was the supreme realist, knowing his job was to defend the
United Kingdom and prevent the possibility of the Germans launching an
invasion. He said he knew full well he could never win the war but he was
very conscious of the fact he was the one man who could easily lose it. By
the time of the Fall of France, Fighter Command had been depleted in
strength because of the squadrons going to France to support the battle
there. Dowding's initial establishment was fifty-two squadrons – that was
the absolute minimum that was considered necessary for the defence of
the United Kingdom. He was way down in strength when the time came
for fighting the battle and that was a thing he was always fighting for, to
maintain at least his basic, initial establishment of fifty-two squadrons.

ANTHONY EDEN

Personally I think Hitler was right not to attempt the invasion. I suppose
the only outside chance would have been in June/July, before we got

anything in order as far as the Army was concerned, if he could have then put one hundred thousand men ashore and attempted to march on London or something. But then how could he do that? He hadn't the ships to take them. If you think it took us four years of tremendous effort with all the resources of the United States behind us to prepare for the invasion of France, it's hard to see how Hitler, occupied still with defeating the main enemy on land – France – could find the resources to switch quickly to attack Britain. He could only succeed if he had command of the air, which he never got, and if he got command of the sea, which he never got either, and, thirdly, if he could build such an armada of ships that he could bring all the supplies and munitions and artillery and all the rest across with him. And none of those things were possible for him.

COLONEL ADOLF GALLAND
Luftwaffe Jagdgruppe 26

Göring's task, as he felt it, was to establish the Luftwaffe's superiority over the intended invasion area, and he had influence in all the steps of the various phases of the Battle of Britain. In the first phase he ordered that only fighter units should overfly England and force the RAF pilots to attack fighters against fighters. This did work for a short period, but then the Fighter Command held back British units from fighting. The next step was that the High Command ordered that some bombers should go along with us and should drop bombs, and, by doing so, would force the RAF Fighter Command to present itself in the air. This also worked for a certain time. Also at this time we made some low-level attacks on British bases. But the big step would have been the whole strength of our bombers escorted by our fighters attacking the British fighter bases, and I believe that this was a quite successful operation but it was a mistake that we did not continue for a longer time, attacking bases, depots, plants for engines and for fighter fuselages.

FLIGHT LIEUTENANT WRIGHT

The last week in August, the first week in September were the worst for us because that last week in August the Germans had been pounding the airfields mercilessly and 31st August was probably our worst day. Fighter Command was very nearly on its knees and Dowding was very conscious of that, and he was wondering how much longer he could hold out, because he was still having to face the problem of denying the Germans air superiority and yet here they were knocking the airfields to pieces. Any man under that strain would start to show it, and by the first week in September he was showing signs of strain although he was in complete control of himself. The day after the visit of the King and Queen, 7th September, an invasion alert was issued and all that day things were remarkably quiet and all of us were beginning to wonder what the devil was going to happen next. Then, late afternoon, the Germans launched the heaviest attack we had ever known – but the attack didn't go to the airfields, it went to London. So we were able to pull ourselves together, repair things and, most important of the lot, it gave the pilots more of a chance for a little rest.

WING COMMANDER 'MAX' AITKEN
601 Squadron RAF

We didn't think the Germans had a chance. We had fought them over France, over their own aerodromes. We knew that the Hurricane and Spitfire were as good as anything they had got, we knew our morale was as good or better than theirs and when it came to fighting over our own homeland, if we had to get out we'd be all right by parachute. And of course we had the biggest asset any Air Force ever had, which was radar. Radar really won the Battle of Britain because without it we would have been doing standing patrols and with the limited number of aircraft and limited number of pilots you couldn't have done it. As it was we could wait on the ground and then radar would watch and through various controls we'd be told to take off when the Germans were over Calais or over Boulogne and so we wasted no petrol, no time, no energy. In fact we could sleep in between sorties and then we'd take off and would be directed towards the German formation and given height, distance and their numbers, which was very important. So we'd go into battle feeling fine and fresh and fit and we would be at an immense advantage, we'd have the advantage of height, we'd have – well, we didn't have larger numbers, naturally they were far greater in number than us – but each squadron knew exactly what it was doing. We were controlled from the ground; we were never lonely.

FLIGHT LIEUTENANT WRIGHT

As soon as he knew where the aircraft were coming from and how many there were, he would immediately pass instructions to the sector stations for them to be scrambled. 'Scramble' being the code word that was used for just getting to the air, they would immediately take off without any instructions about what they were to do, but the moment they were airborne the sector controllers would then give them instructions, where they were to go and the height at which they were to fly. The pilots still were under control by the sector command and the very elaborate and sophisticated radio telephone called the RT. RT control from the ground and the fighters that were airborne were strictly under control until the leader of the formation could see what he was being directed towards. The moment he saw the incoming raid he would say the famous word 'tally-ho' and everyone would shut up and get on with it. The Germans came sailing in and always found something in their way; it might be a very small formation, but something was always there.

COLONEL GALLAND

The first fact was that the RAF losses we reported were from time to time overestimated. And our High Command made the mistake of discounting all these losses from the inventory of the RAF, and very soon there came these negative figures. Secondly we were confronted very soon by the British fighter-control system based on radar, which we didn't have at the time, and this radar system and fighter control were very effective. The next argument can be used that the defence on central lines is easier than attack from a wide radius. The defence took place over their territory and we had the Channel with a lot of water in it between our bases and the targets. Secondly our range was very limited and could only cover a small part of the British Isles, including London. But over London we could only stay for ten minutes to come back to our bases. So this limited range of our fighters, the escort, was perhaps the main point which prevented an effective air offensive against Britain. Without any doubt the British fighter pilots fighting over England defending their own country showed extreme bravery, and their experience was very high: their morale, and the material performance of their fighters was about equal to ours.

SERGEANT PILOT RAY HOLMES
504 Squadron RAF

I think we were just getting on with the war as one would play a game of rugby or cricket – to win. That was all and if you just played your hardest the other man had to come down. I don't think there was any worry about losing at all – we were out to win.

WING COMMANDER AITKEN

Although there were a lot of aircraft about suddenly, when you were fighting a particular man, him in his machine and you in your machine, the sky became empty and you didn't see anyone else, you saw nothing except this one man you were trying to shoot down and he was trying to shoot you. It was just one against one and sometimes you knew he was very good, sometimes you knew he wasn't so good and so you could assess the situation fairly closely as to whether he might be lucky to hit you but otherwise you can get him.

SERGEANT PILOT HOLMES

We used to say we must shoot down these German bastards and I think we built up a sort of synthetic hate against them, but I think it was a bit artificial. We were after the aeroplanes, at least personally that was my view. I wanted to shoot an aeroplane down but I didn't want to shoot a German down, I really did not. We did hear stories of Germans shooting at our fellows in parachutes and we thought that was pretty horrible, but we weren't sure whether it was true or not. I know I had an experience of a German aircrew getting draped over my own wing; he baled out of a bomber and got caught on my wing with his parachute and I was jolly careful to get him off as easily and as quickly as I could by banking the aeroplane and shaking him off. I was very glad when I heard he'd dropped down in Kennington Oval safely. So I had no feeling of wanting to kill that fellow personally.*

WING COMMANDER AITKEN

I'd say there was no chivalry at all – you mean between the German Air Force and the British? I'd say absolutely none at all, not as far as I was concerned. I hated them, they were trying to do something to us, to enslave us, and I wasn't going to have anything of that if I could possibly avoid it. I would say there was none, but I know there seems to be some of it about now, these days. But not from me – never.

SERGEANT PILOT HOLMES

I don't think anyone ever considered that he would be killed, that was something which was just put at the back of your mind. If it was not, then you'd have got the jitters and have been very worried. If a fellow did go missing it was just, 'poor old so-and-so's had it' and that was that. Inwardly of course you'd feel it tremendously if you lost a pal but you didn't dwell on the subject at all. It couldn't happen to you.

WING COMMANDER AITKEN

LMF [Lack of Moral Fibre] was a very unfortunate situation, a horrible thing which was that a pilot really packed it in and said I can't go on. They all said may I go to training. Well, no – if a fellow said I don't want to do any more fighting there was only one thing to do and it was done with absolutely no thought at all. He was taken away from his squadron that day, he was taken away from the Air Force that day, if he was an officer he was stripped of his rank and he was put into another service or into the Home Guard or something. We could never keep on anybody who faltered for one moment, because you know faltering is a very catching business and if that had happened in any way it would have been quite wrong. Therefore there was this horrible thing LMF – it became a bit of a joke, you know people saying I think I'm suffering from it, but the fact

---

* The German pilot later died of his injuries.

of the matter was that it could have become a disease unless it was stopped. Sometimes you could tell a fellow was going to get killed. Yes, you could – he sort of lost it. When you're tremendously keen on something you're much better than when you're rather holding back, and the fellows who were tremendously keen generally came through.

COLONEL GALLAND

We didn't know at the time why he changed to London: we had only to obey orders. I believe today that Hitler and Göring wanted to make use of their advantage of having the capital of the enemy in the range of their fighters, which could therefore escort the bombers. On the other side Berlin was far out of the effective range of the RAF at this time and in addition the effect of an air raid against a big town has been overestimated. Nobody knew at the time how much was needed to destroy a great part of the town. Perhaps Hitler and Göring hoped that they would force England to negotiate after these attacks. It is difficult to decide which motive really had priority, but it is a matter of fact that this switch to London from military targets changed the situation of Great Britain and Fighter Command considerably.

SERGEANT PILOT HOLMES

After your first attack if you're lucky enough to see one or two that you can go for, and if you've broken them up then that's what happened, you chase them and if they turn for home you let them go because our strict instruction was that we mustn't chase anybody over the Channel because if we came down in the Channel there's a pilot and an aircraft gone. The main thing was to break up the raids and save our own aircraft. And so thirty-six Dorniers very quickly became two or three on which you're focusing your attention. I followed two or three and made attacks on each one of them and ultimately used up all my ammunition. Then I hit the tail of the last one and he came down on Victoria Station and I came down on a rooftop in Chelsea.*

---

* Holmes calculated that he could sever the thin tail boom of the Dornier 217 with his wing and that his Hurricane would survive the impact. He was right only on the first count.

COLONEL GALLAND

The Battle of Britain during daytime became more disorganised and finally it was stopped. After a short time the Luftwaffe Command changed over to night attacks by the bombers only and the fighters were ordered to carry a bomb, and about a third of our fighters had to drop bombs in daylight, while the other two-thirds were escorting the bombers. Both fighter bombing and night bombing had never been practised, and therefore the effects were very low.

ANONYMOUS MALE EAST ENDER

Pub interview in Canning Town, east London

My flat overlooked all this area, looked down the river and across the river to the City, 'cos there's the Surrey Dock there, and I'm going to say this much – in my opinion he should have continued that type of bombing in daylight 'cos he was hitting everything of consequence, shipyards, gasworks, oil farms, everything of consequence, you know, all the bombs were dropping in the proper target area. So he only wasted his time when he came of a night-time, when he couldn't see what he was throwing them at.

ANONYMOUS MALE EAST ENDER

Pub interview in Canning Town

Just over the road from here was an oil bomb that set the house on fire and more or less blew it to pieces – the house is now rebuilt, as you can see for yourself over the road. From there we had other duties and went to the pub, the Liverpool Arms in the Barking Road, where we found that the proprietor had had his head chopped off with the glass and was laying in the forecourt, and big hole in the road where an ambulance had gone down and killed the ambulance driver and attendant. And I would like to say this – bombs were streaming about this particular area and the old women and people went out to put those bombs out, even in the road which was a silly thing to do, they could have let them burn themselves out. But they just had the spirit in them that they had to do something about it, and the old women – some of them are in this pub tonight – went out and they did a magnificent job of work.

MR OVERLANDER

Pub interview in Canning Town

They expected a tremendous number of civilian casualties, dead, and all the schools and playgrounds were turned into emergency mortuaries with stretchers and things of that sort to put the bodies on. But the thing that surprised the authorities, owing to the policy of Anderson shelters and things of that sort, was that very few of the people themselves were injured but there was a tremendous damage to property, all these little houses at the least blast fell down, and it was a question of putting people in schools and things of that sort, of turning out the auxiliary fire brigades and people of that type to give the people, where they could, at least sleep.

ANONYMOUS MALE EAST ENDER

Pub interview in Canning Town

Many of the casualties that happened in the early part of the Blitz need not have happened if they had accepted the help and advice of the authorities. There must have been thousands and thousands of Anderson shelters stacked up in depots up and down the country where people said they weren't going to have their gardens destroyed, they weren't going to have them in the house at all.

ANONYMOUS MALE EAST ENDER

Pub interview in Canning Town

The day I was hit was October 13th, 1940. About ten to eight I said to my wife and my in-laws, 'Well, I'll be off now,' and I just walked out the door. Lovely, big three-floor houses they were and I just walked up the approach road about twenty yards from the church which was our air-raid post and suddenly there was – shh – nothing, I heard nothing and I fell flat on my face. I picked myself up, I turned around and all I could see was just a grey curtain hanging down the middle of the road, about twice as wide as this pub. It was just a brownish-grey curtain hanging there and I thought, My God, something's happened. So I staggered down to the post and I said to the post warden, 'Jim, I think something's happened up at the Prince of Wales.' When we went up there and when we saw it I said,

'Christ almighty, the family's down there!' And there it was – we were there, about fourteen of us all on this big row of houses, and it was just one bloody great hole.

ANONYMOUS MALE EAST ENDER
Pub interview in Canning Town
The whole of Holborn was ablaze; the buildings were falling down. Cheapside was not so bad but all around St Paul's there were buildings ablaze. One thing that struck me as absolutely typical, the Lord Mayor of London was walking along, quite unconcerned with his umbrella and bowler hat, along Cheapside.

ANONYMOUS FEMALE EAST ENDER
Pub interview in Canning Town
The shelter where we used to go used to be what we call 'under the arches' and at the end of under the arches was a bigger archway and there'd be a canteen in there and this was run by Father John Groser of Stepney. He used to run this canteen and run dances so we all used to have half an hour, an hour up there and all. He used to come through selling coffee or cocoa or tea and what have you and keep us all happy in the shelters, it was one big, happy family.

ANONYMOUS MALE EAST ENDER
Pub interview in Canning Town
It was a very light attack on the first day and in this small and very narrow street the bomb sort of slid down the front of the houses and we went down there all in our newness ready to serve and we got some of them out, and then we saw this dear old lady sort of staggering around and all she had on was just half of what should have been a nightdress. It was the top half and she was completely in a daze and we said, 'Go and get something on, Ma,' and we didn't want to go and help her, obviously. So she said, 'Oh, I'll go in and get something,' and when she came out she'd got her hat on.

ANONYMOUS MALE EAST ENDER
Pub interview in Canning Town

One of the biggest morale builders in the East End of London was Joyce, Lord Haw-Haw. He used to come on the radio every night about eight o'clock and predict where the bombs were going to be dropped. He'd say, 'Well, tonight we're not going to Stepney, we may drop a few on somewhere else,' or something of that sort, and it so infuriated the people, the people were so angry about him, I mean, he actually done more good than he did harm.*

ANONYMOUS MALE EAST ENDER
Pub interview in Canning Town

A big morale booster was the Women's Voluntary Service – the WVS. These ladies came down to the town hall in 1939 and the town clerks and people of that sort were very perplexed what to do with them and they found them an office, but when the Blitz started they certainly proved their worth. They went out with mobile canteens right in the middle of the Blitz; the following day they had their clothing centres open. People who had lost everything were fitted up with clothes and then taken along by the WVS and be given a cup of tea and a bun, then taken along to the assistance people who doled them out £10 or £20, whatever the size of the family was. Really, from the start these ladies done an excellent job. For example one lady from Poplar was a Miss Gretton, she was one of the brewery family and she'd led a very, very sheltered life – but she had guts, that woman.

J B PRIESTLEY
English author and broadcaster

One interesting thing, you know, is that on the whole women took it better than men. I think because men hated their helplessness – they couldn't do anything back – whereas women are more used to this extra

---

* William Joyce was born in 1906 in New York. A leading figure in the British Union of Fascists, he fled to Germany in 1939 to avoid internment and broadcast for the Nazis to Britain throughout the war. Declared British on a flimsy technicality he was hanged for treason in 1946.

suffering without any aggression following it, so the thing didn't get on their nerves as it did on men's nerves.

MR BUTLER

London air-raid warden

Some of the worst things I think was when there'd been a direct hit and someone had blown into little pieces and you had to pick that up, put it in sandbags, label it where it came from, where we found it, and by that they used to more or less identify all these people, who they were and where they came from. Sometimes we'd get two hands, two left hands, or two right feet. Well, you'd know full well that if you got two on the same side there were two people that had been killed there. I think that's about one of the worst things that you had to do and it took a man with a very strong stomach to do it, I can assure you on that.

GEORGE HODGKINSON

Coventry town councillor

People seemed to choose the kind of shelter that suited their disposition. Some favoured going under the stairs or the domestic surface shelters which were made available to them and of course there were the street shelters made for the purpose of affording protection for people on the move, in the street, they could dive into these shelters. One old lady when her priest went round to comfort her said, 'Well, I just read my Bible a bit and I says bugger them and I goes off to bed.'

FLIGHT LIEUTENANT WRIGHT

We had no defence against the night bombing. The night-fighters, although they had a wonderful promise and this AI – Aircraft Interception, which was an airborne form of radar – fitted into night-fighters, we hadn't had it for a long time and at the time of the Blitz it was not working. We had it first in Blenheims, a comparatively sedate aircraft, the magic box, the black box, all sorts of mysterious names we had for it, because it was a great secret. But during the Blitz itself we had no defence. Heavy demands were made on the single-engine fighters trying to see in the dark, they couldn't see anything at all, it was very much a hit-or-miss proposition.

COLONEL GALLAND

The night raids of our bombers were sometimes very successful, as in Coventry; on other occasions they had a minimum of navigation equipment, they didn't have radar and they were forced to navigate in daylight, and weather conditions always changed. It depended mainly on the first attack by the leading unit: when this unit hit the target, the following bombers could easily hit the target also. It was almost by accident whether night-fighters would be effective or not.

GEORGE HODGKINSON

As chairman of my own street fire-guard organisation I had to go on the street to be ready with buckets and stirrup-pump and so on, ready to snuff out any incendiaries that were round about. We lost one neighbour and her mother and we were under the bombs all night, our family, eleven solid hours. We got a landmine exploded within a few yards of the house: it ripped through the house hooking the curtains to the window frames, took the roof off, the tiles falling on to the pavement and you could see the stars through the building. We were in a rather desperate state at the end of the night.

MR BUTLER

There was an Anderson shelter and apparently there was a little girl inside. Her parents had gone round the corner to visit their friends or relations or something and the shelter was more or less caved in and covered with soil. I got down into the shelter and there was this little girl about fifteen or sixteen and her mouth was full of soil. Naturally I got hold of her hand, which is our job to console these people and try to quieten them down. She was in a pretty bad state and I cleaned her mouth out; she laid back and as she was catching her breath, sort of breathing heavily, some stupid devil walked over the top of the shelter, soil came down and went back in this girl's throat and as she squeezed my hand like that she just faded out. Now I had the feel of that girl clenching my hand for weeks and weeks and weeks. I could never forget it and I don't forget it now.

FLIGHT LIEUTENANT WRIGHT

I remember one time Dowding was going through a built-up area that had been very badly blitzed and houses and flats hanging out in all directions and things flung around, it was then that he expressed a feeling that might sound a little stilted – he said he was appalled at what he considered was a dreadful intrusion into the privacy of the lives of these people.

COLONEL GALLAND

Hitler decided to attack Russia, but nevertheless he continued with this attacks against London and Great Britain with reduced strength. In April 1941 Hitler assembled all the commanders in France and he told my friend and myself that it was done in order to camouflage the offensive against Russia; so the last raids can only be considered as a cover for the beginning of the Russian campaign.

GWEN BUNT

Plymouth housewife, night of 22–23 April 1941

The children, Raymond and Sheila, were both asleep. I usually put them into bed about seven. When the sirens went I called my mother, she came down the stairs and said, 'I'll take Raymond up.' 'All right,' I said, 'I'll take Sheila.' And we called Mrs Todd, that was the lady upstairs, and she came down with her three children and we went to our respective cupboards. I sat on a little tiny chair, put Raymond at my side and I held Sheila in my arms. They were still asleep; they never woke up. When the bombs fell I'm sure I heard the one that hit us – I could hear the screeching of it as it fell and then I knew no more. I must have rallied round because I heard my father say, 'Oh, I think your mother's had it.' I didn't answer him, I said, 'Oh, Sheila's all right, she's in my arms.' I went to put my hand out to see if Raymond was all right but I couldn't feel him, my arm was high up like and of course we was buried, and I said, 'Oh, I can't move.' Anyway, someone took Sheila from me – I could feel that – and then I felt whoever it was carrying me put me over his shoulder and I seemed to rally round again and I could feel myself being carried out into the air and the next time I knew I was in hospital when I came to. Later

I learned that my mother was dead, and the two children were, and Mrs Todd was killed – she was expecting a baby any hour – and two of her children. One of her children must have run out but I never heard of him from that day to this.

EMILY THOMAS
Plymouth housewife, night of 22–23 April
The children had been with us and then, like children do, they wanted to run around, and they ran to another part of the shelter – you know, the shelter runs into different compartments. They hadn't been gone not five minutes before that shelter had a direct hit where the children were. That's one of the awfullest things I remember and of course we were stunned, we were shocked, and there were several men there, my son-in-law was there with my husband, and of course all the men dived to try to get the children but they couldn't because there was too much masonry. My husband went back to our place and got some crowbars that were lying in the garden and they tried to lift this heavy masonry but they couldn't. By the time they got through to them, well, by the time they got through to the children, they had died.

ARTHUR BOTTOMLEY
Trade-union leader and Walthamstow borough councillor
There was a Captain Blaney who was a bomb-disposal man and one night when I was the Civil Defence Controller he came to me and he said there was a parachute mine that had come down. Well, the instruction given us was that we shouldn't touch them, it was a matter for the Navy. And Blaney said, 'Look, I'm going to tackle it,' and I said, 'It's not your duty, you must leave it alone.' He called me a white-livered cur and this rather challenged me and very foolishly the Chief Inspector of Police, Captain Blaney and myself went to this power mine and he defused it. Everybody else who's approached one was blown up, so we were jolly lucky. But he was reprimanded – he was reduced to the rank of lieutenant and he became very troubled and upset about it, as you can imagine. Not long afterwards he borrowed my car and I saw his sergeant and said, 'Is my car

back?' and he said, 'I'm sorry to say Captain Blaney is not coming back.' 'What happened?' He said he was defusing a bomb and he failed to notice two others there and it exploded – up he went.

ANTHONY EDEN
Foreign Secretary from December 1940

President Roosevelt sent his Republican opponent Wendell Wilkie over to this country in 1941 at the time when there had been a good deal of Blitz activity. And I remember he came to see me at the Foreign Office and he asked me what advice I could give him as to how to find out what people in this country really thought about the war. 'Well,' I said, 'ask them.' And it so happened that we were coming out of the Foreign Office there was a man working away at windows which had been broken in the night, on top of a ladder, and Wilkie went up to him and said, 'How do you feel about the war?' The man looked slightly astonished and said, 'What do you mean?' Wilkie said, 'Well, do you want to go through with it,' and the man said, 'Hitler ain't dead yet, is he?' If I'd have laid it on it couldn't have been a better answer. And that, Wilkie told me long after, was a view found throughout the country and therefore if Britain did hold on and did work her way through, immense credit of course to Winston and his leadership. But immense credit is also due to the British people, because it was their victory.

CHAPTER 8

NORTH AFRICA
AND THE BALKANS

In 1940–41 events in the Balkans and North Africa were intimately linked. After the Fall of France the Italians concentrated their troops in Libya on the Egyptian border, and invaded British-held Egypt in September 1940. Beset by the logistical problems that were to prove a feature of desert war they advanced only as far as Sidi Barrani, where they dug in. In November the Greeks defeated an Italian invasion and drove it back deep into Albania. On 7 December 1940, under the overall command of C-in-C Middle East, General Sir Archibald Wavell, the Commander of Commonwealth Forces in Egypt, Lieutenant General Henry Maitland Wilson, launched Operation Compass. Major General Richard O'Connor's attack destroyed the advanced elements of the Italian Army at Sidi Barrani, and Wavell then withdrew the 4th Indian Division for service against the Italians in Ethiopia. The offensive continued: after capturing Tobruk on 22 January, O'Connor sent the 7th Armoured Division on an uncharted route across the bulge of Cyrenaica and on 7 February 1941 cut off the entire Italian force at Beda Fomm, compelling it to surrender. Shortly afterwards he was ordered to halt at El Agheila and Wilson was appointed to lead a Commonwealth Expeditionary Force, its troops taken from O'Connor, to reinforce the Greeks in anticipation of a German reaction to the defeat of their Italian ally. The pro-Axis government in neighbouring Yugoslavia was overthrown in late March, but in April the Germans raced through Yugoslavia. By the end of the month they had driven Wilson's force out of Greece to Crete, and they took Crete itself by airborne assault in May. Meanwhile Lieutenant General Erwin Rommel, who had made his reputation commanding a panzer division in France in 1940, had arrived in Tripoli with a small armoured force soon called the Afrika Korps. He defeated the British at El Agheila on 24 March; on 7 April he captured O'Connor and Wilson's replacement in Egypt, Lieutenant General Sir Philip Neame, and by 15 April had recovered all of Cyrenaica except Tobruk, which was besieged until 27 November 1941. The see-saw of war in North Africa had begun.

ANTHONY EDEN
British Secretary of State for War

Chief of the Imperial General Staff Field Marshal Sir John Dill and I had a meeting, I think it was early July, and we decided the only place we could fight the enemy was the North African desert; there was nothing else. We couldn't hope to make a landing in France in any foreseeable future, therefore couldn't injure the Germans that way. The two alternatives were bombing and fighting in the Middle East. As to aircraft you realise the difficulties – because the Germans and the Italians had the inner lines, they could shift their aircraft with the greatest of ease through the north of France down to Greece or anywhere. We, on the other hand, had to go all the way round the Cape with almost everything, with all the delay that entailed.

BRIGADIER JOHN HARDING
Chief of Staff to General O'Connor, Commander Western Desert Force

There had been no light at the end of the tunnel at all since the withdrawal from Dunkirk. I think for political and above all morale reasons – the morale of the people of this country and the standing of our positions round the world – it was terribly important from this point of view and indeed from everybody's point of view to show that we could hold the Germans.

PRIVATE BOB MASH
Engineer, Nile Army

We actually made dummy tanks, dummy guns, and from the air when reconnaissance planes came across it just looked as though we had a really good, strong army. I've known the time when we've blown up rubber tanks, put them in position, taken them down in the evening, taken them three or four miles further away, blown them up again and lay them there, and from the air it looked as though we had plenty of tanks. Just the same as on the Canal Zone anti-aircraft guns, every other anti-aircraft gun was a wooden one.

ANTHONY EDEN

What we needed for the battle to have any chance, according to Maitland Wilson, who was going to be in charge of the battle, was what were called 'I-' tanks in those days, infantry tanks, heavy, rather slow-moving animals, which would act as fortresses to move forward and to reduce Sidi Barrani. And Wavell, quite rightly, was tremendously security-conscious, a lot of gossip always in a place like Cairo, and he didn't want anybody to know anything. So I wasn't allowed to telegraph Winston, give any hint of what might happen until I got home. But at the same time Wavell did want these I-tanks and so I had to send a telegram, very masked and complicated, saying to Winston please don't ask questions and please don't argue or anything but please send us some I-tanks. Which I must say, grandly, he did at once. Because we didn't have too many of these things and they were very important. But apart from that, the battle was fought on Wavell's resources and brilliantly fought, there's no question of that.

LAWRENCE DURRELL

Press officer, Cairo

Wavell had an extraordinary weakness for poets and poetry and was in fact at that moment doing an anthology and a treatise on generalship, which is one of the more amusing and one of the most sensitive books I think ever written by a general. He was a frequent visitor to the Anglo-Egyptian Union. A side of him was withdrawn, not exactly morose but he had a wall eye, and wall-eyed people give a feeling of dryness and moroseness. A bit gentle, nice, we liked him very much. He was a great addition to the circle and he used to come down very modestly, and at the time he was, I suppose, deep in plans to mop up the Italians. It never showed and he always had an anthology of verse under his arm.

LIEUTENANT COLONEL RONALD BELCHEM

7th Armoured Division

General Wavell will go down in history as one of our most competent generals of the Second World War. Indeed it's known that Rommel told his son that General Wavell was a military genius. General Wavell, remember, was Commander-in-Chief of the Middle East, stretching from the Persian Gulf right across to Malta. And for this enormous responsibility the resources at his disposal were meagre indeed, not only on the ground but also in the air. Probably only the Navy was able to afford the scale of effort that the situation demanded. But working on interior lines General Wavell, who was a great strategist, managed with these meagre resources to liberate Ethiopia, to defeat the Italian forces there and in Somaliland.

ANTHONY EDEN

Churchill was delighted when success came along. It was a very trying time until it did because I could show him on the map what we hoped to do, but Wavell quite rightly never would be too optimistic in what he said. He'd always play it down to get more help for this or that, which was rather trying if you were at the London end hoping great things, wanting great victories for other purposes apart from the actual battle. But of course Churchill was delighted when the results came in and they were wonderful. If any of my listeners have military ambitions, I would strongly advise them to avoid holding a high military command in the first two years in the British Army. Better wait until the stuff begins to come along, which I am afraid in the last two experiences was after the third year or later.

MAJOR GENERAL RICHARD O'CONNOR

Commander Western Desert Force

We started out to do a five-day raid. My resources were only two divisions, the 4th Indian and the 7th Armoured divisions, whose morale was extremely high and they were very well trained. The enemy, on the other hand, had a vast numerical superiority, something in the nature of eight to one, but their morale was low and they had no interest or enthusiasm for the war at all. We therefore felt that we had to do something to knock him off balance and prevent him using that vast superiority against our small numbers. In this we were helped because his method of defence was this: he had a series of these fortified perimeter camps and we decided that we would attack one and one only. As they were so far apart we felt sure they would be unable to support each other and we would be able to deal with this one by itself. Therefore, in order to get a better result, we decided that by night we would move our main forces round between two of these camps until we came right to the rear and then to attack from the rear, which would be the last place he would expect to be attacked, and then the surprise would be complete.

BRIGADIER HARDING

General O'Connor's instructions were to inflict such heavy losses on the Italians to destroy their potential for the invasion of the Delta, and his tactics were to get in behind the camps in which the Italian forces had entrenched themselves and to take full advantage of their fortress-minded deployment and to knock off the camps one by one, at the same time inflicting very heavy losses on them. Eventually this opened the way to an advance which again he exploited to the full. He was a commander who was always looking for an opportunity for bigger and better things and he certainly saw this, appreciated it immediately and took advantage of it.

LIEUTENANT COLONEL BELCHEM

Although they greatly outnumbered us numerically and in other respects, our equipment was probably superior. Secondly their training was very elementary: they were not trained for desert operations, the Italians, neither were they clever at night. Most importantly their morale, although apparently high, was a synthetic morale inspired by repetitive propaganda and one was very conscious that if they suffered a defeat this would probably peel off like a plastic wrapper, which in fact was the case. But they had, for example, no tanks worth paying much attention to and I speak with feeling for the Italian crews because I was myself with an Italian tank regiment in Italy for a period before the war. O'Connor undertook an operation that was due to last about four days, which was the limit for the available tanks, which were nearly worn out, and for our administration in terms of supplying water and fuel and ammunition. He achieved complete surprise, got behind the Italian positions at Sidi Barrani by a night march and in the morning Italian resistance collapsed. O'Connor's great achievement was that by using captured vehicles and captured dumps of water and supplies he was able to maintain this four-day battle into an offensive lasting over a period of weeks and resulted in taking him as far as Benghazi and indeed beyond to El Agheila.

LIEUTENANT PAOLO COLACICCHI
Italian Tenth Army

Your army in Egypt, although considerably smaller than ours in number, was certainly better trained, better equipped especially in transport and tanks and armoured cars, and also had at the top generals who were certainly more aggressively minded than ours, so of course morale sagged even more. The armoured car acting as an OP [Observation Post] for the artillery had a tremendous effect on our men because they couldn't see the enemy. We could just see something glistening on the horizon, which was the armoured car, and then you'd fire a few shots and it would move a couple of hundred yards and readjust the fire of your batteries and this shook very much our Libyan troops. We had two divisions of Libyan troops who had, some of them, fought very well in Ethiopia, but these men must see the enemy to fight well. You can't put them in a fort and say hold it, and all day keep them subject to artillery fire, which they can't see where it comes from. They turn to their white officer and say, 'What about it, why can't we fire back?' And you say, 'Well, we haven't got the guns,' and they say, 'Well, then, they're stronger and this is very bad.'

MAJOR GENERAL O'CONNOR

I wasn't really surprised. I thought we'd do it, I thought we'd surprise them. We dominated no man's land and so they really didn't get their patrols out in the way they ought to have. The relative difficulty was getting right this night march between the two camps, which were only twenty to twenty-five miles apart. But they didn't hear us: we had aeroplanes in the air to make a noise all the time so they never heard our movement and it came as a complete and absolute surprise to them.

ANTHONY EDEN

Many unkind things have been said about the Italians and I think some of them are unfair. There was a brigadier commanding an armoured brigade or support group in the line next to the Italians at Solum or somewhere whose name was 'Strafer' Gott. He afterwards became quite famous and had he not been killed would have had command of the Eighth Army. I'd known him for some time and he came in with the others to talk to us in the desert while I was there and said something which impressed me at the time. He said it's not fair or true to say that the Italians are not brave – what it is, is that they are not properly trained. And I should think that was right. Mussolini pushed these people out indifferently trained and they were expected to go and fight these battles in desert conditions for which you have to be trained.

MAJOR GENERAL O'CONNOR

We had a great disappointment because the morning after Sidi Barrani I received information that the 4th Indian Division was to be withdrawn and that the new division, the 6th Australian Division – which was very good, I must say, when it came – wouldn't be ready for action for another month. That meant that the impetus of our pursuit would vanish and the enemy would be alerted and it would no longer be possible to surprise him. In fact we were back to rather below square one, but we managed and we did take Bardia after a considerable fight and Tobruk after a lesser one and advanced our line to Derna and then we had to come to the great decision: whether we were going to follow the enemy up along the Benghazi road or go right across the El Akhdar desert, come right across the line of communication of the Italian Tenth Army and to stop them escaping. And this, after a very hard fight, we successfully did, thanks to the marvellous work of the 7th Armoured Division, and we really liquidated the whole Italian Army.

ANTHONY EDEN

There was a school of thought which believed in the autumn of 1940 that during the winter Hitler would assemble, as he could have done no doubt, a formidable force with a view to launching an attack on this island in the spring. In the event he wasn't thinking of attacking us, he was thinking of attacking Russia, which opened up an entirely new perspective in the war. I don't pretend that after Wavell's victory we in London realised that there might soon be a Russo-German conflict – but we did think that if it were possible to bring certain Balkan countries into conflict with Hitler then the consequences might be really unforeseeable.

LIEUTENANT COLONEL FRANCIS DE GUINGAND
Joint Planning Staff, GHQ Cairo

O'Connor, who was commanding the Western Desert Force, had captured Tobruk and Benghazi, and his force had gone well south of Benghazi and at that moment Rommel and the Germans hadn't really started to come into North Africa. I was under the Joint Planning Staff in Cairo and always trying to look ahead and produce plans. We had to show that it was perfectly feasible, with the transport resources and air power and the Navy, that this desert force would get to Tripoli and mop up the remaining Italians. Army Headquarters produced similar studies and came to the same conclusion and O'Connor wanted to go ahead to Tripoli, he told me that himself. At that moment Churchill had a great idea of intervention in Greece because everyone knew the Germans were going to invade Greece at some time, and he wanted to offer a British expedition. The Prime Minister of Greece Ioannis Metaxas, a very strong character, and his Chief of the Armed Forces, Alexander Papagos, who was the hero of the Greek people after his victories over the Italians in Albania, but he would have nothing to do with it. And Papagos said the Allies clean up North Africa first and then we'll think about other operations. One of the reasons for intervention in Greece, Churchill had in mind, was to try to persuade Turkey to come in on our side, which would have been tremendous. Personalities change the course of events and Metaxas died, heart attack or something. And another Prime Minister took over, nothing like such a strong man, and Churchill got on to him and

Wavell was told to denude the Western Desert and reduce the forces to the minimum and to prepare an expedition force to Greece.

LIEUTENANT COLONEL BELCHEM

The decision to go to Greece was a political one and from the point of view of a professional it was a military nonsense. It may have been necessary for Great Britain to help our Greek allies at that time, even though the Greeks did not seem to be particularly enthusiastic about it, but militarily I can only express an opinion from a cold professional angle. Firstly, if you think of the position in the air we simply had not got any comparable Royal Air Force contingent to enable us to hope to succeed in Greece; whereas against us, limited only by the number of forward bases available, the Germans were able to concentrate the whole of the Luftwaffe. Under those conditions we couldn't hope to maintain our position alongside the Greeks, who were themselves very poorly and very sparsely equipped. Yet from the overall point of view of the Commander-in-Chief Middle East the military situation was that the diversion of resources to Greece included the 6th and 7th Australian divisions and the New Zealand Division and part of a Second Army division, taken away from General Wavell in Africa, virtually the whole of the fighting formations which were ready and equipped for operations. Therefore by going to Greece we endangered our entire position in the Middle East.

BRIGADIER HARDING

I was all against it. I thought it was a great strategic mistake and I think there was considerable misunderstanding between High Command in Cairo and government in London. What they were really intending to do in Greece, to me it was disastrous. The opportunity that was lost was really of holding Rommel right in the early part of his advance, preventing him from ever getting within striking distance of the Nile Delta.

MAJOR GENERAL O'CONNOR

I'm quite certain that if we had advanced immediately we could have pushed them out. We had good information that there were very few people in the way. I have this letter, an extract that I'm going to read, from Hitler to Mussolini at the time of the fall of Tobruk, when our own Eighth Army was in retreat. It reads as follows: 'If at this moment the British are not pursued to the last breath of each man, the same thing will happen as when the British were deprived of success when they had nearly reached Tripoli.' That seems to me a good-enough indication that we could have got there.

ANTHONY EDEN

With Greece the position had been complicated by two factors, the first that we gave Greece a guarantee, I think before the hostilities began, and the second was that although the Greeks superbly repelled the Italian attacks, they did ask for air help from us, and we had a number of squadrons and ground troops with them in Greece way back before there was any question of the Germans taking part in the Middle East. So in a sense we were largely committed. And the view of the War Cabinet and the Defence Committee at home and of the Chiefs of Staff was that we should, if the Greeks were going to defend themselves against the Germans, we should bring them what help we could. And Dill and I were sent out to Cairo to look into this business. We had appalling weather, we were badly held up and when we reached there in our flying boat I remember saying, 'What are we going to do, supposing Archie Wavell and the other Commanders-in-Chief think it's wrong to go to Greece?' I think Dill said, 'Well, let's jump that one when we get there.' We found Archie there at the landing stage and after a brief introduction he suddenly drew us to one side and said rather solemnly, 'You've been a long time coming,' and I said, 'We've been as quick as we could – it wasn't our fault.' He said, 'I hope you don't mind what I'm going to say, I don't think I ought to waste time and I've begun the movement of troops and the concentration to enable us to go to Greece.' We did all think the same.

BRIGADIER HARDING

I think Wavell allowed himself to be over-pressurised from London in launching operations before he was fully ready for them. I think he was also misled by the Intelligence appreciations at the time who underrated first of all the capability of the Germans to put down forces across the Mediterranean and across North Africa, and then they underrated again the power and strength of the German armoured formations and their anti-tank capabilities.

COLONEL SIEGFRIED WESTPHAL
Rommel's Operations Officer

The German troops who brought the order to go to the desert were very surprised and they had no time to prepare for this new war theatre, but I think they acted very reasonably; many of them did suffer homesickness but the fighting reaction was not influenced by it. Yes, the Germans are a continental people, and we never had in mind to fight outside Germany. I was, in the years between 1935 and 1938, in the first Operational Department of the German General Staff in Berlin. One day came to me a gentleman of another department to speak with me about the maps we would take with us in wartime, and he proposed maps of North Africa and I said to him that is nonsense, we intend not to have warfare in North Africa and this map would not be very useful for the troops, and I declined. Later on when I came to the desert I had to suffer about very bad detailed maps and therefore we were very busy to get in our hands British maps, which were excellent. And Rommel always not with Italian or German maps, only British maps.

ANTHONY EDEN

Many things weren't as expected, but one result did come through – that was the Yugoslav coup d'état. In fact we were just on our way home thinking there was nothing more we could do. At Malta we got this message and we decided to go straight back to Athens to see what we could arrange for contacts with the Yugoslavs, and as we got into the flying boat came a message from Winston, 'Please go back to Athens at once' – minds with a single thought.

LIEUTENANT COLONEL DE GUINGAND

Churchill then sent Eden out to visit Athens and I was the Staff Officer appointed to produce what resources we had available, which we could send to Greece. It didn't look very impressive, however we all survived that and we had a momentous conference at the King of Greece's palace outside Athens, and the King of Greece sitting at the head of the table, with the Prime Minister one side and Papagos on the other. I was called in at the right moment to explain what forces and resources we could send to Greece, and I was actually there when Eden asked Wilson to inform the King of Greece and his Cabinet, his views as to whether we'd be successful if we intervened. Wilson got up and made a most optimistic statement, that he felt we could hold this line and northern Greece and prevent the Germans from getting deep into Greece. I was absolutely shattered because all our studies in ground-planning staff had shown that it wasn't possible – you'd never get the forces and sufficient strength there in time before the Germans would be there.

ANTHONY EDEN

There's the extraordinary thing about Stalin and his approach to the Yugoslavs immediately after the coup d'état: Stalin offered them a pact of mutual assurance. I was amazed because until that moment Russians had taken every precaution not to give Hitler any excuse for attacking them, and yet there they were deliberately flouting him. Hitler was furious at the Yugoslavs, he called it Operation Retribution and if I'd been Hitler at that moment I'd have said, 'Well, we know which side they're on.' Stalin's answer to me, when I asked him a year or more afterwards why he did it, he gave a double answer, he said, 'Because, in the first place, we knew by then that we were going to be attacked, and in the second place they were fellow Slavs and we wanted to encourage them.'

CAPTAIN HANS-OTTO BEHRENDT
Intelligence Officer on Rommel's Staff
One of my favourite Rommel stories is when in the port of Tripoli in February–March 1941, Rommel told my friend Lieutenant Hundt, an engineer, 'Here you can build me a hundred and fifty tanks.' The man looked stupefied and Rommel told him, 'Don't you have timber here in the harbour and canvas of sails to make a hundred and fifty covers for

Volkswagens? So you can give me a hundred and fifty tanks.' Those 'tanks' misled the British in the first campaign.

PRIVATE BOLZANO
Italian Army
One day I stood on the road near the sergeant of panzers and I ask him, 'Tell me the truth – how many working panzers you have now still?' And he said, 'This morning we report seven but the truth is,' he whispered in my ear, 'we have sixteen – but if Rommel knows that, he attacks immediately.'

CAPTAIN BEHRENDT
Rommel was much loved by the Italian simple soldiers because he cared more about them than anybody else in the desert and they called him 'Santo Rommel', I have heard them say this. Rommel himself once said they have other than military virtues and he liked the Italians because they admired and saluted him very nicely, whereas the Germans were not so ready to do this as the Italians. I think that Rommel's criticism of some Italian leaders was also decisive for this Italian esteem, the esteem of the simple soldier towards this German general.

LIEUTENANT COLONEL DE GUINGAND
During the meantime when we had denuded the desert, Rommel had landed in Tripoli, not very strong, but in accordance with his character dashed forward eastwards with the very meagre resources he had there. And absolute chaos reigned, our forces started tumbling back towards Tobruk and we were getting no news in Cairo whatsoever. Wavell sent for me and said, 'Will you go up with my personal liaison officer and try to find out what is happening and see O'Connor and persuade him to hold Tobruk?' I found an Australian division in absolute state of exhaustion and all lying around the place in Tobruk, had several days without sleep and I couldn't find O'Connor. After many hours I found Brigadier Harding who was absolutely magnificent; exhausted, he was holding the fort and he behaved in a simply amazing and wonderful way. He said certainly they would try and hold Tobruk.

LIEUTENANT COLONEL BELCHEM

Wavell's decision to hold Tobruk at the time of that retreat was the greatest single factor in enabling him to hold Rommel at the Egyptian frontier and the great risk created by the intervention in Greece was overcome.

MAJOR GENERAL O'CONNOR

It was a great shock to be captured. I never thought it would ever happen to me – very conceited, perhaps – but it was miles behind our own front and by a sheer bit of bad luck we drove into the one bit of desert in which the Germans had sent around a reconnaissance group and we went bang into the middle of them.

BRIGADIER HARDING

I was following behind O'Connor and Philip Neame when they got captured and I found myself with no general at all and joined forces with General Moorshead who was commanding the Australian division and together we tried to sort things out, but it was pretty chaotic. At the same time we sent out search and rescue parties to see if we could find out what had happened to O'Connor and Neame and the people who were with them, but it took us a little time to sort things out, and it wasn't until Wavell came up and came into Tobruk and brought with him General Lavarack, another Australian and two Staff Officers, and sorted the whole thing out and left General Lavarack in command, and we really got the situation under control again.

ANTHONY EDEN

Air Chief Marshal Sir Arthur Longmore, from the air point of view particularly, ruled out any further advances along the coast towards Tripoli because of the growth of the German air activity from Sicily, which would have been very formidable at that time if we'd gone beyond Benghazi – at least that was his view and of the other Chiefs of Staff.

MAJOR GENERAL O'CONNOR

It was a question, really, of whether or not we could go on and do both Tripoli and Greece, but Tripoli immediately. If we could do Tripoli immediately it still left all the options open for doing Greece if we wanted to. Some of my friends say, oh, yes, you could have got to Tripoli all right, but could you have stayed there, could you have stood up to the bombing that you would have got from Sicily? My answer is that Rommel stood up to the bombing by the British when his line was extended, his line of communication extended right the way from Tripoli to Alamein, and he was there for a number of months and stood up to it, and if he could do it so could we. The time to have done it was straight away, the same afternoon. That would have been the battle finished. We could have gone on: we had an Australian brigade ready that was coming in by vessel, and we could have used them. I entirely blame myself for not having done this. I think it was quite inexcusable – I ought to have.

BRIGADIER HARDING

It's always rash to hazard a guess but I think not very far off it. It would have taken tremendous time and resources to have driven Rommel out of North Africa, but certainly I think we could have driven him back to a point, to a position where it would have been difficult. With the increasing air power at the disposal of the Allies it would have been difficult for the Germans to phase a further offensive with any prospect of reaching the Delta.

LIEUTENANT COLONEL DE GUINGAND

When I got back from Greece I was absolutely convinced that evacuation would have to take place even if we got the forces there, and I discussed with the Joint Planning Staff plans for evacuation and I was told by Wavell to stop any work on that and not to mention the word. I felt so strongly that I saw the Naval and Air Commanders-in-Chief and put it to them and they said they felt that they would like us to go on planning the possibility of evacuation, which we did. I eventually went over to Greece to tie up with the Air Force and the Navy various details for evacuation, that is after we had sent the troops over.

ANTHONY EDEN

We had agreed with the Greeks for certain withdrawals, which they said they could make at our first meeting. In the event they couldn't withdraw troops from Macedonia and expose Salonika, and they didn't bring their troops back from Albania to the extent which we expected. That meant we were not strong enough on the Aliakmon Line. At any rate it didn't alter the balance sheet in the final result and I think the argument that, in war, you take action which you think may have some positive results, but you can't really see beyond a certain distance, and if you're likely to come a cropper.

JOHN COLVILLE

Assistant Private Secretary to the Prime Minister 1939–41

Wavell was one of the few soldiers who Churchill did not know personally but he had heard him spoken of with admiration on all sides, and so he persuaded Lord Rosebury to bring Wavell to Chequers and he made very little impression on Churchill because he was a shy man. Nevertheless Churchill had heard his praises sung so frequently that he took him on trust and Wavell then commanded the Middle East. This trust lasted for a time but Churchill lost faith in Wavell, first in the spring of 1941 when Rommel got as far as Alamein before Wavell's intelligence had even regis- tered the fact the Germans were in Africa and they captured General O'Connor and two other high officers. Churchill thought it incredible. The second thing was Crete: he thought it important that Crete should be held at all costs; if we lost Crete we lost our bases in the eastern Mediterranean. And he kept telegraphing Wavell, 'Surely you can spare a dozen tanks for the defence of Maleme airfield,' and Wavell replied that he had no tanks: they were all having their tracks mended or having their engines greased and he couldn't spare even a dozen. Crete was lost, it was a great disaster, upset everybody in the House of Commons, the country – it was a low point for us in the war. Colonel Laycock who at this time was a comparatively unknown officer but was a friend of Churchill's social acquaintances was brought to Chequers for luncheon. And as he'd been to Crete, Churchill listened with great interest to what he had to say. And there came the moment when Laycock said, 'I really believe Crete could have been saved if only we could have kept the airfield – if we'd just had a dozen tanks we could have held the airfield from the Germans.' And Churchill's eyes opened wide and I felt as if I could hear a nail being hammered into Wavell's reputation and coffin.

ANTHONY EDEN

One has to admit that we didn't attain the objectives we'd hoped for. We weren't able to conduct, with the help of the Yugoslavs, any effective campaign in the Balkans. We lost Greece and many brave men, and more were captured, and we lost Crete too. So in that sense the balance sheet was much against us and it was a depressing time at home as well as for those responsible for the campaign.

LIEUTENANT COLONEL BELCHEM

The philosophy of combined operations between the Royal Air Force and the Army had not evolved and this was probably because there was not a sufficiency of Royal Air Force to prompt the evolution. But it's more diffi-cult to understand in the case of armour. Manifestly at the battle of Tobruk the very heavy armoured losses we sustained indicated there was something wrong with the handling of the armour and perhaps one would have expected General Wavell to have summoned an armoured expert to be his right-hand man at that time.

ANTHONY EDEN

At the minimum, I think, you put the delay which the battle of Yugoslavia and the battle of Greece entailed on German plans, that was four weeks. You would certainly be in a very unpleasant situation if the Russians had had to stand another month of good weather at least before 'General Winter' came to their rescue.

LIEUTENANT COLONEL BELCHEM

General Auchinleck certainly had his problems.* Firstly he was manifestly unlucky in his choice of subordinates: General Cunningham had done

---

* In July 1941 Churchill ordered that Wavell should exchange commands with General Sir Claude Auchinleck, C-in-C Indian Army.

very well in Ethiopia but conditions in the desert were very different; then General Ritchie afterwards justified himself in his operations in Normandy and elsewhere, but at the time that he assumed command of the Eighth Army he was completely unready and unprepared for such a responsibility. As a result, for the second time Auchinleck had to go up to the desert at a moment of utter crisis, had to relieve General Ritchie and again take personal command of the Eighth Army at a moment when we were in full retreat and when even Mussolini was already in Africa with a white horse, waiting to lead the Italian columns in a victory march through Cairo.

CHAPTER 9

BATTLE OF THE ATLANTIC 1940–41

Following the capture of the French Atlantic ports, the young German U-boat commanders enjoyed what they called 'the first happy time'. It was the heyday of 'aces' like Günther Prien, Joachim Schepke and the most successful of them all, Otto Kretschmer, interviewed below. Admiral Dönitz was at last able to put his 'wolf-pack' tactics to work and the effects were devastating. In October 1940 Convoy SC-7, with only four small escorts, lost twenty of thirty-five ships, seven of them sunk by Kretschmer. In February 1941, the Admiralty moved the headquarters of Western Approaches Command from Plymouth to Liverpool and on 6 March Churchill proclaimed the 'Battle of the Atlantic'. Only now was RAF Coastal Command brought under the operational control of the Royal Navy. The counter to the wolf-packs were permanent escort groups, the most famous led by Captain 'Johnny' Walker, but it was the escort group led by Captain Donald MacIntyre that on 17 March 1941 killed Schepke and captured Kretschmer in the battle for Convoy HX-117. Elsewhere, the same day, Prien's U-47 was lost with all hands. The Germans were reading the British naval codes and it was not until HMS Bulldog recovered an intact German Enigma machine from U-110 on 9 May that the intelligence war began to turn in favour of the Allies. In June the rapidly expanding Royal Canadian Navy took over escort duties to the mid-Atlantic and the advent of technical innovations – high frequency direction-finding (HF/DF), short-wave radar sets and side-firing depth-charges to create a wider pattern – greatly increased escort effectiveness. Against which the Germans were equipped with increasing numbers of the reliable, long-range Type VIIC U-boat and, although most convoys were steered around their patrol lines, merchant-ship losses continued at well above replacement levels: 1,345 (4.6 million tons) against twenty-four U-boats sunk in 1940; 1,419 (4.7 million tons) against thirty-five in 1941. However, merchant-ship losses peaked between October 1940 and April 1941.

LIEUTENANT ERNST VON WITZENDORFF

U-boat officer, achieved first command (U-121) in March 1942

I must say in this time we were young naval officers and we were interested to do our duty and to be successful. When we attacked in daytime looking through our periscope, or attacking in the night being on the surface, we saw these big merchant ships like animals creeping over the sea then we were eager to sink them and we didn't think on those poor merchant seamen which were on the merchant ships. But later on when we have been successful we thought about them sometimes and we had a bad feeling. But it was our duty in the war, and what could we do?

CAPTAIN GILBERT ROBERTS

Western Approaches Staff, Liverpool

We were aware that their intelligence was for some reason good, but I myself put it down to very superior hydrophone equipment that the U-boats had, probably being able to pick up the noise of the convoys' propellers up to, oh, eighty or a hundred miles. But in addition I knew that they would place their U-boats in a line across at right angles in the expected path of the convoy and this line with, say, five U-boats could be a hundred miles from end to end and so against a good hydrophone very little disguise of the position of the convoy could be effected. It was only after the war that we knew they were breaking the codes and they knew very well the time of leaving port of the convoys and in addition how many escorts would probably be with them and how many merchant ships were in each convoy, including tankers.

LIEUTENANT DESMOND PIERS

Royal Canadian Navy, commanding sloop HMCS Restigouche

Half-hour by half-hour the size of the waves mounted until within about two hours after the gale struck we were in rather desperate straits. The huge waves rolled on board although we were bow on to them. A huge wave would come along and the bow of the destroyer would climb up the wave and as we got past the fulcrum of the ship down would come the bow into the trough with a tremendous bang, the tail of the ship would go shooting up and the officers would be thrown out of their bunks and crockery off the table and everything. This is a typical North Atlantic storm. Well, we were so pounded by this gale and one of the first things to happen was our mast came down, with just the sheer strength of the wind and the rolling and pitching and the waves, the whole of the foremast came down and the shroud, the guy wires on the mast fell across the siren wires between the funnels and caused both sirens to roar. In the midst of this howling gale in the North Atlantic just about sunset, this was a terrible sound. However losing the mast wasn't so serious except losing the wireless aerial, but this was soon replaced by a very confident petty officer. The next thing to happen was the aft funnel was swept away, which was a little more serious because it put out the fires in the aft boiler room and then of course the cargo began to shift on board and we found that the rivets were giving way under the forrard magazine and we were flooded after the Carley float [a life raft] had torn adrift and hit the quarterdeck and sheered off the top of a hatch and the aft end of the ship filled up with water. So here we were flooded forrard and flooded aft, one funnel down, lost our mast and the ship filling up with water. The only thing we could do in circumstances like this – the pumps couldn't compete with it – was to turn out every member of the crew to bale her out with buckets.

LIEUTENANT COMMANDER OTTO KRETSCHMER

Sank forty-six ships (273,000 tons) all except two in U-99 *between April 1940 and March 1941.*

I think it was November 1940; it was the first time that there were enough submarines in the North Atlantic to practise doing the tactics of the wolf-pack. A few months earlier I was the only submarine in the North Atlantic and now there were about seven or eight. I remember there was a signal that a convoy was coming in from America to England and that its position was not known and Dönitz ordered all the submarines there, on the west of Ireland, to form a sort of recce line. This was a stationary recce line, and when the first submarine to sight the convoy made its contact signal the recce line would dissolve automatically and every boat was free to go in to the attack. Well, I was the southernmost boat of the line and Convoy SC-7 passed through the middle of it. I tried to get in and attack as darkness came, tried to get though the escorts into the convoy – which was my own peculiarity of attacking – and failed the first time because they saw me and shot star shells and I go away again. But for the second time I succeeded and was inside the convoy going up and down the lanes, looking for the most important, valuable ships and had the opportunity to expend all torpedoes – I had twelve in all – during the night. Not all of them hit, some of them failed, I don't know why in every case. You know, we had some bad experiences with our torpedoes and they should have hit, all of them, because the distance was very close. This was really the first time that these tactics could be experienced by all of us and also by Dönitz himself, who of course only knew it from peacetime training. The whole night was successful and was called the 'Night of the Long Knives' because so many ships were sunk.

LIEUTENANT ROBERT SHERWOOD
Royal Navy, commanding corvette HMS Bluebell

The attack on SC–7 commenced in the same way as previous attacks. It started with one ship being torpedoed but very shortly after that it became clear that we were in for something different because other ships were torpedoed and I suppose roughly by midnight the whole area was in a state almost of daylight by the ships burning. There was at this stage no coordination; we hadn't arrived at that position in escort duty where group formations would give us set patterns of anti-submarine attack and we were left to our own devices to assume whatever tactics we considered suitable for the occasion. I could see ships in various stages of sinking, some on fire, some not, and other ships being silhouetted by the light of the ships that were on fire. I did actually go at one stage into the convoy with a view to attempting to find submarines if they were there. I never did find any but one of the merchant ships had a shot at me so I decided it was probably as well to get out of there again. I have a recollection of a Dutch ship, the funnel painted in the Dutch colours – the Holland–America Line – and I can see that ship now, silhouetted against the light of another ship burning close by, and I think that ship actually did stop to pick up survivors from the other ship and was sunk herself. It was certainly a new form of attack and obviously we realised very quickly that there was more than one submarine involved and this was a new departure for us, a completely new departure. I think we envisaged simply single submarine attack and we thought that these chaps working on the surface – which we knew they were doing of course – would never attack in more than single units because they would get in each other's way and might even torpedo each other.

CAPTAIN W EYTON-JONES
Merchant Navy, SS Ben Vrachie, *sunk 13 May 1941*
Actually I thought we saw a glimpse of the flashes in the distance during the night and I thought it could be a submarine so we took evasion tactics and at daylight we saw it no more. So I went to sleep on the settee and just after daybreak I was hurled off by a terrific bang. I looked out aft from the bridge and saw the gun platform going under, so I realised we were practically half-blown to pieces. I went back and I got the naval box with all the naval secrets in, shut them and threw them over the side, made sure they sank right. I went back to try and get in the chart room but the door had jammed – I lost my coat and all my papers. I looked out from the bridge again and I saw the port boats were blown to pieces. The starboard boats, the men were there trying to cut one adrift. The forward boat was lowering away but unfortunately it overturned and then I thought there was nothing else for it. I saw the ship going up, the stern going under the water and I got as far as the fore rigging, trying to let go a raft and she went up on end and went backwards and I went down with her. I had a life jacket on one arm, which I didn't have time to get on, so I went down with the

ship. A lot of people say you had a tremendous amount of suction but I wasn't aware of it. After a bit I came to the surface, I saw a lady passenger's face coming up and I tried my best, but every time I got her face above water she shouted, 'Save me!' and went back under. After twenty minutes of hard swimming I got her on to some wreckage, then I looked around and saw the one boat that had got away with about a dozen men in it, and after a bit they came along and picked us up and we went through the wreckage, which was scattered all over a good square mile.

PILOT OFFICER WILFRID OULTON
RAF Coastal Command

With the exception of the Sunderland flying boats, a very small number, all the other aircraft except the Anson were lash-ups, they were borrowed from entirely dissimilar functions in order to do this job in Coastal Command. I even had a flight of biplane Tiger Moths doing convoy escort, if you can imagine anything more ridiculous. Secondly the navigation aids were not there; it was entirely dead-reckoning navigation and whereas an experienced navigator can look at the sea and estimate the wind and where he's likely to be in an hour's time, this is very difficult for a new boy. So without navigation aids, with inadequate experience and with training which was not specifically adapted to the job, navigation was a very serious problem. And since the point to be navigated to, the convoy, was often equally at error, it was no wonder that we failed to meet many convoys. And on return it was no wonder that aircraft would wind up perhaps twenty or thirty miles from their airfield and very often fly into a hill instead of getting back home safely. So lack of equipment, lack of training and unsuitable aircraft were certainly a handicap at the beginning of the war, and indeed throughout the war.

CAPTAIN EYTON-JONES

We picked up what people we could and then I saw the submarine surface. He went round picking up cases out of the water – general cargo, possibly spirits, food and so forth. And after a bit he backed down through the wreckage towards us. A man came on the conning-tower, the man I took as a commander, a squat little bloke and he looked down on us and then he shouted, 'What ship?' One of my crew, unfortunately to my mind, shouted back, 'Queen Elizabeth.' I though this is probably where we get shot or in trouble, but somebody gave the true name of the ship, the *Ben Vrachie*. They looked at us, circled round for a bit, they laughed at us and went away to the north-east. And we were just left there floating among the wreckage. We went round to get what gallons of water we could, a few tins of biscuits, then after having a good look round we said there's only one thing for it, to try and get out of this if we can. Halfway between Brazil and North Africa. The only thing I could think about was to try and get to land as near as possible so I set the course to the northeast. All we had was the one lifeboat, which was made for forty-eight people; we picked up fifty-eight. There wasn't really enough room for people to sit down, the boat was leaking badly, it had been on the chocks for some time. You had quite a bit of trouble getting the crew to move so you could bail, and you bailed for nearly two days until the wood of the boat started to swell and tighten up. After that it wasn't so bad.

CAPTAIN ROBERTS

I was visited by a Squadron Leader Selby, who was later killed, who told me a great deal about their difficulties and I told him about ours and we resolved together that this lack of liaison should stop. And it was only a day or two of my time and his that we devised, with the help of my own technical-school staff, a set of very simple searches which could be executed by a single word given to an aircraft which would be sent to succour a convoy, even for an hour or two in the Atlantic. And this word sent to the aircraft would get the aircraft to do exactly what the escort commander wanted. He, the escort commander, being in full possession of all the local intelligence, which an aircraft above and perhaps just having arrived certainly wouldn't know.

CAPTAIN EYTON-JONES

The worst days were when there was no wind: the sun was terrific. We cut up a lifeboat cover which was in the boat for the men to put over their heads with their life jackets to keep the rays of the sun off them. We started off by giving four ounces of water, two ounces in the morning and two at night, and one biscuit. That went on for some time and then we got a couple of squalls at night-time but we were only able to save a little bit of water, and that was only by spreading the mainsail out flat and you could hear the men underneath it sucking it with their dry lips trying to get them a bit more moist. But they behaved remarkably well, they were damned fine men. The second day we saw a ship in the distance; they didn't see us.

PILOT OFFICER OULTON

You'd be called from your bed typically at three o'clock in the morning, raining and cold and walking through mud to get some food, to get briefed, to go out in a dinghy to your flying boat, get the covers off and get started up, taxi away down a flare path and perhaps hazards in the flare path, an odd boat that shouldn't be there or a box, then to fumble your way out through perhaps Milford Haven Head and out into the Atlantic. This in itself was no mean task and even today many aviators would take it pretty seriously. Then came the problem of delicate navigation to locate the convoy or to establish a patrol line in the right area and then would come perhaps eight hours of dreary ploughing up and down constantly looking for something for which you looked yesterday and the day before and which wasn't there today either. And at the end of that time, with perhaps a break if you had a convoy and had some communication with the convoy, then you'd have to come back again in the dark, often in bad weather, perhaps at two hundred feet under low cloud, raining like hell, and find your way back into your own flophouse again. Tie up the boat, into a dinghy to shore, a debriefing by a lot of querulous intelligence officers who wanted to know why you hadn't done something quite different and then to bed perhaps twenty hours after getting out of bed in the first place. And then twenty-four hours' rest and do it all over again, and so carry on year after year.

CAPTAIN EYTON-JONES

At one time there was a lot of noise on the boat. They were Chinese and I said, 'What's all the bothery?' They said, 'Number-one cook go crazy.' Eventually he jumped over the side with a life jacket on and after a wee while, we got him back again. And later that night in the dark he jumped again; we didn't get him back because the sharks got him. We saw the splashes and the crashes. And then a Chinese steward, he died. We had to throw him over the side, that was all we could do and the sharks tore him to pieces too. It's one thing I remembered in my dreams for many months seeing those dreaded sharks following us at the back, day in day out, about ten or twenty feet away.

CAPTAIN PETER GRETTON

Royal Navy Escort Group Commander

Again, the lessons of the First World War were that the right place for aircraft was around the convoy in escort. But the airmen much preferred to go out on long sweeps looking for U-boats: it gave them the feeling of the offensive, somehow. But in fact it was quite useless. It was like looking for a needle in a haystack and eventually this was appreciated and the aircraft used to escort the convoys instead.

CAPTAIN EYTON-JONES

About the tenth day we saw an aeroplane – still didn't see us though we had our sails up. On the morning of the 13th somebody shook me and said, 'Hey, Captain, we see lights,' and I looked round and I saw some green lights which looked to me like Brighton Pier. So I said, 'We'll burn a flare.' A few minutes later they burnt another flare and after a bit I saw the green lights getting closer, more visible. After a bit I saw a red light above the green and then it dawned on me that it was a hospital ship. They got alongside and we boarded that ship, which we found out afterwards was the *Oxfordshire*. They put a rope ladder over and the crew tumbled up; they nearly went mad with excitement. Eventually I was left in the boat with only the lady passenger. I said, 'Would you send something down that we can send the lady up with,' because the lady was very weak and so they put a sling down and two men came down and we hauled the lady on board. Then they sent a sling down hooked on to the boat and hauled it on board. After thirteen days when you couldn't lay out or even sleep decently I thought it the most wonderful thing to lie down in the scupper under the bulwark. Then all of a sudden, 'Hey, there's another bastard down here,' and two students picked me up and asked, 'What are you doing down there?' They hustled me along to the canteen down into the hospital bay and they put all our men, fifty-six at that time, into bunks and they were all whistling and shouting, almost hysteria, and then some of the sisters from the hospital came round with cans of tea, buns, it was the most wonderful drink we'd ever had, because we were practically dehydrated. In the thirteen days you didn't perspire, nature completely stopped, and the average loss of a man per weight per day was about two and a half pounds. How long one could have survived I don't know, but we'd sailed five hundred and thirty miles in those horrible conditions and survived within a hundred miles of Sierra Leone, and all I had to go by was the pole-star, using my finger to think how high it was above the horizon.

CAPTAIN ROBERTS

When I first went to Liverpool I got hold of a number of escort commanders and I asked them what they did when a U-boat attacked by night. The answer in most cases was, 'Well, what can you do? It's a very difficult thing and we can't see them.' The radar of course in those days was very elementary and we had very few sets, but in fact there was one escort commander who had the idea, which is still absolutely relevant, that when an attack of which there is no warning takes place all the escorts should do the same sort of thing on a planned schedule at exactly the same time, so that it had the maximum effect over the broad ocean around that convoy. This of course was then Commander Frederick 'Johnny' Walker in the little corvette *Stork*. His escorts, on the word 'Buttercup', went away from the convoy, thinking that the U-boat would then be chasing away from the convoy having fired a torpedo, but I thought it cannot be they are outside, they must have been among them. I talked to C-in-C Western Approaches Admiral Noble about this and he agreed. I said I will set up an operation which will be based on the fact that when they fire they are inside the convoy. This was called 'Raspberry' and for some time it was quite successful.

LIEUTENANT COMMANDER KRETSCHMER

When I was depth-charged I had to go to the surface because water was coming into the boat and everything was over. I couldn't move and was lying in a large patch of oil listing to starboard and being fired at by two destroyers from the port side – without success, I must say – so there were waterspouts all around the boat. Their forty-millimetre pom-poms had fuses against aircraft so they didn't harm the boat very much, only the paint was off, but still the aft part of my boat went under and that part of my crew which was on the aft deck was thrown into the water and I couldn't do anything about them. I wanted to give them every chance to be picked up and go into captivity and this I could only do by asking one of the destroyers, which was my friend Donald MacIntyre, about four o'clock in the morning, my Morse lamp sending the signal that part of my crew was floating in the water, and I asked him to pick them up. He drew alongside these people and lighted his searchlights so I could see through my glasses their heads and how they went aboard.

CHAPTER 10

BARBAROSSA

Operation Barbarossa started with the invasion of the USSR on 22 June 1941 and ended on 5 December with the German Army on the defensive in the face of determined Soviet counter-attacks. Stalin had ignored all indications that an attack was imminent, including strongly worded warnings from the British. Some Russian historians suggest that Hitler correctly anticipated an imminent Soviet attack to seize the vital oilfields of Romania and that some, at least, of the early catastrophes that overtook the Red Army were the result of being concentrated forward for attack rather deployed in depth for defence. The Germans, however, had grossly underestimated the ruthless adaptability of a Soviet regime they had expected to collapse like a rotten building once the door was kicked in, as well as the mobilisation potential of the Red Army and the extent to which patriotic fervour against the invader would submerge the hatreds and divisions within the Soviet Empire. The basic premise of Barbarossa was that German forces would have won complete operational freedom within five to six weeks following the collapse of the Red Army. When this did not occur Hitler lost his nerve and first weakened the central thrust towards Moscow in order to pursue economic-strategic goals in the south, then halted an advance on Leningrad in the north that might have succeeded in order to bolster the central front. The Soviets, meanwhile, had learned from Richard Sorge in Tokyo (see Chapter 2) that the Japanese would not attack and brought west the Siberian Army, well-trained and far better equipped for winter fighting than the Germans. The pattern for the rest of a war that was characterised by almost unimaginable cruelty and sacrifice on both sides was set by the staggering fact that by the end of 1941, despite having lost four and a half million soldiers (equivalent to the entire German Army) and half a million square miles of territory with seventy-five million inhabitants, the Soviets took the offensive and sustained it through the winter.

MAJOR GENERAL WALTHER WARLIMONT
Deputy Chief of Wehrmacht Operations

On 29 July 1940 I first heard about Hitler's intentions to go to war with Russia, after the French campaign and the triumphant victory. We were of a good mood since we believed that Chief of Operations Staff General Alfred Jodl would come and announce promotions for his Staff Officers too. But this assumption soon vanished when he arrived with a very closed face and ordered that the doors were shut up and sentries had to be before these doors. And when we were sitting all together, all the five officers including him, without any introduction he started to tell that Hitler had resolved to go to war with Russia. Was a great shock for all of us and we at once began to raise our objections against this, asking him how it would be possible to protect the German life against the British Air Force when the bulk of German forces would have been shifted to the east, and what at all should be the aim of this new campaign after a treaty had been closed just one year ago, and many more questions. He answered to all of them but none of his answers could persuade us that Hitler's intention was to the well-being of the German Reich. Finally he said, 'We have to take in mind that in the short or long term it will be necessary to go to war with Russia in order to crush Bolshevism. At most it is better to begin the war as soon as possible because now we are at the height of our military strength and it will not be necessary to cause the German people to another war within a short period.'

DR GRIGORI TOKATY
Lecturer at the Zhukovsky Academy of the Soviet Air Force

First of all we were not ready to start a war, we were weak. Stalin wanted to gain time and at the same time to direct Germany against England. The other aspect was that while doing this he displayed his complete mistrust to the British – the British warned us, that must mean that they try to put us against Germany – that's the main reason he neglected the warnings. I belonged to a leading military academy and naturally the process of war in the west used to be discussed daily. We were not fools; we knew what was going on. We anticipated that Germany will turn against us sooner or later. As far as the general public was concerned the Soviet Telegraph Agency Press made two denials that German aircraft tried to fly over our territories, and these incidents created a mood in Moscow. One must remember that Russians are Russians, Moscow is Moscow; you have rumours more than anywhere else, and rumours are usually inclined to exaggerate, so there were really bunches of population that thought immediately tomorrow we'll be attacked. People kept this under the surface: we did have a centralised propaganda machine which did not allow any other public statement, and central propaganda said there is no danger, so everybody kept quiet. But there was great unease.

SIR JOHN RUSSELL
British Minister in Moscow

I think the people in Russia always had a fear that the Germans might be going to attack them. There's a very deep-lying mistrust in the Russian people for the Germans, going way back through history. But the government, the Soviet government, was so determined not to admit the possibility that any speculation about it was suppressed.

HANS KEHRL
Nazi industrialist

We had the greatest trade agreement we had ever had and the Russians delivered promptly and from an economic point of view everything seemed to be in order. I personally made negotiation with them for putting up a synthetic-fibre mill in Russia and the treaty was signed by the 15th of June 1941 and the first ten million marks in gold were to be shipped on the 1st of July 1941.

MAJOR GENERAL WARLIMONT

I was convinced before the war started that it was a great disaster, a great wrong. Even after the campaign in Poland my conviction didn't change because on 3rd September, the third day of our going to war, the Western Powers had declared war on Germany. After the campaign in France in 1940 my conviction became uncertain, but when I heard one or two months after the armistice with France that now Hitler was to go with Russia, the old conviction came up again and it was at this moment that I changed the place of living for my family, moved them from Berlin to the place where are today.

CAPTAIN EKKEHARD MAURER

German Army

The morning of 22nd June 1941 my battalion commander and myself, I was his Adjutant, at the time were in our foxholes very close to the barbed wire and just before the artillery barrage began he whispered over to me something like, 'Don't ever forget 22nd June 1941 at three-fifteen in the morning.' Then he paused for a moment and said, 'Well, I don't think I have to tell you not to forget because you won't forget it anyway. At this very moment the worst decline, the worst disaster of German history in many centuries, is going to begin.'

DR TOKATY

I think the right mood was deep depression, deep disillusionment, so many people simply cried. Through the 1930s we were told that the Red Army will never fight on its own territory and the very first shot will be made on enemy territory, then suddenly on the 22nd we were told the enemy smashed right down our forces. People couldn't understand how this could happen. Within a few hours I'd been talking to a person who worked inside the Kremlin and he told me that inside the Kremlin they were really frightened because that we were not prepared, that our armed forces had been wiped out and there was nothing to stop the Germany Army. About one month after the war started the government issued a secret order, demanded to begin evacuation of the main strategic centres at once at any cost. It gave a clear impression that the government did not believe that they will be able to stop the enemy, so we have panic and the frightful feeling that we will be defeated very deeply rooted in the centre.

We anticipated that the Germans would arrive here and we will be unable to defend Moscow.

SIR JOHN RUSSELL

From June 1941 until October 1941, when the government evacuated Moscow and went down to Kuibyshev, it was a funny sort of atmosphere because the shock of realising that the Germans had betrayed them was sinking in and of course the Soviet government had to do a great adjustment and we, from being a hostile or semi-hostile foreign capitalist power, suddenly became friends, and the second 'Fascist–Imperialist' war suddenly became the 'Struggle for the Defence of the Motherland', and there was a great deal of adjustment, psychologically, to be done all round.

AMBASSADOR W AVERELL HARRIMAN
President Roosevelt's Special Envoy to Europe

After the meeting when the Atlantic Charter was issued Roosevelt and Churchill agreed that there should be a joint mission. Churchill appointed Beaverbrook and Roosevelt myself, and we went together to Moscow and we both agreed to give a certain amount of aid to the Soviet Union. A great deal of it came out of Britain because what we might have given to Britain we diverted to Russia, so it was an extremely generous act on the part of the British government – but it was important for Britain to keep Russia in the war. There we saw Stalin, we had three long talks with him and then the great banquet happened. At first Stalin was very rough with us. He said, 'The paucity of your offers proves that you want us to be defeated in the war.' But after he'd finally gotten everything he could out of us he said, 'This is very generous,' he was very complimentary about what we were trying to do and he gave us this big banquet. That was in early October 1941; the Germans were very close to Moscow but I gained the impression that Stalin was going to hold out – he was a great war leader in spite of the horror of his tyranny. He had tremendous spirit and gave confidence to the Russian people.

DR TOKATY

Stalin showed himself as the supreme leader of the whole war effort to the public on 3rd July 1941 when he made his first war speech and for the first time and for the last time addressed his countrymen, very gently, very beautifully. Everybody repeated it since then. I think he realised by this time his mistakes and tried to correct them.

ALBERT SPEER

Hitler's Chief Architect

Now Hitler took over from the Army so many commands, he was the highest in command and he was in command of the whole Army. And more or less he was also in command of the Armaments Office because he told me details of the armaments and this compelled him to have another itinerary of the day. The day was now filled up from morning to evening with the different duties he had to do because the decisions had to be made and the map of the situation was there and had to be shown to him, if he liked it or not. And I think this made a change in Hitler's whole system, health system, he was getting more and more – he was no more approachable. He was getting more and more a man without any possibilities to discuss. I think he was also getting some numbness and some of the liveliness went out of him. He was in some way – I have the experience of being a prisoner for twenty years – he was in some way behaving like a prisoner. Hitler hadn't had any vacations in this whole period; he never stepped out because he thought without him all would be wrong.

COLONEL HASSO-ECCARD FREIHERR VON MANTEUFFEL

Battalion Commander, 7th Panzer Division

The first stage of the Russian campaign were going according to schedule and the plan worked out but in the end of July came a halt at the autobahn in Moscow. And I was with my division and we asked why and were informed that Hitler have a new order, Directive 33, the main failure of the Russia campaign in 1941. Hitler gave an order to disperse the forces. At the beginning of the war against Russia, on June 21st, we had a main objective Moscow, but now in July he ordered in another direction. One Army Group would go south-east and another to take cities first, then attack against Moscow. During August we faced the empire of mud and in beginning of October of snow. But the dispersion was the main failure of the campaign and when Hitler ordered to attack Moscow at the end of October we had not sufficient forces to attack.

DR TOKATY

Ordinary people lost any regard for the authorities and the authorities themselves were utterly sure that Moscow will be taken and they were unable to do anything else but to swallow lots of insults, sometime direct attacks on the security forces' automobiles, just to stop top-ranking secret-service officers and shout insults at them without any fear. The real patriotic part of the population found itself united. I don't think any attempt on the part of the secret services to continue their traditional lines these days would lead to anything we could possible imagine today. I think it would be a revolt. We could not afford any kind of revolt these days because the Germans were next to Moscow. Yes, we hated Stalin; very many people began to speak openly against the Party. But we could not contemplate revolt because that would mean weakening our position. Everyone with a keen heart used to say, never mind who, Stalin or the devil himself, number one is not to allow the Germans to take our town. Nothing was allowed to interfere with that and the secret service realised that and behaved accordingly. Although the official history denies it I was there, I saw it; my colleagues and everybody else was looting – but I wouldn't say there was widespread looting. It's extremely interesting that the Soviet population displayed another quality, highly disciplined attitude to the situation. There were certain parts of the population which tried to begin preparing themselves to serve the new masters when they come, but they were in a very limited scale. Literally hundreds of thousands of women and people with children, old men, were digging defence lines at the very same time outside of Moscow. Hundreds of thousands of ordinary people, without being mobilised, doing everything possible for their town, for their history.

MAJOR HANS HINRICHS
German Army engineer

It was completely different from France and, of course, from the desert area. France had a very dense road network, there were only a few woods and the population of France was rather indifferent. There were no ambushes. It was really a war in a very civilised country. In Russia we had very few roads and these became rather muddy already in September. You couldn't diverge for a moment in Russia because of the large woods and of course the many rivers and streams you had to cross without bridges or river-crossing installations. I, with my engineer company, built more than a hundred bridges on the way to Moscow.

DR TOKATY

When the country found itself face to face with the enemy, with the danger look in the eyes, something else appeared among us. Religious feeling just appeared in the midst of nowhere and that helped to unite the people. Religion, the church, suddenly joined the ranks of those who opposed the enemy and after that was natural that nobody even dared say a word against the church, an ally. We were driving through Moscow and suddenly we stopped after a dreadful night and suddenly I walk along my train. I thought everyone must be dead asleep and I heard somebody singing about the defeat of Napoleon, a very patriotic song which glorified the eternal values of Russia, that which never dies and I don't think it will ever die. Russia is too big a place to chop off just in one go.

ALBERT SPEER

Of course I hadn't much knowledge of what the German people was thinking because in a system if you are on a higher level you are quite a distance to the people itself – I heard only from some officials of administration who said they were very poor conditions in Russia and that there was a catastrophe of the transport. Of course I realised too from the newspapers, which said the advance had stopped. I was bothered about those situations and in November 1941 I offered Hitler to use about thirty thousand of my workmen, which were working on these huge peace buildings in Berlin, for to rebuild the transport system in Russia. But Hitler still didn't want to be convinced of his defeat in Russia and he hesitated for a few weeks until he gave the order that his workmen in Berlin are to be shifted to rebuild the Russian transport system.

ANTHONY EDEN

I was leaving from Scapa Flow with Ambassador Maisky and Sir Alec Cadogan, my Permanent Secretary, in a cruiser called HMS *Kent*. The weather was appalling and it was the only time in the war I got flu. I went to Invergordon and was anxious to get on board the destroyer and get to the cruiser as soon as possible and sail. And to my slight indignation I got a message from Winston saying I must talk to him on the telephone. That meant a long march to a shed where the telephone was, so I asked if it was really very important, because I wanted to get on board if it wasn't, and the message came back that it was of the utmost importance. This was Winston telling me about Pearl Harbor. So then I said to him, 'Well, what do we do now?' He said, 'I'm going to the United States,' and I asked, 'Do I go on to Russia?' He said, 'Certainly, you can't not go. Stalin's expecting you. It would make the worst impression. You go to Russia and I'll go the United States and we'll feed our telegrams to each other,' which is what happened.

DR TOKATY

Stalin gave a speech on 6th November from an underground station, a very good speech. He said, 'Hitlers come and go, but people remain' – and we used to say, 'Stalins come and go, but people remain.' The next morning he received the parade in Red Square and we could see that in spite of all his shortcomings, Stalin rendered a great service to the USSR by that presence because it showed the Supreme Commander does not run away and that is very important in critical times. Secondly he made a speech about Lenin which showed that Stalin retained his nerve. That sense spread at once into all the armed forces, all the commanders began saying, 'Stalin himself hasn't lost his nerve, he is sure – let us fight,' and that made a tremendous impact on the battle qualities of the armed forces.

ANTHONY EDEN

Stalin himself was always a tough negotiator, imperturbable, unyielding, ruthless, but I have a regard for him as a leader and a statesman despite all the cruelties that I have no doubt he did perpetrate. We had difficult discussions because he wanted me to give all sorts of commitments about the post-war period, which I wasn't in a position to give. But it was typical of him that he knew then, with the Germans a few miles from the gates of Moscow, exactly what he wanted to get at the peace table. And he wanted to get it into my head as soon as he possibly could, and if possible get a commitment from me, which he didn't get, to back what he wanted. And what he wanted above all was the security of Russia, never mind anybody else's particular interests in the matter. Max Beaverbrook had been there a little before I went out, with Harriman, on a purely supply mission, and he'd done a very good job in making the Russians understand that we were prepared to play our full part fairly with them. But I've no doubt the Russians had a lingering suspicion, and they ought to have guilty consciences. During the period we were alone they did absolutely nothing to help but they did a good deal to help the Germans. And so perhaps they did suspect that we would play the same sort of game they'd played, do very little, the minimum, and leave them to bear the burden. But gradually I think they realised that wasn't so, and not because of any great generosity on our part. It was due to the fact that it was very much in our interests that the Russians should make as fine a show as they could against the Nazis.

MAJOR HINRICHS

The conditions became very bad during the period end of October to early November, when the mud period set in. And particularly bad for mechanised forces once we had the first frost in the middle of November. My company was mechanised; we had large lorries carrying one section and these lorries stuck in the mud – frozen the next morning, could not move at all. Within a period of two or three days we had to improvise mobility by requisitioning horses and wagons.

LIEUTENANT HEINRICH SCHMIDT-SCHMIEDEBACH
German artillery

The mud froze to irregular hard waves and we had horses. I was the platoon commander with two three-inch guns and this frozen mud was very bad for the horses. And the carts, they were often demolished only by movement, not by shooting, so we had doubts that our material would be in a position to march towards Moscow. At first it was not so bad, perhaps fifteen or twenty degrees under zero and there was no danger for our weapons. But suddenly at a certain point the rifles didn't shoot any more. This was the turning point in the winter war, I think, and it was the greatest point for the soldiers. The lubricating oil we had was not suitable for this sub-arctic winter, but the Russians had the real lubricating oil for their weapons.

ANTHONY EDEN

Towards the end of my stay I was allowed, after a lot of pushing, to go to the front, or near the front, and that taught me a lot about the war on that front because I saw some captured German prisoners. That was about the most pathetic thing I'd ever seen because it was ice cold and none of them had a decent overcoat at all, hardly even a pullover of any sort. And there they were dragging their shirt cuffs down over their hands to try to keep warm. They thought I was a Russian officer or a Russian politician and began to complain to me about the cold, not surprisingly. There was little I could do for them but seeing those youngsters – they'd mostly come from the Sudetenland – there in those conditions made you realise how unprepared the so-called perfect Hitler machine had been for a winter war in Russia. And I remember saying to Winston when I got back, 'They can't be all that good because I can't believe we would have sent divisions into Russia at this time of year without something, some form of overcoats.'

ALBERT SPEER

We were all quite happy about the success of the German armies in Russia and the first inkling that something is wrong was when Goebbels made a big action in the whole of Germany to collect furs and winter clothes for the German troops, and then we knew that something was happening that was not foreseen.

ANTHONY EDEN

The Russians were avid in their demands: tanks, aircraft, raw materials, aluminium, wanted them all and I don't blame them for wanting, they were carrying the main burden of the battle in those days, but to get them to them was a problem and our shortages were very real. And I always feel that perhaps in this country we forget too easily the tremendous contribution of our Merchant Marine, protected by the Royal Navy in those convoys to Russia. The conditions were so terrible, the cold, and yet they got through after heavy losses sometimes. The Russians certainly never understood: partly they didn't understand the problem of the whale and the elephant again [a sea power versus a land power], what it meant, how difficult it was, partly perhaps they didn't want to understand. I had many arguments with Stalin about these convoys. Once we virtually had to stop them because we considered he wasn't treating our sailors the way they should be treated and he retaliated that our sailors were not treating his people properly, which was not true.

ALBERT SPEER

Because Dr Todt was responsible for the whole construction work in Germany I was with him around Christmas 1941 to discuss how my workmen should be used. This time Todt was very depressed and he told me that we shall certainly lose the war because not only physically but also psychologically the Russians are much stronger than the German soldier. I was shocked because I knew that Todt was rather an optimist.*

---

* Fritz Todt (1891–1942) joined the Nazi Party in 1922 and was Hitler's first Armaments Minister. Speer became the second after Todt was killed when his aircraft exploded on 8 February 1942.

COLONEL MANTEUFFEL

My division, which was a panzer division, was the only unit which crossed a bridge within thirty miles of Moscow. We cannot see the capital because of the mountains but we could ride with electric train to Moscow and took the bridge, which had not been demolished, in the night of 27th November 1941. I hoped that was a great success for the whole Army. Some hours after I put my feet on the bridge and my troops were going on towards the hills that were north-west of Moscow I heard from my radio operator that no troops came after my division, and because I command no reserves we have to retreat.

ANTHONY EDEN

It was obvious from our first tough conversations, at which Ambassador Sir Stafford Cripps was present too, that we were going to have plenty of trouble in the future. My general view was the sooner we could get down to discussing these matters with the Russians the better. Because as the war progressed, as we were confident we would win it, so it was likely the Russian demands would become more formidable and if we could pin them down it would anyhow strengthen our position for argument later. But of course one couldn't move in any of this except in agreement with the United States, which is what I told Roosevelt then, and also in consultation with the Dominion governments who were all in the war at the time. I think the Russians were doubtful as to what our attitude really was. We had been a year in the war already and the Russians had certainly done nothing to help us in their time. On the contrary, they supplied Germany with a great deal that Hitler had asked for, materials of various kinds, in order, presumably, to try and buy him off, to delay the moment of his attack on them. So it would be natural that they were suspicious, but I think gradually they got to understand that we were in the business completely with them. Churchill's broadcast after Russia was attacked was a masterpiece in that respect and I'd been with him in Chequers the night before and discussed this, and we'd agreed I should go and see Maisky and speak to him in exactly the same sense, which I did. I think the Russians were gratified; they began to feel perhaps we really would help. But then, of course, they wanted everything.*

AMBASSADOR HARRIMAN

The question of wartime strategy was a matter of concern; General Marshall wanted to make a cross-Channel operation a major effort and so back as early as 1942 we were talking about what might be done. There was a misunderstanding of American Chiefs of Staff and the British capability. I think you had twenty-six divisions but they were only twenty-five to forty per cent equipped and in no sense in a position to engage immediately in warfare. So when it was finally decided to postpone that Second Front, which Stalin had asked Eden for when he went to Moscow in December 1941 to relieve the pressure on the Russian Front, Churchill decided that he'd better go and see Stalin himself to give the news that there could be no Second Front in Europe, but there could be one in Africa. I worked with him and Churchill had some very tough talks with Stalin in August 1942. That was the time Stalin accused the British of being cowardly in their action. Stalin said never before in history had the British Navy turned back, and once the British realised the Germans were not supermen they would have the courage to fight. You could imagine this did not go down well with Churchill and, I think in one of the most brilliant speeches he ever made, answered Stalin and he told what the British had done within their resources and were prepared to do. And in spite of his annoyance he never did ask Stalin where he was with the Second Front when he made his deal with Hitler. He kept his temper. There was an old interpreter with the British Embassy who tried to interpret but Churchill had a bad habit, from an interpreter's standpoint, of making long statements. I would have thought that to translate Churchillian English to Russian would be very difficult at best. In any event he was trying his best and seemed to be

---

* Sir Stafford Cripps (1889–1952), when Ambassador to Moscow in 1940, found his warnings of an imminent Nazi attack treated with disdain by Stalin. He returned to Britain in 1942 to demand ever greater sacrifices on behalf of the USSR.

stumbling along. Churchill pushed him, 'Did you tell him this – did you tell him that,' and at one point Stalin put his head back and roared with laughter. He said, 'Your words of no importance, what is vital is your spirit.' And that exchange, the brutality of Stalin and the manner in which Churchill took it, laid the basis of this wartime relationship. Stalin, in my presence, toasted him, 'My comrade in arms during the war, a man of insatiable courage and determination' – but he added, 'in this war'. I think he knew quite well there would be very little in common between them at the end of the war.

ANTHONY EDEN

From the first Stalin was eager for the Second Front and I don't blame the Russians for doing that – they were sustaining a terrific burden from the German attack. On the other hand it was quite impossible at any time, though we had endless conversations, to make him understand the difficulties of an operation across the sea. The elephant just couldn't understand the whale's limitations of operation and I suppose to some extent the whale was impatient with the elephant for not understanding. It was a constant source of trouble until eventually the landings in Normandy put an end to the dilemma as far as it existed in Stalin's mind. He was quite clear in his mind as to what he wanted: he wanted us and the Americans in due course to agree on what should be the main terms of the peace settlement that ended the war. What concerned him was the security of Russia and he wanted to be quite sure what had happened to his country should not happen again, regardless of what the effect of that would be on the feelings of some of his neighbours.

SIR STAFFORD CRIPPS
Speech given at a 'Russia First' rally, 1942
The Soviet Union has no idea and no wish to interfere in the internal affairs of any other country. I know that from the lips of Stalin himself.

CHAPTER 11

PEARL HARBOR

In 1940–41 the Roosevelt administration inched towards active participation in the European war and at the same time forced the British government and the Dutch government in exile, whose hopes for eventual victory now lay entirely with the USA, to join in a campaign of increasing diplomatic and economic pressure on Japan to abandon its war on China. Although the Japanese began their 1904–5 war with Russia by sinking the Russian Asian Fleet in harbour, the principal US naval base in the Pacific at Pearl Harbor was completely unprepared for the Japanese attack of 7 December 1941. As the attack was so politically advantageous to Roosevelt, suspicions about his complicity have never abated and as late as May 1999 the US Senate voted to annul the 1942 censure of the Hawaiian Fleet and Army Commanders because they were denied vital intelligence available in Washington. The truth is that the threat was incorrectly evaluated because of racialist underestimation of the Japanese (itself a crucial factor in creating the climate for war in Japan), and because of a generalised assumption that if the Japanese did attack, it would be southwards to seize the oilfields of the Dutch East Indies. This made it all the more inexcusable that the principal American deterrent, the heavy bombers based in the Philippines, were destroyed on the ground ten hours after the attack on Pearl Harbor. There could be no doubt, however, that the attack would provoke American rage, so there was a strong element of justified incredulity in the American reaction to the attacks. Germany and Italy did Roosevelt the further favour (so often ignored by historians) of declaring war on the United States four days later, but only Japanese Americans were interned. Until the Japanese carrier force was crushed at Midway in June 1942 Roosevelt's greatest problem was justifying a 'Europe First' policy to the American people. The Doolittle raid on Japan in April 1942 was a harbinger of the fate that awaited Japan and a gesture to show that something was being done in the Pacific.

CHARLES BOHLEN
US diplomat

Roosevelt began to see during the Thirties the dangers that were looming in the world with the rise of Hitler and militaristic Japan, and he felt that the interests of the United States were directly connected with these developments. Our interests clearly lay on the side of the democracies against the totalitarian states but he was very conscious that the instinctive feeling of the American people was just against sending our boys abroad to fight on foreign battlefields. The best illustration of that was in 1937: he made a speech in Chicago in which he proposed rather a mild solution and the reaction he got from the political public was very short and very negative. So we had this problem all the way through the late Thirties and even the early Forties, up to the time of Pearl Harbor.

AMBASSADOR W AVERELL HARRIMAN
President Roosevelt's Special Envoy to Europe

I don't know anything about it until I went in March 1941, but Roosevelt, almost immediately after the attack on the Low Countries in May 1940, began to move. He was there for the deal, for the destroyers, and then he had a defence committee; we had a partial industrial mobilisation and then the extraordinary piece of legislation which was Lend-Lease, proposed in December 1940, became law in March 1941. Under that he was authorised to take action after Hitler's attack in the Low Countries. The President did everything he could to give aid to Britain, and my instructions were very simple and brief: they were to contact the British government and find out what we could do to help Britain short of war, and we began at once doing all sorts of things which were not really neutral under the literal interpretation. We were repairing British naval vessels in American ports and we escorted your convoys across the Atlantic as far as Iceland and we transferred two million tons of shipping.

The battle for the Atlantic was raging when I first came over, about ten per cent of your ships were being sunk, and it didn't take much of a mathematician to figure out it was becoming increasingly difficult.

NORMAN CORWIN
American 'Poet Laureate of the radio'
It was a stroke of absolute imbecility for the Japanese to have bombed Pearl Harbor because that unified the United States. Many of the war measures such as steps to give aid to Britain when she was standing alone used to squeak by in Congress. Even programmes of armament, of military preparedness, got through Congress on very, very close votes – one-vote margins in a total of four hundred to five hundred votes – so that there was considerable division which represented a strong current of isolation. There was a strong anti-British feeling in certain parts of the country; it was felt that Britain was trying very hard to drag us into its war and that the war was none of our concern and that we could simply twiddle our thumbs and it would all go away. But this only furthered the isolationist attitude which Republican Senator Henry Cabot Lodge and the rest of his colleagues, who voted down our participation in the League of Nations after World War One, had established during the days of Woodrow Wilson.

LIEUTENANT COLONEL ALBERT WEDERMEYER
Author of the US Army's strategic 'Victory Program', known as 'Germany First'
The American people were repeatedly told by the President in fireside chats and in official announcements that the administration was doing everything within its power to avoid involvement in the war. This could be interpreted as deceit, but subsequent to the war and as information has become available to me concerning the policies and actions of President Roosevelt, I have decided that he may have known better than those who opposed our entry into the war where the best interests of the United States lay.

AMBASSADOR HARRIMAN
We did things entirely against the rules of neutrality such as repairing naval vessels in and convoying ships. They were very close to warlike acts on our

part, but there was no indication that they provoked Hitler. Japan, I believe from the record, appears to have been provoked by Roosevelt's declaring embargo on the shipment of oil and scrap-iron – they resented that very much. Roosevelt indicated that as long as they were going south through Indochina into Indonesia, that we would not supply them. That seemed to have an influence on the Japanese decision to attack, but I don't know of any indication that our act provoked Hitler. Hitler accepted them and didn't seem to care to bring the United States into war, but suddenly at this moment he declared war. There was no agreement I understand between Hitler and the Japanese. Interesting psychological action on his part, which relieved Roosevelt of his difficulties.

JOHN McCLOY
US Assistant Secretary of War

It's difficult for me to say how close we were but I've no question that the trend was towards an intervention in the war and I'm inclined to think it would not have been far removed. It did take the Pearl Harbor incident to consolidate opinion and bring us into the war, but I feel there were steps that were developing, to be sure somewhat comparable to the steps that took place in World War One. I think with the moves that Mr Roosevelt was making – the Cash and Carry Programme, that he had agreed the protection of the convoys, the destroyer deal and one thing and another – which would be apt to produce an incident that would set war off. The trend of public opinion generally throughout the country was towards an intervention, I think. It was not only the aggressive attitude of Hitler that caused concern but his excess in the Jewish affair, and the general body of opinion was shocked.

CHARLES BOHLEN

I think the Neutrality Act was really a desire to prevent the United States being drawn into war, which the isolationists felt was none of our business. I think they were wrong and I think the American government thought they were wrong, but it was a very definite problem. Roosevelt saw the thing clearly and did what he could to help move public opinion along, but certainly without such an event as Pearl Harbor it was very doubtful that the opinion would have been moved to the point of taking positive action except under extreme provocation.

COMMANDER MINORU GENDA
Japanese naval airman, planner of Pearl Harbor attack
Admiral Isoroku Yamamoto told Vice-Admiral Takijiro Onishi the idea of attacking Pearl Harbor and I was instructed by Vice-Admiral Onishi to make a study of it. This was not an official order because I was not under Vice-Admiral Onishi's command. I was Chief of Staff of an entirely different unit but we had close relations from before and so Admiral Onishi asked me, because of our special personal relationship, to make a study of attacking Pearl Harbor. It was felt that in case of war, if Japan were to fight in a conventional way there was little hope of winning. Therefore the idea was to strike against the US Pacific Fleet in the Hawaii area simultaneously with the start of the war. There were three difficult points in attacking Pearl Harbor. First was to keep it a secret, as if the Americans found out that the Japanese fleet was approaching Pearl Harbor they would be immediately counter-attacked. The second point was what course to take in the approach to Pearl Harbor; the possible routes included a southern route from Truk Island, a central route that passes the Midway Islands and a third to pass south of the Aleutian Islands. The point was which of these three to select; many things had to be considered – the weather, the size of the waves, the visibility. The third point concerned the attack, the actual attack itself: would it be possible to conduct a torpedo attack? This was a very big problem, because if this were not possible the raid could not succeed. We had to figure out how to make a torpedo attack in the shallow waters of Pearl Harbor.

COMMANDER MITSUO FUCHIDA
Japanese naval airman, strike leader at Pearl Harbor
The most difficult problem was torpedo launching in shallow water. The lesson of the British in attacking the Italian Fleet at Taranto, I owe it very much the solution in the shallow-water launching.

COMMANDER GENDA

I am asked that question very often, whether we received any hints from the British Taranto operation. But we did not.

PRIVATE GEORGE ELLIOTT

Radar operator, Hawaii

It was shortly after seven in the morning that we picked up this large flight of planes and fellow radar operator Lockhart at that moment thought that the machine was out of kilter because of the large blip we were receiving from a hundred and thirty-nine miles out. After verifying the equipment and the information it was showing we decided it was a flight of planes coming in and we sent the information to Private MacDonald, who was the switchboard operator at the Information Centre, and of course it being after seven everybody had left because our problem – the malfunction Lockhart and Elliott were sent to resolve – had been over. MacDonald said that there was nobody there that could do anything about it and I left word to see if he could find somebody who would know what to do, and to call us back. A little later this Lieutenant Tyler called back and Lockhart answered the phone and in essence was told to forget it. I might add that at that particular time we were expecting a flight of our own B-17s from Marchfield, California, to reinforce Hawaii and whether this influenced his decision I don't know. They came in fully armed but with no ammunition on board and those that weren't shot down were forced out to sea where they ran out of gas.

LIEUTENANT KEN MURRAY

Staff Officer, Pacific Fleet Command

My first knowledge of the attack was when I was awakened by the sound of bombs dropping and the roaring of aircraft all around us. I ran out and saw immediately that they were Japanese planes and there was this fellow standing next to me who said, 'Boy, it certainly looks real, doesn't it?' And I said, 'I'm afraid it is,' and I went back in, dressed and went over to my office. I happened to be standing next to the Commander-in-Chief, Admiral Kimmel, and we were glumly watching the havoc that was going on. Suddenly he reached up and tore off his four-star shoulder boards, which indicated his rank and title as Commander-in-Chief of the Pacific Fleet, stepped into his adjacent office and when he came out, realising that he was going to lose his command, he had donned two-star Rear-Admiral shoulder boards.

GUNNER'S MATE TOM COMBS

Heavy cruiser USS New Orleans

We were taking power and steam from the dock since we were alongside for repairs and somebody in the confusion had cut our power and steam lines, so everything had to be operated on manual. We had only one battery that we could use, which was the port five-inch battery, so we started using it on the aircraft as they came in. The low-flying torpedo planes all came over the hill and down towards battleship row so we were able to get some pretty good shots at them even though we were in manual. We had to pass ammunition by hand, and we had a young chaplain on board, at the time he'd been aboard less than two months. His name was William Maguire and as far as a battle station was concerned he didn't have one; he was primarily concerned with crew morale. So he was marching up and down the gun-deck saying, 'Praise God and pass the ammunition.' This has been credited to song writers but Chaplain Maguire actually said it that day, a day of confusion and terror for most of us.

MARINE RICHARD FISKE

Battleship USS West Virginia

He had a real thick moustache and as he flew over he kind of smiled and looked at the ship and flew over towards the hangar over there and laid his bombs. The second group of aeroplanes peeled off and one came at us. They were torpedo bombers and one of them hit us and blew me over towards the other side of the ship. My battle station was up on the bridge with the captain so I went up there and as I looked around I saw the *Arizona* blow up and she just sort of rained sailors. I wasn't very scared at this particular time because I couldn't imagine that this was happening to us: it just wasn't real; it seemed like a nightmare. I didn't really comprehend the impact of it until afterwards when I swam ashore and then I realised, my God we're at war.

LIEUTENANT MURRAY

During the attack itself I had no sense of fear. It didn't appear it was real and they weren't shooting at me. I was not frightened until that night when the USS *Enterprise* planes came in and all hell broke loose when we let go with everything we had around here. Of course during the daytime you couldn't see the display, but at night with the tracers and the shells bursting, that was when I became frightened.

COMMANDER GENDA

If we had been able to locate any American carriers we would have sunk them all. There was no mistake about it: our biggest target was the aircraft carriers and the fact that we were not able to locate any carriers was most fortunate for the United States. I don't know how much confidence Admiral Nagumo had. I can say that he was very concerned, but that's because he was not from the Air Arm, he was a torpedo man, therefore he was an amateur as far as air operations were concerned. Admiral Nagumo is dead now; I don't know whether he is in hell or heaven, but it's not possible to go there and ask him.

AMBASSADOR HARRIMAN

I was in England in December and Churchill asked my daughter and myself to Chequers. It was my daughter's birthday, we were having dinner, it was entirely a family party. Every evening at nine o'clock the Prime Minister wanted to hear the BBC news. The butler brought in a small radio which Harry Hopkins* had given him and there was some rather unimportant news: the battle was not going very well in the Middle East, and other things of little importance. Suddenly there was a stop and the announcer

---

* Harry Hopkins (1890–1946), Roosevelt's friend and Chief Diplomatic Adviser, was instrumental in getting the $50 billion Lend-Lease programme through Congress.

said a dispatch had come in: the Japanese have attacked Pearl Harbor. And then he went on and said, 'The something band will play Thursday night at the Savoy Hotel.' And I was startled. Commander Thompson, the Naval Aide to the Prime Minister, said, 'Oh, no, Pearl River,' and I said, 'No, Pearl Harbor.' The Prime Minister had been rather quiet all evening and suddenly slammed the top of this little radio down and jumped to his feet. As he went towards the door John Martin, his Private Secretary, came into the room and said the Admiralty was on the wire. I went with him to the room and it was true. Churchill immediately called up Roosevelt on the telephone and got a description of what went on. Roosevelt said, 'Now we're in the same boat together,' and Churchill said, 'Yes, I will go to the House of Commons tomorrow and declare war on Japan.' President Roosevelt acted more slowly because Hitler was in his mind the main enemy and if he declared war on Japan the concentration of all our energies would have been against Japan, and the American people were naturally aroused. For some unexplained reason Hitler declared war on the United States, which relieved Roosevelt of all his difficulties and then he made up his mind that the defeat of Hitler was by far the most important to achieve first. He was the most dangerous of enemies, and Roosevelt was very skilful in keeping American public opinion directed towards Europe, although we did have a very major operation in Japan and a very successful operation after we recovered from the tremendous blow of the loss of a very substantial part of our navy at Pearl Harbor.

JOHN McCLOY

The morning after Pearl Harbor the nation was at war in a sense of great determination, 'Let's go, who do they think we are' sort of attitude, but it was a long way before we began to get really industrially organised to the point we later reached and there were a good many headaches and a good many bungles that we made during that period. An intense warlike attitude was developed very rapidly and it wasn't very long before we were really ticking in terms of munitions output. Early on, thanks I suppose to the shock that Pearl Harbor gave us, this was truly a nation at war immediately after that disaster took place. There was stepped up activity and there was a tension in the air that hadn't existed before, but generally speaking the methods and the manner of government of Mr Roosevelt didn't change greatly. I was always in the military side, the War Department, and there were many things the White House was interested in. Mr Roosevelt's tendency was to let the professionals handle the conduct of the war. On very broad matters of strategy of course he had views, but he was much less apt to interfere or to cast his influence on the generals and so I don't think there was a marked difference in the atmosphere or the general method of conducting business in the White House after Pearl Harbor.

GEORGE BALL
Associate General Counsel for the Lend-Lease programme
All doubts were resolved overnight not by Pearl Harbor so much as by the very curious and quite stupid decision of Hitler two or three days later to declare war on the United States. I can tell you that if Hitler had not made this decision, if he had simply done nothing, there would have been an enormous sentiment in many parts of the United States that the Pacific war was now our war and the European war was for the Europeans and we should concentrate all our efforts on the Japanese. Let me say that in those first two or three days it was a terrible anxiety for those of us who felt very keenly that what was happening in Europe was the affair of the United States as well as the Europeans and that we really had to intervene.

REAR-ADMIRAL LORD LOUIS MOUNTBATTEN
Chief of Combined Operations
Within a week of Pearl Harbor, Churchill went to see Roosevelt, to discuss future Allied plans. Subsequently General Marshall and later General Eisenhower came over to see the British Chiefs of Staff. They wished to get their troops ashore: they had this large army, they knew I was planning the invasion and they wanted to take part as soon as they possibly could. I tried to point out it would take time but they were very impatient and General Marshall kept saying, 'If you can't find room first, we shall end up by being drawn into the Pacific.'

DR JOHN KENNETH GALBRAITH
Deputy Head of the US Office of Price Administration

I was having a sleep Sunday afternoon and one was always tired in those days, hoping always to get over the fatigue of the day and the week. I was awakened by one of my colleagues saying the news has just come over the radio that the Japanese have attacked Pearl Harbor, and I got up and went to a meeting and I found that my superior, who was in charge of all the civilian operations of the War Office, was away so I was sent to the great meeting of the wartime leaders that convened in Washington on the night of Pearl Harbor. I remember my sense of mission going to that meeting – we had seen the war coming, it was today and here was the hour and here was I attending the meeting with the other great men who were in charge of the nation at this critical hour. All these phrases went through my mind. Then we got to the meeting and it was one hell of a disappointment because nobody could think of anything to say or do. Somebody invented a phrase – this is going to make raw materials east of Suez very scarce – and Donald Nelson, who was later put in charge of the war effort, he got somebody to come up with a great book of strategic raw materials and it seemed like a good idea to go over that and see what materials were threatened by the Japanese. Everybody was coming in during the course of this summons in sport jackets and some had tennis shoes on, and it became terribly evident that nobody had any real information as to where these strategic commodities came from and eventually the whole discussion boiled down on the question of kapok. It was clearly listed as a strategic material, it evidently came from that part of the world but nobody could think, for God's sake, what this stuff was used for. The whole evening left me with a sense of grave disappointment, and I have never expected since then that I would ever be hands-on with history.

PROFESSOR VANNEVAR BUSH
Chairman of the US National Defense Research Committee

In twenty-four hours, no problems were involved, the country turned around absolutely. Before that time this country was pretty divided and there was a pretty hot argument whether we needed to get into it, whether we should, whether our interests were really involved and so forth. After Pearl Harbor all opposition disappeared overnight. I think Roosevelt was convinced for a long time before Pearl Harbor that we needed to get in. He did everything he could, but he didn't have a united country behind him till Pearl Harbor – then he did.

JOHN McCLOY

Internment of the Japanese wasn't only War Secretary Stimson's decision. It was Mr Roosevelt's decision pressed to a large degree by Earl Warren, who later became the Chief Justice of the Supreme Court and who was then Governor of California, and West Coast Commander General John DeWitt, who felt that after Pearl Harbor, with tensions such as they were on the West Coast, that it would be very awkward indeed to permit the Japanese to remain as they were, not only because of the danger of sabotage or espionage, but because of the high state of feeling against the Japanese at that point. There was a very important element of protection in this and there was a good bit of legal argument at the time as to the justification for doing it, particularly in respect of American citizens. There was an old English law on this subject, which rather influenced some of the decisions, and the thought was that for their own protection and for the general good – as barn burnings had already taken place – they had better be picked up and put into a safer community. I have a feeling that we probably exaggerated the likelihood of riots or destruction. Very shortly after they were picked up and put into these camps, they relocated and out of it came the organisation of those Japanese units which served so well in the Western theatre that the sentiment of antagonism towards the local Japanese entirely disappeared.

ISAMU NOGUCHI
Japanese–American artist and landscape architect
In America there are so many people from different parts of the world and to hate people, as apparently war requires, involved the possibility of hating your own people, the question of who you were going to select to hate the most. In the First World War the Germans were hated thoroughly

and there was a great deal of discrimination and harassment of the Germans. In the Second World War there were three nationalities, the Italians, the Germans and the Japanese, and so a Foreign Committee was formed of the United States Senate to investigate what should be done about the people of these nationalities in this country. They went to the West Coast among their investigations and made enquiries among the Germans, the Italians and the Japanese, supposedly. I went to some of their meetings and was very struck by the strong representation of the Germans and the Italians. The Japanese were a convenient sort of symbol of the enemy and for those of Japanese extraction in this country to be suddenly recognised as being something to do with the enemy made them terribly anxious and of course they were harassed because they were the most convenient scapegoat around.

JOHN McCLOY

There was no question there was hardship and I took part, as others did, in trying to get compensation for them for the losses they'd suffered and there was a substantial appropriation for their distress and the inconvenience they suffered. But there was no misery, no brutality. Administration of those camps were under the supervision of a man who was a very fine liberal, humanitarian individual and who was very sensitive to their needs.

EDISON UNO

Japanese–American teenager

Amazingly there was very little bitterness because in 1942 most Japanese–Americans felt it was an act of patriotism to cooperate with the government, therefore they did everything possible to minimise the bitterness or the hardship that we might run into. The authorities treated us with some kindness and consideration but more important was our cooperation with the United States government. We felt that it was an act of civil obedience and loyalty to prove to our country that our incarceration was truly a mistake, a mistake that some day they would admit had been done against their own citizens.

LIEUTENANT COLONEL JIMMY DOOLITTLE

USAAF pilot who led the raid on Japan that bears his name on 18 April 1942
The idea of taking off a land plane with the tail down was somewhat foreign to the Air Force types. It was a Navy technique we had to learn and during training one chap stalled off and crashed. He was not hurt. We had only one real worry and that would have been a dead calm. The carrier would have been able to make perhaps thirty knots; under those conditions taking off from the carrier deck would have been, at best, precarious. In the event there was a thirty-knot wind, the carrier was able to make twenty knots into this wind so we had an effective wind of fifty knots across the deck.

RICHARD TREGASKIS

War correspondent
The Doolittle raid was terribly important towards psychological effect. It was a big surprise to the Japanese – the last thing they expected was to have American bombers appearing over Tokyo, even if it was such a small force. Surprise is such a great weapon in any military operation, but I think the psychological effect was the main thing about it and of course you have to give those Doolittle flyers an awful lot of credit. They were almost suicidal in their net dedication because it was a very risky kind of thing.

MARQUIS KOICHI KIDO

Lord Keeper of the Privy Seal
I don't think any particular measures were taken but it was a great shock to the Japanese people when American planes had bombed Japanese soil.

TOSHIKAZU KASE

Principal Secretary to the Foreign Minister
When the Doolittle raid was conducted that produced a consternation because the military repeatedly assured the public that the Japanese sky was impenetrable. When this alleged impenetrability failed it naturally produced a reaction of discrediting the capability of the military command.

LIEUTENANT COLONEL DOOLITTLE

The actual damage done was minimal. We were sixteen aeroplanes each with one ton of bombs. In later stages of the war the Twentieth Air Force under LeMay was sending out five hundred aeroplanes, each of them with ten tons of bombs. However, it did have some advantages. We had had nothing but bad news at home so it was the first good news our folks got. It caused the Japanese to question their warlords who had informed them that Japan would never be attacked. Most important of all, it caused the retention of aircraft for the protection of the home islands that would have been much more effective had they been able to go south, where the fighting was going on.

MARQUIS KIDO

The Emperor had no alternative but to approve the execution of the captured Doolittle pilots because the Army had conducted a trial and decided on the execution. I can only guess that those who played a major role were executed and the others spared.

JOHN McCLOY

I think that generally public opinion had the feeling, as we say in baseball, that the big league was in Europe and in the United Kingdom, where the chief menace was, where the chief enemy had to be met and opposed, and there's where our chief energies were applied. There was some sentiment on the West Coast towards the other concept, the Pacific emphasis, but I think that was not too pronounced. Moreover I think that our military had this idea pretty far advanced in their thinking. There were elements in the Navy that were thinking in terms of Pacific war – most of their training had been taking place in the Pacific, the big naval bases had been moved from the Atlantic to the Pacific and it was natural that they should be thinking in terms of their effort in that part of the world – and, as well, General MacArthur was out there. But in spite of all that I think the general body of opinion supported Mr Roosevelt's feeling, which didn't mean that we should go to sleep in the Pacific. Relatively shortly after that we were involved there in the Battle of Midway, one the great battles of history.

REAR ADMIRAL LORD LOUIS MOUNTBATTEN

Roosevelt said, 'Only one thing, the battle of Midway's just taken place. The bounds of naval power begin to be redressed and I think we can do an operation based on Australia with the American marines, American aircraft carriers and so forth. Ask Winston if he can let me have a couple of British carriers and the destroyer screen to go with them.' I said I certainly would.

DR GALBRAITH

Nothing in Pearl Harbor caused the people to dislike Roosevelt or to love him more. One of his great enemies before Pearl Harbor was Thomas Girdler, who was head of the Republic Steel Corporation. He was the most venomous of Roosevelt's enemies. After Pearl Harbor, maybe even before, when there was need for steel expansion, he was one of the pragmatic types who came down, made his peace with the New Dealers and showed how Republic could expand its steel plant – at the public's expense, let me say. But I remember Tom Girdler saying, 'I'm prepared to do this and I'm prepared to do it where you won't get similar action from the stuffed shirts' – he meant the US Steel Corporation, which was much larger. But, he said, 'This doesn't mean I love you. This doesn't mean I've changed my mind about Franklin Roosevelt.'

CHAPTER 12

FALL OF MALAYA AND RETREAT FROM BURMA

The planned defence of Malaya and Singapore relied on 355 front-line aircraft and a strong fleet to defeat any invasion before it could establish itself on land. In December 1941 there were only 158 second-rate aircraft, as well as the new battleship, Prince of Wales, *and the old battlecruiser* Repulse, *which sailed without air cover on 8 December and were sunk on the 10th. The Army totalled approximately 140,000 men but was a heterogeneous assembly of two Indian Army divisions and late-arriving reinforcements from Australia and the 18th Division from Britain, none of whom was trained or equipped for jungle fighting. With only 55,000 men Lieutenant General Yamashita repeatedly outflanked British positions the length of the Malayan peninsula and assaulted across the Johore Strait to land on Singapore Island on 9 February. Although he was desperately overextended he now controlled Singapore's water supply and the morale of the British troops had been eroded, as had the will to resist of their commander, Lieutenant General Percival, who surrendered unconditionally on 15 February. Along with a string of other defeats. the fall of Singapore struck an irreversible blow to European prestige in the Far East. Perhaps 25,000 Indian Army soldiers joined the Indian National Army and fought alongside the Japanese against their previous comrades-in-arms in Burma. Even before the capture of Singapore, Japanese forces attacked into Burma from Thailand and forced the Salween river line on 31 January. The 17th Indian Division was constantly outflanked and after the premature demolition of the bridge over the Sittang river on 22 February lost most of its equipment, organised defence of Burma was effectively over. The British destroyed the port and oil terminal in Rangoon but were harried out of the country and were only able to make a stand along the mountain ranges that mark the India–Burma border.*

LIEUTENANT COLONEL ICHII SUGITA
Battalion Commander, Japanese Army

I did not know what the abilities of British soldiers in the jungle, but I believed from the history of the First World War that your officers and the men are tough enough to fight against enemies.

MAJOR GENERAL JOHN SMYTH, VC
Commander 17th Indian Division

The fundamental reason why we failed in Malaya was that we were stretched to the limit at that time in our war with Germany and Italy and there simply were not the trained men, air forces and ships that we should have supplied to meet the Japanese attack. The plan for the defence of Malaya was based entirely on the Air Force and there were to be some 355 first-class aircraft with the Army protecting their bases and their aero-dromes. The idea was that they should attack the Japanese while they were at sea and destroy them or damage them before the campaign started. The priority of arms and equipment for Malaya, at that time, was very low. They were only number four after Great Britain, the Middle East and Russia. Also with regard to men, the first priority for India – and India supplied most of the men – was the Middle East and Malaya only came second, and that was the same with the Australians. Some of the Australians that arrived in Malaya had never even fired a rifle, so we did feel very much a second eleven against the very highly trained and strongly supported Japanese. The Chiefs of Staff at home thought that Singapore Island was quite indefensible against an enemy that had complete command of the air and the sea, and that is why the defence had to be well forward, on the mainland of Malaya. And from the start, of course, we were thrown on to the defensive. One of the reasons, of course, was that the Japanese employed three hundred tanks – we hadn't any tanks at all –

but it was really the employment of the hook around our defensive positions, which was their main method of operating by sea or by land, which made it so difficult for our ill-equipped forces.

CAPTAIN TERUO OKADA
Intelligence Officer, Japanese Army

In Japanese infantry training most of the training, apart from riflemanship and digging trenches, is on bayonet fighting and night fighting, all the time. I think this night-fighting training was most useful in the jungle where conditions are fairly similar. We got this experience in China where the Chinese Army could press us during the day, but we knew that at night as soon as we withdrew all the bullets from the guns and went into the night fighting with cold steel we could drive them back, always. We had the confidence and I think this came from training, training, training on the night fighting and the bayonet fighting.

PRIVATE WILLIAM CRUICKSHANK
Prisoner of the Japanese

My particular lot, the 18th Division, we left England known as a crack division in the British Army at the time. We weren't actually meant for Singapore or that area at all; we were meant for the Middle East. We were trained for the Middle East, and when we were thrown into the jungle without the proper equipment, without the proper arms as well, that came as a shock. But when we found that we were absolutely cut off, there was no method of fighting back at the end, there was no method of evacuation; it was a terrible shock. I, personally, when we were told to lay our arms down, I just cried like a baby, I think more with temper than anything else, to think there was nothing we could do.

DAVID MARSHALL
Malayan member of the Straits Settlement Volunteer Corps

Somebody picked up this diary that had been thrown away. It turned out to be the diary of a young British soldier who had come from England by ship via Cape Town and it was peppered right through with remarks like,

'Had lecture today on dangers of snake bites in jungle. Browned off. Lecture this afternoon on drinking water from streams and rivers, danger to kidneys and liver. Had lectures on insects and mosquitoes and malaria in jungle, danger of jungle animals in tropics. Browned off.' I can't remember all of it but it was a fairly extensive diary kept up almost every day, and when I finished it I realised that poor boy must have been frozen stiff with fear and had really lost the battle psychologically before it began, because going into that jungle he was afraid of all the unseen terrors and only too glad to get away. It made me believe what may have been a completely false story that the Japanese commander would sneeringly tell us when we were in the camp, that they didn't have to fight the British troops with bullets. All they had to do was hang fire-crackers on the rubber trees and set them off at night, and you'd see the British troops scurrying like rabbits. Of course we told them we didn't believe it, but frankly after reading that diary I don't think it improbable.

CAPTAIN OKADA

We are always taught camouflage from early stages of training. There were many things we don't like in the jungle, leeches and all kinds of things, but I like the jungle and it did not have the fear that it seems to have had for some Allied soldiers. I would have thought that with the Allies being in such an area long before us they must have completed ways of training or manoeuvres in the jungle long before we did.

HARRY MILLER
British civilian in Singapore

Pearl Harbor was a bit of a shock, the fact that they were capable of launching such a massive operation and succeed beyond all dreams in sinking much of the American fleet. Nevertheless there still persisted the idea that this was a fluke, that they had taken the Americans by surprise, the Japanese airman was a short-sighted, rice-eating individual flying a death-trap of an aircraft and certainly not a very fast one. All that was disproved, of course, very, very soon when they came into Malaya and started dominating the air and we realised that the Zero aircraft was a superb machine and that the men in them were superb fighters and that we in Singapore – in Malaya – didn't have anything in the way of aircraft to match up with the Zeros.

MAJOR GENERAL SMYTH

The Japanese Air Force gained such a tremendous superiority over the whole of Malaya in the first forty-eight hours that movement was made extremely difficult. Percival's idea was to oppose the Japanese as they landed but that didn't come off – they were able to land in Thailand and we would not break Thai neutrality, so we were at a disadvantage from the start.*

CAPTAIN OKADA

Our training would be the normal training, for instance we had no special training for desert fighting in north China – we did get sand glasses against sandstorms but that was about all. We got mosquito nets against mosquitoes but there was no special training for specific jungle conditions as such. The jungle is not such a terrible place. Our clothing and the food we carry, you see we can live on rice, salt and sesame seeds and salted fish, this can keep a soldier going a long time, also we can find many things in the jungle to eat. And especially when the enemy aircraft come the jungle can be very friendly to you.

HARRY MILLER

The bombing in Singapore started with a vengeance somewhere around four o'clock on the morning of 8th December when the bombers appeared.** Singapore was still lit up with street lamps and it was a fine moonlit morning so they had the whole city at their mercy. They dropped their bombs on an air base but also into the heart of the city, leaving their calling card, so's to speak, and that produced about thirty-three dead and about a hundred and twenty-five wounded. It hit Chinatown; it really hit

---

* Lieutenant General Arthur Percival (1887–1966), Commander-in-Chief Malaya 1941–42.
** The same day as Pearl Harbor – the International Date Line intervening.

the heart of the city. After that there was quite a lull because their targets were elsewhere, in northern Malaya, but as they moved closer the attacks became more frequent. It was after they crossed the causeway that the intensive air strikes on Singapore began and the last three days before it capitulated was a sheer hell of concentrated bombing and artillery and the Japanese aircraft were rarely out of the sky and there were none of our own aircraft. There were artillery duels between our fellows and theirs, but with the Japanese bombers overhead and the Japanese fighters our gun crews became their targets and they were knocked out one by one.

LIEUTENANT COLONEL SUGITA

We took Singapore in sixty-five days; we made a surprise attack, so we made a great success. Your forces are not so aggressive as we expect them and, one other point, they had not fortified along the coast the northern part of the island, so we easily attacked and occupied the northern part of Singapore. We do not expect that British forces should be surrendered according to our demand, which I prepared beforehand. I was surprised but we respected them going to surrender.

DAVID MARSHALL

All the time we believed we were going to be rescued at the last minute. The British Empire had a tremendous psychological place in our lives: its strength, its massiveness and the need to protect Singapore not for the sake of the people of Singapore – we recognised that – but for the sake of maintaining the British Empire. It was important to maintain this pivotal military centre, which was the naval base for the Far East of the British Empire, for the protection of Australia, New Zealand, Hong Kong and the financial and commercial interests of the Empire.

HARRY MILLER

The fighting soldier fully expected that in view of the situation that existed there would be another Dunkirk from Singapore. Fighting morale was very badly hit by the lack of any of our aircraft and it was one of the most serious aspects of the war at that particular time; it really contributed quite a lot to defeat. There came a time when there just weren't any more ships coming into Singapore to pick people up. So the Europeans, the great mass of civil servants and municipal and business people who were there, realised that they were in for a pretty sticky time. Morale was pretty high, nevertheless, perhaps higher among the civilian population – and I include the Asians in that – than among a certain element of the fighting forces. It wasn't just the Australians, it was anybody who came back from the fighting front, leaderless and completely giving up. They just threw their rifles into canals or drains along the side of the road and moved rapidly into the city, sheltering among the civilians, finding refuge in one of the big buildings and refusing to be moved out of it. It was a pretty oppressive spectacle considering the fact that Asian and European civilians were still fighting the war in their own way, in the sense of manning first-aid posts, casualty stations, fire brigades and all the other essential services.

LIEUTENANT COLONEL SUGITA

We prepared the plan, but it was the first time for us to have such a meeting and when the news from the front that the ministers came to the headquarters of the 5th Division they did not know how to deal with them. I was asked by the headquarters of the brigade to meet your ministers and we talk about how to surrender but your ministers do not say 'surrender'; they want us to come to Singapore headquarters to talk with the High Commissioners. But according to our plan we want some pressures on our side. Then we departed and returned back to my headquarters to report our meeting and then we went to the front and I saw the place where we met later. So the conference was held at about 7pm and they had little idea how to deal with their own, I guess because they're not enough time to prepare for the meeting and they had little knowledge of surrenders, because the Staff Officers did not expect surrenders so soon. They believe the British Army stay and fights against us, so they had not enough knowledge about the detail concerning the meeting. General Yamashita wanted to get an answer from the British side. And there were possibles: General Percival wanted to keep some troops in Singapore to keep order and peace within the city, but we wanted the British Army disarmed all over.

HARRY MILLER

It was the morning after the surrender and I had gone back into the city just to see what was happening, and almost unostentatiously we were being taken over by long lines of Japanese troops, unkempt, bearded, squat and bandy-legged individuals who came shuffling and slouching in. Extremely tired men, grim-visaged. They set up barricades at strategic points and then stood beside them and one thought – Well, was the great British Army beaten by runts like these? And by golly we had been beaten by them.

LIEUTENANT COLONEL SUGITA

We were so surprised because we expected your forces about fifty thousand and we found about one hundred thousand prisoners, so it was just over twice what we expected.

MAJOR GENERAL SMYTH

I don't think any country could have been more unprepared for war than Burma was at this particular time. The government was unprepared, the civil organisation and the people were unprepared and the defence forces practically did not exist. And this was all the more remarkable when one realises that Burma was taken over by the War Office for defence purposes in 1935 and did nothing about it at all. The priority for arms and equipment for Burma was very low indeed and when the war started the War Office very callously handed the unwanted baby back to the Commander-in-Chief in India.

LIEUTENANT COLONEL WILLIAM JAMES
100th Indian Infantry Brigade, Burma

I went to Burma from India with an independent Indian brigade before there was any thought of a Jap invasion. At the time I went over, which was in 1941, I personally was disappointed because I'd hoped to go to the desert and at that time one never thought the Japanese would be so foolish as to take on the Allies. It was merely an independent brigade going into a very peaceful country in which there were two British battalions, one was based just south of Rangoon and the other was up in the hills, and there were of course the Burma Rifles.

MAJOR GENERAL SMYTH

Wavell of course had become a national hero when he defeated the Italians in the desert at the beginning of the war, but then of course he had a series of disasters against the Germans in Greece, Crete and against Rommel in the desert. Anthony Eden said that he'd aged ten years in one night when he was defeated by Rommel. So he was at that time a very tired man and he very much wanted a rest. Now Winston Churchill, who was a law unto himself over these military appointments, insisted on exchanging Auchinleck with Wavell. The Viceroy of India protested, the Secretary of State for India protested and most of all Sir John Dill, the Chief of the Imperial General Staff, protested very strongly. He went to Winston about this and he said that Wavell was essentially a Westerner and knew nothing about the Far East, and Auchinleck was essentially a man in the right place as Commander-in-Chief in India. He deprecated the exchange very much, but it took place. Wavell had one marked characteristic which was a very great disadvantage to him the whole way through the Malayan and Burma campaigns: he had utter contempt for the Japanese as soldiers and that led him into all sorts of difficulties. To start with he refused two Chinese divisions that had been offered to him by Chiang Kai-shek, which was a disastrous blunder – he spent the rest of the campaign trying to get them back. And then it was a great mistake him sending his Chief of Staff in Delhi, General Hutton, as Burma Army Commander. Now Hutton was an excellent Staff Officer – he was the man in the right place in India – but he was quite out of place as a battle commander and I'm sure he would be the first to admit that. The Chiefs of Staff were against this appointment and so was the Viceroy and eventually they persuaded Wavell to accept Alexander in place of Hutton, but that was not until the 19th of February and of course Alexander arrived really too late to make any marked effect.

MAJOR MIKE CALVERT

Pioneer British jungle-warfare expert

When Burma was attacked I was given the job of forming the Bush Warfare School out of all sorts of headquarters staff plus my own staff. And because the Japanese tactics were to do right or left hooks around the British, who rather stuck to the roads, we kept on finding ourselves used as the only force to oppose those hooks. Also we did a raid down the Irrawaddy in a paddle steamer: we were a hundred men and I had recently returned from Australia and brought back Australian bush hats, so we pretended we were the advance guard of an Australian brigade from the Middle East and we kept a Japanese regiment entertained with only a hundred men for two or three weeks.

MAJOR GENERAL SMYTH

Wavell called me up to see him on the 28th of December 1941 at his house in Delhi and told me then that two brigades of my 17th Division, which I thought were on their way to Baghdad, had been diverted at sea and they had gone to Singapore, which came as a great shock to me, and then he said that he wanted me to go to Burma with the remaining brigade to form a new 17th Division. But in all our conversations that we had that afternoon it struck me that he didn't anticipate that Burma was in any immediate danger at all. And then during the operations when I asked him to speak to my brigadiers and staff, when we'd been hanging on by our eyelids for several days against two Japanese divisions, I expected him to say, 'Well done, stick to it,' that sort of thing. But the whole gist of his remarks were that he didn't think the Japanese were any good and therefore we, by implication, were worse.

MAJOR CALVERT

The main thing was the Japanese had experience. They had been fighting in China and the Chinese is a good foe. They were fanatical, they were tremendous patriots and once they were told to do a thing they got on with it and did it. They instilled the fear of God in everyone by the fact that in a rapid advance they were told not to take any prisoners, so any prisoners they did take, they shot. The Japanese were not equipped with a mass of trucks like the British Army so they did not have to use roads and they were trained to march and travel light. They were also taught to fire their weapons effectively and not to put down barrages of massed automatic weapons.

MAJOR GENERAL SMYTH

The Sittang disaster undoubtedly was the cause for the loss of Rangoon and the loss of Burma. Quite briefly what had happened was that we had been withdrawing towards the broad Sittang river with one long and narrow railway bridge, and it was quite obvious that what we wanted to avoid at all costs was being caught by the Japanese in the act of crossing this river. Therefore on the 12th of February, which was crisis day, really, in this Burma campaign, I sent my Chief of Staff to see Hutton and I told him that if I was to get my division across the Sittang safely in time to prepare a proper position on the far side I must start immediately. But Hutton was under great pressure from Wavell that I was not to withdraw under any circumstances because Wavell and Winston Churchill were trying to persuade the Australian Prime Minister to allow two Australian divisions to land in Rangoon and they wanted to see the 17th Division stuck out on the map well in front. On the 19th, General Hutton came forward and allowed me to withdraw but faced with two Japanese divisions and a far superior Air Force it was by then going to be a desperate race to get anyone at all across the Sittang.

MAJOR W S BOLLER
British Army in Burma

When we made our last retreat from Rangoon we had travelled about twenty miles before we were held up by a small Japanese platoon. We had the 7th Brigade and other regiments trying to break through but it took several concerted attacks before we did. Anyway, we got through there and when we arrived at a hill station in Burma, we stayed there about ten or fifteen days, then we had to embark into various vehicles and make our way into India. Then we had to abandon the vehicles and we walked day after day for miles and miles and sometimes without food, water or anything of the sort.

MAJOR GENERAL SMYTH

It was a crushing disadvantage to me in the 1942 campaign that I hadn't got a wireless set which could contact my air support in Rangoon and therefore, believe it or not, the only thing I could do was to tap into the railway telephone line, get the babu [clerk] in the post office in Rangoon and try to persuade him that it was vitally important for me to be put on to the Air Force headquarters. That was really the reason why, in our withdrawal to the Sittang, we were terribly bombed, badly bombed by the RAF as well as by the Japanese Air Force, simply because they had not been properly briefed as to exactly where we were.

MAJOR BOLLER

The overall impression I had of that horrible trek out of Burma was that it seemed to bring the best and the worst out of people. Some people who I'd looked up to and respected, I found I couldn't respect any more because they became entirely different on that march. In fact they felt – I felt – that it was a question of survival of the fittest and in actual fact it was. If you didn't look after number one you just didn't get out, you just didn't get anywhere. I found that many people wanted to fight and quarrel and look for the best thing they could find for themselves and they couldn't care less for anybody else, and this went on all through the march and it left a very bitter taste in my mouth.

MAJOR GENERAL SMYTH

The great advantage the Japanese had over the British and Indian troops, in this campaign, was that they were trained and equipped for the job, whereas our forces had no pack rations, no pack wireless and no pack transport, and therefore we were entirely supplied by lorries and were very much road-bound. The Japanese were trained to get through the jungle, they were lightly equipped and lightly armed and they specialised in wide enveloping movement through the jungle where if necessary they could live on the villages, being rice eaters. Later on in the operations I was sent the Yorkshire Light Infantry, a very fine battalion, which I was very glad to have, but a note arrived with them that I was to use them in wide encircling movements in the jungle. I cable back to Army Headquarters: 'Presume Yorkshire Light Infantry can live on rice,' and a very indignant cable came back, 'On no account must the Yorkshire Light Infantry be given rice.' Well, there you have it in a nutshell – they could move through the jungle and live on the villages and we couldn't.

LIEUTENANT COLONEL JAMES

Coming out of Burma in 1942 we were falling back behind our retiring Army and there was nothing one could do with one's casualties except hold on to them and do what one could with them. It was tragic because we had severe burn cases, in excruciating pain and if we'd been able to evacuate those casualties by plane into India, in a matter of hours, the majority of those cases would have been saved. As it was the majority were lost. It was not until the Wingate operation that casualty evacuation by air came into its own thanks to the Americans. They had light planes, the [Stinson] L-1 and L-5, and they were evacuated right from the very front lines to the larger airstrips where they were taken by larger planes, the [C-47] Dakotas, and flown back to hospitals in India. In a matter of two or three hours a chap who was badly wounded or extremely ill was lying between sheets in a base hospital and I don't think the British Army had ever known that kind of evacuation before that time and from then onward in the Fourteenth Army it became pretty well routine and it was life-saving. If it hadn't been for that, our mortality rate would have been much higher than it was.

MAJOR GENERAL SMYTH

What is not generally known, and most people would be astonished if they knew, is that we hadn't any Mepacrin [malaria tablets] at all, and one of my battalions had four hundred cases of malaria and therefore they couldn't move at all because they'd not got sufficient men to carry the sick.

LIEUTENANT COLONEL SUGITA

According to the Geneva Convention we treat prisoners of war fairly, but after the war is going on we faced very difficult conditions concerning the food, and the war itself became severe. I don't think so much about treatment of the prisoners of war as you told us. They said Japanese Army treat them badly but ask a soldier and he say no. There are a jungle zone and very short of food, which were not prepared beforehand, and lot of the soldiers very short of food and they had to face difficult fighting. At the end of the war they unable to fight as soldiers in peacetime. A lot of officers and men were dead not only because of Japanese treatment but also because short of food and hardworking. After war it is good propaganda that Japan made bad treatment of prisoners of war.

CAPTAIN LEWIS BUSH

Pre-war English teacher in Japan, captured at Hong Kong
You must remember that to the Japanese in those days a prisoner of war was regarded as worse than a criminal, because first of all no Japanese could conceive of being taken prisoner of war. If he were, he would be robbed of his civil rights for the rest of his life. Every Japanese soldier in Burma or any other theatre of war nearly always had a hand grenade or something to polish off his own life if he were in danger of being taken prisoner, or to bite off his tongue. They were even taught how to take their own lives by their superiors. And so this fact alone meant that we, who had surrendered honourably by order of the Governor of Hong Kong, we were completely at the mercy of people who had no conception of human rights, let alone the Geneva Convention on the treatment of prisoners of war. Of course there were exceptions; after the war many of my comrades and I have said that if it hadn't been for the good ones we would not be alive.

CAPTAIN OKADA

The Chinese, we understand them because they're much more simple. It's hard to explain, but you see if they caught you they cut off your head and you caught them you cut off their heads. Also in the meantime we could exchange information through our scouts and there are cases when they sent us bags of peanuts saying, 'To the Imperial Japanese Army let us have good fighting next year as last year'. So there was a certain understanding. But fighting the Allies was a different matter – the ground rules you may say are not so simple. I never could understand why certain regiments would die for their beliefs or for their country under a foreign officer. You had Indian regiments with British officers and this we could not understand. We felt the British officer was a good fighter although the ones we captured they always said to me, 'We will win the war,' when I interrogated them. Now this I could not understand because here is a man who has surrendered and he still says, 'We will win the war'. We could not understand because if we are fighting to win the war we will fight until we die.

LIEUTENANT COLONEL SUGITA
In the Western countries it is not shame to surrender their responsibilities; it is quite different from those in Japan. I don't know exactly but most of the soldiers that were told that we should not surrender, they despised surrenders of those officers and men.

PRIVATE RONALD FRY
Prisoner of the Japanese on the Death Railway, Burma
At one time we said to a Japanese officer what you could do with here is an elephant, you know to move the trees, and he said, 'I've got all the elephants I need – you are my little white elephants.'

PRIVATE H R OAKLEY
Prisoner of the Japanese on the Death Railway, Burma
They hated us for what we were, because we were white or British. They considered that they were above everybody, that they were the better people, and they would reduce you to lower than an animal if they could, any time. After we left Singapore we were transported to Siam – Thailand – and then we arrived at these sites where we had to put up bamboo huts and so forth, and then we were immediately put to work laying this railway line, which started at Kanchanburi and ran for three hundred miles.

We was marshalled out every day on various working parties and we had to build a bridge at Tamarkan. We had to do pile driving, which consists of a huge weight with about fifty men pulling ropes and dropping this thing down on the pile, which drove it into the bed of the river, which you were doing from the time you started till the time you left off. That was one task – the other would be forming chains by passing baskets of soil from one man to another all day, shoring up embankments and so forth.*

PRIVATE CRUICKSHANK

They'd pick on someone who'd done a stupid little thing, didn't bow to one of the guards for instance, and they'd stand him outside the guard-room in the blazing sun and take great delight in pricking him with a bayonet point to make him stand upright to attention if he started to droop, that type of thing. They'd always laugh about it – oh, they could laugh – and yet they couldn't understand when they found us laughing under the conditions we were in. That's one thing we beat them at: they just couldn't understand how an Englishman after, say, a year of hell with them could still laugh and joke, and this was where we always had them beat.

PRIVATE FRY

The latrines were concrete foundation and so everything that was in there turned to liquid. In no time the top was just an absolute sea of maggots, and when it rained they overflowed and everywhere you trod was maggots. One chap was in such a bad way, I think it was cerebral malaria, that they found him with his head down there – he'd committed suicide.

PRIVATE CRUICKSHANK

We did hit back in our own ways. The Japs would make us build their huts whenever we moved to another place and we were all covered with lice, bugs, everything under the sun. We'd spend maybe one hour of our three

---

* About half the 100,000 Asians and 16,000 of the 60,000 Europeans employed as forced labourers on the Thailand–Burma railway died of overwork, malnutrition and disease.

hours' rest picking these bugs and lice, put them in tin cans or anything we could find, and when we finished their huts we used to scatter the damned things in their huts. This is one of the ways that we could hit back at them and we used to love it. It used to give us some form of entertainment: we'd talk about it afterwards and this is what would make us laugh, this type of thing.

CAPTAIN BUSH

One of our men, I think he was a private in the Middlesex Regiment, he managed to make a tunnel from his hut in our camp to the Japanese Army canteen and over a period got away with thousands of cigarettes, chocolate bars and all kinds of luxuries in the way of soaps, which he was selling around the camp to fellow prisoners. Now he was caught and we expected of course that he would be beheaded in public, because if you blinked your eyes on morning parades you would get a bashing. But this chap was taken up before the Japanese military court and he was ordered to be kept in camp for six weeks – he wasn't allowed to go out on working parties with his comrades. And this chap appeared with a placard on his front and another on his back which simply said, 'I am a thief,' in English and Japanese. A Japanese guard came to me and said, 'Oh, Bush-san' – that means Bush captain – 'this is a terrible punishment for this poor man, how terribly humiliating.' This astonished me but the fellow stayed in camp for six weeks, the guards gave him portions of their own food, they gave him cigarettes. He'd never had such a wonderful time in all his life as a prisoner of war.

CAPTAIN OKADA

After the final surrender we were a working party and the British officer in charge of the guard caught some of our men peeing against a wall and he called us and said these men must be punished. The punishment was to put stones in their knapsacks and make them run around the courtyard many times. After this happened two or three times we complained to the British officer and said we would like to punish our men ourselves, so he said that would be all right on condition it was done in front of him. So next time we had our people to be punished we lined them up and the colonel in charge beat them up, in fact out of the five two fell down because they were beaten so badly. The British officer then said that our mode of punishment was very cruel, but we said, no, our men prefer this because it's much quicker, it does not waste time, the man does not miss his meals, he's back on duty right after he recovers and he'll recover quicker.

MAJOR GENERAL SMYTH

I feel, and I think my troops will always feel, bitter that all the blame was put on them. I think that the bad thing about both those campaigns is that – although defeat was inevitable in those circumstances – the blame should have been put in both Malaya and Burma on the unfortunate troops who had to carry the can.

CHAPTER (13)

BATTLE OF THE ATLANTIC 1942–43

The figures for merchant-ship and U-boat losses tell the story of how the Battle of the Atlantic was so nearly lost, thanks in part to the US Navy's obstinate refusal to adopt convoys in 1942, granting the U-boats their second 'happy time' off the American coast, and then won by Allied technological advances, tactical refinements and sheer numbers as the massive US ship-building programme gathered pace. In 1942 the U-boats sank 1,859 ships (8.3 million tons) for the loss of 86 of their own; in 1943 they sank 812 ships (3.6 million tons) but lost 242. The turning point of the campaign was the battle for Convoy ONS-5 in late April and early May 1943, so well covered by The World at War *interviewers, in which twelve merchant ships were sunk but eight U-boats were lost and a further seven were forced to withdraw because of battle damage. On 23 May Admiral Dönitz, who lost his youngest son, Peter, on U-954 in the ONS-5 battle, recalled all his U-boats from the North Atlantic. The closing of the air gap in the mid-Atlantic by long-range bombers, allied to the new airborne centimetric radar, was probably the most significant tactical contribution to the Allied victory, but strategically the greatest German reversal came in June 1943, when the Royal Navy introduced a new system of encypherment that defeated German attempts to break it, although Merchant Navy cyphers remained an open book to them. Meanwhile, from July 1943 British cryptographers at Bletchley Park were consistently able to read signals sent by the Kriegsmarine's four-wheel Enigma cypher machine, which had totally defeated them from February to December 1942. During the Battle of the Atlantic approximately 3,500 merchant ships (14.5 million tons) and 765 U-boats were sunk with the loss of seventy-five per cent of all operational U-boat crews, the highest loss-rate of any of the armed forces engaged in the Second World War. It is a curious fact that of the ten top-scoring U-boat commanders only Günther Prien, who sank* Royal Oak *in Scapa Flow in 1939, was killed in action.*

ADMIRAL KARL DÖNITZ

Commander-in-Chief of the German Navy from 30 January 1943

In 1942 when the German warfare still was successful, there lacked a further development of the submarine weapon. The reason was the regular use of Anglo-American planes against the German U-boats in the Atlantic ... The result was that submarine manoeuvrability on the surface was diminished, to the disadvantage of the operational and tactical use of the submarines. Secondly we learned the Anglo-American warships and all of the planes could find the position of the German submarine every time; this had become possible because they had made a short-wave radar instrument so the submarine could be attacked at night by a plane which the submarine could not have seen before.

PROFESSOR VANNEVAR BUSH

Director of the US Office of Scientific Research and Development

Of course it was pretty gloomy after Pearl Harbor but it didn't take long for it to recover and how strange to look back on those days. I knew all of us who were in the middle of it knew that we were very close to losing that whole damn war on account of the submarines. We nearly lost the first war that way and so we nearly lost the second war. I don't think the people in this country had any idea that we were so close to the rim, but we were.

LIEUTENANT PETER-ERICH CREMER

Commanding U-333, May 1942

Before I was going to the American coast I had an attack from a Liberator; I lost two and a half metres off my bow. I went very close to the shore and the destroyers were protecting the steamers and tankers on the sea side so I picked out the biggest one and torpedoed him. Only one torpedo tube was still in action so I was obliged to shoot through one tube and must re-load the torpedo after torpedoing one ship. So I sank four ships in one night: the destroyers were running with full speed on the wrong side of the convoy and I could get out without the destroyers having seen me.

COMMANDER PETER GRETTON
Escort Group Commander 1942–43

We had tremendous disappointments at the start when we found that a bomb or a depth-charge had to be let off within a very few feet of a submarine before it did any serious damage, but we soon got much improved explosives and some improved anti-submarine weapons. Looking back, it's quite clear that one was inclined to forget at the time what our people were doing and the things like the high-frequency direction-finding sets, which we had in the ships and ashore and which let us fix the position of U-boats wherever they were in the Atlantic, were a tremendous advantage and the Germans never seemed to rumble to what we were doing there. In addition we got the ten-centimetre radar set in early 1942 and this let us detect submarine periscopes at quite short range, and the conning-tower of a submarine at quite reasonably long range, and this made a great difference too.

LIEUTENANT CREMER
Commanding U-333, *6 October 1942*

Some submarines were staying near Freetown [Sierra Leone, West Africa], because the convoys were coming from America to Freetown with transports of goods and soldiers, and they hadn't seen much ships so I was obliged to look in the harbour; so I went very close to this port and the destroyer I met [corvette HMS *Crocus*] had radar installed on board. We didn't know during this time that they had radar so he had me on his screen and with full speed ahead he rammed me for the first time. When I saw him it was too late to dive. I tried to torpedo him but the distance, one hundred and fifty yards, was too close and the torpedo wouldn't explode. So I tried to get a bigger distance between the destroyer and the U-boat and he was shooting during one hour or two hours with machine guns. My sailors were on deck and I tried firstly to take the sailors in the boat because I did not know how much they were wounded. An officer next to me was dead and another officer he had a bullet through his throat and I had got a bullet in my chest and I had some thirty shell splinters in arm and leg and a bullet in my head. After the sailors were in this boat to escape I was sailing with very low revolutions so the enemy had the impression the boat was sinking, and when he came very close I got full speed ahead and then he rammed me two or three metres off the stern and then I dived.

ADMIRAL DÖNITZ

We still had in 1942 and in the beginning of 1943 great success on the U-boat warfare. Some wolf-packs attacked a convoy on March 1943 in the Atlantic and sank twenty-one ships and only one U-boat was lost but this defeat of the Anglo-Americans had its consequences. It accelerated the use of warships with, on board, all possibilities of anti-submarine weapons, and they had an instrument with which they could take the bearings of a U-boat when it made a wireless message. By this and also radar instrument they could find and track the positions of the U-boat and then attack it. But the breaking down of the German submarine warfare in May 1943 happened because the German submarines had lost the operational and tactical quality of surface manoeuvrability.

PROFESSOR BUSH

At the height of the submarine war there were about forty ships being sunk for each submarine that was being sunk. The Germans were building submarines faster than they were being sunk. We were losing ships faster than we were replacing them and it looked very bad indeed. Six months later the ratio of sinkings had dropped down to nearly one to one. What had happened in the meanwhile? The British introduced their anti-submarine rocket [Hedgehog] in the Bay of Biscay, which was a magnificent weapon against the submarine. I saw it tested in Britain and it scared the hell out of me – terrifying. Americans introduced Fido, which was a target-seeking torpedo. You dropped one where a submarine submerged and the torpedo would hunt it out. Soon there would be the radar which could pick up a periscope. A dozen weapons came in right at that time and it changed the tide, and also the introduction of hunter-killer groups. And on that, the British were ahead of us, largely because US Fleet Commander Admiral King was stubborn on that particular subject.

SQUADRON LEADER WILFRID OULTON
RAF Coastal Command

Bearing in mind the fact that we were two people separated by a common language, I don't think we could have done very much better than we were doing at the time. The Americans had their problems too and they weren't going to believe everything we said without trying it out for themselves. Certainly things could have been better, but whether they could have been better in the light of the political history of the time, I doubt very much.

ADMIRAL DÖNITZ

Very late, in the beginning of 1943, the number of German submarines began to approach for the number I had asked for before the war. It had become too late, for the problem of timing was of great significance in the Battle of the Atlantic. We had to sink as many ships as possible before our Anglo-American opponents could develop an effective anti-submarine defence and could replace the merchant ships which had been sunk. For this reason it was of strategic importance to deploy submarines economically. This principle was that submarines had to be sent into action where every submarine every day could sink the greatest tonnage of the enemy's ships. This also meant that German submarines must not be used for any other purposes: their main strategic purpose was to sink as many ships as possible in the Atlantic. Other seas, for instance the Mediterranean, had their importance but they were only of secondary importance in comparison with the Atlantic, and the German use of U-boats in this or other seas had to be weighed against the disadvantage of having fewer boats in the Battle of the Atlantic before any order was issued. But this was not always calculated; the use of German submarines for other purposes hampered

German success in the Battle of the Atlantic in the first three and a half years of war.

SQUADRON LEADER OULTON

I was fortunate enough to get command of the first well-equipped aeroplanes for the job, Halifaxes, diverted from Bomber Command and equipped with the new centimetric radar. I had command of this squadron for about a month on the 31st of May 1943; we were carrying out offensive patrols in the Bay of Biscay. We'd gone off before dawn as usual and were on patrol when suddenly in the middle of eating a sandwich I saw something odd ahead, which turned out to be a U-boat [*U-440*]. We stalked it, that is we climbed up into cloud to get nearer, and then dived and carried out our attack at very low level, fifty feet, and crossed the U-boat, dropped a stick of depth-charges which exploded correctly, and that would ultimately have been the end of the story. But it was a very tough U-boat and we came round again and carried out a second attack with the remaining depth-charges and the U-boat was still there circling gently and firing at us whenever we came close enough.

COMMANDER GRETTON

Commanding Escort Group, Convoy ONS-5

My group had been running for three or four months during the winter in very bad weather and we had done very little until the convoy before ONS-5, which was HX-231. We had a big battle [4–7 April 1943]: we lost twelve merchant ships but we sunk three submarines, and at that time this was considered all right. Then we had a rest in harbour and sailed again to escort ONS-5 westwards across the Atlantic. ONS-5 was a rather small and very slow and of course unladen convoy, and we had a lot of trouble. The weather was very bad, the ships got disorganised and south of Iceland after three or four days we had several attacks by submarines, most of which we drove off successfully [*U-386* and *U-528* damaged], and only had one ship sunk. Then after a spell we had a long series of very bad gales indeed, combined with a little nip into the ice pack off Greenland, and at this stage my ship was running short of fuel. I couldn't fill from the tanker because of the weather and I had to leave on the 3rd of May. It was a decision I've always regretted, but I had no idea that forty-eight U-boats were building up ahead of us in the way that later they were shown to be.

SQUADRON LEADER OULTON

I signalled for help and began to home in other aircraft. The first to arrive was another Halifax of my own squadron and he, poor chap, the first time in his life he'd seen a U-boat, there it was, and he went in to attack and he was a bit nervous and he missed it, the first time and the second time. So he went home, no use him staying. A little while later I spotted a Sunderland and flew over to it and formated and tried to indicate to the captain that he should attack my U-boat but he wasn't interested at first; but eventually I got him to come around, he saw it, did a double take and dived on the U-boat, attacked it but not fatally. So another time passed and I saw another aeroplane, another Sunderland going by, and this was an Australian – you know how very individual they are – and this chap didn't want to get mixed up with an RAF aeroplane and certainly not with a Halifax. He wouldn't have anything to do with me but in the end I shouted and banged my microphone and pointed down and flashed on the signal lamp and crowded around him until in the end he saw the U-boat and went in to the attack.

LIEUTENANT HARTWIG LOOKS
Commanding U-264

I torpedoed two ships each with two torpedoes and one of the ships after the explosion of the torpedoes another big explosion happened on board the ship, perhaps the boiler also exploded, and in our glasses during the dark night we could observe that this ship was sinking very quickly. Then I turned around with the submarine to fire the stern torpedo but it had a malfunction and ran straight on the surface with a big, white, shining wake. As it didn't run with the exact speed this torpedo passed the target ship behind the stern and came to the second column of the convoy and hit there another steamer, but I couldn't observe any result, just the explosion of the torpedo, because at that time one of the escort vessels certainly picked me up and got contact with me so I was forced to submerge. This escort vessel depth-charged me for some minutes and then joined the convoy. I had the chance to reload two of the bow torpedoes and after about one hour I surfaced again and proceeded on the last bearing of the convoy and I was once more successful to get contact with the convoy and I did just the same as the time before. I proceeded on the port side of this convoy to a position where I had the chance to attack and once more was lucky by slipping through into the gap between two of the escort vessels and closing to the port column of the convoy and both torpedoes hit the target ships and then the escort vessel was alerted and close in about one thousand metres distance and I had to disappear. I got once more depth-charges for about one hour without hitting me but this happened just before dawn so I had no more chance to find the convoy during the darkness, and of course now we had the daylight coming up and I had to stay underwater for a longer time.

CAPTAIN RODNEY STONE

Merchant Navy, SS Gharinda, *Convoy ONS-5*

I was having a cup of tea because there hadn't been an alarm for over an hour – I mean it was as bad as that, if you've got a clear hour it's not too bad going. Normally when you're in command if you get an hour or two hours' consecutive sleep you're very lucky. You've got your clothes on all the time; you never take your clothes off. Well, I got up on the bridge and a ship on my port beam got it in number-five or number-four hatch and she went down very quickly indeed. I didn't see the actual explosion, I arrived a moment after it happened but I looked around first to see if anything else might be in the vicinity because that's somebody else's ship, not mine. But having looked round I looked back and saw the captain when he jumped from the bridge into the sea. There was a lifeboat near by, I know that. Well, I couldn't stop and pick him up and I suppose it was a matter of half a minute when I got one myself, I believe from the same submarine, which hit me forrard of the bridge in number-one hatch. It blew my derricks clean over to the starboard side – you know, those huge steel things – it blew them over as if they'd been bean sticks. I ordered abandon ship and all the crew went to stations – the boats were turned out, you keep them turned out you see – and the boats were lowered and one boat of the six was dropped bow-first because one of the sailors, his hands were probably numb with cold, let go of the rope. That didn't matter because any three boats could have taken my crew. They were all Indians except two or three Chinese and I never gave any orders in English at all. There was no sign of panic at all, I'm pleased to say.

LIEUTENANT COMMANDER ROBERT SHERWOOD

Commanding HMS Tay, *took over escort of Convoy ONS-5*

The crew of the *Gharinda* were all rescued without getting their feet wet. Her captain, a man called Rodney Stone, was sitting in the stern of his boat and I looked down from the wing of the bridge and I could see him sitting there with the biggest gun I've ever seen between his knees. I remember saying something to him about it – I trust it wasn't loaded – but he got it on board and he still has it as far as I know.

CAPTAIN STONE

I did the quickest run around the ship I've ever done in my life to make sure that nobody else was on board and then I went down the ladder to the lifeboat – I suppose I was about three or four feet above water level. I'd got all my boats in a line, which made it fairly easy for Captain Sherwood on HMS *Tay*, who didn't have to go from one boat to another, all dotted around the place. That was something we were taught – if you get sunk get all your boats together and keep together, because if an aeroplane looks for you it's much easier to find a bunch of boats than one solitary boat. I had one of my rifles, which I was very proud of, with me and didn't want to lose it. The only reason I had it was because I'd been cleaning it and I grabbed it as I went down those few steps. Sherwood did ask me if the damn thing was loaded and I said no it wasn't. I was picked up very unceremoniously by the scruff of the neck and thrown on the deck – the same as the rest of my crew and my officers – and I went forward and made myself known to Captain Sherwood. My only casualty was the Third Officer who went over the side into the drink – he sat on the gunwale after I'd told him not to. We pulled him out almost instantly and he couldn't speak, he was so bloody cold. So he was picked up, thrown on deck and taken straight down to the *Tay*'s engine room, otherwise he'd probably have frozen to death. I don't know the temperature of the sea water but I think it was below freezing at the time, because we'd just come out of the ice floes.

LIEUTENANT RAYMOND HART
Commanding HMS Vidette, *Convoy ONS-5*

I'd just been out some two thousand yards to a particular contact and given it a pattern of depth-charges [*U-514*, damaged]. Sweeping back to my station I was just reducing speed to eight or ten knots when I got a very firm Asdic contact about eight hundred yards from the nearest ship in the convoy. My immediate reaction was to increase speed and give it a five-charge pattern straightaway to keep the chap's head down – it would put him off his stroke if he was going to fire torpedoes – but I was short of depth-charges at that stage. Conditions were perfect, the night was relatively calm, a bit of fog, but perfect for a deliberate attack, so I decided to do a deliberate attack with our forward-throwing weapon, the Hedgehog, which as you probably know threw twenty-four bombs ahead of the ship and the bombs only exploded if they made contact with a submerged object. We had to fire by voice pipe because the bad weather which we had encountered before had upset the electrical communications. I gave the order to fire when I thought we'd approached the right spot and some literally few seconds after the bombs hit the water we all saw two vivid flashes as the two bombs hit the U-boat [U-630]. If I remember rightly one of them was on the port side and one of them just on the starboard side of my bow. This was quite an exhilarating moment and I think I remember striking the First Lieutenant on the chest and the next thing we heard was from the Asdic operator and the Asdic officer that there were noises of a submarine breaking up. Well, we'd seen a tremendous kerfuffle in the water and the bow of the ship was virtually lifted out of the water as we went over the spot where we'd hit the U-boat.

LIEUTENANT-COMMANDER SHERWOOD

Somewhere in the region of ten o'clock the attacks started and they became fast and furious. It was not an attack as we had known it in the past – escorts were reporting submarines coming in, ships being torpedoed – and this was of course absolute hell; it was the first time it had ever happened, certainly least to me. Shortly afterwards there were reports that submarines had been hit and presumably sunk. Must have been pretty late in the night when I asked *Vidette* to come back in, which she did, and on the way she ran into a submarine and that was another one gone. Of course this was very distressing to me because all I was doing was sitting there putting marks on a chart as the actions took place and not getting any action myself. But I suppose thereby lies the tale that the more exercise you do between ships of a group produces better answers.

SQUADRON LEADER OULTON

As soon as he appreciated the situation the Australian immediately went into the attack, and because he was going to have a very rough time with the heavy deck armament of the U-boat I flew slightly ahead of him and gave him cover with my machine guns. He went in and dropped his depth-charges perfectly, they exploded and then there was a tremendous orange and blue explosion and when that subsided there was nothing but wreckage, the U-boat had gone and a lot of survivors in the water. So I flew round and dropped out Mae Wests [life jackets] and dinghies in the hope of getting some of the survivors. I knew there was a British escort group about a hundred miles away and then my wireless operator intercepted what was clearly traffic between Brest and Junkers 88 fighters coming out to the area, so I thought we'd better go home.

LIEUTENANT LOOKS

I thought we would have a good chance for the next night because we picked up quite a lot of signals from other submarines getting contact to this convoy and so we thought that this convoy would be absolutely dead during the night. Then suddenly dense fog came up, we could only see fifty metres, not more, so it was nearly impossible to find the convoy again. I submerged for one period to listen with my hydrophone but we couldn't find the ships again, and staying on the surface during the dark time, now in dense fog of course, it was very dangerous. I was nearly rammed by one of the British escorts, it passed just five or ten metres behind the stern using his searchlight but they couldn't see anything, as we couldn't see more than just the shadow of the destroyer passing our path and then disappearing in the dense fog. I submerged because it was not so nice to be in such close contact with a destroyer and this escort vessel turned around and depth-charged me for about one or one-and-a-half hours without result. And then I thought it was useless to try to find the convoy because underwater the submarines at that time were merely sitting ducks. We were very slow using our electric motors underwater and so we had no chance to find the convoy again, and as I was running out of fuel I decided to go back to the base the next day.

COMMANDER GRETTON

Well, of course, I was delighted by the battle for ONS-5. One felt that the long training we had – we had slogged at training and really practised our manoeuvres and various dodges – had paid off and we were beginning to get on top. As a result after a very hectic week in St John's, Newfoundland, there was a lot of alcohol consumption and much writing of official reports, then we sailed for the next convoy, SC-130 [11–26 May], on top of the wave and despite the fact that we had a very heavy battle with about twenty U-boats: we sank three of them and we didn't lose a single ship. Dönitz in his book says that after SC-130 and another HX convoy which was coming across about the same time as us, he felt it was no good going on and withdrew from the North Atlantic.

SQUADRON LEADER OULTON

The RAF as a whole had nothing like enough aeroplanes and it must have been very difficult to apportion the resources. And I think that on the whole they didn't do too badly in sharing it out fairly. Surely, if there had been more aircraft, more Liberators allocated from America, then we could have improved the situation much earlier and saved the lives of a lot of seamen. But I don't think it would have brought the war to an end very much earlier. D-Day would not have been much earlier whether or not the Battle of the Atlantic had been won six months earlier or not.

ADMIRAL DÖNITZ

Another heavy disadvantage was the breaking down of submarine warfare, which happened in May 1943, which until this time had prevented the sea powers from having enough ships to carry out landing operation on the Western European continent. In consequence of the defeat of the submarine the Anglo-American invasion of Normandy on July 1944 was now a success and now we knew clearly that we had no more chance to win the war. But what could we do?

LIEUTENANT CREMER

The beginning of the end is the year 1943 when Captain Walker had trained the escort crews. After each attack you get depth-charges at least twelve or fourteen hours, and then it's a terrible stress not only for the sailors but also for the commander. Water comes into the boats, there's no electricity, there is no more hydraulic, there's only the possibility to handle the controls by hand and there's no possibility to give messages to the stern or to the bow except by voice. These twelve hours, everybody of course, after every attack, has to do a lot to repair, and this gives a little help not to think. But during the time when the destroyer is coming the propeller revolutions are changing in the frequency so you could know when perhaps two or three seconds later comes the depth-charges. This is a very bad moment for the crew and they are looking at their commander, how are his nerves and at his face, and it was also for him not too easy. It is very nice now, twenty-five years later, to talk about it but during that time it was always the death before the eyes. From thirty-six thousand sailors we have lost thirty-two thousand, so you can imagine it was a terrible sacrifice.

CHAPTER 14

BATTLE OF THE PACIFIC 1942–43

The Imperial Japanese Navy's (IJN) Commander-in-Chief Isoroku Yamamoto had hoped, at best, to 'run amok' for a year before US industrial power began to overwhelm Japan. However, the IJN was first checked in the Coral Sea on 4–8 May 1942, simultaneously with the surrender of the last outpost of the US–Filipino Army in the Philippines. General Douglas MacArthur, the Commander-in-Chief, had been ordered to leave in March and set up a new South-West Pacific Command based in Australia. Australian forces under his command inflicted the first Allied defeat on the Japanese Army at Milne Bay, on the eastern tip of New Guinea, in early September. Before that, however, the Americans had broken the Japanese naval codes and on 4–7 June the IJN's all-conquering carrier force was destroyed off Midway Island in an ambush set up by US Fleet Commander Chester Nimitz. On 7 August the first of seventy-eight amphibious landings by US forces during the Pacific War was made to seize an airfield on Guadalcanal in the Solomon Islands east of New Guinea and immediately came under intense attack by land and sea. The Americans held on and the campaign became a prolonged battle of attrition, in which the IJN lost many irreplaceable ships and aircraft before finally evacuating the island in February 1943. Their hope had been to interdict communications between the United States and Australia from the air base on Guadalacanal and another on Betio, the main island of Tarawa atoll in the Gilbert Islands. In May 1943 the Americans encountered unexpectedly vicious resistance when recovering Attu, one of two Aleutian Islands lost to the Japanese in June

1942, and in August mounted a massive operation to retake Kiska, only to find the Japanese gone. In 20–24 November 1943 tiny Betio became the most crowded place on earth when the Americans assaulted it with 35,000 men against a Japanese garrison of 3,000 Marines and 2,000 pioneers. Many valuable lessons were learned, but many more remained to be learned.

MICHIKO NAKAMOTO
Hiroshima schoolgirl

I thought, always I had thought America was a very, very big country and Japan is very small and what's going to happen, that was my first thought. Well, naturally Japan was winning and every day we had over the radio all the victories and the whole nation was very excited and the thought I had at that time when I heard the news about the war was immediately all the victories over the radio all day long so we are quite excited and it was almost like a festival. I didn't even doubt about the news when they were always talking about the victories and then the sad news began to be heard over the radio and we were very sad but of course we had to believe what we were hearing. I can't remember correctly by order about the battle of Midway, battle of the Solomons and all South Pacific areas. Japan was beginning to pay much sacrifice although it was always said we sank many ships, we attacked so many aeroplanes, but at the same time we lost our soldiers, we lost our ships; so I don't recall precisely news of the battle of Midway but I remember it was very sad news and always when news began with very sad Japanese music, very immediately we knew it was bad news.

AMBASSADOR W AVERELL HARRIMAN
President Roosevelt's Special Envoy to Europe

There were people who wanted to go to the Pacific first: all the Pacific states [of the USA] were more interested in the Pacific war; some military opinion was that we should fight this war first. Roosevelt did everything he could to bring public opinion to his view [that Germany should be beaten first]. Those who were involved in the war demanded more, the Pacific was almost an endless demand; war production was very limited in the beginning. It wasn't until considerably later that we had adequate for both fronts, so one side or the other had to sacrifice and also we had to balance off the requirements of our allies, Britain and the Soviet Union. I think Roosevelt handled public opinion extremely skilfully.

TOSHIKAZU KASE
Principal Secretary to the Foreign Minister
Most people were surprised by the extent of the victories achieved by the Navy and Army in the initial phase of the war. There was a torchlight parade night after night, but I was basically sceptical because having lived years under German Blitz in London, having witnessed at close quarters the war in Europe, I knew that victory amounts to little when the war is likely to be dragged on.

COMMANDER MINORU GENDA
Japanese Navy Air Staff
The British and American troops were not as well trained as those of Japan. In this respect I think that the Navy, particularly its air arm, had no equal in the world at that time. I was in Britain before the war and saw the ability of the Americans when the war started and my impression was that in both countries their ability was below that of Japan. As for strategy, there was not much to choose between the two sides.

PETTY OFFICER SABURO SAKAI
Outstanding Japanese naval fighter pilot (sixty kills)
Frankly speaking, Japan had already used up a great part of its resources in the war against China, therefore I personally did not think that Japan would be able to win. In fact I was surprised because the war unfolded so easily in favour of Japan. At the same time, when the other side's counter-offensive got started I felt apprehensive.

PROFESSOR VANNEVAR BUSH
Director of the US Office of Scientific Research and Development
For most of the war the strategy of the Pacific was an American strategy. It had to be: the British were there, but a very minor part. But as far as

the war in Europe was concerned, the strategy was worked out jointly with genuine joint discussions and consideration. The decision was made early that Europe came first and it was a decision in spite of the fact that we got the devil knocked out of us in the Pacific for a long time. Now the Navy protested at being left way under par in the Pacific and it did put us up to very heavy casualties, but I think the country in general agreed with the decision that the real threat was in Europe.

NAOKI HOSHINO
Japanese Fascist ideologist

We were told only part of the Midway story; the Navy did not tell us the other part. What we were told was that one aircraft carrier was sunk and one was severely damaged. Since there were four carriers involved in the battle, the way we heard it three had come back, but the Anglo-American side was saying that all four had been sunk and there were similar reports in their newspapers. This left some doubt in our minds and we pressed the Navy for more details, but they stuck to their original announcement. As to when we learned the whole truth it was three years later after the war ended, at the War Crimes Tribunal we learned that four carriers were sunk at Midway from the official documents presented by the United States. If four aircraft carriers were lost at Midway it means it was impossible for Japan to pursue the war effectively any further, so from that point on the military never let us know the real situation. As a result of investigations conducted after the war ended it was found out that the Navy had reported the truth to General Tojo shortly after the Midway battle and he ordered that this being an important matter it must never be revealed to others. Tojo, being the kind of man he was, probably intended to reveal the facts bit by bit as time went on but the war proceeded at a fast pace with Japan going downhill and there was no opportunity to make the facts known. So Japan's subsequent battle plans were made on the wrong assessment of its own strength.

COMMANDER GENDA

I think the big reason the Midway battle did not go well was because Japan was not wary enough. The Americans knew in advance that Japan

Interviewee Anthony
Eden behind the Big
Three at the Teheran
conference, 1943.
(*insert*) Sir Anthony
Eden, then Earl
of Avon, being
interviewed for
The World at War
in 1971.

Admiral Karl Dönitz, then
head of the U-Boat army,
congratulating U-boat crew,
1942. (*insert*) Interviewee
Admiral Dönitz in 1971.

Squadron Leader Max Aitken during the Battle of Britain, 1940. (*insert*) Sir Max Aitken interviewed in 1971.

General Sir Harold Alexander and interviewee Brigadier John Harding in the desert, 1942. (*insert*) Lord Harding in 1971.

Hitler and his gang in the early 1930s.

First Quebec Conference, August 1943 – Churchill and Prime Minister Mackenzie King of Canada stand behind President Roosevelt and Governor General of Canada, the Earl of Athlone.

Night pageant, Berlin to mark Hitler's 50th birthday, 20 April 1939.

Stage management – Hitler addressing the Reichstag following the Fall of France, 1940.

Churchill and Lord Privy Seal Sir Stafford Cripps on HMS *King George V*, October 1942. 'Former Naval Person' was the *nom de guerre* used by Churchill in his correspondence with 'Potus' (the President of the United States).

Normandy 22 July 1944 – Churchill with Montgomery, Lieutenant General Guy Simmonds of II Canadian Corps (left) and Lieutenant General Sir Miles Dempsey of British Second Army (*rear*).

The Battle of Britain, 1940: the workhorse Hawker Hurricane (*foreground, above*) attacked bombers such as the Junkers 88 (below); while the Supermarine Spitfires (*background, above*) took on the escorting Messerschmitt 109s (*below*).

Barbarossa, 1941 – devastation for the Byelorussian peasantry.

While the German mechanised spearheads clattered on ahead the bulk of the army followed on foot and most supply columns were still horse drawn, like this one near Leningrad, autumn 1941.

Mud slowed the German offensive of 1941 and winter brought it to a grinding halt. The flag is for aerial recognition, not patriotic fervour.

would attack Midway, therefore the United States was ready and waiting. And we got trapped in the net. The biggest reason for the failure was that the secret leaked. The Americans had obtained Japan's secret code in Guadalcanal – no, in the Solomons or somewhere like that – salvaging it from a sunken Japanese ship. After Midway we won and lost some engagements but we didn't win as many as before and the defeats began to outnumber the victories. Therefore Midway was the turning point.

MARQUIS KOICHI KIDO
Lord Keeper of the Privy Seal
I guess it was from the Midway naval battle. In that battle Japan lost four large aircraft carriers; this tilted the naval battle against Japan. From then on Japan was on the defensive, therefore I think the Midway battle was the turning point.

RICHARD TREGASKIS
War correspondent, Guadalcanal
All the Pacific fighting was bitter, really, because the Japanese were in a kind of suicidal attempt to hang on, but the thing about Guadalcanal that was really bitter was that this was the whole strength we had. We had such a tiny fraction of America's forces, money and man-power resources. Ninety per cent went to Europe and we had such a tiny little thread of existence down there. It was our first offensive in the Pacific and we went in with only one division and no air power – except the Navy supplied some air power when we went in – but for a long time we had no air power so that the desperate thing was that we had so little to work with. When I was there only a few days – I was one of the first people to come ashore at Guadalcanal – we'd had some desperate battles and we had lost four cruisers, one of them the *Canberra*, the Australian cruiser, so it was very discouraging and all the ships were leaving. Landing-force commander General Alexander Vandergrift called me in and said, 'A lot of people are saying this may be another Bataan and now is probably the last chance you'll have to leave.' And so I thought and thought and struggled with my conscience, such as it is, and eventually after watching the ships leave one by one decided to stay.

TOSHIKAZU KASE

When our Army begun to suffer at Guadalcanal, and the Navy at Midway, I thought the time had arrived for preparations for an early termination of hostilities. I thought I had to evade the Military Police and to see the movement, and effort, in utmost secrecy, even at the Foreign Office. The group formed to prepare for this movement included the Private Secretary to one of the key members of the High Command in shaping military operations plan, and he was at one time Private Secretary to General Tojo as War Minister, so he was in the know about the intentions of the Army High Command.

RICHARD TREGASKIS

I think the salvation of the Guadalcanal campaign is in an anecdote about probably the greatest single hero of Guadalcanal, Lieutenant Colonel Merritt Edson. He was the head of the 1st Marine Raiders and they say about Red Mike that he had every medal the Marine Corps could give except the Purple Heart and that was the one he deserved most. He had never been wounded and never was till he died. But he was very smart and stubborn and clever. When he was summoned to consult about the situation, General Vandergrift didn't believe the Lunga Ridge would be attacked but Edson said this is where the Japanese will attack, this is their first major attack, and that's where they came. Red Mike had only the remnants at that point of his 1st Raider Battalion and the 1st Parachute Battalion, which had been through the worst of the Guadalcanal fighting to that point. And it so happened that this main attack by the Japanese came right through his bivouac where he was with his troops, who were supposed to be resting. And so they drove right through them and those people hung on and Red Mike went around and personally talked to all these guys who were falling back and he would say to them, 'The only difference between you and a good marine is you're going in the wrong direction.' So he held that whole business together and held that ridge until some supporting troops came up. But the main point of this dramatic episode is that it shows how on Guadalcanal there never was enough and what we had was so badly shot up that it was only through miracles that they could survive. Just nerve and, well, guts.*

MAJOR GENERAL J LAWTON COLLINS
Commander 25th Infantry Division, Guadalcanal

My division was sent down from Hawaii to go into Guadalcanal to relieve the 1st Marine Division and another Army division that had established a bridgehead on Guadalcanal, having driven off the Japs – killed off a good many of them. But a stalemate had developed and Admiral Richmond Turner, who was in command down in that area, wanted my division turned in to Guadalcanal to lead the offensive of the 14th Army Corps to break out of this stalemate, which we did.

LIEUTENANT COLONEL ICHII SUGITA
Japanese Army

Before the beginning of the war, I felt by myself that the war against America and England would be a very hard war, but I went to Guadalcanal and I found out that the tide had turned against us, especially after the failure to attack at the aerodrome in Guadalcanal on 24th or 25th October.

MAJOR GENERAL COLLINS

It was jungle fighting, but not entirely because Guadalcanal is a rather rough volcanic island and the ridges were covered normally with tall grass that grew eight or ten feet tall. In the earlier fighting by the Marines and the Army Division there, this grass has been burnt off so the ridge lines were clear and the jungle was down in the valleys, very heavy. But in my attack, which was designed to envelop the south flank of the Japanese position there, we stuck to the ridge lines so our troops in the initial fighting went along the ridges in relatively open country. It was very tough fighting because these ridges were not very broad and furthermore the Japanese

---

* Edson received the Medal of Honor for his epic defence of the Lunga Ridge with 800 men against an attacking force of about 2,500 on the night of 13–14 September 1942.

were tough fighters and they never would give up. We had isolated a Japanese regiment as a strong point and they fought until we actually had to annihilate them. We used loudspeakers after we had surrounded them and tried to persuade them to surrender but they wouldn't. They were gallant fellows, no question. Not very skilful at times, but tough fighters and this made it difficult.

ROBERT SHERROD
War correspondent

Nimitz was a much quieter man who had a great deal more strength than MacArthur. He was much stronger and better prepared for war, and the Pacific was essentially a naval war, you can't get away from that. MacArthur tried to pretend that it was not mostly a Navy war and it made for a great deal of conflict during the war. Sometimes there was overlapping. Once during, I think it was the invasion of Leyte, we caught ten Japanese destroyers and both of them put out communiqués on it. MacArthur simply said yes, we sank them all, and then we [Nimitz's staff] said we sank six and damaged four, which was correct of course. It was like MacArthur was determined to beat Nimitz with his communiqué; he'd sink to such petty things as that.

MAJOR GENERAL COLLINS

MacArthur had practically no troops when he withdrew from the Philippines. He went down to Australia and the fighting was initiated by Admiral Nimitz from Hawaii. We went up the islands leading to New Guinea and this could better be controlled under naval command, that is unified command with a naval commander, and he had the airmen and the army troops under his control. So we had unified command in the initial phases. Then when MacArthur began to come in later, in the drive to the north from Australia, he ran the show in the western part of the Pacific. Admiral Nimitz was a very able man and a very wonderful chap personally, no problem getting along with Admiral Nimitz. And the same was true with admirals Halsey and Sprague and the other naval people. I was not under MacArthur's command but there was no difficulty that developed as far as I know. I think that it worked out quite satisfactorily, the coordination. By the time the latter part of the fighting was on, I was in Europe, so I had no personal experience in this regard.

ROBERT SHERROD

I was conditioned by what I had gone through in the invasion of the island of Kiska where we landed thirty-five thousand troops – thirty thousand Americans and five thousand Canadians – to do battle with the Japanese who as a matter of fact had been evacuated in a very clever move a few days before we made the landing. Nonetheless, once the wheels started rolling the full thirty-five thousand were landed and the only casualties were some American units that started shooting at each other, I think they killed about thirty and wounded about ninety.*

MARINE JOE HRUSKA

2nd Marine Division, Tarawa

I was at Pearl Harbor during the 7th December attack and I was in Guadalcanal, so I was exposed to warfare prior to this engagement. To me Tarawa was just another part of this war. We were briefed, of course, before the landing and it really didn't mean nothing to us, nothing really exceptional, nothing at all. It was just going to be another phase, another battle, another day in the life of a marine.

COLONEL DAVID SHOUP

CO, 2nd Marine Regiment, Tarawa

We didn't have too good an idea how many they were. We knew they'd been shipping Japanese in there and they'd been digging holes all over the place, but sometimes you can't tell. You might dig four holes for one soldier to fool the other fellow. We had this wonderful aerial photo of the island, which gave every position; it's absolutely unbelievable, I still have a copy of that map in which every foxhole showed up, every tank

---

* The invasion of Kiska in the Aleutian Islands in August 1943 was as described, but in the earlier invasion of nearby Attu the 2,500 Japanese defenders fought to the last man and inflicted 4,000 US casualties.

trap, every gun emplacement. From that we drew wonderful maps so that every squad leader had a map of his section, which showed what he was going to be confronted with, how many positions, how many guns and how many tank traps and all that but not how many people. Aboard ship one evening we were even going around the island and counting the toilets.*

ROBERT SHERROD

Tarawa was the first step in the drive across the Pacific aimed at taking air bases from which Japan could be bombed. The bombing by B-29s, we knew even at that stage, was not going to be successful from China and it never was successful. So the drive was to break the inner barrier of Japanese defences and to do this we had to skip from one island to another, from one chain of islands to another. skipping most of them but taking certain key islands for air bases. The strategy was rather simple – the carriers went ahead and bombed the islands and the amphibious forces followed up. We were hoping all the time that the Japanese fleet wouldn't come out in enough strength to stop the drive, as it might have several times.

CORPORAL EDDY OWEN

2nd Marine Division, Tarawa

With the information we had before we went ashore we didn't figure there'd be too much opposition because we'd been told that they were going to drop all these bombs, they were going to drop seventy-two daisy-cutters, and in fact I believe the terminology they used was the equivalent of two destroyer-loads of high explosive would be dropped on the one square mile island. Well, we thought we'd just walk in, get a star on a bar, you know. So really the first time that I knew they were firing at us I was still on board and we were watching the bombardment, explosions, and we saw stuff hitting the water and we all thought it was some kind of large fish. Then all of a sudden someone screamed and we all dived into the paint locker, and I went ashore with two skinned knees because I happened to

---

* Colonel Shoup won the Medal of Honor leading the assault on Tarawa.

be on the bottom. By then of course we realised that there was opposition on the beach, as we had been told before we went in. We had been briefed, I believe, that there were eighty-four pillboxes around the perimeter of the airstrip and of course each one had a machine gun in it.

COLONEL SHOUP

We had no air bombardment. It was planned but the bombers that were supposed to come and hit the place and put down the daisy-cutters and just eliminate these buildings and all the trees to make it easier for us, they never got there. We got some later but it was not very much. You never have enough air support but the thing was by the next morning I'd gotten some requests out to the Fleet Commander for naval gunfire and bombardment in some particularly tough areas. There's nothing more effective than a five-inch or an eight-inch shell that lands in a foxhole – that's pretty damned effective, that's the end of that outfit. But if it lands twenty-five yards away, you wish it to hell.

ROBERT SHERROD

I've seen a lot of men who refused to go when they were ordered to. I spoke to Colonel Shoup about this and during the battle an officer came up to him and said, 'Colonel, I've got a thousand men out there and I can't get them to follow me across the airfield' – which was a very hot place to go, anyway. And Shoup said, 'You simply have to go and take as many with you as will come, and if it's only ten men that's better than nothing.'

MARINE PEDERSON
2nd Marine Division, Tarawa

We were told they were Imperial Marines and we were told there were quite a few over five thousand. We were told they were going to receive blockbusters before we got there, which we didn't see.*

---

* The defenders under Rear-Admiral Keiji Shibasaki were 3,000 marines, plus 1,000 Japanese and 1,200 Korean Pioneers, of whom 17 Japanese and 129 Koreans survived.

ROBERT SHERROD

I was surprised when we found the boats would not go over the reef and we, except for those who could go in the limited number of amphibious tractors, would have to wade in to the beach, which was something like seven hundred yards and a very long wade indeed with machine-gun fire and mortar fire falling all around you. I felt very thankful to be alive considering the difficulty of getting ashore and the number of men I had seen killed. I was with half a boatload that crawled in under the pier, which somehow or other didn't have a lot of Japanese under it shooting at us, as they had before. So we managed to crawl towards the beach under the pier until the last hundred yards or so where the pier was solid under the water, and I felt a hundred times going in that I would never make it.

COLONEL SHOUP

I'd read a great deal about it, listened to the British people who were down there telling us about the tides and all that and we had estimates of the depth of the water over the reef. Our problem was that the LCVPs [Landing Craft Vehicle, Personnel – aka Higgins boat] always drew a certain amount of water and of course the question was would there be that amount of water. We arranged to get a certain number of amphibious tractors which would take the men in to the beach, unload and then, hypothetically, come back out to the reef no matter if there was one foot of water or none and pick up another load and bring them in. Well, that's wonderful except the Japanese were in this battle too, and they didn't permit such a high percentage of these amphibious tractors to come back – they shot them up at the beach.

MARINE PEDERSON

I saw a lot of bodies floating on the water, a lot of marines and they still had their packs on. They had the worst of it, really, out in the water, because they came in on the Higgins boats and they were dropped in pretty deep water. Some of them were fortunate enough to get to the pier, others weren't and they died right there in the water. The first, second and third waves were very fortunate because they were all in armoured amphibious tractors and the AmTracs all got to the beach. There were quite a few of them knocked off but at least the rest got to the beach and they got their men off. But then the fourth, fifth and sixth waves were in Higgins boats and they came up short because the reef was there and as they couldn't go no further they dropped their front and the marines got out, and the water was above their heads.

MARINE HRUSKA

We went in on regular old Higgins boats. At that time there wasn't too many half-tracks or AmTracs or whatever you call them and we had nothing but plain old Higgins boats, the old-fashioned plywood boats. We got up in the morning, had breakfast early and there was no commotion, no disturbance, no nothing, except that this was going to be no more than an exercise. And then of course when we went in to the island we discovered it wasn't going to be a drill. We discovered it when the ramp of the Higgins boat was dropped and we looked for a shore that wasn't there. We were quite some way out from the beach, far enough to the point where you couldn't see the beach for the turmoil of warfare, the smoke, the fire, the bombs, and we actually couldn't see the shoreline at all.

ROBERT SHERROD

People were always being shot just next to you, it seemed. After I'd got ashore and was leaning against the small sea wall – it was only four feet high and made of coconut logs banked with sand – and soon after I got ashore a marine came by and he cheerfully waved at a friend of his and all of a sudden he spun around with a bullet straight through the head. I suppose he was five feet from where I was at the time, but this was the danger unless you bent low and almost crawled along the beach. During the first night the Japanese did swim out to this old hulk of a freighter which had been sunk some time before and also to the disabled tanks and tractors hung up on the reef and opened up on our people, so the people coming in the second morning took the heaviest casualties because they

were getting it not only from the front but from the sides. Very courageous thing the Japanese did – they were all killed, of course, but they
caused a great deal of damage before they were.

MARINE PEDERSON

Out of this particular pillbox, or from behind the pillbox, came an
Imperial Marine with a Molotov cocktail and I killed him. I continued on
to the pillbox – until you throw your charge you usually go behind the
pillbox – and there was also an Imperial Marine there, and I was not
prepared for him and he was not prepared for me. He ran, thank God. Of
course if he had been prepared for me, I would have been dead.

ROBERT SHERROD

We found that the man who had been shooting at people along the beach,
such as the marine who was killed right in front of me, the sniper was in
one of these devilish bunkers they had built. There was only a small slit at
the top of a coconut log and we didn't assume that a Japanese would be
crazy enough to be right in there. Finally Major Crow said, 'Hey, that
shooting is coming from in there, fifteen feet away,' so a marine threw a
hand grenade in and another one came up with his flame-thrower. The
Japanese ran out at that time but they caught him with the flame-thrower
and incinerated him. You can't have a lot of sympathy for him after you've
seen him kill a man within five feet of you. It was the idea of a killer being
killed, and the method of the killing did not make a great deal of difference to one's thinking at the time.

CORPORAL OWEN

By the third day the smell of death was terrible. Every day as the tide came
in there was one navy corpsman that had been killed and when the tide went
out they'd leave him hanging over the superstructure of the pier but we
were afraid to get him because there were Japanese under there, we knew
that. Finally, as some of them were captured – we were trying to capture the
Japanese and take them back aboard ship for interrogation – finally, one
night, we had to go and get this corpse so that we could bury it.

ROBERT SHERROD

The island was one square mile we thought; actually after the war we found it was only half a square mile. So if you can imagine nearly six thousand dead men on an island as small as three hundred acres, and considering that it's one degree from the equator and the amount of heat, you can imagine the smell that got within a day or two of all this rotting flesh, it was a terribly oppressive thing. I don't know anywhere in World War Two where there was such a concentration of death. I believe there was in the trench warfare of the First World War but certainly never again did I see such a concentration of death as there was on this tiny little island. The other thing that was so impressive, that is besides the very heavy casualties, was the speed with which it all happened – it only lasted seventy-six hours.

COLONEL SHOUP

We learned many, many things, which were later adopted in the procedures, and also gave warning to all other forces about what was likely to happen, and what had to happen if you were going to be successful. Many things had to be done better and naval gunfire had to be made a little more accurate and heavier, and maybe fired parallel to the beach instead of over the top of the landing force, so that you get a better chance for your shells to be effective. Also some of the smaller things which may not have added up as a tremendous thing but were very helpful. For example the Japanese came out on the beach when our tractors came in and threw grenades in. Well, the men that are down in the tractor have no chance to kill the Japanese – maybe the fellow that's running the tractor, if he hadn't already been knocked off or he becomes so fearful that he's out of action in effect. So the Japs will slip out and throw grenades in our tractors. Well, as you know our people get decorated for picking up a grenade and throwing it back but this is not so easy when you're six feet deep in a tractor. Well, as a result of that one of the things we did was we put chicken wire on top of the tractors and when someone threw a grenade instead of going into the tractor and exploding among the troops we could throw it off.

CHAPTER 15

VICTORY IN NORTH AFRICA

While many would agree with Lord Mountbatten's judgement that Bill Slim (see Chapter 28) was the finest general the Allies produced during the Second World War, Bernard Montgomery was entrusted with by far the greater part of British resources and consequently received much the most publicity during and after the war. Everybody in Britain followed the fortunes of 'Monty' and the Eighth Army, and church bells were rung when they won the grinding second battle of El Alamein in October–November 1942. Winston Churchill broadcast a cautiously worded welcome: 'This is not the end, it is not even the beginning of the end – but it is, perhaps, the end of the beginning'. The World at War interviewers were interested mainly in Field Marshal Erwin Rommel, conditions in the desert and the allegedly chivalrous nature of the fighting, so I have had to dredge items such as the Allied landings in French North Africa on 8 November from interviews dealing primarily with other matters. Elsewhere, the massive Soviet counter-attack at Stalingrad on 19–20 November was doubtless a more significant turning point, but thanks to Hitler's belated decision to pour men and resources into North Africa, more than 150,000 Axis soldiers became prisoners of war in Tunisia on 13 May 1943 – 60,000 more than the miserable German defenders of Stalingrad who surrendered to near-certain death on or around 30 January, the tenth anniversary of Hitler's rise to power. The North African campaign was free of the atrocities that were a feature of every other theatre, chiefly because it was not fought among the civilian population so there was only a very limited amount of what we now evasively call 'collateral damage'. But it is also the case that the Italians who made up the bulk of Rommel's army were generally decent folk, and their deadlier allies behaved far better here than elsewhere, probably because there were no SS units in Rommel's army. But as several veterans testify in the following pages, it was not the 'clean' environment many believe it to have been: the essence of war is always brutality.

MAJOR-GENERAL WALTHER WARLIMONT
Deputy Chief of Wehrmacht Operations

I would not say the campaign in North Africa was considered a sideshow by Hitler or anyone else. Hitler had consented to this expedition of German troops only after, and on account of, the Italian collapse in December 1940. In the Western Desert, based on Rommel's unexpected successes and in connection also with the German campaign in Russia, far-reaching plans came aiming at such high goals as cutting off the British lifeline with the Empire and their oil supplies too. An opportunity of this kind always remained far from being realised since Rommel's troops were much too scarce in number and we were not able to reinforce them because of the steadily growing requirements, particularly on the Eastern Front, because of the predominance of the British fleet in the Mediterranean and because of our eventual failure in the east.

MAJOR-GENERAL FRANCIS DE GUINGAND
Chief of Staff to generals Auchinleck and Montgomery

Churchill was in some political difficulties at the time, things were going against Britain and naturally the morale of the British people wasn't all that good. Everyone was wanting some victory or some stimulus and some help, therefore it was essential that on the one front where we were fighting, the desert front, we should produce some concrete results. And he was determined that we should have that and he was going to give us all the resources he had available in human reinforcements and also material. And so we did feel the Prime Minister was a hundred per cent behind us, which he was, and he did the most amazing things, forcing through convoys with tremendous loss to get equipment to us.

GENERAL WALTER NEHRING
Commander Afrika Korps in 1942

I was never convinced that to reach a major success in the Western Desert might have altered the outcome of the war. Our forces were too weak, our supply in the Mediterranean was too dangerous and plentiful in losses and therefore never sufficient for victory. Our military operations in North Africa were only of secondary interest to Hitler, who was concerned mainly with the hard war against Russia. Finally the German forces in North Africa were only a lost lot sacrificed by Hitler.

COLONEL SIEGFRIED WESTPHAL
Operations Officer to Field Marshal Rommel

I think that Hitler had no interest for the situation of the German soldiers in the front line. But the situation of the German soldiers in the Eastern Front was incomparably more bad than the German soldiers in the North Africa desert. We were not a main thing; the eyes of Hitler were directed every day to the Russian Front, the deciding front, and our role was not so important. He was content if we had no difficulties and he couldn't help us if we were in very bad situations. Yet he did send us what we needed in supply, but he was not able to guarantee that this supply came from the continent. He was helpless in this situation like we too.

LAWRENCE DURRELL
British author and wartime press officer in Cairo

Auchinleck was absolutely charming but an extremely sedentary man. He had no real personality, he was handsome and personable and quiet in a Scots way but he hadn't any, you know, for a critical moment you need a bit of rhetoric, a bit of panache and a sort of 'Charge, boys, charge' thing – and he hadn't got that precisely.* The people who had it, like General Harding, were not in evidence and were commanding detachments in the desert and being shot up. It's sad about Wavell because he had that. His orders for the day were inspiring and you needed that inspiration.

---

* General Sir Claude Auchinleck, C-in-C Middle East July 1941–August 1942.

MAJOR GENERAL DE GUINGAND

I was Director of Military Intelligence at the time but the Commander-in-Chief of the Middle East used to always take me up to the desert with him when he went, and I was there during the tremendous panic that took place when we had to retreat from the Gazala line and to hold Tobruk, which we failed to do. I had never seen such chaos; it looked like you'd never be able to save the situation. I've never seen the desert road crammed with every sort of vehicle, every unit muddled up higgledy-piggledy, no one knew what was going on. Luckily our Air Force was stronger than the enemy's, otherwise I think we would have been routed. We got back to El Alamein hoping that they had taken precautions beforehand to prepare defensive positions, that there was somewhere for us to go to, but it was touch and go for several days. One wondered whether we'd ever be able to hold the front and prevent Rommel from getting into Egypt and Cairo itself. He was running into supply problems but he found a tremendous lot of supplies like petrol and transport in Tobruk and during that time Auchinleck relieved Ritchie of his command and took over personal command of the Army himself. I saw that take place, and I thought he pulled things together magnificently and eventually the front settled down. We made one or two half-hearted attempts to try counter strokes but there wasn't enough force behind it and Rommel began to run out of supplies. Men were tired and the thing stabilised and then we had to begin to plan for eventual battle in El Alamein.*

NORMAN CORWIN

American 'Poet Laureate of the radio'

The early grumbles were against involvement in somebody else's war. We felt that this was a war made in Europe for Europeans and that it was none of our business and we had better stay out of it. There was even a senti-ment – I remember this being expressed – to the effect that England would

---

* Of the surrender of Tobruk on 21 June 1942 Churchill wrote, 'This was one of the heaviest blows I can recall during the war. Not only were the military effects grim, but it affected the reputation of British arms. Defeat is one thing; disgrace is another.'

fight to the last American. I was actually involved in an effort by radio to countervail, to counteract that sentiment. Much of it was inspired by … I do believe there was a fifth column at work, but there has always been blatant anti-British sentiment in certain sectors of the population. It had a chance to flourish and to be developed when Britain met reverses not only in Europe but in Africa. When they lost Tobruk and suffered reverses in the desert, the sentiment was whipped up more than it had been before.

REAR ADMIRAL LORD LOUIS MOUNTBATTEN
Chief of Combined Operations

I remember Roosevelt said, 'It seems to be an awful waste of time that we should be pouring divisions into England and you take out the same number of divisions, say six divisions, to fight in Africa. Would it make more sense if we sent out divisions to fight in Africa?' I said, 'Of course it would. How do you propose to send them?' He said, 'Round the Cape, join up with the Army of the Nile and fight our way back west.' I said, 'Why don't you send them straight there, right from the Atlantic ports and into the western Mediterranean ports?' 'Yes', said Roosevelt, 'I remember Winston reminding me about Operation Gymnast, which is your plan, isn't it, for that operation?' I said, 'May I tell my Prime Minster this? Because you see the important thing from your point of view is that you've got a lot of brave but entirely unblooded, inexperienced soldiers. But having got ashore, in which you're bound to succeed, they won't then try and push you back. This gives you a chance to consolidate and from there you have many options open to you.' He liked that very much and said I could tell the US Chiefs of Staff when I saw them.

COLONEL WESTPHAL

You succeeded in summer 1942 finally to stop the exhausted rest of the German Army that reached Alamein, and that was absolutely the deciding point. I think the German Army in the desert has never fully recovered from this exhausting campaign, which did begin on 26th May and ended in El Alamein. Besides, it was absolutely unknown to us that you had built up a strong position at Alamein.

PRIVATE ROBERT REED

2nd New Zealand Division, Eighth Army

We had been through Greece and Crete, we had been chased out of the desert on several occasions, we'd had several terrific reverses where we'd lost everything, lost many men. But never at any occasion did I realise, or thought, we were going to lose the war. I can't give you any reason why I didn't realise we could have lost the war, but I knew we were going to win.

MAJOR GENERAL JOHN HARDING

Commanding 7th Armoured Division

Rommel was a brilliant tactician, a great opportunist and a very fine leader on the battlefield. He was very quick to see an opportunity and seize it and his forces responded. He had his army trained and poised in such a way that he could almost immediately take advantage of any opportunity that he saw, exploiting a limited success.

GENERAL NEHRING

The biggest advantage of the German forces in the Western Desert prior to Montgomery's arrival in August 1942 was that they had a skilled commander. Rommel and his troops were both tested in war, 1939 to 1940 in Poland and France. On the British side, experience in war was at the time missing, but the British generals and their troops were learning it well and quickly.

PRIVATE RUHI PENE

Maori member of the 2nd New Zealand Division, Eighth Army

All Field Marshal Rommel's men were good, they were real fighters, we admired them just like I think they admired us – why else invite us here today?* As a matter of fact at one stage of the fighting Field Marshal Rommel was admired that much and idolised by our troops that they had photos up in their tents. Then word came down from our general to the officers to pass on to all the men to cut this business out of idolising the man.

---

* Interview conducted at a reunion of Afrika Korps veterans in Germany.

LIEUTENANT PAOLO COLACICCHI
Italian Tenth Army

Rommel himself became a sort of myth to the Italian soldiers just as much as to the German soldiers. In fact one regiment, the Bersaglieri – they are the ones with a lot of feathers in their hats – fighting out of Tobruk baptised Rommel 'Romolito', which in Italian means little Rommel and also refers to Romulus. This was a Roman regiment and they liked him, and on one occasion he even put some of their feathers in his own colonial helmet and wore it because he was pleased with them.

MAJOR GENERAL HARDING

Rommel became a bit of a hoodoo yes, but personally I don't think I ever felt it. I remember taking special measures to try and destroy this image of infallibility and invulnerability, that in some people's minds sprung up as a result of Rommel's success. What I call psychological and propaganda ones, instructions to commanders, papers issued on the subject, but mainly by word of mouth and by examples from commander to commander, and so down to the troops.

LIEUTENANT COLONEL RONALD BELCHEM
7th Armoured Division

Obviously the Rommel legend had an adverse effect on morale because General Auchinleck issued a most extraordinary directive to his generals saying that by all means possible they had to repress the idea that Rommel was a magician or a bogeyman. I don't think one should over-emphasise this – Rommel's name, and it was a good name – was built up by the fact of his own personal mobility on the battlefield. He had a flair for being at the crucial point at the right moment, to give orders on the spot and so forth, and incidentally he got a great write-up from our own press correspondents. But if there was a danger of Rommel's legend causing inferiority complexes among our own people, this was really a reflection on our own leaders. It implied lack of confidence in our own tactical commanders and lack of confidence perhaps in our own equip-ment. But I don't think one should over-emphasise this because even after the [May–June 1942] defeat at Gazala and the retreat right back to Alamein the fighting formations were not licked – they were bewildered.

MAJOR GENERAL HARDING

I can remember being told by representatives from London that the two-pounder anti-tank gun mounted in the Crusader tank was about the best weapon there was. It wasn't, because it couldn't really destroy a German tank at all. On the other hand, it did take us a long time, longer than perhaps it should have done, to appreciate the fact that in modern war with armour and air power it is a combination of armour, infantry, artillery and engineers, the whole thing supported by air power, and this took us a long time to learn.

COLONEL WESTPHAL

In the first time of the African campaign we had the advantage to have better tanks, but then from month to month the British on the other side became stronger and stronger, and the equipment and ammunition became better. So the only advantage we had at last was perhaps sometimes a tactic more mobile than the other side. The task of the German Africa Army was only to bind a lot of troops of the other side so long as possible and in this manner help the Eastern Front and to cover Italy from a landing operation. I have never the meaning that we would have the possibility to occupy Egypt or to reach or cross the Suez Canal. Younger people than I were quite more optimistic and were influenced by some great success we had in these two years – I was always not pessimistic but of a critical nature, and I think it was quite good.

LIEUTENANT COLONEL BELCHEM

I think the main problem was disparity of tactics. We had been trained to fire on the move, to execute a sort of cavalry charge on tracks, and to handle our men that way. The Germans had studied this problem much more than we between the wars – and also, of course, Rommel had experience from northern France and so had many of his tank crews – and they appreciated that the tank's best action against his enemy is to wait for him to come on, sitting in a hull-down position, and that if they're caught in the open to decoy the enemy on to their anti-tank guns and not to hurl themselves at a brick wall, and that their real objective is to find a weak spot and to pull themselves through it. But above all armoured forces must be ready to concentrate quickly in overwhelming force at the right point. I think in this context one must think of radio – I don't think that the higher commanders in the early part of this campaign really understood that mobile ops cannot function efficiently without first-class radio communications – and over and over again you'll find instances where the command man was not on the air at the crucial moment. As a German report said, 'At no time and at no place did the British High Command feed in concentrations of their available resources at the critical point.'

COLONEL WESTPHAL

Finally what was the deciding point for us, the defeat at El Alamein – but I think we had crossed the Rubicon like Caesar when we went to Egypt. I had made the plan for the conquering of Tobruk, and this plan ended up by having taken Tobruk. We would send some reconnaissance battalion to Sidi Barrani and stay with the mass of the Army via near Bardia and the south of this place. Not to go with the mass of the whole Army to Egypt because we had the opinion that the distance from the ports Benghazi, Tripoli and perhaps Tobruk would become too big to guarantee our supplies. But in the moment of taking Tobruk I was wounded in Germany and Rommel saw the only opportunity to beat the Allied Army for ever and pursued them, and Hitler agreed. If I would have been present at the time I would have fought for stopping at the Egyptian border, but I don't believe I would have succeeded.

LAWRENCE DURRELL

I think everybody, whether they were British or Egyptian, felt that our worlds were floundering and the prospect that Mr Hitler might be in charge for the next fifty years was not something to appeal to anybody.

PRIVATE NOEL GARDINER

2nd New Zealand Division, Eighth Army

We thought that this character Hitler had sort of got loose and the show was getting out of hand and something had to be done about it. We were right out in New Zealand, it seems incredible, twelve thousand miles away, but it doesn't alter the fact that we are of British stock and we'd been involved in the First World War to fight this battle of democracy. We think that's the best way of life – that people, all things being equal, should be able to please themselves provided they don't give offence to anyone else. We think that's what we're fighting for, to be left alone and not to be dominated like Hitler was domineering people, and we thought it was a worthwhile proposition.

PRIVATE TOM FITZPATRICK

9th Australian Division

We thought of El Alamein as very much a united Empire effort. We spoke of Empire in those days and now it's the Commonwealth, but I'm old-fashioned and I still think of it as the Empire. We realised that the battle of El Alamein was going to be far too vast for the 9th Division, we had to think in bigger terms than that, but we didn't regard ourselves as a small cog in the wheel – we thought we were a pretty big cog in the wheel, I think that's an Australian characteristic.

PRIVATE PENE

It was a Commonwealth war, of course, that's why we joined up. I mean the UK was in trouble and the automatic thing was to help them out and also to try to keep the war away from us. That was the thing – keep it away from our children, our families, but mainly to support England at the time. I think it was an all-out effort by the Commonwealth, as it should have been.

PRIVATE JOHN McGEE

Infantry, Eighth Army

It could be possible that I got captured today, or my company got captured, and while we're moving out to a rendezvous with the Germans our people would come up and relieve us and away we'd go, and then they, the Germans, would be the prisoners.

LAWRENCE DURRELL

There's the thing [Sir Arthur] Bryant brings out in his Peninsular War book, the thing that Napoleon noticed, the British fox-hunting man was the thing that astonished the French. Not necessarily the fighting man but the fox-hunting attitude, and the Eighth Army had that in class and they also had a war that was mobile, it was like dodgems. I mean it was fifty miles forward, fifty miles back, re-form and attack, and people would do the tally-ho act. So it gave a liveliness to all the rest, which was stagnation – Europe was stagnation and despair, blackness. There was light and you could fall back and if you got a lucky flesh wound or even if you had a desert sore you could get a weekend off and in fifty-five minutes you were back in Cairo, teeming with lights, you rang up people, you went out to dinner and you had a flask of whisky, and on Monday morning you were back in the line.

COLONEL WESTPHAL

I think we have fought this campaign according to rules coming from the tradition of Prussian and German Army in the nineteenth century and the same was the case on the other side. Furthermore we had no difficulties with the Arabian population, there were so few they didn't disturb us, and we had no towns and no cities, or very few so that we could handle the warfare like an open campaign. There were many differences between fighting in the desert or fighting in Europe. The greatest advantage for us in North Africa we had not to fear the cold in the winter-time, and the further one, the population. And a great disadvantage was the great distance from Europe and disadvantages of supply. Supply had to go to Italy by train, from Italy by ship to North Africa and the Allies had superiority in sea and air, therefore we never had reliable supply, fuel, ammunition, food, cars and so on. Another disadvantage was, in the desert we had no possibility to cover before the eyes of the enemy: we had no woods, we had no trees, we had no villages and every man who has been in wars remembers that if the other side shoot with artillery, he always had the feeling he personally is the target of the enemy.

LIEUTENANT COLACICCHI

I would say that we Italians in Africa got better as the war went on. The Italian is very quick to learn, our units improved and of course up to a point the example of the Germans helped. But by the time of Tunisia when the war in Africa was finished, as far as we were concerned, I would say we gave a pretty good account of ourselves.

MAJOR GENERAL HARDING

If you can have a good place to have a war I suppose it was a better place than anywhere, because you were not handicapped by the movement of refugees, or by the problems that arose from demolished towns and buildings obstructing roads and railways. It was wide, open country, you could move about and you were not obstructed in any way and if you had to do that sort of thing, it was as good a place as any to do it. We had a horror after being in the desert of ever getting into buildings again.

MAJOR GENERAL DE GUINGAND

If you've got to fight, got to have these horrible wars, I suppose the desert was one of the best places to fight because there was ample room for manoeuvre: you could go all over the place, you could use mobile forces comparatively easily and you had no large towns, cities and few civilians and therefore it was a much cleaner type of warfare than when you got into civilised and populated Europe. The civilian population suffered terribly and we had to destroy cities, communications, towns, harbours and the lot. It had its disadvantages because there was no cover for us at all; you were absolutely exposed to enemy air and ground forces. It was jolly hard at times, it was very cold at times and you had these frightful dust storms, which were very unpleasant things to live in.

COLONEL WESTPHAL

On my side I remember well the very good camaraderie, and the fair treatment of our soldiers by the other side. I remember the storm dust who endured three or four days, because it was for us absolutely shelter against the enemy reaction, enemy bombing and this dust storm in the Italian language was *gibli*, we called it that.* But I can remember in the same manner the many flies, one fly had in one year nine million children, and I can remember the very salty water and the most things we had not like the other soldiers in Europe.

LIEUTENANT EMILIO PULLINI
Folgore (Lightning) Parachute Division

We arrived to northern Africa in very good condition because we had very tough training in southern Italy for a couple of months, on difficult ground and very hot climate too, and I think that when we arrived we were very fit. Unfortunately in the desert the conditions were very much not the same as we had in Italy because we arrived in the middle of July and immediately we were taken to the battleground, and that was rather a sudden change, and there were some things we did not like very much, flies mainly and a very hot sun which was above us all day long. It was very uncomfortable to spend all day lying in foxholes from sunrise to sunset just covered in flies and doing very little because we had no chance of doing anything else.

PRIVATE BOB MASH
Engineer, Eighth Army

Flies were terrible but there was one dreaded little animal that I didn't like, and that was the scorpion. A scorpion could be very dangerous because it had poison in its stinger in the tail. A scorpion would never give himself up, would rather kill himself than surrender.

PRIVATE PENE

Flies were a nuisance, a bad one. At Alamein the particular ones we had to deal with fed on the dead – the dead weren't far away from us, a matter of a few hundred yards from our company – and they fed on the dead and then came round trying to feed on our water and food. At one stage we weren't allowed to kill them because the smell from them interfered with

---

* Actually Arabic.

our stomachs and caused upsets. They wanted water just like we did and they would dive-bomb our tea and of course would float on top of the tea, and the only way to get rid of them was not to tip it out, it was to sieve the tea with your teeth and just blow it off. They also liked jam: we had plenty of that on our bread and we did this sort of thing [gestures] but of course one or two flies go in there and we had to spit it out – that's how friendly they were.

PRIVATE REED

My father served in the First World War in the desert and I had a fair idea what to expect. I thought the conditions in the desert were quite good. As the summer came along it got very hot in the day but the evenings were cool and I didn't find the conditions at all harmful to me physically. I enjoyed my days in the desert.

LIEUTENANT HUGH DANIEL

Eighth Army dispatch rider

Obviously a lot of people did become lost but the organisation of an army is such that every endeavour is made to ensure that things work on set lines. You have your four defence lines and you have your lines ranged behind, then you have your lines forward for communication. These, in the desert, were marked as clearly as could be with old tins, any bits of discarded material, or cairns of stones were built and placed. Maps had been produced, very accurate maps from some splendid survey work done in the ten years before the war. We therefore had points of reference on the maps, the wells known as 'birs' from the Arabic name. The tracks used by the nomads weren't particularly evident but they were marked on the map, so for a person who could read a map well and was within the confines of the Army area there was no reason to get seriously lost. We had prismatic compasses, we had sun compasses, we had maps which gave us the night sky – Cassiopeia was our favourite constellation, which gave us the pole-star. So I don't think we were particularly worried.

MAJOR GENERAL DE GUINGAND

The Eighth Army at that time were rather disillusioned, didn't know where they were and what they were doing wrong. When Montgomery arrived he took a grip immediately; you suddenly felt here was leadership. One of his finest hours was when he ordered a conference of the Staff on the very day he arrived; he told me to get everyone together on the Ruweisat Ridge. He talked to us all and he was very spectacular, the effect was simply incredible. He told us that the bad days were over and he was now determined that it was going to be a success. All plans for going back from the position we were in at El Alamein, I had to burn the lot. He said, 'Now the order is that everyone stays where they are and fights where they are and dies where they are.' Then he told us that Churchill was giving him and Alexander instructions to kick Rommel out of North Africa, we were going to get additional resources of men and material, and he was specific about the sort of discipline in the Army. Before he arrived the Army Commander gave an order of instruction and you found that some of the subordinate commanders used to query it and say they didn't think they were going to do it, they thought of a better way of doing it. He said that's got to stop, what he called no more belly-aching, and if there were any doubters about the plans which he initiated then they'd better leave the Eighth Army.

LIEUTENANT COLONEL BELCHEM

Montgomery immediately, as quickly as possible, started going round all the formations of the Eighth Army and gathering people around him to talk to them and to radiate this confidence, which he was capable of doing. And he also used the press and the radio and gimmicks such as his hats to help stimulate his image and to get himself known to everyone, which he did, and incidentally accepted by everyone. Perhaps the hat gimmick first arose when he was visiting the New Zealand Division and it was very hot. He borrowed a hat with a broad brim and he realised that the New Zealanders appreciated seeing him in one of their hats, so before he went to the Australians he borrowed an Australian hat to go in, and with the tanks he borrowed a beret. I think he decided the beret was the most distinctive headdress and incidentally one of the easiest to handle, and it was by this headdress that he became well known. He introduced an entirely new philosophy, namely that before going into a major new offensive operation everybody, including if you like the nursing orderlies in the hospital, should know broadly what was the commander's intention in the coming battle, so that everybody could feel he had a part to play in achieving that object. Incidentally, in the fighting line their initiative would be developed within the framework of what the boss wanted to accomplish and this paid enormous dividends.

COLONEL WESTPHAL

When I came back to the Army in the beginning of August 1942 the situation at El Alamein was very difficult because the supply became more and more bad. The reason was that Tobruk was not a port for commerce ships, but only a port for warships, therefore the usefulness of Tobruk for the supply was very few. We had a much longer distance for the supplies from Tripoli and even from Benghazi, therefore we reconsidered the possibilities and realised that it was a mistake to go to El Alamein. We realised too, especially in regard of the Italian troops who were not motorised, that we should step back to the Bardia line. But we were absolutely clear that Hitler would never agree with this plan, and we tried to make the best of it: we erected many minefields before the front – which was useless.

MAJOR HANS HINRICHS
German engineer officer

In Russia the fighting is a war of infantry and of single tanks. In the desert the fighting is characterised by the opposition of tanks in larger quantities and of air support. Air support, for instance, did not play a considerable role in Russia, at least not in the central part where the troops had enough cover. In Africa, air superiority was all-decisive. In Russia you saw the individual enemy soldier, in the desert you hardly saw the British tanks.

LAWRENCE DURRELL

It's a very funny thing, a battlefield, it's extraordinary how inanimate the whole thing seems. There was a little bit of an action going on in the right-hand corner of some sort, for the rest there were people lying about smoking. It's one of the very singular things that films and books don't bring out, although I think Tolstoy perhaps is an exception, of a battlefield where nothing seems to be happening, the action is always somewhere in another corner and it's a decisive thing. And then they ask you if you were there.

LIEUTENANT PULLINI

At the end of the battle of El Alamein we were left there without transport because we were paratroopers and had very little transport of our own. So far as I know the majority of the German troops withdrew before us and not much transport was left for us.

LIEUTENANT COLONEL BELCHEM

When viewers see the pictures of El Alamein battlefield they will see these wide areas as flat as a pancake and therefore let us bear in mind that Eighth Army had to assault, had to cross, this very open desert into defensive positions organised, sited and developed over a period of months under German direction with three belts of interlocking defensive positions. The minefields were up to five and a half miles in depth and behind them stood the 15th and 21st Panzer divisions. While admittedly we had superiority of forces and Air Force by anyone's standards, under these conditions the assaulting force was obliged to be considerably superior to that of the defender.

MAJOR GENERAL DE GUINGAND

Alex showed Montgomery a signal he'd just had from the Prime Minister saying we must attack in September and that it was absolutely essential. Alex said to Monty, 'What shall I answer?' and Monty said, 'I'm not going to attack in September.' So he said to me, 'Freddie, give me your pen.' He wrote in his very clear handwriting and said, 'Send this to the Prime Minister.' The first point he made was that Rommel was attacking on 31st

August and it would cause delay in our preparations, secondly that training and getting used to the new tanks and equipment would take longer
than September before we were ready and he finished up saying if we are
forced to attack in September it will probably fail. If we wait until October
then it will be a complete success. And he said, 'Alex, send that off to
Winston,' and Alex read it and said, 'Yes, I will,' which he did. Any Prime
Minister getting a document like that from the military commanders, he
couldn't go against it. If he forced us to attack in September and it failed
then there it was on the record that the principal military authority had
said it would fail.

MAJOR GENERAL HARDING

The landing in Algeria was a long way off, it took quite a time to reach
even within striking distance of Tunis and I doubt if they'd have got there
as soon as they did but for the defeat of Rommel at El Alamein and the
subsequent advance of the Eighth Army. I think the two fronts were too
far apart for that to be effective. You can't win a war, much less a
campaign, without defeating the enemy. If Rommel had been able to leave
small containing forces facing us in the desert and used the whole of his
force against the First Army and the Americans who landed with them,
then I think it would have ever got to within striking distance of Tunis.

COLONEL WESTPHAL

At Alamein Hitler did not allow the retreat from El Alamein in the direction to west. But we didn't obey, we pursued the retreat and that was the
only possibility – to stand about six months in North Africa to cover the
southern flank of Europe. If we had obeyed this, to stand at Alamein,
defend every piece of soil of the desert, we would be surrounded and
captured by Montgomery two days later. But sometime God in heaven did
help us, we had heavy rain in Nile Delta and therefore the Air Force could-
n't start, that was our luck. Otherwise the Army would have been
destroyed before we could reach the Halfaya Pass.

MAJOR GENERAL HARDING

As far as the High Command was concerned there was, just before the breakthrough operation was launched, a question as to whether or not there was sufficient resources left to break the German front and to make a hole big enough to allow pursuing forces to get through. A battle like that was a battle of attrition and it was fought, rightly, in a way in which you had to continue the offensive until you had broken the enemy's power of resistance, and this does take time, especially under those sort of conditions.

COLONEL WESTPHAL

It was very funny: we had only one road from El Alamein through Mersa Matruh, Bardia, Tobruk and Benghazi, and on this one road we marched. At first the German division then following a British armoured division, then again a German division followed by another British division. But they did not attack us and we couldn't make anything because we had no petrol.

MAJOR GENERAL HARDING

I was actually in favour of pressing on all-out, hard as I could go and as fast as I could go. On the other hand I think Montgomery was very conscious of the fact that we had already been twice up and twice back and he was determined not to be pushed back for a third time. A defeat then or a failure to exploit the success of Alamein would have had very far-reaching consequences on morale and confidence and on the general position throughout the war. I think he was right – I thought he was overcautious at the time but looking back at it all, I think he was right to be cautious and maybe there was something between the two views.

CHAPTER 16

STALINGRAD AND THE EASTERN FRONT

*During 1942 the Red Army was rebuilt under new leadership, including offi-
cers imprisoned during the Tukhachevsky purge who were released to replace
the Stalinist yes-men who had led the Army to defeat in 1941. Britain agreed
to divert some American supplies and equipment due to her under Lend-Lease
and in 1941–42 the Royal Navy fought twenty-one convoys through icy seas to
north Russia. The struggle between the Nazi and Soviet regimes reached its
climax when a German thrust towards the Caucasus oilfields led to the battle
of Stalingrad (August 1942–February 1943). Including all operations along
the flanks of the salient, the Germans and their allies suffered some
800,000–900,000 casualties and the Soviets approximately a million. The last
German effort to regain the initiative, at Kursk in July 1943, destroyed such
a large proportion of German armour and ground-attack aircraft that they
never recovered. In an offensive second only in size to Barbarossa three years
earlier, on 22 June 1944 the Soviets launched Operation Bagration on the
Byelorussian front, where the Germans had thinned their line to send units to
counter the Allied landings in Normandy. The Soviet advance was halted at
the outskirts of Warsaw in August–September while the Germans crushed a
heroic uprising by the Polish Home Army. Stalin refused to permit Allied
aircraft to stage through Soviet-held territory in order to drop supplies to the
Polish patriots and the advancing Red Army – admittedly over-extended at
the end of its offensive – did not support the Poles, who suffered heavy losses. The
Soviets did not enter the ruins of Warsaw until January 1945, when they
launched the final offensive that took them to Berlin.*

The Eastern Front claimed the lives of over five million Germans and their allies, including perhaps a quarter of a million Soviet citizens who joined them, plus 10 million Soviet soldiers and as many civilians, although even today these figures remain a matter of dispute. Stalin had probably killed at least as many more, in purges or as a result of hasty 'collectivisation' in the 1930s, and Russia has arguably never really recovered from this double genocide. Both world wars were conflicts, on a gigantic scale, of economic and industrial as well as military strength. In neither would Germany be defeated until the heart had been ripped out of her Army. In the First World War this occurred chiefly on the Western Front, as too many French, British and Dominion war memorials testify. In the Second, it occurred chiefly (though of course not exclusively) on the Eastern Front, and it was the Red Army that paid the exorbitant price.

ALBERT SPEER

Hitler's Armaments Minister

Already in 1942 there was important group of officers, which later on belonging to the plot of 20 July, opposed to Hitler's military policies in Russia. That meant they wanted to think about defence policy, to build small fortifications along the Russian line, to build the defence as strong as possible and not waste the tanks ... and so on in a long offensive. On both sides only a few were still in action and those few were fighting each other, but all the other tanks, thousands of them, were lying lost somewhere in Russia and couldn't be transported back any more. The idea of the generals was if those tanks could be spared for defence, approximately five times more Russians would be necessary to launch successful attacks than the defender has. And the losses for the man who is leading the offensive in warfare is much higher than those of the defence, as long as the defence doesn't break down. The estimation was that Russia couldn't afford to attack because in the long time they would be exhausted before they are winning back the whole country. This was the idea of the generals, and I think it proved to be the right idea.

COLONEL GENERAL NIKOLAI LOMOV
Deputy Head of Operations, Red Army General Staff

Throughout the period of the war and especially in 1943–45, most indicative were the great number of troops in the Soviet Army. The number did not fall below six million people – that is in the active Army – who were deployed on the Soviet–German front from the Barents to the Black Sea. So, of these six million people, in spring and summer in the four Ukrainian Fronts [in the Soviet Army an Army Group was a 'Front'] there were about two and a half million people. It goes without saying that these forces were backed with the requisite equipment – tanks, planes, etc. In 1941 at the beginning of the war there were about two thousand tanks, then already in 1944 there were twelve thousand tanks, modern tanks, T-34s, and self-propelled artillery platforms. Our artillery was also in very good order. It must be said that the German defence was very strong and a very high density of artillery was required to break through this defence – this density reached more than two hundred pieces of artillery per kilometre of the front.

PRIVATE ALBRECHT SCHIMPF
German Army

In Russia there were no signposts to mark the way, no streets like in Western Europe, and to find our way we had to set the frozen bodies of horses along the snow roads to find the way during the snowdrifts. Certainly it was a very macabre sight but it was only to find the roads because there were no points to find, no house, no cottage, no tree, always wasteland, snow and snow.

CAPTAIN EKKEHARD MAURER
Infantry, German Army

The Russian soldier was a very robust and hardy soldier, well used to those climatic conditions. Sometimes we got terribly angry because for instance we had to leave behind or just drop our arms, machine guns or what have you because they didn't work any more, and the Russians just grabbed them, we saw sometimes, put some winter oil on them and used them against us. The Russian soldier was also probably more prepared for man-to-man fighting – most of those divisions actually were composed of Asiatic people. Our soldiers being Western European people did not like this man-to-man fighting so much, they were more relying on our automatic weapons, on using their brains.

MAJOR HANS HINRICHS
Engineer, German Army
We were attacked by a Soviet company in the early morning at approximately thirty-five degrees below zero. This company attack was repulsed and the Soviet soldiers remained motionless about ten hours lying in the snow and in the evening they attacked again with the same spirit.

OLGA RYBAKOVA
Leningrad housewife
Well, naturally, we felt very depressed when we heard about the suburbs of our city being taken by the Fascist troops. But still we thought and we hoped that all these defeats would be only temporary, just as they were a hundred and forty years ago when we had the invasion of Napoleon troops.

ALBERT SPEER
During my visit to Kiev I was of the same opinion as the generals with whom I was together quite often, that the whole movement of partisans in Russia who just started this time was caused by the treatment of the population. Even Goebbels, it's well known at this time, he was for better treatment of Ukrainians, mainly because he thought if they get some, if the situation is eased and they get some national pride, then possibly they could be won over even to fight the Stalin system. There was one very old church which was blown up, but I was told that there was, it was an explosion of some munitions magazine I found out later, that it was done by the gauleiter who was in charge of the Ukraine.

PRIVATE SCHIMPF

I think the war is very cruel, but which war is without cruelty? And it was especially cruel if the Russian soldiers they are drunken when they attacked. One night I had to make a counter-thrust to win back the position of another company and we found the chief of this company badly wounded and upon him a drunken Russian soldier cutting off the face.

OLGA RYBAKOVA

The most terrible time was December 1941 because I think until August we had commercial shops so we could buy something and it was a great help for us. We even could buy caviare, but then the commercial shops were closed. The blockade began. And in September–October it was still passable, although already in October a great friend of my mother died. It was the first death that we heard of. But in November it was began to be cold and the rations were shortened, became less and less food, and the end of November, December and January were most tragical times. Firstly it was cold – minus forty – then the famine, the hunger began to be felt and people began to starve and die from cold and undernourishment. Most deaths came when the end of February and March. When I went to the shops to receive the ration for my family and for some friends living in my house, when I went on the way there I found I had to pass dead bodies and then on my way back some more bodies were lying – if I passed on the way there two bodies, on the way back there were four.

ANTHONY EDEN
British Foreign Minister
They were very difficult about it and there were endless discussions and arguments. Churchill went very boldly on that visit himself to Moscow to try and explain matters to Stalin and had a very tough time of it and in October 1943, when we had our first Three Power Conference in Moscow, I asked Churchill to let me have [Chief Staff Officer to the Prime Minister General Sir Hastings] Ismay with me with the authority of the Chiefs of Staff to put the whole position to the Russians, because

I was quite sure that the moment we got to Moscow they wouldn't want to discuss whatever thing we were supposed to discuss, but would say, 'What about the Second Front?' – which is exactly what happened. Ismay and his American colleague, US Military Attaché General Dean, did a great job and that, I think, did a great deal to disabuse the Russians of some of their suspicions. After all we were there several weeks and during that time the explanations were pretty well continuous, not only at the conference table but in private conversations and at meals. After that the Russians became more understanding, but they were always apprehensive if we were going to postpone the date a little and Molotov or Stalin would say, 'Let's not change the dates.' It was natural; they were sustaining pretty heavy casualties themselves. They were tough and difficult and there was a period when Winston stopped sending personal messages altogether because he thought that it wasn't any good. But you expect that sort of thing to happen. I think considering what one knows of the characteristics of the three countries, their forms of government, their way of life and everything about them, the fact that we managed to keep the alliance at all in reasonable shape was quite commendable.

MAJOR GORONWY REES
Combined Operations Staff Officer and D-Day planner
Curiously enough, and this was a thing that afterwards I really remember, I now remember with a kind of horror, one of my great friends of that time was [Soviet spy] Guy Burgess, and I used to see him a great deal during the whole of this operation. And afterwards I wondered why on earth, you know, how absolutely terrible, I could quite easily have given him some indication as to what was going on.*

---

* Rees confessed on his deathbed in 1979 that he had been a Soviet spy in association with the 'Cambridge Five'. Thanks to their activities and those of traitors in the Roosevelt administration, including Alger Hiss, the Western Allies had no secrets from the Soviet dictator.

TOSHIKAZU KASE

Japanese diplomat

The success of Nazi Germany in the European theatre affected the younger officers until before Stalingrad, which coincided with the first defeat the Japanese Army suffered. Many young officers became disillusioned with the German military efforts after Stalingrad.

PRIVATE WILHELM HOFFMAN

Sixth Army at Stalingrad, diary entries

11 September. Our battalion is fighting in the suburbs of Stalingrad. Firing is going on all the time. Wherever you look is fire and flames. Russian cannon and machine guns are firing out of the burning city – fanatics! *16 September.* Our battalion plus tanks is attacking the grain elevator. The battalion is suffering heavy losses. The elevator is occupied not by men but by devils no bullets or flames can destroy. *18 September.* Fighting is going on inside the elevator. If all the buildings of Stalingrad are defended like this none of our soldiers will get back to Germany. *22 September.* Russian resistance in the elevator has been broken. Our troops are advancing towards the Volga. We found only about forty Russians dead in the elevator. *26 October.* Who would have thought, three months ago, that instead of the joy of victory we would have to endure such sacrifices and torture, the end of which is nowhere in sight. The soldiers are calling Stalingrad the mass grave of the Wehrmacht.

PRIVATE ANTON BOSNIK

Russian defender at Stalingrad, extract from a letter

We moved back occupying one building after another, turning them to strongholds. A soldier would crawl out of an occupied position only when the ground was on fire beneath him and his clothes were smouldering.

ALBERT SPEER

My brother was in Stalingrad and personally I tried everything to bring him out by plane. The man in charge of the whole air forces around Stalingrad promised me to do his utmost to find him but he couldn't be found any more. Göring's assurance that he could supply the besieged city from the air was just one of this things which happened quite often in Hitler's surrounding. People were afraid telling the absolute truth and they wanted to please him with something which was cheering him up, and Göring saw Hitler in a desolate, depressive mood so he made his promise possibly without asking his generals before.

LIEUTENANT REINER
Fourth Panzer Army at Stalingrad, extract from a letter
Stalingrad is no longer a town. By day it is an enormous cloud of burning, blinding smoke, a vast furnace lit by the reflection of the flames. And when night arrives, one of those very hot, noisy, bloody nights, the dogs plunge into the Volga and swim desperately to gain the other bank. The nights of Stalingrad are a terror for them. Animals flee from this hell. The hardest stone cannot bear it for long. Only men endure.

ADOLF HITLER
After-dinner speech, Munich, 8 November 1943
I wanted to get to the Volga, at a particular point where stands a certain town that bears the name of Stalin himself. I wanted to take the place and we've done it. We've got it, really, except for a few enemy positions still holding out. Now people say why don't they finish the job more quickly? Well, I prefer to do the job with quite small groups. Time is of no consequence at all.

GRAND ADMIRAL KARL DÖNITZ
Chief of the German Navy
The defeat of the Battle of Stalingrad made to a high degree the whole of our situation much worse. It was clear that we still could not hope to win the war against Russia. By such a victory Hitler had hoped to make our possession upon the European continent so strong that British sea power could not see any advantage in pursuing the war against us. He hoped that in the circumstances we would get a good peace with our enemies in the West too.

COLONEL IVAN CHISTYAKOV
158th Guards Artillery Regiment

The special thing about Kursk was the number of troops involved, more than two million people, fifty thousand tanks altogether, about ten thousand aeroplanes, weapons, mortars – everything was bring prepared for the battle of the third summer. We should congratulate our Party organisations, our political workers and our officers. They prepare the troops very thoroughly to resist the German attack, explaining the new techniques and equipment of the enemy and what our government had given us. At Kursk the Soviet troops displayed great heroism as you would never find in any other army. No capitalist army will find such heroism as our Soviet soldiers showed. The heroic advances of our troops were very great, it was mass heroism. Lenin said that Soviet people would produce not one hero but hundreds of thousands and this true. The people who we freed greeted us everywhere with salt and bread as their saviours from this Fascist slavery.

MAJOR GENERAL WALTHER WARLIMONT
Deputy Chief of Wehrmacht Operations

Hitler at that time used to speak of a large gap which had remained there – gradually there was more gap than front and eventually more front than gap but that took all the time until the end of September. Then the Russians followed this breakthrough into three large bridgeheads and particularly at Bryansk, which became the starting place for the winter offensive. On the northern part of the front the Russians penetrated into the Balkan states and approached the frontier of East Prussia where Hitler had his headquarters. Things developed in the south where the Russians had penetrated Romania, the main source of the German petrol supply, and opened the way further to the west into Hungary and to Bulgaria thus endangering the whole of the German troops in the south-east – two hundred thousand men. In the fall of 1944 they followed into Hungary and came close to Budapest and on the main front they pursued their success further on to the German frontier. In the north the advance led to the German Army Group being enclosed leaving almost twenty-eight divisions in Poland and never could break out until the end of the war. The Russians' winter offensive penetrated deeply into Germany no more than about fifty kilometres east of Berlin and in the south approached Vienna.

COLONEL GENERAL LOMOV

The Soviet High Command was expecting to begin the attack in the second half of January and were making all the necessary preparations – equipment, supplies, troops. But, as is well known, in December 1944 the German Command made an attack against the Anglo-American forces in the Ardennes. In connection with this and related complications Churchill turned to Stalin with a request for help from Soviet forces in this difficult situation. The Soviet High Command replied that the attack would be speeded up and in fact the operation which has been prepared for later actually began on 12th of January. This had a very positive effect on the position of the Anglo-American troops and the Germans were forced to stop their attacks and in the Ardennes the situation stabilised. It was a successful operation in spite of the fact that the Soviet forces had to attack earlier than intended.

MAJOR GENERAL WARLIMONT

The effect on morale is hardly to be esteemed by me because at that time I was at the headquarters in East Prussia which General Jodl compared between a concentration camp and a monastery. The immediate strategic situation was much more important. Hitler had special inclination to save Hungary much more than our own country so he was inclined to send the few reserves he still had. We had to assemble them in Hungary. Another important consequence was that the Greek armies in the south-east were about to be separated from any possibility to retreat to Germany. At the beginning Hitler was prepared to give the permission to other retreating movements from there. These were endangered by warfare in Yugoslavia, which made it still more difficult to come through.

GENERAL ALEXEI ANTONOV
Red Army Chief of Staff

Our Red Army started in the direction of Berlin. Fifth Guards Army was commanded by me, very lucky, we were the main group that advanced to Berlin. Beginning in January, interesting events shows the good feelings of our Soviet government and of the English troops. In Ardennes, difficult situation for the English Army, Churchill asked Stalin to speed up the attack by the Red Army to help the English attack from the west. We received the order for a forced march, virtually running night and day, to prepare attack. We were lucky to be ready by 14th January to Warsaw and then onwards to the Oder attacks and counter-attacks south of Warsaw. But we overcame these blows. Twenty heroes of the Soviet Union, soldiers and officers.

MAJOR GENERAL WARLIMONT

The main reason for keeping the German Army in Finland has been thrown away already in later 1943 when the siege of Leningrad had to open up because we couldn't hold it any more. So the Russians had free access from that time. This retreat was much easier than on other fronts because it had already been prepared. Defence under Marshal Mannerheim remained friendly to the Germans and they support the retreat wherever they could. Hitler tried to impede the retreat by demanding that we had to keep up the occupation of the area. Speer came in and told Hitler that it wasn't necessary, that there were enough stores of nickel in Germany, and so this impediment was set aside also.

Z T BOKIEWICZ
Polish Home Army, Warsaw uprising of August–September 1944

The German troops were in completely chaotic retreat and when you went into one of the main streets of Warsaw, which ran from east to west, you could see the German Army retreating with all their belongings and the units were mixed. The soldiers had on their faces – they were afraid and they were completely dishevelled and in a terrible state. The Russian Army was approaching Warsaw and we could hear the gunfire in the distance and then they stopped and it was a great surprise to us because they were so near. In fact during the second part of the uprising they were just across the river and there was some contact with their units. They were the units of the Polish Army, which was part of the Russian Army, and General Zygmunt Berling of that Army sent some observers and one of the battalions was actually landed on our side and took part in the fighting, but because the soldiers were recruited in Poland a few weeks before they were inexperienced in street fighting and they were almost completely annihilated.

ALICJA IWANSKA
Student involved in the Warsaw uprising
I feel that Poland was betrayed by the Allies, that the Allies behaved in an opportunistic way towards Poland. Most of us feel that way, that they could have taken more chances themselves in order not to betray their Allies. So naturally we got extremely disappointed, but there is something in the Polish national character, you know, we're just optimistic and we do not give up friends so easily. So we feel that we still have friends among those Allies and that one day they would help us during some other peace negotiations, in some other situations where it may be easier for them to help us or maybe if they would decide to take more chances.

LIEUTENANT GENERAL HASSO-ECCARD FREIHERR VON MANTEUFFEL
Commander of Panzer Grenadier Division 'Grossdeutchland' February– September 1944
After the landing to north France and absolute Allied air supervision not only on the front line west of the Rhine but over the whole of Germany, there was no doubt that the fortress of Germany lay open. Lack of personnel, material replacement of all kinds, the lack of tanks – it was impossible to replace the heavy losses. There we have no operational reserves on the front of the battle theatres and no battle theatres. The weakness of the Italian alliance became public; my doubts were increased by the setback of the attack of my own Army [to break through to troops

trapped in Kurland] in September 1944. In four days three tank brigades were wiped out because they were absolutely unprepared for such an attack. The defeat was catastrophic both on material terms and had an effect on morale. The losses could not be made up, so was unable to keep arms filled, to reinforce exhausted attacking forces. Before the beginning of the offensive the morale of the German attacking forces was as high as could be expected, and this compensated for comparative weakness in weapons and in armour and manpower. After the defeat, we could not go on fighting at all.

WILLY FELDHEIM
Hitler Youth

I was a member of the Hitler Youth and in 1945 I was fifteen years old. As the Russians came through Poland to the border I felt I had to do something because the Russians are coming and this is my homeland. And so I went back to the military training camp and there, after maybe two weeks, came a commission of Army and SS and asked for Hitler Youths to form a special force anti-tank brigade and we would shoot tanks with a kind of bazooka, a small one. Mostly we had to go backwards, we had to go back and then we came in the Berlin area. It was early in the morning and we had to hold this area of very small gardens and wooden houses, we had to defend this line. I had the right corner with three other guys and had to go back to my battalion chief for some ammunition and I was very close to the wooden house and about thirty or forty metres from the street and I hear a very, very big noise and four Russian tanks were coming with Russian infantry on top. I saw some of our young boys, they jumped out of their holes and they were shooting to the tanks and destroyed one of the tanks, and others were shooting with their guns and killed all the Russian soldiers. And the Russians must have been in a sweet factory because they had all their arms full of sweets and chocolates. They were falling on the street and all the little boys – because everybody in our unit was fifteen or sixteen – they were running on to the street for the chocolate and the sweets.

MAJOR GENERAL SIEGFRIED WESTPHAL
Chief of Staff to Commander in Chief West
The German soldier was exhausted, he had only one desire, to end the war, but he was willing to fight further on because to cover the rear of the Eastern Front.

DR STEPHEN AMBROSE
American historian
There was a great celebration at Torgau where they met, dancing and embracing, exchanging of gifts – very happy times. The United States during the war had been propagandised into seeing Russia as a democracy, a land of freedom-lovers with essentially broad social aims about the same as those of the West, which seemed to make sense since they were clearly an enemy of the Nazis and we were an enemy of the Nazis, thus it appeared we had a great deal in common. The leaders, especially the British leaders, and most especially Churchill, never agreed with this view, but this was the view of most of the ordinary soldiers and the citizenry of the United States. I don't know how people felt in Britain about the Russians during the war, but in the United States we had the attitude that it would be quite possible to get along with the Russians after the war in the creation of a better world. The vacuum in central Europe had been filled by Russia and American and, to a certain extent, British troops, and we could now decide the fate of Europe, create a Europe that would no longer disturb the peace but which would be dedicated to democracy and material progress, a better life for everyone.

SECOND LIEUTENANT WILLIAM ROBERTSON
US Army
Everybody was very happy and a good deal of celebration was going on right at the river bank. There must have been a platoon of Russian troops came forward; they had schnapps and we toasted each other's success, we toasted everybody else's success. The Russians were overjoyed, we also; there was handshaking and back-slapping and exchange of souvenirs.

I have a Russian watch and somebody else's wedding band and I lost my watch, I lost all sorts of insignia from my uniform. I have a Russian cap ornament as well, a lot of this. The Russians were fascinated – by this time they'd gone across to the west side of the Elbe, wandering through the town – they were fascinated with the Jeep. They would commandeer vehicles as they were going so they had a motley type of equipment, and they were very interested in the Jeep, so at that point we thought it would be best to take some of them back with us to establish a meeting at noon the next day for our regimental and divisional commanders to meet.

GENERAL ANTONOV

We were full of feelings. Our first feelings were ones of vexation for the German people. We saw destroyed towns, destroyed streets, squares, white flags in the windows, we thought how awful a disgrace and tragedy the Fascists had inflicted on the German people. We walked and thought about the unhappiness the Soviet people had delivered us from, having defeated the Fascist Germany under the leadership of the Leninist Communist Party. On 9th May in the sports area of Treptow Park the Commanders of the Corps took part in the victory demonstration. After all we had suffered in the preceding four years, it is written in detail in my memoirs. It is a good thing that people write down in books what they suffered at the hands of the Fascist aggression.

DR AMBROSE

The war ends on 8th May and within two months the Soviets gave up more than two-thirds of the city to the British and Americans and of course gave up a part of the city to the French. So the first thing they did was to live up to their agreement that Berlin would be a tripartite occupation and, eventually, four powers. I think the thing that stands out was that the Russians lived up to their agreement to let the West into Berlin after they had paid the price in blood for capturing it. Most estimates are a hundred thousand casualties to take the city. The Americans hadn't gone as far into the zones that had been assigned to the Russians as the Russians had come into zones assigned to the West. The Russians had to do more pulling back than the West did. Eisenhower at the very end of the war refused Churchill, who wanted 'to shake hands with the Russians as far into the east as possible' in order to use territory that was taken in Germany and that was already assigned to the Russians for trading purposes.

CHAPTER 17

STRATEGIC BOMBING: ROYAL AIR FORCE

Britain's part in the bombing campaign against Germany was a product of strategic thinking dating back to the First World War. It became the only way of striking back at Germany after the Fall of France, and area bombing was repeatedly endorsed not only by the Chief of the Air Staff Sir Charles Portal and Prime Minister Winston Churchill, but by the Anglo-American Joint Chiefs of Staff. It was not, then, the independent creation of its most active protagonist, Air Chief Marshal Sir Arthur 'Bomber' Harris of the RAF's Bomber Command. Remarkably, some of the most vocal critics of Bomber Command clamoured for a premature invasion of Europe, even though as Albert Speer observes in the following pages – and as Stalin himself acknowledged – the bombing campaign constituted, in itself, a Second Front. It was brave of The World at War *series to challenge the pious assumptions that held almost unchallenged sway in the 1960s, but as late as 1992, when a statue of Harris was unveiled outside the RAF's church, St Clement Danes in London, it had to be placed under twenty-four-hour guard to protect it from vandalism. I met Sir Arthur near the end of his life and it struck me then, and remains my conviction today, that he was the victim of the same sort of sleight of hand by which the political elite diverted blame for the shocking losses of the First World War on to Field Marshal Haig and his generals. It is grotesque to blame service personnel compelled to redeem the errors of politicians for the casualties they incur and inflict. One may also fairly wonder about the ethics of those who only voiced objections to the bombing campaign once it finally began to kill more Germans than it did Commonwealth aircrew, and who so strongly advocated as an alternative the sacrifice of countless Allied lives in a premature invasion of Europe.*

AIR CHIEF MARSHAL SIR ARTHUR HARRIS
Commander-in-Chief of RAF Bomber Command
Night bombing was necessary because we had no armament that could face up to fighters in daylight, we only had the .303 machine guns. You can't really put a .303 machine gun against fighter cannon, which is the sort of thing that the Germans learned in the Battle of Britain.

GROUP CAPTAIN 'HAMISH' MAHADDIE
RAF Bomber Command Pathfinder Force
We started with a very small, compact Air Force of quite experienced people – but experienced in the basic flying sense, not to any degree in wartime flying. So we had to learn from the very first day and this was a very expensive business in aircrew and aircraft.

AIR CHIEF MARSHAL HARRIS
There was hardly any Bomber Command to be efficient at that time. They had few aircraft, they had no navigational aids at all and if you try to be with no navigational aids in daylight it's a bit difficult, but in the darkness it's impossible. The first of the navigational aids arrived just after I got to Bomber Command. What had happened before then was no surprise to me at all, it wouldn't have surprised anybody who's ever flown an aeroplane in the dark or in the daylight. People talk a lot about picking out targets and bombing them, individual small targets – in the European climate? I've come to the conclusion that people who say that sort of thing not only have never been outside, but they've never looked out of a window. We've had in the past two months a very nice mild English winter – how many occasions, looking out of the window or walking out in the garden, could you see up to eighteen to twenty thousand feet? Maybe on two or three days at the most. On how many occasions can you guarantee that you could see down through it, four or five hundred miles away in the other end of Europe? That was the

situation – there was no possibility of hitting individual targets consistently until we'd got the navigational, electronic aids that would show those targets up in the dark or through clouds.

MAJOR WILHELM HERGET
German fighter ace with 58 night kills
I did night-fighting from January 1942 and in the beginning you came very often during the full moon and during moonlit times. And that was bad because when the moon was there we could easily see the bomber but the bomber could see us exactly as easily. You had to know what you were attacking, that it was a bomber and not another Messerschmitt or a Junkers 88. I followed a Ju 88 for twenty minutes thinking it was a Lancaster and got very close before I saw it was a Ju 88. I saw underneath only four exhaust flames and thought, Ah, four motors. Nearly a terrible mistake, but that's how it was.

GROUP CAPTAIN MAHADDIE
In the first bombing year, into 1940, three bombs in every hundred got within five miles of the aiming point but not very much more. It wasn't very much better for the next two years until it was quite obvious that we could not find German targets in the face of increased German opposition and all the devices that the Germans had invented by that time. So we had to have a very highly professional look at the method of navigating to the target, then identifying the target and then leaving the load that was carried on the target.

AIR CHIEF MARSHAL HARRIS
People easily forget the fact that for over a third of the year we could hardly get in Germany at all because there wasn't any darkness that would take you any further than the German north coast. So if you started on a system of targets you find yourself confronted by these very short summer nights, you can't get to the far distant ones. If you succeed in knocking five out of six, and the sixth one is a very important one, you spend the whole of your time standing by to try and get a favourable opportunity to

get at the sixth one, then the nights got too short again, all the first five that you got at would be rebuilt and you had to start all over again.

ALBERT SPEER

Hitler's Armaments Minister

In some way the most important mistake was to get us accustomed from attack to attack to the heavier bombing. If there would have been a longer time between raids and you would have done with one stroke, very heavy bombing, then possibly the result on our morale would have been heavier.

AIR CHIEF MARSHAL HARRIS

I never engaged in these idiotic pamphlet-dropping exercises. They only served two purposes really – they gave the German defences endless practice in getting ready for it, and apart from that they supplied a considerable quantity of toilet paper to the Germans.

GROUP CAPTAIN MAHADDIE

At the time the Chiefs of Staff were almost committed to carving up Bomber Command as we knew it. It wasn't a very big force, just a few hundred aircraft, but the majority of the aircraft were obviously destined for the Navy through Coastal Command and the majority of the remainder would have gone to the Middle East. Harris devised this 'Thousand Plan' – he scraped up a thousand aircraft, not only from his command but he begged and borrowed them from every command, and he was able to demonstrate with that one raid on Cologne how valuable strategic bombing could be to the war effort.*

MAJOR HERGET

About your British pilots – I really can say they were more than brave, and what they did in reality helped you win the war. Once when they won the

---

* The first thousand-bomber raid, on Cologne, took place on 30–31 May 1942. Bomber Command itself only achieved a front-line strength of 1,000 bombers in June 1944.

Battle of Britain, when only the pilots of the Spitfires and the Hurricanes were defending their country, and the next time the bombing campaign because they were destroying in the night, which was very harmful because the people couldn't sleep. The difficulty in what you had to do at first was starting as early as possible, flying one after another – we had it very easy, we could just shoot down one after another. So you made the bomber stream shorter – in twenty minutes they were gone.

AIR CHIEF MARSHAL HARRIS

There was no greater risk than putting up a thousand than there was in putting up twenty or thirty, except the proportion of casualties would probably be less, and that proved to be the case. I was trying to show them what could be achieved with something approaching an adequate force, and that it would be achieved without abnormal casualties. Actually the casualties turned out precisely the same as my operation-research people said would occur, and they were considerably lower than anybody else expected. The risk would be heavier sending over fewer machines for the defences to compete with. One of the main ideas of sending over the bigger attack was to overwhelm the defences, and that's exactly what occurred.

FRAU CHANTRAIN

Cologne Red Cross

When the sirens sounded everyone went into air-raid shelters and it was a short attack. The sirens sounded about ten o'clock and in half an hour Cologne lay practically in ruins – I came out of the air-raid shelter and Cologne was a wall of flames. I tried to get to my station but it was very difficult to reach it because Cologne was built with pretty narrow streets and the balconies were on fire and falling in the streets. The digging parties hauled the dead people out and laid them at the side of the road. Those who had been killed by high-explosive bombs were propped up, their skin was a grey, pallid colour and their hair stood off their heads like wire nails. And of those who had died of incendiaries you could only find bits of bone, which were gathered up in washtubs, big zinc baths. The cruellest thing was when you had a friend in these houses; you saw the bones lying there or you knew they were underneath. That was unbelievably horrible. Mothers came to me who had themselves very severe burns who were scarcely capable of life, with their children in their arms, and begged for help. We saw it was pointless – the children were beyond help. The soldiers on leave from the front came and asked after their relatives and you had to tell them they are dead – your wife is dead, your children are dead, your grandparents are dead.

ALBERT SPEER

We really didn't expect in 1942 such a heavy raid would take place. We were only used to smaller attacks and when I got the news that about thousand bombers were attacking Cologne it was incredible for us, but it was accepted afterwards and we tried to convince Göring who didn't want to believe it. In Cologne the morale of the people was not shattered too much, it was more like shock, a shock which passed away.

GROUP CAPTAIN MAHADDIE

If you couldn't get the German worker in his factory it was just as easy to knock him off in his bed, and if his old Granny on the seat by the door got the chop that's hard luck, it doesn't bother me in the least. I'll tell you what bothers me a lot more, which is four or five million Jews that were pushed into gas ovens. Something that also affected me and lasted me throughout the war was Rotterdam, an undefended town that burned for ten days and was the first route marker that Bomber Command ever used. You'd see those fires from the Humber, or you saw them from the Wash, and that was a pretty terrific thing to watch a city burn for a week.

AIR CHIEF MARSHAL HARRIS

My interpretation of Point Blank* was to bomb individual targets when we could find them, and hit them. It was to give first priority to the

---

* Directive issued by the Joint Chiefs of Staff in June 1943 'to accomplish the progressive dislocation and disruption of the German military, industrial and economic system and the undermining of the German people'.

requirements of the Army. Area bombing very often took place because we were trying to find some particular targets and the Americans themselves would be the first to admit that very often their bombing was area bombing. I contend that we did just about as much accurate pin-point bombing when we could, when conditions served, when the navigational aids were there to make it possible, just as much as the Americans did.

ALBERT SPEER

I know that there is much argument about this question of bombing was a good or bad. One can't overestimate the results of the bombing attacks enough, because what is always forgotten is that we were forced to build up a strong defence and all these anti-aircraft guns which were stationed in every town, because we never knew what town would be the next. We had all the ammunition stocked there for a heavy air attack of several hours: they had to shoot for several hours, and not run out of ammunition. But apart from that, the damage done was diminishing my production I should say by twenty or thirty per cent and that much more output of tanks or ammunition and of U-boats and so on, of course, would have been, for you, quite visible counter action.

AIR CHIEF MARSHAL HARRIS

The majority of people in this country were only too glad to see Germany get a dose of what she'd been handing out to everybody else, hoping she would get away with it. Obviously you always get some people that object to anything. After all a lot of people, including myself, have the strongest objection to war. People talk about morality and war – tell me some action of war that is moral? People say you mustn't do anything to civilians – good Lord, what's happened to civilians in every besieged city of the past? Haven't they always been starved to surrender and bombarded into surrender? What's the difference between bombarding them with guns and bombarding the cities where they're manufacturing the weapons and ammunition?

GROUP CAPTAIN MAHADDIE

Before we had H2S [ground-mapping radar first used in January 1943] we had extremely good navigators, selected navigators, and this was the essence of the whole Pathfinder thing. These navigators were able to get much closer to the aiming point than we had previously. Then we laid great lanes of flares, hundreds of flares, and even if we missed the aiming point we could identify some very positive feature on the ground like a lake or a bend in the river, and from there we could creep on to the target and put flares down, different-coloured flares. Then later on we got target indicators and they fell to the ground looking just like a bunch of grapes or a chandelier. The Germans called them Christmas trees.

ALBERT SPEER

I was often on the flak tower to see the air raids and the most impressive was perhaps the helplessness you felt that all the anti-aircraft guns which were shooting didn't reach the planes. The planes you could see in the searchlight, but they followed the raid undisturbed and then you saw what we called the Christmas trees that was the sign of the Pathfinders and then you saw the blast of bombs very far away and you knew then that there had been something disastrous to us.

AIR CHIEF MARSHAL HARRIS

The effectiveness of the first Hamburg raid was due to at last getting permission to use something we'd had in the bag for a long time, which was known as 'window' – the dropping of clouds of aluminium paper strips, which completely upset not only the German location apparatus but also their gun-aiming apparatus. Later on in the war, we had a similar argument trying to get the magnetron valve released to us. We could have done much better if we'd had it released much earlier, but we got it in the end. That was an essential aid to bombing small targets under the weather conditions which normally prevailed. There's always reluctance, and very wrongly placed I think, on the grounds that if you spring a surprise on the enemy he may make one himself and come back at you with it. War isn't done that way. If you've got something that's a surprise, use it before the other fellow's learned how to, because you can be quite certain that if you're being very clever over some electronic gadget, the enemy are not such fools that they are not probably on the same lines and likely to have the same thing or something even better coming up in the lift shortly.*

BEN WITTER
Hamburg journalist

I was standing in my house and looked for a moment through the window. I heard no sirens but it was no longer night, it was light as day and as I saw this the first bombs began and I took my parents into our cellar, which was not reinforced and it seemed as though its walls were moving all the time. When we didn't hear any more bomb explosions I climbed up the stairs of the cellar and found that the roof was on fire and with the help of other people put it out. Then I went on my bicycle to the editorial office and couldn't see anything because the daylight which the so-called Christmas trees had created was over and it was night again and there were clouds of smoke. The next day people made a pilgrimage to this part of the city and were very curious. They thought it was the heaviest attack but then came even heavier attacks. I didn't go on my bicycle again but by car and I saw people running away, they were burning like torches and our car was jolting over dead people. Because of the heat the bodies had shrunk and we thought they were children, but they were adults. This attack was concentrated on an area where many working men lived but which also contained a lot of factories. The whole area was crossed by canals and most of the people tried to leap down into them but the water was on fire. It was burning because very many small ships had exploded and oil had been released into the water and people who were themselves on fire jumped into it. Some kind of chemical must have been in it because they burned, swam, burned and went under.

---

* Between 24–25 July and 2–3 August 1943 Bomber Command mounted four major raids on Hamburg. More than 40,000 were killed and more than a million survivors fled the city.

ALBERT SPEER

The population after heavy attacks like Hamburg were extremely shocked, but the shock is not going above a certain degree. I think this degree is overridden by events, when people can't take any more they're just getting numb, there's no more psychological reaction, and when I was seeing them going through the streets in the morning to work they were going like ghosts, they looked terribly bad but in some way like automata they went there. I had this experience mainly in the Ruhr valley where almost every night there were bombing alarms for weeks and weeks and only when it was pouring rain they maybe had one night's sleep. But work went on there in spite of that, morale was still there. But one can't say it was morale – it was German.

MAJOR HERGET

Colonel Hajo Herrmann had the idea of using bomber pilots on Messerschmitt 109s to fly at night because they knew about instrument flying, but a bomber pilot is not a fighter pilot and when he is looking mainly at his instruments he is not looking outside. We were fighters, we were looking outside the whole time. The instruments even in the night-time didn't interest me. I watched them when I was starting and when I was landing, but during the whole flight only to see if I was flying in the right direction. 'Wild Boar' was good if the weather was good but it was wrong to order them to fly in the 109s when the weather was bad, when they were landing in the wrong place or they jumped out. They jumped because they didn't know where they were or they didn't know how deep the clouds were. Very many pilots died because they didn't jump.*

FLIGHT LIEUTENANT WILLIAM REID, VC
61 Squadron Bomber Command, night of 3 November 1943
Although I was hit in the shoulder it just felt like a numbness, you know, hit with a hammer and not painful or anything. I didn't see any sense in

---

* Wild Boar, a response to the Hamburg raids, involved German fighters attacking by the light of burning cities or flares dropped by higher-flying aircraft. It was abandoned by the end of the 1943.

saying I was wounded in case they all thought, He'll pop off any minute now. We flew on again and set the same course but I had no windscreen in front. In some ways this was lucky because my head had been cut up above the helmet and it was bleeding pretty badly, but the cold air coming in – it was minus twenty-eight degrees – froze it up, made it chill up quickly, so it stopped bleeding. I thought it was flak but the rear gunner said, 'Oh, no, it was an Me 110,' and I thought at the time, You should really have said right away. Well, the next time it was again just as startling and trying evasive action we probably lost about another two thousand feet and we couldn't talk because the intercom was shot away. There were some shells going off which I found out later had gone right down the plane and made quite a number of holes in the plane and they hit the magnetic compass and the giro compass. The trimming tabs had been shot off the plane and this meant that you had to hold the stick right back. Well, because my shoulder was wounded this arm was pretty weak and the engineer held it with his other uninjured hand and so we combined to keep the plane straight and level.

WYNFORD VAUGHAN-THOMAS
BBC radio reporter, Berlin raid 3 September 1943
The night comes down and suddenly you take off and in the dusk you go tearing down the runway and you rise and slowly you circle. You still have your riding lights on and far off in the distance a single searchlight guiding you, moving back and forth, and you look behind you and the sky is full of fire coming up to join you. Aircraft rendezvousing in the sky and then the flood started to pour out away into this mystery of Europe. From there on all lighting went out and you could see back in the night sky, rising and falling behind you, the wings of other Lancasters. You got nearer and nearer the searchlight screen right along the Dutch coast and suddenly you were among it. In those days nineteen thousand feet was terrific; we were wearing oxygen masks and as we had on board a four thousand-pound bomb we couldn't get much higher and so you had to go in among these waving searchlights. And honestly I felt like a shrimp moving among luminous seaweed, and up the beams came pumping the flak.

MAJOR HERGET

I saw the bomber very late and I tried to attack, but I was much too quick. I had about double the speed and could only dive and go underneath and then – how to brake without brakes? You had to wait until the plane came along again and I had to fly so slow until the Handley Page could overtake me that I nearly could not handle my Me 110 any more. Then I saw the Handley Page and I was more than surprised when I saw something like a big cannon coming out from underneath and it was pointing at me, so I thought they must have seen me and now I must shoot as quickly as possible. This I did and then the plane exploded because it was full of bombs and then I fell from six thousand five hundred metres and I nearly had to jump out of my plane because I was spinning around all the time. I said to my navigator, 'If we pass two thousand metres then we jump out. I'll tell you, I'll give the order.' We had just passed the two thousand-metre mark on the altimeter when the plane went into a vertical dive and I took the stick and tried to get it out of the dive by force. In the meantime the moon came out and I saw already the tops of the trees when I was able to pull out and climb again. If you have to leave the Messerschmitt by parachute there are two tails, which is difficult if you are spinning. I know very many pilots who have lost an arm, a leg or were dead from hitting the tail. So I was very happy to be still alive and after that I was telling all my pilots never, never to attack the bombs in the body – shoot in the motor.

WYNFORD VAUGHAN-THOMAS

You look and behind you could see the whole sky clearing and a mass of black specks following you. Ahead, in a bullring of light, you could see the whole of the Berlin searchlights and again this awful moment when you crawled in among them, the whole thing was a light nightmare, there were tracer bullets going past you, there was flak coming up and we were dropping the big cookie and the ritual took over. You could hear the captain chanting, 'Steady,' and then of course, 'Bombs away.' You followed it down, it was as if honestly a jewel had been thrown on black velvet, it sparkled, it shone. The whole of Berlin looked the most beautiful dazzling sight you ever saw until you realised this was civilisation burning below you. And in that moment, a slow East Anglian voice came on the intercom saying, 'Fighter attacking, sir.' The whole aircraft seemed to be filled with fumes and the captain calmed the whole thing down, the heroism of coolness. The East Anglian rear gunner had it absolutely taped and the captain held the whole crew together. You saw the tracer of bullets drop right below the nose and another burst of gunfire and the cool voice saying, 'Night-fighter shot down.' Everybody shouted, 'Isn't he lovely, there he goes,' and he went down like a burning piece of oily waste rag and my eye went lower down and it fell into this festering mess below, and suddenly the other side of the bullring came up, cloud came round again and I realised I'd been through Berlin.

ALBERT SPEER

I don't know how much, how strong you would have been if you could succeed really in destroying Berlin, which is a large area, much larger than any other town in Germany. Theoretically if you would have succeeded in destroying Berlin as you did with Hamburg it would have been disastrous for Germany, I think that is certain. Berlin did suffer heavy raids but this was like bombing several towns, because I was in Berlin at this time: if you had a bombing on one part of Berlin the other part was not involved, the distance was too large.

AIR CHIEF MARSHAL HARRIS

The casualties in the Battle of Berlin were no more than we would have suffered if we'd gone anywhere else in Germany. People seem to forget that Bomber Command fought a thousand battles during the war and you can't succeed in every one. I'm not saying the Battle of Berlin was a defeat or anything like a defeat – I think it was a major contribution towards the defeat of Germany. After all we didn't like when six hundred acres of London went up the spout – six thousand acres of Berlin went up, and Berlin's a much smaller city than London.*

---

* The 'Battle of Berlin' ran from November 1943 to March 1944, when Bomber Command came under the command of General Eisenhower in preparation for D-Day.

PILOT OFFICER NOBLE FRANKLAND
RAF Bomber Command

The people I fought with in the war were in my view all heroes: they were tremendous believers in what we were trying to do. There was an amazing spirit of dedication to the task in hand; this was very moving and a tremendous inspiration. Whose idea it was you can never trace, but it was a sort of infection, and this applied to people who came from all over the world, and Bomber Command was an extraordinarily cosmopolitan sort of command. By the time I was in it about forty per cent of it came from overseas, mostly from New Zealand, Australia and Canada, but also from many other countries, and not all British. There were lots of Czechs and Poles serving in Bomber Command and the spirit of dedication was moving.

GROUP CAPTAIN MAHADDIE

Despite the fact that Harris didn't come and see us and hand out cigarettes or anything else, he sent the most amazing signals. One I'll always remember, and this was something you read out to your crews at briefing, this one said, 'Tonight you go to the big city' – that's Berlin – 'you have the opportunity to light a fire in the belly of the enemy and burn his black heart out.' Well, after the crews stopped cheering a thing like that they didn't want aircraft. Just fill their pockets with bombs and point them towards Berlin and they'd take off on their own.

AIR CHIEF MARSHAL HARRIS

There were high losses on one occasion, on a Nuremberg raid, but on other occasions the losses were not more than we expected, everybody expected, including the crews themselves. And they were the sort of losses that the ground forces had put up with in the first war, and the only reason they didn't have to put up with [them] in the second war [was] because of the bombing of Germany and the tactical bombing in front of them. And if you want confirmation of that ask General Montgomery – he knows. The boys we had were the pick of the litter and they were just full of guts and they deserved credit for what they did, and they get precious little credit for it.*

ALBERT SPEER

Hitler's reaction to the bombing was typical for him, he always wanted to see somebody else is responsible for a failure and not him, and so in this case it was Göring who was responsible. And more, he really started to attack Göring for the failure of the air defence and I was sometimes present when he really shouted at him and was telling him that it's disastrous how he failed. But of course Göring was not so responsible. Of course the output of our industry was at its highest peak in July 1944 but that was due to the steel reserve and then the output topped and in September/October we were at the end of everything. I wrote several memorandums to Hitler in which he was told we can't continue any more. He usually said, 'You will do it' and 'I think it's not as bad as that' and 'We had many situations before which were very catastrophic and we pulled through, we will pull through this situation too.'

GROUP CAPTAIN MAHADDIE

My own interpretation of weaving was very slight. I liked to let my gunners get a good look but I didn't like to get too far off course. I just banked slightly to give the gunners a good view underneath; I moved off maybe ten degrees to port or starboard during this manoeuvre. The corkscrew was much more violent. I was discussing this with Willy Herget in Germany recently and this did put the night-fighters off because you made a very violent manoeuvre, activated by the gunner himself. If he saw a fighter closing in he immediately said, 'Corkscrew port' or 'Corkscrew starboard' and then you threw the aircraft into a quite violent corkscrew manoeuvre. Just imagine you're following round a quarter of a mile radius tunnel and you went down and then up and followed the corkscrew motion right around until you lost the fighter.

---

* Ninety-five of 795 bombers were lost during the Nuremberg raid of 30–31 March 1944.

MAJOR HERGET

Usually I only had two successes in one night and then I landed, but that night I was in the middle of the bomber stream, I was flying through the propeller wash and my plane was shaking and so I dived on the first plane in front, the next to the right, the next to the left. I was shooting between the two motors, it was a Lancaster, and to the left another Lancaster, I shot again between two motors, only a short time, sometimes I needed only four to eight bullets until the plane was burning. I had five successes against aircraft with bombs on the way to Frankfurt and now on the way back I found another three. The last one was the hardest because the Lancaster saw me because I came from the direction of Frankfurt, which was one big fire. I came from right underneath and was firing in the body until it crashed to earth. At that time I was thirty-three years of age and I was not able to climb out by myself, to get out of the plane. They had to lift me out.*

FLIGHT LIEUTENANT WILLIAM REID, VC

617 Squadron, July 1944

There was a tremendous noise and this stick of bombs came down through us from above. One of the bombs went through the port wing and the engine started to fall off and then another bomb must have gone between the cabin and the mid-upper gunner because it severed the controls. The rudders went sloppy and I shouted, 'Stand by to bail out' and then, 'Bail out' and the plane started to fall. Chunky Stewart, my engineer, handed me my parachute and then he took his own and headed into the front bay to bale out. You just open the hatch and drop out. By this time it was spinning down and this tremendous noise of engines getting faster and faster and I couldn't get out of my seat. I tried to open the side window, although the props are quite close to you there, but I couldn't get out of there either and then I forced the stick forward and got out of my seat and I remembered the dinghy escape hatch which is above the pilot, behind, and as I turned the handle in the dinghy escape hatch the whole nose must have come off because the next thing it was quietness and I was falling through the air.

---

* Herget's unique eight kills in one night took place on 20–21 December 1943.

STRATEGIC BOMBING: ROYAL AIR FORCE

MAJOR HERGET

I was shot down in the night of 14–15 June 1944 by a Mosquito, burning, sitting three minutes in the burning Ju 88 and not being able to jump out. If you're sitting in a burning plane it's a horrible feeling and I was praying to the Lord and asked him if this was my last minute. Then a voice said to me, 'If you believe, no' and in the same second my mechanic could open the door to the ground in the Ju 88 and we could all jump out.

AIR CHIEF MARSHAL HARRIS

What we've always claimed in the service was that we had asked originally for a first line of four thousand, with which we could knock out Germany. When we got down to the real bomber offensive it really only lasted for a year, with one quarter of that number. I know people say today, 'Bombing will never achieve what people will claim for it.' There was a long period in the peace when the people went about saying bombing can never sink a battleship – look what happened to battleships, what did any of them do except sink under air attack? They said bombing could never win a war – well, two bombs defeated Japan. It's quite true they were atom bombs but the atom bomb is only the equivalent.

URSULA GRAY

Dresden resident, post-war wife of author J Glenn Gray
The only idea was to get out in an open space and our house was situated close to a beautiful area called The Great Garden, which had lovely old oak trees, three hundred years old, and beautiful little pavilions. By that time already there were buildings falling apart and you had to make your way over stones and rubble and killed people and you just didn't care – you stepped on whatever you could just to get out and away from it all. Many other people already had gathered. They had the same idea, to get away from the burning houses, from that ocean of fire and bombing, and huddled up under the trees. While we were sitting there they sent bombs which kind of illuminated the city in red and green and for a moment it was a very strange picture. I will never forget it: it looked like the windows of a cathedral. After this raid was over the city was just an ocean of fire,

thousands and thousands of people killed, killed right beside us, around us, and screams and smells. The most gruesome picture was the nakedness of the people killed by the bombing: the tornado or the air pressure of the bombs had apparently torn their clothes to shreds.

AIR CHIEF MARSHAL HARRIS

It could have been more effective if we'd had the number we'd always asked for doing the job, and if we hadn't had so many diversions. But the diversions up to a point were necessary – everything in the aid of the armies was first priority and very rightly so. I'm quite sure of one thing, with the lesson of Japan in mind, it could have been fairly simple to knock Germany out without an invading force. Whether that would have been the proper thing to do in those circumstances I don't know, because maybe the result would have been that the Russians would have finished up sunning themselves on the beaches of Spain and Portugal.

CHAPTER 18

THE HOLOCAUST

The mass murder of Jews – and of Jehovah's Witnesses, Freemasons, itinerant gypsies, homosexuals and other 'undesirables' – began with the deprivation, disease and brutality of the ghettos of eastern Europe and slave labour camps like Dachau, Sachsenhausen-Oranienburg, Bergen-Belsen and Buchenwald. In addition, more than a million Jews, together with non-Jewish Polish intellectuals and Soviet Communist officials, were massacred by mobile killing squads (Einsatzgruppen). What distinguished Nazi genocide from the Japanese and the Soviet equivalents was the industrialised slaughter known as 'The Final Solution', ordered by Hitler in December 1941 and organised at a conference of senior Nazi administrators held at the Wannsee Villa in Berlin on 20 January 1942. Following the Wannsee conference the remaining ghettos in eastern Europe were wiped out by mass executions and deportations while some nations allied to, or occupied by, the Germans also deported their Jewish citizens. Many thousands died of suffocation and thirst in trains taking them to the new extermination camps, all in Poland. The ultimate death factory was at Auschwitz-Birkenau, where four gas chambers could take two thousand people each compared to the ten chambers holding two hundred each at the next worst camp, Treblinka. The interviews conducted by The World at War *team included the bitter testimony of the Slovak Rudolf Vrba, one of only five men to escape from Auschwitz, and the self-criticism of the Italian Primo Levi, who finally could not bear to continue living with his survivor guilt. There is a kernel of foul truth in Josef Stalin's aphorism that one death is a tragedy, a million a statistic, and the jolting memoirs in the following pages seek to keep the matter personal. At a time when the fate of Germany hung in the balance, the Nazis devoted*

enormous resources and ingenuity to killing millions of helpless people who
posed no military, political or economic threat whatever, and they continued
doing so until the last days of the war. You cannot read what follows and
doubt the fundamental evilness of Hitler's regime.

ALBERT SPEER
Hitler's Armaments Minister
Hitler often mentioned his hating the Jews and he gave many examples already in the early time when I was with him. And I should have been warned that he is serious about it because he proved to be serious about other things he predicted too, for instance when he was trying to be the superior nation in Europe. I can't say that I neglected it, it's more or less cowardice, it was just to avoid something which is coming up to me, which would force me to make decisions. And I was running away from my responsibility, which was now as a human being.

ANTHONY EDEN
British Foreign Secretary
There had been too much evidence of the persecution of the Jews before the war began in Hitlerite Germany and then as the war progressed some horrifying reports began to come out. At first it was very difficult to assess their accuracy and they were so horrible it was hard to believe they could be true. By the latter half of 1942 the evidence was so extensive that one could hardly fail to give credit and as a result of that we did get in touch with other governments, the United States in particular and the Russians, to exchange information and to discuss what we could do. We decided that one of the things we must do was to make a joint statement in each of our capitals at the same time declaring what our information was and what this horror was which was being perpetrated, and also make plain our detestation of it, and our determination that those responsible for it should be punished when the war was over.

SIGMUND WELTLINGER
Member of the Berlin Jewish Council set up by the Nazis
They were very friendly gentlemen who said, 'You are a Front Soldier, nothing much will happen to you. Perhaps you will be home again by this

evening but just in case take the most necessary things with you, your shaving things, washing things, whatever you need.' So I went with them and believed it too. But when I came to Sachsenhausen-Oranienburg camp outside Berlin I was immediately taught different. We were all shoved together with clubs and blows and had to stand in even ranks to be counted. Because I had been a soldier I didn't find that all very difficult but the others who didn't fall in quickly were beaten immediately. The most terrible thing was when somebody grabbed hold of a big, strong man and he said, 'Don't grab me.' The guard said, 'What, I shouldn't grab you?' and he gave him a blow and this man was immediately overpowered by three SS people. A block was brought and he was bound fast to it, and the camp commandant said he was sentenced to twenty-five lashes. Then a giant man came, an SS man with a huge ox-whip, and started to beat him. At first the man only groaned a bit but then he begged them to stop. The commandant said, 'What do you mean, stop? We'll start all over again from the beginning.' But after three more lashes the blood was spurting already and salt was rubbed in the wounds, or pepper – I don't know any more. The man was dragged away, unconscious or dead. We never saw him again.

HERTHA BEESE

Berlin housewife and Social Democrat

We knew that the concentration camps existed. We also knew where they existed, for example Oranienburg just outside Berlin. We sometimes knew which of our friends were there and we also knew of the cruelties in them right from the beginning. We heard what happened in those camps. I cannot say who the source of the information was, I can only say that one person passed it on to another and that we believed it to be true – I mean those of us in the Resistance. I don't think that the general population would have believed it all had they been told, or had they heard about it from somewhere. The camps were so cruel that one simply could not imagine that anybody could be so bestial if oneself was decent. We knew that lampshades were made from human skin, we knew that people starved to death and that newborn babies were hidden.

WYNFORD VAUGHAN-THOMAS

British journalist

One morning as they were being marched a Russian prisoner broke ranks and seized a pole and he ran to the electrified fence, and in a terrific effort, he leapt it. They were so astonished, it was the last thing they expected and they couldn't open fire. He got off into the forest and was lost for three days. But then with the use of dogs they roamed the whole countryside and they caught him and brought him back. They reported this to the SS. Himmler wouldn't believe it and they said, 'Right, come and see for yourself,' and they asked this chap would you repeat the jump and promised him his freedom. Hitler, the whole of the SS brass hats came to watch it, they re-staged it. They put him in the front, handed this man the pole and with a tremendous effort he cleared it. They took a film of it, photographed it and brought him back. Himmler shook him by the hand and then they took him out and shot him.

GRAND ADMIRAL KARL DÖNITZ

Commander-in-Chief of the German Navy

The biggest mistake of Hitler, I have to say the main fault, was that under his government these terrific exterminations of men happened, which went on behind the backs of the German nation, which would never have tolerated them, but the government kept these crimes completely secret from the German people. They were done through a small number of officials and primarily in the east outside Germany. There's no doubt that the German people knew almost nothing of the annihilation of the Jews. Such an action is not proper, human being could not imagine, that is why they could not have the slightest suspicion that such a thing could be done at all. I heard of these annihilations for the first time in the beginning of May 1945 in the American soldier's newspaper *Stars and Stripes*, which I had brought to me from the headquarters of Eisenhower. Immediately I demanded from Eisenhower that the highest German law court should prosecute these crimes, but Eisenhower did not answer my demands.

AVRAHAM KOCHAVI

Lodz ghetto and Auschwitz survivor

We ran out of food in the house and one day my mother, may her soul rest in peace, asked me to go down to the bakery and stand there the whole night in order to get a loaf of bread the next day. I got up in the middle of the night and went down to get into the queue. When I arrived there were already masses and masses of people standing in line. At dawn a Pole, who was *volksdeutsche* [ethnic German] arrived with a rifle slung over his right shoulder, a band with a swastika on his left arm. He was supposed to keep order so that everyone should receive bread. Among us there were children, non-Jews, Poles, running around. They dragged that same *volksdeutsche* over and pointed at each person saying, 'That's a Jew, that's a Jew – *Das Jude, das Jude, Jude*' – so that these people would be taken out of the line and not get bread. My turn came. I turned and saw that the boy was a friend with whom I played. I said to him in Polish, 'What are you doing?' His answer was, 'I am not your friend, you are a Jew, I don't know you.' That same German with the swastika band was standing before me. I saw that he was a neighbour of ours and I spoke to him in Polish. His answer was in German: 'I don't know Polish, I don't know you.' He forcefully took me out of the line where I was waiting for bread and slapped me.

RUDOLF VRBA

Jewish Slovak

The star was important because those in the general population who took the whole Jewish discrimination as a joke, suddenly when they were visiting, speaking to a Jew on the street, were subject to enquiries from the Fascist organisations, to be exposed perhaps as Jews, perhaps as people who are not aware of their national identity. And so a certain division between the Jews and the non-Jewish population because it was risky to speak with a Jew in the street, because he could be labelled as a plotter against the regime with the Jews, who's plotting against the new era free of Bolshevism and Anglo-American Jewry.

DR ROBERT KEMPNER

Member of the American prosecution team at Nuremberg

One thing I was missing – when did Hitler give the order to eliminate, or to liquidate, as he said, the Jews. Prosecutors have to have luck, that's the main thing. One day the team working on the Foreign Office files in Berlin sent me a whole batch of documents and the file had in the back the note: 'Final Solution of the Jewish Question'. One of my analysts read it and said to me, 'By God, now we have it,' and I said what do you think we have? We had discovered the organisation meeting for action how to kill the Jews and the Protocol about the Final Solution, which was called on 20th January 1942. All the men, the second men of the ministries, were assembled together with Gestapo boss SS Lieutenant General Reinhardt Heydrich with his, let's say, Executive Secretary SS Lieutenant Colonel Adolf Eichmann, who put the Protocol together. And there you could read that there were eleven million Jews in occupied Europe and that they had to go through with a fine-tooth comb from west to east, first to put them to labour and if they are no longer able to work, and I underline that, then they have to be liquidated. It is interesting to say that we discovered the Protocol not in time for the first big trial, only two or three years later when I prosecuted members of Hitler's cabinets and diplomats who participated and executed this programme. I put it into my desk so that others shouldn't see it right away, so that it should not become known before I had talked to all the living participants of this conference. Some said they were away, others said, 'I just went out of the room when this killing point was read,' and others said, 'I didn't hear anything, I can not remember.'

DR WILHELM HÖTTL

SS official in the Reich Security Main Office (RSHA)

I should like to describe Eichmann, so to speak, as a transporter of death, as a man with, basically, a small brain and an incredible organisational talent. He succeeded first of all in getting out the Jews who wanted to emigrate – two-thirds of the Austrian Jews were saved by this. And in exactly the same way he succeeded, later, once the extermination order was in force, to get the Jews into the extermination camps. And Himmler was in some ways an Eichmann type, perhaps on a somewhat larger scale. He did not have a great mind either, but he had exactly the same devilish organisational talent. Eichmann did everything he was ordered to do. He was possessed by carrying out his duty: he had a certain inferiority complex; he had not achieved much in his life before he was in the SS and wanted to show how clever and hard working he was. And that was the bad thing about him and to the same extent with Himmler, too, who after all as a poultry breeder on his chicken farm had not been at all successful and also wanted to show what a great chap he was.

ANTHONY EDEN

After some negotiation and near the end of 1942 I made this statement in the House of Commons, which I must say in dramatic effect far exceeded anything I had expected. It's a strange place, the House of Commons, you never quite know how it's going to react, but it was just exactly everything one could have prayed for. Jimmy Rothschild just got up and said simply, 'Mr Speaker, is there any way this House can express feelings unanimously about what we've been told?' And the Speaker, Algy Fitzroy, got up and said, 'It is for the House to rise if it wishes to express its feelings.' And the whole House got up. I remember Lloyd George coming to me afterwards and saying, 'In all my years in Parliament, I have never seen anything like this.'

AVRAHAM AVIEL

Polish–Jewish survivor of the Radun ghetto massacre, Poland, witness at the trial of Adolf Eichmann in 1961 – 7 May 1942
We were all brought close to the cemetery at a distance of eighty to a hundred metres from a long, deep pit. Once again everybody was made to kneel. There was no possibility of lifting one's head. I sat more or less in the centre of the town people. I looked in front of me and saw the long pit then maybe groups of twenty, thirty people led to the edge of the pit, undressed probably so that they should not take their valuables with them. They were brought to the edge of the pit where they were shot and fell into the pit, one on top of another. At the same time I saw that the group

of people that had dug the pit, about a hundred or less, were being taken out of the pit in the direction of the road, of the town. From afar I could make out the figure of my big brother and then, as if by a strong tie binding me to my brother, I decided to run to him. I hardly had a chance to say goodbye to my mother. She no longer held my hand, she no longer tried to keep me from going.

RIVKA YOSELEVSKA

Polish–Jewish survivor of the Hansovic ghetto massacre, Poland, witness at the trial of Adolf Eichmann in 1961 – August 1943

When we arrived at this place, we saw naked people standing there already, so we thought maybe they are being tormented, perhaps there was still hope we would remain alive. To get away was impossible. I was curious to see whether anybody was below that hill where the people had to stand and I made a quick turn. I saw three or four rows, twelve people already killed. My little daughter asked, 'Mother, why are you wearing your Sabbath dress, they are going to kill us.' Even when we stood near the ditch she said, 'What are we waiting for? Come let's escape.' Some of the younger ones tried to run away. They hardly managed a few steps, they were caught and shot. Then came our turn. It was difficult to hold the children, they were shaking. We took turns. Parents took the children, took other people's children. This was to help us to get through it all; to get it over with, and not see the children suffer. Mothers took leave of their children, the mothers, the parents. We were lined up in fours. We stood there naked. Our clothing was taken away. My father didn't want to undress completely and kept on his underwear. When he was lined up for the shooting and was told to undress, he refused; he was beaten. We begged him, 'Take off your clothes, enough of suffering.' No. He insisted on dying in his underwear. They tore his things off and shot him. Then they took mother. She didn't want to go, but wanted us to go first. Yet we made her go first. They grabbed her and shot her. There was my father's mother who was eighty with two grandchildren in her arms. My father's sister was also there. She, too, was shot with children in her arms. Then my turn came. My younger sister also. She had suffered so much in the ghetto, and yet at the last moment she wanted to stay alive, and begged the German to let her live. She was standing there naked holding on to her girl friend. So he looked at her and shot them both. Both of them fell, my sister and her girl friend. My other sister was next.

COLONEL KARL WOLFF
Waffen-SS, Himmler's Chief of Staff

At Minsk I was forced by Himmler to watch an execution of about a hundred partisans among whom were also a great number of Jews, because they were the couriers for the Resistance in this extraordinary partisan war. I said, 'It really is no business of mine, this is nothing to do with the Waffen-SS, it's a police affair,' and then he said, 'You are fortunate enough to be in the very closest circle, so as to speak at King Arthur's Round Table, you must also learn what we have to expect from our troops since we are now involved in a life and death struggle with such a brutal power. You must see this happening at least once.' Not to go into too many unnecessary details an open grave had been dug and into this these partisans, who had not even been condemned by a proper hearing but had merely been taken by numbers, they had to jump into this and lie face downwards, and sometimes when already two or three rows had been shot they had to lie in the people who were already shot and then they were shot from the edge of the grave by members of the ordinary police, not, of course, the SS. While he was looking on, Himmler had the deserved bad luck that from one or other who had been shot in the head he got a splash of brains on his coat and I think it also splashed into his face and he went very green and pale. He was not actually sick but he was heaving and turned around and swayed, and then I had to jump forward and hold him steady and I led him away from the grave. To the commander of this small action group, SS Major Brasdfisch, I said, 'It serves him right that happened to him. It's quite right that he should see what he is ordering his people to do.'*

---

* Wolff's words betray him: he states that the SS were not the executioners but then says the commander of the death squad was an SS officer.

AVRAHAM AVIEL

I began jumping over the heads of those sitting near me. I jumped and fell, jumped and fell. I didn't care what would happen. And so, I don't know how, by some miracle they didn't notice me. I managed to reach the edge of the road at the rim of the ditch. I lay down and was afraid to get up and continue lest they notice me. Standing near me at that moment was Zelig, the carpenter of the town. He was a skilled worker and worked for the Germans in the Gestapo. He held a special certificate providing that he had to remain alive, he and his family. Altogether there were ten such men who had certificates at that time. He was holding this certificate in his hand and wanted to take out his family whom he had noticed in the large group being led to their death. At that moment a German came up to him, and thrust a revolver in his neck. I heard a shot. He turned dark all over, and continued saying, 'I have a certificate.' The German fired another bullet into him and he fell down near me, half a metre away. I waited a little and then continued crawling back to the road. I succeeded in reaching the group which was part of those digging the pits. At that moment a German approached and asked me, 'Who are you, what are you doing here?' I had a certificate to the effect that I was a sort of locksmith. I said to him, 'I am a good locksmith, I am a blacksmith,' and he went away. I remained there, lying down. I went forward towards my brother and I joined him in this group. My mother was killed – she was shot together with all the other Jews in the pit. Only afterwards did I learn that I had been the only one who somehow managed to escape.

RIVKA YOSELEVSKA

Then he got ready to shoot me. We stood there facing the ditch. I turned my head. He asked, 'Whom do I shoot first?' I didn't answer. He tore the child away from me. I heard her last cry and he shot her. Then he got ready to kill me, grabbed my hair and turned my head about. I remained standing and heard a shot but I didn't move. He turned me around, loaded his pistol, so that I could see what he was doing. Then he again turned me around and shot me. I fell down. I felt nothing. At that moment I felt that something was weighing me down. I thought that I was dead, but that I could feel something even though I was dead. I couldn't believe that I was alive. I felt I was suffocating, bodies had fallen on me. I felt I was drowning. But still I could move and felt I was alive and tried to get up. I was choking, I heard shots, and again somebody falling down. I twisted and turned, but I could not. I felt I was going to suffocate. I had no strength left, but then I felt that somehow I was crawling upwards. As I climbed up, people grabbed me, dragged me downwards, but I pulled myself up with the last bit of strength. When I reached the top I looked around but I couldn't recognise the place. Corpses strewn all over, there was no end to the bodies. You could hear people moaning in their death agony. Some children were running around naked and screaming, 'Mama, Papa.' I couldn't get up. The Germans were not there. No one was there. I got out naked covered with blood from the corpses whose bellies had burst. I got to my feet to see that horrible scene. The screaming was unbearable, the children shouting; I ran over to the children, maybe my daughter was there. I called out 'Markele' – I didn't see her. I did not recognise the children either. All of them were covered with blood.

AVRAHAM AVIEL

We decided that we had nothing more to do in the ghetto. We could no longer look at the faces of those who had shot our dear ones. We couldn't look at the paths which were drenched in blood, and we resolved to escape from the ghetto. We hoped that perhaps father was still alive. We did not know whether he had succeeded in escaping or not. We wandered around, alone, in the forest for a few days, we managed to make contact, we learned that Father was alive and then we joined him. He had succeeded in fleeing from those who had to dig and who had revolted; they were fired upon and he managed to escape. At the time about seventeen persons, who had revolted and had succeeded in escaping, were saved. We went to establish the first contact with the partisans who were then beginning to organise themselves. The first operation the Jewish partisans carried out against the Gestapo was roughly two weeks after the slaughter, an operation by young Jews. They went out and, at a short distance from the pit, they laid an ambush for the gendarmerie which was in the village, for the Gestapo head of the town – if I am not mistaken he was called Kopke; they managed to wound and also to kill some of them.

RIVKA YOSELEVSKA

Further off I saw two women standing up. I walked over to them. I didn't know them and they didn't know me. We asked each other for our names. At the far end a woman shouted for help with outstretched arms and asked to be saved, to be pulled out from the corpses, she was suffocating. We walked up to her, Ita Rosenberg, and pulled her out of the mass of corpses who were pulling and dragging her down and biting her. She asked us to pull harder; we didn't have any strength left. We struggled all night long and all day screaming and shouting. Looking around, we saw Germans again and people with hoses and shovels. The Germans ordered the gentiles to pile all the corpses together in one place. So they did. A lot were still alive. The children were all running around in the field. As I was walking I saw them and went over to them. The children were running after me and wouldn't leave. I sat down in the field and remained there. The Germans came and helped round up the children. They left me alone. I just sat and looked. There was no need for much shooting at the children. They fired some shots and children fell down. The Rosenberg girl begged the Germans to let her live; they shot her, too. The local people went away. The Germans drove away. They left the truck with the belongings standing there overnight. When I saw they were gone I dragged myself over to the grave and wanted to jump in. I thought the grave would open up and let me fall inside alive. I envied everyone for whom it was already over, while I was still alive. Where should I go? What should I do? Blood was spouting. Nowadays, when I pass a water fountain I can still see the blood spouting from the grave. The earth rose and heaved. I sat there on the grave and tried to dig my way in with my hands. I continued digging as hard as I could. The earth didn't open up. I shouted to mother and father, why I was left alive. What did I do to deserve this? Where shall I go? To whom can I turn? I have nobody. I saw everything. I saw everybody killed. No one answered.

STEFAN SOLARCZYK

Polish resident in Auschwitz who took part in the construction of the camp

I was working on a locomotive on the narrow-gauge railway. They were moving large cobblestones and some SS surrounded the group. One of the SS picked up one of the stones and threw it into a prisoner's back. I saw him hit the prisoner's spine and his spine was twisted. The prisoner was lying on the ground motionless and he went up to him with a large pick handle which he laid on his neck, put one foot on one side and the other on the other. His legs twitched for a moment or two. There were also shootings. I was particularly struck by one SS man who had a boy from Krakow, he was his favourite: he let him go and bathe and go in the water during the summer. One day he just sort of began shooting live rounds at him. The boy swam off and he shot into the water near him and then hit him with the effect that he sank.

LANCE CORPORAL RICHARD BOCK

SS guard at Auschwitz-Birkenau

A block chief could even decide the life or death of a prisoner. I remember not just once but often when a Sonderkommando [prisoner work party] went past a block chief would call out to the kapo [prisoner trustee] very fiercely, 'Kapo, come here.' The kapo came over and – boom – he hit the kapo in the face so hard that he fell over, and was just about to put the boot in when the kapo got up very fast – if he was lucky. And then he said, 'Kapo, can't you beat them any better than that?' and the kapo ran off and grabbed a club and beat up the prisoner squad quite indiscriminately. 'Kapo, come over here,' he shouted again. The kapo came and he said, 'Finish them off,' and then he went off again and he finished the prisoners off, he beat them to death. Wherever you looked – beatings, blows and more blows. It was particularly bad at Auschwitz in 1941. Clubbed to death, clubbed to death wherever you looked. Today I would not condemn any kapo I knew. I often talked to kapos, and a kapo had to beat and club to save his own life.

DR KONRAD MORGEN

SS investigating magistrate

In Berlin they recognised that these were not individual cases but as they said in the higher SS circles, 'The whole area of the concentration camps is a pigsty.' It's wrong to think that a commandant could do as he pleased; it was quite the opposite: the prisoner should be treated strictly but justly. To torment people, harm them and harass them, to exploit them and then even kill them, that was not permitted, and every commandant when he entered the service had to sign the Führer-Command Number One and that read, 'Only the Führer and Reichschancellor shall decide the life of the enemy of the state'. That is why the top SS leadership was shocked and enraged by these abuses which I had exposed and they demanded punishment. So far nobody had succeeded in finding out anything really concrete in this area; it was so shrouded in secrecy that the police or law courts had been unable to see a way through. I heard one story about a district attorney in Dachau who dared to go into the concentration camp about the death of a prisoner and the camp commandant had ordered some hand-grenade practice very near the district attorney, and he got the point and stopped his investigations. But now an officer in uniform came with orders direct from Himmler personally, so they couldn't do anything against that. I got the job of investigating all big and punishable acts in concentration camps, and all the other police and legal authorities were instructed to hand all such cases over to me.

ALBERT SPEER

My view was a more technical one. I heard from my leading technicians that those people from the concentration camps was falling sick after a short while, and this was not possible for our production because when some workmen is falling sick, then the whole assembly line is disturbed and it needed six weeks or more to get him from apprentice really to the workman. In those six weeks was necessary another man, a skilled workman, to introduce him to his job and his time was lost too. So we objected and said it must be better nourishment and they must be treated better, they must have better housing and partly I think we succeeded. I read now that even Paul Hossler [Commandant at Auschwitz, then Belsen, hanged in 1945] gave orders from 1942 on for better nourishment of the concentration-camp inmates. When I visited the V-2 factory in the Harzburg mountains they were working in caves. I tried to do the utmost; it was a question mainly that there was no housing since they were living in the caves. I ordered some barracks should be built but then I myself dropped ill, just a few days afterwards, and I wasn't really again in my office until May 1944. After that I saw to it again and had some medical care for them and I heard that the things were better, were improving. Of course my only task was to produce as much as possible and I didn't look to the left or to the right what was happening there. I was just glad if I could get along with the things which I was responsible for and didn't bother for the responsibilities of other offices.

DR MORGEN

In Berlin the Reichs Criminal Police Office had obviously not been informed of my previous history because if they had I cannot imagine I would get a commission for a job which took me to Buchenwald. It may have been because one hands over the most unpleasant and difficult jobs to the new boy, so that he can prove himself or perhaps come to grief over it. I heard a whole string of unbelievable stories, among others that these SS officers at the time of the Jewish action way back in 1938, the infamous Kristallnacht, had quite unashamedly lined their own pockets, and had exploited the Jews. I was so enraged and shocked at all this, that I had the feeling something must be done about this. Obviously none of these local people here had the courage to do anything, but they all encouraged me and offered to support me. Then I took matters into my own hands: I went to the Weimar banks and without anyone asking me whether I had any orders to show, but just because I had a uniform on, and handled myself accordingly, I got all the accounts of the concentration camp – the private accounts of the SS Colonel Karl Koch. I went through them and I was able to establish that a sum, about a hundred and five thousand marks, had been embezzled by Koch and he had spread this very cleverly over various accounts, official, semi-official and also his private accounts. And that set off a whole avalanche because all those people who had been afraid of Koch, and they suddenly saw that there was a higher power still than even Koch represented, and they suddenly saw he was sitting in prison now and had no power any more. They all gave evidence against Koch and I didn't just establish embezzlement in his case but murders as well.*

WILLI HILSE
German railwayman at Auschwitz

Just before the exit of the camp after Auschwitz station a shunting train was standing and it happened that the engine was standing on the level crossing and the personal car of a high SS officer was standing at the level crossing. This man was drunk out of his mind and he kept shouting at the sentry who was standing at the gate, 'Shoot, shoot, shoot at him!' He didn't do it, he didn't take any notice at all. Meanwhile I had come up on my bicycle and stood in front of this SS officer's car and I said, 'The engine driver' – it was Polish personnel – 'will not move until he has his orders to move because a shunting train can only move forwards or backwards when he gets his orders from the shunting overseer.' You can imagine that this SS officer in his car was going wild and kept on shouting, 'Shoot, shoot, shoot.' I went over to the engine driver and said to him, 'You have nothing to fear. I will take full responsibility whatever happens. Should the SS officer attempt to get up on your train, push him down.' It didn't go that far but the SS officer jumped down from his car and went over to the SS sentry and tried to tear the rifle out of his hands, but the SS sentry grabbed his rifle and ran off. After a while the coupling of the train was complete and the signal came from the shunting chief. Then I said to the SS man, when the train had gone past and the level crossing was free, 'Please, now you can drive on.'**

DR MORGEN
What triggered my investigation was an Army postal packet sent back home from Auschwitz and the customs had opened this packet and found

---

* Thanks to Morgen, Koch was convicted and executed in April 1945.
** Later in the interview Hilse identified the officer as SS Lieutenant Colonel Rudolf Höss, hanged on the gallows next to the Auschwitz crematorium in April 1947.

there were one or two kilos of gold in it. And it was dental gold and then nobody could work out how this dentist had got hold of so much gold and I was supposed to go down there and find out what was behind it. As I had this job to do it was explained to me that the concentration camp of Auschwitz-Birkenau had a very special and particular role, the extermination of the Jews, the so-called 'Final Solution' as the code word put it. I heard, which was at first inconceivable, that human beings were being intentionally gassed and reduced to ashes and to judge by the quantity of dental gold, must mean hundreds of thousands of dead that this gold had been taken from. After I heard all this, I immediately set off for Auschwitz, I didn't even know where it was, I had never the name Auschwitz before and I found it on a map as Oswiecim, the Polish name, and I saw that it lay in the Upper Silesian industrial area. One morning very early I arrived by train and was very curious to see what sort of place it was, and somehow or other you had the feeling that a place where such incredibly ghastly things were happening on such a huge scale that it would somehow exude a frightful aura, that there would be something peculiar about it. But, no, there it was, a perfectly ordinary, grey, miserable, dirty industrial town. It was all perfectly normal, you didn't see anything of the concentration camp either. I was picked up in the commandant's car, and a few minutes later I found myself face to face with Commandant Höss. The man Höss is one of the strangest men I have ever met. I could describe him best if I say he was a man who seemed to be made only of pure stone, hardly a trace of emotion, hardly a movement. He spoke very softly, very ponderously, slowly, deliberately and I explained my business to him and asked him to show me, the whole concentration camp including his extermination machinery. Then he gave me a chap to guide me round and we made a very thorough tour.

DOV PAISIKOWIC

Russian–Jewish survivor of Auschwitz

There was a French actress, Jewish. She was very pretty. One SS told her to undress in front of him. She refused; he forced her to undress. She began to undress but did not want to take off her underclothes. He forcefully tore them off, so she took a shoe and with the shoe hit the SS man on the forehead. His forehead started bleeding and while he was taking out a handkerchief to wipe his forehead she took his revolver from his holster. That same moment all the SS ran out. This French girl had only the revolver, no SS tried to fight her. They brought machine guns and shot into the room where people undressed. They all shot but none of them dared enter the room as the woman had the revolver. Real heroes.

DR MORGEN

One always thinks that people who do such terrible things must be marked in some special way, but they were mostly people who enjoyed a good sleep, had a good appetite and who in their behaviour and bearing were indistinguishable from the rest of the world. They were quite normal human beings. However, I did not understand this intimacy between SS extermination personnel and Jewish assistants – helpers. I was sitting in my guard room and there was an SS non-commissioned officer lying there on a couch and was making no attempt at all to behave like a military chap, but was quite unconcerned about an officer like me coming in – and a very pretty young Jewess was baking potato-puff cakes and sprinkling them liberally with sugar and served them up to him on his couch. And he ate them lying down like Nero in Rome, surrounded with his harem.

YAACOV SILBERSTEIN

Jewish teenager at Buchenwald and Auschwitz

We were supposed to go in October 1942 from the transport straight to the oven but two minutes before we were to be sent Lieutenant Colonel Höss, the commander at Auschwitz, arrived and said, 'These Jews are not going to the crematorium. They have a trade and came from Buchenwald.' After that we were taken with no selection and put into showers. Those who came from Buchenwald were put to work in building. When we arrived we saw how the Jews were running to the electrified fence. There they stuck. They were tired of life; they could not continue in this fashion.

DR MORGEN

I arrested the Gestapo chief [SS Second Lieutenant Maximilian Grabner, hanged 1948] immediately and accused him; I was also able to bring evidence of crimes committed by Höss. Höss had started a love affair with a Czech female prisoner and made this girl pregnant, and that was reason enough for him to attempt to kill her. And he did it in a particularly horrible way. It had to be done discreetly and so I found this woman in a standing bunker, that was a cement construction in the cellar, very small and you to crouch right down to get in there and this woman was standing there for days and weeks naked, and hardly got anything to eat, only when sympathetic prisoners smuggled something to her, and I arrived just in time to save her. I immediately took her out of the camp and got her to a Catholic hospital near Munich and then when she had recovered her strength, she told me with great difficulty the story of her suffering. This woman's fear of Höss was indescribable.

RUDOLF VRBA

The Jewish council provided the German authorities with my photograph, my description, et cetera, and finally I ended up where others ended up, in the train, except that I had been a bit damaged in the face and the body until they got me there. We were put in a sort of transit camp and because in the camp there was a strong force of young people, resistance was divided by dividing the camp with one part promised that they will work on the spot and stay in Slovakia, whereas the other part goes into the unknown destination. Because of course I have been a naughty boy who tried to avoid his duty to the state and to the Jewish nation by my lack of discipline – because instead of obeying and doing what others do I tried to cross the border towards Hungary into Yugoslavia and became the shame of the Jews by my lack of discipline and understanding – it was decided that it would be better for me if I go to the place where discipline will be taught to me.

AVRAHAM KOCHAVI

There were twenty or twenty-five cars in every train like that and it had taken a long time until the Germans pushed multitudes into the train.

I heard terrible cries. I saw how people attack other people so as to have a place to stand, how people push each other so that they could stand somewhere or so that they could have air for breathing. It was terribly, terribly stifling. The first to faint were children, women, old men, they all fell down like flies. Father was standing next to me and all of a sudden I see that he is falling, he has collapsed. With all my strength, as much strength as I had, I tried to lift him and bring him to, but I didn't succeed. Then I found a piece of wood on the floor of the car; I got up and began to beat with the piece of wood – it was a club or something – people who were standing around me in the car so that they would make room for father, so father could get up. I remember that I did not care about the suffering of others, their cries, their threats, only that father should get up, that I should not remain alone.

RUDOLF VRBA

In the gas chambers was transported thousands of people from Bohemia and when they were gassed in the pocket of each of them was a ticket in which the German authorities promised them that on their arrival everything will be done that they should rejoin the members of their family – which were gassed in the same gas chambers a year before. So that promise was kept.

RITA BOAS-KOUPMANN

Dutch–Jewish teenage survivor of Auschwitz

I was afraid, yes, like a dog in a burning house is afraid, mostly because of the smell which was a terrible sweet smell. It had something to do with burning hair and burning chicken. I only know that I was thinking they are burning chickens; I didn't know the chickens were people. When we arrived it was the 6th of June and I remember one of the prisoners spoke to me, 'You have bad luck because the English arrived in France and you go out to the crematorium.' That's all what she said, and I was thinking what exactly is a crematorium? And I asked her, 'What do you mean crematorium?' and she said, 'Look' and then she pointed to the flames. 'You are going through the chimney, that's where you'll go through.'

PRIMO LEVI

Italian–Jewish chemist at Auschwitz III (Monowitz), a labour camp

I wrote a book about my stay in Auschwitz, and a chapter of my book [*Survival in Auschwitz*, 1958] has the title 'The Submerged and the Saved', in Italian *I Sommersi e I Salvati* [later the title of his last book of essays, published in 1986]. The Submerged as a rule are those who did not keep afloat, they did not carry the first shock and after one week of concentration camp were already lost – not materially lost but with no hope of survival. They were called 'musselmen' in the concentration and they were lucky to lose almost completely their sensitivity. There was also another way of losing your sensitivity and it was the opposite one – to climb, to be a social climber in the camp. Many particular qualities were needed to do that. You needed to understand German very well, to be very shrewd and to be very free of every solidarity with your mates.

RUDOLF VRBA

The gentle or the brutal technique for unloading trains depended on conditions. If the SS knew many transports are coming it was brutal, but if there was only one transport it was much more interesting than sitting in the barracks so they might grant you the gentle technique: 'Ladies and gentlemen, we are so sorry for the inconvenience, which was caused by some idiot who organised this journey. We are awfully sorry, just look at this mess. How do they treat people like this? Would you please get out and please don't get in touch with these criminals [Jewish inmate working parties], they are placed here only for taking the luggage. And if you have got unmarked luggage and are afraid it might get lost then take it with you, but if you have names on your luggage don't worry, we are keeping a good eye that none of those criminals can take anything away and our German honesty, about which I hope you have got no doubt, is a guarantee that all your property will be given to you. Please don't make us any trouble so that we can give you water and allow you the basic sanitary conditions to be restored after this dismal journey.' Looking around at excrements and urine and blood around the wagon and pretending they don't realise what has happened, and there's a lot of humour and so the prisoners come out.

RITA BOAS-KOUPMANN

I remember that came a little girl who was dressed like a little SS woman in boots and a green outfit with a whip and we said, 'Look, this girl, she's from Friesland.' And she said, 'Hello, you are from Friesland, all of you? You go to gas chambers – they sent my parents to gas chambers as well.' She was not touched at all and said it the way I said it now. You know what happened to that girl? She was a little beautiful girl and one of the SS women took her like a little daughter, I don't know why, and she built a little SS woman out of her.

LANCE CORPORAL BOCK

Holblinger said to me, 'Richard, are you interested in seeing one of the actions?' I said, 'Yes, very interested indeed' and he said, 'I'll take you with me this evening.' We drove out to Birkenau, not to where the ramp was later but where the train stopped on the big slope. It was a transport from Holland and the Dutch Jews who came to Auschwitz were very elegant and rich. He parked his ambulance there and I sat in it pretending to be the co-driver. Then they drove them all off in a lorry to Bunker One where there were four big halls. The halls did not have a proper roof, just a sloping top. At first Holblinger did not have anything to do. Then they went into the hall and the new arrivals had to get undressed, and then the order came, 'Prepare for disinfection'. There were enormous piles of clothing in there, and there was a board running around so that the piles did not all collapse. And the new arrivals, the Dutch people, had to stand on top of this great heap of clothes to get undressed. Lots of them hid their children under the clothes and covered them up then they shouted, 'Get ready' and they all went out, they had to run naked approximately twenty yards from the hall across to Bunker One. There were two doors standing open and they went in there and when a certain number had gone inside they shut the doors. That happened about three times, and every time Holblinger had to go out to his ambulance and they took out a sort of tin – he and one of his block chiefs – and then he climbed up the ladder and at the top there was a round hole and he opened a little round door and held the tin there and shook it and then he shut the little door again. Then a fearful screaming started up and approximately after about ten minutes it slowly went quiet.

DOV PAISIKOWIC

Several minutes later the SS company sergeant major arrived. He was the head of all the crematoria. He received us very nicely and said, 'Here you will have enough to eat, but you will have to work a lot.' The doors were suddenly opened to the gas chambers. People, naked people, started falling out. We were all frightened, no one dared ask what it all was. We were immediately taken to the other side of this house and there we saw hell on this earth – large piles of dead people, and people dragging these dead to a long pit, about thirty metres in length and ten metres in width. There was a huge fire there, with tree trunks. On the other side fat was being taken out of this pit with a bucket. We remained almost unconscious and we did not know what to do in such a situation, but we had no alternative and we had to immediately begin working. Four people would take hold of one dead person but the SS came and said, no, each one of you will take one. He showed us how, with a simple walking stick, to take one under the chin, to put the stick on the neck and drag the dead to the pit as one would drag a rag or a piece of wood. At the pit there were still others who pushed the dead into the pit.

LANCE CORPORAL BOCK

They opened the door – it was a prisoners' Sonderkommando who did that – then a blue haze came out. I looked in and I saw a pyramid. They had all climbed up on top of each other until the last one stood at the very top, all one on top of the other and then the prisoners had to go in and tear it apart. They were all tangled, one had his arm down by another's foot and then round it and back up again and his fingers were sticking in someone else's eye, so deep. They were all tangled, they had to tug and pull very hard to disentangle all these people. Then we went back to the hall and now it was the turn of the last lot to get undressed, the ones who had managed to hang back a bit all the time. One girl with beautiful black hair, a beautiful girl, was crouching there and didn't want to get undressed and an SS man came up and said, 'I suppose you don't want to get undressed,' and she tossed her hair back and laughed a little. Then he went away and came back with two prisoners and they literally tore the clothes off her then they each grabbed an arm and they dragged her across to Bunker One and pushed her in there. Then the prisoners had to check where the small children had been hidden and covered up. They pulled them out and opened the doors quickly again and threw all the children in and slammed the doors.

DR MORGEN

The experience of Auschwitz was a terrible one for me and I had planned to cross the border and go into Switzerland. But then on this long journey I reconsidered it all – if you go and tell them all this, who will believe you? I could hardly believe my eyes and ears when I saw it all for the first time and something where there has never been anything like it before, and it all seems absolutely impossible anyway – how should I prove it? And I was genuinely afraid they would just say to me, 'He's an agent provocateur, a spy or a madman.' I just couldn't imagine any positive result from it. It could only lead to me or my parents having to suffer an awful lot, pointlessly too since I could not change anything. But I said to myself, even if I can't get those who are responsible for this extermination of millions, I can at least bring the executives to justice in so far as they deviate from the path of so-called legality and act on their own initiative to enrich themselves, to cover up crimes, or out of power-mania, or whatever all the reasons were for violating prisoners. For that I could bring them to justice, to shut these monsters up and put an end to their activities. I kept trying to arouse an examination of it all, but how can you change a system, particularly when there's a war going on?

WYNFORD VAUGHAN-THOMAS

A pile of women's bodies, an enormous pile, you have probably seen the photographs, but the smell and the horror of it. There were little children playing touch around the pile of these bodies and that was the final, horrible end. In the huts typhoid, everything, had broken out and you couldn't hear yourself speak for the death rattle. There were people lying on top of each other, sick, vomiting, withered bodies crawling on their hands and knees. I went into one area where they had to seal it off because of typhus; through the wire came what I thought were broken twigs, they were the arms of people and the voice, the croaking sound of voices that had withered at the roots, and I'll never forget it. Sometimes you wake up at night and you hear sounds and you think you're in Belsen again, that horrible, awful sick smell and the final indignity of taking the human body and bulldozing it as if it was worth nothing. You were surrounded by this neutral pine forest and I can't look at Christmas trees sometimes without remembering Belsen behind it. It was sealed off in this dark north German plain and you felt you'd reached the cesspit of the human mind.

ANTHONY EDEN

Auschwitz was very long range as far as our people were concerned, and certainly until the later stages in the war I should imagine out of range. There are some Jewish organisations who feel to this day it would have been good if we could have bombed Auschwitz. I don't really know how it could have helped anybody even if we could have done it. You can't bomb with that accuracy, it certainly would have killed a lot of people, and then of course it was in enemy territory and even if as a result of the bombing some people had got out, they would have been in a hostile country – where could they have got to or was there any real hope that they could have escaped? I hardly think so. We decided against it, and we didn't even ask Bomber Harris to consider the project. So we may have been right or wrong, but that was how the decision was taken. As one considers all the possible alternatives one comes back to what was the main thing to do, which was to win the war, not disperse our effort more than we absolutely had to. It was only by winning the war that we could hope to save the lives of any unfortunate Jews who were still survivors from the terrible and unforgivable treatment to which they were subjected.

DR STEPHEN AMBROSE

American historian

Jews realised overwhelmingly that when push comes to shove a Jew can only look to another Jew for support. This gave a tremendous boost to Zionism, which had been an important force before the war among world Jewry but not decisive in the way that it was to become after the war. The only solution for the Jews was to have their homeland back and so they took it. The Jews had moral capital piled up in the West upon which they could draw for a long time. It seems to be running out, but immediately after the war the West had a very guilty conscience about what had happened. Had Hitler not attacked Poland and instead concentrated his efforts exclusively on eliminating Germany's Jews, it's perfectly evident the West would have allowed him to do so. He could have killed all Germany's Jews and no one in the West was going to raise a finger to stop him.

RITA BOAS-KOUPMANN

We were brought to freedom in a train, not with those SS people but with soldiers, old-men soldiers. They told us you are lucky, you go to Sweden and Hitler is dead. One of the girls said, 'Hitler is dead, now I'll see my daughter again.' She never had told us during all the years she had a daughter. We couldn't believe we were free until we saw for the first time of our life English soldiers. Then I knew we were in Denmark and the people from Denmark were running to the train with bread and cigarettes and I remember that one woman took out her lovely white shoes and gave them to me. I took of course the shoes in my hands but my feet were not clean and I was sick – but I like to say I came out of the war with a pair of white shoes.

DR ADOLF GAWALEWICZ

Polish–Jewish lawyer and Auschwitz survivor

I had to drink urine in the wagon. A couple of months later, on the yacht of a rich Swedish lady, I drank a glass of champagne. Then I told her that our generation had to note in their lives enormous contrasts such as between drinks – urine and champagne. This was received, rightly, with disgust although at the time the joke seemed to me excellent, excellent.

This was already the first contact with the fact that what we went through will be difficult to understand even for our contemporaries, and much more difficult for the generations that have already no personal experience from those days.

YAACOV SILBERSTEIN

Rabbi Frankforter had one wish. He gave me his will. He said, 'You see what they are doing with us day in, day out. They are finishing us. I will be the first victim here, as I am a rabbi. This is why they will want to finish me before the rest.' He asked me to do one thing. He blessed me and said, 'You are still young and you will remain alive. I have only one request for you that you should never let people forget. Tell everyone what they did to us at this small camp, in Buchenwald. Wherever you go tell this, also to your children so that they should pass it on.' This is why I insist on it even today – 'To remember and not to forget'.

CHAPTER 19

CASABLANCA
AND TEHRAN

One of the least explored of the major themes of the Second World War is the degree to which the Americans, deliberately or accidentally, pursued policies that ensured Britain would be completely exhausted by the end of hostilities. President Roosevelt's formidable wife, Eleanor, once said that he did not think, he decided, and he announced one such unilateral decision at the closing press briefing of the Allied conference at Casablanca in January 1943. The conference had been dominated by the better-prepared British, and from it emerged a joint plan for the allocation of mainly US resources within the framework of a 'Germany First' policy. Without discussing his announcement with Winston Churchill or even his own Chiefs of Staff, Roosevelt announced that the war must end with the unconditional surrender of the Axis powers and their allies. No policy could have been better designed to ensure that Germany and Japan would fight to the bitter end and that, consequently, American hegemony would be near absolute in a shattered post-war world. Later, at the meeting of Roosevelt, Stalin and Churchill at Tehran at the end of November 1943, Roosevelt sought to ingratiate himself with the Soviet dictator by snubbing Churchill. Ironically, Stalin respected Churchill as a brave man and an honest opponent, and despised Roosevelt for his disloyalty. Roosevelt's outlook and that of several high-ranking Soviet sympathisers in his administration was born of their naïve belief that Communism was simply a more drastic version of their own Progressivism. This aspect of American policy, decidedly awkward in the light of the ensuing Cold War, was airbrushed out of post-war history. It is evident that the Americans were, quite understandably, not interested in fighting to preserve the British Empire, and attitude surveys of US troops fighting in north-west Europe testify to a wider cultural gap between them and the British than we some-times like to imagine. In this context we should perhaps let the great Lord Palmerston speak for Roosevelt: 'We have no eternal allies and we have no perpetual enemies. Our interests are eternal and perpetual, and those inter-ests it is our duty to follow.'

REAR ADMIRAL LORD LOUIS MOUNTBATTEN
British Chief of Combined Operations

At Casablanca the British and American Chiefs of Staff arrived first; we had three or four days entirely alone before Churchill and Roosevelt turned up. It didn't go very well, we took up positions, the British with Alanbrooke as our spokesman were pressing for a continued Mediterranean strategy; we were there, it was the obvious thing to do. The Americans wanted to land immediately in France, and engage the Germans on the mainland of Europe and also to give more pressure to the Pacific. All the arguments that Admiral King developed for the Pacific we developed for the Mediterranean, and it was about the third day we agreed a paper on facts, and alternatives and possibilities. Admiral Cook, who was the Director of Naval Plans for the Americans, had absolutely nobody on his staff who knew anything about landing craft at all, so I lent him all my combined operations staff and helped him produce the position paper. The position paper worked miracles and we began to see a way through. By the time we met Roosevelt and Churchill we had five priorities. Priority one was unquestioned security of sea communications – if we lost the Battle of the Atlantic we'd lost the war and all escorts, all anti-submarine aircraft, a great effort was to be put into that. Priority two was to continue aid to Russia – obviously if Russia was out of the war then we'd be in a bad way too. Priority three was that the British proto-col in the Mediterranean prevailed and the Americans agreed that they would not withdraw their land forces from the Mediterranean, a great saving of shipping. Priority four, called Bolero, was the continued influx into England of American forces and the operations into and out of

England by them, which included the possibility of the capture of Guernsey before the main invasion. Priority five was the Pacific. There was no question of holding back resources that were needed so everybody was happy, and the President and the Prime Minister were very pleased with our work.

LIEUTENANT COLONEL ALBERT WEDERMEYER
Author of the US Army's 'Victory Program', also known as 'Germany First'
My still vivid impression of the British delegation at Casablanca, the Prime Minister and his military chiefs, concerned their skills in negotiation – they were really very good. They were a team with a game plan and well rehearsed in the plays. They maintained the initiative through all stages of the discussion because they had formed clear ideas of their objectives and they had coordinated the political and the military factors and worked out detailed proposals. By contrast, our own American team was not well prepared and I was the responsible individual. Our basic political and military aims were vaguely conceived and there'd been little opportunity for our military chiefs to talk to the President and obtain his approval for certain aspects of our strategy. Our various Service Chiefs were not even in accord on many issues. Although I disagreed with some of the British positions at that time I wholeheartedly admired their performance in negotiating. Later, when Chief of Army Staff General Marshall heard about this – as he noted this in the course of the discussions – he approved of certain changes that I recommended, which greatly improved our planning and negotiating in subsequent conferences.

ADMIRAL MOUNTBATTEN
Well, it took quite a while to persuade them to come round. Alanbrooke was a brilliant, decisive man who spoke rather too quickly for the Americans to follow always. Didn't always win his arguments by his manners. I think what really happened was that their great man Marshall was brought around by Sir John Dill, who had been sent over to represent us with the Americans.

LIEUTENANT COLONEL WEDERMEYER

Sir Alan Brooke was sometimes a little curt in his reactions to General Marshall's suggestions and it was perfectly apparent to those who attended. Fortunately Sir John Dill, noting that the situation was becoming tense and that nothing constructive could be accomplished, suggested that we all break up and have a cup of tea, and everyone enthusiastically agreed. Sir John Dill enjoyed great esteem and confidence among Americans. His pleasing personality and tact as well as his penchant for low-key diplomacy gained many friends during the war among American political and military leaders. Perhaps as a result of this Casablanca incident an unusual comradeship and personal friendship quickly developed and maintained throughout the war between Sir John and General Marshall. The affection and respect in which Sir John was held in this country is recognised by the fact that he is the only foreigner buried in our Arlington National Cemetery, where an impressive equestrian statue marks his final resting place.

BRIGADIER GENERAL IRA C EAKER

Commander Eighth Air Force, USAAF

I had a message one day from Commanding General Arnold to meet him in Casablanca the following day. I did not even know there was a Casablanca conference in the works but I took a B-17 and flew down and General Arnold told me that the Prime Minister had secured an agreement from our President Roosevelt that the Eighth Air Force would discontinue daylight bombing and join the RAF in night bombing. I said to General Arnold, 'This is a tragic error. Our crews are not trained for night bombing; we'll lose more people coming into this misty island at four in the morning than we will over German targets; our planes are not properly equipped for night bombing and besides we'll permit the Germans to go into the factories in the morning. If we continue this compound effort day and night we'll keep them from working around the clock, and with our small bomber force we'll keep a million men standing on the West Wall. Think how many divisions that will deny the Eastern Front and to our own forces when we cross the Channel.' Well, General Arnold said he'd been hopeful that I would feel strongly about it. He said, 'I think you have a better chance than any of the rest of us to convince Prime Minister Churchill.' The next morning at ten o'clock when I went to the Prime Minister's villa he said, 'I'm not sure you're aware of it but I'm half American.' And he said, 'The tragic losses your gallant crews are sustaining has led me to suggest you join Air Marshal Harris with the night effort, because his losses are considerably lower than yours.' Well, I said, 'In my year's service in Britain, Mr Prime Minister, I have learned that you always listen to both sides of the case before you make a decision. I've set down here in a memorandum one page in length the reasons why I think we should continue.'* He said he would read it and sat down on a couch and invited me to join him and read it very carefully and very deliberately. When he had finished he said, 'Young man, you've not convinced me you're right but you have convinced me that you should have a further opportunity to prove your case. When I see your President at lunch today I will tell him that I withdraw my request that you join the RAF at night bombing and continue to give time to your present effort.'

ANTHONY EDEN

We had our difficulties of course – one, the American instinct I suppose, in view of their constitutional position, was not to get involved in any commitments too early. The Russians' instinct was to try and get everything done or anyhow their claim set down very clearly at the earliest possible moment. Probably we were somewhere between the two but over the French business, our difficulties particularly with the Americans were considerable and that led the Russians to make difficulties about the French too. I still think the French should have been there, and our arguments with the Americans about de Gaulle were endless and I think the Americans were quite wrong about it. My view simply was that de Gaulle was there and he was the symbol of French resistance, even though we might not like some of the things he did or wanted to do.

---

* Eaker was well briefed: he knew that Churchill greatly favoured one-page memoranda.

DREW MIDDLETON
American journalist

Most of us had been brought to Casablanca from Tunisia and Algeria. We spent two days in a rather comfortable hotel and then on the afternoon of the third day we were taken out to the garden of the building in which the main conference had been held. Mr Churchill was there, the President was carried in and they sat down together side by side and began to talk. Mr Roosevelt began by saying that when he was a young man the great reputation in the American military was General Grant, who had once sent an order saying he would accept no terms but unconditional surrender, and that these in fact were the terms the Allies or the United Nations wanted to present to their enemies. He then went on as though he did not understand how important a statement he had made. Mr Churchill looked considerably surprised at this and in later years he told me that he had been surprised, that there had been no discussion between them beforehand and I think to the end of his life – I know to the end of his life – Mr Churchill felt that it was not the best way to present the Allied position to the enemy. However, as he said then and later, he was Mr Roosevelt's ardent lieutenant and he would go along with it.

AMBASSADOR W AVERELL HARRIMAN
President Roosevelt's Special Envoy to Europe

I don't know how Roosevelt decided on that question of unconditional surrender. I know that he sprang it on Churchill at this press conference but I don't know whether he did that intentionally or by accident. He brought it out in a way that wasn't fully understood, that there couldn't be any terms of surrender, there had to be unconditional surrender, but he spoke about peace and the Federal General Grant who said [at the Confederate surrender], 'Your officers can take your side arms and you may need your horses for ploughing.' In other words, he showed a certain generosity about what he intended it to be, but that never came through. I had dinner with Churchill that night in Casablanca and he was very much upset that this had been sprung on him without consideration. On Roosevelt's side it was perfectly true that the Joint Chiefs of Staff had discussed it from the military standpoint and had agreed that it was a good thing to do, but Churchill thought there should be political consideration given. Now whether Churchill wasn't consulted because Roosevelt was afraid that Churchill wouldn't agree I don't know. Roosevelt had a habit of doing things like that, he didn't like unpleasant arguments and sometimes did things without consultation, which occasionally made Churchill quite angry. That's when [Roosevelt's Chief Presidential Adviser] Harry Hopkins came in to smooth things out. I was opposed to it, I felt that it would lead to the Germans holding out longer. Stalin at first was opposed but later on very much in favour of it – I think it became clearer that he was afraid that the Germans would surrender to our side on the terms which would be far more favourable to us than to him. Our Chiefs of Staff were always afraid Stalin would make a deal again with Hitler. I knew that was utterly impossible, the breach had been so great.

ANTHONY EDEN

It was originally Roosevelt's idea and, as you know, originates from the American Civil War, but we were told about it in advance actually, though I think Winston was taken aback by the actual moment of the announcement. I'm sceptical whether it had much effect either on Germany or Japan, but we were troubled in the Foreign Office about its possible effect on the satellites and we did raise, quite soon after Casablanca with the Americans and the Russians, the question of whether we couldn't deliberately cut the satellites out of the unconditional surrender treatment altogether. The Russians soon agreed about that; interestingly enough the Americans were more difficult because they didn't want to put any conditions on what their President said, but eventually they agreed too that in any propaganda to the satellite countries there'd be no mention of unconditional surrender.

CHARLES BOHLEN

US diplomat

My personal objection to the doctrine of unconditional surrender which was produced by President Roosevelt at the Casablanca Conference in

1943 was that it seemed to almost ensure that the war would go on to the very bitter end, that there was no opportunity left for any possibility of revolt against Hitler inside the Third Reich. And it would seem to prolong war unnecessarily. The Soviets sent us a note in which they voiced some objection, for the same reasons I'd indicated, to the doctrine of unconditional surrender and the State Department supported it and sent it over to the White House. But it came back rejected by Roosevelt who had fixed in his mind that the surrender of General Lee to General Grant at Appomattox Court House was unconditional, which I don't think historically it really was. I don't know why he advanced it. I imagine one reason was to do with fighting a coalition war: one of the ways of keeping anybody in the coalition from making any moves or tentative proposals to the enemy was to commit themselves to war to the bitter end.

DREW MIDDLETON

I think that there was a legitimate argument that this would make the Germans fight harder, that it would be used by Dr Goebbels and others to inspire greater resistance once we got into Germany. It was also said that because of this there would be very little chance of an opposition movement developing to Hitler. That, I think, was proven by history to be untrue – there was an opposition movement, even then. I think first Roosevelt wanted to reassure the Soviet Union, secondly he wanted to reassure people in Europe who might at that time be having second thoughts about who was going to win – and I include in that Vichy France – and thirdly, I think he meant it as an inspirational message to our own people. We were not going to – that there were not going to be further compromises, that the West meant to fight the thing to the end and win it completely.

GRAND ADMIRAL KARL DÖNITZ
Commander-in-Chief, German Navy
In consequence of the defeat of the submarine, the Anglo-American invasion of Normandy in July 1944 was now a success and now we knew clearly that we had no more chance to win the war, but what could we do?

At the conference of Casablanca when the Allies fixed that Germany would get a peace only by unconditional surrender, by this decision it was clear that there could no longer be an independent German government. Germany would be ruled in the coming years of peace by the victorious Allies and for this purpose Germany should be divided into four pieces. And of course our military fronts had, by a capitulation, to stop where they were standing. The soldier had to stay, they had to give their armament, their weapons and had to go as prisoners into the hands of their enemies. For instance three and half million German soldiers on our Eastern Front who in this time were still standing far inside the Russian frontier had to become Russian prisoners. After all, we believed that the war would be lost in the summer of 1944; we could not give the advice to end the war by unconditional surrender. This demand of the Allies that Germany had to surrender unconditionally was a political mistake.

DREW MIDDLETON

I think the [American] defeat at the Kasserine Pass in February 1943 had a very good effect. One thing, of course, it got rid off a lot of second-rate officers, secondly it brought the troops face to face with the fact that this was going to be a long war and a tough one, and that the Germans were very good. Armies never learn from other armies; they have to learn by themselves and a lot of the tactics we used disastrously at Kasserine were those the British Army had used equally disastrously two years before in the Western Desert, and then discarded. I think it helped our Army, and it also made them realise – because the British came down from the north and did help – that this was going to be a cooperative effort and that we couldn't win it alone. Also it got the average GI accustomed to the fact that there was going to be one battle after another and that they weren't going home every time a city like Algiers fell.

LIEUTENANT GEORGE GREENFIELD
British Army officer
The first knowledge we had of the Tehran conference resulted in an absolute fiasco because a cable had arrived at the GHQ in Baghdad and it

was marked Top Secret and Confidential and signed by some former naval person [Churchill's wartime code name]. The Orderly Officer who was on duty that night and who had a camp bed in the main operational office was a regular soldier – a very stuffy man who was always telling the temporary officers and gentlemen just how they ought to behave and how regulars behaved. The dispatch rider arrived in the middle of the night and produced this fantastic, very secret hush-hush cable, which of course was in an envelope. Half awake and half asleep he put it on the desk but unfortunately he pushed it under a blotting pad. The result being that thirty-six hours later the secret cable that was supposed to go to the Commanding Officer was still lying under a blotting pad on somebody's desk. I think some office cleaner eventually discovered it.

CHARLES BOHLEN

Churchill and Roosevelt had made a number of attempts to get together with Stalin and it only came to fruition at the time to decide military matters. The real purpose of the conference was to agree on a date for the cross-Channel jump for the Allied armies and to coordinate with the Soviet offensive from the East. Each of these three men were as different as could be. Churchill was an extremely attractive individual with a great zest for living, which was very pleasant to watch. Roosevelt was an exuberant man – in foreign affairs, where precision is so important, he was inclined to deal in improvisations and would try to make decisions based upon the circumstances as they developed at the conference. Stalin was always very reserved, very quiet and behaved very well with the foreigners. He seemed to know his dossier very well and be in complete command of any situation. I know nothing about what the Soviet method of work was, how the delegation operated when they were in private. Tehran was a very small conference and Roosevelt insisted on it being kept informal. Rather than set the agenda, any discussions revolved around the question of setting a date for the Second Front. Mr Churchill was never against the idea of a cross-Channel jump but he had grave apprehensions of fixing a date. The date was fixed within one week at Tehran without regard to the state of the Nazi defences. He had in mind the difficulties of amphibious operations, also I think he was very conscious that the British had really one great asset left and that was the Home Army, and he was very much afraid that if the Nazi defence was sufficiently developed you'd have a great bloodbath. The Channel would swim red with blood: he kept talking like that all the time. But the United States Joint Chiefs of Staff had always held the view that the way you were going to end the war was to go right for the throat of Germany across the Channel. And the Russians were very anxious to have our armies come to grips with the Germans to relieve the pressure on them in the Eastern Front. Once Churchill came around, as he always did, he came around wholeheartedly, I don't think with any afterthoughts. The main accomplishment of Tehran was military and in that sense it was the most successful conference that we ever had with the Russians. There were some political discussions after dinner and at luncheon but no decisions actually were made.

ANTHONY EDEN

Both the Moscow conference between Foreign Secretaries and at Tehran between the heads of government the atmosphere was better than it later became, and probably for the simple reason that the Russians at that time militarily had not become so far advanced that they felt they could absolutely insist on whatever the things were that they required, because they hadn't the command of the situation. But we did manage to settle some things in Moscow, for instance rather astonishingly there was agreement about the restoration of Austria's independent life between the three of us and eventually that was carried out and Austria to this day fortunately still leads her independent and natural life. If you look beneath the surface in Moscow, there were differences in outlook and approach: there was Soviet Foreign Minister Molotov harping all the time on the Second Front, and there was US Secretary of State Hull who wanted a rather grandiloquent but a fine declaration about the rights of free nations and how they should behave to each other. And I was trying to get an arrangement for post-war Europe. At least the machinery which would enable us three powers to discuss how we wanted to shape the post-war Europe, and we were following our own particular thoughts and wishes, and they did progress a little bit each of them. But there was not all that close a meeting of minds.

LIEUTENANT GREENFIELD

The great event as far as I was concerned was Churchill's birthday party. When Stalin arrived he had fourteen picked Georgian bodyguards who rushed into the British legation and shooed everybody out of the way and lined the steps up from the drive. In the meantime wooden ramps had been built for Roosevelt and beforehand a bunch of tough guys with guns obviously under their armpits came all around the place, pushing Churchill out of the way and looking under cushions and divans and heaven knows what. And there was Churchill in a dinner jacket looking absolutely calm, smoking a large cigar, with a very bored sergeant of Military Police standing twenty-five yards away, looking vaguely into the distance. Stalin arrived in an enormous black bullet-proof limousine, just came out, gave the most perfunctory glance at the guard of honour, came up the steps very slowly and just gazed at Churchill. Churchill came halfway down the stairs to meet him and Stalin just stood and looked at him in a very cold, evil sort of way. Then he walked straight on up past him, more or less left him with his hand extended, straight up past him and into the main hall. We all felt it was a really calculated insult.

SIR HARTLEY SHAWCROSS

Chief British prosecutor at Nuremberg
Stalin said that he thought fifty thousand of the German General Staff and officers should be gathered together and summarily executed. He wasn't joking. President Roosevelt thought he was and said, 'Oh, well, perhaps forty-nine thousand.' But Churchill said that he'd rather be taken into the garden and shot at once than be a party to such an iniquity. But the Russians persisted almost to the end in saying that there should be no trial: these men were criminals and they should be immediately executed the moment they were caught.

AMBASSADOR HARRIMAN

Roosevelt had a feeling that there was this antagonism, which had arisen because Churchill had been the sponsor of the British intervention in the Revolution after World War One. And he felt it might be possible for him to go a little bit further with Stalin because of that. He was very anxious to see Stalin alone, but Churchill wasn't at all keen to have something being done behind his back. It wasn't a question of lack of confidence but Churchill didn't want to be cut out of anything. Actually, as it turned out, Churchill saw Stalin more frequently than Roosevelt – he saw him twice alone, I was representing the United States in both those cases but Roosevelt only saw Stalin at Tehran and then again at Yalta. He did have private talks but he wanted to give Stalin the idea that he could talk to him without Churchill, and Roosevelt was very keen to establish the United Nations.

ANTHONY EDEN

I wasn't particularly conscious that at Tehran there were differences with the Americans about Poland, but there were so many differences on the merits of the thing between us – there was reluctance on their part to talk about Poland because of the political dynamite with an election pending. I wouldn't have thought there was wrangling in front of the Russians, I don't recall that. There was even some humour sometimes, of which Stalin was perfectly capable. I remember one evening, after all the discussions were over, we'd been dining together, I think FDR was the host and there was just FDR, Stalin and Winston, Molotov and I and Harry Hopkins sitting round this table having coffee afterwards. Winston, funnily enough, soberly but firmly, said, 'I think God is on our side – at any rate I've done my best to make Him a faithful ally' and Roosevelt looked a little bit astonished at this statement but didn't comment. It was translated into Russian and Stalin said, 'Yes, I'm sure that's correct and of course the Devil is on our side because everybody knows the Devil is a Communist and God, I've no doubt, is a very good Conservative.' I thought that a pretty good impromptu reply.

AMBASSADOR HARRIMAN

Because at Tehran most of the concentration was on military action, it was then that agreement was reached that the Second Front would be undertaken. Stalin was pressing for the appointment of the Supreme Commander; somehow that came in his mind if the Supreme Commander was appointed, that committed both. It was tentatively agreed that General Marshall would be the Supreme Commander. When Roosevelt got back to Washington it was strongly advised not to let General Marshall leave because he was such a vital force in every aspect of our military action and he decided on Eisenhower. I was given the task of telling Stalin about this change; I was quite stirred, I felt that this would mean that Stalin would think that there was a hedging of the commitment to Tehran, but not at all. Stalin said Eisenhower is a general of experience particularly in amphibious warfare. He didn't think it was any of his business who the general was as long as the man was appointed and so after Tehran there was no doubt in Stalin's mind as to the Second Front coming about, it was a question of when. In the meantime there were other military activities which were being considered by the British and Americans. The Chiefs of Staff were working on those questions when we were at Casablanca; it was decided to go to Sicily and then to Italy. Churchill wanted to cross into the Balkans and go to Vienna, and that was considered a diversionary move. Our Chiefs had different relationships to the President than the British Chiefs who are recognised as advisers to the British War Cabinet; whereas Roosevelt is the Commander-in-Chief, they have direct relationships. Over the years the British soldiers had been trained to realise that war is a political expression and somehow our Chiefs got the idea that Churchill had some Empire and post-war Empire considerations, and that wasn't true at all. What he had in mind was a settlement in Europe which would be workable, in which the hopes and aspirations of the people of eastern Europe could be attained and it would lead to a chance of peace.

CHARLES BOHLEN

Churchill and Stalin more or less agreed on the Curzon line and tentatively agreed on Poland's frontier, but that produced a certain amount of confusion later on because there were two rivers there. Churchill meant the eastern and the Russians took it to be the western. Roosevelt did not participate in that particular discussion because he had told Stalin that he was coming up for re-election again in 1944 and he didn't feel it proper for him to offer any opinion on any Polish matter at that time. We had brought some rather carefully prepared maps of Poland and the British delegation was operating on a map torn out of the London *Times*, a little flimsy piece of paper. I finally said to Roosevelt, 'Can't we offer them this map of ours which is a much better map?' and he said yes. I took it over and gave it to the British, and Stalin looked at it, and then came over and said, 'I see this map was made with Polish statistics,' and I replied to him that I don't know that there were any others in existence at that time.

AMBASSADOR HARRIMAN

People say Roosevelt thought he could use his personality to get Stalin to do things. I think that's wrong; what he felt was that if he could establish a basis of mutual understanding during the wartime period that would last into the post-war period. He knew the differences in the system and the greater difficulties, but he felt that in time this arbitrary rule would not last, and it wouldn't be possible to keep two hundred million people under his complete control. Roosevelt was a religious man and he thought that the Russian people were religious and they would change. If only we could have cooperation during the period after the war, that it might lead to a change in Russia and a permanency. He was always afraid that the personal antagonism between Stalin and Churchill would interfere with that.

LIEUTENANT GREENFIELD

Of the three great leaders I think in a way Stalin was the most impressive, although that may be in a negative sense. Roosevelt struck one – and I'm speaking out of a period as a junior officer, some thirty years ago – as being a big fixer, the man who worked in the smoke-filled rooms and so on, very jovial and glad-handing. Churchill was of course Churchill and

I had seen quite a lot of him during the war so I knew him or knew of him well. But Stalin I had never seen before. He was a tiny little man about five feet four inches in height, very grey – his hair was almost white and so was his very bushy moustache. He had the most cold, poker-player's eyes, very dark, lustrous – small but lustrous eyes one would say – very dark brown, almost black, a very fixed stare and a very immobile, hard face. It's not fanciful to say that there was an aura of cruelty about him, most remarkable, and I noticed he exchanged notes with people who had exactly the same expression: very hard, very composed. A most cunning and cruel peasant.

CHAPTER 20

ANGLO-AMERICAN RELATIONS

The fact that American and British geopolitical interests were often divergent did not greatly impinge on the conduct of the war at the practical level. There were moments of cultural abrasion and many illustrations of George Bernard Shaw's aphorism about Britain and America being 'two countries divided by a common language'. However, US Lieutenant General Lucian Truscott summed it up well: 'British and American soldiers invariably got on well together, and it was only among the higher echelons that friction developed between the Allies. All in all, British and Americans held each other in mutual respect; they were worthy Allies who fought well together.' At a time when more Britons than ever before are indulging in the anti-Americanism that has become such a feature of politics in Europe, it is perhaps as well to remember that not long ago one of the many Commonwealth war cemeteries in France was vandalised by someone who left a message that the British should take away their garbage. In international relations, as Ambrose Bierce put it, to do a favour is often to make an enemy because the beneficiaries, anxious to be relieved of the burden of gratitude, will submit the motives of the benefactors to forensic examination in an effort to prove that they were not altruistic. Because my words of introduction to the last chapter could be read in that light, it is appropriate to follow them with some of the material available in The World at War *transcripts – little of which reached the broadcast programmes – that reminds us of the instinctive affinity that existed between Americans and British, and the enormous patience each had at times to exercise with the other in the complex joint pursuit of their common cause. At the same time the manner in which institutional concerns dictated US strategy, in particular with regard to the invasion of Europe, and the American philosophy of overwhelming rather than solving problems, are themes not without resonance today.*

ANTHONY EDEN
British Foreign Secretary

There was of course the big problem of Anglo-American relations, where Churchill played this very key part throughout. It's been said, and perhaps there's some truth in it, that he was perhaps over-anxious to keep in step with FDR, on the other hand a little incident happened one evening which illustrated Winston's mind in that respect. For some reason he wanted to call a meeting of ministers on the afternoon of Christmas Eve in 1942, and I protested vehemently so he moved it to the morning. After the meeting Attlee and I had luncheon with him alone. We were talking about the war and Winston said this to us: 'I want you to understand the key importance of FDR. After all, if I was eliminated or even if all three of us were eliminated, there would still be responsible men who would carry on the battle and see us through to victory. But in the United States, if anything happened to FDR where is the man who could carry on as things are today?' And that, I have no doubt, was in Winston's mind all through, particularly in view of the system in the United States where the Vice President was not in the picture and there was no obvious successor. And that explains a large part of it. On the whole our relations were good, despite all the many difficulties. On the military side, of course, the man who contributed enormously to this was Sir John Dill, our military representative in Washington, and his relations with General Marshall. When Dill died America paid this unique compliment in their whole history, of asking that he should be buried in Arlington cemetery with the American war heroes.

DR STEPHEN AMBROSE
American historian

The British Empire and the greatness of the British as a nation was dependent upon her physical separation from the continent and on the very wise British foreign policy in the eighteenth and nineteenth century, of which the most outstanding part was that the British paid others to do the fighting for them. You see this most clearly in the Napoleonic Wars – the British Treasury is used to support the Prussian armies and to support the Russians to fight against Napoleon. So Britain emerges from the Napoleonic Wars in a very strong position thanks to the geographical accident that there is an English Channel. In the twentieth century, technology overcame the Channel and Britain is now part of Europe and very much involved in Europe's wars. And the United States becomes the offshore island and in World War Two was very wise indeed – what we did was pay the Europeans to do our fighting for us.

ANTHONY EDEN

I used to reflect sometimes in my more depressed moments that whereas the Russians could be amoral – for instance in their attitude towards the Poles and some of their neighbours – so our American friends could be exaggeratedly demoral, at least where American interests were not directly concerned, and we were somewhere between the two. And one of our constant troubles and differences was of course about Free French leader de Gaulle.

AMBASSADOR W AVERELL HARRIMAN
President Roosevelt's Special Envoy to Europe
In meeting with Stalin, Churchill was concerned about Poland. Poland and Eastern European countries had governments in exile and hospitality with the British in London. Roosevelt was interested in the longer term, wanted to get the United Nations started, and he realised President Woodrow Wilson had made a mistake waiting until after the First World War to propose the League of Nations. He wanted to get the Americans committed during the war and he also wanted to get Stalin committed. But Roosevelt accepted Churchill's objectives and Churchill accepted Roosevelt's objectives. Both men had one primary objective and that was to keep the Russians in the war, and to get the Russians to play the maximum level they could. Roosevelt, I think before we got in the war, hoped

that we could limit our action as much as possible to Naval and Air Force participation. He didn't want to have American boys back in trench warfare which he'd known so well in World War One.

ANTHONY EDEN

De Gaulle and the future of France was one of the most constant sources of argument between us and our American allies. My view was that de Gaulle was the symbol of French resistance and that as such he must be, as soon as was possible, given the authority we would have given to our French ally, and it was for the French people to deal with him afterwards, if he had to be dealt with, and not for us. However, the Americans – some of it was personal, FDR certainly didn't like de Gaulle – I thought the Americans were unfair to him and unfair to the French, and perhaps not over-eager to see France restored to a position of importance after the war. At any rate that was our chief difficulty and Winston, who could himself be impatient with de Gaulle, often had a difficult position to argue with Washington.

PROFESSOR VANNEVAR BUSH

Chairman of the US National Defense Research Committee
The White House became the place in which all orders on every subject emerged, and it became the centre of an enormous structure fighting a war. The way in which that happened in this country was extraordinary. The President was a far more powerful man in time of war in many ways than even the Prime Minister – his cabinet has no power, he's simply appointing his representatives, his power becomes almost absolute in time of war and no one's questioning it. I think Roosevelt used his power with great discretion. I don't think he ever interfered improperly with his military men – they made mistakes, but he kept the power. The military part of the Allies worked together with such mutual confidence and such integration of efforts in that war, and that was centred on the Combined Chiefs of Staff. It wasn't a piece of decoration, that's where the great decisions were made and that operated with great skill. I think Sir John Dill deserves the credit for a good part of that movement.

ANTHONY EDEN

For us it seemed a very strange system. FDR of course was the President, the supreme controller of foreign policy and more, in a sense, than the Prime Minister is here. And under him was his Secretary of State, Hull – a very revered figure – and Sumner Wells, the Under-Secretary. Wells was very close to Roosevelt and Roosevelt used to act a lot through Wells. And then there was a curious situation that Hull and Wells were hardly on speaking terms. I remember once when I was on official visit to Washington during the war, and Hull was giving me a farewell dinner. I'd been staying at the White House and I went round the State Department to say goodbye to people I'd been working with, said goodbye to Wells and said casually, 'Of course I'll see you tonight at dinner,' and he flushed up and said, 'I haven't been asked.'

AMBASSADOR HARRIMAN

Churchill and Roosevelt's first wartime meeting was immediately after Pearl Harbor. Churchill came to Washington with his Chiefs and Beaverbrook was there too, and that started this wartime relationship. I think no two heads of government could ever work as closely together. It was interesting – there were different personalities and different proce-dures. Chief Presidential Adviser Harry Hopkins played an extraordinarily important role in interpreting one to the other and whenever there were rough edges, smoothing them out. I was involved to some extent because I was in London, Hopkins in Washington, he saw all my telegrams and we worked closely together. But Roosevelt had his problems. We were in the first meeting with Beaverbrook to get our military and industrialists to raise their sights; he was quite anxious that we should have rapid mobili-sation, he wanted to have minimum of human life and maximum use of munitions, so he got Beaverbrook to estimate how rapidly we could mobilise. It was agreed that Britain had taken too long, doing it step by step. Beaverbrook came out with this idea that we ought to get a hundred thousand aeroplanes, fifty thousand tanks and as many guns, and Roosevelt took that and announced it without consulting his Chiefs. They were furious, couldn't be done, but Roosevelt had a habit of doing things, establishing a principle without consultation, then just sitting there. There wasn't anything they could do and they had to come through with it. They did, with some pain and possibly some loss; at the same time it was achieved. The Americans all thought Beaverbrook had just pulled the idea out of his head. He didn't actually, he had some very skilful men who analysed the two countries and actually they were close to being right.

REAR ADMIRAL LORD LOUIS MOUNTBATTEN
British Chief of Combined Operations

In June 1942 Churchill asked me to see Roosevelt and then the US Chiefs of Staff to explain our difficulties, which were not a lack of desire but a lack of physical capability to do a landing. The Americans had no special combined-operations organisation, had nobody with any specialised knowledge, and none with any experience. They knew that I certainly wouldn't do anything to discourage them. I first talked to Roosevelt with Harry Hopkins. Roosevelt said to me, 'My overriding need is to find a way to deploy the hundreds of thousands of young Americans that have now been trained in the Army to go and fight, and I'd like to do it this year.' I said, 'I don't think that's on.' He said, 'When I spoke to Winston we had a general agreement that there would be an operation in readiness, a sort of sacrifice operation if the Russians fared very badly. Have you looked into that?' I said, 'I certainly have and I can tell you right away it isn't on. The Germans have got twenty-five divisions and with the number of landing craft I've got now I couldn't put more than just over four thousand troops in the first flight. I couldn't get more than perhaps six divisions ashore with great luck and they'd make no difference at all. The Germans would not have to withdraw one division in Russia to compete with that. But if we fail, as I'm afraid we should, they then would have all those divisions ready to go against Russia, and they'd be much worse off.' Well, this discussion went on for a long while. He didn't take that lightly, it took an hour or two to convince him, then he said, 'All right: suppose the German morale cracks, what have you got ready?' I said, 'We have an operation called Sledgehammer now being planned and with two months' notice we could send in troops, because of course then it would be on the assumption that Germans would not be resisting us in the same way. But that's not anything to rely on.' 'No,' he said, 'I know it isn't. My nightmare would be if I was to have a million American soldiers sitting in England, Russia collapses and there'd be no means of getting ashore.'

ANTHONY EDEN

The Americans were very much dedicated to the concept of attack across the Channel, and they had given some undertakings to Soviet Foreign Minister Molotov when he was in Washington going far beyond what we could do, and we were embarrassed when Molotov got back and showed us what he's been told. We said it wasn't possible. But I think the Americans got to understand that an early cross-Channel attack was just not on. And if we were going to do something soon as a joint effort on land, the only place we could do it was North Africa. So the Americans came to the same conclusion and there were things that attracted them about North African landings. They could make landings from the Atlantic, which the Americans always liked to do, rather than within the Mediterranean, which was mainly our responsibility. They were certainly wholehearted once they started with it and perhaps had accepted that this meant a delay in crossing the Channel.

LIEUTENANT COLONEL ALBERT WEDERMEYER

Author of the US Army's 'Victory Program'

At the beginning of the war the British strategy was essentially defensive, providing for limited air and naval operations and for an economic blockade of Europe. Aware of their limited means at that time they could not conceive of a major operation of the magnitude of Normandy unless and until the military and economic power of Germany had been greatly reduced. Even after the United States entered the war in 1941, the British still retained the general concept of peripheral operations. For example, they planned for the employment of Americans in the attacks against Europe from the south, the British from the north and the Russians from the east. Army Chief of Staff General George Marshall was determined to concentrate American offensive power into the British Isles, which after careful analysis he established as the logical place from which to conduct an invasion. Some planners recommended an attempt to establish a lodgement on the Continent in 1942, however, this seemed premature prior to appropriate preparations for such a big operation. General Marshall, as well as his staff, of which I was one, insisted that the planning and concentration continued to ensure maximum strength for the decisive invasion in 1943. So when these military considerations were out of the way along came the politicians, Prime Minister Churchill and President Roosevelt, who were determined to initiate operations in considerable force [Operation Torch in North Africa] as soon as possible. And why? Well, from the political viewpoint they recognised that they could not justify to their people and to the Russians any extended delay in sending strong military power against the enemy.

JOHN McCLOY
US Assistant Secretary of War

There were times when threats were made. I think it was probably only once or twice. I recall General Marshall made a threat, 'Well, if you don't go along with us on our effort to get to grips with the main challenges in Europe we'll have no alternative but to move to the Pacific.' That always put Mr Churchill's wind up and usually you got more support for another major effort. I think those were just intermittent flare-ups. Mr Churchill had a very real fear towards getting ashore prematurely on the European continent, he had very vivid memories of the sacrifice of a British generation in World War One – Passchendaele, Somme – they are always nightmares to him. His tendency was to try to avoid that or certainly not go ashore before we were ready for it. I think we probably could have delivered our strength a little earlier than we did on the main front. After all the passion that had been aroused after Pearl Harbor we just had to get ashore someplace and we had a tremendous urge to participate. In view of the British attitude that we were not prepared to go into the main theatre, we looked around for another spot to express our strength and it turned out to be Africa. We thought of it as being something of a diversion, but I think it did have an important effect and certainly it was timely. I think it would have been very awkward indeed if we hadn't gone at that point and thereby expressed ourselves, our strength, our energies.

ADMIRAL MOUNTBATTEN

I stayed in the White House with Roosevelt and we had a bout of long conversations before I saw the Chiefs of Staff. Bit awkward, but still I had to start with him. In the Pacific the American marines and the American aircraft carriers, as they built up, would probably be enough to carry on the war in the Pacific but he pointed out that Admiral King was asking for more and more resources to be drawn into the Pacific. I pointed out that surely the American Navy with the marines and their aircraft carriers could do all that was wanted provided they had enough resources, but I did go and see Admiral King privately afterwards to point out that he really must provide the sailors to man the landing craft in Europe. I said, 'I know you can't afford to give them from the regular Navy but the civilians are now joining. Instead of putting them in khaki as soldiers, put them in blue as sailors and they'll have the responsibility for getting our Army ashore' – and he liked that idea. That helped the whole thing to go through.

CAPTAIN GORONWY REES
British planning staff for D-Day

I think you can say that as far as the planning was concerned Normandy was an essentially British operation. Of course we had American officers with us and they worked very closely with us, but the original conception of the plan was a British one and the detailed planning of it was also, I would say, about ninety per cent British. But in the course of it one had to learn to work with the Americans and this was not an easy thing. Their methods of planning and their methods of conducting war are really terribly different from ours, and one had to learn an entirely different language in order to talk to them from the one used normally when speaking to British colleagues. They used an enormous amount of paper, they used three men where we would use one and they were, in strange ways, a very cumbersome military machine. You have to explain, everything has to be explained in detail, over and over and over again, and you can't simply take anything for granted with them. And this was quite a difficulty at first I think, but we all got to know each other in the end and then we got to speak each other's language.

MAJOR GENERAL MARK CLARK
Deputy Commander, Operation Torch, later Commander US Fifth Army in Italy
I had gone to England in 1942 with Ike. We were both major generals, he was in charge of planning in Washington and I had the training end of it, and General Marshall sent us over to England in the early spring of 1942 and that's when we were taken in tow by Mr Churchill. Pug Ismay and Dickie Mountbatten and all those fellows became fast friends of ours and mine; I admired them all. I didn't meet Alexander at that time but Mountbatten and Ismay were pretty well the right-hand men of the Prime Minister and they were the men we worked with. I thought they were fine, they helped us tremendously.

CAPTAIN REES
Well, there was this fundamental difference between the way we make war and the way the Americans make war. We were always conscious of how very small our resources were. We knew for instance that if we lost a division it would mean a disaster to us. Whereas the Americans were quite prepared to produce another division – there's an infinite number of divisions in the pipeline. And they regarded people as expendable in a way that we didn't, not only men but also material, because again our resources were very limited and we simply could not afford to waste things in the way that the Americans could. On the other hand they showed great advantages in the sense that the American's equipment produced material that was beyond our means and their engineering instruments could perform feats in a time and at a speed which we could never dream of.

MAJOR GENERAL KENNETH STRONG
General Eisenhower's Chief of Intelligence

I think the British were very slow to realise that the main effort for war in Europe lay with the Americans. I think the British press was probably slow as well. I think people forget the great weight of divisions and supplies and so on were American. This in many ways was a sad thing for the British and Eisenhower was well aware of this shift of emphasis. But he was very devoted to Churchill: he was a very great friend of our country and one of the greatest friends I think we could have had, and when it came to any sort of point where we could be given the benefit of the doubt he always favoured us on the whole.

WYNFORD VAUGHAN-THOMAS
BBC radio journalist

I arrived in Italy as General Montgomery left. That may be a coincidence. He was going to look after the Second Front and I was going to look after the Italian Front, and I was invited to have a briefing with him, along with other war correspondents, so he could just give us a little word of encouragement before he left. He came briskly out of his caravan, it was a damp blowy day and the rain was coming down. It was quite clear that we were going to be stuck in those mountains for a very long time and he said, 'One thing I'd like to say, I'm going to other duties at home, but I want you to remember the troops have got their tails well up.' The American behind me said, 'Excuse me, General – what's up?'

MAJOR GENERAL CLARK

The fellow that I did most of my business with during the war was Alexander. I called him Alex and he called me Wayne – my name is Mark Wayne Clark and Ike always called me Wayne, so all my friends over there called me Wayne. I liked Alex from the start. I found that he was capable, kind, knowledgeable and very fair. You could talk very frankly with Alex and he'd talk frankly to you and you'd come to a decision. We struck up a very great friendship and he had with him Brigadier General Lemnitzer, who I had taken over with me on my staff as my artillery officer, and we assigned him to John Harding, who was Alex's Chief of Staff, as a sort of American go-between so that if things started to go bad he could trot back and forth and straighten us out. So with Lemnitzer being the diplomat and the capable fellow that he is, things worked very smoothly.* All the time I served under Alexander, and that was not only when I was in the Fifteenth Army Group commanding the Fifth Army but later when Alexander moved up to theatre command and the British government saw fit to ask my government to let me command the Fifteenth Army Group, which was all British. So all the time Alex was my boss. I admired him deeply; I still do.

WYNFORD VAUGHAN-THOMAS

I remember a marvellous arrival of General Clark's Chief of Staff and he said, 'General Clark's got fifty-seven different bands and you're going to listen to every one of them.' And I said, 'What about this problem?' He said, 'Sir, in the American Army we don't solve our problems, we overwhelm them' and that's exactly what they did.

ANTHONY EDEN

I expect the Americans were suspicious of ulterior British motives; it would have been very curious if they hadn't been. I think mainly they were worried that we should drag them into what they call the Balkans, which in their language was quite a wide term, and certainly they were not in favour of what we should have liked to have done, which was the further advance up Italy and to have tried to get Vienna. They didn't want that, they wanted this concentration on France and they had their way. But that I think was their chief suspicion of us, and I suppose to some extent they thought we were always concerned for our own interests in different parts of the world, which no doubt was true. There's nothing very evil about that.

MAJOR GENERAL STRONG

Gradually, as the American resources grew, the number of divisions grew. In the end, they had something like four times as many divisions in the field as

---

* General Lyman Lemnitzer was Supreme Commander of NATO 1963–69.

the British had. Then they got more and more influence. Whereas in North Africa they were extremely complimentary to Montgomery's Alamein operation, as they felt themselves stronger and stronger, and more competent, they became from time to time rather critical of the British. They were critical about the slow progress of the British in Sicily, Italy, and when it came to the beachhead landing in Normandy, which was directly conducted by Montgomery under Eisenhower, and he did a magnificent job there. Eisenhower once said to me, 'I don't think there's any other chap could have got us ashore like Montgomery did,' yet as time went on they became more critical and thought Montgomery was slow and hesitant. It's not absolutely true, but that's the impression they got. And therefore this element really enters into the feeling that perhaps Montgomery was not quite the man to carry it out even if it had been possible.

MAJOR GENERAL FRANCIS DE GUINGAND
Field Marshal Montgomery's Chief of Staff

I think if you compare the relationship between, say, politicians and generals in the Second World War with the First World War, and between generals, there's no comparison – it was marvellous in the Second World War. Look at Churchill, he kept virtually the same Chiefs of Staff the whole time. In the First World War they were appointed and displaced and there was a terrible lack of confidence between politicians and the Service Chiefs – and there was an awful lot of bickering and jealousies between the commanders themselves. I don't think that really existed in the Second World War. Monty was very good, it was his team, all the people who served under him knew exactly where they were and they never tried to bounce any of their colleagues at all. And until the Ardennes thing in 1944 the relationship between Monty and American generals was reasonably good.

MAJOR GENERAL RONALD BELCHEM
Twenty-First Army Group Staff

I remember very well a night that Eisenhower came to stay at Monty's headquarters while we were in Germany. After eating our 'K' rations, Ike was telling his amusing stories of his childhood in the United States and they were on completely good terms together. Professionally, obviously, there arose differences between them from time to time because, if you will allow a broad definition, Eisenhower was a political general whereas Montgomery was a cold, calculating, ruthless combat general. It's very seldom that a general is both of these categories at the same time – the combat man sweeps aside any factor other than those concerned or help-ing to win the war as quickly as possible with the minimum casualties. The political general has a rather different task. He's dealing, shall we say, with public opinion, he's dealing with Roosevelt, with Churchill, with de Gaulle and things of this kind. He's also concerned with holding together a team which inevitably includes a number of personalities who could be difficult. In this case he was concerned with Bradley, Patton, Montgomery, the air commanders and sometimes Bomber Harris. It's a different problem that he has and therefore he cannot always agree with the much more direct approach of the combat general. I think perhaps Eisenhower was some-times too diplomatic with Montgomery, because whenever he was firmly of an opinion and said, 'Stop – there's no further argument about this,' Montgomery stopped and concurred because that was his professional training. Indeed he once put it in writing to Eisenhower – 'Once a decision is taken there's no more argument.'

MAJOR GENERAL STRONG

I was one day with Eisenhower in his caravan and there he'd been discussing this problem of the British leading the advance into Germany, and a telephone call came through from the Prime Minister and he answered it. Then he laid down the phone and said, 'Look here, this is a dilemma. I'm being urged to use the British in the front line as a spearhead, and here the Prime Minister telephones me and says to me for goodness sake we've had losses in North Africa and Italy, there's a great deal of war weariness home in England. Spare what you can, save what you can. This is a very difficult problem – how am I going to do one and at the same time save British lives?'

PROFESSOR BUSH

Between American and British scientists I don't think there ever was a war in history in which allies got along as well together as in this last one, and the relations between every part of the American and the British scientific effort was cordial. There remained disagreements at times, it wouldn't have been human if there hadn't been, but they were friendly disagreements and we worked together in great shape. I don't think there was any disagreement that hindered progress. At the beginning our relations with the military were rather distant. The military in both countries did not realise that the time had come for a great revolution in weapons and that they had to have particular interest in what the scientific fellows were doing. Later on it became close. When we first started all our men were introduced to the military's scientists, we did that throughout the war. Some of them were good, tough engineers, but they all had to be scientists and they had to accept them on faith. Towards the end of the war we had gotten to respect one another both ways and we could work in harmony and every group we had working on any subject, proximity fuses or radar, was made up of civilians and military, young military men particularly, who knew what was happening in the field and what was needed and what would work and what wouldn't, sat with the civilians and they worked together. And that happened on both sides of the Atlantic.

CHAPTER 21

ECONOMIC AND SCIENTIFIC WARFARE

When The World at War *series was shown the Official Secrets Act was still a powerful tool of censorship and nobody then dared speak about the breaking of Axis cyphers, arguably the most significant operational-technological achievement of the war. The first crack in the dam was Frederick Winterbotham's 1974 book* The Ultra Secret, *but some information uncovered by Allied cryptographers was so embarrassing that it remained classified for decades. It was not until 1995, for example, that a Senate commission forced the release of material that showed how comprehensive Soviet wartime penetration of the US government had been. Another vital scientific achievement was the invention of the cavity magnetron at Birmingham University in 1940, which permitted the development of the airborne centimetric radar that was crucial to the outcome of the Battle of the Atlantic, as well as to accurate night navigation and bombing. In combination with the proximity fuse, another British invention given to the United States in 1940, it spared London the worst of the V-1 attacks in 1944. The fact that Britain could not herself develop these inventions (or the research into the atom bomb, handed over in 1941) and put them into large-scale production points to the single most important factor in the crushing of Nazism and Japanese militarism – the enormous surge unleashed by the war in the US economy. Despite considerable duplication of effort and profiteering on an epic scale, not only did it build and supply an American Army of millions and the largest Navy and Air Force in the world, it was also the indispensable financier and supplier of both Commonwealth and Soviet war efforts. Surplus capacity explains why production peaked in Germany as late as mid-1944 despite devastating bombing – but Germany did not begin to mobilise until it was far too late, and when it did the Byzantine nature of the Nazi regime, mistaken labour allocations and cultural constraints prevented it achieving its full potential.*

PROFESSOR VANNEVAR BUSH
Chairman of the US National Defense Research Committee
Scientific discoveries revolutionised the ideal of warfare completely and by the end of the war all we thought we knew about the ideal war at the beginning was obsolete. It's the only time in history that ever happened and it can't happen again, because before the war there was a great stock of technical knowledge built up ready for use, but which had never been applied to military things and, of course, therefore there was a great blossoming of new ideas and new devices.

CAPTAIN PETER GRETTON
Naval Escort Group Commander
Scientists used to analyse attacks by aircraft, attacks by certain ships on submarines and statistics on convoy work and that sort of thing. And they would produce new ideas on the use of ships, on the use of aircraft and the whole tactics of convoy defence, which I think revolutionised the whole affair. I think the most dramatic example was that the scientists early on studied the size of the convoys and they soon discovered that if you doubled the number of ships in a convoy, in order to provide the same protection – the same degree of protection – you only had to increase the number of escorts quite marginally. So by increasing the size of the convoys considerably, this released escorts for other duties, in particular to forming the support groups which were later so extremely important in the Atlantic.

ALBERT SPEER
Hitler's Armaments Minister
[Hitler's Reichsminister] Bormann was not an obstruction to my work in the first time when I was Minister, he was the reverse; he supported me because as it's well known Bormann was trying to diminish the influence

of the strongest one and I diminished in this time the influence of Göring. Göring was, more or less by my activity, no more the head of the four-year plan and of course Bormann liked it. But then when Bormann found out that now I am the strong man, he of course tried to do the same thing to me. There was no unanimous handling of the things, everybody of the big stars of Hitler's government were doing things of their own. It would have been better if the leading men would have been brought together now and then to discuss problems. It didn't happen. Hitler was preferring to have these discussion with every single man in leading positions and then to make his decisions, and often it was the man who was there first who got the decision and the other men who were late had to see how to get along with this decision. As long as I was on very good terms with Hitler, as was the case to the end of 1943, I was always mostly the first one to come to Hitler and get my orders and so the others had to see how to get along with them. But afterwards it was getting more and more difficult because I was no longer his favourite.

CAPTAIN GRETTON

The Germans had some very high-class scientists indeed, and excellent engineers, but they didn't achieve the results they ought to have done. Firstly, I think, because they were mucked around and the Nazis kept changing the priorities, and secondly and most important I don't believe they were ever allowed to take any interest in the operational side, as opposed to what happened to us, where the scientists were made to feel full members of the operational team. I believe this, more than the question of weapons and devices, was the reason why the Germans fell so far astern in technological matters.

ALBERT SPEER

Hitler was more and more convinced that he doesn't need any more advice of anybody and he made the decisions by himself without listening to experts. He didn't even come any more to headquarters: he didn't like to see them any more, and the decisions were made which were preventing the highest output possible and we had so many types of tanks that the supply of spare parts was almost an impossible question. We had so many parts, so many different ammunitions for so many different guns, that the logistic problem was no more possible to solve.

PROFESSOR BUSH

There were a number of reports from the Academy of Science about an atom bomb but it was the British report that really made everybody feel that after all it probably could be done. Of course we way underestimated the time and the money that would be required. But the first real conviction that the job could be done came from the British report.*

ALBERT SPEER

I was enthused by the V-1 rocket because it was such a wonderful technical device, and I also thought it will be a strong weapon but was disappointed when I heard that the warhead of the missiles only carried a very small load of explosives, and that the cost of such a missile compared with what it's bringing as an explosion to the enemy is not worth the effort. We could do, with the same material and the same workmen, we could do better. Hitler was dreaming of attack of a few thousand missiles at once and he said there should be stocked and then with one big blow he will start his offensive. And it turned out that in the end it started very slow, they were just firstly a few and the next day there was another few and then there were five or six or ten every day and not more, because by then the war was already in a stage that Hitler ordered everything into immediate action.

PROFESSOR BUSH

The project that involved the greatest technical difficulties? You would have to put the atomic bomb as one of the greatest. But the next I'd put the proximity fuse and after that radar, and particularly centimetric radar. Of course you people are ahead of us on radar but when we got going we

---

* The British MAUD Committee, drawing on the research of emigré German scientists, produced a report on the feasibility of a uranium bomb on 15 July 1941, an advanced copy of which was sent to Bush. He waited until he received an official version in October before taking it to President Roosevelt.

produced the short-wave radar, which was an enormous advance, and the Germans never got it. Proximity fuses, when they first presented that to me, it came up on appeal because some of my people had turned it down as impossible. I talked to four fellas and finally said to them, 'I think it's impossible on the face of it but I will not stop if you four guys think it can be done, go ahead, waste your time, beat your brains out trying to do it.' But think of what they proposed to do – to take a radio set as big as a baking powder can, put it in a shell, fire it off so that they press down its support with the force of a ton, it would contain thermionic tubes, little glass tubes with filaments in them and they'd expect them to be in operating condition after it had gone out of the gun. It was out of this world, yet they did it, and I think it was the greatest technical accomplishment.

MAX AITKEN
Son of Minister of Production Lord Beaverbrook

My father was a master of propaganda. There was the pots and pans drive where everyone was asked to give up pots and pans and railings, and ex-Prime Minister Stanley Baldwin didn't give up his gates but most other people gave up everything they could in the way of metal. We pilots knew that you couldn't make aircraft out of pots and pans but it was good stuff, it brought the people to realise that the situation was desperate. And I believe the response to the pots and pans drive was tremendous. They had piles and piles of pots and pans, not knowing what to do with them, but he, as I say, he was a great propagandist and enthused them. They didn't like him much, the air marshals didn't like him and I don't think the manufacturers liked him for a start. But he did enthuse them, he worked hard and when I say hard I mean hard. He wouldn't have any weekends; any chairman of an aircraft company who was going to play tennis he'd get him off the tennis court at once and bring him in. He had an uncanny knack of knowing when people in the aircraft industry were taking time off. He said the pilots have no time off, the pilots flew all weekends, and they were tired, and they flew at Christmas and they flew at Easter and New Year, and therefore he couldn't see why anyone else should do it.

OLIVER LYTTELTON
Minister of Production 1942–45

There had only been one Minister of Production before, who was Max Beaverbrook. Otherwise the Ministry of Supply dealt almost entirely with Army matters, the Ministry of Aircraft Production with the Air Force and the Admiralty with its own thing. The two new ministries, of Supply and Aircraft Production, in neither department that I can remember had there been a minister who had been on the battlefield. And this is one of the central difficulties of war production: you've got to have equipment which industry can produce and which is as near the tactical requirement of the Air Force or the Army as you can get.

EMANUEL SHINWELL
Trade-union official and Labour MP

I don't hold any particular brief for the late Lord Beaverbrook. I knew him well, knew him very well indeed, often had conversations with him, often was associated with him over the Second Front before he became a member of the government. But I would say this in Beaverbrook's favour – if he had not been made Minister of Aircraft Production it would have been disastrous. Of course he upset things, he went in and turned the whole thing upside down, disturbed people, incensed people, did all the things he shouldn't have done according to the critics – but without Beaverbrook it's doubtful if we could have got through.

DR JOHN KENNETH GALBRAITH
Deputy Head of the US Office of Price Administration

In the late Thirties part of the CIO was under left-wing leadership and in the days of the Nazi pact with Russia there was foot-dragging on the part of some of the union leaders.* I think this could easily be exaggerated but there were strikes and there was a certain lack of enthusiasm on the far left.

---

* The Congress of Industrial Organizations (CIO) split from the established American Federation of Labor (AFL) in 1938. The two organisations merged again in 1955.

But from 22nd June 1941 the left-wing unions became very enthusiastic and started talking about no-strike pledges and, generally speaking, the big production unions got their back into the war pretty strong. Walter Reuther of the United Automobile Workers was, though very young, a very strong militant figure in seeking to develop production against the Nazis. So I wouldn't put the unions on a par with the businessmen. The businessmen were a drag but so were the unions, certainly after the attack on the Soviet Union – and I'm not saying this was true of all the unions, just a few under left-wing leadership – but from that time on they were a pretty affirmative force.

ALBERT SPEER

Of course a man who is producing the arms is very powerful man in every country who is leading the war. I was not as powerful as I would have liked to be because in my hands were only the armaments production for the armies, but not those for the Navy and for the Air Force and not the general war production. This was leading to some failures in production because of course the whole production must be put together. I tried first in vain to be the boss of the whole thing, and succeeded very slowly in the length of time, the latest thing was in May 1944 when I got the production of the Air Force. It's astounding for everybody who didn't live in this system to hear that it was divided in many districts, in thirty-two districts, and if the head of every district was a gauleiter he was a strong political man and had the power, the absolute power, in his district. He was only subordinate to Hitler himself, so when my orders didn't please one of the gauleiters possibly they weren't carried out.

DR PAUL SAMUELSON
Member of the US War Production Board
One thing we learned, and this was a surprise to most of us, we all thought the Nazis were very good organisers of the economy. After the war, when we went on our bombing surveys and got all the records, it turned out that they didn't even know what the gross national product was. They were never even on a two-shift basis in the factories. The

democracies of the world, once they set their mind to it – and I am think-ing primarily of the UK and the United States – we did a better job of mobilisation than ever the totalitarian states did. I think they were done in by it.

ALBERT SPEER

Industrialists who were advising me told me at the very beginning of my office in 1942 that the great difference between Great Britain and Germany was that in Great Britain the women are mobilised to a very high degree. They gave me the percentage of women working in Germany in this war and they gave me comparison to the women working in Germany in the First World War, and it was quite obvious that women were almost not used for war production. So I tried to get the women in war-production machinery but it was opposed by Sauckel, who was in charge of all the labour – he was in some way at the same position as Bevin [Labour Minister Ernest Bevin] in England.* Sauckel denied it and the thing came to Göring and Göring flatly denied it too, then it came to the decision of Hitler and Hitler also said no, the women must be preserved, they had other tasks, they are for family, they have to rear their children and it would spoil their health and their morale if they are working in the factories. I think it was a general line of the whole system, it started with the thatched roof, which was propagated everywhere, it started with fostering the old customs and so on and so on. There was a long list of things which didn't match the technical age, which were on the contrary going more to the past, and those things were, really made it impossible to push through armaments production as I wanted to do it.

DR GALBRAITH

The one great thing we had, the one great thing that Britain had, and very little point has ever been made of this, was that the tables of the social accounts, which were new in those days, for business and others, allowed us to see exactly what we were investing in civilian goods, capital goods,

---

* Fritz Sauckel (1894–1946) was Hitler's *de facto* Minister of Labour.

what we were putting into war production – and the Germans had no such figures. And those of us who were concerned, who saw something of the German economy towards the end of the war, were awestruck by our greater knowledge of what we were doing.

ALBERT SPEER

Looking back of course I see that is, was, one of the big mistakes of our warfare to use foreign labourers. But not only now, also in the time when the things were decided, my leading industrialists and me we had the opinion that the rule that production can be done is with German forces, mainly with the women. But Hitler denying it, we were, I was too, compelled to ask Sauckel for deported labour. In the first time there were not so many arguments because I was of the opinion too that I need the workmen and that even if they are coming against their own will, it's a necessity to me, so I supported Sauckel and in the Nuremberg trial when I was in the dock I made a statement saying again what I did.* At first Sauckel was quite successful and brought to Germany hundred thousands of foreign labourers. But then he got in trouble because the people who were drafted in France, for instance, they didn't want to go any more to Germany, or more they didn't want to go in the beginning, but now they resisted really with some risks, went away and were joining the Maquis, the French Resistance. Generals who were in charge in France at this time were saying that Sauckel is more or less supporting the French Resistance with his systems. So we found out, together with the Production Minister of the French government, that it would be much better to occupy those French workmen in the French production and to charge them with consumer-goods production, while I am in Germany changing consumer-goods production into armaments production. We just started with this, with difficulties because Sauckel was opposing me and had the help of Bormann, but we got along.

---

* Speer's acceptance of culpability on the forced-labour count at Nuremberg was sufficiently nuanced for him to avoid the fate of Sauckel, who was hanged.

DR GALBRAITH

The business community regarded Roosevelt, at minimum, as a major deputy of the devil and Roosevelt was deeply suspicious of the businessmen, so the people who were associated with mobilising for war were divided. Some of them felt that their main purpose in being in Washington was to put a curb on the Socialist excess of the New Deal. Some of them were uneasy about being there. They had something of the feeling that the people who worked there were playing in an orchestra in a brothel. There was also a great unwillingness to convert from civilian industries. There was a feeling that war production would be a very unprofitable business, would lose markets for automobiles, for tyres, for chemicals and so forth and there was a very great reluctance to take the plunge into the production of war goods.

OLIVER LYTTELTON

It's very easy to win battles with tanks that can't be produced and if you ask the ordinary run of General what he wants, he wants eight inches of front armour, he wants a high-velocity gun, capable of forty-five miles an hour over rough country and absolutely reliable. Such an animal can't be made. In the Air Force they used to introduce modifications – say a new bombsight that weighed twenty-eight pound more than the last one – and this starts altering the whole design and hundreds of modifications have to be put in, the wing, the ribs have to be strengthened and so on. So you want a synthesis between tactical requirements and what is possible from the point of view of production.

ALBERT SPEER

We succeeded quite well with tank productions, in fact we produced five times more tanks in July 1944 than in February 1942, but one must compare to see the whole picture that the output in 1942 was a very low one, and the output in 1944 was, compared with the production in United States or in Russia, the normal one. I wouldn't say it was a minor one but it was a good output and also if I think of the air attacks, everything was against the highest production in Germany. But we could have done more without the changes Hitler always ordered – but Hitler was representing the Army wishes and a Production Minister has to fulfil what the Army is asking for. Of course we were all sticking together, and we had many talks about it and we tried, almost with intrigues, to attack Hitler's opinion from different sides and were winning other officers who were coming with experience from the fights to tell Hitler. Well, he changed his opinion maybe for a few days, but afterwards he jumped back again, and it was mainly the question that he wanted the heaviest tanks possible, which now were so slow that the tanks of the other side were far superior to them.

DR GALBRAITH

Washington in the 1930s had been a place of great excitement. I was not there much during the 1930s but many young people had come to be part of the Roosevelt revolution, part of the New Deal and then, after Pearl Harbor or even before Pearl Harbor, it became the Mecca for every kind of talent and non-talent. It was the scene, and everybody who was there had an enormous sense of his own importance when we all felt we were carrying the fate of the world on our shoulders and didn't hesitate to proclaim that fact at any given moment. One saw everyone you'd ever heard of in the streets, in the restaurants. It wasn't a place of great gaiety but on the other hand Washington never is. It was a very interesting time, and I think there's a tendency if one is winning, that is common to both Britain and the United States, to behave in a crisis with a certain panache, a certain style and everybody wanted to prove that he can take on very serious tasks of the period without being too gloomy about it.

PROFESSOR BUSH

We started on this side a year and a half before Pearl Harbor and gradually, through Harry Hopkins, Roosevelt himself who saw the picture, we had an organisation here for the development of new weapons by civilians going for eighteen months before we got in. We also had a complete interchange with Britain way back there, the form of organisation was a simple one. The first national office was later made the Office of Scientific Research and Development. The change came when the military machine was joined to it and through that all the work funnelled, it was a single paramilitary organisation getting its money from Congress. On the other hand the British – I never did understand the British organisation and I'm not dead sure they did either. But it was not in paramilitary form, it was in the separate military branches and joined together largely by committee. We had the unitary organisation, which is far better.

DR GALBRAITH

There was a certain enthusiasm in Washington for making people suffer. I think most of us who were associated with it felt a certain amount of suffering on the part of the American business community was good for its soul and I think that was probably disliked. And then, as everywhere else, there was great dislike for disrupting the accepted patterns of life and when you shifted the corporation from producing automobiles to tanks, or when the Ford Motor Company had to become the producer of the B-24 bomber – which it did very inefficiently for a long time – this interrupted comfortable patterns of life, which many people didn't like. Then there were the shortages. Though on the whole the people took the shortages rather well. I think there is the same tendency to accept shortages that existed here in Britain, with one exception: people were very resistant to gasoline rationing. Clothing shortages, food shortages, coffee, sugar, people would accept – but there was no form of rascality, chicanery, thievery and larceny which people wouldn't engage in to get extra gasoline. That was the one form, that was the kind of rationing which was really terrible to administer in the United States.

DR SAMUELSON

The first problem was that we had a head of stagnation, what we call the Great Depression, and so most of our business community said we couldn't expand our production very much. It was a perfect controlled experiment of modern science – you wouldn't think that was possible in economics but it was: the followers in America of John Maynard Keynes versus the business community.* The Keynesians said the American economy had lots of slack, it will get the orders and there will be a

---

* John Maynard Keynes (1883–1946), influential British political economist who proposed an interventionist role for government that shaped Western economies for a generation.

secondary multiple in response, there will be a vast expansion in output, and so build big plants. The business community generally said, 'Oh, no, we're practically at capacity now.' Well, Franklin Roosevelt decided in favour of the Keynesians and when he announced fifty thousand planes everybody thought the man had lost his senses. Well, of course, we didn't get fifty thousand aeroplanes in a month, but a couple of years after Pearl Harbor the American economy reached levels just about what had been predicted by John Maynard Keynes himself in visits here and by his followers in this country.

OLIVER LYTTELTON

Maynard Keynes had an effect in the government circle as he would have in any circle. He had a brilliant brain but he didn't get his way enough. In a curious way this applied more to the Americans than us. People got frightened of this colossal intellect and the Americans were terrified of him. They thought that any minute some unarguable point was going to be raised by him, and US Treasury Secretary Henry Morgenthau was frightened of him, he really was.

GEORGE BALL

Associate General Counsel for the Lend-Lease programme
Lend-Lease was a novel conception and the more immediate problem was to get people to understand what it was. In this, I think Mr Roosevelt's very simple analogy of lending your neighbour a hose when there's a fire was the most persuasive kind of simple illustration so that people could understand it. The biggest problem the programme had, of course, was the allocation of materials. Should we give it to the United States armed forces, or should we send it to the Pacific theatre, or should we turn it over to our European allies or to the Soviet Union after the Soviet Protocol? There was a long period of delay when we simply weren't keeping up deliveries and President Roosevelt got quite exercised about it and really began to put great pressure on the bureaucracy to meet the commitments.

DR GALBRAITH

This was the first war where radio was important – there was no question that quick access to mass opinion was a matter of great utility. In something like the freezing of rubber-tyre stocks, the announcement of sugar rationing and the announcement of coffee rationing, you could very quickly get the explanation through to the whole population. It was very important in propaganda terms for the keeping up of the war spirit. Roosevelt used it for that purpose and used it with great skill, as did Winston Churchill – Roosevelt I think with less skill than Winston Churchill, but I think he was an apt student. In World War Two, censorship was surprisingly unimportant. We had no powers of censorship in the Office of Price Administration so we had to keep our rationing intentions secret, but we had no protection from leaks and after 1943 we no longer kept our production figures secret. Ships, aircraft and so forth were so large it seemed simpler just to let them be known and we learned after the war that they were on the whole discomfiting to the Germans. Hitler prohibited the citing of American production figures within the German bureaucracy and said they were faked. So the only really important restrictions on the media were the news of impending battles, military actions, the invasion of North Africa and so forth. I think that in retrospect one is surprised how liberal the reporting was. I would say that governments, when they're winning a war, tend to be much more conscious of the importance of the freedom of the press than when, as in the case of Vietnam, they are losing the war.

GEORGE BALL

One of the possible defects of the American system is that the executive branch, the President, does not have control over fiscal policy as in the case of Britain. We have a Budget Message to the US Congress and that's more or less the end of it. It simply makes proposals with regard to taxation, for example, and the Congress wasn't prepared to vote the kind of taxes which the President felt were absolutely necessary. This greatly contributed to the inflationary forces as we began to gear up for production and we got into some serious problems until that could be brought under control through an enormous bureaucratic operation.

DR SAMUELSON

You might have thought that inflation would have been a major problem because in most countries in most wars it's always been a major problem. But very early when we mobilised we put in rationing and although there was a small amount of grumbling it's amazing how well the rationing system worked, although if the war had lasted another five years I won't answer for the consequences. Probably when you hear the name John Kenneth Galbraith you think of his books *The Affluent Society* and *The New Industrial State*. Well, among connoisseurs like myself it's the book you don't read that's the most intriguing: it's the book he wrote after the war about our wartime-rationing system. He was the Deputy Administrator of our price controls and he called it 'the disequilibrium-equilibrium system' and let me tell you how it worked. It really was a charm, too bad that it had to be in terms of war. You could get as much employment as you wanted and families which had never had any money at all were suddenly having lots of money. Now you'd say that with all this money and limited supplies of civilian goods the balloon would really go up in terms of inflation. But what happened was that all the things that you spend money on and enjoy – automobiles, durable consumer goods – were completely unavailable. There was only one thing available and that was savings, so people put their money in bank deposits, half their money in War Bonds. As a result we not only financed the war without too much disruption of the price levels but also came away with a nice nest egg that prevented the post-war depression which lots of economists – I'm one of them – predicted.

DR GALBRAITH

The cliché has it that Pearl Harbor brought a great change and there was a change, no doubt, but it wasn't dramatic and there was a stepped-up sense of urgency, but some of the same old businessmen were there, some of the public-relations types and what really happened, I suppose, was the organisations got better. But I didn't notice anybody any less interested in making money, anybody more interested in conducting a war in any spirit of business sacrifice. I was in charge of price control and probably I had a somewhat jaundiced view of the whole situation because most of my time was spent by people proclaiming to me how greatly their patriotism would be enhanced and how much more energetic they would be if they could just have a little more money.

DR SAMUELSON

There was a famous wartime picture of Sewell Avery, a great tycoon of the last age who was the head of retailer Montgomery Ward and who had brought it out of the Depression, being carried out of his office by two American soldiers in uniform because he wouldn't comply with the War Labor Board. Well, he learned where sovereignty lay.

DR GALBRAITH

Those years were ones of considerable social progress. The notion of equality of sacrifice – well, it was never realised in fact – but it became in some degree established and so that there was at least a bad conscience after the war about extreme inequality. It certainly committed the United States much more strongly to the idea of full employment. It was seen that it became a cliché that if you can give a man a job to produce war material, then surely you can give him a job to produce civilian goods, and I suppose the most important single result was that since the war was being conducted by a government very sympathetic to trade unionism, there was a very widespread acceptance of the trade unions among businesses which previously had been very anti-union. If they were going to participate they had to take the unions along with it; this one of the reasons why the businessmen, in the early months of war, dragged their feet.

CHAPTER 22

HOME FRONT

Several wartime episodes did not reflect well on politicians in Britain, most notably the demands by prominent leftists like Sir Stafford Cripps, Aneurin Bevan and Michael Foot that as soon as the Soviet Union was invaded by Germany, British lives should be risked in an invasion of Europe that would, at that time, certainly have failed. Nor did the war prevent inaccurate sniping from the press. On 5 March 1942 the Daily Mirror *printed a cartoon produced by the columnist William 'Cassandra' Connor and his friend Philip Zec that showed a sailor clinging to wreckage with the caption 'The price of petrol has been increased by one penny'. Labour Minister Ernest Bevin and Home Secretary Herbert Morrison were infuriated by the implication that they were conniving at profiteering and demanded that the* Mirror *should be closed down. At Churchill's urging they settled for summoning Cecil King, the proprietor, and giving him the dressing-down of his life. The* Homes Fires *episode of the series permitted King to represent the incident as an attack on the freedom of the press by Churchill and in the same vein portrayed Bevin's legal action against a strike at the Betteshanger colliery in Kent in January 1942 as unjustified repression, obscuring the fact that strikes over wage differentials and 'who does what' were as much a feature of wartime Britain as they were of its post-war industrial decline. 'Churchill's speeches rang less true these days,' affirms the soundtrack. 'The hopes of the British people were moving away from Churchill,' it continues. Away from the Conservatives, most certainly: but the throng that cheered itself hoarse on VE day, 8 May 1945, when Churchill appeared on the balcony of Buckingham Palace, and continued to do so wherever he appeared during the 1945 General Election, suggest that the electorate did not so much vote*

*against Churchill, but in favour of change. I believe that many of those who
cast their votes in 1945 remembered what had happened after 1918. Then, too
many of the men who had fought so hard for 'a land fit for heroes to live in'
came home to face unemployment, and there was a firm determination in
1945 that the same thing should not be allowed to happen again.*

LUCY FAITHFULL

Child evacuee organiser

When the evacuation scheme was first announced by the government and
it was explained to the people what the evacuation scheme was, this
posed the parents with the most terrible and cruel dilemma. And particularly for the women – the men knew they must stay in London – the
women had to decide whether to go out with their children under five or
whether to stay in London, whether to keep their schoolchildren with
them or whether to allow them to go out. No one should think that this
was an easy decision – why not keep your children with you, which is the
natural thing to do? But against this was the terrible thought that there
was going to be gas, that there was going to be terrible bombing and
death, and the children would be maimed. And by and large, with of
course notable exceptions, parents did decide to send their children out
and I always feel that probably they did this knowing the teachers, and
knowing that their children would be in the charge of the teachers whom
they knew and whom they respected. When the train drew out a kind of
stillness came in the train when the children realised they were leaving
parents behind, and they weren't parents who were waving gaily to them
but parents with tears streaming from their eyes thinking they'd never see
their children again. Then, in the train, a liveliness would break out; then
there would be the arrival at whatever place they were going to. Then
they would be herded into some hall, then the foster parents – the people
who were going to have children billeted on them – would come to the
hall and some of them were wonderful, some of them would just take
children for the sake of the child. Sadly, others would choose children
and then there would be the terrible situation that at the end one or two
unattractive children would be left, and I can remember one case when

nobody would have this child and there was this terrible sense of loss on the child's part.

OLIVER LYTTELTON
President of the Board of Trade 1940–41
I had a medium-sized country house near Rye and I went into it very carefully indeed, and I came to the conclusion on my wife's advice that we could take eleven children, something like that. And thirty-one arrived with their two junior nurses, I think. They were pretty dirty and two of them had impetigo. I put them into a large room – you've no idea, I'd no idea that such things existed in England – they relieved themselves all over the carpet and the place was a shambles. Well, you might say that I ought to have known that this sort of thing happened, but when their parents came down to see them on Sunday in motor cars I realised things were different. I mean, I wouldn't have thought that parents would have allowed a child to become lousy, or with impetigo and relieve themselves on the carpet and at the same time have a smart motor car.

LUCY FAITHFULL
Then when no bombs were dropped and the Phoney War was on, parents didn't see why they should be without their children and the children certainly wanted to be back with their parents, and of course there was a great flow back. Now it could be said that this was a wasted experience but I don't think it was, because when the bombs did drop and the war really started, as you might say, in earnest, children went out with not quite the apprehension that they did in the first instance.

J B PRIESTLEY
English author and broadcaster
By May 1940 the people of this country felt they had to fight and fight hard. I don't think most people realise that the British called up a larger proportion of their population for war service than any other country. Far more than Nazi Germany, women and all. The summer of 1940 has stayed in my memory as a very exceptional summer in Brighton. It was rather hot

and what I wanted to do in the *Postscripts* broadcasts was to relate the little homely things I'd noticed, like ducks on a pond or a pie in the shop, breakfast and so on. The theme was the war and the way people were taking the war. I think if the *Postscripts* were popular, as I believe they were, it was that tying up of the big war theme to the small, homely things that gave them their popularity. We were really alone. Certainly I don't think now that Hitler was ever really determined to invade this island, but we didn't know that then. And the eyes of the world were undoubtedly on Britain. Now this was important for two reasons – first, immediately, because of the war but also for another thing I brought into those *Postscripts*, which was that you could never keep things as they are. I always remember a play Daphne du Maurier wrote called *The Years Between* about an officer who didn't want any changes, he was just fighting for the world he had in 1939. I don't blame him, but it's a curious notion because after a war there must be changes. I mean either they'll go one way or they'll go another way and either they'll be worse than they were in 1939, or better. This was my own view, and so I expressed the view that we were fighting the Nazis but we were also fighting in a sense for our better selves. We were fighting for a better Britain and this made the broadcasts popular to a good many people and made them very unpopular with some other people. But they were under the illusion that you can keep things in one place, and you can't.

RAB BUTLER
President of the Board of Education 1941–45
One of the great features of my Act was the settlement of the religious issue. Over half the schools were church religious schools, and over half those were out of date. I brought in this idea of putting three-quarters or seven-eighths of them under the council, which was highly controversial, but if I hadn't done that, you would have trouble now. You have no trouble with Roman Catholic schools and no trouble with Anglican schools and all the rest are under the council. I think it was a great achievement because that had alarmed Churchill in 1902, when he'd had the religious controversy which made education so bitter. The Roman

Catholic hierarchy came round and were very distinguished, nearly always dressed in their robes when they saw me, with a little chaplet hat on the head and those crimson robes, makes you sit up if you're only dressed in a poor old suit like I am. And I argued with them and told them they'd get more. What astonished me about the meeting with Peter Amigo, Archbishop of Southwark, was that his cathedral had been bombed and his palace had been bombed, and there was no proper means of keeping out the chill winter air. He was dressed in full canonicals and I climbed up a staircase which had not been bombed, so it was possible to go up it. He was sitting there and he said, 'I can never agree with politicians' and as he'd been nominated by the Roman Catholic hierarchy to talk to me I thought this was a bad start. He then suggested we might pray, so I said I was quite ready to because I was also a Christian, and little by little we began to get on terms. But he wasn't exactly friendly to start with and nor was Cardinal Archbishop Arthur Hinsley.*

MICHAEL FOOT
Left-wing journalist

When the Russians came into the war, were brought into the war by Hitler's attack on Russia, we started – and it was organised partly by the Soviet Solidarity Society, which was predominantly Communist of course – a Second Front campaign was organised in which many of us participated, many of us who were not Communists like myself and Frank Owen, who had been editor of the *Evening Standard,* and Aneurin Bevan. Of course we were also stating a view which was the same about the Second Front and about support for the Russians which Beaverbrook [Foot's employer] himself was expressing inside the Cabinet when he was there. Anyway we started a campaign in the country in which we advocated this and undoubtedly we had Secret Service – or whatever it was – people sent to our meetings.

---

* Although endlessly controversial in the post–war years, Butler's patiently negotiated Education Act, 1944 was probably the best solution possible to what had been one (and at the time of writing still remains) of the most intractable problems in British politics.

DINGLE FOOT

Liberal MP and Parliamentary Secretary to the Ministry of Economic Warfare
In the first war you had to give coupons for restaurant meals, but in the
second war the Ministry calculated that the more people ate out of their
homes the better, because in fact less food is consumed. They therefore
wanted to induce people to eat in restaurants and particularly to eat in
canteens, and for that reason quite deliberately meals taken outside your
home were exempt from rationing. The great difficulty we discovered was to
get a great number of British workers to eat in canteens and many of them
insisted on going home even though it meant eating up the family rations.

OLIVER LYTTELTON

It was quite simple – the difference between rationed clothes and free
clothes is four hundred and fifty thousand workers, simply that. I came to
the conclusion when I looked at the manpower that this was a necessary
thing. Winston was opposed to it because he held a rather simple, straight-
forward view that the civilian population which kept up its morale the
longest would end up the winner. I told him that I thought the population wanted to do something, particularly the women, after Dunkirk,
wanted to feel they were part of the war. 'How dare you tell me what
public opinion is, where did I find you?' he said to me, that sort of thing.
So I said, 'Well, all right, I still think that' and when it came off and people
were glad to be a little bit shabby and felt that they were doing their stint,
he was absolutely delighted and announced to everybody, 'Here's somebody who taught the Prime Minister something he didn't know.' That's a
very engaging feature there – most people don't like it at all when other
people turn out to be right.

MICHAEL FOOT

There wasn't a tremendous protest about the suppression of the *Daily
Worker*, chiefly because that took place during the period before the
Russians came into the war. But at the time when the subsequent threat
was then made to the *Daily Mirror*, the *Daily Worker* case was brought up
with it because the action against both was done under Regulation 2-D.

As subsequent matters have revealed, the government was very near the complete suppression of the *Daily Mirror*, which would have, undoubtedly, caused a tremendous ferment because the *Mirror* was the spokesman for the feeling of many people up and down the country, and expressing it probably much better and more openly and much more bluntly than many other newspapers. Moreover the threat to the *Mirror*, which so nearly succeeded, did have an effect partly in emasculating the *Mirror* – I don't say completely emasculating it – but certainly the tone and temper of the *Mirror*'s criticisms of the government were modified and of course it had an effect on newspapers throughout the rest of Fleet Street. But I must say that if anybody looks at the papers of those days they will see that the government ministers – everybody – were bitterly criticised in the general press and even more in individual weekly newspapers like the *Tribune* or the *New Statesman*, so the idea that there was any general suppression I think is false.

TOM DRIBERG
British Independent Labour MP and later Soviet spy
I think Britain was freer than any of the other countries, probably, within the war. We had the rights of Parliament reserved, which was something, but it wasn't a free society in other respects. There was censorship but one newspaper had been suppressed, the *Daily Worker*, and the *Daily Mirror* had been warned that it might be suppressed, so it wasn't a free society in that way and of course, perhaps necessarily, we were locking up people without trial, the Fascists and people it was believed would be pro-Hitler and pro-Nazi if Hitler invaded. [Leader of the British Union of Fascists] Sir Oswald Mosley and his wife spent most of the war in Brixton prison – that's not part of a free society, imprisonment without trial – but it was agreed to at the time, under the pressures of wartime necessity, by pretty well everybody, including myself.

DINGLE FOOT
Sir Oswald Mosley was a very sick man, he'd been interned for a number of years without trial and I would have thought anybody who was in

favour of civil liberties would be glad to see him released, whatever his views might be. This wasn't the universal view and you even had the National Council for Civil Liberties making a nonsense of its own name by resisting his release.

CECIL HARMSWORTH KING
Proprietor of the Daily Mirror

The shares remained absolutely steady, sales remained absolutely steady, the only man who thought it was going to be shut down was Churchill. When it was brought up in the House of Commons, on the whole the House came out on the side of the *Mirror*, more or less. They didn't like the *Mirror* but they weren't going to have it suppressed. And after that we trimmed our sails a bit and the government forgot their foolishness. I was told at the time that the relevant episode was earlier. The country was covered with posters of Churchill and underneath it said the word 'Victory'. After we were thrown out of Singapore under conditions which did the war direction no credit at all we got a former member of your [Communist] Party to write a piece in which he said, 'There's a victory yourself, Mr. Churchill' and that was said to have annoyed him more than the loss of Singapore. After that he was looking for an excuse to suppress us and the cartoon was just what he thought a suitable occasion.

TOM DRIBERG

Things were going very badly in North Africa. Independent candidates were beginning to be put up to challenge the official coalition Cabinet because there was a party truce and if a member died or retired, his seat went automatically to the party who had held it. From about 1942 Independents started challenging this fix and one or two of them got into Parliament. Several friends said they thought I should consider standing. A month or two later, listening to the radio at night I heard that the Conservative Member of Parliament in the constituency in which I lived in Essex had died and I thought it was a chance and I took it. I hadn't the faintest idea how to be a candidate, I didn't belong to any party, didn't know the electoral law. First I went to see my employer, Lord Beaverbrook.

I was working at the *Daily Express* and he was a bit sceptical and the only advice he would give me was that I must wear a hat: British people will never vote for a man who doesn't wear a hat: He was completely wrong, as on so many things: I didn't wear a hat and I got in. On polling day – this was before the age of public-opinion polls – Beaverbrook was giving a lunch party in London; he said that according to his best advice from his man on the spot in New Malden [Essex], I was going to forfeit my deposit. In fact I won by a two-to-one majority.

ANTHONY EDEN
British Foreign Secretary

When Tobruk fell on 21 June 1942 Churchill was in Washington and the American press carried alarmist reports of the state of the government at home and possible votes of censure. Winston rang me up, I suppose about midnight his time, to ask what was happening, whether the government was still in office and what was going on. And I was able to tell him as far as I knew nothing had happened except that this motion had been tabled, which he'd have to take. By then Russia had been attacked and Pearl Harbor had taken place, so though there might be a rough passage there was very little doubt how the whole business would come out in the end and that there would be an Allied victory. The debate wasn't all that formidable for a number of reasons it's not worthwhile going into here, and once it was over the government was in comparatively calm waters. I was Leader of the House part of that time and there's a difficulty, in wartime: everyone nominally supports the government, all parties do, but that doesn't prevent quite a few people in each party suddenly thinking they want to be critical and that it wouldn't endanger the government. But from outside it looked as though there was much more criticism than probably there was and in itself it was healthy. It is remarkable, really, that during a war we were able to continue the conduct of Parliament like that with critics, some of them very formidable ones, saying whatever they wanted to say in public session or secret session.

TOM DRIBERG

I remember two persons in particular who were very helpful, both Christian Socialists. Although an Independent, I'd always made clear that I was a socialist and one of them was vicar of the famous socialist stronghold of Flaxted. The other even more interesting one was Jack, who was a person in the constituency and secretary of the Braintree local Labour Party, Braintree being the principal stronghold of Labour votes in this largely rural, largely Tory constituency. So he was in a bit of a dilemma because all the parties were officially supporting the coalition government. But I wouldn't have got elected if it hadn't been for the thousands of Labour votes and he came out and formed the committee in Braintree which promoted my candidature, for which, needless to say, he was removed or had to resign from the secretaryship of the local Labour Party, quite correctly in the bureaucratic sense. And then there were all sorts of other people. I daresay a few Tories voted for me because there was universal uneasiness about the war, they thought it was time for some fresh blood and then the Communists were supporting the war effort, Russia was in the war by now and the secretary of the local Communist Party also got expelled from his party for supporting me. He came out on the evening of poll and testified in the most dramatic way at a meeting in Braintree market square, because he had just heard the Conservative candidates had said that what was going wrong in North Africa was because too many supplies had been sent to Russia. The most dramatic event, which was a national tragedy, was the fall of Tobruk, which certainly pinpointed the need for changes pretty high up in the armed forces, if not in the government. I think Tobruk fell about three or four days before polling day in the election and it was a tragedy and we felt it was such, but nonetheless I'm bound to admit that it probably greatly added to the number of votes we got.

DINGLE FOOT

Secret sessions of Parliament did serve a particular purpose; it didn't mean of course that the government revealed any state secrets or military secrets. Obviously you don't do that to six hundred people, even though they are Members of Parliament. But it did enable the criticism of the government to be expressed much more freely than it could have been done in open debate, in which of course if somebody made an outright attack on the government that of course assisted the enemy propaganda, it was helping Dr Goebbels, and therefore people found it far more convenient to make their attack in secret session.

TOM DRIBERG

The impact, as so often with these great Parliamentary occasions, there was a bit of an anticlimax when you get there, and in this case the anti-climax came instantly in the opening speech of this ineffable old Tory, Sir John Ward, because he made this fantastic suggestion that there should be a Supreme Commander of all the armed forces who should be none other than the Duke of Gloucester. But there was a roar of laughter and a howl of disappointment from various parties in the House, and from then on the debate never really recovered its momentum. Although Nye Bevan and various others spoke very forcibly in support of the motion that 'This House has no confidence in the central direction of the war', which was a direct attack on Churchill, in the end Churchill won it very easily.

MICHAEL FOOT

I went to the debate because it was soon after the fall of Tobruk and the whole situation was extremely serious and the motion was going to be moved by Lord Milne on behalf of the critics, because the critics embraced some on the Tory side and some on the Labour side. Well, Lord Milne started off his speech by suggesting that one of the ways we could deal with the situation was to put the Duke of Gloucester in charge of the military forces of this country and I'm afraid this did not conduce to the effectiveness of his speech. It looked as though the whole vote of censure was going to be blown up in derision and so Aneurin Bevan got up in the most awkward circumstances on the second day to try to repair this situation. There was not the slightest doubt that the whole place was shaken by what he said, partly of course because his criticisms fitted so closely with what many people in the House of Commons knew to be the truth of reports from the front and partly because it merged into a general misgiving, which was widespread in the House at this time, about the general strategy of the war. He concluded the speech by emphasising demands about the Second Front – which was not so widely shared in the House of Commons, although of course it was shared by many strategists, particularly in the United States.

RAB BUTLER

We had very few home civil Cabinets in the war. We had this committee under Reconstruction Minister Lord Woolton, which really did splendid work; it finally approved my Education Bill. It launched the bill of the Health Service and Beveridge's plan, it launched the whole of the post-war housing plan and the Insurance Bill which the Labour government introduced in 1946 – also some very powerful Labour men were on it: Bevin, Attlee and Morrison. Churchill didn't take much interest really but he was pleased to support the Reconstruction Committee. He had a great regard for Bevin and he was pleased to support any social reform that Bevin supported. Bevin was a most remarkable man because, practically uneducated, he managed to deal with everything, including the whole foreign affairs of the country, and he was one of our greatest helps on that committee, and Lord Woolton was a very good chairman. We had two or three Conservatives on it, a man called Oliver Lyttelton was very bright and helpful, and then that sinister figure Lord Cherwell we used to call 'The Prof'. He represented Churchill on the committee and hurried off to tell him the news after every meeting because Churchill wanted to know how we were going to go in for nationalisation. And we had a proposal by Herbert Morrison to nationalise the electricity industry and that's where the coalition government stopped and they couldn't get agreement on that. But Herbert tried to get us to agree to nationalise electricity, which after all we agree to now. The Conservatives felt we mustn't go too far in wartime on the home front and we'd already gone a long way because the Health Service is one of the biggest things in any country in the world. There has never been a plan like the Beveridge Plan and it was all planned in that committee.*

MICHAEL FOOT

Defence Regulation 1AA [banning strikes in essential services] was introduced by Labour Minister Ernest Bevin with the support of the whole of the official trade-union movement, but here again Aneurin Bevan understood better the ferment outside and there was a massive unofficial strike among the miners because they felt they were being extremely unjustly treated. That was not understood by the official leadership of the miners or by the official leadership of the Labour Party as a whole. This regulation was introduced by Ernest Bevin to try to deal with the kind of threat of strike action that, as he was saying, was incited by unofficial agitators. Aneurin Bevan poured scorn on what was said and argued that the official leaders of the unions didn't understand what the rank and file were thinking and saying.

'BILL'

Betteshanger Colliery striker

There were several of the local residents, and particularly some of the troops, they were jeering and sneering at us, but little did they know that at the time we were manning this pit twenty-four hours a day, with the Home Guard, troops and ourselves, and many of us worked and stopped at the pit here twenty-four hours a day, so that in one sense we were patriotic in the safeguarding of the interests of the other capitalist owners. I don't think Churchill would have interfered. I don't think he wanted us to go to prison – I think he wanted us to stay here and guard his property, because it was his property after all, it wasn't ours.

---

* The report by Sir William Beveridge (1879–1963), published in December 1942, provided the blueprint for the Welfare State legislation of the post-war Labour government.

LIEUTENANT HUGH DANIEL
Eighth Army dispatch rider

I'm sure it was at the time of Alamein, or a little before, there was some industrial dispute in this country concerning the miners, the details of which I've never followed up. But when this was reported it did cause tremendous distress because at that time I remember being with the 50th Division, Tyne and Teesdale, and these lads from the north-east were really baffled. They were fighting hard and enduring hardship and they couldn't understand how back in this country, when even Russia had come into the war, they couldn't understand how the miners could be squabbling back home when everything was needed to push the wheel round.

TOM DRIBERG

There were lots of Jews serving in the Polish forces stationed in Britain, this was a good deal later, early in 1944 when the British forces were getting ready for D-Day and they didn't want any trouble in the rear, and so there were some difficulty about these unfortunate Jewish soldiers. They were being persecuted in the Polish forces stationed in Scotland and about one hundred of them deserted or went absent, came to London to hide in the East End and sent a message to me and I went to see them. It was a very dramatic moment in a darkened hall in the black-out, groping one's way through East End Lane to find this obscure hall, and great tension in it, as these hundred and twenty men sat around. I couldn't see them properly and they told us of the appalling persecutions to which they were subject and the constant insults. Again and again a man would say that one of his supposed mates, the Polish soldiers, would say to him, 'When we land in France, one bullet for a German, one for you, bloody Yid.' So we had to take this up in Parliament and there was quite a tussle about this, but the War Office gave way rather reasonably and rather quickly and agreed that because of the impending D-Day they agreed to transfer all these men *en bloc* to the British Army and they settled down very happily.

ARTHUR BOTTOMLEY

Trade-union leader and Walthamstow borough councillor

There was a lowering of morale and near panic in Dover towards the end of the war, but this was understandable: Dover had been bombed and shelled every day for four years. To the rest of the country the war was over, but to Dover and Folkestone and those areas it was not. Dover got a particularly heavy bombardment and I had to go down and explain to them the reason why they were suffering was because the German guns on the French side were so heavily fortified. If the Canadians who were there had made a frontal assault, thousands would have been killed. I'm very glad to say the people in Dover and elsewhere accepted this and I want to pay tribute to the people of Dover and Folkestone – they knew more about the war than any other people in this country, including the fighting men, because they had a battle on their doorstep every day.

JOHN ROGAN

Air Navigator, Eighth Air Force, USAAF

The most vivid memory I have of World War Two was not a combat experience. I remember the sights in the Underground in London where many of the children were sleeping against the walls and we were told that some of them had stayed there for periods of weeks and hadn't even gone up to see the sunlight.

LUCY FAITHFULL

There was a small survey done when the war was over in the London area and a number of children who had been evacuated for the duration of the war were seen and assessed and a control group of children who had remained in their own homes in London and had therefore not gone to school, had slept in the Underground with their parents at night, had not had school meals or school milk. These two sets of children were assessed together and as far as it was possible to make the assessment the children who had stayed in their own homes in London with all the apparent disadvantages were taller, were heavier and were emotionally more balanced and happier children than those who had been in billets in the country for the duration of the war away from their homes and families.

MICHAEL FOOT

Aneurin Bevan was always getting into trouble at the Party meetings where the majority supported the leadership of Attlee and [Ernest] Bevin and those who were members of the coalition government. But Aneurin Bevan understood better than most of them – and they were deeply occupied of course in their tasks in the war – he understood the ferment that there was outside. There was deep, widespread radical ferment that was illustrated in the election victory for the Labour Party in 1945. Bevan had prophesied that victory and was confident it was going to happen when most of the others did not believe it was possible. Indeed, Bevin and Attlee wished to sustain the coalition government after the war and it was largely the awareness of the ferment in the country, and of how radical it was and how Labour could put itself at its head, which Bevan realised, which destroyed the possibility of the continuance of the coalition and gave Labour the chance to get independent power.

RAB BUTLER

In my day education wasn't chartered as being so expensive, but the Beveridge Plan was mentioned in millions, and Churchill got very worried and his two Chancellors of the Exchequer, Sir Kingsley Wood and Sir John Anderson, were equally critical. And that's why the Beveridge Plan was delayed after my bill, that's why education came first.

LUCY FAITHFULL

During the whole of the evacuation period I think that in the field of child care and in the field of family life we learned more than we perhaps would ever have learned otherwise. I think that the great mix-up of different types of people in different areas, town and country to the forefront, underlined a tremendous need in the country overall, and I think therefore that the evacuation was the impetus to social legislation following the war.

CHAPTER 23

OCCUPATION AND RESISTANCE

The episode Occupation: Holland 1940–1944 *was among the best of the series because, like all good historians and journalists, its makers let the interviewees tell the story. I have combined their excellent research with material collected but not used in the earlier episode* Inside the Reich: Germany 1940–1944, *which hardly deals with Germany at all – it is mainly about Stalingrad, perhaps because the episode on Stalingrad eschewed interviews altogether. This was unfortunate, because the question of German resistance to Hitler's malignant regime is one that has yet to be fully integrated into our understanding of the war. Although at first Hitler's undoubted popularity was the principal obstacle to any attempt to remove him from power, there can be no doubt that Franco-British appeasement followed by the ineffectual Phoney War and the collapse of France made him seem magical. Later, the policy of unconditional surrender announced at Casablanca made even officers who hated all he stood for shrink from overthrowing him.*

There was another even more discreditable theme. It began with the kidnapping in November 1939 of two British Secret Intelligence Service (SIS) officers at Venlo, near the Dutch–German border, where they had been lured by SS Colonel Walter Schellenberg posing as a disaffected Army officer. The two officers had with them a list of all SIS agents in Germany, who were rounded up. From this, in part, stemmed Allied refusal to credit all subsequent approaches by the German Resistance. Secondly, thanks to failures by Special Operations Executive (SOE) desk officers, German counter-intelligence was able to play the 'England Game' using captured

Dutch SOE agents to send false messages back to London, which led to the death of fifty-four SOE agents and the dismantling of organised Dutch Resistance. The culpability of the British officers was covered up and the resulting, unjustified, suspicion of the Dutch led to them not being consulted in the planning of the disastrous Arnhem operation (Market Garden) in September 1944.

ALBERT SPEER
Hitler's Armaments Minister

The way I was going along with Hitler is much more complicated. I can't say that it was a direct line. I was realistic about the outcome of war and of the situation and I did think in a realistic way to prevent the worst. But on the other hand Hitler was still there and his ability to mesmerise people I think was also working with me, so my behaviour was in some way schizoid. I didn't behave like a normal man who would have said, 'This man I can't work with any more.' I was working against him, I was plotting many things against him, but after a while I was again with him. It's almost not understandable this behaviour without knowing what power Hitler had over his surroundings.

HERTHA BEESE
Berlin housewife, Social Democrat

I once took in the baby of a school friend, because both parents had been leading Communists and had been taken away. The baby had not been with me for an hour before they arrived to search my flat, 'Whose baby is this?' I replied honestly that this was my friend's baby who had been arrested as a Communist leader. When the mother sent me clothing for the baby it had become known immediately and my flat was searched again. They asked what was in the parcel and I replied, baby's clothes. Well, they could hardly have taken the baby away from me – what would they have done with it? But maybe years later they would even have done that. Then they left, embarrassed, but warned me they would come back. Who was watching us, informing on us? When I returned from Bernau by bicycle, sure enough the gauleiter arrived only

General Erwin Rommel during Auchinleck's Crusader
offensive in the Desert War, November 1941.

General Bernard Montgomery before El Alamein.

On the Eastern Front.
An Arctic convoy,
Winter 1941–42.

Panzers cross the
steppe, 1942.

Germans are marched into captivity after surrender at Stalingrad.
Most of these men would die in captivity.

The devastating raids on Hamburg, July 1943. Speer told Hitler that six more such raids would end the war.

The USAAF's first raid into Germany was on the Focke-Wulf factory at Marienburg on 9 October 1943.

Interviewee, then Air Marshal Sir Arthur Harris.

It wasn't only the SS – German Army massacre of Jews at Katowice, Poland, 8 September 1939.

Massacre of the Mizocz ghetto by an Einzatsgruppe, 14 October 1942. Interviewee Rivka Yoselevska survived an identical atrocity.

A forced show of unity between Generals Giraud and de Gaulle at the Casablanca Conference, January 1943.

Never forgiven: de Gaulle is not pleased as Paris cheers Churchill, November 1944.

Changing of the Guard: Attlee, Truman and Stalin at Potsdam, July 1945.

Carnage on the beach at Iwo Jima, 19 February 1944, with Mount Suribachi looming in the background. The raising of the flag on top of it four days later created one of the iconic photographs of the war.

Brigadier Orde Wingate (*centre*), interviewee Mike Calvert and others during the first Chindit expedition, Burma.

General Sir William Slim, 'Bill' Slim or 'Uncle Bill' to his many admirers.

(*right*) End-game in Europe: German soldier advances in the Battle of the Bulge.

(*below*) Comradely reassurance, Juno Beach.

GI next to the death train that evacuated 3,000 prisoners, most of whom died, from Buchenwald to Dachau in April 1945.

Some of the SS guards shot out-of-hand by American troops who liberated Dachau on 29 April 1945. Others were beaten to death, with the participation of camp survivors.

SS Lieutenant Colonel Rudolf Suttrop, Dachau Adjutant, hanged there 28 May 1946.

an hour later. Somebody must have seen us returning and must have informed on us immediately. It seemed we were surrounded by invisible evil spirits, who watched and betrayed us.

DR OTTO JOHN

Lufthansa lawyer under Klaus Bonhoeffer, older brother of German Resistance Pastor Dietrich Bonhoeffer

The network was gradually built up. In the beginning it was a close circle around the Bonhoeffer family with connections within Berlin and outside Berlin to university professors, to doctors all of high academic standing, liberal-minded and at heart anti-Nazi for moral more than for any other reasons. Later on they were joined by officers from all quarters, particularly conservative officers and generals of the First World War who were afraid that Hitler would lose the war. It was my job at the beginning of the war, once I had been introduced into the circle of Hans von Dohnanyi, who was the son of the Hungarian composer Erno Dohnanyi, it fell on me by chance because I had so many soldier contacts in Berlin, so I was making acquaintances here and there through trusted friends and was able to establish contacts between people who by tradition were not really friends at the beginning but in front of Hitler they got together.*

LIEUTENANT EWALD-HEINRICH VON KLEIST-SCHMENZIN

Surviving conspirator of the July 1944 bomb plot against Hitler

It's extremely dangerous in a dictatorship to do something against a dictatorship and it was very easy to lose your head. And most people like their own head pretty much. Furthermore, I think a person who has never lived in a dictatorship can't understand the power of propaganda. If you just hear always the same, if you read in every newspaper the same and you have very few possibilities for other information then you become very

---

* Dr Hans von Dohnanyi (1902–45) was a senior official in the Reichs Ministry of Justice, later seconded to the Abwehr (German Military Intelligence), where Hans Oster had attempted to warn France and Britain about Hitler's intentions before the war and which under Admiral Wilhelm Canaris became a hub of Resistance activity.

impressed by the things which you are told. And it's very difficult to have – to make up your own mind, to be critical.

DR JOHN

People in general just didn't think much. Life was easy for them, lots of work had been provided for them, exports were blossoming and they were just well-to-do people but without thinking about what was going on politically. One should also note that what the Nazis did behind the scenes was very well covered – I mean it wasn't easy at all to find out what was going on. Our group was very well informed because Hans von Dohnanyi was the Personal Assistant to the Minister of Justice and through him we had access to all information which one could possibly have in Berlin from the circle around Hitler.

HERTHA BEESE

In the flat underneath ours lived a Jewish family. The only reason they had not yet been persecuted and taken away was that the father was Italian and belonged to Mussolini's party. But when we ourselves faced more and more difficulties the wife began to feel insecure and was scared that they might take her away despite the Italian connection and she therefore left. So their flat became empty and I begged that it should not be handed over to the landlord since we still hoped there would be a total collapse and we would all be rid of our difficulties. I looked after the empty flat and one night, it must have been around midnight, the doorbell rang. I opened and there stood in front of me a Jewish couple. This was how I began to help persecuted Jews. All of a sudden I had entered an invisible circle of people who smuggled Jews about. As soon as one hiding place had been detected they were quickly passed on. They would always move about by night. I have never found out who it was who sent them to me in the first place. Some decent people. The problems started with the feeding of the Jewish people since they neither had food-rationing cards nor very often any money. So we in turn had to make use of friends who exchanged their smoking cards for the odd potato or bread, or a friend would come and leave a bit of food. But all this was so illegal that names, sources or contacts had to remain unknown.

DR JOHN

There were friends of ours who'd been arrested and we knew their families were watched, friends of theirs were watched and the telephones were tapped. Since 1943 we were aware that the next morning the Gestapo would come. One couldn't tell how people in prison would stand up under interrogation. We expected to be arrested, all of us to be arrested, because we couldn't tell whether or not they had been tortured and had given away names. So from that time onwards we really had to be afraid of the next morning – it was said that with the milkman was coming the Gestapo.*

RITA BOAS-KOUPMANN

Dutch–Jewish teenager

My oldest brother, he knows a lot about politics, but my parents and the rest of the family didn't know so much. What they heard from Germany they didn't believe and they didn't like even the Jewish people coming from Germany because the things they told us were so horrible. And we didn't like them, you know why? We were not rich at all and they, they had better houses than we had, admittedly because they came to Holland with money. It sounds crazy , but we were not so very alarmed – we didn't believe all the things they said. My brother, I mean Eddie, the oldest one, came to our house in the days the war started and said, 'Come with me, let's try to escape.' And I remember my mother said, 'I must wait for the man who brings the laundry. What would you want me to escape from? I want to stay in my house and you have to do with politics, not me. What should the Germans do to me?'

PRINCE BERNHARD OF LIPPE–BIESTERFELD

Son-in-law of Queen Wilhelmina of the Netherlands

What I remember vividly was a feeling of complete frustration because I took my wife and the children over to England and I was absolutely

---

* Pastor Dietrich and Klaus Bonhoeffer were arrested at the end of 1943, as were Hans von Dohnanyi and Josef Mueller who had collaborated on a dossier of Nazi war crimes and of resistance plans passed through Pope Pius XII to London. Admiral Canaris and Hans Oster were dismissed from the Abwehr in January 1944 and later executed.

certain at the moment that I left that I would come back the next day. Of course we'd been fighting for three days and I took part in some of the actions in and around the palace, extraordinary enough as it may seem. I made friends with the boys that were guarding my mother-in-law and the family and I said that I'd be back tomorrow. And the next day as it happened the bombardment of Rotterdam had taken place so after my mother-in-law arrived in England I had only one feeling – I wanted to get back. I was lucky, thanks to some friends, that I managed to get back on a destroyer to Dunkirk and from Dunkirk to Zeeland and to see the rest of the fight there. Then I had to make my way back to England and after that we thought what can we do to continue, how can we start training the new people that will come from all over the world?*

COMMISSIONER HIEJENK
Amsterdam police officer
When the Germans crossed the bridge into Amsterdam across the Amstel there were lots of people and the most terrible thing was that among those people were a lot of them who brought up their hands in the Hitler greeting, so that you knew that they were happy for the Germans to arrive. There was nothing more terrible than to see that, to see Dutch people greeting the German troops. Another terrible thing that appeared was that several Dutch people you had trusted now turned out to be on the side of the Germans. That was the nastiest and most terrible moment that I as a policeman have experienced.

DR LOUIS DE JONG
Announcer on Radio Orange
The Netherlands government, in July 1940, was the first government-in-exile which got a broadcast programme of its own. This programme was called Radio Orange because the symbol of the Royal House of Orange

---

* Prince Bernhard was a German aristocrat who had been a member, for convenience, of the Nazi Party and the SS Cavalry Corps before marrying Crown Princess Juliana in 1936.

was of great importance to the people in occupied Holland and so we started on 28th July 1940 with a stirring speech by Queen Wilhelmina. Conditions of broadcasting were difficult at the time not only because of the war going on, the bombing of London, but also because at first we had very little news from occupied Holland. So early in 1941 when there was a danger that we were running out of texts – the news at the time was always broadcast by the BBC European Service – we decided to start a political cabaret. I remember that we looked in all the gramophone shops in London for old Dutch records, because we used the tunes of these records and put new words to the tunes.

JETJE PAERL
Singer on Radio Orange

They had a programme every week but I wasn't in it every week. But my father wrote the songs every Saturday night and he used to listen all during the night to hear if there were any new things happening in the war that he could use, especially news that was not broadcast or was not talked about in occupied Holland. So for instance the first meeting of Churchill and Roosevelt, he wrote a song about that. And he took very often well-known songs that everybody could whistle, and made political – if you can call it that – words on it, anti-German war songs, so that the next day when people were walking in the street or cycling they could whistle this song and everybody would recognise the tune and would think, Oh, he's listened to Radio Orange too. That gave a kind of togetherness of anti-German feeling.

EDDI CHRISTIANI
Orchestra leader

The Germans give out a bulletin to everybody who was playing music, to every singer, to everybody who was actually in the business, that first of all it was forbidden to play any kind of music that was composed by a Jewish composer or an American composer or a British composer. You can imagine – no music of Gershwin, no music of Cole Porter, no music of Irving Berlin and so on and so on. Even it was forbidden to play sway Dutch music and people dancing on that music. It was allowed for the Dutch people to sit down in a hall and just listen to music, but no dancing. It was also forbidden to make show with your orchestra. For instance it wasn't allowed for a trumpet player to play a muted trumpet, like Duke Ellington, or to croon. It was forbidden for a trumpet player or a saxophone player to make a movement of his instrument like swaying, it was forbidden to play a higher note than a C, a rhythm C, because it was all negro music and they say in Germany negro was the music of the devil and we are now a cultivated people, so were the Germans, so we had to play proper cultivated music. But we musicians who liked to play a good sway tune we find always a way to fool them. I can't say the Germans were a stupid people aside from that because in the past they make good music and they composed very good light music too. But we don't like the way they treated us, you know, because we are free birds and if you forbid a free bird he like to find a way to show. Just before the war we learned the song 'In the Mood' and we translate it and during the whole occupation we play 'In the Mood' and there were many Germans who believed it was a Dutch song.

RITA BOAS-KOUPMANN

I think the alarm started when Jewish people had their card with a 'J' on it. That was the first time they marked you, you had your identity card you had to carry with you and what was special was the 'J' in it and you were marked because anybody could ask for the card.

DR BRUINS SLOT
Dutch–Christian Resistance
The mistake we almost all made in Holland, apart perhaps from a few, is that we signed a declaration that we did not have any Jewish blood. You must understand we are, Holland is, a country that hasn't been at war since Napoleon. We were completely taken by surprise and psychologically we were completely broken, and perhaps you might understand the devilish system in principle but you could not see all its consequences. You must not think that all the Resistance fighters have done everything right. I don't think so at all, but it was only very slowly becoming clear.

MR VAN DER VEEN
Dutch–Christian Resistance

In November 1940 the Jewish professors of the technical university were sacked and we protested in the form of a strike. Then the university was closed and not opened until next year in April. So that was the beginning – you couldn't do your normal study programme and then you were politicised a little bit by identifying with the oppressed in the form of the Jewish professors.

B J SIJES
Dutch Resistance, Amsterdam

There were demonstrations on the birthday of Prince Bernhard at the end of June 1940. People took the opportunity to express their anti-German feeling in that way. There were demonstrations against the dismissing of Jewish civil servants and university professors. Then students went on strike in November 1940 and there are street fighting against the Dutch Nazis in summer and autumn of 1940. The economic conditions were getting worse and young workers were threatened with forced labour in Germany. And when the Germans began to terrorise the Jews living in the centre of the town, where the most poor of them were living, the Jews organised themselves in battle groups. These were the first battle groups in occupied Holland and they got help from non-Jewish workers. In another part of Amsterdam, a more wealthy part, Jews helped by non-Jews started a fight against a detachment of the Gestapo. As a reprisal the Germans arrested on Saturday and Sunday the 22nd and 23rd of February in a very brutal way more than four hundred Jews between twenty and thirty-five years. This caused immense indignation and on Monday 24 February everywhere and especially in the factories people talked of the outrage that took place in the Jewish quarter. The next day, 25th February 1941, the first anti-occupation strike in history broke out, more than one million people were involved in it.

GERBERN WAGENAAR

Dutch–Communist Resistance

It was the biggest demonstration, the protest of the people against the persecution of the Jews, that spread so enormously among the population, because those feelings were very strong, that it became a general strike. It was a demonstration against the Nazis, against the Nazi occupation, against the persecution of the Jews … Thousands in a closed group marched through the streets of the centre of Amsterdam while the Germans with tanks circled around them. They didn't have any weapons so they found their weapon in marching and singing the Internationale.

COMMISSIONER HIEJENK

There were Jews who under the threat of the Germans had to betray other Jews. The way the Germans put the pressure on those Jews to make them betray their fellow sufferers is something I don't want to talk about because that was really vicious. I know of a case when someone had been shot by the Resistance, a doctor, but I won't tell you his name. This doctor was very gifted and talented and this man had betrayed several of his fellow kinsmen, betrayed to the Germans but so badly that the Resistance had to kill him. That's one case – but another more difficult case is a Jew who betrayed several people. He is shot down and he is hit in the belly and wounded like this he is taken into a Jewish hospital. So the Jewish doctor is obliged to treat this Jew who had betrayed his fellow man to the Germans, and he had to try to keep him alive, and that is a very difficult decision.

DR SLOT

My main reason for joining the Resistance were not nationalistic reasons. I joined the Resistance because I recognised the devil in the National Socialistic system. It is the most perverse barbarism we have known in the course of history. I reached this conclusion by reading a book by Herman Rauschning, *The Revolution of Nihilism*. I would like to add that Herman Rauschning has been a National Socialist, he had been a governor for Hitler in Danzig, but at a certain point he saw through it. Then he wrote this book, which shows very clearly how perverse this National Socialism was.

MR VAN HALL

Dutch banker who ran an illegal welfare organisation to help victims of the Occupation

It was simply that you couldn't stand it, what was happening around you, and you said I'm not going to take it. I'm a rather stubborn man at times, all members of my family are the same, and we couldn't have it that these people marched around and did the most awful things in our country. Now if we'd been in your country we would have served in the armed forces, but that was impossible of course. Some Hollanders left Holland and went to England and it often took them a very long time, but I was an older man and that didn't come up. Furthermore I was involved so much in this business and I thought it was very important, but I felt just like your soldiers must have felt. The only thing is we didn't carry guns – but we did it in another way.

MR VAN DER VEEN

In that time you had seen such terrible things that you felt the very integrity of your being as a Christian was at stake. In reacting to this situation we should make ourselves available for the oppressed and take the risks that come with it. I felt that being in the hands of my Lord was the special equipment to be available for the dangerous jobs that had to be done. I was not married, I had no children and of course it's a question of character and temperament, partly, but I felt that I could take that risk. There are certain limitations to what the Germans could do to you if you are in the hands of the Lord. They can shoot you, they can kill you, but the relationship with Christ goes beyond the possibilities of German police and therefore I felt free. There was taking care after me, if that is English. You felt free to be available for other men and I said to my girlfriend when we discussed it, 'As Christians we can't make a point of the risk that you accept by doing the dirty job.'

ANONYMOUS ROTTERDAM WOMAN

I was working in a café–restaurant in the kitchens as a cleaning woman and there was also a man, a very nice chap – I got on with him very well. One morning it was freezing and he comes in with his collar down and I say to him, 'Oh, Tom, aren't you cold? and I grab his collar and I put it up. And then suddenly as I fastened it up I feel this little triangle, the little NSB [Dutch Nazi Party] pin. I got a terrific shock and he got a shock himself because he never would have thought that I would touch his collar. But he was still a nice guy because after that I would call him 'Dirty Black Dog' and he would just reply 'Orange Goat', just like that.

DICK WOUDENBERG

Teenage son of a prominent Dutch Nazi

It was very difficult for me to go to a normal Dutch school because my father was a well-known man on the one side but I think on the other he was a hated man. And it is not very nice for a young boy to have a hated father. There was a possibility in the first year of the war to go to Germany to this National Socialistic educating institute and I was very glad to have this possibility to switch. I was very glad to leave this country, then. In a very short time I was educated in this SS thinking – a great Germanistic empire and there was no reason for me to think about Holland and the Netherlands. This war had to be won and I was too young, but when I had the age I had to be a soldier to fight for this country, to give it its place in the greater Germanistic empire. And then it went so far that we could leave behind a situation that was too old, that little, small country was an old fact in history and we came to the new situation – this great new Germanistic empire.

PETRONELLA ELDERING

Dutch Resistance

I think it was quite a vital thing, you know, it was the best way to live during the war to do something against the occupier. It was something that made you happy that you could do it, it gave you a feeling of being, not brave but just doing something worth while. You see, you just had to do it.

MR VAN DER BOOGARD
Dutch factory worker

After the disaster of May 1940 the Germans took our officers of the Army to prison camps. Later on most of the officers were sent away home. I don't know exactly the reason but in the end of April 1943 they said that all the officers of the formal Dutch Army must go back to the prison camps. Well, we did not like it, but what will we do, what can we do? So here in this factory some people said we will go on strike, don't work any further. We phoned to everybody, you know we had many connections all over the Netherlands at that time. Elsie knew everybody and so she phoned to say we are going home, we don't work any longer and we will go on strike.

GERBERN WAGENAAR

What drove me personally, and I think all of the other people, we were driven by a terrific hate because we'd never experienced anything like that in Amsterdam, that many people just because they were Jewish, that those people – women and children and there was no exception – that those people were just arrested and knocked about. So you almost got a feeling to see someone in the water so there's not really anything left but to dive after him to get him out. You don't ask yourself is it clean or is it polluted, you are filled with anger. I'm still absolutely sure it helped to relieve their fear and terror, the depression and the despondence, that it helped cheer those people up. But we've only realised that afterwards – at that moment it was sheer hate.

ANONYMOUS ROTTERDAM HOUSEWIFE

When the doorbell was rung, two Germans, they both came up the stairs and one stayed at the top of the stairs, the other came into the room. He looked all over the room and the two men who were there had to get dressed and come with them. And we, being women, crying of course, both of us, one woman with the baby in her arms and the other one hanging on to her skirt. And I can still recall vividly the one German who was inside the room, he was crying and the tears were streaming down his face and he said, 'Oh, I'm so terribly sorry I'm not alone,' that is to say I would love to help you but I can't do anything because there is another one with me. He couldn't do it but he would have tried very hard to leave those two men there because he thought it was terrible. And that was the first time I'd ever seen a German cry, and to see him really cry, big tears down his face. He was terribly upset.

ALBERT SPEER

None of my thoughts about assassinating Hitler succeeded and such ideas have something ridiculous if they don't succeed. I am quite aware of that – I only wanted to state how far Hitler was forcing one of his followers in the end of the war by his attitude, that he was forcing him freely to think about killing him. One can see in the end of a person sometimes his whole life, and in my opinion the end of Hitler showing us what the whole thing was like. It was more an idea to kill Hitler, but that can't be compared with what the people around Stauffenberg did because they were doing it for a very high ethical level and this was not the case for me.

MAJOR GENERAL WALTHER WARLIMONT

Deputy Chief of Wehrmacht Operations

My disillusionment had begun early during the otherwise so successful campaign against France; at many instances during the campaign against Russia, when Hitler dispersed the German forces on our march to the south of Russia, to Stalingrad, with all the consequences. So there was not much to get disillusioned about later, all he did then in my opinion was no more military leadership, it was just despair, obstinacy against everything which went wrong.

DR JOHN

Claus von Stauffenberg was wounded in Africa, he had lost his left eye, three fingers of his left hand and his right hand altogether. He came to Berlin to do Staff Officer work in the High Command of the Home Army and this placed him in a position to be near the original conspirators. He came to Berlin in October 1943, before that he'd been in hospital and before then he'd been in Africa. Now he was a very intelligent and able

Staff Officer and he realised nothing would be done unless someone really went into it and saw to it that things were properly prepared in a General Staff manner. I never forget a friend of mine, a captain of the First World War who was working in intelligence, he came to me and said, 'Otto, we've got a young man who's come in and he's the one who will do something.' In the end it did turn out that he did take action. Originally he was only the planner but then he became aware that there was no other chance for any other officer to get near Hitler, which he could do because he had to report to Hitler's headquarters and attend conferences there. This enabled him to get really near to Hitler and then to make the attempt, which he did on 20th July 1944. I was prepared since November 1943 because since March 1942 it was my particular job to try and establish contact in Madrid and Lisbon with the governments of the United States and England.*

MAJOR OTTO-ERNST REMER
Commander of the Berlin Guard Regiment, July 1944
The whole conspiracy was organised in a dilettante fashion. They had especially overlooked the fact that the German Army was fighting for Germany and for Europe and wanted to win the war. Every German knew that if Hitler was assassinated then the war would be lost and nobody could hinder the Russians to invade Europe. In addition to this the preparation of the putsch was insufficient. One had to know the mentality of the German Army and know that the overriding duty was to the oath of loyalty. Any putsch such as Stauffenberg's had to succeed in killing Hitler because it was to him that the oath was sworn. This could not be achieved by cowardly placing a bomb in a corner – he should have had the courage to use a pistol and shoot Hitler. This is what a real man would have done and I would have respected him. On the contrary one of the main conspirators, General Erich Fellgiebel, who was in charge of suspending immediately the central news office in headquarters, when he heard that Hitler was alive

* John made contact with British Intelligence when posted to Madrid and escaped to England after the failure of the July Plot.

419

went straight to the leader and congratulated him on his survival. These are things that I, as a soldier, cannot understand.

ALBERT SPEER

Those of 20th July plot I saw quite often. My job as Armaments Minister brought a weekly contact with them because they were all my clients in some way. When we discussed things they were very bitter, but never about how far they wanted to go; they were just showing me that organisation is very low, that many things could be done to make things more effective and so on. It was found out a few days later that there was a list of new government which was drafted by those who plotted. It was found I was Minister, in this new government, for Armament. Luckily enough behind my name was the question mark, which was proof that I was not involved in the plot. If Stauffenberg could have succeeded in killing Hitler, in my opinion things could have taken quite another course because when, for instance, in Vienna the gauleiter was taken over by an officer and a few soldiers and was arrested for a while, there was no countermeasure, they just behaved like sheep and let themselves be arrested, which I wouldn't have believed before. And the same thing happened in Paris where the whole of the Gestapo was arrested without taking any defence measures. So if Hitler would have been killed I think there would have been really a chance for the men who made the plot of 20th July to come through.

GRAND ADMIRAL KARL DÖNITZ

On 20th July 1944 I was at my post of command to the north of Berlin; towards noon I was called by telephone by my communication officer in Hitler's headquarters in the province of East Prussia. He told me that it was necessary that I should come as quickly as possible to Hitler's headquarters; the reason, why I should come, he did not tell me speaking by telephone. When I arrived by plane in the late afternoon I was instructed at once on the aerodrome what had happened. Who belonged to this Resistance organisation and which reason and project it had I did not know at this time. About my opinion which I have today, on this question,

I have written in my book. There's no doubt that the persons who made this attack were morally right.

MAJOR GENERAL WARLIMONT

I couldn't say that the July Plot had any effect on Hitler's ideas; he just kept to this illusionary idea that it would be possible to resume the offensive in the West as soon as possible. But his relations to the General Staff had never been particularly good because they were in his National Socialist Party eyes a flock of intellectuals or defeatists. And from July on this opinion deepened to a suspicion to almost every General Staff Officer as an adversary of his regime and even his person.

LIEUTENANT COLONEL RICHARD SCHULZE-KOSSENS
Waffen-SS

Hitler and all the people who were at the headquarters were shocked by the attempt and later on Hitler has spoken about the July Plot and he never understood that Stauffenberg or another officer, or a general, didn't want to risk his own life to kill him, but rather preferred to risk the lives of some of their own comrades who were present at the military conference when the bomb exploded, and some of them were killed or injured at this time. There were hundreds of officers who came into the headquarters and they could have the possibility to kill him when they wanted – if they risked their own life.

ALBERT SPEER

I was in the room when Goebbels was counteracting the July 1944 plot and I was discussing with him some facts, that Himmler was not to be found. They tried everything to find out where he stays because he was Minister of Interior and he was chief of the whole SS, and it was up to him to fight this plot. But obviously he was hiding somewhere and the same happened with the SS troops, a small number which were in Berlin, they were just as if they couldn't be there. And then late in the night Himmler showed up when everything was finished. Goebbels asked him, 'Where have you been?' and he had some phrase, 'Well, it's better you stay away somewhere far, in a lonely place so you can't get involved in it because you can't erect the countermeasures much better if you are not in the middle of it'. But Goebbels obviously didn't believe him, he mistrusted definitely Himmler this day. I had the same feeling.

DR JOHN

Later on in the night of 20th July 1944 about midnight the announcer said soon the Führer will speak to the German people. I laughed, 'Oh, nonsense, he can't speak, he's dead.' Then I thought that they, the Nazis, had at their disposal a voice being able to imitate Hitler, as we had one at the ready if need be. Then I thought that the imitator would talk but actually at three or four minutes to one o'clock he started talking and I at once recognised his voice and I was flabbergasted that he should be alive.

CHAPTER 24

STRATEGIC BOMBING: US ARMY AIR FORCE

The summary report of the September 1945 US Strategic Bombing Survey (USSBS) was to a degree influenced by the revulsion felt by some of its members to its subject matter. It differed, too, in some respects from the compendious final report of the USSBS. The World at War *episode* Whirlwind: Bombing Germany 1939–1944 *reflected the summary report, whose Director, George Ball, and Chief Economist, John Kenneth Galbraith, were among those interviewed. The survey started from the premise brought into the war by the USAAF about the greater accuracy of daytime over night bombing – no longer true in 1945 when the RAF could bomb as accurately by night as by day – and in the transcript we can see how US Lieutenant General Eaker became exasperated by his interviewer's attempt to get him to revive the false dichotomy. As noted by Air Chief Marshal Harris in an earlier chapter and by General (then Colonel) LeMay in this one, critics of night bombing are inclined to overlook the matter of cloud cover, which blinded the USAAF's highly accurate Norden bombsight. The Eighth USAAF also came to the European theatre wedded to the concept of the self-defending bomber formation, with the B-17 Flying Fortress carrying so many gunners that its payload was half that of RAF bombers. The theory was harshly disproved in 1943 and the USAAF could only return to Germany once the bombers could be escorted all the way by the long-range P-51 Mustang fighters of the Ninth USAAF, after which Luftwaffe fighters were obliged to rise to the challenge of the Eighth and were massacred by the Ninth. Thanks to meddling by Hitler, the jet-powered Messerschmitt 262 fighter, which none of the Allied fighters could intercept, entered service a year or two later than it might have and made no great impact on an already lost situation. Perhaps the least cited passage from the USSBS summary report reads, 'These attacks left the German people with a solid lesson in the disadvantages of war. It was a terrible lesson; conceivably that lesson, both in Germany and abroad, could be the most lasting single effect of the air war.'*

LIEUTENANT GENERAL IRA C EAKER

Commander Eighth Air Force, USAAF

I am aware of the effort on the part of some historians and some leaders of other branches of the services to denigrate the bomber effort, but I would think now they've been pretty well answered by the Germans. Mr Speer and without exception all the senior German commanders accredited the air effort with their destruction. From Rommel and the African campaign all the way through to the end, all of the principal German commanders since the war have accredited our air effort with their defeat.

ALBERT SPEER

Hitler's Armaments Minister

The bombing offensive of the Royal Air Force and of the American Air Force was doing tremendous harm and we could see that one day we should collapse if it was continuing, so it was a question of death or life to get again air superiority in Germany. In the opinion of General Galland, who was an expert, it was absolutely possible in time, because even if in shooting down one bomber in daytime he was losing three or four fighters, the pilots mostly were saved but the whole bomber crew was in our hands and what was needed in the production on the other side for one bomber was much more than our losses. We could utilise the material too, so it was almost sure that if we would have enough fighters in Germany – and Galland was building up a thousand fighters just for the home defence – that one day there would be a battle in the middle of Germany with about eight hundred or so American bombers and quite a lot would be shot down. But it never came to that because Hitler didn't understand this thing, he didn't want to understand, and he ordered when we were just finished, he ordered the whole

STRATEGIC BOMBING: US ARMY AIR FORCE

thousand fighters to go to France to fight the invasion. They weren't even trained for this task so after a few days, a few weeks, nothing was left of them. They could have won the battle over Germany, which would have been as important as the success of the invasion. The same was also with night-fighters against your Royal Air Force bombers. It's quite well known that those who were there already did much harm to the British bombers and if they could have been multiplied, if we would have three or four times as much of the night-fighters, possibly you would have been compelled to stop the whole attack on German towns.

LIEUTENANT GENERAL EAKER

RAF daylight bombing failed because they did not have bombers that were equipped as our Flying Fortresses were and they didn't have sufficient quantity. They only had a hundred heavy bombers when I arrived over here and we were not successful until we had several hundred heavy bombers equipped for daylight work. No one will ever get me to fundamentally disagree with the work of Sir Arthur Harris and Bomber Command. I thought it was well led and superbly executed.

GENERAL ADOLF GALLAND
Commander of the Luftwaffe fighter force
German fighters were fighting all around the world and we could never concentrate our complete fighter strength in Germany or central Europe. Also from the beginning of 1943 the German lack of fuel has resulted in the reduction of training time, which had reduced the capability of our crews and our fighters considerably. The air superiority and the quantity were increased both by the American Air Force and by the Royal Air Force and finally the range of their fighters had been extended so far that even Berlin and East Prussia were in the range of the American fighters. The American fighters on some raids did fly all over central Europe and landed in Russia and they did fly over Germany and landed in Italy. In addition the performance of our fighters, both Messerschmitt and Fokker, were not increased by the extent of the performance of the English and Americans, especially in altitudes over twenty-five thousand feet.

ALBERT SPEER

Hitler was once, when Galland and me were there, he was very angry when he got news that the fighter pilots didn't fight courageously enough in France. Of course he didn't want to realise, which was well known, that the British and American fighters had better speed and were superior as pilots. So he told Galland in a rage, the whole fighter force are good for nothing and we are producing only now anti-aircraft guns and the whole production of fighters will be stopped.

DR JOHN KENNETH GALBRAITH

Member of post-war Strategic Bombing Survey

In 1944 the German war production went up and went up quite rapidly until September 1944 – thereafter it tapered off and began to decline. It had its effect when we were right on the frontier of Germany and when not only the bombers but the tactical aircraft could patrol the roads and railroads, and greatly reduce the mobility of the German forces. When it became possible to bomb and bomb again the oil plants, this in turn created a shortage of oil which undoubtedly had a further effect on the mobility of the forces. At that time we exaggerated the effect of the air attacks. Roosevelt set up the Strategic Bombing Survey, of which I was a member, because he had become suspicious of the Air Force claims. The suspicion showed that Roosevelt had mastered the first principle of warfare – naturally suspect what air generals tell you. The effect was to minimise the impact of the bombing; the clearest case was on the fighter, the German aircraft industry, which was attacked in February of 1944 and had a forty or fifty per cent increase in production in March of 1944.

ALBERT SPEER

I had the same experience with our Air Forces. They claimed to have bombed a synthetic rubber plant in Russia and it would be out of action for a year or longer and then our experts had a look into the matter and said it would be repaired in a few weeks' time.

LIEUTENANT GENERAL EAKER

We were very hopeful that we could demonstrate the effect of strategic bombing and we were all conscious of the tremendous part that Lord Trenchard had played in its development.* We had watched his experiences from World War One and he was the patron saint of air power in this country, as he was in yours. We always felt that the independent status that the Royal Air Force had made it much easier for them to make decisions on equipment and on strategy and tactics, whereas we had to present our case to the Army General Staff.

AIR CHIEF MARSHAL SIR ARTHUR HARRIS
Commander-in-Chief, RAF Bomber Command

I said to General Arnold before they came in the war, that if they were going in for daylight bombing they would have to have much better armament than they had in the Flying Fortresses at that time.** That was when I went over to the States, before the war, and was allowed to go and look at one of their Fortresses. They had hand-held guns in blisters and I told them, 'For goodness sake you must have steadier guns than that if you're going to fly in daylight,' and we offered to give them our target designs.

MAJOR WERNER SCHROER
Day fighter ace with 114 kills

The Americans normally flew in groups of three and then in various levels, and coming from behind we tried to get one of them by a long-distance attack, to get it separated and to hit it in the wings or somewhere in order to reduce the velocity of the plane and have it separate from the other two, and then it was much easier to get them. This was effective in the beginning and later on we tried to attack them from the front, but you could only use experienced fighters for that because of the difficulty in escaping afterwards through the formation, because you had very little time to shoot, hit him and then escape.

---

* Marshal of the Royal Air Force Hugh, Lord Trenchard (1873–1956), Chief of the Air Staff during the First World War and founder of the RAF.
** General of the Air Force Henry 'Hap' Arnold (1886–1950), Commander of the US Army Air Corps from 1938 and the USAAF 1941–45.

LIEUTENANT COLONEL JAMES M 'JIMMY' STEWART
Commander 703rd Bombardment Squadron, Eighth USAAF

The fighter, he was the bogeyman in this tremendous, vicious defence that they mounted. The flak, although it got much more serious in the latter part of the war, for some reason I always felt that the odds were better in your favour with flak. The fighter, though, had eyes and in a great many instances the fighter had a pretty competent pilot at the controls, and when he latched on to you, you were in trouble.

LIEUTENANT GENERAL EAKER

When I first went to Harris's headquarters in February 1942 and explained to him our plan and our hope for the build-up of cooperative attacks against the German defence industry, he said very frankly, 'I don't believe you can bomb by day, I think your losses will be too heavy. The German anti-aircraft and fighter defences on the West Wall are too strong. We've tried it and we couldn't do it.' What he referred to, of course, was that General Arnold had given him a small number of Liberators and he'd sent them out on day attack as single planes and they'd been badly shot up. But, he said, as time went on, 'If you could do it, it would be very fortuitous, it would help my night effort, it would keep all the defences on twenty-four-hour alert, it would prevent them going on to factories to make weapons. It would be very good if you could do it and nobody will hope stronger than I do that you succeed and I'm going to do everything possible to support your effort.'

AIR GUNNER JOHN COCHRANE
Eighth Air Force, USAAF

I think it was generally understood that the combat tour was twenty-five missions because it was anticipated that you'd be dead by that time, so there wasn't any point in asking you to stay around any longer. I don't say that the fear was an acute one, that you went around trembling, but it was pretty well felt that our chances of surviving were not particularly good. But after all, it was what we felt we had to do and I felt that if you were going to die that was about the best way to die. I'd much rather die in an aeroplane than in the mud on some battlefield. But my observation was that morale was very good. I think that was partially because you had a definite limited tour, and you knew that if you lucked it out and survived the tour, you went home. I think it's very important to give a human being some goal or some target to aim for, and to know that he'll get relief after that.

LIEUTENANT GENERAL EAKER

We never had a morale problem with our crews. Of course after severe losses any group had a temporary period of reaction from it – human beings always react like that. And I must tell you that one of the reasons I think our morale was sustained is that shortly after I joined Air Marshal Harris, understudying the British effort, he told me, 'We have found that you must give any soldier or sailor or airman a chance for survival. I strongly recommend that you fix a period, a number of missions and then let your crews rest, or go home to join your training effort.' I worked out twenty-five missions at an early date, and the reason I arrived at that was that we began to show a pattern of two per cent of total loss with all our missions. Well, that gave a crew two per cent over twenty-five missions, which gave a crew a fifty per cent chance of survival, so I held to that twenty-five mission level for as long as I was at Eighth Air Force.*

AIR GUNNER COCHRANE

I think that combat flying is so impersonal that you don't get that intimate sense of loss if you see an aeroplane shot down that you'd have if your buddy on the battlefield had his head blown off right within arm's length. But I know of two fliers who developed a fear of flying to the point that they simply declined to fly any more and they were transferred out. I have no idea what happened to them, whether they were court-martialled or simply reassigned because of some medical justification.

---

* Bomber Command had a thirty-mission tour of operations, which could be repeated.

MAJOR SCHROER

I told new pilots not to attack from behind in a direct attack but to move the plane up and down to confuse the rear gunner. I even told them to close their eyes in order not to see the tracer ammunition, which could frighten. I don't know whether I did the same, but I always tried to get as close as possible in order to have a better chance to hit it. The gunners started shooting their tracer ammunition I think at about one thousand metres distance, to get rid of their own fear.

MAJOR STEWART

I think the most complicated part of it was the assembly, that is getting together different Groups from numerous airfields that were situated all over East Anglia, lots of times in marginal weather, getting them into formation, getting them at one point at a certain time. At each one of them, each Group had its own time to arrive at that position and the formation of the bomber stream, in other words getting yourself ready for attack. This always seemed to me the most difficult and the most complicated part of the mission.

GENERAL GALLAND

Hamburg was the first example of the very successful combined operation of the American and British air forces. The Americans during the day and the English during the night-time – this has been called round-the-clock bombing. Also Bomber Command adopted a new tactic with countermeasures against our system, our radar was blind, and also they adopted the bomber-stream tactic, compared to the isolated bombing going on close to the targets. Both methods put our night-fighters in a completely new situation and the effect was that the night defence was absolutely minimal. The attack led to a compact mass attack on Hamburg, which was extremely effective, and this mass attack caused very big fire storms. Losses were very high and this time it was absolutely clear to everybody that by now we had to change to air defence as first priority. Göring was completely convinced to do so and tried to convince Hitler. Hitler, who was always in favour of attacks and against defence, decided completely against everybody's intention and he decided to build more bombers and attack England. This has been a terrible mistake but Hitler decided by his own and nobody was able to convince him to the contrary.

COLONEL CURTIS LeMAY
4th Bombardment Wing, USAAF

One of the frailties of the human mind is always trying to find a sort of miracle or short way of doing something to get the job done without much effort. This was, of course, the goal of our intelligence people, always looking for a target that if you just destroy this one target it'll be the key thing that will cause the enemy to collapse and the war will be over. They discovered the ball-bearing industry, the main part of which was at Schweinfurt – a large part of the ball bearings of Germany were made there. They forgot that they were getting a lot of them from Sweden and other places, so an attack on the ball-bearing industry wouldn't knock out a very vital cog in the German war-making machine.

ALBERT SPEER

When you hit Schweinfurt first it was to me like a nightmare getting true, because I was often thinking that bombing one of our bottlenecks of the armament industry would be much more effective than the bombing of cities. And one of the aims I always considered was bombing the ball-bearing industry, and really two attacks on Schweinfurt industry you did much more damage than you ever did before with all the ground bombing. We thought first that we are now at the end of our efforts for armaments industry. But I had a very good representative, Tessler, and he did this all means not only the repair but also the replacement of ball bearings with other devices, which could do the job not as good as the ball bearing but it could be done, and then we found that there were stocks in the Army and so stocks could be used too, so we could bridge over the lack of ball bearings for several months until we had repaired the damages. Of course we were frightened that there will be other raids on Schweinfurt and really there were other raids but too late. If you would have repeated those raids shortly afterwards and wouldn't have given us time to rebuild then it would have been a disastrous result.

MAJOR SCHROER

We didn't expect an attack coming that far into the country without fighter escort; we were very astonished at it. If you had a Group of twenty-seven planes and you don't know how many planes are joining you for a combined attack, twenty-seven planes is not much to attack hundreds of bombers. Besides it was very difficult to find out whether the fighter planes we were seeing were our own fighter planes or were Allied planes and there was very much concern and the attack could not be executed in the way it should be because of the fear of [P-47] Thunderbolts in the back. But later on we found out and we were informed by our ground station that no enemy fighters were there, so it was easier. But the trouble by that time was the long distance we had to fly to get to the bomber formations. Our detour to Frankfurt took almost all our petrol reserve and we have twenty minutes left and we all had to land in Frankfurt to get the fuel and later we didn't succeed in finding them again. My squadrons didn't – others did.

COLONEL LeMAY

The first raid on Schweinfurt was to be a combination attack with Schweinfurt one target and the Messerschmitt plant at Regensburg another. The plan was that my Division and the 1st Division would go in with fighter escort as far as they could. I would attack the Messerschmitt plant and then go out through the Brenner Pass and land in North Africa. That would mean that I took on the German Air Force on the way in. But the 1st Division coming behind me by ten, fifteen minutes or so, would come in relatively free because the main fighter force had been expended on me and would be on the ground rearming and refuelling, but they would have to fight going out. That was the plan. At the time the attack was launched the weather was good over the target but miserable in England. I managed to get my Division in the air because we'd been prac-tising instrument take-offs for some time but the fighters did not get in the air and the 1st Division did not get in the air until an hour and fifteen minutes later. This placed the Bomber Commander [General Eaker] in a position of having to make a decision of aborting the whole operation or going under very adverse conditions. We'd been waiting so long for the weather for this important target that he decided to go. So we went in.*

GENERAL GALLAND

Schweinfurt had been the result of very good conditions in favour of the German fighter command. The American escort fighters were not able to follow the bomber over the target, they had to turn back about the area of the Rhine and we were able to intercept the bomber stream with most of our fighter units.

ALBERT SPEER

When in 1943 ball-bearing industry in Schweinfurt was attacked heavily with the American Air Force I thought that we couldn't continue our war production because for every armament it is necessary to have ball bearings. But to our good luck, the Americans and the British didn't continue for strategic reasons too, they had too high losses, as I see nowadays. Then the second time it happened on a much larger scale when on 12th May 1944, the Eighth American Air Force bombed oil plants in the middle of Germany. These plants were, we thought until then, are protected because they were too far away and the fighters couldn't accompany the bombers, but they did. This day I just was on the airfield to fly to see the damage done; I told my closest man in the planning office, the leading man of the planning office, with this the war is definitely lost, and I wrote a memorandum to Hitler in which I stated that after September 1944, after a few months, we shall run short of fuel because our stocks will be used, and the supply of new production of fuel is absolutely insufficient to the tanks and also to the planes. But Hitler just said I trust you are getting along; you did get along so many times, in increasing production when we thought production had been decreased, and possibly you will do it this time again.

---

* In the Schweinfurt–Regensburg raid of 17 August 1943 LeMay's Wing (not Division) lost 24 of 146 B-17s and the 1st Wing lost 36 of 230. A further 87 were damaged beyond repair and 95 suffered lesser battle damage. Losses on this and other missions caused Eighth USAAF to wait for the long-range Mustang fighter before venturing deep into Germany again in 1944.

DR GALBRAITH

The question of whether a more complete concentration on the oil targets would have shortened the war is really unanswerable. The RAF would have had to attack them in the daytime because the attacks were very imprecise at night – the losses would have been heavy. And this would have enabled the Germans to concentrate even more energy on the regeneration of the oil plant. They had half a million working on it; it might have been a million men because they wouldn't be repairing transport and other things. Most of us felt that concentration on major targets and hitting them day after day and week after week was the sound tactic. But I would be hesitant to reach a final conclusion because the overriding fact is that air-power bombing was a much less effective thing than was imagined at that time, and we've been learning in Korea and Vietnam ever since how ineffective and limited its effect is.

ALBERT SPEER

But again here it happens that you didn't repeat it as fast as we were frightened of and so the repairs could take place and we had at least the small part of the whole capacity once again for production. In October–November 1944 new raids were on the oil industry and those raids were so successful that production was almost nil. The stock of gasoline for the Army was running very short: we had no more for instance to train fighter pilots for the fighters; the tanks were almost no more able to move but just short distances. For instance the Ardennes offensive was supposed on gaining large stocks of gasoline off the Americans, otherwise we couldn't succeed to get deep into the country, even if they had succeeded in breaking through.

DR GALBRAITH

Had the power plants been attacked this could have been disastrous but we might well have found out that the speed with which those were put back would be similar to the speed with which the aeroplane fighters were put back, or the speed with which the oil plants were put back. One just doesn't know how great the regenerative process would have been until it was experienced. It was almost my hunch that had the central power stations been taken out this would have done more damage but we might only have discovered that the Germans were very good at putting those back.

MAJOR GENERAL WALTHER WARLIMONT
Deputy Chief of Wehrmacht Operations
In headquarters one didn't notice very much, but I had some connections with the people when I came to Berlin in September 1944. All the lives in Germany were dominated by the Allied attacks, nobody was safe from air attacks here.

LIEUTENANT GENERAL EAKER
I think the greatest thing we did was destroy the Luftwaffe, making it possible for the subsequent sea and ground operations to be successful. You may recall that when the British were doing sweeps over the German airfields in France they didn't respond – they said why go up and get shot down, because the Spitfires outmanoeuvre us. The same way when we began to go over with our long-range fighters against their aerodromes: they'd move their planes off the aerodromes under the trees or into the autobahns, and bring them back when our fighters had left. The only reason, the only way in which we could bring the German Luftwaffe to engage with us was to do something that was causing them great damage, and Hitler and Göring forced them to respond to our bomber effort because we were cutting up their industry. And that's why we sent our fighters with our bombers, because it gave our fighters a chance to engage the enemy fighters when they came up after our bombers.

COLONEL JOHN MEYER
Commander 487th Fighter Squadron, Ninth USAAF
Just as I was starting down the runway I saw a lot of flak off the edge of the field. I called our control and asked him if there were any other aircraft in the area and he said no there weren't. At about that time I saw a Messerschmitt 109 that was headed directly at me, but I was still on the ground without flying speed and anybody who flies knows that an

aeroplane is a pretty clumsy instrument when it's still on the ground. So that's memorable in the sense that I saw there was nothing I could do and my view was that I'd had it. Fortunately for me this German pilot saw a C-47 just at the end of the runway so instead of continuing his attack on me he pulled up with a wing-over and started shooting at this C-47, which put his tail right in front of me just about the time I got airborne. I pulled the gear up immediately and had my sights on him and shot him down before the wheels had fully retracted in the well.*

AIR GUNNER COCHRANE

I think perhaps my most vivid recollection is the first time [8 March 1944] that my Group went to Berlin. After we had dropped our bombs there's a manoeuvre as you turn away, one Group has to cross above the other, and the Group on top dropped their bombs right smack on to our squadron. We lost one aeroplane and that was a terrifying memory and an incident that I'll never forget.

MAJOR SCHROER

I had two Fortresses and one Mustang in two-hour fight on a Berlin raid. But this was a very good attack as far as our fighters were concerned. We had at that time, for one of the very few times, managed to assemble a quantity of more than a hundred fighters in one formation and attack the American bombers with that strength, which had never happened before. And I was in front of that formation and I had the best chances.

GENERAL HASSO-ECCARD FREIHERR VON MANTEUFFEL

Commanding Fifth Panzer Army 1944–45

The population of Germany, especially in the big cities and in the industrial areas, the houses and rooms were destroyed, the family were separated, no fuel or coal for heating, the food supply was insufficient,

---

* This engagement on New Year's Day 1945 ended with the 487th shooting down 23 of 50 German fighters that attacked their airfield in Belgium during the German Ardennes offensive.

they received no mail by their dependants who were on the front line. The propaganda machine by Goebbels and the promise of Hitler's new weapons, improved aircraft types and submarines and the increase production of German industry – expectations for this were raised to a higher pitch therefore failure was all the greater.

GENERAL GALLAND

We have lost one good opportunity when we discovered that we had a fighter which was superior by at least 100 miles over other enemy fighters. This had been the jet fighter Me-262, which came so late because Hitler at the beginning of the war had not allowed long-term developments to continue. He has ordered that all developments which in one year's time would not be ready to be used in operations should be dropped from the drawing board. And this had led to a very limited effort only to continue the development. When in 1943 it became know that enemy superiority was increasing tremendously in air power, only at this time Messerschmitt got the order to show the proof of this jet fighter. But then Hitler made a second terrible mistake. He ordered that this superior fighter should be used as a Blitz bomber and not as a fighter. We have lost a good opportunity to stop at least the daylight raids in good weather conditions. More than twelve hundred Me-262 had been used but only a very small number had been used as fighters and the effect of the Blitz bomber was about zero.

ALBERT SPEER

You succeeded in November 1944 to besiege the whole Ruhr valley by just striking on the transport. There is a memorandum of Hitler from November in which I am telling him that now the oil industry is as much as no more existing for us, that we have no more coal transports for the other parts of Germany and that without coal the other industry will cease to produce. And this was really true. You can see it on our own production: production was highest peak in July and then it dropped very quickly to only a percentage of what we did in the utmost in the peak of our production.

GEORGE BALL

Director of the US Strategic Bombing Survey

We came up with a rather complicated set of conclusions which I don't think were agreed, at least not with the same degree of enthusiasm, by everyone on the Board. By and large one of the most effective things that the bombing had done was to force the German Air Force into the sky in order to defend the targets in Germany and this enabled the Allies to kill the German Air Force, which gave command of the air to the Allies for the invasion of Normandy. This was fully indispensable. The second thing was that much of the bombing we had done was not as effective as it might have been because of the great over-supply of general-purpose machine tools in the German economy. Sometimes we only succeeded in rationalising production, which was otherwise out of phase. By June of 1944 German war production was three hundred per cent of what it had been in 1939. Beginning in June of 1944 when we began to strike the hydrogenation plants which produce the synthetic gasoline, the whole situation began to change and this has been made clear by Albert Speer, who I interviewed with some of my colleagues in May 1945. Then in September 1944 we started the massive bombing of the Rhineland and the effect of this was to disrupt production enormously, not so much by smashed-up plants and knocking down a lot of bricks and mortar but by interrupting the movement of supplies and goods within the plants, that is from one building to another on the little railroads that they had, and the thing finally ground to a considerable halt and the Germans were in terrible trouble by the end of 1944.

ALBERT SPEER

This was in November 1944 and again there is a memorandum to Hitler which is still in the files, and I told Hitler that the Ruhr valley is blocked, which meant that we haven't had no more supply of coal for other parts of Germany, that the production of parts and of steel parts in the Ruhr valley didn't come to the factories in other Germany, so the production in a short while would be nil. Then we introduced a new system: we said we shall try to complete tanks and guns as much as possible with the parts which are already there, distributed over many factories, and all the factories had to report to central offices what parts they have and then we shifted parts around and could get along. But I had to give Hitler a list of what he has expected, and I told him there are the last weapons you are getting, then it's finished because without the Ruhr valley we can't do it any more. I gave him a second memo in 30 January 1945 and told him, said things have gone worse and said he can only get so and so many weapons, and in this statement was a sentence running like: 'With this the war is lost even if the courage of the German soldiers is superior to the soldiers of the others.' And this was distributed, six copied to the General Staff, to the six departments of the General Staff of the Army, and Hitler first has no reaction at all, he didn't ask me to come. For a few days I didn't know what his opinion is and then he asked me together with my deputy and he told me very bluntly that's not up to you to tell me the war is lost or not lost, that's my decision; you can tell me what your situation on your field is and no more. And if you do it again I won't accept it any more. He was quite angry and turned to my deputy and continued talking with him and I was sitting at the side.

URSULA GRAY
Dresden resident, post-war wife of author J Glenn Gray
The third raid was by the Americans and they concentrated on strafing people. There was no defence, we had no defence at all, and they concentrated on getting these people who were trying to save their lives and get out into the suburbs and go into the country. All the people who were gathered on the meadows along the river, they went right down and strafed the people and killed them one by one. It was such a terrible feeling because you were so helpless. Here was this machine above you and it hit you or it hit the next one and there was no defence.

LIEUTENANT GENERAL EAKER
I don't agree there was overkill. There may have been in Dresden, but bear in mind we'd been asked by the Russians to destroy that great railroad complex because most of the German weapons and supplies and

reinforcements going to the central section of the Eastern Front were going through there. Well, we lit some fires one afternoon and the British sent a thousand bombers over that night and we followed up next day with a thousand bombers, and of course it created a great fire which killed fifty thousand or so Germans – but it eliminated that great bottle-neck that we were asked to destroy. No commanders knew what amount of resources the weather and other things would permit you to get on that target. It was always better to put up more than you needed in order to saturate defences than to send not enough and suffer heavier losses and not accomplish your mission, and have to go back.

CHAPTER 25

THE ITALIAN CAMPAIGN

Veterans of the Italian campaign felt that they had as good a claim as the men in Burma to be considered the 'Forgotten Army'. There was a good case for not invading Italy at all, and another in favour of a wholehearted commitment of the men and resources available in the Mediterranean to leapfrog rapidly up the Italian peninsula. It is harder to justify what actually took place: an invasion foisted by the British on the reluctant Americans, who regarded it at best as a strategic distraction to draw German troops away from France in preparation for the main invasion of Europe, and at worst as a scheme designed by Churchill and his generals to postpone the Normandy landing still further.

The last Axis troops in North Africa surrendered on 13 May 1943, the conquest of Sicily was accomplished between 10 July and 17 August, and the Italians overthrew Mussolini on 25 July. The first Allied landings were made on 3 September: Italy surrendered on 8 September and on the following day the Allies landed in strength at Salerno, only to be viciously counter-attacked by the Germans. Naples fell on 10 October and then the Allies reached the formidable German Gustav Line behind the Sangro, Rapido and Garigliano rivers, whose strongest point was the town of Cassino at the mouth of the Liri valley, one of the few in Italy that runs along rather than across the peninsula. In January 1944 a landing was made at Anzio to the north, intended to outflank the Gustav Line. Instead it was ferociously counter-attacked and became an increasingly miserable beachhead until, in combination with a major assault on the Gustav Line in May, the Allies were at last able to break out. Controversially, US Lieutenant General Mark Clark chose not to trap the Germans falling back from the Gustav Line and went for Rome, which he entered on 5 June, the day before D-Day in Normandy. Clark makes it clear, in the pages that follow, that, whatever the orders of British General Alexander, his military superior, he had political top cover for his action. Another eleven months of grinding combat followed, with the terrain always strongly favouring the defence, before all German forces in Italy surrendered on 2 May 1945.

LIEUTENANT GENERAL MARK CLARK

Commander US Fifth Army

The whole thing was – they were Churchill's babies. I was a great admirer of his and I think they were good babies. He decided that we should go from North Africa, he sold it to Roosevelt and then we did it. I can see him now at his map and at his persuasive way, with his pointer, pointing out the soft underbelly of the Mediterranean – and after we got there I often thought what a tough old gut it was instead of the soft belly that he had led us to believe.

TOM DRIBERG

British Independent Labour MP

Aneurin Bevan always attacked Churchill for his North African and Italian strategy: Churchill had spoken of Italy as being the soft underbelly of the Axis. Nye pointed out after we'd been there for some months fighting slowly up, that it wasn't the underbelly at all, it was the hardcore or the carapace or whatever word he used. He was always very good at words too.

LIEUTENANT GENERAL BRIAN HORROCKS

Commander XIII Corps, Eighth Army

Monty was in charge of the invasion of Sicily but the plan for it was made in Algiers because Monty was still fighting in the desert. When he got it, he didn't like it and he changed the plan at the last minute. This caused fury in Algiers and they summoned Monty to come along and explain why he'd made all these alterations. So he flew in and when he landed at the airport [Major] General Bedell Smith, who was Eisenhower's Chief of Staff, was waiting for him. Monty said cheerfully, 'I suppose I'm a bit unpopular up here, aren't I?' Bedell looked at him and said, 'General, to serve under you would be a privilege, anywhere. To serve alongside you is not too bad. But, General, to serve over you is hell.'

MAJOR GENERAL KENNETH STRONG
Eisenhower's Chief of Intelligence
There was a big difference of opinion between the Americans and the British about how the war should be fought. The British believed that after they'd captured Sicily and landed in Italy the right strategy was to push through Italy, through Yugoslavia, through the Balkans into Germany, link up with the Russians and destroy the German forces in that way.

DREW MIDDLETON
American journalist
By then the troops had reached the point where they realised that the Italians were not the main enemy, that there were still a lot of Germans around and it was going to be tough. Combat troops after a certain period become extremely sceptical and cynical about statements by their Commanders-in-Chief and really, you know, the fellow in the rifle company doesn't look beyond his company commander. That's his leader and in some cases if anything else comes down, well, fine, I'm interested to hear it but we've got to take that bridge and Captain So-and-So is the man who will help us take it, not General Eisenhower sitting back in headquarters.

MAJOR GENERAL STRONG
On 18 August 1943 I was suddenly told that I must leave at once for Lisbon with the American Chief of Staff, [Major] General Bedell Smith, in order to meet Italian emissaries who were coming to talk about Italian armistice conditions. When we met them General Smith said, 'We've come to give you the armistice terms,' whereupon General Castellano said, 'That's not why we came here at all, we came to discover how we could join with the Allies in clearing the Germans out of Italy.' Bedell

Smith said, 'We can't discuss that, we'll do it later – I'll read you the armistice terms.' Castellano asked some questions and then retired to discuss them. It was quite clear that one of Castellano's main objects at this conversation was to find out what the British plans were, where were they going to land and how strong they were going to be, because this would determine the Italians, about the attitude they would adopt. And we decided we couldn't tell them that, it was too dangerous, too many lives at risk.

MAJOR GENERAL FRANCIS DE GUINGAND
Montgomery's Chief of Staff

The Italians surrendered and it was anyone's guess what the effect would be. I think most of us felt that the Germans would withdraw right out of Italy to the passes of the north, but in the event they didn't and so it looked a very difficult job because we knew the Italians' hearts were not in the fighting. It took us ten days to prepare ourselves to cross the Straits of Messina, and we got all our artillery geared up to cover us and the Air Force geared up to cover us, and the Navy ready and really it was a pretty thing but there was very little opposition when we got over. Then the real difficulty started when we got there and the terrain was completely different to the desert, which is flat, easy country to manoeuvre over. When you got to Italy there were these numbers of small rivers that were running down from the backbone of Italy down to the sea, which created bottlenecks every few hundred yards, and the Germans were blowing up all bridges. It meant a most laborious business of having to push the enemy rearguards out of action and then having to build bridges, get our people across and then come over the hill and find another ruddy bridge gone.

GENERAL SIEGFRIED WESTPHAL
Field Marshal Kesselring's Chief of Staff

Hitler and the High Command had no hope that the forces in southern Italy could survive a combined operation of the American Fifth Army and the British Eighth Army in a landing and therefore Hitler was happy that we could defend the Apennines, and that was the reason the Army Group B, under the command of Field Marshal Rommel, was in northern Italy in order to take this position. But the position in the Apennines was twice longer than the smallest position, south of Rome in the Abruzzi. We made this proposal to defend south of Rome because we were sure that we could survive the capitulation we expected from the Italians, and we have proof of that because we got all our divisions out from Sicily. Nevertheless the railroad and the roads were destroyed by air bombs and we have very few of petrol, so Hitler didn't believe us and all our requests for reinforcements were without any answers. If I did speak with the German High Command I got only answers good for a naughty child, but not for a man who has a strong task. After the Italian capitulation and the landing near Salerno it seemed they were right but Hitler did change his opinion and he ordered that Army Group Kesselring had to defend south of Rome and that the Army Group B who was behind us had to go to the Western Front.

MAJOR GENERAL STRONG

We were preparing the land at Salerno and Eisenhower was very anxious indeed that he should get the maximum cooperation possible from the Italians and this is the reason that he insisted, or pressed very hard, that this armistice should be signed. We hadn't awfully many troops, General Castellano told me that we needed at least fifteen divisions if we were going to make a successful landing. We had four or five divisions but we couldn't tell Castellano that. If we could drop them near Rome that would cut the German communications and probably, with the assistance of the Italians, capture Rome. When the time came the Italians got cold feet. They said if you drop parachutists there we cannot support them: the Germans have taken away from us all our vehicles, all our petrol and we are absolutely immobile, and therefore they will be destroyed before they can do anything. I think myself that it was a pity we cancelled the operation. General Eisenhower sent a man up to Rome, one of his trusted officers, to find out the situations there and he reported back to Eisenhower and said the operation was not feasible. I think it's a great pity it was postponed; I have a feeling that it could have succeeded and that the Italians would have given us more support in Rome than we thought. But General Eisenhower said he had to take the point of view of the man on the spot, who said the thing was not possible.

DREW MIDDLETON

I think there was great exhilaration, yes, but more than that confidence. They knew their weapons, they knew their commanders, they thought they could do it. But my point is that the surrender of the Italians did not lead them to think that Salerno or anything else was going to be easy – they knew it was going to be hard.

MAJOR GENERAL STRONG

When we landed at Salerno the Germans had been suspicious for some time that it was a possible landing place. It was the most suitable. It would've been much better if we could've gone further north and cut the lines of communication nearer Rome. Admiral Cunningham, who was the naval commander at the time, wanted to sail up the Tiber to Rome but the Air Forces said, 'You can not carry out those operations except under an air umbrella, the support of the air, and the furthest north we can give you the support of the air is at Salerno.' And that is why Salerno was chosen. Of all General Eisenhower's battles that is the one when I think we were nearest to a tactical defeat. We knew the German troops were there, we knew that we would be attacked by them, and we knew the risk was very great. But when the time came it required the intervention of all the Air Forces, it required their intervention to save us at Salerno, and indeed one of the commanders there had got as far as considering that he might have to take his headquarters out of Salerno and back to Sicily again.

MAJOR GENERAL JOHN HARDING
Field Marshal Alexander's Chief of Staff
The purpose was to me quite clear: it was to pin down, to use up, exhaust as much of the German military strength as possible in order to give the maximum support to Overlord, and the subsequent operations in the north-west. Certainly that was always in Alexander's mind.

LIEUTENANT GENERAL CLARK

Ours was more or less a secondary role, you might say, an unglamorous role. You might compare it to the guards of a football team who take the tacklers out so the fleetbacks can run and make a touchdown. We were holding, and drawing into Italy all the troops we possibly could to keep them from interfering with General Eisenhower when he made the main show in Normandy, so that our role was to hold enemy troops, to keep them there, to chew 'em up and prevent them from fighting in other places.

MAJOR GENERAL HARDING

I don't know that the difficulties of fighting in the mountains were fully appreciated by people who thought of Italy as a place of sunshine and fine weather. I don't think they appreciated in any way the problems that arose, particularly the logistical problems, the movement problems from the effect of heavy rain and snowfalls in mountainous country, which was not very well roaded. I remember once a fairly distinguished Member of Parliament coming out to look at the front and we had a Member of Parliament on the Alexander staff and I told him that he'd better take his colleague out before dawn to make sure that he got wet through and that he had to help him push his Jeep out of the mud at least three times, and not to bring him home until after dark. And he had no difficulty in carrying out his instructions to the letter.

LIEUTENANT GENERAL CLARK

The terrain of course was – you couldn't have worse, it wasn't terrain that was susceptible to the use of armour. It wasn't until we got to the Po valley that we could really turn our armoured units loose. We had to use their armoured infantry as infantry and the tanks as artillery pieces.

PRIVATE WHITMORE
Sherwood Foresters
Oh, terrible, terrible it was. It was worse than being in the Peak District of Derbyshire. The village people of southern Italy are very crude, no toilets, no nothing. What I can remember, there were houses they lived in,

would have a bed in that corner and a couple of nanny goats sleeping in this corner and a few fowls in that corner and that would be it. The road would lead up into the hills out of the village, a lane sort of thing, and each side of this lane was absolutely swarming with flies on human excreta. I've never seen anything like it, there were no toilets anywhere and possibly I think that was why so many of us were sick.

MAJOR GENERAL HARDING

The Monte Cassino monastery is the keystone from a tactical point of view to the entrance to the Liri valley, which is the easiest and best approach from Naples to Rome. It stands very prominently on the eastern flank of the Liri valley and it would be out of the question to advance in strength up the valley on the way to Rome leaving Cassino in the hands of the enemy. I think it was necessary to bomb it from a point of view of the morale and confidence of the troops. Everybody thought the Germans were using it for military purposes. Whether or not they were remains of some doubt, but they claim they weren't. As far as we were concerned it was the general belief on that front that the Cassino monastery was being used for military purposes by the Germans, and that being the case it's part of my military philosophy you must not put troops into battle without giving them all possible physical and material support to give them the best chance for getting a success. That being so it was necessary to take out the monastery for those reasons. It proved to be illusory, because the ruins of the monastery buildings gave a better position to the German forces, which the 1st German Parachute Division which was stationed there took full advantage of, than the buildings themselves if they'd remained erect.

LIEUTENANT J GLENN GRAY

US Army Intelligence
It was at the very beginning of our entry into the line in front of Cassino. We were a very green division, well trained but inexperienced and like many cruelties in the war it was somewhat unintended. Our soldiers were accustomed to giving food to the hungry, shivering civilians and some order came down that this was illegal and improper. The civilians gathered

with their tin cans with wire handles, and we discovered the rather horrible spectacle of having to throw food in huge cans into this dirty mud. An Italian winter, with these youngsters, even old men and women standing around watching us, was the rather grim introduction to the war for me in the winter of 1943–44. At first I was horrified and wrote in my journal about how hard a man's heart is. But like everything else I got used to it and managed to eat my fill – at first when we were giving the food to the civilians, many of us ate only half our lunches or suppers.

MAJOR GENERAL STRONG

It was very necessary to draw as many German forces as possible away from the Anzio area and therefore the decision was made that in conjunction with the Anzio attack there should be an all-out attack on the main front, on what they called the Gustav Line, which would gradually draw away those German divisions which were likely to oppose us at Anzio. Planning for this was mainly carried out by the American Army Group in Italy, but in January 1944 the Prime Minister, who was recovering from pneumonia, came to Marrakesh. Lord Beaverbrook was with him and I had to attend two conferences about the plan and I listened to him with great trepidation, to the statement that we would manage to penetrate the main front. I said that I didn't think this attack would be successful enough to do what they wanted. The Germans had spent endless effort in fortifying the Gustav Line with concrete pillboxes and every form of defence and I said I didn't think we'd penetrate it. So the Prime Minister listened to what I said but the plan went on as had been decided upon. And afterwards, when it was all over, he invited us to have a glass of sherry with him and he called me over to him. He said, 'You mustn't be disappointed if we don't take notice of what you say, but you are right, it's your right to call attention to the seamy side of this business.' People who had opposed the Prime Minister in the past had got into trouble, but I heard no more about it.

MAJOR GENERAL HARDING

I've got a very vivid recollection of that occasion: a stylish room, everybody sitting round the table with the Prime Minister in a dressing gown with a cigar resting over the top of a wine glass, Beaverbrook sitting next to him, and all of us round the table making our contribution during the course of the discussions about Anzio. Admiral Cunningham said that the operation was fraught with great risk whereupon the Prime Minister retorted, 'Yes, Admiral, of course there are risks but without risks there is no honour, no glory, no adventure,' which shut the Admiral up completely. Honestly, no admiral of the Royal Navy could possibly admit that he was not interested in honour, glory or adventure.

LIEUTENANT GENERAL CLARK

I wanted to go into Anzio with all Americans or all British, one or the other, because when you take in a British division and an American one you're complicating your communications and your supplies and every-thing else. But that was turned down because they thought that if it was a failure each nation should share the blame equally. I went in with two and a half divisions, which was totally inadequate but that's the way the ball bounces in war. You do what you're told or they'll get somebody else to do it.

WYNFORD VAUGHAN-THOMAS

BBC radio journalist

We were all assembled before the landing for the usual conference; we were to be briefed by the Corps Commander, Major General John Lucas and he appeared. I was a bit surprised, he wasn't quite the dynamic leader I expected, he smoked a corn-cob pipe and he was known to the troops as 'Corn-Cob Charlie', and he kept on quoting Kipling on every possible occasion. Some of Kipling's quotations didn't seem to work out later on. Anyhow, there was this rather nice, kindly fellow with a white moustache and he sat down and he briefed us. There was no map behind him because the Americans didn't believe in maps – the French never looked at maps, the Americans brought maps but didn't study them, the English lived on maps.

GENERAL WESTPHAL

When the Allies landed near Anzio in beginning of 1944 there were only two battalions and some very old-fashioned batteries at the coast for defending. If the Americans had realised the situation they could stay on the evening of the landing day in Rome. We had some feeling that new landings either south or north of Rome or Livorno or Genoa or on the Adriatic Coast were to be expected and we had given in December a general order to all troops what they have to do in any case of landing. When I was awaked in the morning of this operation at three o'clock I had only to say and give orders. Then came the troops from northern Italy, from southern France and from the front of the Tenth Army in the rear of Cassino and so we were able to build up a new front against the landing troops under the command of the American General Lucas. Then we got many forces from Germany too, but the counter-attack did fail because the very bad weather and because we had made a too strong attack line, but not large enough, and then the troops had not the possibility to use the opportunities. I was very anxious we would have too great losses and I proposed to end the counter-attack. Perhaps if I had not done so we could reach the sea.

WYNFORD VAUGHAN-THOMAS

The trouble basically was, I think, Lucas did not really believe in the operation. Of course we didn't know it at the time, no soldier when you go into action is ever told the full thinking behind the piece of action or he'd never go near the place. But it was quite clear afterwards that the Americans were torn between whether to back this sort of thing whole-heartedly or to hedge on it. Now the higher command in America I'm sure never believed in the whole Italian business. They wanted to play it small but you can't tell an Army general 'we're just having a holding operation, toddle along quietly and don't get yourself killed too often, don't run any risks but keep the enemy under pressure'. You can't conduct war that way and Lucas was caught between these two awfully contradictory views. The British on the other hand were innocently convinced that we were going to land, lever the Southern Front loose and drive on to the Alban Hills, hold them to make certain that the Germans panicked and then up would come the Southern Front and we'd move to Rome. I had that very firmly in my mind when we landed. I'd no concept we were just going to sit down as soon as we landed and build a perimeter.

LIEUTENANT GENERAL CLARK

At Anzio we got in there pretty much unopposed and established our beachhead and immediately we began to intercept the German radios. We were reading his mail at the time, we'd broken his code as you know, but nobody knew it at the time except those of us in command and I would get every blood-curdling message Hitler would personally send to his commander in Italy: drive us into the sea and drown us, and so forth. Hitler seized upon this as an opportunity to really give us a slap in the face. He ordered Army Commander von Mackensen to go in and set up an Army headquarters there, he ordered eight divisions in. He was able to take three away from the British front on the Adriatic and bring them in immediately, one and a half from Yugoslavia, from France, from Germany and he built up a tremendous force. We had the mail, we had the orders, and if we had pushed on out to beat him we would have been severely defeated and cut off completely. So we had to dig in on a line that was the maximum we could hold as a bridgehead and await the onslaught, which came within three or four days because his build-up was very rapid. I moved troops in just as fast as the landing craft could get 'em there, but I didn't have unlimited troops to move in. Those who said we could have stepped out and gone to the Alban Hills – well, we might have gotten a detachment to the Alban Hills but you'd have said goodbye to them because the build-up against us was too fast and too severe.

WYNFORD VAUGHAN-THOMAS

When dawn broke we'd got complete surprise, we captured a German in his pyjamas in a farmhouse. He came up rubbing his eyes and got ready to shave and we surrounded him. Along the road there came this marvel-lous drunken car, swaying back and forwards, it was full of the most happy

Germans who'd had a night out in Rome and they were staggering back, and they couldn't believe they were captured and they kept on embracing me, until finally we put them in the clink too. There wasn't a single shot fired at us basically. You looked out and you saw the troops flooding ashore, it was a most extraordinary sight, and there was a great feeling of exaltation sprang up. I remember then getting into a Jeep and I drove up the main road to Rome, and we came to a spot known as 'the Flyover', it was crossing with a bridge on it, where a side road went across the main road to Rome. We all thought that after a quarter of an hour brew-up and on we'd go, but we waited for hours and then a dispatch rider said consolidate. We never went forward from that particular spot for two weeks. It was the biggest shock of my life. I thought at least there would be flying columns sent out to break up the German resistance, even if we lost them we could have driven on to their headquarters. It wasn't an area that they had prepared defensively and if we'd had four or five tanks what chaos you would have created behind the lines. There was no plan to spread chaos, no plan to confuse the Germans. We came, we saw, we conquered – but we stayed where we were.

MAJOR GENERAL HARDING

I don't think it was carried out with sufficient vigour and aggressively in the early stages of the landing. My experience of combined operations goes back to the First World War in Gallipoli and there one learned that there is a moment after the initial landing when the enemy is in a state of uncertainty and doubt, and an opportunity which is a very fleeting one occurs. I think probably the same thing happened at Anzio, there was an opportunity for exploiting the original landing. I don't think it was seized – what the reasons were it's difficult for me to say.

LIEUTENANT GENERAL CLARK

The enemy build-up was four or five times as fast as I could build up, so that although General Lucas could have moved further from Anzio he would soon have been met by an overwhelming force. He would have been defeated, no question about it, so we had to dig in on the biggest perimeter we could possibly digest and wait for the onslaught, which came. I remember that the first time I directed that our heavy bombers come in with close support it was a touch and go situation up there.

WYNFORD VAUGHAN-THOMAS

Every aircraft they could spare in Italy came over for three or four days. It was known as saturation bombing and I remember watching one of the great raids coming over and you felt the earth had come to an end – it spouted in front of you, it shook, it shuddered and occasionally one went behind – when a soldier hears about precision bombing he digs a very deep hole and hides in it. On this occasion I thought there can't be a living German, the whole landscape heaved. There were wave after wave of these huge bombers coming over and the astonishing thing is about three-quarters of an hour later the Germans rose out of all this mess and came hopping towards us again. They didn't get very far, but the fact is that they survived it and were able to mount an attack.

GENERAL WESTPHAL

The German counter-attack at Anzio failed because exceptionally bad weather which made impossible to moving the armoured cars and the artillery and the training of the troops who was not as strong enough for succeed. Nevertheless, we were very near to the sea, but at that moment, we had no reports from the first battalions who attack and I was very anxious that we would have too big losses, and I proposed to Field Marshal Kesselring to end this attack.

WYNFORD VAUGHAN-THOMAS

I still to this day don't understand German tactics, but they went back to the First World War, bringing in unit after unit, and there was a moment when you actually saw them leaving their lines like those old films of the Somme battle, and falling down as our machine guns took them. Anzio was the nearest approach to World War One that I've ever heard in the last war; we even had trenches afterwards. But on this assault it was like the Somme all over again and they came over a moon landscape complete with wrecked tanks, abandoned Jeeps along the road and wire dangling down. The German units would come forward and I was lying looking up and every time the shells came over, crouched down. I think that the biggest memory of battle is when you're lying cringing against the earth or an old piece of broken brick, anything, and suddenly these little shapes are popping up. There were sounds of ratatats of machine guns and thuds of guns and the guns were screaming over us all the time. The gunfire in Anzio was terrific, it was almost done like a battleship control, every gun firing as one.

SERGEANT BILL BECKETT
Sherwood Foresters

When we was in the line you'd got to send one or two men out of your section to fetch your water and your rations. They used to take a ball of white tape and used to plug into your position and used to trail this white tape to where they'd got to pick up the rations then follow the tape back. Well, in the meantime, a German patrol had come to take the tape and pinned it in his position so you'd carry the rations and water and it was, 'Right, thank you, Tommy, put it right there'. Next morning soon as it's daylight they used to be shouting to you just over the hill, 'Have you got your water, Tommy, have you got your rations?' You'd just peep over and you'd see all your mates lined up getting into lorries.

MAJOR GENERAL HARDING

The situation was that Alexander had committed himself to doing every-thing in his power and using all his resources to the limit, in order to pin down German and Italian troops in Italy – German in particular – to prevent their being moved away from Italy to reinforce the Western Front. He therefore felt his duty to continue the operations against Cassino. After one or two more abortive attempts to drive the Germans off the Cassino monastery hill and to get up the Rapido valley, I came to the conclusion that the German strength and particularly the skill with which the German commanders were able to manipulate their troops on the battlefield, the advantage they were able to take from their tactical train-ing and organisation to carry out effective blocking and laying operations in that difficult terrain meant that we would never have succeeded in breaking the Gustav Line unless we launched an offensive on a wide front from Cassino to the sea. The plan was to make use of our superiority in armour, artillery, the air and in infantry on the main front. At the same time to make use of our position at Anzio to fox the enemy to where the main assault was coming and to prevent him from moving quickly from the Anzio front to the main front and vice versa.

SHERWOOD FORESTERS

Group interview, Nottingham pub

We got closer together, the longer it went on the closer we became, because we knew there was only one way out of it, and that was into the sea or get out the other way ... And it did happen, eventually we got out the other way ... After three months it was demoralising what was seen, I'm telling yer ... It was every night, every night everybody was hunting Germans, everybody was out to kill anybody. You used to go out – I used to go out on me own, creeping, to kill. We was insane ... Yeah, I think we did become like that, we did become like animals in the end, eventually ... Yes, just like rats ... Yes, oh yes.

WYNFORD VAUGHAN-THOMAS

We got into a marvellous position, we broke into the hills and then we were going to get across the German line. We got to a little place called Artina and I could see down below in the Valmontone the German Army desperately trying to get through it, the Göring Division moving up through the vineyards below us and we had 'em. If we'd only chucked in the full weight of our Army right nobody would have got out from further south in Cassino. I can't understand to this day why he switched the attack because Mark Clark was no fool. It's quite true that he whipped the sign outside Rome for his bathroom but otherwise he was a damn good general, and he had to keep the Americans fighting although they didn't really have their hearts in it. But for some reason he pushed us through the hills instead of cutting across the German line. Maybe he wanted to get into Rome before the British, but anyhow the Germans were able to pull out.

LIEUTENANT GENERAL CLARK

I took heavy casualties in coming over the mountains and there was no chance, in my opinion, for me to have cut the Germans off. First, they're too smart – they wouldn't have remained in a position where I could just attack on their flank and defeat them, they had other access roads from the south leading to the north. But the main reason I couldn't do it was that I couldn't attack to the east from the bridgehead without taking all the hills that were heavily defended by the Germans, who would have debouched into my flank and raised havoc with me. I would have suffered heavy casualties if I had attacked to the east without taking the Alban Hills and I didn't have the means to do both.

MAJOR GENERAL HARDING

If I may put it diplomatically, I think General Clark was overwhelmed by the wish to be the first into Rome, which he would have done anyhow. I think that's why he suddenly went contrary to what Alexander had intended to do. The intention was that the break-out from Anzio, to direct it on Valmontone to cut the main route by which the German forces would withdraw. The whole concept of the operation from Anzio was with that intention. By diverting his axis to advance from almost due east to north-east he missed an opportunity of cutting off some forces, but he was attracted, I think, by the magnet of Rome.

LIEUTENANT GENERAL CLARK

But don't think that Rome didn't loom as a very interesting prize in our path. When the President came to see me, President Roosevelt in Italy, he said, 'I'm not sure that you can extract yourself from the battle but I'm going to be in Sicily and I'd love to see you.' I went down to see him and he handed me a letter and said, 'I didn't think you could come and I've written you a letter.' In it is how anxious we were to capture Rome, to liberate Rome. And I had been told by my government, by General Marshall, of the approximate time of Ike's cross-Channel landing and of the hope that I could capture Rome before, because it would be quite a blow to the Axis if these two could be coordinated.

WYNFORD VAUGHAN-THOMAS

Well, the liberation of Rome was the last Roman holiday on a big scale, I suppose, in history. I arrived at dawn and first of all people came rather anxiously out in the streets. You don't know who's going to liberate who, I mean you can easily lose your watch if you come too soon to greet the liberators. You've got to let the gallant defenders of freedom go back and the bringers of the new freedom arrive and it's a very nice thing to know when to come out of your cellars.

BILL MAULDIN

American cartoonist with Stars and Stripes

Thinking of the poverty of Italy and the destruction of its cities and villages, especially in the south, reminded me of a dog that had been run over while running out to bite the tyres of a passing automobile. I had the feeling, certainly most people did at the time, that Mussolini was an opportunist and was trying in a sense to get on Hitler's bandwagon and grab all the loot he could along the way, and just dragged his country into it. The Italians are not – back in Roman days they were different – but they're not the world's greatest fighters. It's one of the things I love about them, really. But they love parades and I think this was where Mussolini got his support – he gave everybody lots of parades and it's terribly impressive, I'm sure, to stand in Rome or Milan or wherever and see all these glittering robes and troops go by and feel the world is yours and you could do just about anything. The fact is that Mussolini saw a bandwagon going by and tried to jump on it, and they got run over.

CHAPTER 26

D-DAY IN NORMANDY

Thanks to the all-star 1962 film of Cornelius Ryan's great reportage The Longest Day *and, more recently, Steven Spielberg's* Saving Private Ryan, *the Allied landings on the Normandy coast on 6 June 1944 may well be the most celebrated episode of the Second World War. The planning of Operation Overlord and Eisenhower's bold decision to accept the advice of his chief meteorologist and launch the invasion in the sole window of opportunity provided by fickle English Channel weather was dealt with well by the episode entitled* Morning: June–August 1944. *However, the programme used only anonymous voice-overs to describe the landings themselves: one of the great pleasures of this project has been to put names to some of those voices. The interviews unfortunately did not cover the left flank, so this introduction must suffice as the only mention of the British 3rd Division's landing on Sword Beach and the drop of the British 6th Airborne Division, which silenced the gun battery at Merville and captured the bridges over the River Orne and the Caen canal, the latter still known as 'Pegasus Bridge'. In military history attention inevitably goes to the places where things go badly wrong and on D-Day that was Omaha Beach, where a combination of terrain well-suited for defence, the best German troops on the attack front and the requirement to land with only minimal time for bombardment led initially to a bloody stalemate. One of the first break-outs from the beach was accomplished by a company commanded by Captain Wozenski, interviewed below. General Collins, whose VII Corps had a relatively easy landing at Utah Beach, mentions in passing that the US 82nd Airborne Division was scattered like confetti inland from his beachhead but managed to capture the bridge over the Mederet river, the inspiration for the climax of* Saving Private Ryan. *The character portrayed in the film by*

Tom Hanks gets in a jibe against the 'over-rated' Montgomery. Montgomery was in operational command of Overlord from start to finish, and, whatever his personal flaws, its success owed much to his practical good sense.

MAJOR GORONWY REES
Combined Operations Staff Officer

I got involved in the [August 1942] Dieppe operation really by accident and found myself deeply involved in the planning of it, and it was a most appalling disaster. I think everything that could go wrong went wrong with that operation and the result of it was that by the end we were most powerfully impressed by the dangers and the hazards of any kind of combined operation on that kind of scale – we'd never attempted to do a combined operation on that scale before, and really nobody knew how to do it. And this was why, in fact, it was worth doing because if we hadn't done that operation then I'm quite sure thousands of lives would have been wasted in the D-Day operation. We learned so much from Dieppe that I think it was quite invaluable as far as the final invasion was concerned.

ANDRÉ SENATOR
Mayor of Asnelles, Normandy, inland from Juno Beach

We had waited for four years for that day to come and we never thought that the landing would be done here on our coast, although we thought that would happen in the north of France because you know there's a hundred miles between our coast and the southern coast of England. So we never thought the reason of the landing here is the condition of our beach, which is a beach of sand, but hard sand. You remember the failure of Dieppe was because the tanks couldn't get out of the beach, the beach is made of stones and stones were rolling under the caterpillars of the tanks, while here you can drive cars and of course tanks on the beach, and the soil of the beach is good.

ADMIRAL LORD LOUIS MOUNTBATTEN
Chief of Combined Operations

To prevent the enemy from building up reinforcements so quickly that he could push you back in the sea, you had to do two things. First, you have

coastal defences, and the Air Force had to have very special conditions of cloud amount and heights, so that when I come to put them together I found they might have to sit about for one hundred and twenty or one hundred and fifty years before they got the operation launched. I found that in one year the chances of them getting those conditions was going to be about sixty to one against.

BRIGADIER RONALD BELCHEM
Twenty-First Army Group Staff

It was accepted by all that Normandy was the best compromise location for this invasion. The disquieting thing that happened between the beginning of what we might call combat planning in January 1944 and the invasion in June was that after Rommel assumed command of this sector in France he began to build up the strength of the defences in Normandy, on the beaches, from the point of view of pillboxes, guns and the like. The discrepancies in relative strength between the German defences in, shall we say, the Pas-de-Calais and upper Normandy in January–February were very apparent, but there was an enormous acceleration in the strengthening of the defences in the Normandy peninsula going on right up to the time of the landing.

SERGEANT LEO GARIEPY
Canadian Tank Commander, Juno Beach

We knew exactly, we had known for months, what the beach defences were like, what the town was like; we had a photograph of the town, we knew the town, not by a map, we knew the town by photography where each crew commander had a photograph of the town that had been divided in twelve rectangles, we knew the streets by their names. I broke forty walls to get to the German headquarters, I knew it was going beyond each house, I knew where there was potatoes, I knew where there was cabbage, I knew where there was turnips – I knew where I was every inch of the way. We were so well informed about the defence. We had been trained about Juno for a long, long time. The only thing we didn't know about Juno prior to D-Day was that Juno could have been in Greece, Italy,

Spain. We had no idea where Juno was, we only learned on the night prior to D-Day where Juno was, in Normandy.

PRIVATE ARNOLD LEVIN
16th Regiment, US 1st Division, Omaha Beach

You can get so scared that you're not scared any more and I think that's what happened to me. We were psychologically trained as well as militarily trained, which is probably more important, really, because we were trained to such a point that you do everything by instinct. We give the British a lot of credit for that because we did spend some time at a British assault centre, I think it was a place called Barnsley. We spent a lot of time there. Miserable place but the training was good – and after it was all over the food was awful.

SAPPER JOE MINOGUE
Royal Engineer in a flail tank with 50th Division, Gold Beach

We began to suspect that this business of rendezvousing at Le Hamel twenty minutes after the actual landing was only a blind and they really thought we'd all be killed. To some degree this was heightened when the Divisional Commander – he was [Major] General Percy Hobart, who must have been about seventy – one day when we were waterproofing near Southampton Water, popped his head under the tank and said, 'We're expecting seventy per cent casualties, you know, but if any of you chaps get there I'll see you the day after D-Day.' And indeed he did.*

SERGEANT GARIEPY

The DD Tank is an ordinary Sherman, modified and called DD because it stood for duplex drive; you could drive it at sea as well as on the land. They were modified in Birmingham by adding a shelf, which we call the deck, around the circumference of the tank at the upper-track level. The

---

* Major General Sir Percy Hobart (1885–1957) trained the Mobile Force (later 7th Armoured Division) in Egypt and was recalled from retirement to form 79th Armoured Division RE with specialised tanks, known as 'Hobart's Funnies', for the Normandy landing.

shelf was about fourteen or eighteen inches in width, on which was riveted a rubberised canvas that rose nine feet in height all round the circumference of the tank. This canvas was held rigid by thirty-two inner tubes and when the inner tubes were inflated the canvas was rigid. We displaced more than thirty-two tons of water, the weight of the tank, which gave us buoyancy. Two propellers were synchronised with the tracks and when the tracks turned so did the propellers. This gave us propulsion; to give us direction the propellers were mobile fifteen degrees to the right, fifteen degrees to the left, steered by the crew commander standing on top of the tank because someone had to see over the screen to direct the tank.

MAJOR GENERAL COLLINS

The 4th Division had never participated in an amphibious operation before and a very important part of their training was some exercises at Slapton Sands in southern England. To me it was highly profitable because one of the things I was concerned with was whether we were going to be able to get these amphibious tanks ashore without them being swamped. This was a British design; the tanks had a canvas body around them but when they went off the LST [Landing Ship, Tanks] were inevitably going to scoop up some water as they went down the ramp, particularly if the weather was bad. So I went personally in with those tanks and watched this performance and in consequence I decided to put them as close to shore as the Navy would do it. There was always the danger that ships would be hit by gunfire, but I made them put off about four to six thousand yards offshore and despite the rough water we were able to get practically all of our tanks ashore, whereas on Omaha Beach they were put way offshore and most of the tanks foundered.

SAPPER MINOGUE

For tank men I think there were two main fears, one is the danger of being trapped inside a tank that's on fire and the second one, because we were soldiers and because we were used to being on the land all the time, was our fear of water. Really, I think we were more terrified of being drowned in that damned tank than anything else. One thing we did do to pass the time was to get a hacksaw and cut about thirty pounds of valuable metal from inside the turret of the Sherman tank that we had, so that if there were any fear of drowning two of us in the turret could grab the driver and co-driver and pull them into what we thought might be some kind of safe haven, in which they could just shoot through the turret top.

MAJOR GENERAL COLLINS

We had a number of conferences at General Omar Bradley's headquarters at Bristol and then we had a final show at St John's in London, which was supervised by Montgomery and in which the Army Commanders all along the line, the British and the Canadians and ourselves, outlined our plans and the Corps Commanders all spoke there also. We had a big map laid out on the floor and we stood in front of the map. Mr Churchill was present at that, it was a very dramatic thing, and then following each of our presentations Monty would ask us questions as to what we would do under various circumstances. I found it fascinating and profitable.

GROUP CAPTAIN STAGG

Towards the end of May the date for the actual invasion was fixed for 5th June and during that time, just as the whole of General Eisenhower's forces were assembling round the coast of these islands, there seemed on our weather charts to be nothing but a series of depressions with almost winter-like intensity. As the time went on the seriousness, the ominousness, of the whole situation got worse until by Saturday night, 3rd June, it became obvious there would certainly be a storm in the Channel area on the Sunday night and Monday. General Eisenhower, at that meeting, decided to hold the operation. On that Sunday morning, 4th June, after three days of tremendous tension, we were completely uncertain what could happen. Then, miraculously and mercifully, the almost unbelievable happened: during the Sunday we spotted from two reports from the Atlantic that there might just be a slight interlude between the two depressions off western Ireland.

LIEUTENANT RAY NANCE
117th Regiment, US 29th Division, Omaha Beach

We were loaded on trucks and proceeded to the port of embarkation, which in our case was Weymouth in southern England. We'd travelled this way once before on a dry run and there'd been nothing along the road, but this time there was so much equipment parked along the road and in the fields that it seemed the whole island would tilt and slide into the Channel.

SAPPER MINOGUE

I would say that the success of the actual invasion was simply down to the fact that the soldiers were so glad to get off the landing craft and to escape the seasickness that they were just ready to go anywhere by that time. But it was a fantastic sight to see so many ships of all shapes and sizes heading down the Channel and all going one way. I think anybody who saw that sight couldn't fail to be impressed by the organisation that must have gone into it.

GROUP CAPTAIN STAGG

If that interlude could be long enough and if it arrived in the Channel at the proper time, it might just let the whole thing get started again. When I reported this to General Eisenhower's staff during the afternoon they seemed to be very pessimistic about it, they didn't think it could be started again. But by the evening my own confidence in the forecast for this quieter period had so increased from further reports that had come in that I convinced General Eisenhower. The next morning, early on 5th June, they met again to confirm this decision and when I could tell them that we were even more confident than we had been the previous night, the joy on the faces of the Supreme Commander and his Commanders after the deep gloom of the preceding day was a marvel to behold. It was in the early hours of Monday, 5th June, General Eisenhower made his final and irrevocable decision for the operation to go forward again, round midnight that night. As it turned out that Tuesday, 6th June, when D–Day actually took place, was the only day in the whole of June on which it could have been started. The day before was too stormy and the period a fortnight later was the stormiest of the whole month. The Germans seemed to be caught unawares, whether they didn't spot this interlude coming along or whether they didn't think it would last long enough to be of any use to General Eisenhower we don't know, but they certainly didn't expect General Eisenhower's forces at that time.

BRIGADIER BELCHEM

The only formations that managed to gain their D-Day objectives, or approximately so, were on the British side the 50th Division in the Gold sector and on the American side General Collins's Corps at the base of the Cotentin peninsula. In other areas we fell short. Tanks got south of the Bayeux road but we weren't able to follow them up with infantry and it took some months before we captured the city of Caen. The main problem actually on D-Day was the American Omaha Beach. Throughout D-Day the situation there was extremely critical and it demonstrated in the event the wisdom of using highly experienced divisions in this sort of operation. The 1st American Infantry Division, which was one of the top Allied divisions, did a magnificent job in holding on in the Omaha area, bearing in mind that when they landed they found the German defence division at that particular part of the coast was holding an anti-invasion exercise, so they ran straight into a formation deployed to stop exactly what they were trying to do.

PRIVATE GEORGE ALEX
101st US Airborne Division

After we all got in the air and circled some part of England for quite some time waiting for the rest of the aircraft to get off the ground and get together we felt this was it, this is for real, we're going. It was about three hours, something like that, by the time we all took off and got in the air together and as the time was getting closer, because you'd got to get there just before daybreak, you're getting nervous, getting butterflies in your stomach and you're wondering, What am I doing here, why did I ever come, why did I volunteer? You're worrying if you're going to get hit by your own people again, like for instance when we dropped into Sicily our own Navy shot us down when we were flying over the beaches and that was almost the end of the Airborne at that time. Someone would get sick in the aircraft and they'd pull their steel helmets off and start getting the heaves and then everyone else down the line would follow suit and everybody is heaving, dry heaves, and waiting to get out of that aeroplane, hoping that the moment would come right away to get out of that place because it stunk. And of course we all managed to pitch our gas masks out, we didn't want to carry that around our necks all the time and the English Channel must be full of gas masks. When the time came to go, when that green light went on and out the door we went, we didn't hesitate one moment we were so happy to get out of that thing.

MME THÉRÈSE BROHER
Resident of Sainte-Mère-Eglise, inland from Utah Beach
It began day before D-Day, it was in the evening of the 5th, about nine o'clock. We went at first to go to bed and we heard planes and they dropped lights. Many colours in the sky, it was wonderful. And we heard other planes coming so we set out for a shelter, but bombs dropped all round the house and we went under a table in the kitchen. We were frightened and we thought that will probably be it for us, and it lasted about one hour – we did not know exactly because all clocks stopped. And bombs dropped, we were frightened, and at last it was the end of the bombardment. And we heard crickets, funny noises, we did not dare to go out and then we saw two men with all kinds of weapons around their body and one of them came near us and he told us in French, 'We are Americans.' It was a very good, big surprise and we had at home a bottle of white wine that wasn't broken and my father was so happy he gave that bottle to the first American soldier he saw.

MAJOR GENERAL COLLINS
The 82nd did seize the bridge across the Mederet, which was very helpful. But their drop was scattered almost from the base of the Cherbourg

peninsula up to the city of Cherbourg itself. This resulted in confusion to the Germans as to just where the attack was going to take place because they couldn't believe that it could be so scattered, and this did tend to slow down their reaction to where the landing was actually taking place and therefore it was an advantage.

MICHEL DE VALAVIELLE
French farmers, resident inland from Utah Beach

I was here in my farm when the landing happened. We were having in the farm a German battery of artillery with 88-millimetre guns and when the American people came we were afraid. We don't realise what has happened during the night, many, many planes, and I go to the farm and see an old woman who was just coming from the beach and told me the sea is dark with ships, and some time after a German soldier came here and he was having a prayer book on which it was wrote, Murphy, Michigan. He told us it was a prayer book of a paratrooper, so we realised it was the landing. The German obliged us to stay a long time in the house while they were fighting with the American soldier; the fight was during the beginning of the day until about twelve. At that time the American soldier began to approach the house. I go out first to tell him Germans were gone and there was nobody except French people in the house. He took me, I suppose, as a German soldier and so I was wounded by the American soldier. When they realised their mistake they took me immediately and I was the first Frenchman wounded on the beach in a hospital. So it was unforgettable view of the D-Day for me.

LIEUTENANT PATRICK DONNELL
47 Commando, Royal Marines, Gold Beach

We expected a clear beach with an indication as to exactly how we should proceed. We were even told the Military Police would be there to greet us. Our job was to land immediately behind the first wave of the 50th Division and pass through them, swing to the west, and capture a small port called Port-en-Bessin, which was halfway between the British beaches and the American beaches. About a mile off the beach we realised that the thing was not at all as we had expected. My commanding officer waved to us to turn to the left and at that moment a German battery on high ground beyond Arromanches got their sights on to us and started to pick some of the craft off. Of course these craft sank in deep water and very few of the men actually got on to the beach. Most of them were rescued and taken back to England. It became obvious to us as we proceeded further along the beach eastwards, in the wrong direction from what we had originally intended, that the beach itself was in a considerable state of chaos and ultimately it became a matter of each craft for itself. On the run-in, other craft ran into underwater obstacles and mines, and of the fourteen craft that set off, only two actually returned to the parent ships. I was pretty concerned about the German battery because it had considerable accuracy, but just as we turned and they began to pick us off a destroyer saw the situation and began to fire at the guns, and anyone who's ever experienced naval gunfire knows it's a terrifying thing because of the very high velocity and I think this shut the Germans up so that we lost only two or three craft in deep water. The other craft were lost closer to the beach. One of them went over a mine and the front half of the craft with the personnel in it went straight up in the air. That was not a very pleasant sight. The sea was quite a different colour when that craft blew up.

CAPTAIN JOHN FINKE
Company Commander, 16th Regiment, US 1st Division, Omaha Beach
There was a great deal of confusion, in fact we didn't realise what some of it meant. For instance we thought there had been a lot of aircraft shot down because the water was covered with these bright orange life rafts. But they were actually the survivors from the tanks, we called them DD [duplex drive] tanks. They had a canvas thing and they swam in the water and used the motor of the tank to push themselves by means of a propeller. Well, I think ninety-nine per cent of them swamped, that is went down in the drink, and the tank crews had been able to get out in most cases and into these orange rafts, which we didn't realise the meaning of until we got ashore and found that all these tanks that were supposed to be with us

weren't there. They later brought in a few of what they called wader tanks, which were unloaded at the water's edge. They had been waterproofed and they could move up the beach, but there were very few of those actually.

SERGEANT GARIEPY

The retaliation, very, very mild, they were firing, and machine-gunning at us but not heavy at all. Of course you must understand that the DD Tank in the water looks like a little, very unharmful canvas boat; there's only about fifteen inches of rubberised canvas that shows. It's only when we're coming out of the water, that's when they realised there were tanks, but by then we were a little too close to their heavy-calibre guns on us and they were firing over our heads. No, the tanks lost at sea were through rough sea not by enemy action; there may be one or two that was sank by mortar but the big opposition was the sea, the condition of the sea, not the enemy.

CAPTAIN EDWARD WOZENSKI

Company Commander, 16th Regiment, US 1st Division, Omaha Beach
At Slapton Sands in England when we were rehearsing we had nine landing-ship rockets. They would trigger off a rocket at a time until they walked down the water and hit the beach. Then somebody would pull the master switch and a thousand rockets would take off per ship in a fantastic display, they would just churn up the beach. In the real show they were drawing some shore gunfire and we saw the rocket ships taking some evasive action and somebody panicked and pulled the switch. And we saw this tremendous display but I'll bet my bottom dollar that there wasn't one rocket that came within a half a mile of the beach. Nine thousand rockets, the most beautiful display you ever saw in your life, and I swear to God I didn't see so much as a hand-grenade crater within a half a mile of the beach. Of course we expected great things of the Ninth Air Force too. We'd been briefed with their pilots, John Finke and I were both briefed. He had Exit E-3, and I had responsibility for Exit E-1, and each one of those exits was to get one hundred and eighty-six tons, the figure stays right in my mind to this day, one hundred and eighty-six tons of dive-

bombing by the Ninth Air Force on Exit E-1 and the same thing for John Finke on Exit E-3. To this day, I don't know what happened. As I say, I didn't see so much as a hand-grenade crater anyplace.

SAPPER MINOGUE

I was the gunner of the tank and I had a forward view until such a time as I was asked to do a 360-degree traverse to blow the waterproofing around the turret ring. And in the forward view I saw that the three tanks in front of us were not doing too well. The first tank had stopped because its commander had been killed, the second tank had been a bit too close to him and had slewed slightly to the right and hit a clay patch on the beach and the tank behind him, they had a hit in the petrol tank, or rather on the side of the tank, which had set the thing on fire, and we saw the crew busily scrambling out. This did not do a great deal for our confidence.

COLONEL JAMES SINK
116th Regiment, US 29th Division, Omaha Beach

As we went in we were … just at the left were two LCIs [Landing Craft Infantry] – this is a military ship that carried about two hundred men who landed by a couple of ramps that dropped down over the bow of the ship on each side – and one of them carried our headquarters, the other half of my unit, which was to take over my mission if I failed. And as we were preparing to come in and beach, on our left we saw this tremendous explosion aboard the craft and everything went up in smoke. We found out later what had happened: the top side of the landing craft was loaded with flame-throwers and the Germans got a couple of rounds into this and set them off. Of course the pressure in these things went off like a firebomb, more or less like a bomb attack from an aeroplane, and it enveloped the ship in flames. Although we did see a lot of men jump off the ship to escape, quite a few were caught inside and burned up. The commander of my landing craft didn't say a word to me and just turned our craft around and headed back to sea. It took some persuasion on my part to get him to come back and land, and when he did he brought us back about three hundred yards to the east of where we were supposed to land.

PRIVATE ROBERT KOCH

116th Regiment, US 29th Division, Omaha Beach

In my particular ship the first man, who was a sergeant, raised up to see how far we had to go to reach land and was struck right in the forehead by a bullet and fell back dead. He was the first man that I had ever in my life seen dead in any combat. We were about three hundred feet off the beach when our ship got hit so we had to swim in, and the water was approximately twelve feet in depth so when you went off you were over your head. When I arrived on the beach, believe it or not the only thing I had was myself – my rifle I'd dropped in the water and I lay there and thought to myself, What am I going to do here, am I going to wrestle or fist-fight or what? But the other boys had come along and some of them, my buddies, had been shot and were laying near me and of course I took their rifles and their belts and moved along.

SAPPER MINOGUE

Chaos? Well, one landing craft had been hit in the engine room and the five tanks on it spent the whole day facing out to sea until the tide turned and they could come in. And chaos, if you like, was this whole business of Le Hamel, which we'd been told was held by a German platoon, and when it finally fell about four o'clock in the afternoon there was so many men came out of it that it must have been the biggest platoon that the German Army ever mustered.

PRIVATE LEVIN

I was with my CO and saw that fellow Robert Capa, the internationally known photographer who took the picture that appeared on the front of *Life* of a man caught in an obstacle. Now we started to go after him but as we started out we caught some small-arms fire and went back in, and we figured that he was probably better off where he was, there was no sense getting people killed.*

---

* Robert Capa (1913–54), Hungarian-born war photographer, took 108 pictures at Omaha Beach, of which only eleven blurred frames survived a laboratory error.

CAPTAIN FINKE

We had a great deal of difficulty getting the men to move. There was great deal of enemy fire and they would take cover behind some of these obstacles that were there to catch assault craft. They were about the size of a ten- or twelve-foot telephone pole with a teller mine on the top of it. The whole area was just full of these obstacles. Any port in a storm. People would just try to take cover behind one of these poles. Well, it didn't provide any cover so you just had to force them to move no matter how you did it. It had so happened, I had sprained my ankle in the marshalling area and had to go ashore carrying a cane instead of a rifle. I used it to very good effect to just whack people until they moved. And it was not much fun, obviously.

PRIVATE KOCH

We finally did make it to the bottom of the cliffs where we had more safety, because the Germans couldn't fire their machine guns straight down and they couldn't also fire their rifles down because they had to expose themselves over the cliffs, which would give us a chance to get them. Now we remained in that position for – well, I would say it was a lifetime but it was about four to five hours – and then one of the other companies of, I think it was of the 115th Regiment, that had come in after us, they had fortunately come in at a better position and came around, came up on the cliffs and they'd taken over. And they greeted us and told us to come on up and we were very thankful to see them. In our original company that went in at approximately 213 men, eight hours after we were on the beach there was only 38 of us that were fit for continued duty, and we lost most of them from the water-line to the bottom of the cliff.

SAPPER MINOGUE

When we reached the first corner there was a dead German there and he was just like something from a film, because he was young, he was huddled up and his helmet had fallen off, and he was very, very blond. As we turned this corner I was told to clear the waterproofing off the machine gun and I began to fire down this deserted road. At the very moment that I began to fire, probably about one hundred and fifty yards ahead, three of our own infantrymen burst though a hedge at the side of the road and suddenly one of them fell as though he'd been hit and the other two dragged him back. I've often wondered in the whole of the intervening twenty-eight years whether in fact I was responsible for any injury or death that poor bloke might have suffered.

CAPTAIN WOZENSKI

I think the greatest unsung hero of World War Two was Sergeant Streczyk, one of my platoon sergeants. To the best of my knowledge he was the first one off the beach and it was the path that he took that I picked up. The rest of our battalion followed and then later on I think almost the whole Corps went up that path. As I told this character Cornelius Ryan,* I'm climbing the bluff and I see Streczyk coming down because he's happy to see me and he's got a grin on his face. And I say, 'My God!' as he puts his foot on a teller mine right in front of my nose. I'm climbing up the cliff and he puts his foot on a teller mine. He says, 'Don't let it worry you, it didn't go off when I stepped on it going up.' We got up to the top of the cliff and we found just one of our weapons that would fire. I landed with one hundred and eighty men and eight officers, counting myself, and I had a head count and I counted thirteen men, one other officer and myself. And one weapon, one M-1 rifle, would fire. So we put that man on guard and the rest of us sat down and cleaned our weapons, first echelon maintenance right on top of the bluff. Shortly thereafter I ran into John Finke, I think he had come up and gone off to my left toward his goal, and somebody had winged him through the helmet. He had blood streaming down all over the side of his helmet and I remember my telling him to get his ass back to the beach.

---

* Cornelius Ryan (1920–74), author of the enormously successful *The Longest Day* (1959) about D-Day and *A Bridge Too Far* (1974) about Operation Market Garden (Arnhem), which were made into major films in 1962 and 1977 respectively.

LIEUTENANT NANCE

You could see your friends, people you'd served with for years, floating face down or face up. It was a beautiful day, the sun was shining, planes overhead – and snipers in the cliffs, if you can call that beautiful.

COLONEL SINK

I don't think I was frightened – I was scared, and I think when you're scared you really are more alert. It's like you're playing a game with somebody – you're going through the woods, you've got a gun and he's got a gun – who's going to shoot first? I guess it's more like a duel – you know you're going to spin round and pull the trigger first.

SAPPER MINOGUE

We were aware that we had been very, very lucky indeed that for us it had been a kind of glorified exercise and that none of our fears had fortunately materialised. But we also realised something else: that we would never, no matter what we were called upon to do, be quite as afraid again. It was the whole business of the invasion, we'd been preparing for it for months and months and each of us had been building up little secret fears that we might not survive it.

MAJOR GENERAL COLLINS

In order to save casualties after we had the experience of heavy fighting through the bocage [thick hedgerow] country it was decided to precede the attack by a tremendous bombardment and this would take place in front of my Corps. I was directed by General Bradley to prepare the plans for the attack, which would break out the bocage country and get out into the open a bit. The bombardment started on 25th July with some three thousand planes dropping bombs just in advance of our troops. In the initial planning we had asked that the fighters and bombers come in parallel to our lines so that they would be sure not to have bombs fall short on our troops. Unfortunately they came in at right angles and we had many shorts and took some casualties in our own troops. The weather was not too good so the attack was called off after only perhaps an hour, and was rescheduled for the next day, but the same thing occurred then. We took about six hundred casualties, including one of our senior Army Commanders who was there as an observer.*

SERGEANT GARIEPY

We were bombed quite often by mistake. We had a saying in the Army that when the British bombed the Axis took cover when the Germans bombed the Allies took cover. Well, when our cousin Americans bombed, every-body took cover.

BRIGADIER BELCHEM

Hitler refused permission to his generals to withdraw, when the position was impossible for them, behind the Seine and the Loire, which a professional would have done. On the contrary, he made them remain and fight it out in Normandy and indeed made the Germans counter-attack the enveloping movement of the Americans. This was frustrated firstly by the Americans on the ground, and secondly, of course, you cannot successfully launch a major offensive operation, particularly an armoured operation, without at least local air superiority – which the Germans didn't have.

MAJOR GENERAL COLLINS

After we made the breakthrough west of Saint-Lô, we headed south, parallel to Patton and then we had to defend to the left, because it was a natural thing that the Germans would try to cut off Patton's line of communications at Avranches. So we anticipated that a major counter-attack would be launched at Avranches. The First Army's job was to prevent that breakthrough and my corps, which was on the right flank, was to turn to the west and the real battle took place at Mortain, where we held against the concentrated German attack for several days. The troops of Patton were now spreading out towards Brest and through France, and part of the First Army was then to seize the south end of the

---

* Lieutenant General Lesley McNair (1883–1944) was Commanding General, Army Ground Forces, responsible for the training and equipment of troops for overseas deployment.

pocket. The Germans had only one way to get out and that was towards Paris and if we could close the open mouth of this bag, by the British and Canadians coming down from the north with the Americans coming up from the south, then we could pretty nearly end the German ability to continue the war in France. Unfortunately for a variety of reasons the attack coming down from the north was slow and laborious. Had they been able to move faster we might have trapped more Germans in the Falaise pocket. Very little of their equipment got out but quite a number of Germans were able to escape towards the Seine river and this was too bad. I think that Britain had been in the war for much longer than we had and had taken very heavy casualties, and the Americans were fresh and they had practically no casualties. So while we were anxious to drive forward and were not too concerned about the casualties as long as we could get our objective, it was natural that the British and Canadian forces did it in a more orderly, pacing way.

BRIGADIER BELCHEM

There were very great practical difficulties in closing the Falaise gap quickly and it was difficult for one side, the British–Canadian–Polish, to appreciate the point of view of the other side, the Americans. We were coming down from the north, from the congested, bombed and difficult areas of the Caen sector, and the Germans facing us on the north side of the corridor they were trying to keep open for their escape were in areas where they had been fighting against us for three months or more. The Americans were coming up to meet us from the south, more open country and against much less prepared and organised German resistance.

CHAPTER 27

BATTLE OF THE
PACIFIC 1944–45

Following the loss of four fleet carriers at Midway in June 1942 the Imperial Japanese Navy (IJN) did not sortie in force for two years, by which time the gross industrial disparity between Japan and the USA had made the outcome of the war a foregone conclusion. The Japanese Naval Air Arm was ground down at Guadalcanal and annihilated in the battle of the Philippine Sea (the 'Marianas Turkey Shoot'), when the IJN also lost another three carriers. The remaining carriers were used as decoys and sunk at Leyte in October 1944. The Philippine Sea battle came about because the IJN had to try to prevent the Americans from seizing Saipan and Tinian, the southern Mariana Islands, which brought the Japanese mainland within range of the USAAF's new B-29 bombers. Political considerations, plus ferocious inter-service rivalry and a desire to restore American imperial prestige, led to a second offensive being mounted in General Douglas MacArthur's south-west Pacific area to recover the Philippines. The two most savage small-island battles, at Peleliu in September 1944 and the northern Mariana island of Iwo Jima in February 1945, were fought to cover MacArthur's flank and to gain a base for P-51 fighters to escort the B-29s respectively. Hindsight suggests that both, as well as MacArthur's reconquest of the Philippines, were strategically irrelevant and that Admiral Chester Nimitz's central Pacific drive, his submarines and the USAAF, would have won the war without them. Starting at Leyte, Japanese pilots began to employ the 'body-crash' technique on a large scale, taking the name kamikaze (Divine Wind). For the remainder of the war about 2,800 kamikaze sorties sank or irreparably damaged more than 70 Allied ships and damaged about 330 others, killing and wounding nearly 10,000 Allied personnel, the majority of them in the 82-day battle for Okinawa in April–June 1945. This was to be the last island invasion prior to the assault on the Japanese mainland and some 130,000 Japanese soldiers and about half as many Okinawan civilians died, against 13,000 dead, 36,000 wounded and nearly 25,000 battle-stress casualties among the American forces. The suicidal ferocity of the resistance on Okinawa was a crucial factor in the decision to use the atom bomb in September.

ROBERT SHERROD

War correspondent

The contrast between Tarawa and Eniwetok [February 1944] is what you would expect after we had learned a great deal about amphibious warfare. At Tarawa we were just starting, it was our first action against a defended beach, and Eniwetok was fifteen weeks later. We had learned at Tarawa that three thousand tons of bombs was not enough, particularly when it's the wrong type, when it's fragmentation instead of explosive, for instance. By Eniwetok we had forty thousand tons of preliminary bombardment and bombing, and we didn't have there the problem of the coral reefs, because central Eniwetok is not a coral island so our landing boats could get ashore all right. We had new equipment such as the Army DUKWs, pronounced 'ducks', which are trucks rather than tractors, not treaded but running on rubber tyres. Marvellous machines, especially for bringing us material – equipment of various types, food, water and so on. So we were well prepared for Eniwetok, which was a different type of island. It was hilly, even mountainous in a small way, it was eight square miles instead of the half square mile we had at Tarawa, but we still did not realise the extent of the difficulty that we were going to have with it. They were awfully good at digging into those ravines, tunnels forty, fifty even one hundred feet long with a great many exits to them. They were hard to get out, you needed a number of weapons – the flame-thrower was always good for clearing caves. You used Bangalore torpedoes, hand grenades, you even used bulldozers. Not many people realise that the bulldozer was a weapon in World War Two. We armoured the bulldozers and used them, with cover from the air of course, to close up the vents in the caves. There must have been thousands of Japanese who suffocated to death across the Pacific because their caves were closed by bulldozers.

MARINE SERGEANT WILSON COOKE
Iwo Jima

We used everything available – demolition charges, flame-throwers and what not – but the Japanese were so well entrenched and had been there for so many months preparing the islands for defensive situations that if you blew one entrance another would open up, and they had tools inside with which to work themselves back to the surface. They had sliding doors to close off so that the flame-throwers wouldn't get them and exhaust the oxygen. So it meant simply that men went in, active men, and you killed them underground. It was just that rough.

MARINE LENLY COTTON
Okinawa

Our platoon was – other than the one that could vote – they were all under twenty. Ninety per cent were nineteen or younger, there were as many below eighteen as above, five or six that were sixteen, including myself, and one that was fifteen that I know of personally.

ROBERT SHERROD

The decision on the approach to Japan, now that we knew the end of the war was approaching, was taken in July 1944 at a meeting in Pearl Harbor between President Roosevelt, General MacArthur and Admiral Nimitz. This was the only time MacArthur left his own area during World War Two – actually he never came back to the mainland. MacArthur and Nimitz made their presentations without their staffs and at the end of it Roosevelt told MacArthur he accepted his version and therefore we would approach Japan by two routes – MacArthur's from the south-west Pacific up to Leyte, and Nimitz across the central Pacific – of course by then we were already in the Marianas – on up to Iwo Jima and Okinawa. Their forces would converge at Okinawa and the invasion would take place from there. I think you have to say politics were involved. Roosevelt was having a difficult election in 1944, when he ran for his third term against Thomas Dewey, the Republican, and MacArthur was a threat to him, always. MacArthur had a great following among the common people in the United States, particularly among the right-wingers, and he of course was a Republican. So I'm sure you could speculate sensibly that Roosevelt let MacArthur have his way because it did eliminate him as a factor in the election of 1944.

MARIANAS TURKEY SHOOT
JUNE 1944

ENSIGN ROY 'BUTCH' VORIS
Fighter pilot on the USS Enterprise

They'd picked them up on radar now and it was apparently a strike that we'd not had any intelligence on. It was a major wave and I would think it would be somewhere around two hundred to three hundred Japanese fighters and dive bombers and torpedo planes. They were somewhere between twenty-five and thirty thousand feet, that was way above our normal operating altitude in those days and so we climbed to intercept them and here we saw them coming and they had already started their run in and were heading downhill, picking up speed. And I remember the fighters criss-crossing over the dive bombers and the torpedo planes and we just went full throttle and came right on top of them, just a trail right on down. So were able to work the attack force for a period of about a hundred miles, one at a time, nibbling away at them and by the time they had traversed that last hundred miles I don't think more than a dozen of them, of the Japanese planes, ever reached our Task Force.

BATTLE OF SAMAR, LEYTE GULF
OCTOBER 1944

SEAMAN GEORGE SMITH

Flight-deck crewman on escort carrier USS White Plains

Someone yelled at me, 'You'd better get your helmet and your Mae West on, because here come the Japs,' and at about that time I heard an explosion on the fantail. First I thought it was one of our own planes exploding back there and I looked up and saw all this tin foil falling, this tin foil to jam our radar and of course it was general quarters and everybody manned their battle stations and then they started shooting, trying to get our range. Our skipper turned the ship where the shells landed, he was zigzagging, then we started to lay down smoke but they pulled in pretty fast on us, they caught one of the carriers back there [USS *Kitkun Bay*] and they sank it. They got so close we could see the Japanese flag flying. This was a running battle of about two hours and we were going between these two islands and the Japanese thought it was leading to a trap so they broke off the engagement.

CAPTAIN TADASHI NAKAJIMA

Commander Mabalacat base, the Philippines, organiser of first Special Attack Unit (Kamikaze)

The first attacks took place against the American carriers in Leyte Gulf. The reason why this development took place was that if the Americans succeeded in landing on Leyte and then set up air bases then they would cut us off completely from oil supplies and the United States would force Japan to its knees. Now, why were fighter planes used in these Special Attack forces? The reason was that Japan had fewer and fewer bombing planes, attack planes, and we had to rely on fighter planes. However, of course, fighter pilots were not trained in bombing attacks and therefore it was felt that the only way to solve this was to have these fighter pilots ram themselves, plane and body together, into the enemy ships.

SEAMAN SMITH

At about two o'clock that afternoon we were still at battle stations in a formation of four carriers because they'd sunk one in the morning and at the time we didn't know it but we were attacked by kamikazes. We thought they was dropping bombs on us because one of the carriers off the port side there [USS *St Lô*] took a direct hit and after that we saw a plane come down and hit them and we knew we was under attack by suicide bombers. They hit this carrier dead centre and as we went by men were abandoning ship and as we got beyond it the whole ship seemed to explode and there was nothing there. And at about that time on our own ship a kamikaze came in on us and went in just like a regular landing. I guess he was trying to sneak up on us like one of our own planes coming in. As he started to drop in the skipper seen what he was doing and turned the ship hard port. Well, the men on the starboard side they swung their guns around and shot across the flight deck, hitting the kamikaze, and he winged over and dropped on the other side of the catwalk into the water and exploded with debris showering up on to the flight deck.

LIEUTENANT FRANK MANSON

Crew on Allen M. Sumner-class destroyer USS Laffey

I was on the bridge of our destroyer in a bay in the Philippines and these shiny planes appeared over us and they dived on two of the destroyers and hit them. I turned to my skipper, who was a veteran of the South Pacific, and said, 'Captain, did you ever see anything like this in the South Pacific?' He said, 'Hell, no, I've never seen anything like it,' and he put on flank speed and we started to turn in a tight circle – he thought that was the best manoeuvre.

IWO JIMA
FEBRUARY–MARCH 1945

MARINE JACK STEARN

We didn't expect much opposition because there was going to be a tremendous bombardment by the Fleet and the Air Force. The Air Corps had been bombing continually for over a month. When we began to get close to the island it was during the night and I came up on deck to watch the excitement. It was a beautiful sight to see these different ships of war firing at the beaches, the flashes, the roar, the tremendous power that seemed to overpower the island. Then it began to get late so I went below to get myself some sleep before we had to land. And coming up for the landing the firing was still going on and you could see the flash – well, it was day by this time but you could still see the flashes from the gunships, the battleships and cruisers and destroyers, and you also could see the strikes of the rounds of artillery on the beach, a lot of flames and a lot of dust.*

MARINE SERGEANT COOKE

It had been bombed for seventy-odd days by the Air Corps and prior to going in we shelled it for two days and we'd found this normally suppressed anything on the beach from former operations, that is Saipan in the Marshalls, etc. I went in on Blue Beach with the 24th Marines and when we hit the beach we moved about – oh, possibly three hundred yards in – just as far as they, meaning the Japanese, decided for us to go and then they turned loose with everything they had, so they pinned us on the beach itself. So we spent the first night, we meaning my company, spent the first night on the beach. We did not go in – we could not go in, we tried an attack and it did not work. The next morning at daybreak my company, that was Charlie Company – and Bravo Company, which was in front of us was shot off the hill, unfortunately by some of our planes and a hell of a lot of Japanese – we relieved Bravo. We were committed and we stayed committed for twenty-six days after that. I have a picture taken on Iwo of my company. There's sixteen of us left out of two hundred and seventy that went in.

---

* Lieutenant General Tadamichi Kuribayashi (1891–1945) put all his guns and almost all his garrison in buried bunkers and caves, with the result that the preliminary bombardment left the defences essentially untouched.

MARINE CORPSMAN HERMAN RABECK

The other islands were just normal islands but this thing looked like something out of godforsaken. As you hit the island it was – if there's ever been hell, this was it. There wasn't a living thing anywhere in sight. I would say that forty to fifty per cent of the men I got close to were dead. I was actually hopping over bodies and you never could tell who was alive and who wasn't because everybody hit the ground and stayed there. There was a little incline and everybody clung to the incline because the fire was that heavy and everything that hit the beach was blasted out of the water as fast as it hit it. In fact our own men were blasting ships out of the water to make room for more guys to get in, it was that bad. The whole line of the shores was just one mess of debris, of LSTs and LCTs [Landing Craft Tanks] and God knows what else that tried to get up on the beach, stopped at that point and couldn't get back. They just blew them right out of the water's edge so we couldn't get any wounded off the island. It was just one of the biggest messes I have ever seen. I don't know who the beach master was but he had the roughest job of any man I've heard of because there was absolutely no way of getting boats in or out without blasting your way in, one way or another.

ROBERT SHERROD

I remember walking along the beach and seeing how many people had been killed during the night, and the splattered arms and legs and guts and blood you found all along. The casualties were horrible. I described one battalion that was commanded by a captain because all the other officers had been killed or wounded. Several battalions had over one hundred per cent casualties, that is counting the reinforcements that came in against the original baseline, of course, and you'd find such things as not a single officer remaining in a regiment, except perhaps one, with the rank of major or higher. It's the only battle in the Pacific War when our casualties were the same as the Japanese, although the Japanese were all dead except a few hundred that surrendered, and ours included dead and wounded.*

---

* Actually they were greater: American losses were 8,700 killed and 19,000 wounded, while except for 216 who surrendered, the Japanese garrison of 21,000 was killed.

CORPSMAN RABECK

Our own shells were pretty accurate – we had no problems on this particular island with our own shells, we had enough to contend with the
Japanese shells. They were too damned accurate, they were unbelievably
accurate, they just lobbed in like clockwork, rhythmically patterned, one
after another, just bounced right in there and they didn't miss anything
that was in sight. That spotter up on Mount Suribachi had everybody in
his line, couldn't miss, we were sucked in beautifully.

MARINE LIEUTENANT CLAYTON EASTON

The thirty-first day was just as bad as the first one. They could reach us
any time with anything they had. Their fire-control plots, their gun cables,
their gun controls were blocked off to where they could fire at any inch of
the island at any time. It was just a fact that you put two and two third
divisions of marines in, and then put the Japanese there, if a bullet hit the
island anywhere it had to hit somebody.

MARINE GEORGE SLATTERY

One thing that impressed me about Iwo was the underground noise, the
rumbling that used to go on under the ground. You'd hear this rumbling
all through the night and the ground was warm – you see, this was a
volcanic island. We heard this noise underneath and there were people,
marine officers, who were convinced that the Japanese were digging
underneath us and were going to blow up the whole island or that something awful was going to happen.

MARINE SERGEANT COOKE

Iwo is volcanic, as the world knows, I'm sure. Well, with the bombardment that occurred on this particular island the entire vegetation was
gone, gone completely, and you'd waken in the morning before the shooting would start and you'd look out across this expanse of no man's land
and it was bubbling and seething with steam coming out of the ground.
In fact we had to use cardboard from the ration packs to put down in the
foxhole so that your ass wouldn't burn up when you were using the hole

to protect yourself. Now my reaction was that if there's a hell I'm living through it now so I don't have to worry about going to hell any time in the future – I've been there.

CORPSMAN RABECK

The ash was almost like quicksand and in fact when I finally got hit they had to dig me out by shovelling with their hands, because it covers you that fast. It would just cover you right up and just drift in. That's the way the ash actually was – it moved, it was alive, and if you didn't move fast enough it covered you up.

MARINE SERGEANT COOKE

We had lost so many people, my CO he just came round and said, 'Cooke, you're company commander. We'll talk about commissioning you later.' So with that I accepted responsibilities I'd not had before and it started to get rough because I saw more of the picture than you could on a platoon front. From platoon front to company front you got about four or five hundred more yards, so the realisation came to me that we could have taken a licking then, a bad licking. We came very near to doing that particular thing, we found out – of course much later.

MARINE STEARN

I was on the island a total of six days and it seemed like six thousand years. I couldn't differentiate between night and day because everything kept going, the fear that was always there, the shelling that was always there, there was no place to really go back and relax a bit and then come back forward and say OK we're going back into it again. You were always in it, wherever the heck you went you were always in it.

CORPSMAN RABECK

This was about the fifth day and I was standing on board the ship completely taped up. I had practically a straightjacket on to keep me from bending because I couldn't support my torso, but I was up on top and one of the boys started to holler, 'There goes the flag,' and I don't care where you were on the island, you could see right up to Suribachi and the flag was raised and everybody started to howl because we figured the island was secure. It was far from secure – we had a long way to go yet – but it was nice to see the flag up there anyway.

MARINE JOHN GREET

Most of the time we had to use flame-throwers to get them out, they were buried so deep. Very few of them came out on their own and when they did, usually the one in front he'd come out with his hands up and the one behind he'd come out with a grenade.

MARINE C S AXTELL

We were heavily attacked that night and some measure of the infiltration is that there were twenty dead enemy within ten yards of the colonel's foxhole. As the morning sun came up we started to pull out of our foxholes and relax a bit and one of the West Virginia boys – he was a tall gangly fellow, very dry humour – he was sitting against a stone wall with his knees up under his helmet as we used to sit quite often, when one of the enemy ran out on top of the stone wall and held a small explosive charge to his abdomen. A chunk of his torso went spiralling into the air and came down on John's knees with the absolute posterior devoid of any clothes staring him right in the face. And he looked at that and he says, 'God, have I been hit that bad?' And that was the trigger that released the tensions of the previous night and there were several of us that were perfectly useless for as much as an hour – we just lay there on the ground in convulsions.

MARINE GREET

Sometimes we got them out by coaxing, if we got one that could speak English. We found quite a few of them over there and they'd lead the rest of them out. But they were very sceptical, they'd got the idea that we were going to torture them, like they did to our boys I guess. We saw some pretty terrible sights over there.

MARINE SLATTERY

One thing we found out about the Japanese throughout the war was something that couldn't be written about during the war, which was that once a man had surrendered he had sort of written himself off. If you see what I mean, he was disgraced anyway so he was likely to tell you everything he knew. It was quite unlike interrogating prisoners in any other war that I ever heard of.

MARINE RICHARD COLEMAN

I was always taught to hate them, to detest them, that they were the animals and we were the men. By the same token we were taught that they would die for the Emperor and we weren't taught to die for our President. To come up against an individual who wants to die, or who doesn't care about dying, is a tough thing to combat in your mind. We wanted to live, we wanted to kill him and survive.

OKINAWA
APRIL–JUNE 1945

LIEUTENANT COMMANDER DONALD GARY

Fleet carrier USS Franklin, *19 March 1945*

By the time I got back to my battle station and then further aft the lights were dimming and smoke was pouring through the ventilation system, and everyone it seemed was going toward a given compartment that had a light and it's like moths where they go to the light – you were groping in the dark so you go where the light is, and that's what I did and that's what about two hundred and eighty-five other fellows did. There we found ourselves reasonably smoke free but with only one little cup of ventilation through the skin of the ship. So there we were, all of us afraid and just stood by while the terrific explosions from the topside just rocked the ship. There were explosions from the seventy-two other planes on deck and they were blowing up. It was our own bombs that at that time made us more afraid of what the eventual outcome was going to be. We were trapped for about an hour and a half and during that time the list on the ship grew greater and all in all everyone was just waiting to die, it was that bad. But suddenly something stirred in my mind and I knew a way out. I stood up and declared myself, told them I knew a way out and if I could get there I'd get back for the rest of them. Five times I went back, I got them all out too.*

CAPTAIN NAKAJIMA

At the beginning we were able to select from the large number of people who volunteered. But as the war situation deteriorated and when the attack planes had to take off from Japan proper, when Japan itself was under threat of attack, we needed a large number of Special Attack Force pilots. And then it could be that not all of them were volunteers but may have included those who did not actually desire to volunteer and those who were sort of dragged in by their comrades and persuaded to volunteer.

LIEUTENANT MANSON

When the five-inch guns opened the plane is out about maybe five or six miles, that's when you see the big puffs, and then when the forties open you see smaller puffs and they're getting within maybe one mile or two miles and then when the twenties open they're less than a mile and you know there's an explosion imminent and you just hope it's not against your ship. But you really don't know because you can't tell what the pilot's going to do at the last minute, whether he's going to veer off, what his judgement is going to be like, whether he's going to try to hit the water-line, whether he's going to try to hit the bridge, or whether he's going to hit your ship or one close by. But it's a human bomb, that's what it is, and it's got a man's brain in it.

CAPTAIN NAKAJIMA

When the Special Attack pilots' cause was set up and if time was available then we did have special ceremonies. But, in general, the feeling was that

---

* Almost uniquely, at this stage of the war, the *Franklin* was hit by two conventional bombs. Lieutenant Commander Gary was awarded the Medal of Honor.

it was natural for these pilots to take off and attack the enemy and there was no special, no important ceremony put on.

LIEUTENANT MANSON
USS Laffey, *16 April 1945*

The first four planes we were able to shoot down but I believe it was the fifth plane that hit us coming in from the stern, and once they'd hit us and made a ball of fire and a lot of smoke, why of course they had something to aim at from up there and from that point forward we had a holocaust on that destroyer, fire and explosions and shrapnel. This attack went on for seventy to ninety minutes and was the most sustained and continuous attack against a single ship of World War Two. There were twenty-six planes that made suicide attacks against our ship and seven of the planes were shot down by our gunners and fifteen managed to miss the ship and we were actually hit, direct hit, by four. We had two that grazed the ship and did some damage but there were four that plunged right into the after part of the ship.*

MOMOKO YONAHA
Okinawan girl conscripted into medical service with the Japanese Army

It was at dawn on 19th June that I finally reached the Yamashiro mountain. I hid in the mountain all day but from the air the American bombers kept bombing us and we were also subjected to strafing attacks and also heavy bombardment from the warships lying offshore. Many who were beside me died. I somehow survived and when night came I was afraid to stay any longer in the mountain and I walked down towards the coast. I was walking along the beach and met other people until finally nine of us formed a group. All around us the soldiers and the inhabitants were running helter-skelter, here and there, obviously confused. We got into a small air-raid shelter more to get out of the rain than anything; we found

---

* The *Laffey*, now a museum ship in Charleston, South Carolina, is thought to have taken five direct hits. After running repairs, she sailed back to California under her own power.

four soldiers who had taken shelter there. From the beach we could hear the US Army calling on us through loudspeakers, they kept shouting, 'Come out, come out.' Whoever it was spoke a very beautiful Japanese. They were telling us, 'We will not inflict any harm on women and children and old people, so please come out,' but we had always been taught that we cannot ever become prisoners of war so we did not lend our ears to the invitations. I had already decided to die and one of the soldiers had a hand grenade and he said, 'Let's all commit suicide,' and we all agreed. And once we had made that decision I felt a great relief and calmness came over me. Just while I was waiting for the soldier to pull the pin, suddenly one of the soldiers took out a sword and started waving it around. 'You women and children get out,' he said, 'you shouldn't die here.' We were quite taken aback by this, by the sudden, loud shouting, so we stood up and stepped backward. Of course the air-raid shelter in which we were hiding was very small so one step back and we were outside. We looked up and there we saw a US soldier pointing a pistol to us, gesturing with his pistol to come out. This is how I managed to survive.

MARINE COTTON

I hear crying and there's a dead Japanese woman with a baby with sores all over him and so I give him some water and some K-rations and wanted to take care of the baby, and at about that time I see a head pop up out of the ground and I see it's a woman and child and they're down this cave. Well, I'm not too happy about crawling down into a cave where there's probably a huge complex of them. At that time a tank comes round and sees that I've got a cave and I'm trying to have this Japanese talk these people out of there. Anyway, these people don't want to come up and the tank wants to throw a round down there and all. With women and children down there, there's no reason to do this and if there are some soldiers down there let Military Police or what's coming behind take care of them. There was four of us and I don't recall whether it was five or six prisoners we'd got. They were down to their loin-cloths, they just wanted to be taken prisoner. Fortunately the word was out to try to show kindness and so we gave them all our water and whatever we could. There must have been a thousand eyes watching us, because when they seen this here comes soldiers piling out of every nook and cranny, and the next thing you know there's four of us and we have hundreds of prisoners. And a few of them, thinking about their honour, start using the grenades on themselves, just committing suicide.

ROBERT SHERROD

It was right at the end of the battle. These were people who had been indoctrinated with the fear that they would be killed or tortured by Americans and so they chose suicide – jumping off these high cliffs at the southern end of the island. I don't know if anybody tried to count them but there were hundreds of them because of the bodies we found days afterwards around the island. These bodies marching along in the water, it was a horrible sight to see. It was the great crowning horror of all the sights, something we never believed could happen even though we'd seen suicide attacks before. But the useless destruction of babies and children – some people threw their children over the cliff and then jumped after them – was something that was horrid for the Western mind to comprehend.

LIEUTENANT MANSON

There were a number of individual experiences aboard ship that you can't get out of your mind, and you remember them every time you think about the kamikaze days. One man, he was in a forty-millimetre mount and he had been fighting against quite a number of planes that had come in, but we had been hit in his area also two or three times, and all of a sudden, with nobody understanding why, he just yelled out, 'It's hot today' and jumped over the side, and that's the last we saw of him. Had he stayed on board he might have survived but of course we couldn't find his body or anything after that. But it was an unusual type of reaction. He stayed with it just as long as he could until he broke, and then that was the end of his fighting. Every man has his breaking point and the kamikaze, I would estimate, probably tests that breaking point more than any other form of combat.

CHAPTER 28

RETURN TO BURMA

Japan's principal strategic purpose in Burma was to cut American supplies to China along the Burma Road, built in 1938 by Chinese labourers from Lashio in northern Burma to Kunming in Yunnan Province. Supplies continued to flow by air from the huge air-base complex at Dinjan in Assam, and the objective of the last Japanese offensive in the theatre, stopped at Kohima and Imphal by the Anglo-Indian Fourteenth Army in 1944, was to cut this supply line while they simultaneously conquered the Chinese coastal areas from which the Americans had hoped to bomb Japanese cities. Allied strategy was to keep China in the war at any cost because, poor though its performance in the field might be, Chiang Kai-shek's Nationalist Army tied down half the Japanese Army. During the dry season 1942–43 the British attempted a counter-attack in Arakan that was driven back to the Indian border. Early in 1943 Brigadier Orde Wingate's concept of a long-range jungle penetration supported from the air was tested in the first Chindit expedition, with mixed results. The appointment of Mountbatten as Supreme Commander South-East Asia in August 1943 finally gave General Slim's Fourteenth Army the support it needed and in the dry season of 1943–44 another offensive in Arakan met with greater success. A second, much larger, Chindit expedition was conducted in support of a drive from the north by Chinese forces under the American General Stilwell to open the way for a road from Ledo in Assam through Myitkyina to connect with the Burma Road. Following the Japanese defeat at Kohima–Imphal the Fourteenth Army swept forward, operating through the monsoon, outmanoeuvring the Japanese at Meiktila and Mandalay and finally capturing Rangoon on 3 May 1945. Considering the political, logistical, topographical and climatological conditions under which it was fought, Slim's Burma campaign deserves to be considered among the greatest achievements by any British general in history.

ADMIRAL LORD LOUIS MOUNTBATTEN
Supreme Allied Commander South-East Asia

Accidentally, we were forced to try and reconquer Burma the wrong way round from the north, which had absolutely no access at all, through mountainous jungle. We invested air supply on a big enough scale to enable them to go on fighting in the centre of Burma. In fact it was the greatest military land victory of the war against the Japanese. We counted over 190,000 Japanese corpses and God knows how many more were mutilated and wounded and withdrawn. That was the single biggest victory against the Japanese anywhere and really showed what British military might was like.

COLONEL ICHII SUGITA
Japanese Army in Burma

At the beginning of the war the British used horizontal attack, but in the later operations they used vertical tactics and surprise and they had a lot of time to prepare for the attack. The British Army had air superiority so it is far easier for them to use air power and change the tactics.

BRIGADIER JOHN SMYTH, VC
Major General Commanding 17th Indian Division during the retreat from Burma, retired in November 1942 in his permanent rank of Brigadier

As regards their training and their worth as soldiers, there's no doubt that the British troops and Indian troops that Bill Slim had in 1944 were every bit the equal of the Japanese because they'd been properly trained and properly equipped and were supported with a far superior Air Force, with ability to transport troops. The jungle was a great enemy to untrained troops and a great friend to the trained troops. And the Japanese made every use of it; they were adept at using the jungle to their advantage. As regards the monsoon, that really came into Bill Slim's part of the campaign, the second campaign in 1944, when we decided to use the monsoon and to go on operating through the monsoon, which came as a very great surprise to the Japanese and was a great factor in our victory.

PRIVATE JOE HAMMERSLEY
Fourteenth Army

I had malaria seventeen times. The last time they thought I had spinal malaria and I was put in isolation for ten days then taken out and put with the rest of the troops that had malaria. When they thought I had spinal malaria I couldn't walk and I couldn't even move my arms and I was getting inoculations all day and every day, three times a day for ten days. I had a lumbar puncture, which I wouldn't advise anyone to have, and I was in hospital exactly twenty-one days and then came out and went back into action. I'd been in action again for about five weeks and I was taken out with dysentery. I was in hospital for four weeks with dysentery and went back into action again and I was in action until the war finished at Rangoon.

LIEUTENANT J K OWENS
Staff Officer, Fourteenth Army

We operated in country in which there were a lot of mosquitoes and there was always the danger of malaria, and we ran into patches of scrub typhus, which was very difficult and something for which we soon learned you had to nurse people on the spot. Even if you carried them back and got them on to those little L-planes and flew them out they usually died on the way. I must say that when we did have big troubles with scrub typhus in the Kebaw valley a number of nurses, British and Indian, volunteered to come forward, right forward, to nurse the troops there and then on the spot, which saved a great many lives.*

PRIVATE BERT REEVES
Fourteenth Army

I would say that the monsoon not only affected people physically but also morally. Because of the constant rain if you went to strike a match to light

---

* Scrub typhus is a disease communicated by flesh-boring parasites called chiggers.

a cigarette you'd find that your box of matches had disintegrated and so also had your cigarettes. In this, and in many other ways, it is really a moral disintegrator to a human being as well as the physical aspect of it, which is sloshing through mud, living in mud, lying in mud and sleeping in mud, drinking in mud and eating in mud. That was the monsoon in Burma as I recollect it – just a nightmare.

PRIVATE HAMMERSLEY

The dampness of the jungle used to bring the leeches out. They used to go up through your gaiters on to your body and they'd go all over your body and they'd blow themselves up with blood and then fall off. But if you caught them before they fell off you had to burn them underneath, so they went up and pulled the black spot from your body, the sting, otherwise they would leave black spots all over your body.

PRIVATE JOHN HOWARD

Fourteenth Army

Bully beef, or corned beef as it's better known, tended to go very greasy in the warm sun. It would melt into a mass like porridge but cook did marvellous exercises with it, presenting it in different guises. He would cook it in some flapjacks, cook it almost like hamburgers, he would put batter around it; he would present it in many guises of stew so that we could in fact absorb the stuff. But it still became intolerable.

LIEUTENANT OWENS

The British troops, you could hand out their ration of [the anti-malarial drug] Mepacrin and they took it. They knew they would go yellow and didn't like it awfully much – nor did I – but the Indian troops firmly believed this rumour about becoming impotent if they took Mepacrin and it was necessary to hold parades in which the Indian sergeant majors used to march up and down the ranks and the troops had to stick their tongues out.

MAJOR MIKE CALVERT
Pioneer British jungle-warfare expert

I first met [Brigadier Orde] Wingate on my return from the Henzada raid. I came into my office and there was a short, squat officer sitting in my chair. I said, 'Who are you?' and he said, 'I'm Wingate,' and I said, 'Well, I'm Calvert and that's my chair and I'm commandant here.' He said, 'I'm very sorry,' and he got up and I gave him another chair. I didn't know who he was, I didn't know the name Wingate. Then he started to talk and he asked me about Henzada and drew information from me, and then he took me for a walk and I started to listen. I was training guerrillas and I had tried to learn as much as I could about guerrilla warfare from books and from other men who had fought as such. And then I came across Wingate. I found he was miles ahead of anybody I'd ever heard of or spoken to. One must remember that at the time, at the beginning of 1942, apart from Tobruk in the Middle East, British forces had never held a position under attack for more than three weeks. Morale was low and we were confused and we were trying to take on the world. Then there came Wingate with set ideas, determination and optimism. He had a tremendous belief in the British soldier, not quite such a belief in the British officer because he reckoned that often they'd been trained wrong. And he believed that with proper training and with his own zest and conviction the British soldier could beat anyone in the world.

BRIGADIER SMYTH

The dilemma that constantly confronted our troops, both in Malaya and Burma, was with regard to these enveloping movements of the Japanese, which was their stock in trade. And the dilemma simply was, should we stay put and be cut off from our supplies and ammunition, or should we at once withdraw. That dilemma faced the British and Indian troops all through both those campaigns and it was obviated by Bill Slim, as he told me he was going to do, in the 1944 campaign, by being able to air-drop supplies and rations on the troops when they got cut off, and so that didn't matter.

PRIVATE WALLY NEW

Fourteenth Army

In the Arakan the Japanese were well dug in, in these strongpoints. I think they had sort of near hospitals and everything in there, women and all I should think. Really, they was well dug in, I mean we used to get practically on top of their bunkers and they would fire from there but our fire had no effect on them at all, and we had no air support at that time. My battalion, that's the 1st Battalion the Royal Berkshire Regiment, brigaded as well with the Durham Light Infantry and the Royal Welch Fusiliers, and I can remember we went into the attack just before dawn and the Japanese sort of allowed us to get right on top of their wire, concealed wire they had, even on top of their bunkers, and as soon as we got there they opened up through the slits of their strongpoint with machine guns and mortars. They had these seventy-five-millimetre guns, which were sort of a whizz-bang effect, not like the big, old shells you could hear coming over and duck for cover. No sooner you heard the report they were upon you and many of our lads got killed or wounded in this attack and we could just make no progress at all. The attack was called off and we had to go back to our original positions. When we got back the next day the Japanese, who were real jungle veterans, had encircled us there and we had to pull back further, where we relieved, I think it was the Lincolnshire Regiment, and of course digging in again in this hilly jungle. The same old thing happened again, patrols went out and many of our chaps got bayoneted and the Japs suffered casualties as well but it wasn't a major great big battle like it was in Europe, more close fighting on these patrols. Well, eventually, they encircled us, got on top of us again and we had to withdraw back to the coastline where our brigade headquarters was.

CAPTAIN NEVILLE HOGAN

Burma Rifles

I was in the first Burma campaign on the retreat and I went back with the first Wingate expedition [February 1943] and in the second [March

1944] and later with 77th Brigade and their Brigadier Calvert, 'Mad Mike' Calvert, as he doesn't like to be known. I was a townsman and the jungle for me was absolute hell, especially in the first Wingate expedition when the jungle was a friend to the Japanese but our enemy. In the second expedition we made the jungle our friend – in other words we used the jungle and its cover and for ambushing, etc. We used the jungle in many ways but in the first expedition, and in the first Burma campaign, we were scared of the jungle.

PRIVATE HOWARD

I wouldn't like to say that we were frightened of the Japanese so much as we were not so well trained at the beginning. They had the advantage of ten years of war in China prior to coming to Burma whereas we started from scratch. But we learned very quickly. We probably felt no purpose in the early days so there was a sense of not being fully confident – this changed in early 1944, probably with the advent of Lord Mountbatten and Bill Slim, when for the first time it was decided to stand firm at the Chindwin [river] and we then felt that there was a sense of purpose, that we were going on, we weren't going forward a few yards and moving back a few yards, we were going forward with a sense of purpose and we were going to win. I think that was the time we decided that we were as good as the Japanese, if not better.

MAJOR CALVERT

People have often asked me about the type of man required. I found the British soldier has the staying power – he may not be the best attacking troop in the world, he's not terribly good at pursuit and he doesn't like hitting a man when he's down. But for staying power he is, I think, one of the best in the world and for this operation you needed both the physical and mental staying power which would win in the end and which was kindled by the jokes of the British troops which kept one going again and again.

PRIVATE BUCKTHORPE

Fourteenth Army

I thought the Japanese was one of the best fighters in the world. They would fight to the end and they wouldn't give in – in fact we used to find them strapped to trees so that they wouldn't drop and they could fight to the last.

PRIVATE NEW

When we were in the jungle at night, I mean you were probably in your foxhole. There used to be two of us in a foxhole at a time, and it might be quiet for some time and then all of a sudden you'd hear a heck of a noise going on, you know, banging of cans and shouting, 'Where are you, Johnnie, where are you, Johnnie?' and that sort of thing. And you used to think well this is it, there's going to be an attack coming in. But we had been previously warned not to take much notice of this and nothing would probably come of it. It was a bit nerve-wracking, though.

CAPTAIN HOGAN

The Japanese were animals but great soldiers; their battle drill was fantastic. You couldn't help but admire them. If they were ambushed they were at you in twenty to thirty seconds. Then pounding you with their mortars and in frontal attacks – nobody could beat them, I think, they would just come on and on and on.

PRIVATE HOWARD

Fighting the Japanese was totally committed war. There was no question of heroics or chivalry in the sense that one read about prior to the war in the Biggles books. We were totally committed to killing as many Japanese as possible, prompted by the fact that we knew from experience that there had been atrocities and we were always fearful of that fact and didn't want to take, or be taken, prisoner. And so we were fully committed to war, probably more so than in any other theatre.

PRIVATE HAMMERSLEY

Many a time we've seen the remains of a tortured prisoner and it wasn't a very nice sight to be seen. They used to torture them so much. They used to pull their fingernails out, they'd castrate them, things like that. We had an English nurse, I should say she must have been raped five or six times before they let her go and she was dead when we found her. They'd torture you until you gave them the position of your own troops. We could hear the prisoners screaming. Whether that was done for our benefit I couldn't say but you could hear the prisoners of war screaming.

MAJOR CALVERT

The first Wingate operation took place in 1943. It was initially to accompany a general advance into Burma but the general advance was cancelled. However, Wavell wanted the expedition to go forward so it was rather like a testing operation. We went in seven columns across the Chindwin and we averaged 1,500 miles march. My own column of Gurkhas plus British commandos – a few of them – we got on to the main Japanese line of communication, their railway, and we blew the bridges in five places and I blew the rail in about seventy different places. We got back fairly intact but many of the other columns got caught and about one third of the force was lost. This was a raid and its tactical-strategical effect was not great. Its main effect was on the morale of the British and Indian troops. Our forces were not picked men, they were ordinary British and Gurkha battalions and the rest of the Army said, 'By God, if these people can do it, we can.'

CAPTAIN HOGAN

Even if you went downhill you knew you had to go uphill again and we were carrying sixty to seventy pounds on our backs, especially after an air-supply drop, five days' rations plus arms and ammunition. It was – really I cannot explain – you think would it ever end? It just went on and on and on and the rain and of course the fear that you would be ambushed or attacked, and hungry – I was young then and I was always hungry. The thought that you would get wounded and have to be left behind was always in our minds. I saw chaps having to be left behind with a hand grenade, pistol, flask of water and rations, just propped up against a tree. It was a terrible thing to have to leave somebody but many came back after the war who had been left behind. The villagers looked after them, the Naga tribesmen, absolutely marvellous. Took them in and looked after them. I know of chaps who were left in the first Wingate expedition; we picked them up in the second.

PRIVATE HAMMERSLEY

We were in the jungle all the time. We had this Naga man, who knew the jungle better than we did, as a guide and they can take you through the jungle and you wouldn't know where you were going and the Jap wouldn't even know you were there because the Naga, they were born in the jungle, grew everything in the jungle and lived up in the hills. They knew the jungle just like reading a book and the Japanese wouldn't know we were in the jungle because the Naga would be out in front of us and he could spot the Jap before we'd ever know he was there. The Japanese took Naha hill men as prisoners because you see there's two clans, the Nagas and the Chins, and the Chins were for the Japs and the Naga were for the British.

MAJOR CALVERT

I had wounded crossing the Chindwin. I left them at a village and I wrote a note to the Japanese commander saying these were men who have fought for their king and country just as you are fighting. They have done well and I know with your great sense of honour you will look after them. Those men I've met again and they were looked after by the Japanese, who respected them.

PRIVATE DENIS GUDGEON

Captured at Chindit

I was taken down to a camp in Rangoon and there I was interrogated. They threatened to give me the 'water cure', that is pouring buckets of water into you. They obviously already knew quite a bit about Wingate and they respected him very much. In fact I remember the day in 1944 when the Japanese guards came rushing in saying, 'Wingate chinto,

Wingate chinto,' which meant Wingate was dead. And it could have been General MacArthur himself or Viscount Slim had been killed – they obviously held him in very great regard.

LIEUTENANT OWENS

As a Staff Officer I didn't have full practical experience of jungle fighting at close quarters very often, but one was very conscious that there's no front line in jungle warfare, that in fact the enemy can and do get behind your lines, particularly at night. So you are never quite sure whether the sounds you heard were your own patrols coming back or someone else's coming in. From time to time small units of signallers a quarter of a mile away from you would be scuppered in the middle of the night and eight or ten chaps would just disappear completely.

COLONEL SUGITA

We went through Singapore to Burma: it was 20th April 1944 when we left Japan and we arrived at Singapore about 25th April. At that time the headquarters was optimistic about the operation, the headquarters of Burma also optimistic. But I found it was a very pessimistic future because they told us the operation would be a success but I told them we had not air superiority, we had a hard supply and already the operation was carried out about forty days. In the past we had Malaya in operations sixty-five days. If we had a hard experience and we unable to succeed in forty or fifty days, if we are unable to achieve that result, I told them that the operation would be unsuccessful. I went to middle of Burma and I found out that it was very hard for Japanese to get success in operations. At that time the soldiers and officers I met spoke of adverse conditions especially due to short supply on the spot and they believed that they are unable to succeed.

PRIVATE LEONARD BROWN
The Queen's Own Royal West Kent Regiment
The siege of Kohima was a battle that I don't think could ever be fought in any other conditions throughout the world. The terrain there was

mountains on three-quarters of the area of Kohima and one road running through Imphal to Dimapur; this was the main road to India and we were told by our colonel, Danny Laverty, that this was our objective and this was where the Kents was going to stay. We got in some trenches and before we knew where we were, the Japanese was there. They had big guns, they had everything; we had machine guns, rifles and a couple of old 1914–18 war guns. They attacked us at the tennis court and it was just like playing tennis – the area from one side of the tennis court to the other was the positions between the Japanese and the platoon I was with. The fighting I saw was literally hundreds at a time coming towards us. Their manpower strength just pushed us back from one trench to another, which was roughly ten feet behind us. They kept over-running us due to their manpower and the lads I was with, we gradually pulled back until we were in one small perimeter, I would say less than half a mile, and in this perimeter we stopped the Japanese Army. After the first seven or eight days the ammunition and the food was running out and the water was almost nonexistent. Every day Danny Laverty said, 'Hang on, if you let go India's falling.' Eventually, I believe on the thirteenth day, we were told the 2nd British Division was on the outskirts of the perimeter and on the fifteenth day they broke through to get us out.

CAPTAIN TERUO OKADA
Intelligence Officer, Japanese Army in Burma

Imphal being such an important junction spot we thought it would be very difficult, but Kohima was something we never expected. The British and their allies put up a very strong fight there. I think that surprised everyone. In Burma we were fighting various people. The Chinese don't count much, you know, if it's five to one it's a fair fight, less than five to one they always run away. The Burmese levies in the British Army were not much use, I think, but of course it was the Fourteenth Army we were fighting all the time and although they put up some good battles in the initial stages we were pushing all the time. Kohima being a small place we did not expect the resistance they put up. We just hoped to cut them off but the resistance was such that we could never completely isolate them.

The main thing that stuck out was they had better supply, supply drops, which we had not imagined in the beginning.

PRIVATE HAMMERSLEY

Sometimes the Japs would be about five or six yards in front of us and it would be hand grenades and rifles, but sometimes they used to come – they could speak English as well as we could – and they'd call out, 'Over here, Taffy,' or, 'Over here, Bill'. You'd get up and bang, the Japs had you.

LIEUTENANT OWENS

The Japanese were very tough, devoted fighters and they were beaten, I think, not because of lack of courage, of which they had plenty, but they didn't have the same ability that we did for regrouping after they were defeated. If they lost their officers and had no instructions they were really lost, whereas the good old British sergeant or the Indian havildar was deemed quite capable of carrying on and doing something, even if there were great losses and he'd lost all his officers, and seemed quite capable of getting back to base on many occasions. The Japanese were very tough indeed, in fact when we first made contact with them near Kohima our soldiers turned round and said to us, 'What the hell did you tell us about these little bastards,' because in fact these Japs were over six feet high. This was because we met the Japanese Guards Division first of all. It was about six months before we could take a prisoner, and during that time of course we picked up a number of Japanese who'd been badly shot up and it was quite necessary in our little field hospitals to tie their hands down, because if you didn't do that they tore at their bandages, opened their wounds and literally tried to commit suicide that way.

PRIVATE BROWN

I hated the Japanese then and I do now. As soldiers I think they are very good but to torture prisoners – that's not soldiering, that's butchery. There was a clean fight that we fought at Imphal against the Imperial Guards of Japan. I've known stories, and I know they're true, that when the white flag went up from our side the Imperial Guards let the boys go

509

and pick the wounded up, and in return when the Imperial Guards put the flag up then their boys went out. After that there was no give on either side – they didn't give us a chance and we didn't give them a chance.

LIEUTENANT UKIKURO HONDA

Japanese Army in Burma

The Fifteenth Army had three divisions: the 334th Division, known as the Umi Division, was to attack Imphal from the south first, the 31st division was to take Kohima and the Matuli, or 15th Division, was to attack Imphal from the east. The Umi and Matuli divisions were to surround Imphal and cause its fall. Our unit was the 3rd Battalion of the 17th Infantry Regiment of the Matuli Division, with two companies, three anti-tank guns and machine guns. Our role was to cut off the Imphal–Kohima road, used by the Indo-British Army as a transport route, at Mishan. When we arrived at Mishan we took them by surprise. With the death of only one soldier we destroyed two strongholds. After that we were ordered to join the attack on Imphal and advanced to Kanglatongbi. The Indo-British forces were greatly reinforced from the air and there was a great increase in enemy tanks and infantry to our front. Our battalion was told to hold Kanglatongbi at all costs and we clashed almost daily with enemy tanks. Thanks to the bravery of my men, the anti-tank guns and the topographical advantage we were able to hold off the Indo-British forces and we destroyed close to twenty tanks.*

ADMIRAL MOUNTBATTEN

It was about the fiercest fighting of the war. I sent the 2nd British Division down to support the fighting at Kohima, and they went into Kohima. The front line was on either side of the District Commissioner's tennis court. They stood shoulder to shoulder. Where they were killed, they were buried. Out of three British infantry brigades, two brigadiers killed, two

---

* Mishan and Kanglatongbi are villages between Imphal and Kohima on the Dimapur road.

of the brigadier replacements seriously wounded. That's what the fighting was like in Kohima. My Chief of Staff, Sir Henry Pownall, asked me one day, 'Supremo, are you sleeping all right?' I said, 'Yes, very well, aren't you?' He said, 'No, I can't sleep.' I said 'Why not?' 'Do you realise we've got an entire Army Corps cut off, every exit in the Imphal plain – we've got a Japanese division on all three exits. We're running out of munitions, we're running out of supplies, we can only put in a certain amount by air – if we can't open communications by the end of June, they'll have to surrender. It'll be the greatest disgrace to British arms.' I said, 'Who's responsible, you or me?' He said, 'You are.' 'Have we done everything that we possibly can?' He said, 'Yes, we have.' I said, 'Then let me do the worrying and you do the sleeping.'

LIEUTENANT HONDA

The Japanese Army's target date for taking Imphal was 29th April, the Emperor's birthday, but when 29th April came there was still no decision on the battlefield. I think it was around 10th May that I began to become pessimistic. We received orders to retreat towards Bukuru when the Imphal road was lost. It was raining very hard, we had many sick and injured men, we were out of food too. The roads and the passes that could be used leading to Bukuru were mostly occupied by Indo-British forces, therefore going by the map we marched along river and valleys. We ate tree buds and searched for rice, for food. After a week or ten days we finally arrived at Bukuru. It took about another month to the Chindwin river, therefore from Mishan to the banks of the Chindwin river I think it must have taken about forty-five days. There were six hundred and fifty in my battalion when we started the retreat – two hundred and forty had died in battle. About two hundred and fifty died of sickness and wounds between Mishan and the Chindwin river, about a hundred who crossed the river also died. I came down with a very severe case of malaria. I was unconscious for about ten days and had no appetite for about fifteen days. All my hair fell off too.

PRIVATE HAMMERSLEY

The troops really thought they were forgotten because any time we got an English newspaper there was never any mention of the Fourteenth Army. And mail from home, we got a letter around every four months and we just thought that people had forgotten that we were there. We had nothing from home such as recreational equipment or anything that was any use to us and the troops thought they had really been forgotten – that was not just my division, it was right through the Army.

VERA LYNN

Popular singer known as 'The Forces' Sweetheart'

My songs spoke of a better time ahead and I think also reminded them of home. It brought them a little bit nearer and linked them with the loved ones that they left behind, and I think the accumulation of the feel of the songs at that particular time built up to a strong feeling that they've never forgotten and always remember. Once I'd been there – and the boys were talking to me wherever I went – it came out that they were the Forgotten Fourteenth. They were short of everything, they said, and the entertainment was very small and they never even seemed to get their cigarettes. Because this was a very important point, when I got home I was to see that they had more cigarettes sent out to them. They really thought they were the Forgotten Army and I think they probably were.

CHAPTER 29

WESTERN EUROPE

The sub-text of the episode entitled Pincers: August 1944–March 1945 *was subtly emphasised by a picture of a knocked-out tank with 'America First' written on the side. The pincers in question were the break-out from Normandy and the Red Army's near simultaneous destruction of German Army Group Centre, but lack of interview material has obliged me to include the latter, Operation Bagration, in Chapter 16. This chapter covers Montgomery's attempt to end the war in 1944 with an imaginative but poorly executed operation in September to outflank the German West Wall through Holland. He hoped to seize the bridges across the three broad rivers to his front using two US and one British airborne divisions (Market), while XXX Corps made a lightning armoured advance along a single axis (Garden) to Arnhem before hooking south into the Ruhr valley. The Americans were bogged down in obdurate fighting in the Hürtgen forest and the advance halted to overcome an acute problem of logistics overstretch, not relieved until the approaches to the great port of Antwerp were cleared in November.*

Hitler became obsessed with Antwerp, first bombarding it with hundreds of V-1 and V-2 missiles and then making it the strategic objective of Operation Wacht am Rhein, the last great German offensive of the war better known as the Battle of the Bulge. The aim of the offensive was to divide the British Twenty-First Army Group from the US Twelfth Army Group by driving through the Ardennes, as in 1940. The attack fell on a thinly held part of the Allied front and achieved some penetration, but failed to capture the supplies it needed and was destroyed once weather permitted Allied air supremacy to manifest itself. In the course of the battle

Eisenhower put Montgomery in charge of US forces north of the Bulge, and at the end nearly sacked him because of some boastful statements amplified by the British press. The Canadian First Army fought a bitter battle to outflank the West Wall through the Reichswald in the north in February–March 1945 while in the south the US First Army seized the Rhine crossing at Remagen on 7 March. In April, Montgomery's set-piece Rhine crossing at Wesel involved the largest airborne operation in history and the war in Europe ended six weeks later.

MAJOR GENERAL SIEGFRIED WESTPHAL
Chief of Staff to Field Marshal Rundstedt

I was, together with Rommel, already convinced after the defeat of Alamein that the war was lost for Germany. The reason for this conviction was the strong superiority of the Allies in ground forces, in air and naval forces and superiority in materials. The most deciding point was of them the Air Force. But in the summer 1944 this conviction was strengthened by two events: the useless loss of the whole of the Army Group B in the centre of the Eastern Front with about twenty-two divisions only, on the stubbornness of Hitler, and then the defeat in Normandy.

MAJOR GENERAL WALTHER WARLIMONT
Deputy Chief of Wehrmacht Operations

The situation in August 1944 as we saw it from headquarters, in the west we had just lost almost the whole Army of Normandy at Falaise. Our armies were retreating towards our frontiers, Paris was lost on 25 August and there seemed no possibility to remedy this situation any more. In the east the great collapse had taken place on 22nd June, the third anniversary of the beginning of the war against Russia in 1941, and this advance of the Russian Army was still going on towards the German frontiers from the east. In Italy just the same picture, retreating German armies up to the north of Florence and in the air and sea warfare, enemy domination.

WYNFORD VAUGHAN-THOMAS

BBC radio journalist in the invasion of southern France

We were prepared to sell our lives dearly. We'd thought that the Germans would resist and a great wave of smoke went in and the barrage went down. We leapt into the warm water, it was my birthday, 15th August, and we were near St Tropez. When we reached the sand I said, 'This is it, they're going to open up any minute.' Suddenly through the mist there came a Frenchman and he carried a tray of champagne glasses and we all stopped – quite clearly, utterly unexpected. He smiled and turned to me and said, 'Monsieur, welcome, but if I venture a little criticism you are somewhat late.'

MAJOR GENERAL WARLIMONT

The tactics of Hitler under these circumstances was not at all modified; he apparently had forgotten what he had said in late 1943 when the invasion was to be expected: 'If we do not repel invasion we have lost the war.' Now there was no word any more about having lost the war, he just went on as before. The principles were: hold what you have, never give up anything voluntarily and try to regain what you gave up. He had no idea of the real situation of the day. The 19th August he announced that every occasion to take up the offensive in the west again had to be used and on the next day Hitler gave his first orders for an offensive, already thinking that the German armies in France, just beaten on every side, would be able to take up an offensive thrust against the right wing of Patton whose Army at that time was in advance towards the Rhine. And he thought it would be possibly sustained by the German Army, which came up from the Mediterranean coast. Nothing came of it, it was impossible of course.

WYNFORD VAUGHAN-THOMAS

There came a moment when the French Army paused for a moment and I remember dear General Alexander Patch saying to me, 'Mr Thomas, you know a little bit more about the French. Why aren't they advancing?' I looked at the map, at the beginning of the Burgundy vineyard country. They were studying it because it would be tragic if they fought through the great vineyards of Burgundy – France would never forgive them and they paused. A young officer arrived and said, '*Courage*, my Generals – I've found the weak spot of the German defences: every one is in a vine-yard of inferior quality.'

LIEUTENANT J GLENN GRAY
US Army Intelligence

Near Vienne, in a town near by, the civilians were taking revenge on girls who had slept with German soldiers. The common thing was to shear their heads and march them through the streets and everybody beat them. My friend and I took a walk through the town and we saw people beaten, some being killed, but many of them simply rejoicing in this first hour of liberation. A group of rejoicing Frenchmen about twenty yards ahead of us were marching down the street when a slim young girl detached herself from them and ran to me directly, so rapidly that I didn't know what was going on, threw herself in my arms, kissed me on the mouth and spun out of my arms and disappeared into another crowd.

MAJOR GENERAL KENNETH STRONG
General Eisenhower's Chief of Intelligence

Although we had taken some time to break out of the bridgehead, longer than we thought, once we got out the Allied troops advanced at tremen-dous speed and outran their supplies. The only port available was the port of Cherbourg, which really wasn't in full working order yet, and the remainder of the supplies were coming mainly over the beaches. Those who were in close touch with the situation said nothing really could be undertaken on a grand scale against Germany until more ports were avail-able, more particularly the port of Antwerp.

MAJOR GENERAL FRANCIS DE GUINGAND
Field Marshal Montgomery's Chief of Staff

After we broke out of Normandy all supply had to come from the beaches or be carried by air, and that restricted the amount of supplies that could be given to the Army Groups and they found often they couldn't do what they wanted through lack of supplies. I think a lot of historians will now say that this wasn't sufficiently appreciated by the Supreme Commander, who didn't put sufficient pressure on Twenty-First Army Group to clear Antwerp. We got to Antwerp pretty quickly, but there was an enormous delay before the Scheldt was cleared to allow shipping to come up to Antwerp, and so that still meant that all supplies had to come through the beaches and by air.

LIEUTENANT GENERAL BRIAN HORROCKS
Commander XXX Corps

Monty argued that the German Army had a really bad defeat in Normandy and this was the moment to really hit them. What he advocated was a strong drive up the coastal plain with the right on the Ardennes and the left on the coastline, day and night, never letting up, never giving them time to recover. Of course he would be in command of this and we'd go right through, bounce the crossing of the Rhine, come around behind the Ruhr and the war would be over in 1944. That's what he thought. Eisenhower said, 'No, I don't like this, it's a pencil-like thrust and you're not touching a lot of the troops which are in France. I propose to advance on a broad front right up to the Rhine and then do a crossing of the Rhine and finish the war there.' That was perhaps safer, but it meant that the war wouldn't be finished in 1944.

MAJOR GENERAL STRONG

It's important to remember what Eisenhower's task was. He was told that he had to undertake operations to aim at the heart of Germany and to destroy the German armed forces. He then had decided to advance from a broad front, north and south of the Saar and Ruhr, and make an envelopment attack into Germany. When we broke out the Germans were in considerable confusion and Montgomery thought that was the opportunity of inflicting a decisive defeat on them, so he said to Eisenhower, 'Get me all the troops I want, give me all the supplies, give me all the support, lend me American divisions and I then can go on, by one thrust I can get to Berlin and I can end the war.' I was present at a conference at

Eisenhower's headquarters, there were ten British and ten American officers round that table when this proposal was discussed and not one of those ten officers thought it was a good idea. The man who was chiefly against it was the Supply Officer: he was British, John Gale, very capable, had known the Americans in North Africa, and he said, 'It's quite impossible, we haven't got the supplies to do it, even if we ground divisions and take their transport away, we simply cannot do this.'

LIEUTENANT GENERAL GERHARD GRAF VON SCHWERIN-KROSIGK
Commander 116th Panzer Division

When we went into our own country at Aachen I tried to find a way of ending the war as quickly as possible. We found in Aachen a quite revolutionary situation: the whole population was very upset against the National Socialist government, hoping that the Army would help them and take over power in the town. Which we did, and so the whole population of Aachen became very happy to have the protection of a military commander and that the Nazis had left the town. I tried to use the orders of Hitler for staying with my division and defending Aachen to the last, to use this order to stay and be overrun by the Americans. By this way to open a large hole in the front line and helping Field Marshal Montgomery to advance very quickly, and to occupy the Ruhr basin before the end of 1944, which would mean the end of the war. But unfortunately the Americans did not advance further. They stayed before Aachen and made no attempt to occupy the town. That was not an understandable pause, and very disappointing.*

MAJOR GENERAL STRONG

General Eisenhower said that Arnhem failed because of the bad weather, but I think it really failed because we hadn't taken sufficient account of the German resistance. At that time people were convinced the end of the war was near, that the Germans were demoralised, but it wasn't actually true; it may have been true somewhere, but not all. As regards the German resist-

---

* In early September General von Schwerin-Krosigk was relieved of command.

ance three things happened which were unfortunate for us. One was that just before Arnhem we discovered that there were elements of German armoured divisions refitting and getting new tanks not far from Arnhem. The second was that a copy of our plans was captured with one of the first officers who landed among the parachutists and this was whisked off to the German commander on the spot and from then he had all the information of what we were trying to do. And the third, and this is the most important, was that the local commander was Field Marshal Walther Model.

MAJOR GENERAL DE GUINGAND

If the German armour had not been met at Arnhem we would have got a bridgehead across, but it's anyone's guess whether having got that, with the bad weather setting in and winter coming along, whether we'd have been able to do anything more than achieve an expanded bridgehead over the Rhine and maintain that for several months during the winter. One knew from experience how magnificent the Germans were at retrieving a critical situation. That's one of those great question marks, whether if we had been completely successful at Arnhem it would have really succeeded in defeating the enemy in 1944.

MAJOR GENERAL WESTPHAL

I became in the beginning of September 1944 Chief of Staff of the Supreme Commander West, Field Marshal von Rundstedt. We had three Army Groups with together eight Armies, but no troops. The kernel of all reports, demands and discussions with General Headquarters was the demand for stronger reinforcements but we didn't get any answer. On 24th October I was ordered to come to Hitler, his headquarters in East Prussia, and he told me and the Chief of the Army Group in the centre that we would get end of November or beginning of December strong reinforcements. He named twenty infantry divisions, ten armoured divisions and a lot of special troops and he promised that we would be supported by the Air Force with about three thousand planes. But we were totally surprised that these were not intended for the defence in the Western Front. Hitler said that the possibility of building up a new front against the Western Allies was nearly a miracle and he had the opinion that miracles didn't repeat themselves. Therefore he had the opinion to attack and this plan for offensive in the Western Front had been developed in every detail in the headquarters.

MAJOR GENERAL DE GUINGAND

In war you can't be strong everywhere and therefore Eisenhower had to decide where he was going to be strong, where he going to be weak and he assessed the situation in the Ardennes sector was extremely difficult country, particularly in winter, snow and ice, trees and forests, and therefore he decided to thin down the Ardennes sector. The German preparations were brilliantly carried out under Hitler's control and it had produced these great armies with very well-equipped tanks, what air power they had available and everything had been prepared for this event. We really didn't have any certain knowledge that there was such a large force had been pulled back ready to conduct an offensive. Very shortly before the Ardennes campaign was launched there was someone in American intelligence who began to suspect that was something was cooking, but the Americans did not take him very seriously, and so it came as a complete surprise.

GENERAL HASSO-ECCARD FREIHERR VON MANTEUFFEL
Commander Fifth Panzer Army

The Ardennes offensive was Hitler's idea in December 1944, worked out by Chief of Operations Alfred Jodl by order and attraction of Hitler personally. Overall objectives were Antwerp and Brussels and he order two armies, First Panzer and Sixth SS Panzer Army, to break through the Ardennes in a concentrated attack and quick at once to Antwerp. And the cover of these two armies was the responsibility of the Seventh Infantry Army under General Brandeburger. Hitler hoped that with its intention to effect a blow against the coalition and to split three armies, the First American Army, Second British and First Canadian, and to capture them. And he explained to myself in November in headquarters that by 11th or 12th December he hoped a military and political falling, to a collapse of this coalition. He hoped furthermore to change the whole situation on our West Front in Germany's favour because Montgomery could be cut off from the rest of the alliance and especially to cut off their sources of supplies, which were lying and built up east of the Meuse for the attacking the West Wall and to their drive to the Rhine. After this attack in the Ardennes he had intended other attacks on other sectors of our West Wall. He explained that Antwerp and Brussels were something of a risk and might be beyond the capacity of the forces available and their conditions. Nevertheless he had decided to stake everything on one card because Germany needed the breathing space, a defensive struggle could only postpone the decision and not change the general situation for Germany.

MAJOR GENERAL WARLIMONT

I am astonished that even today, thirty years after the war, you ask me what Hitler's role was, because Hitler was in everything from the beginning, particularly after the disaster at Moscow in 1941. It was he who ordered the offensive to drive to the coast at Antwerp. It was he who demanded, after looking out the first planning preparations, that the left wing had to be enlarged and from the right wing of the offensive had to be opened up a second attack as soon as possible. On this old basis, regardless of every modification of weapons and what else had gone on in the meantime, Hitler ordered the same kind of procedure as in 1940 during the Ardennes offensive. And there was a last moment – there had to be bad weather. Even he was convinced that it would be impossible to perform an offensive of this kind under the pressure of the British and American Air Force.

MAJOR GENERAL WESTPHAL

I think the health of Hitler at that time was not good, he had to bear the consequences of the plot of 20th July and he was the origin of the plan to attack, not the OKW [Supreme Command of the German Armed Forces]. It was a deciding role. When we came back we studied the possibilities to reach Antwerp and we were convinced that this was not possible with these forces, and we reported that this big solution was not possible to carry out. We proposed a little solution in the rear of Aachen, the first German town who had been conquered by the Americans in October. They offered attack from both sides and this was possible with the divisions we had to expect. And we compared with the game of bridge: the plan to conquer Antwerp was like 'grand slam' and the plan to attack both flanks of the American troops was like 'little slam'. Unfortunately Hitler didn't play bridge and we had the possibility to destroy ten to fifteen American divisions, a quarter of all American forces fighting in Europe, but a few days later came the answer, 'This operation is unalterable in every detail.' But we didn't resign, we sent a new proposal basing on the situation near Aachen; it was declined again. Then we had the opportunity to speak with Jodl, the Chief of Operations Staff of Hitler. He had the same opinion like we but he was too weak to persuade Hitler. Then I asked Rundstedt to go personally to Hitler because Hitler had respect for his personality, but he refused. He said he had often spoken with Hitler without any success. Hitler used monologues for one or two hours about theme and there was no solution to get. Finally on 2nd December we did meet Hitler in Berlin, in the Reichschancellery. Field Marshal Walther Model, the commander of the Fifth Panzer Army, the SS leader Sepp Dietrich and me tried a fourth time to persuade Hitler for this reasonable, only possible plan, but without any success.

MAJOR GENERAL DE GUINGAND

The final objective Hitler had in mind was the capture of the port of Antwerp, which would cut off our supplies. There was a subsidiary objective, which was to drive a wedge between the Allied forces and produce the situation where he might be able to negotiate peace with the Allies and not have to submit to unconditional surrender. He didn't achieve them and I don't think he had a chance of achieving them. He was frightfully lucky that he had the very bad weather conditions which he wanted, there was fog and blizzards, and when the attack opened they made a very deep penetration and they reached the Meuse and never crossed, and there was nothing actually between the Meuse and Brussels, our main headquarters.

MAJOR GENERAL J LAWTON COLLINS
Commander US VII Corps

The German offensive in the Ardennes was really their last gasp and Hitler was directly responsible for it. He had ordered a rather grandiose plan which was going to end the war from the German point of view and it was designed to break through this very broken country in the Ardennes, through which the Germans had gone before, so they knew the area well. They were going to break through where the American defences were very light, cross the Meuse river and then head for the port of Antwerp, which was our base port. If it had succeeded then the British and American forces would have been separated and the main base port for the whole northern half of the armies would have been lost and the war would have come to an end. Actually it was too grandiose a scheme, the German officers knew that it couldn't work, but they were forced under the system to do their best.

GENERAL MANTEUFFEL

We have reliable data about the strength of the enemies and we were informed that the forces to the other side of the hill were relatively weak. Reports of our front-line troops confirmed this data as a quick way through of our forces because they would not be expecting a German attack here and at this time. I went to the front-line troops disguised as a colonel of infantry and was there for thirty-three hours. The Americans one hour after darkness went to the villages to their rooms, or to their girls, but there were no cover between their positions during the night. And it was this manner I proposed to Hitler, so I formed strong troops and we went up, I think five o'clock in the morning, we slipped through the positions of the Americans.

MAJOR GENERAL STRONG

Some of the American divisions that were holding the area were new and not all that well trained. We knew that the Germans had a reserve army, that they were preparing for some sort of operation. It could have done several things and one of them was to come through the Ardennes. People who went up behind the American lines found a good deal of confusion. I don't think that confusion lasted very long – the attack took place on the Saturday morning and General Eisenhower made his plan for dealing with the attack on the Tuesday morning at Verdun and from then on I think he had the whole situation completely under control.

PRIVATE JOHN LOVELESS
US serviceman in the Ardennes

When we went from England, across France and through Belgium, I think most of us felt that we were just gradually going to get into the action. That was reinforced by the fact that we were going over what they called the Blue Road rather than the Red Road. The Red Road was to take the troops into the areas where the fighting was more pronounced and the Blue Road was into a more or less quiet area, which was simply preparatory to getting to the front line. So we were somewhat hopeful and cheered by the fact that we were going over the Blue Road, but of course it didn't make any difference because of the German offensive.

PRIVATE HENRY BROTH
US serviceman captured in the Ardennes

We really didn't know that we were going to be captured until we were broken down into smaller units by the Germans and they surrounded us and sort of backed our particular group up on to a hill. Then we realised that we had to surrender or that was it. The lieutenant went down and made arrangements with the German officer in charge and came back and told us we had one hour to dismantle and destroy our weapons, or dig holes and bury whatever we wanted to bury, and be ready to come off that hill within one hour.

SS COLONEL WILHELM OSTERHOLZ
Battalion Commander Sixth SS Panzer Army in the Battle of the Bulge

As a simple soldier you see more of everything on the road, you have to think there are more divisions than there really are. Therefore we had the feeling that this build-up of force might enable us to reach the final objective, which was Antwerp. And the weather was foggy, and the American and British air superiority didn't matter in that kind of weather. And in addition to that we had for support a whole artillery corps, we never knew such type of artillery support, and therefore we believed we would be successful. It was almost the same area where we had attacked when war against France was waged, and we knew that area and you know that soldiers are a little bit superstitious and everybody believed that we could repeat that rapid advance we had in 1940.

MAJOR GENERAL COLLINS

There were two key points from the American point of view, one was at St Vith and the other was at Bastogne. St Vith was what prevented the rapid movement of the Germans in the north half of the Bulge and Bastogne was what delayed Model and much of the German Army in the southern half. We held St Vith for quite a while and finally Monty ordered the withdrawal of the American forces in order to shorten the lines on our north side. Whether they could have held out longer or not will be a debatable question. Fortunately, we were able to hold at Bastogne and a very gallant fight was fought there by my good friend Brigadier General Tony McAuliffe. This plus the splendid fighting that was done by the small units of these two untried American divisions in small-unit actions. They delayed the German advance to the point where we could build up first-class troops on the north side of the Bulge and Patton was able to come up the south and we were finally able to close the gap.

MAJOR GENERAL STRONG

Intelligence knew that the Germans had managed to recover their position and were building up a reserve army which they could use for operations – somewhere, for something. When I told Eisenhower about this he said, 'Will you go and see [General Omar] Bradley and tell him exactly what you think.' I went up twice and Bradley said, 'Yes, I'm aware of this and if Germans do what you're suggesting then I think we can defeat them.' We agreed that the Germans hadn't got enough resources to carry out a full-scale strategic offensive and it would be necessary for them to capture supplies if they were going to be at all successful. Bradley had, in the area of the offensive, moved dumps of petrol, oil and so on, so the Germans couldn't get at them. When the Ardennes offensive took place the weather was extremely bad, there was no air reconnaissance and one had no information of the latest movement on the German front, and when they did attack they attacked with almost twice as many divisions as we estimated they would do. It penetrated right through Bradley's army, separated the north from the south and I got extremely worried the Germans might get so far towards Meuse that it would be impossible for Bradley to control the northern flank. When Eisenhower's plan was being carried out, which was to close on both sides of the penetration and cut it off, it seemed to me and to the others that the northern flank should be under one man and there was only one man who was suitable, Montgomery. When the Germans were defeated there was a press conference held by Montgomery in which, not intentionally but by various remarks, he gave the impression that he'd saved the Americans completely.

MAJOR GENERAL COLLINS

My own Corps was up north and we were brought down on the north side of the Bulge which had begun to develop in the Ardennes, comparable to the Falaise pocket. I had good troops and Monty used to come down to my headquarters and would discuss the situation every other day with me and General Matthew Ridgway who commanded the Airborne Corps on my left. I dealt with Monty and we always hit it off well and apparently he thought well of me. But I kept arguing with him that they were never going to be able to break through. The two initial divisions that had been hit by the Germans were new divisions, their first time in action, they were hit by 13 German divisions, but by the time they reached my area we had sealed off the north flank with experienced troops and I told Monty nobody's going to break through these troops, these are top-flight and I was confident that we could hold and then counter-attack. Unfortunately Monty positioned my Corps, which was under his direct command, on the north side of the Bulge instead of near the base. I was way out almost to the Meuse and I argued with Monty and said, 'Monty, you're going to push 'em out of the bag just like you did at Falaise. I ought to be opposite St Vith.' His reply to that was, 'Well, Joe, you can't supply a Corps over a single road.' In exasperation I finally said to him, 'Well, maybe you can't, but we can.'

MAJOR GENERAL WESTPHAL

At that moment when after the failure of the Ardennes, there was no doubt more that we would lose the war totally. I had said to Hitler before the Ardennes offensive that we could only succeed this target if we were able to cross within two days the River Meuse near Liège. Otherwise it would be better to retreat, and Hitler had another opinion. The first time the weather was good for us because we had strong fog, then Rundstedt sent my proposals on the 23rd and 24th December again to Hitler, to go back to the West Wall. But Hitler refused again, and the consequence was that we lost most of the material and many thousand prisoners.

MAJOR GENERAL DE GUINGAND

The Americans fought magnificently. It was an American battle, the British only played a very small part in the northern flank, and they held the shoulders of this great wedge pretty strongly in the northern and southern shoulders and that made it very difficult for the enemy to penetrate very much further. After two days the weather improved enormously and our massive air supremacy could be used, so we went for it hammer and tongs, particularly their railheads and their supply lines, and they began to run short of supplies and so many of their tanks and transports were grounded through lack of petrol.

GENERAL MANTEUFFEL

The Germans who had been deluded into believing in the possible victory now know that defeat could only be delayed. Hitler believed that if his panzer armies could split the rest of the alliance they would accept the stalemate on this front and allow him to switch his strength to the Eastern Front. This assumption was completely mistaken, and the result of the offensive primarily benefited the Russians.

MAJOR GENERAL DE GUINGAND

The Germans cut the Twelfth Army Group in half and left the First United States Army to the north of the Bulge. Bradley rightly made the decision to hand over the American forces of Twelfth Army Group north of the Bulge to Montgomery's command just as a temporary measure, but it was very sound because Bradley didn't have access to, or communications to, his forces north of the Bulge. Montgomery then operated with tremendous efficiency and I admired him greatly during that period. I was with him a lot of the time and I saw the effect this little man had on the morale of the Americans. Calmly he assessed the situations and he helped the American Army to do the right thing when they were very tired and exhausted. But he played a very major part in preventing that offensive becoming a success. For some time Montgomery had been pressing for the appointment of the Land Force Commander. He had said that he was prepared to serve under Bradley and he probably knew quite well that wasn't a feasible situation. He genuinely felt he was the right chap to take on this job and I suppose he got a bit cock-a-hoop with his successes and the British press became very pro-Monty and pro the appointment of Monty the Land Force Commander.*

LIEUTENANT DENIS BEATSON-HIRD

51st Highland Division, Rhine crossing
We clambered into these Buffaloes – they were tanks with the lids off, if I can put it that way – and the route was marked out with dim lamps and you could see these Buffaloes snaking rather like a big anaconda towards the river. There was a tremendous noise going on. Bombing was taking place at Wesel, which was a little further down the river, and the whole of the divisional and other artillery was firing like mad, which was Monty's usual preparation for a battle. The only time I think we really felt worried was when we went down actually into the river, which was a hell of an

---

* A grossly immodest press conference by Montgomery after the Battle of the Bulge almost led to his being relieved of command by Eisenhower, whose outrage was stoked by his deputy, Air Chief Marshal Sir Arthur Tedder. He was saved by de Guingand, who flew to Paris to plead his case.

incline, and one wondered and hoped that the thing would surface and come out on an even keel when we got to the water.

MAJOR GENERAL COLLINS

I went back up to Ardennes and the troops were reorganised, troops that had been brought down from Ninth Army north of Aachen to help us on the north side of the Bulge. They went back and the attack went on from that point, we broke through the Siegfried defences and across the Ruhr and were able to capture successively across the flat German plains. If the Bulge had not taken place, the German reserves which launched the attack were sitting on my right flank and we'd have one terrible time getting to the Rhine. It made it much easier when they were destroyed.

MAJOR GENERAL DE GUINGAND

When one talks about crossing the Rhine, one must acknowledge the fact that Patton's army had already crossed, they had captured the bridgehead. One of those great questions one can ask oneself after the war is whether Bradley and the Supreme Commander could have done better to have reinforced the success of Patton's army and possibly reduce the resources that were made available to the Twenty-First Army Group. Possibly it might have produced a much quicker result. But as far as we were concerned the Rhine was a very wide river, which meant all these obstacles were difficult to cross in war. The whole operation depended upon successful airborne operation over the Rhine and that depended upon good weather in March. We had good weather and the airborne operation was a great success. The Germans were holding one or two small towns, very strongly, but it didn't take us long to expand over the Rhine and really get moving into Germany proper. As an Allied team we were delighted with the success of the Americans and I think the Americans were delighted with any success we had. I don't think there was any jealousy there, I think everyone wanted the ruddy war to finish and the sooner the better.

WYNFORD VAUGHAN-THOMAS

I was with a Scots unit, the Black Watch, and we were supposed to assault the Rhine direct and cross in Buffaloes, it was supposed to be an armoured vehicle that you could ride across the Rhine in a fair amount of safety. We again were able to put the elaborate BBC recording gear in and I had my engineer with me. We got into the Buffalo and there was my brother getting into another Buffalo. My brother became a landing expert with Mountbatten and his job was to go into every one of these landings and study the problems. He looked at me and I said, 'You shouldn't be here,' and he said, 'You shouldn't be here. Who's going to tell mother about this?' I had arranged with the piper to blow the brave lads into battle and this was going to be one of the most symbolic recordings of the war. The banks of the Rhine were about twenty feet high on either side, the Buffaloes had to crawl up and then race into battle. At two in the morning the signal was given and I'll never forget the sight of the Rhine, it was blood red, every farm was burning, the whole place was leaping up and down as if somebody underneath was throwing water up, and I suddenly realised that it was mortar shells, it was the machine-gun fire, and I thought something's gone wrong with the machinery, but apparently it was bullets banging around. There was my brother's Buffalo forging across the Rhine and he was surrounded with spouts and apparently mine was equally surrounded by spouts too. As we crossed the Rhine I said, 'Now the pipes take the lads into battle,' and the piper looked at me, said, 'My pipes they will not play.' They had a bullet through what the Germans called the doodle sack.

CHAPTER 30

YALTA AND POLAND

Although his significance in Britain has been overshadowed by the spy ring known as the 'Cambridge Five', it would be difficult to overstate the importance of Alger Hiss to US politics during the Cold War. Hiss had been one of Roosevelt's key aides, tasked with creating structures for post-war international relations and in particular the United Nations. Although his guilt was not proved beyond doubt until previously secret cryptographic material was released in 1995, it had been clear, from the time of his conviction for perjury in 1950, that Hiss had been a spy for the Russians. His nemesis was the Republican congressman Richard Nixon, whose success in exposing Hiss took him to the Senate in 1950 and to the vice presidency in 1952. Hiss's innocence was an article of faith for a generation of liberal Americans with the curious reasoning that if they admitted his guilt – and that of other New Dealers like Harry Dexter White at the Treasury and Presidential Administrative Assistant Laughlin Curry – it would damage Roosevelt's political legacy. But it was the traitors who had done the damage, and the counter-attack opened the door to the excesses of the House Un-American Activities Committee and of Senator Joe McCarthy.

One result of this polarisation of opinion was a rancorous controversy about the Yalta Conference in February 1945, attended by Hiss, when Poland was allegedly 'sold out' to the Soviet Union. Although Hiss only had a cameo role in The World at War *episode entitled* The Bomb, *towards the end of the series, his interview was one of the longest and, in view of what we now know about him, is an important historical document. There are a few points of subtle mendacity, but more intriguing is his skill in emphasising that the agreements reached at Yalta were the best the Western Allies could hope for. Indeed they were – by 1945 the Red Army's presence had decided the fate of Eastern Europe. But it leaves open the question whether Roosevelt could have obtained a better deal for the Poles and others, if in 1943–44 he had been less keen on an accommodation with Stalin. Perhaps it does not matter now: it did, very much, in the early 1970s.*

DR NOBLE FRANKLAND

Wartime RAF navigator, post-war Director of the Imperial War Museum

Britain went to war to defend the Polish frontiers and the war ended with Poland losing its freedom, its independence, and a lot of people their lives. This is the most tragic irony of the war. The reason isn't far to search – in order to stop Hitler the power needed was so enormous that it had to embrace everybody free of the Nazi creed, including in particular the Soviet Union. And it seems to me there is little doubt that Hitler would have won the Second World War unless the Soviet Union had been part of the Grand Alliance. That being so, the fate of Poland was sealed from that time on. The British and the Americans did their best to secure the Polish position but their efforts were of absolutely no avail.

ANTHONY EDEN

British Foreign Minister, Yalta participant

Roosevelt thought he could do more with Stalin than anybody else and in that I think he was probably mistaken, but it was difficult to get started on the things we wanted to discuss with Stalin. I was very anxious in our Moscow conference to start with the Polish business and [Cordell] Hull wanted to do the same thing. But Hull hadn't the power, he couldn't. I thought it was very strange of a Secretary of State, I didn't see why he couldn't do it, but anyhow we never really got started on Poland as I think we should have done then. Winston was there at the time and told me Roosevelt had said the Secretary wouldn't talk about it because it was political dynamite at home, and this multiplied the difficulties or delays, which I think was the misfortune of it.*

---

* The Third Moscow Conference, among the American, British and Soviet foreign ministers, took place in October–November 1943.

AMBASSADOR W AVERELL HARRIMAN

President Roosevelt's Special Envoy to Europe, Yalta participant

Shortly after Tehran in early 1944, I talked about Poland more than any other single subject with Stalin because it was the issue which was symbolic of other things and in the winter he was very tough about it. I still wanted to agree with Roosevelt's objective of trying to come to an understanding. I became somewhat more concerned in the autumn of 1944 and then in the winter I pointed out that Europe would be in a very weakened condition; there'd be hunger and poverty unless we did more, our food would not be enough, we had to do something to get the wheels of industry going again, raw materials and so forth. I felt that Stalin had every intention of using Communist parties in Europe, I think he would have achieved it if it hadn't been for Truman's initiative and the remarkable cooperation that occurred, as a result of the Marshall Plan, among Britain and the Europeans.

ANTHONY EDEN

The Russians became more and more difficult over the Poles, more determined to get their way. And the tragic business of Warsaw, the failure to help the Poles fighting in Warsaw against the Germans, was the worst phase of the whole business and we were all really bitter about that. And we tried to do all we could, we even flew aircraft from Italy to try and fly in supplies to the unfortunate Poles, but the Russians would have none of it. They just wouldn't do it and one can say that cynically they allowed the Poles to be butchered rather than risk their people, or try to interfere with the process. It's a terrible story. That was where we met our worst difficulties. Churchill and I went to Moscow specially to try and make some progress with the Poles; we didn't get very far. And Warsaw really settled geographically the Polish question because after that the Russians had control and they were going to settle the frontiers the way they wanted; all we could do was to try here and there to get something better for the Poles. And then remained the question of the Polish internal government and that, I'm afraid, we were equally unsuccessful really about, in spite of all we tried to do. When we were in San Francisco, Molotov had sharp arguments with [US Secretary of State] Stettinius and I when the Russians arrested a number of Poles on what we thought the flimsiest of pretexts, merely because they wouldn't cooperate with their nominee. And what in fact happened was that the Russians imposed their nominees upon Poland by force. All that was a sad disappointment until the end of the war, but I cannot to this day see what more either we or the Americans could have done about the circumstances.

AMBASSADOR HARRIMAN

The Warsaw incident was a very great shock to all of us, part of it was a misunderstanding, the fact the Red Army got to the river and couldn't get across, and the Germans moved into two divisions. The Poles rose up without any agreement on the part of the Russians but it was utterly cruel that Stalin wouldn't even try to get supplies in, he refused to let our aeroplanes fly over and drop supplies for several weeks. And finally he did agree. I really had tough talks with the Russian government over Poland, of willingness to help the Poles. It played a role in all of our minds as to the heartlessness of the Russians. Stalin was very suspicious of the underground in Poland, which owed its allegiance to the Polish government in London. On several occasions later on he showed that he thought the partisans were working against the Red Army and against the people he wanted to see and control after the war was over.

CHARLES BOHLEN

US diplomat and Soviet expert, Yalta participant

The British had a record for what is known as spheres of influences and it's a very different thing for you to have spheres of influence, which are a tradition in your history. But overall it reflects the fact that you are a country without real minorities. We have a country that is full of minorities, we had Poles, Czechs, eastern Europeans represented in the United States and therefore it was not easy for us; we always opposed the idea of the spheres of influence. We finally had to come to accept that the Soviet Writ runs through all of the satellite areas up to the western edges of the Russian advance. We weren't a little premature in fixing these zones until we saw how the armies were to come out, and there's some evidence to

German infantry riding on Panzer III tanks in the Desert War, 1942.

A Desert Air Force Hurricane strafing a German tank in Tunisia, 1943.

German soldier house-clearing with a flamethrower during the summer offensive of 1942.

Where it was stopped: the gigantic statue of Mother Russia looms over
the Stalingrad memorial to the Battle of Stalingrad, 1942–43.

The Arvo Lancaster was the mainstay of Bomber Command's night-bombing offensive, 1943–44.

A disastrous failure in the Battle of Britain, the Messerschmitt 110 found a new function as the preferred aircraft of the German night-fighter aces.

Self-defending formations of camouflaged B-17s could not survive over Germany.
When they returned they were provocatively stripped to bare metal with garish
squadron markings, to draw the Luftwaffe up into the guns of the long range
P-51 Mustang, here escorting a B-17 at a post-war airshow.

Note the camouflaged wing panel from an aircraft cannibalised for spare parts used to patch the
flak-damaged port wing of this B-17, photographed near Snettisham in early 1944.

Liberating Europe, the Allies still had to fight for every inch.
A largely Canadian landing at Dieppe in August 1942 was a disaster.

The massive German fortifications in Normandy, 1944.

Grey wolves setting out to sea.

Their prey – a burning freighter sinks in the Indian Ocean.

The Japanese surrender delegation aboard USS *Missouri*, 2 September 1945.
Interviewee Toshikazu Kase stands third from the right, holding a briefcase.

Beached Japanese transport at Guadalcanal.

The victorious Big Three at Yalta. Roosevelt was dying, Churchill was exhausted and only Stalin seemed eternal and indestructible. Churchill had planned to stay on in this resort after the meeting but was so dejected by the talks that he told his staff to get him away from 'this Riviera of Hades'.

Hitler's Gang on trial at Nuremberg, 1945–46. Luftwaffe Chief Hermann Göring, Former Deputy Führer Rudolf Hess, Foreign Minister Joachim von Ribbentrop, Field Marshal Wilhelm Keitel and Senior SS Leader Ernst Kaltenbrunner sitting in front of Admiral Karl Dönitz (in dark glasses), his predecessor Admiral Erich Raeder, Hitler Youth Leader Baldur von Schirach and Labour Minister Fritz Sauckel.

indicate that our leaders underestimated the striking force of the Anglo-American Army that invaded Europe. We got back a good piece of western Austria which had been occupied by the Soviets. I can only say that I think, even from the Soviet point of view, that the division of Germany was regarded primarily as a division intended to keep the troops separate. I don't know when the Russians finally came to the conclusion that they were going to divide Germany.

ANTHONY EDEN

We did discuss with Russians at one of our meetings the possibility of the percentage authority we should regard the other as having in certain countries. The Americans didn't like the idea; it may seem reprehensible now and yet it was practically the only thing we could do and we thought it right to concentrate on those countries where we could. For geographical reasons in a country like Bulgaria, a Slav country, or Romania, which we couldn't reach, or Hungary, which was an enemy power, Churchill thought and I agreed with him that we could not attempt to have more than a limited influence there. So far as Greece was concerned the Russians did play fairly, and when the Greeks were fighting in Athens at Christmas 1944 and Churchill and I went out there, the Russian military representative came to the conference which we held and sat there with his gilded epaulettes, facing the local Communists, and he had quite an effect. So they did fulfil their part of the bargain so far as concerned Greece. And I am not at all repentant about the arrangement we made. Without it we couldn't have intervened as much as we did in Greece and give the country a chance not to fall under Communist rule, which Stalin might otherwise have required to be established there.*

CHARLES BOHLEN

In the first place during the war it was very difficult to predict Soviet policy; on the other hand there was no way of telling definitely what effect

---

* The Fourth Moscow Conference, among Stalin, Churchill, Molotov and Eden, took place in October 1944.

the association with Western Powers during the war, in some form of cooperation, might have had on Soviet thinking. It seemed to be an idea that three powers would consult whenever there was any problems in regard to the occupied areas and I was surprised that the Russians bought it so easily. Whether or not Stalin had in mind the famous deal with Churchill of 1944 with percentage of influence, all I can say is that it never came up at all in any form. Roosevelt knew about it, but there was never any reference to it, at least as far as we were concerned, with the Russians. But it's conceivable that Stalin was operating to some extent on what was expressed in that piece of paper.

ANTHONY EDEN

Latterly FDR was a sick man, no question of that. When Churchill and I met him at Malta, where we'd hoped to have discussion, we were looking forward to meeting FDR when he arrived in this splendid battle cruiser in a wonderful dramatic scene. But when he came to talk – nothing. His daughter whirled him away after dinner and said, 'Now, father, it's your bedtime.' And he was sick but also I think there was this feeling that Roosevelt had, that some Americans had, they didn't want to be ganging up with us before they met the Russians. I'm sure it was a mistake, because any dictatorship in my experience functions better when those it's dealing with are ganged up. At any rate there was one of our difficulties, both that Roosevelt was sick and there was no preparation between us.

ALGER HISS

Director of the Office of Special Political Affairs, Yalta participant
There was no doubt there was a mood of euphoria. The war was going well in the West, the Russians were scoring victories. We rendezvoused with the British delegation at Malta so we got our ducks in a row before we talked to the Russians for a tripartite meeting of Allies. This, looking back on it, was a little strange, but it seemed perfectly normal at the time. The general attitude, in spite of the indications, was not edginess but distance – by the usage of 'we' and 'they', 'they' being the Russians. In spite of what that indicates there was a sense of unity in the curve of the whole development

of Roosevelt's foreign policy since 1933. Yalta was the culmination of Roosevelt's policy – after all the United Nation as a term had been coined long before that. There was a belief, at least on Roosevelt's part, that coexistence was feasible, necessary and desirable. In the intemperate discussions that have come up about Yalta, the idea that nobody could trust the Russians to agree to come to lunch at a time they said was not present at that time. My experiences in all the negotiations I had with them, at San Francisco and again in London when United Nations had its first meeting, was that they were stiff bargainers, but when agreement was reached they were quite meticulous in sticking to the words of the agreement. This had some significance when we come to talk about the terms of the Yalta agreement. It was not my experience with them that they openly, cynically, welshed in any particular kind of phase – they stuck to what had been agreed to, so the real question is what was agreed to? Provisions were ambiguous so they had in their minds the right to interpretations, just as they thought we might have slightly different interpretations, which for me is the gist of the Polish part – the most difficult part of the Yalta agreement as far as the United Nations was concerned. We hammered that out in pretty considerable detail. Concessions were made to us both by the British and the Russians, and it was our show, we were the hosts. So Yalta did represent the culmination of the Roosevelt policy and there was great euphoria. There was a great deal of suspicion, I'm speaking for our side – I don't know about the Russian attitude, I would assume they were as capable of suspicion as we.

AMBASSADOR HARRIMAN

The whole myth of Yalta is that Churchill and Roosevelt sold out to Stalin. The argument was that in areas which the Red Army would occupy as they drove the Nazi forces back into Germany, Stalin was in control and there was nothing that Churchill or Roosevelt could have done physically except try to persuade Stalin. They agreed to nothing except they insisted there should be free elections, that people would be allowed to take their own part. There was an agreement about boundaries but the fundamental principle was that Poland and other countries should be free. Roosevelt's health in my opinion did not play a major role. It's perfectly true that he was weak – he was not able to work long hours, long conferences tried him, he stayed in bed in the mornings – but he took care of himself, he trained himself. These were subjects which he had been considering over several years and he had them fully in mind and he never gave in on anything that he wasn't ready to give in on. So I think there's very little in the fact to justify those who say his health played an adverse role. He was ill, he was a tired man, but a man of great courage and determination.

CHARLES BOHLEN

At the time the Red Army was in occupation of almost all of eastern Europe and most of the Balkans and therefore I think we learned there that wherever the Red Army was they would install a Sovietised system and there was just no argument about it. We did the very best we could on Poland. The British felt very strongly about it, having gone to war on behalf of Poland in 1939, and, although less so, we felt fairly strongly because of the large numbers of Poles in the United States who have intense interest to what happens in their country. Other aspects which are frequently overlooked came out more in favour of the Western side. The voting formula for the Security Council was adopted and also, largely due to the efforts of Mr Churchill backed by President Roosevelt, France obtained a zone of occupation and a seat on the Control Council. Stalin was very much opposed to that. You could tell when he was really worked up about something because he'd got up from his chair and walk up and down behind it several times in the discussion of whether France should have a zone or a seat on the Council.

ALGER HISS

My function was primarily as a technical assistant to Secretary of State Stettinius and to the President on matters relating to the United Nations. We'd corresponded back and forth with Great Britain and Russia about the things left unsaid, particularly the veto power, and we thought we were close to an agreement which could be reached at Yalta. In addition, I served in the Far Eastern Division before I started with United Nations affairs and so I was an extra in case Far Eastern policy questions came up. We had Bohlen and Freeman Matthews on such matters, and I guess that was the team. Harriman of course came, also expert not only on Soviet matters but on Europe generally; we were a pretty small team. I was concentrating on the United Nations; I could be fairly objective about the Polish and other issues. All of us went over all the papers together before-hand. This was a time when position papers were beginning to be popu-lar and we had a session at Marrakesh with Mr Stettinius when we made him do his homework. I left out Harry Hopkins – I can see Harry's gaunt figure and face as we sat round the big table at plenary sessions. Bohlen sat on the President's left because he was interpreter. Stettinius sat on his right, behind was Harry Hopkins. Matthews and I were huddled in the remaining space in the background with papers in front of us, and occa-sionally whispering, occasionally passing notes. And there were pauses for consultation. In the mornings the hard work was done by the Foreign Ministers. All the plenary sessions were held at Lavadia Palace where President Roosevelt was, not because of his illness but because he was the only Chief of State – the others were merely heads of government, so it was protocol as well as convenient. We would try to hammer out in the morning sessions, the three Foreign Ministers and their staff, and after each session it was the duty of the technicians, Gladwyn Jebb and Pierson Dixon were my opposite numbers on your staff, working out the text of what had been agreed to be submitted to the plenary session.*

ANTHONY EDEN

Every morning the Foreign Secretaries had to meet for several hours to try and prepare the agenda for that day, it's much too short notice really, and then in the afternoon the heads of government would also meet with their Foreign Secretaries. So far as we were concerned the hours were appalling, it was almost continuous. And then Roosevelt got himself tied up with an

---

* H Freeman Matthews (1899–1986), career US diplomat; Gladwyn Jebb (1900–96), head of the Foreign Office Reconstruction Department and first Acting Secretary-General of the United Nations; Pierson Dixon (1904–65), career British diplomat.

engagement to meet King Ibn Saud on a destroyer in the Suez Canal and had to leave. It's perhaps a good tactic in a negotiation to summon your train to take you away and to let your opponents think that you're not going to wait indefinitely, but to pin yourself down to an end date really puts you in a awkward fix, so we thought. Churchill and I were much troubled by this tight timetable to which we were working and which suited Stalin I think quite well.

CHARLES BOHLEN

I don't know how carefully Mr Churchill had studied the paper we had to sent on to the British; we sent it to the Soviets also. I was going out in the hall to see them off; Mr Churchill and Mr Eden had quite a discussion over the voting formula, Churchill took the line that after all the countries that had born the brunt of the war should really have the deciding vote and they would take care of the little countries, that the little countries shouldn't be allowed too much voice in things. Mr Eden disagreed quite strongly and Churchill suddenly turned to me and said, 'What is this voting formula of yours?' And I said, 'Well, Mr Prime Minister, it reminds me of a story of the South in the old days and the plantation. The owner of the plantation gave a negro a bottle of whiskey and when he asked the negro the next day how he liked the whiskey, the man replied it was absolutely perfect: "If it had been any better you wouldn't have given it to me, if it had been any worse I couldn't have drunk it."'

ANTHONY EDEN

They were certainly a remarkable triumvirate by any standards. FDR, it was his personal charm which was considerable and his flair as a politician was also considerable, but at that time his health was not good. I remember during one session Harry Hopkins coming up and saying quietly to me over my shoulder, 'I don't think the President's well. I think we ought to wind this up as soon as we can.' So he wasn't on top form at Yalta. Winston, with all his great qualities, but perhaps negotiation wasn't really his strong suit because Winston was essentially warm-hearted and responsive to anybody whom he respected and had an admiration for. In that sense he was a contrast to Stalin who was a cold, cool and a calculating negotiator who knew exactly what he wanted to get and went out to get it, never got excited, hardly ever raised his voice, a cold chuckle or laugh particularly when he thought that FDR or Winston were at odds. He'd get up and walk up and down and rub his hands, but he was a formidable man to negotiate against.

AMBASSADOR HARRIMAN

Yalta was really the highpoint of the relationship between the three men. Victory was in the air and, although we hadn't crossed the Rhine yet, the Germans were in retreat and so there was a good deal more talk about matters in the future, and Poland again became the most troublesome point. And it's interesting that both Roosevelt and Churchill felt they had an agreement with Stalin, both went to their respective legislative group, Prime Minister to Parliament, President to Congress, spoke in very effusive terms. Churchill said that Poland will have the right of self-determination; they were bitterly disappointed that Stalin had broken his agreement. And then there was the agreement for liberating Europe, for free and unfettered elections and they had high hopes that there would be solid cooperation in other fields as well in the post-war period.

ALGER HISS

Basically the impression I had, being fairly objective, was that three highly politicised leaders, Stalin, Churchill and Roosevelt, felt it was essential at that stage of the war that agreement be announced as to Poland. Roosevelt did not want anything like secret agreements, which had bedevilled [President Woodrow] Wilson; they wanted something that should be announced to the world. The Yalta communiqué was no treaty, things not spelled out in detail. Justice Burns, who was present as a supernumerary, I think we were the only people trained as lawyers, and if that had been a treaty there'd have been a whole staff. They came close to precision as their different objectives permitted. I was very aware that both President Roosevelt and Prime Minister Churchill were highly conscious of domestic political issues, they were frank about it, it's in the minutes – Roosevelt saying that Stalin must appreciate his problem with the large Polish electorate in Detroit. Mr Churchill saying Stalin must understand that he had to deal with public opinion, not only in the Commons but throughout the county regarding the Polish government in exile, as a gallant remnant. The nub of the disagreement was there was never a complete acceptance of the American side in a unitary sense of an abolition of the cordon sanitaire which had been set up after Versailles. Those of us most interested in the UN work had early concluded that if any kind of peaceful coexistence was to occur, that had to be done away with, the Russians had to be assured that there was no hidden landmine. And democratic government is a mixture of many forces, in flux at the same time, they rise and fall. Years ago, [American journalist] Walter Lippmann said that American foreign policy moves by one law only, the law of the pendulum swing, but while the pendulum is swinging, those who are espousing policies momentarily predominant are contending with those who know the pendulum will come their way later on – they never give up their position completely.

ANTHONY EDEN

We were not happy about what happened in connection with the Far East, it was never discussed at the conference in the sense of future boundaries or who wished to have what territories and Winston and I were very much take aback when on the last day of the conference, at a luncheon which Roosevelt was giving, we were suddenly told that the Russians and the Americans had come to some agreement about the Far East, disposing of some of the Chinese territories, and we thought that a very bad thing. I was so much against it that I didn't want us to have any part in it and urged the Prime Minister that we should let them make a deal if they wanted to and hold ourselves free. He took the view, we wouldn't have anything to do with the later developments either and though we didn't like it, we'd be better in on it, and see what we could do. But it was a very startling development and perhaps an example of FDR thinking that he could do things direct with Stalin more effectively than with the three of us round the table. I can't help feeling if that had been discussed at the conference end of the agreements, it wouldn't have ended up in the shape which it did.

ALGER HISS

They were seen not only by the participants but by the American public as a whole when they were announced as a vastly successful hopeful wartime agreement, solidifying unity during the remainder of the war and presaging a period of peace. The enthusiasm was tremendous and in view of their later criticism of the Yalta agreement you wouldn't believe what the same people were saying in *Life* magazine. They had some lovely things to say about it then. Once the Cold War was in full blast this became a political dodge to tie dead cats around the neck of the Democrats and all of the participants. Pretty notable Americans like Admiral Leahy, Mr Harriman, Bohlen and high military people including General Dean, who was our Military Attaché in Moscow, uniformly said that this was a successful agreement, we got all we could have hoped and in some cases more. Most people who have studied the text with any objectivity, if they start plotting up who made what concessions, actually the Russians made more concessions than the British. It's almost mysterious as to how the myth of Yalta grew. I wrote a magazine article in September 1955 called *The Myth of Yalta*. Just recently Professor Theo Harris has written a book called *The Myth of Yalta* and his book does show how it developed among Republicans and newspapers who supported the Republicans, and it was amazing, instant mythology. Usually myths take a few centuries to develop; this was done almost overnight, it was ugly. President Roosevelt's health was attacked; the general line was an ailing President, malevolently advised by me among others, sold Poland and China down the river. It's not the impression of those who were present, and I think it's less and less the attitude of the general public. After all, when the Republicans came in under Eisenhower they could no longer say there's no sense in dealing with the Russians, you can't trust them, because they began dealing with them so there had to be some separation of sheep from goats. And it seems to me the Republicans now take a good deal of pleasure in following the spirit of Yalta belatedly by having another President go to the Soviet Union and go to China, which Roosevelt never did.*

---

* The reference is to his persecutor Richard Nixon, President 1969–74.

ANTHONY EDEN

I don't know that our hopes in our hearts was very high, I don't think we could claim more for Yalta than that it was the best arrangement in the circumstances, in the war which was still being waged – that we could make with the war still very much going on, and Russia was still bearing a very heavy part of it. I've never known exactly what happened after Yalta. Certainly things began to sour very quickly and there were some in the Kremlin who didn't altogether like some of the things they'd agreed to. Nobody knows how the Kremlin works and one doesn't know whether there was any truth in that or not. I think it went sour because the military development strengthened Russia's hands and that whereas the Russians had felt it necessary to be considerate of Western opinion at Yalta, a few months later they didn't feel any such necessity because the war was going so well for them. Therefore they swept aside some of the engagements they'd got into. That certainly applied particularly about Poland.

President Roosevelt died of a cerebral haemorrhage on 12 April 1945 and was succeeded by Harry S Truman, who had only been Vice President since 20 January. Truman had replaced the pro-Soviet Henry Wallace, who in 1948 was the Presidential candidate of the Progressive Party, a Communist front, and was described as 'a propaganda parrot for the Kremlin'.

CHARLES BOHLEN

Mr Truman was a man with great powers of decision and the interview with Molotov, which I interpreted in 1945, he was fairly stern with Molotov and shut him up when he began to get into the propaganda explanation about Poland. His behaviour was cold and he merely told him he wished he'd tell Marshal Stalin that we'd like to know when they were going to begin to live up to their agreements. Molotov was more interested in the agreements about the Far East, which had not yet been implemented, but it was a rather unusual interview with a Soviet official. It gave me a certain amount of pleasure to translate rather firm stuff to the Soviets and I think Molotov was not quite used to hearing that. It was not quite as spectacular as Mr Truman makes out in his memoirs.

CHAPTER 31

FALL OF BERLIN

It is unfortunate that Götterdämmerung *has become the standard cliché for the end of the Nazi regime because in Norse mythology it describes a war of the gods that brings about the end of the world. That was certainly the view of Hitler and the hard core of true believers who went down with him, but the term dignifies them by attributing too much importance to their deaths. On land and by sea and air the Germans fought to the bitter end and while one may feel considerable sympathy for the miserable civilians cowering under a rain of bombs, and professional respect for the courage and tenacity of the fighting men, the fact remains that every minute the war was prolonged by the efforts of such as Albert Speer, or by resolute field commanders like Kesselring in Italy or Model in western Germany, meant the death of yet more Jews in the Nazi death factories. All the contradictions in American political and military policy were also brought to the surface in the final months but one cannot fault Eisenhower's logic in not making a dash for Berlin when it was already agreed that it would fall well within the Soviet area of occupation. The interviews conducted for the programme* Nemesis: Germany February–May 1945 *were some of the best in the series, reflecting the makers' fascination with the last moments of this evil regime. Particularly striking are Speer's vivid recollection of the final days in Berlin and Traudl Junge's chilling moment of realisation that Hitler was a hollow man as she took the dictation of his 'Last Will'. The rather gruesome concern with the identification of Hitler's body reflects the fact that in June 1945 the Soviets declared that his remains had not been found, which gave birth to a wave of speculation that he had survived and was being concealed by Nazi sympathisers in the West. It served its propaganda purpose at the time, but*

545

as such things do it acquired a life of its own and has predictably kept conspiracy theorists busy ever since.

LIEUTENANT DENIS BEATSON-HIRD
51st Highland Division

As soon as the Rhine crossing had taken place we felt the war was coming to an end and obviously nobody wanted to get badly hurt and certainly nobody wanted to get killed at that stage. We were all desperately keen to get home fairly soon. There was a feeling of optimism and success – we just felt that this was the end, the Germans were going to pack up and there was nothing really to worry about.

MAJOR GENERAL KENNETH STRONG
General Eisenhower's Chief of Intelligence

Eisenhower still had his main objective, which was to penetrate Germany and to destroy the enemy armed forces. He didn't think that Berlin was a very important objective. What he decided to do was to go straight through to the centre of Germany to the Elbe, go eastwards, join up with the Russians and then to clear the northern flank, north sea ports and to clear his southern flank where there was possible talk about resistance in the Alps. He told Stalin his plan and he got into a lot of trouble for this because the British said he'd had no right to do this, this was a matter of politics or policy and not a military matter. But he always said, 'Here I am advancing, I'm going to come into contact with the Russians, I really must tell them what I am trying to do.' So the British pressed very strongly to him to go to Berlin and he said simply, 'If I'm ordered to go to Berlin, I'll do it, but these orders must come from my bosses who are the Combined Chiefs of Staff in Washington.' His orders were never changed because the Americans were convinced that after the war they could get on well with the Russians. They looked on Russians as being their allies in the future.

PRIVATE JOHN SENEY
US paratrooper

We were told there were some soldiers in a farmhouse wanted to surrender and we walked up in a loose group, not a military type of action, we were just going in informal, and several rounds were fired at us. Then we lobbed a bazooka shell into the house and several soldiers ran out. This one person was running away from me and didn't halt when I fired a round. It went down and when I approached I realised I had shot a girl about eighteen or nineteen years old dressed in something like the Women's Land Army uniform. And we ran into those sorts of situations quite often and we had to shoot some of the German children. It's still hard to say it now, but at that time whenever we captured an SS soldier, if he made it back to a POW camp alive he was lucky. In fact I can say that probably ninety per cent of the ones we came in contact with are buried over there some place.

MAJOR GENERAL FRANCIS DE GUINGAND
Field Marshal Montgomery's Chief of Staff

The Twelfth Army Group were going great guns and things moved so quickly then. The Ruhr was surrounded in no time and that was the beginning of the end and the Red Army were attacking strongly and so we had no fears, it was just a question of time, the Germans would have to capitulate – if it hadn't been for Hitler, it would have capitulated far sooner.

GUARDSMAN BROWN
Scots Guards

Casualties were bad enough at any time but particularly, perhaps, in the last two months of the war. There were men there, you'd been with them for five years, they were not just colleagues but close friends, you knew their families, you knew all about them. And you saw them getting knocked off in the last few days of the war, particularly sad at that time.

GUARDSMAN DUFFIN

Scots Guards

It was a very nasty shock indeed to meet any determined resistance because you felt that the end of the war was so close, and you had almost moved into a dreamlike and unreal situation, you know, towns and villages flew past with no resistance at all, normal countryside with no damage at all. Every day you said to yourself that surely this can't go on, and certainly I think the thought of one's own survival after all this gradually became uppermost in everybody's mind – it certainly did in mine, I don't mind confessing. Then when you did run into any sort of determined resistance, then to me it was a matter of hard anger. What are these – how dare these people prolong the agony any more? The other half was jolly nearly blue funk.

PRIVATE SENEY

We overran a German camp which appeared to have a large number of Jews in it and they were stacked probably four feet high for several hundred feet long in rows. There was evidence that they had tried to bury some of them and some had apparently been cremated in a couple of ovens. There was a village near by with German civilians in sight of the camp. Most of us were quite angry at the time so we had the villagers, from the age of six to sixty, anybody who could walk, digging trenches and burying these dead people laying there. The burgomeister was usually the first one you'd meet, he'd have his sash on, his badge of office, and he would inform us that he was not a Nazi and the town council was not, and then he'd proceed to name all the other dignitaries and we would round them all up and ship them out because then we knew we had all the Nazis.

ALBERT SPEER

Hitler's Armaments Minister

It was my duty to tell Hitler that from the point of view of armament the war was lost and I did it in several memorandums and the harshest one was 19th March 1945, in which I told him very bluntly the war will be finished within four or six weeks, which was the right estimate it turned out later.

And that it is now necessary, at the last minute, to do everything to help the German people for this situation which is now upon the Germans. He obviously knew what was in the memorandum. He said then not to think about the future of the German people, those who were brave they are dead, and those who survive are just cowards.

GENERAL HASSO-ECCARD FREIHERR VON MANTEUFFEL

Commander Third Panzer Army

In March it was very difficult to go through Berlin because all cars and electric trams had built up other objects for barriers in the streets. I needed two or three hours for this fifty kilometres and I came in the bunker under the earth and there was full of crowded officers and Party members, SS men and civilians. I was ordered into a small room and Hitler ordered me to defend east Berlin, the autobahn, and to give him more supplies of food and I answered to have no possibility to give him this because we had stood on the front to defend the Oder against the Russians and they were very strong. I could see this when I go by helicopter over my positions, Russia assembled mass of artillery and Hitler [made no argument].* In the circle of Berlin west of the autobahn, I think fifteen or twenty kilometres, there were troops but not enough equipment. But the west side there is a green park, that was not possible to destroy but they cut all the trees. But the east side, I came from the east side of Berlin, it was all destroyed. I took command of the Third Panzer Army one hundred kilometres east of Berlin and we stood there until 25th or 26th April. But the behaviour of the soldiers at this front line, they're not quite the same as my troops because daily thousands of refugees from East Prussia went over to the border and they were assembled by our troops and it was important they are defended all the way from East Prussia.

---

* Speer's statement that gauleiter Karl Hanke fled Breslau in a prototype helicopter has been generally disbelieved – Manteuffel's testimony confirms that there was such a machine.

GENERAL ALEXEI ANTONOV
Red Army Chief of Staff

The 18th Division of the SS attacked but we managed to hold them down and went further ahead. In the region of Bukov, also a very difficult battle, we took the town. Ever so many nationalities – Italian, French, English, Americans prisoners – were to be found in camps there and we freed them.

PRIVATE SENEY

We had several of our Airborne men return to our outfit from where the Russians had overrun a German camp. They told me they got worse treatment at the hands of the Russians than the Germans. They were subjected to questioning, they were mistreated, they were handled very roughly. Some of them went all through the German camp with their wristwatch but when the Russians freed them they lost them.

ALBERT SPEER

When I came back from the Ruhr valley I gave orders to contradict Hitler's strict general order to destroy everything. I entered Hitler's office and he told me Bormann reported me and 'If you wouldn't be my architect, I would fulfil the consequences which are used in such a case because it is high treason.' This moment I had the feeling that he saved my life and I felt some gratitude to him at this moment and remembered the times in which we both were quite happy about his plans. It was one of his sentimental strokes which Hitler had now and then, even in desperate situations, and I was saved by such. Then the discussion went on and he said, 'I ask you to go on a long vacation, you are obviously overworked and your ministry will be taken over by a deputy.' But I knew that the deputy would do the things I wanted not to have done and I said, 'No, I am quite all right and I don't go on vacation.' Then a strange thing happened, he said you should go, and I said I shall only resign as minister and he told me, 'That's just what I can't afford because for reasons of domestic politics and exterior politics I can't, unless you insist at the moment.' And there I thought the point was one to me. But the discussion continued, now he was giving in a bit. He said, 'Well, if you think the war isn't lost, as you told the gauleiters, then I think you can continue with the work.' But I said, 'No, I can't be convinced,' and he said, 'But do you have some hope that the war isn't lost?' Here was a point where I couldn't say no, if I would have said no I think then he really would have fulfilled what he said to me in the beginning, because it would have meant I am no more his follower, I am against him. So I didn't say anything and he thought that I didn't want to answer this question to avoid difficulties and he gave me an ultimatum, 'In twenty-four hours I expect to have your answer.' Then I turned again to the Reichschancellery twenty-four hours later and really didn't know what to answer him because there was no answer to it. He was standing there – I just got in my mind to see him standing behind you. The situation was won too because his eyes went moist and he shook emphatically my hand and said then everything is all right.

MAJOR GENERAL STRONG

Eisenhower didn't believe that it was worth risking a large number of casualties in order to capture Berlin, which sooner or later he'd have to leave and give back. It would have been very difficult indeed to explain to people why you did this, and then to soldiers why you did this and eventually left the town. If he had been given instructions and orders to take Berlin he would have done it. But those orders had to come from the Combined Chiefs of Staff. At the time when this controversy was going on the British were urging him to go to Berlin, Roosevelt was nearing the end of his life, wasn't really capable of making any decisions and no others came his way except those and he, Eisenhower, carried them out. Suppose he had gone to Berlin, he'd have got entangled with the Russians. I don't believe that our relationship with the Russians would have been any better than we think. People say if we'd gone to Berlin we'd have none of this post-war trouble with the Russians, but I don't think so; I think it's the exact opposite. We'd have had more trouble I think with the Russians if we'd gone there and at the same time the Americans had got another war to fight in the Far East. They were not anxious to get more entangled in Europe than they needed to be. To go and capture an objective which was not a military objective was completely against Eisenhower's best convictions.

ALBERT SPEER

Goebbels behaved first quite reasonably when I told him that it's no use to fight in the streets of Berlin, what is left of the German armies should have a battle outside Berlin, because I told him if Berlin will be destroyed then your whole reputation as a good gauleiter of Berlin will be extinguished, because you too are now responsible for what is happening to Berlin. He approached Hitler with this idea but Hitler then decided that the battle will be in Berlin and all the bridges will be destroyed and that the Berlin population has no value to him, the fight must be to the bitter end. The bridges were not destroyed because I had a meeting with the general in charge of this Army Group and we took the charges out of the bridges before, so they couldn't be destroyed any more. Also people now were reasonable enough not to fulfil all the orders which were given from Hitler's place.

GENERAL WALTHER WARLIMONT
Wehrmacht Deputy Chief of Operations

You may ask how it was possible for a man like me, being as close to Hitler in my position as Chief of Staff, could go through all these years of war and keeping a conviction? Field Marshal Keitel said in Nuremberg relating to this time of March 1945: 'After all our endeavours to change the situation had no effects, we had to go on only for the reason that we were soldiers and had to follow our obligations.'

ALBERT SPEER

Berlin was, in April 1945, more ruins than a town, one could find almost no building which was still intact. And in the middle of it was the old Philharmonic building, well-represented building before the war, which had quite a history of musical events, and this was destroyed too. It was my wish to help the Philharmonic having a concert, I knew it would be my last concert for a long time, perhaps for ever. I invited friends and as much people as possible to go in; we were sitting there in our coats, because there was no heating, it was cold, it was shivering and in this atmosphere of destruction and misery the concert started. I made the programme and we started. Afterwards there were some other pieces of Beethoven, but when I came back from this concert to the Chancellery, very great news, now everything shall turn to the better. I didn't know what it was, Hitler was almost out of his mind and Goebbels was already there, and Hitler showed us the death of Roosevelt and Goebbels was jumping up and saying, 'That's it, that's it.' I was realistic enough, as I proved with my memoirs, that I thought the situation properly, at least in the last month of the war. But those groups around Hitler was unbelievable: they had that was no more rational thinking and they were just convinced that everything will go in the right way and each one was convincing the other one if they went low in spirit. And Hitler was the same, but also sometimes changing his mind from one second to the other.

GENERAL WARLIMONT

I did not stay in Berlin at the time, I flew down to Munich on an aeroplane so I had no impression of the conditions of Berlin itself. I couldn't have overlooked the destruction but I don't think it made any deeper impression on me because I was so sick at that time, I had a concussion of the brains after the 20th July plot. The strongest impression on the German people at that time was still growing demands of the war on almost everybody, so the oldest men were called to go and the youngest ones at the age of fifteen or sixteen years to the Hitler Youth, so it was clear to everybody that there was nothing to be gained any more. The same with the lack of everything from the daily life and those insane orders of Hitler to destroy the water and electricity on which even the plain life of the people had to be sustained. I had only one desire, that the Western Powers might come in earlier than the Russians, because the behaviour of the Russian troops was beyond any imagination in East Prussia.

GENERAL ANTONOV

On 20th April we reached the outer ring road of Berlin and then we fought in Berlin. 301st Division was there. In the evening we stormed the town of Altlandsberg on the outskirts of Berlin, everyone now knew that the Byelorussian troops, including the Fifth Army had reached Berlin. On

23rd morning, members of the Military Council came to me, gave me the task of taking Karlshorst, and to force the Spree. We prepared the artillery and the tanks, we didn't know that Karlshorst would be an historical place where the declaration for capitulation would be signed, we paid more attention to the forcing of Spree. At 1700 our division forced the reach of the Spree by a race on boats. 24th – a very serious counter-attack on the centre of Berlin, the Germans prepared themselves between the Spree and the Landwehr canal, bombed the bridges. I have photos of those bridges, of the Germans in counter-attack, of our people in Treptow Park, how they stormed buildings and barricades across the roads. 27th – we occupied Allianz Square and station and turned towards Gestapo and Ministry of Aviation buildings and the Chancellery; along Wilhelmstrasse and Saarland Strasse there were troops to our left and right. The ring was closing in on the outskirts of Berlin and in the very centre we were getting nearer and nearer to the centre of Hitler's HQ – the Chancellery.

ALBERT SPEER

The situation in the bunker was a fantastic one, an unrealistic one, one can't really describe how the moods went on and off like waves. Sometimes they were all exhilarating, and were thinking well now, with the Western troops coming for the release of Berlin. Goebbels was exclaiming one of the biggest decisions Hitler just made, he is now determined no more to fight against the West, only to the East in Berlin and this will mean the Western powers will join us in our fight against Russia. And then a few minutes afterwards everybody was speaking about suicide and how they are preparing it. Goebbels in some detail of course, saying how he will let his children killed, which were already in the bunker, so one didn't really get a picture which is one sided. It was really a troubled picture I got from this visit. One of the odd things in this last period was those who were in power were still fighting for their power and mainly Bormann was seeing a chance for himself. When Göring was teletyping a message to Hitler and said if he was not contradicting him, he takes over power because obviously Hitler, now encircled in Berlin by the Russian troops, and is no more able at act properly, Bormann made a double meaning to this message. It was quite harmless, it was not such a treachery as Bormann was telling Hitler, but Hitler immediately went in rage and he stripped Göring of all his power and Bormann was triumphant. He was now, it was the peak of his whole career – Himmler was out of the game, now Göring was out of the game, Bormann was the second.

GERTRUD 'TRAUDL' JUNGE
Member of Hitler's stenographer pool

He stood at the table with motionless, expressionless face and his hands on the table board and then he began, 'My Last Will'. Then he dictated me at first his private will and then his political testimony. I must confess that I was at first in a very excited mood because I expected that I would be the first and only one who knows, who is going to know the explanation and declaration why the war had come to this end and why Hitler couldn't stop and why the developments and why the catastrophe. I thought now will come the moment of truth and I was heart thumping when I wrote down what Hitler said. He used nothing new, he came out with old phrases. He repeated his accusations, his revenge swearing to the enemy and to the Jewish capitalist system, and then he announced – in the second part of the political testament – he announced a new government. And then I was like banged on the head because an hour before he had said, 'All is gone, there will be no National Socialist idea any more. Germany is totally destroyed, the people are totally exhausted, there will be no further life in German – in German in the old sense.' And so it was a total contradiction to his own words. Then I finished and I went out and he urged me, 'Please hurry up, to write it in typewriting. Bring it to my room and then join us, I have married Eva Braun meanwhile.' It was another news for me which me very much surprised. I was not prepared for that because I could not think what would be the use of this act, only to die as a wife.

ALBERT SPEER

A few weeks earlier I tried to persuade Eva Braun to go back to Munich but she said, 'No, I stay, I want to go to the end with Hitler,' and when I saw her again in the bunker, the 23rd April, I was together with her, she was the best behaving of the whole entourage, leaving all the men far behind her concerning superiority above the situation. She was not mocking the situation, but she had worked out that she will now go to die with Hitler and possibly this was in some way the peak of her life, to die with the man she loved.

TRAUDL JUNGE

An orderly said, 'Come to Hitler, come to the Führer, he wants to say farewell,' He came towards me and his face was already dead, it was like a mask. He looked at me but I had the feeling that he looked through me and he gave me a shake of my hand and he murmured something but I didn't understand, I had not understand what he said at the last. But Eva Braun who stood beside him and who shook hands to all the others embraced me very heartily and looked at me with a sad little smile and said, 'Please try to get out of here, please try to come to Munich again and give my regards to my beloved Bavaria.' And then she and Hitler shut the door and retired. I had an absolute need for fleeing and I fled these stairs upside the next level and there I found the children of Goebbels. They were totally forgotten, nobody had cared for them and I tried to hold them back, that they wouldn't go down in the other part and be witness to what was happening there. And so I took a book and read them a fairy tale and gave them some fruit. We had a conversation and I was with one ear always hearing for what happened. And suddenly there was a bang, there was a shot and it was obviously within the bunker. The little boy of Goebbels, he noticed, and he noticed there was another sound. He said, 'Oh, that was a bullseye, that was a bullseye.' And I thought, Yes, you are right, that was really a bullseye, and I knew that was the shot that made an end with Hitler and with the National Socialist era and probably with us all.

ALBERT SPEER

Now I was in the middle of the Chancellery, which I had built in 1938. I wanted to see the whole building for the last time, and I went through the Chancellery, through the courtyard, and it was a dark night, but knowing my building so well I could, with my imagination, glimpse every detail of it. This was a farewell to maybe my life's work and the plane was already awaiting me in the big avenue leading to it. It was small, one engine and it was early in the morning. We started, just the pilot and me, the start was a difficult one because this avenue on both sides with high trees and we had to get very quick up in the air to avoid the column of victory standing in the middle of the avenue, and we just passed it. Being a little higher we were conscious the plane was only for daylight action and was always lighted up by the explosions of the engine. We feel very uncomfortable with it, mainly because what we were seeing was all buildings being in fire and shells exploding and gunfire, and only there was one spot in the west where there was absolute darkness. It was a very small spot and we knew that the Russians didn't close their circle yet, and this was our direction.

GRAND ADMIRAL KARL DÖNITZ
Head of State May 1945

When I got the telegram from the headquarters of Hitler, I knew that now I was Chief of the German State. But I knew too that Himmler had opinion that he had the biggest chance to be the successor of Hitler and that's why I thought to be necessary that I spoke to Himmler at once because this man was still powerful, and in the country I had no power at all because the Navy was swimming on the water and he got my demands that he at once had to come to me, but he answered the telephone that it was not possible for him to come. And then I let him see that it was necessary that he had to come and then he came. I didn't know what would be the end of this discussion, it was a question and that's why I put under a piece of paper my revolver on the table. He was sitting down and I gave him the telegram which I have got and which it was said that I am the Chief of State. When he had read the telegram, he got pale and he stood up and bowed and told me please let me be the second man in your state. Then I told him that I have no position at all for him in my state, then he was not content. He spoke against that but he had no success, I didn't change my opinion from that time of discussion. Then I stood up and he had to go, and he went home and I was very glad that the end of the discussion with Himmler was like that because I had the feeling that he wouldn't do anything against me.

GENERAL ANTONOV

The soldiers and officers fought in the Chancellery, Captain Shipavalov's battalion heroic fight with the SS. The heroic woman Major Nikulina [a political worker] together with some officers managed to get on to the roof and ordered the Fascist coat of arms that was there to be taken. Also they took out Hitler's own standard and showed it to me. Marshal Zhukov came and asked where is Hitler? I answered that he had not been found yet, but Goebbels had been found. In the evening the soldiers found two bodies near the bunker, since it was dark I ordered that they should be guarded and strict patrol kept. In the morning representatives of the Commission of the Command came, including an interpreter Elena Rzhevskaya. They took the bodies and examined them and within two weeks they established that they really were Hitler and Eva Braun. That's how the war in Berlin finished for us.

DR FAUST SHKAVRAVSKI

Soviet pathologist

The bodies of Hitler and Eva Braun were burned very much, especially Eva Braun's body. Hitler was less burned but nevertheless one could not say who he was by his looks. His hands and lower legs were totally burned off, the body was very dark, like coal. Part of the cranium just was not there, only some small bits of bone were visible. We looked for other things such as metal inserts or pathological changes – for instance in Goebbel's case, one leg was shorter than the other. In Hitler's case the teeth were important; the thing about Hitler's mouth was that it was filled with what looked like more than a hundred grams of gold. Quite extraordinary. In front of his teeth was a gold band about as thick as a pencil. Hitler had – can't remember exactly, but I think – five of his own teeth, three artificial silicate teeth, which were attached to small pins on a golden base. The rest were all gold teeth. They were very unusual teeth and were therefore very important in the identification of the body.

CHRISTA RONKE
Berlin schoolgirl

We hoped the US Army would come earlier to Berlin than the Russians, but then we heard the Russian artillery coming nearer and nearer and suddenly we saw the first Russian soldiers. They knocked at our door, came in and said if there were German soldiers in the house and asked for weapons. And then they left, but the next Russians were quite different. One of them raped me and other inhabitants of the house. After this my mother and I thought over how to change. My mother changed into an old, ugly woman and I changed into an ugly, sick child. I cut my hair and had a tooth lost here – I looked very ugly. And I was lying in bed when the next Russians came and my mother always said this word, that should be in Polish or in Russian 'sick child', when the Russians returned. Even one Russian soldier felt pity and gave me a piece of bread.

FRIEDRICH LUFT
Berlin civilian

It sounds quite blasphemous but we were lucky having two dead bodies of two women who were living next door. They were killed when we were shelled during the last days of the war and we brought them down and we weren't able to bury them because the shelling was still going on so we put them on the grass here and covered them up with two big carpets. Then we went back into our house again and when the Russians came along and they asked us where are your women, we want to have your women, 'Frau, Frau' they said in German or what they called German, I found the trick to take them to these two dead bodies. I opened the carpet and said, 'This is my Frau here, I can't supply you with any women, these are the only women here.' And the Russians kneeled down, some of them, and made the cross and said little prayers, which was astounding, and got up again and kissed me because they thought I was a widower and gave me presents, gave me cigarettes, gave me bread, clapped me on the shoulder and went off again and got what they wanted probably the next house or on the next street. These were things which happened in those days.

GRAND ADMIRAL DÖNITZ

Now I was Chief of State the programme which I had was clear. I was to end the war as soon as possible and still in this time to save as many people as possible. I wished to help the population of the German eastern provinces who were escaping on land and on the Baltic Sea to the western part of Germany with all means which I could. All warships of the Germany Navy and all German merchant ships which I had were sent to the eastern German ports to fetch these poor fleeing people. I did not want to be obliged to sign a general capitulation including Russia at once, but intended to try to get the first capitulation only with the British and the Americans to win time for the retreat of the German soldiers and population from east to west. The British enemy under the command of Field Marshal Montgomery we got a partial capitulation on 5 May 1945, but General Eisenhower did not agree to my demand for capitulation only with the Americans and he required that Germany capitulate at once to Russia. Eisenhower at least agreed that we got a further period of forty-eight hours before the capitulation was enforced. We did everything to use these forty-eight hours to get the soldiers and the fleeing population to the west. In the Baltic Sea all ships were running without delay, saving wounded soldiers and other soldiers and fleeing civilians. We could bring over the Baltic Sea in the last months of the war two to three million men, the number of fleeing people who saved themselves on land amounted to millions too, and from the military front in the east we could bring 1,850,000 soldiers into the west of Germany. But still 1,490,000 soldiers became Russian prisoners.

CHRISTA RONKE

We went westward some miles and there was shooting and bombing and then suddenly we saw a German soldier coming down from a tree. He didn't know what had happened and we told him to get off his uniform and another minute we saw three German soldiers hanging on a tree – I think they had deserted. And then we stopped at a big villa where some people had done suicides and we lived in the cellar there.

LIEUTENANT J GLENN GRAY
US Army Intelligence

Being a conqueror seems very dubious to me but at the time it seemed quite right, we were convinced of our virtue and of German vice and it was very pleasing. Unfortunately the innocent were in the same position as the guilty. I didn't feel unhappy at all about having to interrogate and arrest Gestapo or even some worse characters, the so-called Security Service people. But totally innocent people were also humiliated in the same way as the guilty. I feel today that this kind of total victory, unconditional surrender, was probably a huge mistake, and we learned the wrong lessons from it, as our recent experience in Vietnam seems to prove. After the war when I became a civilian I began to feel that being a conqueror, a total victor, is quite bad for both and perhaps worst for the victor because he feels unduly virtuous, and I think that conviction has steadily grown since World War Two. We haven't won a war, we haven't lost a war either. If we have to have wars I would sooner see them inconclusive than end with total victory or defeat. It's a harder lesson to learn but perhaps better for the character of both nations.

LIEUTENANT FELIX PUTTERMAN
US Army Civilian Affairs

I would immediately identify myself to all the Germans, to indicate that I was Jewish and that I was not interested in their personal problems, that I was only interested in the services they could provide to keep our troops living at as high a standard of living as possible in a bombed-out community. Most of the troops at first were rather cold but then they began to warm up to the Germans. They found they had much in common with the Germans; the German standard of living was most akin to that of the American troops back home. As a consequence, because they seemed to be cleaner than the other people on the Continent, and for that matter even in the UK, the American troops began to feel that these were really people who lived the same way Americans did and that we had some philosophical differences during the war but in close day-to-day living it was certainly nothing that was dwelt upon in any seriousness.

URSULA GRAY

Refugee from Dresden who later married author J Glenn Gray

We got away by pretending we were French and they didn't touch anybody but German girls. Once I almost made a mistake because the Russians were just like children, they would go into a farmhouse, take everything the farmer possessed and then go out and throw it to other people, all the silver and all the linen. They saw my sister and me with a French tricolour on our bicycles and they threw silver spoons to us. I said *danke* in German instead of *merci beaucoup* and my sister was frightened because she thought now they knew we were not French and they're going to rape us. But they were so happy, so drunk, so child-like they didn't pay attention. So we were not raped, we were not attacked but it's just by sheer accident. I know many of my friends were raped and were pretty badly damaged to their souls and bodies.

LIEUTENANT GRAY

Very close to the end of the war I had a requisition, a very lovely home in the centre of Germany because I knew German. I was always given the unpleasant task of throwing out civilians for our troops and of course I promised them that they would get their own home back. These were not battle-hardened soldiers or officers whom I would have been sympathetic with, these were fresh troops. They drank themselves pretty senseless and began to shoot up the house, I had a great temptation to hold them up with my gun but they were so drunk that I feared they would shoot me. They made a total shambles of the house. I had to break my promise to the German civilians, who were probably no more Nazis than I was. This kind of thing was particularly disillusioning because a lot of our soldiers were wounded, our President was dead, and these colonels were pretending to be playing at war when they hadn't any justification, any real need for a holiday. A kind of corruption of military life which soured me. I still remember it with great anger.

LIEUTENANT PUTTERMAN

Some woman came to me to try to offer me her own services, although she was trying to paint it was something else. I looked at her and I was feeling particularly mean that day – my father was sick and the Red Cross had just told me that my younger brother-in-law had been killed in Germany – and I was about ready to tear anyone apart anyway with my own two hands. I said, in desperation, 'Look, don't bother me – you know you're dealing with a Jew, you don't want to have anything to do with me.' And she looked at me and she said, 'But you are a white Jew.'

CHAPTER 32

ENDURING THE UNENDURABLE

Just as one may see all of Japan's conquests after Pearl Harbor as an attempt to provide defence in depth for the enormous investment made to win an empire in China, so American strategy began and ended with the intention – announced publicly by General Marshall in November 1941 in an effort to deter Japanese aggression – of firebombing the tinder-box Japanese cities. As we have seen, the US plan to establish bomber bases in China was frustrated by Japanese conquest of those areas of the Chinese coast they did not already control. General Curtis LeMay, promoted out of the European theatre to take charge of a new Twentieth Air Force in China, had launched the first precision-bombing attack on Japan with the new B-29 Superfortresses in June 1944, but in January 1945 he was transferred to Twenty-First Air Force in the Pacific. After the capture of Saipan and neighbouring Tinian in July 1944, Tinian became the largest air base in the world and B-29s operating from it also conducted the high-altitude precision-bombing attacks for which the aircraft had been designed. Results were poor and LeMay instituted a policy of low-level area incendiary bombing that burned the heart out of Japan's cities. Two of the few cities still on his list were the targets of atom bombs on 6 and 9 August, after which Japan surrendered, but not without some last-ditch resistance by fanatical nationalists who believed it was better for the entire population to die rather than to bend the knee. The attitude of the Japanese ruling elite is so perfectly captured by Emperor Hirohito's first-ever broadcast that I have included the operative parts of his speech in this chapter. It reveals that the cultural gulf between Japan and her opponents, so significant in the run-up to the war, still yawned widely at its very end.

MAJOR GENERAL CURTIS LeMAY
Commander Twentieth and then Twenty-First Air Force, China and the Pacific

We'd always planned on using incendiaries in the campaign against Japan because the construction used in their cities made them very effective. But in order to use them properly you have to have a minimum concentration of incendiaries to get a good fire started – a minimum of aeroplanes. When we got that number we started, as a matter of fact we started a little bit soon, we should have had a few more aeroplanes. The Japanese seemed to be lacking in low-altitude defences and for that reason I decided to come down low, because we could carry a bigger load from China to Japan at low altitude than at high altitude, and the bombing would be more effective. We tried it and it worked, and of course the attack itself was very effective and seventeen square miles of the industrial area of Tokyo was burned on the first attack.* We then followed that up as rapidly as possible on other industrial areas because I fully expected the Japanese to recover more than they did. We took the armament out of the aeroplanes, with the exception of the tail guns, to allow more bomb load because the Japanese had no effective night-fighter system such as the Germans had developed.

TSUYAKO KII
Tokyo housewife

On 9th March 1945 I felt somewhat severe atmosphere that night and the alarm came, a man came shouting through a megaphone we must shelter in the school but I disobeyed because I thought that school was very dangerous, there were many houses standing around that school, so I ran to the big bridge over the Sumida river and I stayed all night around

---

* The Tokyo fire storm in the night of 9–10 March 1945 destroyed a quarter of a million buildings and killed in excess of 100,000 people.

that bridge. There was no fire at first on my side but the other side was burning and the early morning of 10th March the fire started on my side so I crossed over the other side of the bridge and there it was already burned up so I kept myself rather safely at that place. I thought I could jump into the river at last chance as people had done in the middle of the earthquake of 1923.

MAJOR GENERAL LeMAY

It wasn't until General Arnold's visit to the Marianas that we even thought about the end of the war. And he asked a direct question, 'How long's the war going to last?' We sat down and did some thinking about it and indicated that we would be pretty much out of targets around the 1st of September, and with the targets gone we couldn't see much of any war going on. They still had some capacity to fight, but not the war they had to fight. They had four and a half million men under arms that had never been committed to combat but they had no resources to face the attack that was facing them. We were destroying their oil refineries with precision radar bombing at night and they were hoarding about half a tank in each aeroplane they had left, camouflaged under trees for kamikaze attack against the invasion ... the B-29s were flying at will over Japan and they couldn't do anything about it. As a matter of fact they'd been trying to get out of the war for about three months – they'd asked the Russians to be intermediaries but the Russians had been stalling until they got their war finished so that they could get into the Pacific War before it ended.

TOSHIKAZU KASE

Principal Secretary to the Japanese Foreign Minister

The idea of surrender did not before the war exist in the tradition of Japanese fighting services and even private soldiers preferred just to kill themselves to surrendering. So the idea of surrender meant for a military leader that he had to kill himself for whatever mistakes he committed, particularly with the Emperor.

HISATSUNE SAKOMIZU
Chief Cabinet Secretary
The disposition of the military people, the word surrender never in their dictionary so even the whole country became destroyed, people killed, still they do not want to surrender.

MARQUIS KOICHI KIDO
Lord Keeper of the Privy Seal
On one hand there were people strongly imbued with the Japanese spirit; these people said Japan must continue fighting and it was inconceivable that Japan would be defeated. Then there was a group of people who assess the situation rationally and with cool heads. The younger officers in the Army subscribed to extreme thinking that the nation could commit *gyakusatsu*, which means fighting to the end until all Japanese are killed. But it does not seem that War Minister General Anami was of that opinion. When I talked to him about ending the war he said, 'We should hit the US forces hard on the beaches once, because that would make the peace negotiations more favourable to Japan.'*

YOSHIO KODAMA
Nationalist politician and naval officer
Those who live in modern Japan will find it hard to understand the reason why the Japanese commit suicide – commit seppuku. But if you look at the long history of Japan you will see that whenever your pride is destroyed or when you throw away your pride it is quite proper for a man to commit suicide. The long history of Japan shows that many thousands, many tens of thousands, in the past have committed suicide for these very reasons.

DR JOHN KENNETH GALBRAITH
Deputy Head of the US Office of Price Administration
The Japanese war effort was broken not from being bombed, but from the blockade, as well as from the defeats, from the bypassed armies and the

---

* General Korechika Anami committed seppuku on 15 August.

lost divisions that were bypassed, and the fact that Japan no longer had a Navy. Japan was defeated before the atomic bomb and the defeat had been recognised. The Imperial Council had accepted the defeat and it was merely a matter of finding an avenue of communication with the Allied powers and getting all the bureaucratic element into line.

MAJOR GENERAL LeMAY

I think once you've committed yourself to war – and by the way this is not done by military people, it's done by our duly elected official in government, both your government and mine – once you're committed to war I think then you're committed to completing it and bringing back normal peacetime conditions as soon as possible, which means using sufficient force and everything at your disposal to get it over with quickly. And this always saves lives, yours as well as the enemy's lives in the long run, because in a long drawn-out war you begin to get casualties from the side-effects of exhaustion, deprivation, disease and things of that sort, so getting it over as quickly as possible is the moral responsibility of everyone concerned.

TOSHIKAZU KASE

We knew that to bring about an early termination of hostilities we had to conduct negotiations with our military opponents, but the High Command refused categorically to entertain the idea of talking with the enemy powers. The only great power left out of the enemy camp was the Soviet Union, with which nominally there existed the neutrality pact, and so this was the only window left open for peace. So we argued it out with the military command and we finally start negotiations with the Soviet Union in order to arrive at the final destination, which was Washington and London. We tried to get in touch with Stalin and we thought if one of the senior statesmen was sent with Emperor's personal letter addressed to Stalin, Stalin might receive him, because we thought that Stalin, being an astute politician, might be prepared for a showdown after the war with the democratic powers, particularly America. If he anticipated difficult relations after the war, he might deem it profitable to save Japan from the hopeless situation in which she was finding herself. That was the aim of our efforts directed towards Moscow.

CHARLES BOHLEN

US diplomat and Soviet specialist, at Potsdam

Molotov was there, Mr Byrnes, Secretary of State, myself and the Soviet interpreter and Stalin tossed a piece of paper across the table to Truman saying that they had just received this proposal from the Japanese to send a mission headed by Prince Konoye. Stalin told Truman that his position was to refuse it and Truman entirely agreed with that. What the motivations were from Mr Truman's point of view: he thought that the war was almost over in the Pacific; the atomic bomb had not been dropped when this proposal was made, and that there was no point in getting involved in complicated negotiations.

HISATSUNE SAKOMIZU

After the Potsdam Declaration the Foreign Minister Togo said in the Cabinet meeting that if we want to stop the war now, we must receive this declaration. They don't say anything about Emperor's position so we can stop the war without the question of the Emperor. We can keep the Emperor all right so we better receive this declaration as soon as possible. So many Cabinet Ministers said, 'Let us see the situation for a while,' so we did not receive the declaration. But after the atomic bomb thrown to Hiroshima the Cabinet suddenly decided to stop the war.

McGEORGE BUNDY

Official in the US Facts and Figures Department

The committee studying the atomic bomb unanimously recommended that it be used as soon as possible without warning against a major Japanese military establishment. Only this, Foreign Secretary Stimson thought, would provide the psychological blow which might induce Japan to surrender, although he agreed with some of Truman's advisers that the Japanese should be given an ultimatum which made it clear that they could keep the Emperor.

ANTHONY EDEN

British Foreign Secretary

I'm not saying this to excuse our use of the atomic bomb, because I think we had no choice but to use it, but I am merely saying one must not forget how terrible the alternative must have been and how long it must have gone on and how much suffering it would have created. I can't strike a balance sheet between which method would have cost the more suffering in continuing by the orthodox methods, the ordinary war methods. I don't think that anybody could have voluntarily forgone this possibility of shortening the war, despite the horror of the weapon. We knew about the first and we were consulted, and Churchill and I agreed, and we share full responsibility. We were not, I think, informed about the second.

HISATSUNE SAKOMIZU

We don't expect they use that kind of cruel weapon. We are afraid that they may have atomic bomb but when they succeed to have the atomic bomb I thought they must tell something to us now they've finished the work but Hiroshima happened without warning. I thought that American people very cruel people.

COLONEL PAUL TIBBETS

Commander of the 509th Composite Bombing Group and pilot of the Enola Gay, *which dropped the atom bomb on Hiroshima*

In was a clear, sunshiny day and visibility was unrestricted so as we came back around again facing the direction of Hiroshima we saw this cloud coming up, two minutes and it was up at our altitude – we were at thirty-three thousand feet – and the cloud was up there and continuing to go right on up in a boiling fashion. The surface was nothing but a black boiling – like a barrel of tar, that's probably the best description I can give. Where before there had been a city, distinctive houses, buildings and everything, now you couldn't see anything except black-boiling debris down below.

MAJOR CHARLES SWEENEY

Pilot of the instrumentation-support aircraft at Hiroshima

It takes fifty-two seconds approximately for an object to drop from thirty thousand to one thousand five hundred feet and in that length of time we were able to get twelve slant range miles away from the explosion. A white light just obliterated the whole sky, I'll never forget it. My back was to the explosion of course; however, there was a man in the tail and shortly afterwards I heard him say something which was unintelligible. Shortly thereafter the plane was smacked on the bottom and my bombardier, Captain Clement Behan, turned to me and said 'flak'. There was a little bit of panic in his eyes but I could still feel the aeroplane flying well and we were hit again, and again, each time with diminished force. Inasmuch as Behan had been shot down four times over Europe I had some confidence in his description of flak, but fortunately it wasn't. The man in the tail was describing something that human eyes had not seen before, and these were concentric rings of hot air coming up toward the aeroplane, radiating from the explosion, and these were the things that caused the smacking on the bottom. Afterward we turned back and flew back towards our base fifteen hundred miles away and we saw, off our right wing, the cloud coming up from Hiroshima. This was a cloud that as it boiled up had every colour of the rainbow and at about twenty-five thousand feet the mushroom portion broke off and turned white. We couldn't see the city, it was covered in smoke and as I recall even reconnaissance aeroplanes that flew over there almost constantly for the next two days couldn't photograph the city.

KISHI MATSUKAWA
Hiroshima housewife

A couple of people say, 'Look, parachutes, parachutes!' I looked up and there I saw two boxes, something like boxes hanging from a parachute and coming down. And everybody said, 'Oh, they must either contain some cookies or some canned good – we hope that they don't fall into the sea or the river, we hope they will fall close beside us because if they fall in the sea or the river they will get lost and it would be a great shame to lose all these goodies.' Then in a twinkling of an eye there was a bomb burst and I hurt my head and became unconscious instantaneously. When I regained consciousness it was pitch dark all around me. I tried to stand but I found that my leg was broken. I tried to speak and I found that I had lost six of my teeth, six of my teeth had been broken. I found my face burned and my back burned and like a slash right across from one shoulder to the waist. I crawled to the river and when I got there I saw hundreds of students come floating down the river.

MAJOR SWEENEY

At that moment I felt that the mission had been executed properly and that this just might cause the Japanese government to say, 'We're willing to end the war.' That was what it was all about, ending the war. This was the first time it had ever been used and we knew that it was supposed to devastate a certain area. But in 1945, for example, we knew that Tokyo had been devastated to such a much greater extent that we were told not to even use it as a target of opportunity. So the thing about this weapon was that it did it in a very short period of time. It didn't do as much as Tokyo, but it did it in a much shorter period of time.

KIYOSHI TANIMOTO

Christian Hiroshoma resident

I saw strange flash of light coming through the air even in the bright morning sunshine without any noise. I took couple of steps into the garden and I lay on the ground between two rocks and felt a strong blast of wind, then I got up and found the house behind me was completely demolished and I saw a few people coming out of the ruins here and there. I took one of them to the first-aid station, there I saw many injured people and I began to wonder what happened. I went up to the hillside and took a view of the city and found whole city on the fire. Now I realise it was an attack and then I dashed into the street to get back to the church, which was located in the central part of the city. I encounter a long and terrible line of escapees, all around them they had no cloth whatever on their bodies and the skin from their faces, arms and breast come off and hanging loose.

COLONEL TIBBETS

I never let my personal feelings enter into it. I learned this back in the days when I was flying out of England and bombing targets in Europe. I knew there were people down below getting hurt and I felt that if I let my emotions get carried away and I got to worrying about who's going to get hurt by something like this, then I wouldn't be effective at all. So I had to school myself not to think about it. Now from this point of view I was not affected emotionally; I haven't been up to this day because it was something that had to be done. I was convinced that it had to be done and I was convinced that it was the right thing to do at that particular time.

MICHIKO NAKAMOTO

I knew something had happened to me but I was scared to find out what had happened. I knew one side of my face was injured but I couldn't put my hand to see how much it was injured, I was scared to find out and my arm was burned and my feet were burned and I was wearing a long-sleeved blouse, which we were required to wear during the war, but this was burned off and it left a mark on the arm. Then this lady told me it's better if I went down to the river and washed my burns so I tried to do this, but this burn was something that I could not touch it was so deeply burned and I just couldn't do anything. Until he spoke I couldn't tell which side was his front because he was just burned black and then I hear his voice and that was his front and he asked me what time it was and I think he died very shortly after that. His lips were all swollen and really I couldn't bear to look at him. I just answered what time it was, I thought.

MAJOR GENERAL LeMAY

As far as casualties were concerned I think there were more casualties in the first attack on Tokyo with incendiaries than there were with the first use of the atomic bomb on Hiroshima. The fact that it's done instantaneously, maybe that's more humane than incendiary attacks, if you can call any war act humane. I don't, particularly, so to me there wasn't much difference. A weapon is a weapon and it really doesn't make much difference how you kill a man. If you have to kill him, well, that's the evil to start with and how you do it becomes pretty secondary. I think your choice should be which weapon is the most efficient and most likely to get the whole mess over with as early as possible.

MARQUIS KIDO

In a way it could be said that the atomic bombings and Russia's entry into the war against Japan helped to bring about the end of the war. If those events had not happened, Japan at that stage probably could not have stopped fighting.

TOSHIKAZU KASE

We thought the last chance disappeared when the Russian Army invaded Manchuria, after we suffered destruction by the atomic bomb. The Russians did not declare war until their Army advanced deep into Manchuria, the Soviet ambassador came to hand over the declaration of war at that time. I interpreted the conversation and made vigorous protest against the conduct of the Soviet diplomacy because there existed the Neutrality Pact, which prohibited legally the Soviet Union to undertake an attack on Japan. He was crestfallen, he was cast in a very difficult role.

MARQUIS KIDO

The Cabinet felt that there was no way out but to accept the Potsdam Declaration. But the big question was how to reveal it to the nation. It would be such a shock to the people. Therefore it was announced in the newspaper that the government would disregard the Potsdam Declaration. It seems that this attitude provoked the United States very much.

TOSHIKAZU KASE

The High Command would not have heeded anybody except the Emperor to lay down arms. When Japan entered the war the Cabinet unanimously recommended the commencement of hostilities and in that case the Emperor had no choice but to accept the military commendation. When the war was terminated the Cabinet against itself, that gave the Emperor the chance to intervene and to command acceptance of the Potsdam Proclamation and for a final surrender.

MARQUIS KIDO

Immediately after this meeting [on 9 August] I had an audience with the Emperor; he told me that there was a heated debate between those in favour of continuing the war and those led by Foreign Minister Togo, who advocated a cessation of hostilities. As there was no agreement, Prime Minister Suzuki took the unprecedented step of turning to the Emperor to ask his opinion. The Emperor said he supported Minister Togo's opinion.

YOSHIHIRO TOKUGAWA
Chamberlain to Emperor Hirohito

There was a great deal of difficulty as to the choice of words that the Emperor would use in his broadcast and a decision could not be reached very easily because, after all, the Emperor himself had his own thoughts on the surrender. For example, he felt sorry for the people in the Army and the Navy, who had worked so hard for their country. On the other hand it was felt that if the war were to continue even the Japanese race itself would be completely destroyed, that we would become extinct. It was not until nine in the evening of 14th August that a decision was reached on the message to be broadcast by His Majesty; however, just then the air-raid siren started to sound and it was decided that it would be dangerous for His Majesty to come to the temporary palace where the sound equipment was set up. However, His Majesty was becoming impatient because of the passage of time and we got a telephone call from the Emperor's aide who said the Emperor felt he should come out and hurry up and make the broadcast. And so it was about eleven-thirty that the Emperor came by car to the temporary palace. The recording took thirty minutes but he repeated his recording, that is he made two recordings, so it was after midnight by the time His Majesty returned to the Fukiage Pavilion.

EMPEROR HIROHITO
Surrender broadcast, 15 August 1945

To my good and loyal subjects: after deeply pondering the general trends of the world and the current conditions of our empire, I intend to effect a conclusion to the present situation by resorting to an extraordinary measure. My subjects, I have ordered the Imperial Government to inform the four governments of the United States, Great Britain, China and the Soviet Union that our empire is willing to accept the provisions of their joint declaration. The striving for peace and well-being of our imperial subjects, and the sharing of common happiness and prosperity among tens of thousands of nations is the duty left by our Imperial Ancestors, and I am the one who has not forgotten about this duty. The Empire declared war against the United States and Great Britain for the desire to preserve, by ourselves, the Empire's existence in east Asia and for the region's stability. As to the infringement of other nation's sovereignty and invasion of other territorial entities, those were not my original intent. By now, the fighting has lasted for nearly four years. Despite the gallantry of our naval and land military forces, the diligence and assiduity of hundreds of civil-service officers, and the public devotion and service of one hundred million of our people, the situation on the war has not turned for the better, and the general trends of the world are not advantageous to us either. In addition, the enemy has recently used a most cruel explosive. The frequent killing of innocents and the effect of destitution it entails are incalculable. Should we continue fighting in the war, it would cause not only the complete annihilation of our nation, but also the destruction of human civilisation. With this in mind, how should I save billions of our subjects and their posterity, and atone ourselves before the hallowed spirits of our Imperial Ancestors? This is the reason why I have ordered the Imperial Government to accept the joint declaration. I, from the start, have worked with our various Allied nations towards the liberation of east Asia, and I cannot refrain from expressing my deepest sense of regret to our Allies. The thought of our Imperial subjects dying in the battlefields, sacrificing themselves in the line of duty, and those who died in vain and their relatives, pains my heart and body to the point of fragmentation. As for the bearing of the wounds of war, the tragedies of war, and the welfare of those who lost their families and careers, it is the objects of our profound solicitude. From today hereafter, the Empire will endure excruciating hardships. I am keenly aware of the feelings of my subjects, but in accordance to the dictates of fate I am willing to endure the unendurable, tolerate the intolerable, for peace to last thousands of generations.

YOSHIHIRO TOKUGAWA

After the Emperor returned to the Fukiage Pavilion we went to the next room where the Grand Chamberlain had his office and just at that time the NHK [Japanese Broadcasting Corporation] man came in. He had the two recordings and he had put them into a can and he said, 'Shall I take it back to the broadcasting station?' I said I will take it with me and I put it in this room where I usually stay, it has a small safe where I placed the recording for safekeeping. At three o'clock I was awakened from my sleep and told by the guard detachment that rebel soldiers had come into the palace grounds. I felt I should have to inform the people at the residence of the Emperor and so I started to get ready to leave and as I went out I met the Minister of the Imperial Household and also the Home Minister. So I took them to a safe place underground and I went to the Fukiage Pavilion. On my way back I bumped into the officer who was leading the rebel soldiers but nothing happened and I managed to get back safely. Later I bumped into the officer again and he started to ask me all sorts of questions, but since we had known of the situation the day before we had taken pains to hide the recording, and besides the Home Minister was safe and also the Imperial Household Minister, so I was not worried in the least.*

TOSHIKAZU KASE

The surrender ceremony took place on board the American battleship on 2nd September. I did not like to take part in this ceremony. The Foreign Minister [Shigemitsu] was chosen as the principal delegate, I was sure he would ask me to accompany him to this ceremony and finally I was caught. It was customary in those days for the principal delegate to proceed to the palace and greet the Emperor before starting a mission of importance, so I went to the palace and I prepared Shigemitsu's greetings to the throne. I did not know what to write because I was completely exhausted, my brain refused to function, but I knew that this greeting

---

* The rebel officers led by Major Hatanaka Kenji murdered the commander of the 1st Imperial Guards Division and persuaded some of the palace guards to join them by claiming support from War Minister Anami. After failing to find the Emperor's recording or to broadcast his own message, Hatanaka Kenji committed seppuku.

would be left as a document, would be preserved as a historical piece long after the surrender ceremony. So I collected my wits and wrote something to this effect, it was the substance of the address in the concluding paragraph to the throne: 'We deem it most regrettable that Japan, who has never experienced defeat, is now forced to surrender. But we are determined to make this day a starting point for reconstructing our dear fatherland. We know that that is exactly the Emperor's wish and believing that this is the wish of the throne, we shall bravely face the ordeal of the surrender ceremony and pledge this day be the first step on the road forward to work the democratic of Japan.' The Emperor raised his eyes, evidently to check a tear falling down – that was a very impressive sight for me.

MARQUIS KIDO

When the Americans dropped leaflets demanding surrender I thought that a troublesome thing had happened. The people and the soldiers in all posts all over the country were completely unaware of developments. If they should find out that the government was negotiating peace with the United States then the situation would have become impossible. It might even have led to a revolution, so I felt that we must push things to the conclusion as fast as possible. I think this shows the difference in thinking between Japan and America. The United States probably thought that by letting people know it would have the effect of starting a mass movement for peace, but that is wrong.

TOSHIKAZU KASE

Battleships in three lines, in the forefront as I waited for General MacArthur to come forward, I saw many thousands of sailors everywhere on this huge vessel, and just in front there were delegate of the victorious powers in military uniforms glittering with gold. And most particularly I noticed the Soviet representative, and there was also the Chinese delegate. When I saw the Soviet general I recalled the infamous attack the Soviet Union resorted to as we were crumbling. Then I saw the face of the Chinese; I thought what a pity it was that two Asian nations which should be good neighbours should have fought against one another.

YOSHIO KODAMA

Even if the United States dropped a hundred atom bombs or if they dropped a thousand atom bombs, I felt that Japan should continue fighting to the last man. Japan was undertaking research on the atomic bomb, but it was very small-scale research and they could never have achieved the atom bomb during the war. But if the Japanese had succeeded in developing an atom bomb I am sure they would not have used it in the same way as the United States, they would never have dropped it on a city containing non-combatants.

TOSHIKAZU KASE

The road was very bumpy with holes here and there and we had to move to the battleship. Although I wrote such a brave paragraph nothing made me certain of the possibility of Japan ever emerging as a great power, the destruction was complete. What matters most is the spiritual destruction of national fibre and as I saw our people, they were simply a collection of wonder because the effect of our Emperor's broadcast to finish the war had come as a tremendous shock to the nation. They did not know where they stood and there were wild rumours circulating among the frightened public that the American Army of Occupation would work havoc upon the people at large. I thought nothing was more pitiable then the plight of our people who were collapsing under the shock of defeat. That was understandable but then I was almost despairing of the future of this nation. Twenty-seven years later, now we see Japan emerging a great prosperous nation, democratically, and as I look back upon the day I feel justified with great sense of gratification that what I wrote in the Foreign Minister's greeting to the throne came true and whenever I see the Emperor I recall this scene, which was very painful and poignant. But I know the Emperor himself also with great joy the fact that Japan has re-emerged as a free nation with future of greatness in front of her.

CHAPTER 33

SETTLING
ACCOUNTS

I tend to the view that the entire period between the Franco-Prussian War of 1870–71 and the collapse of the Soviet bloc in 1990 was, among other things, one long European civil war. It is certainly unarguable that the Second World War did not officially end until East and West Germany and the four powers that occupied Germany in 1945 signed a treaty in Moscow on 12 September 1990 that granted full independence to a unified German state. This was in lieu of the peace treaty that was meant to emerge from the conference on the future of Germany that took place in the Berlin suburb of Potsdam in July–August 1945. The third and last of the Big Three conferences saw the sole meeting between Stalin and Truman, who succeeded to the presidency on the death of Roosevelt, and the replacement of Churchill and Eden by Clement Attlee and Ernest Bevin after the Labour Party won the General Election of 26 July. The World at War *transcripts contained so much excellent Cold War-related material that I have sorted the best of it into two chapters. This, the first, covers the period of flux when American foreign policy was in transition from Roosevelt's high hopes for a New World Order based on the United Nations to the proclamation of the Truman Doctrine of containment in March 1947. At Potsdam the Americans took their eye off the European ball because of concerns that the war against Japan would drag on, and got the first hint of how thoroughly their government was penetrated by Soviet agents when Stalin scarcely blinked when told about the atom bomb. Although 'woe to the conquered' is perhaps the oldest and hardest rule in warfare, some would argue that the revolutionary precedents of international law developed for, and by, the Nuremberg War Crimes Tribunal represent the most significant achievement of the Second World War. They are inadequately explained in the transcripts, so I have added the text of the seven principles adopted by the United Nations in 1950 as a reminder that there was right as well as might involved in this greatest of all wars.*

AMBASSADOR W AVERELL HARRIMAN

President Roosevelt's Special Envoy to Europe

Recently the high-powered papers of Roosevelt have been made public and there you can see the very tough exchange of telegrams on both sides between Stalin and Roosevelt, which make it very plain that before he died he knew that Stalin was breaking agreements. The Polish situation was one of them. When we got back to Moscow the commission that was set up of Molotov, the British ambassador and myself was making progress, but then Stalin accused Roosevelt of perfidy in connection with the possible surrender of the German armies in Italy and sent him some very rough telegrams accusing him of being treacherous.

SS GENERAL KARL WOLFF

Governor of North Italy 1943–45

I was understandably deeply disappointed that the highest National Socialist leaders did not stand up and answer for the deeds they had done in the past and they had left those of us who could not be made personally responsible in the lurch. I personally thought it was necessary, with a heavy heart, to volunteer to take Himmler's place on the accused bench in the first big Nuremberg trial. The Americans, however, did not accept my offer because they were worried that I would be called as a witness to the witness stand ... and that I would be questioned by the Russians about the secret of the Italian capitulation, the revelation of which at this point in time was highly undesirable as far as the Anglo-Americans were concerned.* So in order to avoid this they declared me mad and they took

---

* In May 1945 Wolff negotiated the surrender of all German forces in northern Italy with the Americans. The Russians learned about it from the British traitor Kim Philby.

me to the madhouse in Bamburg on my forty-sixth birthday, where I was locked up in a room with sixteen complete madmen with brain damage, paralytics and syphilitics in the last stages. And it was incredibly difficult to survive this time unbroken and to get out of there alive at all.

AMBASSADOR HARRIMAN

There was another issue which was very close to Roosevelt's heart, and that was Stalin did not carry out the agreement we thought we had made to admit our relief teams to contact prisoners of war as they were liberated by the Red Army's advance. We wanted to send them right into Poland and he wouldn't let us do it, and Roosevelt was very bitter about that. Some of the people that I know who agree, talked with him, some of them have written about it. I left as soon as Roosevelt died to go back to see Mr Truman. I wanted to be sure that President Truman understood the position of our relationships because there had been so much folly in the air about the warm relationships that existed with our gallant allies. President Truman was an avid reader, he was a man of very few words, you could carry on a conversation with him in a very few sentences, and I found he'd read my telegrams and understood from those messages the difficulty we were going to have. I didn't have to tell him very much, he asked me some questions but he told me at that time, 'I was not elected President – Roosevelt was elected President. I must understand what Roosevelt wanted to do and carry out what he wanted to do.' So any thought that Truman tried to change Roosevelt's policies was utterly untrue – he tried to do everything he could to carry out what Roosevelt had undertaken to do.

JOHN McCLOY
US Assistant Secretary of War

I don't know who was the first man that told him about the bomb. He wasn't aware of what was going on when he had been Vice President, but Secretary of War Stimson was the first one that really gave him a thorough briefing on what had been done preparing the bomb and what its implications were. He spent a great deal of time with the President on this subject. Mr Stimson was very much involved during the latter part of his term as Secretary of War, this was his main preoccupation – what are we going to do about this, what are its implications not only in terms of the Japanese war but in the post-war period, this great new force that's been introduced into the world. Stimson was quite a religious man. He could be profane on occasion but he was a very devout man and he had a real sense of responsibility for this new force because he really devoted himself to its development and contact with the scientists, so he was anxious to get over to the President all these implications. Mr Truman's reactions were rather stunned, rather amazed, it took him some time to grasp its full implications.

AMBASSADOR HARRIMAN

Stalin was very moved by Roosevelt's death and he felt – he gave an indication that he felt – that the future which they had been building on for the world might be interfered with. He asked me whether Truman would follow Roosevelt's policy and I said I felt sure that he would, and he said, 'Tell him I will give him full support. The world will look upon the situation with the great concern I think.' He was only going to send Deputy Foreign Minister Vishinsky, which was rather a slight, and Molotov objected at once and whispered in his ear. Stalin brushed him aside but said, 'Molotov, will go.' Although Molotov was far more difficult to deal with than Vishinsky personally, I felt it was of some importance as an indication of his concern – interest in – the United Nations.

ALGER HISS
Director of the US Office of Special Political Affairs
The United Nations conference was scheduled for 25th April. On the night of the 23rd Molotov, having come to Washington on his way to San Francisco, had a meeting with Truman and some of Truman's top advisers. By that time those who had been on a leash had been removed from their leashes and they were the chief advisers Roosevelt had in preparation for it. By that time the Polish situation had crystallised: the Russians were moving forward, they seemed to be paying no attention to the kind of provisional government that the British and the Americans had hoped for,

and therefore angry protest were going to the Russians about that. Truman decided to have a showdown – at which he was gifted. On that occasion he accused Molotov in effect of violation of the agreement. This was a strange thing to do in the midst of a war by no means yet won, with an important ally. And it ended by Molotov saying, 'I've never been talked to like this in my life,' and Truman saying, 'Well, if you keep your agreements, you won't be talked to like that,' just like a schoolteacher. Secretary of State Edward Stettinius, who had been present, told me the next morning that he was still shaken and I thought the whole conference was off.

AMBASSADOR HARRIMAN

It was one of the first diplomatic conversations that Truman had and I can only say that Truman used good, solid Missouri language, which was very definite. Molotov had talked to other people that way but no one talked to him that way. So he was very much upset and gave the impression that this was a new voice and not Roosevelt's any more. So I felt it was important to have Stalin realise that there was really no change. Hopkins was the man that Stalin knew, and had a high regard for him because he was the first Westerner that came only a few weeks after the Hitler attack on Russia, and he showed him consideration in the way that I hadn't seen him show anyone else. I suggested to President Truman, and he finally agreed, to send Hopkins who was quite sick and he got up out of his sick bed and went to Moscow. Stalin received him warmly, he was there with his wife and there was a certain good came out of the trip. There were one or two difficulties about the United Nations, which was settled at that time. And so Stalin accepted it as an important gesture. But on Poland, Hopkins thought he had got Stalin to make certain fundamental concessions; they were only superficial, and I was quite sure they wouldn't be of value but Hopkins came home feeling that he had achieved something.

JOHN McCLOY

There was a difference of view in regard to that, I think the predominant view was the sooner we get the Russians into this situation the better. I remember one of the very first meetings I had with Mr Truman, somewhat to my immediate surprise he said, 'I think my main objective now is to bring the Russians into the war [against Japan].' I didn't happen to agree with that. I thought we had the Japanese licked without them and it was no problem bringing them in. There was a number of people who had a very strong feeling that it was necessary to bring the Russians into the war in order to avoid further casualties, but there was another view present that it was really pretty late in the game and the Russian contribution couldn't really amount to very much and we were having already some difficulties with the Soviets in other theatres and why complicate this one in view of the enormous contributions that we had made towards a victory.

DR STEPHEN AMBROSE
American historian

Potsdam was not that concerned about Poland because the Polish question had already been decided by the physical fact that the Russians controlled Poland. The West could make verbal complaints but there was nothing they could do about it, short of going to war with the Soviets, and no one in the summer of 1945 gave it any serious thought at all except General Patton. But that was Patton's bravado and bluster and no one in positions of authority ever took such nonsense seriously. The Red Army would have marched on to the Channel and possibly over to England itself; the end result would have been the Russians would have controlled all of Europe. The West was simply not as strong on the ground as the Soviets.

AMBASSADOR HARRIMAN

Churchill and Eden were there for the early part of the talk, and then the new team came – Attlee and Bevin. So that was somewhat of a break. The discussions were businesslike, cordial, but there were no fundamental agreements that had very much influence on the future. I thought leaving open the Oder–Neisse line was a very great mistake. Stalin wouldn't agree to that and Secretary of State James Byrnes wanted to go home and he made the suggestion of leaving the border to a peace treaty. I thought that was extremely dangerous at the time and I'm very glad that as a result of

Willie Brandt's initiative the Germans themselves agreed to accept the Oder–Neisse line.* It could never have been changed, since the Poles occupied it without war. But they never really got to grips with any of the issues that were troubling us. Truman had the war in Japan very much in his mind. He was still very anxious to get Stalin to carry out his agreement to attack in Manchuria three months after the defeat of Hitler because the American Chiefs of Staff were still saying the war would last eighteen months and we'd have to land American troops on the plains of Tokyo and there would be a million casualties to achieve the objective. They overestimated, this is always the case: the military overestimates the capabilities of the enemy and somewhat underestimate their own.

ANTHONY EDEN

British Foreign Secretary

Truman, whom I respect highly, was entirely new to the business and his approach was therefore less experienced than FDR's and though he tried to make it very businesslike and firm, in fact I think in his very difficult circumstances, the arrangements reached were not those we wanted, particularly about the Oder–Neisse line. When Churchill and I left, we were very emphatic that we could not agree to those arrangements and I know that Bevin, whom I talked to about this at Buckingham Palace when we exchanged offices, was very conscious of how he must stand up against that situation. But in the events partly caused by our delay in being away, we weren't able to hold out against that, and the arrangements at Potsdam were not those that we wanted in respect, particularly, of the Oder–Neisse line.

AMBASSADOR HARRIMAN

Churchill wanted to stand on the Elbe, he wanted American cooperation but Truman was being advised that we had to redeploy all of our forces to

---

* West Germany refused to accept the Oder–Neisse line as the permanent frontier with Poland until Chancellor Brandt recognised it by treaties with the Soviet Union and Poland in 1970.

the Far East and he couldn't have done it. Whether that would have been a wise thing to do, some people say we shouldn't have done it, but what would have happened? The best we could have expected would be some agreement which might not have lasted. They had a free election in Hungary and it didn't last and any agreement made under duress, if it had been successful at all, would have been valueless. Secondly, if we stood on the Elbe they would have not permitted us to move into Austria as they did and Austria would be behind the Iron Curtain. But when I think beyond that, then it would have been clear that we would have been responsible for the Cold War. Instead of that, it's quite clear that we did everything to carry out our agreements and it was Stalin that broke them.

DR AMBROSE

Already Western leaders were deeply suspicious of Soviet intentions, primarily because of the Polish question. Russian actions in Poland and eastern Europe were feeding Western suspicions about Stalin's attentions; by Potsdam the feeling, especially in the States and most especially with President Truman, was that, 'Ah, Stalin is another Hitler.' They didn't think, Oh, we made a great mistake in the war and backed the wrong side – they were perfectly clear Hitler was the greater menace and had to be crushed, and that the crushing of Hitler absolutely depended on the Red Army. Once the vacuum had been created you were faced with the fact that the Americans were demobilising, or redeploying, pulling the Army out of Europe and getting ready to send it over to Japan because they expected at that time to have to invade the home islands for the final defeat of Japan. The British are quite clearly exhausted and not capable of controlling the continent by themselves, and there are three hundred Russian divisions in East Germany and these loomed large in everyone's thoughts.

ADMIRAL LORD LOUIS MOUNTBATTEN
Supreme Allied Commander South-East Asia
The first thing I did at Potsdam was to have a meeting with the Combined British and US Chiefs of Staff to discuss our future operations. I also talked on our combined plan for defeating the Japanese completely. I was

then asked whether I would be prepared to take over practically the whole of MacArthur's theatre so that he could concentrate on the assault on the islands of Japan themselves. And I said yes, but not until I'd really advanced down below, opened the Straits of Malacca and was in a position to take over the files, the Intelligence Officers and the information needed to carry on when the war goes to them. Then I was invited to see President Truman and he shut all the doors and told me in great secrecy the fact that the Americans had an atomic bomb, which they were going to drop very soon, and which he thought would bring the war to an end. He even said the reason for his decision was that this would save thousands upon thousands of Allied lives which would otherwise be lost in that frightful massacre, which would take place on the shores of Japan itself. Then Churchill told me the same thing. He said, 'They will surrender and what are you going to do about it?' I said, 'Well, you've only just told me – I haven't given it a thought.' He said, 'You must go in with your soldiers and you must take possession immediately. How will you do that?' I said, 'Fortunately I have a great operational force at the moment with a quarter of a million soldiers which I'm going to land in Malaya and we're going to seize Malaya and Singapore very quickly.' He said, 'Send a telegram as soon as the bomb drops to your deputy Supreme Commander to sail your convoy at once.' I said, 'I can't do that, they've got to be tactically loaded, it's going to take some time.' 'Nonsense, tell him they can sail on the assumption there'll be no opposition when they get there.' I said, 'May I tell him about the atomic bomb?' 'Certainly not, it's much too secret.' I said, 'They'll think I'm mad if I send him a telegram like that.' 'Discipline, discipline, they mustn't question your sanity, they must do what they're told.'

JOHN McCLOY

I remember I was at Potsdam and the debate that went on there, when we should tell the Soviets about the bomb. I think very early we came to the conclusion we had to tell them, the bomb hadn't really exploded at that point and this was one of the reasons given for not telling – suppose it doesn't explode. So with bated breath we told Stalin about the bomb and waited for the effect. To our great disappointment Stalin seemed to be thoroughly unimpressed with it, we thought he'd be flabbergasted but he just let it pass off. Whether he knew about it already, there'd been some defections, whether he didn't want to show any great emotion in regard to it, I don't know. All I know is he took it very much in his stride and went on to the next item on the agenda. This rather dismayed Stimson because he thought this would immediately be a great Russian rush to sit down and talk to us about the future implications, what the future uses of it were, but he got no encouragement at all.

ANTHONY EDEN

Even after the first proofs of the power of the atomic explosion, some people were quite sceptical about its military decisiveness. I remember Admiral Leahy being in rather that tone of mind. However, it was agreed between us that Truman should tell Stalin of this discovery briefly and Churchill and I knew this was going to happen and we watched the scene with some interest. Just as we adjourned Truman went up with his interpreter to Stalin and told him and all Stalin did was nod his head and say thank you quite gently, and his expression changed in no way. That's how much the Russians had already discovered beforehand, and that's why it was received as a quite ordinary piece of news.*

DR AMBROSE

Molotov raised the question of what happened to the Italian colonies, he wanted to know, and Churchill said, 'We took them,' and Molotov said, 'That's very interesting – who made that decision?' And Churchill said, 'Well, of course, we conquered them, so now they're ours.' Italy of course had been an enemy of Russia, Italian armies had invaded Russia and the Russians had felt that they ought to have some kind of say in what was going to happen to Italy and to the spoils that had been taken. Truman raised an

---

* Eden was referring to the penetration of the Manhattan Project at Los Alamos by Soviet spies Allan Nunn May and Klaus Fuchs, backed by the Rosenberg ring in New York.

eyebrow when Churchill said 'we took them' because the Americans had participated in the process of liberating North Africa, and Churchill then replied that he meant Libya.

ADMIRAL MOUNTBATTEN

Just as soon as Mr Attlee became Prime Minister he sent for me and he discussed what I was going to do. I told him the instructions I'd had from Churchill, which he completely agreed; he then asked me how I proposed to handle the political problems and difficulties faced when such a large part of the world which had been under colonial administration now suddenly being liberated from the Japanese. I told him that my policy would be the same that I had done in Burma, to come in as friends, as liberators, as people who wanted to help them, not wishing to exact retribution and vengeance, and trying to find a friendly way to proceed in the future with the various governments which were responsible for them. He said, 'I entirely agree. Go ahead and do just that, you have my full backing, you have my full trust.' That made all the difference because I don't think I would have quite the same sort of directive from Churchill.

DR KONRAD MORGEN

SS investigating magistrate

After Auschwitz, I could only shudder when I thought about Germany's future, and I said to myself, If we lose the war the our opponents will tear us apart. I could not actually imagine that we would lose the war, although all the signs made it look that way. Despite the criminal tendency of the leadership I had observed in all my investigations, I still did not believe that this same criminal attitude would be turned on their own German people. In their defence, they were certainly obstinate, they were mad and believed that these were their enemies and must be destroyed. But they were enemies – their own people had done everything their leadership had asked of them and made a superhuman effort. When the people at the top have realised we have lost the war, there is no point in fighting any more – why do they go on and ruin the last few remains of Germany? No government can possibly be so criminal.

SIR HARTLEY SHAWCROSS
Chief British prosecutor at Nuremberg

At the beginning of the war I suppose we in England were much too busy fighting for our lives to think what we were going to do if we won the war. But right at the beginning, before the Americans came into the war at all, President Roosevelt warned the Germans that at the end a terrible retribution would be brought against them. And later, in 1942, he promoted the idea of a trial of war criminals, that is to say of the persons who had been responsible for launching the war on the world. As time went on we discussed it – we British at first were not in favour of a formal trial and the Russians were not in favour of it. We came round gradually to the view that there ought to be a trial rather than executive action and the Russians were persuaded to take the same view. Early in 1945, the spring of 1945, it was decided that there would be a trial of those leaders of the Nazi war movement whom we were able to lay our hands on.

ALBERT SPEER
Nuremberg defendant

In the time of Hitler's government we had never chanced to see each other very closely. We were together in parties or we were together at the dinner table in Hitler's Chancellery, but always we were remote. Now after the war we found each other again in a first camp we had to go through before Nuremberg, and we could see new arrivals through a large picture window. We didn't know who's still alive and who is not, because everybody had said he would commit suicide. Now those people were coming up one after the other and we were very closely together. We were starting to talk and somebody said one day, 'It's a pity we haven't had this experience years ago to be together for a long time and have the discussions out.' In this camp I was only a very short time because then I was fetched by car and taken to a camp of the high technicians in the armaments ministry. But afterwards, in the Nuremberg trial, there was a split among those accused in the dock because Göring and the others wanted to start a new myth about Nazi Germany, to give a small platform for Nazi movement, and in my opinion it was absolutely necessary for history's sake but also the sake of the German people, that they get rid as quick as possible of those ideas and go into a new life. Göring and those around him were treating me harshly and didn't speak no more word through the end of the trial.

DR ROBERT KEMPNER
Pre-war Prussian Ministry of the Interior lawyer who fled Nazism
A few weeks after the war I came back to Germany as a member of the American team and assistant to chief American prosecutor Justice Robert Jackson. At that time I took from another agency leave for three months and instead I remained for five years. I started the opening of the doors and I participated in the closing of the known back doors. It was a fascinating experience. One of the biggest helps to us was the German bureaucratic sense – they kept everything and they even made publications and films and a lot of material had been discovered by our Allied search teams, sent in right after the troops went into Germany. Some of the people like General Governor Frank of Poland was so anxious to show his friend Hitler after the war what he has done that he kept his diaries, volumes and volumes and volumes. In fact he had written his own indictment. Other people had also written their own indictments, like the Nazi philosopher and Reichs Minister for the Occupied Eastern Territories, Alfred Rosenberg. We discovered from him folders and folders and folders and he had also written his own prosecution brief.

SIR HARTLEY SHAWCROSS
The purpose was twofold. I was more interested in the second purpose than the first. The first was retribution, the punishment of people who had launched this war against the world – and not only the war, but who prior to the war and during it had committed the most terrible crimes against humanity. The second purpose of the trial was, as we had hoped, to lay down the rules of international law for the future, not only making the waging of aggressive war unlawful, but for the first time making the statesmen who led their countries into aggressive war personally responsible for what they'd done. That was the great innovation of the Nuremberg trial.

Hitherto you could say that a state was guilty of a breach of international law and you could impose some penalty on the state, but no penalty on the individual leaders of the state who did in fact involve it in the commission of illegal acts.

LIEUTENANT J GLENN GRAY
US Army Intelligence Officer

I was always the defender of the Nuremberg trials, a first step in some kind of international court. It was too bad that only the victors were the judges, but I would like to see such international courts after every war. With all the faults of the Nuremberg trials it seems to me they seem to represent a step forward in our rather pathetic attempt to make a better and more liveable world. Obviously lots of my friends disagree with me, but I had a little sympathy for the prisoners in the dock. I would have loved to see Sweden and neutral countries being in the judges seat, but this did not seem to be possible. A rough approximation of justice seemed better to me than nothing at all.

SIR HARTLEY SHAWCROSS

When I first went there I was rather surprised at the appearance of the defendants. I thought, well, if I'd seen these people in the Clapham omnibus I wouldn't have looked at them twice. I think this was true of all of them, except perhaps Hess and Ribbentrop, who both looked pretty miserable creatures, and Göring who looked a very remarkable personality. He'd lost a great deal of weight, he'd been kept off drugs and he was a very much shrunken figure – but nonetheless he was a dominating personality and in a sense all through the proceedings, although he only took an active part in them when he was giving his evidence, he did dominate the court. He was the outstanding personality in the court, and you know sometimes in the course of a long trial like that, lasting over two hundred days, something would go wrong. You would ask a question and the answer you expected would be yes and the witness would answer no, and at that point you had to be very careful not to catch Göring's eye. He was sitting at the corner in the front row, and if you glanced across at him, or caught his eye when there was an incident like that, he would raise his eyebrow or shake his head in a rather smiling way, and it would be very difficult not to smile back.

ALBERT SPEER

When we saw these films in the concentration camps I was almost out of my mind that such things had happened. And it was just too much to get the meaning of it, things which are too high, too much impression to swallow them. I now remember what someone told me in 1944 when he said he never visited a concentration camp, there are horrible things going on. And this I think was worse, I did in my whole life not to have any reaction of this, sign of recognising what was happening with the so-called Final Solution. There was also small other hints and altogether should have led me to some action, but I was silent. I didn't go to Hitler, not to Himmler, not to anybody, and now being in the dock, I thought the only way out is to tell the judges that I not only feel responsible for everything which was ordered in my government including the foreign-worker programme, but also everything which happened during the time I was minister in the government of Hitler, that was all the crimes committed by Hitler.

LIEUTENANT GRAY

A great many soldiers told me that when they raised their hands and took the oath, they absolved themselves of any responsibility for their deeds. I couldn't tell whether this was an elaborate rationalisation or whether it was sincere. The Germans in Nuremberg used the same argument, loyalty to Hitler, their personal oath to the Führer. This is an attempt on the part of the individuals to escape their own shadow and it must be a nearly universal quality. Many of them feel this way; they don't only use it as a rationalisation. I think the burdens of being individually responsible are something we would all like to escape. I must say I never felt this way. I have perhaps too little sense of loyalty but I didn't think President Roosevelt could absolve me from wrong deeds, but I may be an exception here. I think it is a very widespread tendency, especially in wartime, to say my commander is responsible for what I do.

DR OTTO JOHN

German Resistance member who formed part of the prosecuting team at Nuremberg

There was much pretending after the war that for many their oath was a barrier. I mean pretending that they couldn't act against a man to whom they had sworn an oath of allegiance, and we always pointed out to such people, at least those with whom one could discuss the point, we pointed out that Hitler broke his oath so there was no reason to keep the oath towards him. I think it was used more after the war as an excuse than it was factual.

DR MORGEN

You always think the terror can't increase and the disappointments you have in your life can't be worse, and then I had to go through it all in Nuremberg. I had the doubtful pleasure of meeting the man who had been Himmler's Personal Assistant, a very small man, a Mongolian face, very wiry, who was particularly noteworthy in that he rushed round the prison yard like a sewing machine with rapid little steps with a never changing rhythm, without ever showing any signs of tiring, despite the poor food we were getting in prison then. I came from another camp and knew how the American investigators, the CID, was behaving there. Little fish who had been no nearer than a kilometre from a concentration camp were being beaten with chains. They were forced to drink petrol, they put them in hot chambers just to get them to admit to crimes which they hadn't even committed. And I told that to this man and I said, 'The least you can do for your comrades is make a full confession because they are bound to find out in the end what you have done, and the commands you worked out.' They were so cowardly right up to the very end.

LIEUTENANT GRAY

We had war criminals and the Soviets had too. I would have liked to have seen an impartial court trying both sides, extremists on both sides. That would have been an impartial justice and taken away some of the taint of the Nuremberg trials. I think we all have to look forward to an impartial international court. It would do a great deal, I think, to make combatants in warfare much more careful of their actions.

Principles of International Law recognised in the charter and the judgement of the Nuremberg tribunal, adopted by the International Law Commission of the United Nations in 1950.

I.   Any person who commits an act which constitutes a crime under international law is responsible therefore and liable to punishment.

II. The fact that internal law does not impose a penalty for an act which constitutes a crime under international law does not relieve the person who committed the act from responsibility under international law.

III. The fact that a person who committed an act which constitutes a crime under international law acted as Head of State or responsible government official does not relieve him from responsibility under international law.

IV. The fact that a person acted pursuant to order of his government or of a superior does not relieve him from responsibility under international law, provided a moral choice was in fact possible to him.

V.   Any person charged with a crime under international law has the right to a fair trial on the facts and law.

VI. The crimes hereinafter set out are punishable as crimes under international law:

Crimes against peace:

i.   Planning, preparation, initiation or waging of a war of aggression or a war in violation of international treaties, agreements or assurances;

ii. Participation in a common plan or conspiracy for the accomplishment of any of the acts mentioned under (i).

War crimes:

Violations of the laws or customs of war which include, but are not limited to, murder, ill-treatment or deportation to slave-labour or for any other purpose of civilian population of or in occupied territory, murder or ill-treatment of prisoners of war, of persons on the seas, killing of hostages, plunder of public or private property, wanton destruction of cities, towns, or villages, or devastation not justified by military necessity.

Crimes against humanity:

Murder, extermination, enslavement, deportation and other inhuman acts done against any civilian population, or persecutions on political, racial or religious grounds, when such acts are done or such persecutions are carried on in execution of or in connection with any crime against peace or any war crime.

VII. Complicity in the commission of a crime against peace, a war crime, or a crime against humanity as set forth in Principles VI is a crime under international law.

CHAPTER 34

FALLING OUT:
VIEWS IN 1970–72

The World at War *interviews were sometimes more illuminating about the early 1970s than they were of the war itself. The reason why the only non-participant interviewed was the American historian Stephen Ambrose, and why he was used to set the tone for the programme* Reckoning: 1945 … And After *appears to be that in 1970 he had published a well-received account of Eisenhower's war years and also gained notoriety for heckling President Nixon. One can sense a degree of editorial unease in this decision, because the dominant geopolitical fact of the years after the Second World War was that America shouldered the responsibilities commensurate with her power that she had so signally shirked after the First World War. The makers of the series wanted someone to capture that changed reality in a few words and the comments of such as Harriman, Hiss and Galbraith were too wordy to include in an already overcrowded programme. In 1998 Sir Jeremy Isaacs, series producer of* The World at War, *produced American TV mogul Ted Turner's 24-part* Cold War *series, but as the following pages indicate there was enough material collected for the earlier series to merit at least another episode. That would, however, have required the conceptual audacity to argue that the Second World War was not entirely over, which would have challenged the consensus prevailing in the early 1970s. While I am happy to use that argument now, I am not sure, in all honesty, that I would have done so then.*

It seems to me, an individualist rather than a collectivist by sympathy, that one of the greatest historic strengths of the English-speaking world was the old liberal belief that individuals knew better than governments how to live their lives and spend their money. That belief was undermined by the Great Depression and buried deep by the powers necessarily accumulated by governments during the Second World War. Since The World at War *was made many of those powers have receded. Although the view from 2007 is probably no clearer than that in 1973, perhaps the continuing erosion of excessive state power and the restoration of personal responsibility and autonomy will be seen in the future as the last campaign of the Second World War.*

DR STEPHEN AMBROSE

At the end of the war there was a great hope. No one dared to use the words Woodrow Wilson had used in World War One, that this was 'the war to end all wars', but that was the sentiment. There was great hope in the world that this would happen, that this was the last war, that the victors would now be able to cooperate in peace as they had in war, to see to it that the four policemen – as Roosevelt liked to refer to Britain, France, the USSR and the United States – would be able to see to it that there would be no more aggression in the world. That the war had meant something, that it had been fought for something rather than simply against Nazism; something positive, a better world was going to emerge. I suspect even Stalin felt it.

DR NOBLE FRANKLAND

From the point of view of the victors it was purely a defensive war. We had no aims, there was nothing that we wished to introduce, we simply wished to stop Hitler. The war was an extraordinarily simple one, almost uniquely simple, and the victory lay in preventing something, not in achieving anything. That accounts for the very complex situation which arose after the war. They were divided because the effort to stop Hitler was so great it introduced an entirely different power balance in the world. Before the war Britain and France were really leading major powers – or appeared to be, and it's what appears to be that counts. At the end of the war it was evident that Britain and France were now in a sense declining powers and this was due to the strength that was generated in order to stop Hitler. So the whole complex power balance after the war arose from a very negative action, in the sense that war was to stop things, not to start them.

GENERAL ANDRÉ BEAUFRE

I would say that the collapse of the French Army in 1940 has created the collapse of Europe, of Western Europe. Of course afterwards the defeat of Germany completed the phenomenon, but if the French Army had stood as it did in 1914–1918, then the situation in Western Europe would have been entirely different and all the decolonisation would have been entirely different and the position of the Russians and Americans would be entirely different. I think it has been the key event which has produced the history of today, and we are paying today the results of this defeat.

DR AMBROSE

The British had as many problems, if not more, recovering from victory as the Germans did recovering from defeat. What did Britain get out of the war? Not very much, she lost a great deal. Positively she got a moral claim on the world as the nation that had stood against Hitler alone for a year and provided the moral leadership against the Nazis at a time when everyone else was willing to cave in to the Nazis.

DR FRANKLAND

The great effect on Britain was to increase the speed at which the natural course of developments was taking place. The British one might say were a non-imperialistic empire; the British, in acquiring their empire, had been very reluctant to call it an empire. When Queen Victoria took the title of Empress of India there was an outcry, people said our queen being called an empress was ridiculous. She might have declined the offer had it not been proffered by Disraeli, who had a particularly charming way of putting those sort of propositions. It wasn't really a very British idea. We are a trading people and the empire was really a by-product of trade. When the empire served its purpose, created communities, set up trade patterns, it really ceased to have a political significance in terms of an empire. And things would have gradually developed in much the way they have developed, but the war accelerated this.

AMBASSADOR CHARLES BOHLEN

I think the collapse of British power was inevitable, one of the reasons was that nobody, and I doubt if you did either, foresaw the loss of power that Great Britain would suffer following the dissolution of the empire. I know that Roosevelt firmly believed that there would be three great powers in the world, China was one by courtesy, France also to some extent, but I mean that Britain, the United States and the Soviet Union would be the three dominant powers. And when it turned out not to be the case, this was brought sharply to our notice in February 1947 when the British Embassy sent us a note saying they could no longer bear the burden in Greece and Turkey, which led to the Truman Doctrine. And then came the Marshall Plan, which was probably the most successful adventure in which we would jointly engage with you and other European countries, which then necessitated some consideration of security in the area. And that produced the North Atlantic Pact. Those were the twin foundations of American foreign policy which formed our actions in the world since that time.

SIR ANTHONY EDEN, EARL OF AVON

The war transformed the position of the United States in the world. For a long period America lived and grew under the protection of their own law and, it's fair to say, under the protection to some extent of the British fleet, which kept the seas open, and at peace. The two wars, particularly the second, plunged them into this leading world position from which there can be no withdrawal, and one cannot but have sympathy with them and with those Americans who are courageous enough to face up to these new responsibilities. America was founded on the idea that they'd get away from all that in the world, away from the entanglements of Europe and build up their own society. And here they are plunged into all these responsibilities, which they have to carry, and asked to bear the burden financially in a project like the Marshall Plan, and they did a wonderful job for Europe. And now they are finding things turn sour upon them, which is not in any way surprising.

DR AMBROSE

Economists in the United States felt during the war that the big problem was going to be a return to Depression conditions and they agonised over the problem of 'what's going to happen when we demobilise these armies and all of a sudden we are going to have twelve million unemployed again?' What they failed to recognise was that money was being made hand over fist in the United States during the war and there was nothing to spend that money on. So it was being saved and you had this enormous pent-up demand for consumer goods that only American factories could satisfy, not only within the United Stated but for Europe and Asia as well. So at the conclusion of the war, the United States went into a boom that made everything preceding it in America look like peanuts. This is when America really takes off and begins to dominate the world and what we think of as the American lifestyle today begins to take hold in post-1945.

PROFESSOR JOHN KENNETH GALBRAITH

I think it's easy to exaggerate the importance of economic interest in this but there's no doubt that with the passage of time the Cold War became a very great source of comfort and a reward to the military–industrial complex and we are finding how great that reward is now, as we try to reduce the scale of arms expenditure. I think it was more a general feeling that American well-being required European well-being, and vice versa. But by the time the Marshall Plan came, the worst fears of a post-war collapse had passed – 1946 and 1947 were rather prosperous years in the United States.

PROFESSOR PAUL SAMUELSON

The successful mobilisation of the economy by the government was a lesson not lost on anyone and right after the war we passed what's called the Full Employment Act of 1946. Very controversial, but this was the charter that from now on the American economy is not rugged capitalism, it's not laissez-faire, it's going to involve militant fiscal and monetary policy with a planning goal for high employment, for full employment, and we've done a tremendously better job in the post-World War Two period than was ever done by capitalism in its heyday. The expansion periods have been much longer, the periods of recession which we still have with us have been nothing short of anaemic. The one place where we haven't done such a good job is on the price front.*

ALGER HISS

The Yalta spirit disintegrated because of the new forces that had developed during the war, from a period under the New Deal when our industry was prostrate, when big business really abdicated its leadership, it had lost its own self-confidence and it was certainly discredited with the public as a whole. From that period until the end of the war, when a magnificent new industrial base had been created with new captains of industry in control, enormous expansion of the military with new generals and admirals in posts of importance. There was a power vacuum in the world and these people were not going to be denied their crack at it.

DR AMBROSE

In the case of Poland, Stalin simply couldn't allow the Polish colonels, the Catholic Church, Polish landlords to come back and take control. Poland, as he pointed out time and again, had three times in the past generated the gateway for the invasion of Russia. In Greece, for example, with the Greek civil war being waged at the time and the British very deeply involved fighting against the Communists, Stalin quite clearly lived up to the wartime agreement with Churchill and refused to support the Greek Communists. In France and Italy the strongest individual parties were the Communist parties and they had strong moral claims on the nation because they had led the resistance to the Nazis. It would have been possible for the Communists in both countries to raise all kinds of hell at a

---

* To put it mildly – the 'stagflation' of the 1970s destroyed the post-war Keynesian consensus.

minimum and go into armed revolt. One of de Gaulle's greatest fears at the end of the war was, 'Here we've got this resistance, Communist dominated and it's armed – what happens if they go into open revolt?' Stalin could have encouraged them to do so and create chaos in the West – but Stalin didn't want chaos in the West, Stalin wanted the West to recover so it could help Russia recover. And so he cooperated all along the line in France and Italy by telling the Communist parties there to cool it.

ALGER HISS

The signal element of conflict was Poland: other things were pretty well ironed out and that symbolised the Soviet insistence for what Stettinius regarded as security interest. Perhaps the Soviets are more aware of their security than we were. From their point of view the band of containing states must no longer exist. Poland was not going to be an outpost of the West, nor were any of the Balkan countries. They thought they had various agreements about spheres of influence with Mr Churchill: they left Greece pretty much in British hands; they could have certain proportional influences in Hungary, Romania, Bulgaria, particularly Poland. My impression at Yalta was that the Russians thought we had got the substance – not an unreasonable assumption because it was the underlying assumption of the United Nations charter – of co-existence. They could contend their interpretation was not followed by us because we did not allow them to run things as they allowed us to run Latin America. We sent agents in; we were in touch with unhappy dissidents remaining in those countries and our Military Attachés who served in those places were pretty busy about what have seemed to the Russians political matters. So when you have that bone of contention with neither side prepared to give up its position, you can only expect trouble.

LORD AVON

It's conceivable that the change in the American position was taking place before Roosevelt died. I read recently in some American source that there was a last message of his to Winston. A last message which was tougher and endorsing some of the things which Winston had said to him we must do in relation to the Russians. So perhaps a change would have come anyway. Certainly Truman, I know, felt the Russians were not carrying out the terms of their engagements and we ought to tell them so, and do all we could to correct what they were doing.

DR AMBROSE

US journalist Walter Lippmann pointed out the Americans were asking for an awful lot: they wanted to control the areas that their armies had conquered, but also wanted to have a major say/influence in the areas the Red Army had conquered. In 1943 when Italy surrendered the Russians wanted to be part of the occupation, but the Americans and the British systematically excluded the Russians. Stalin originally protested but then eventually he said, 'Ah, I see, a precedent has been set, the principle is clear – whoever occupies a country also imposes upon it his own social system.' The Americans were not willing to go along with that when the shoe was on the other foot. The Americans were demanding a major say in Poland while being totally unwilling to give the Russians any say in areas that their armies had conquered. The Russians systematically followed this principle for the remainder of the war and to the post-war period.

AMBASSADOR W AVERELL HARRIMAN

I had seen a good deal of Stalin during the war and I went up to him and I said, 'Marshal, this must be a great satisfaction to you after all the trials that you've been through and the tragedies that you've been through, to be here in Berlin.' He looked at me and said, 'Tsar Alexander got to Paris,' so it seemed perfectly clear to me, after what I'd been through before, that he had every intention of spreading his influence not militarily but through the Communist parties and he saw Europe wide open. All industry was disrupted – it wasn't only physical damage but there was also vast unemployment, hunger. I'm sure his Communist leaders in Italy and France told him we can take these two countries over. I'm satisfied that he thought that Communism could take over Western Europe either directly or else it would become some sort of glorified Finland under Russian domination. Instead of that Truman had the extraordinary initiative to recognise that something had to be done, and he authorised General Marshall to make his famous 1947 speech. Molotov was invited to the ensuing Paris conference but didn't sense the fact that if he'd stayed in Paris it would have been very difficult. Instead he said, 'We must find out from the Americans what they'll give us, and then divide it in accordance with the one that suffered the most should get the most' – which was Russia. But British Foreign Secretary Ernest Bevin and French Foreign Minister Georges Bidault took the stand and said the American offer was a cooperative, so Molotov left in a huff. Stalin declared war on the Marshall Plan, but there was no doubt in my mind Stalin thought economic conditions were such, he told me once, that there could be a Communist takeover. Communism bred in the cesspools of capitalism and Europe was in an appalling condition. For the United States to take such an initiative was really an extraordinary change. I think Churchill once said that if the United States behaved after World War Two as they did after World War One, Stalin would have challenged the British Channel at least.

DR AMBROSE

Soviet reconstruction could either be by forced savings on the part of the Russian citizenry, who had been through hell, but if you continued to make demands of them, force them to work, provide them with none of the ordinary consumer goods, Russia could rebuild on her own. This was the least desirable choice. A second choice, that worked hand in glove with it, was strip all the areas that you had conquered, just move everything that's movable and bring it back to the Soviet Union. Both of those were solutions that were followed. The third possibility was get investment capital from the United States and the Soviets did ask for a loan, but they were not about to let the Americans come into Russia, that is the enormous American corporations coming in making investments and taking control of the economy. They wanted a loan with no strings. The United States, when they discussed the loan with the Soviet Union, said, 'We want you to open up all of your books to us,' and they weren't about to open their books to the West. So the Russians were forced back upon themselves to reconstruct.

AMBASSADOR BOHLEN

Why the Soviets didn't join the Marshall Plan is not too difficult to discern, I think the main reason was that their system would not permit the kind of interplay that went on during the whole Marshall Plan for the countries that were receiving the aid. And the other thing is they were concerned about losing their control over the eastern Europe countries, which they helped set up, with the exception of Czechoslovakia. The terms of the Marshall Plan as drawn up in the speech were not drawn with the idea of keeping Russians out, but certainly they would not have got through the Congress of the United States just to give out billions of dollars to any country and say, 'Go ahead and spend it the way you want to.' They were really demanding and would require some form of joint responsibilities for the utilisation of this aid. At the end of the war there were considerable shortages in this country, some of which were in the field of materials that we were planning to send to Europe. There were three committees which were looking into the state of the American economy and to see how much we could afford to do, and they came out with plus answers that we could indeed afford it. The Marshall Plan was really pretty heavy going in Congress until the Russians helped organise the Communist coup in Czechoslovakia, and I think that really pushed it over the edge.

DR J GLENN GRAY

I think we felt unduly virtuous as victors in World War Two. We felt we had won because we were in the right, and that has led to unfortunate consequences in Vietnam and elsewhere. We Americans somehow have a feeling that we have a superior kind of virtue. We never fight until we are attacked, we never fight imperialistic wars, we are always the defenders of justice and so on. This again, by means of our policy of unconditional surrender, gave us an undue sense of virtue. It was almost too easy for us. After all, in both world wars America played not a central role or an important role, but all Americans seem to feel after World War Two that without us the Germans would have won. I'm not so sure this is true.

AMBASSADOR BOHLEN

The Cold War is not a new phenomenon in Soviet life: the Soviets began the Cold War on 8th November 1917. The only question is targets, changed from the beginning of the Soviet seizure of power. Virtually until the rise of Hitler you were public-enemy number one, the British Empire was all that was evil and wrong in the world, and a great deal of Soviet policy was geared to that conception. And for a while reality and fiction merged. After the war we were the chief obstacle, as they saw it, to the achievement of certain aims that they were after, we became public-enemy number one. We called that the Cold War because we were the victim of it – a term first used by [US representative to the United Nations Atomic Energy Committee] Bernie Baruch in October 1946, which is an interesting date because it came entirely from dealing with the Soviets over the Baruch Plan for control of atomic energy.

DR AMBROSE

The atomic bomb was tested while Potsdam was going on but there were only two atomic bombs and in 1945 they were used in Hiroshima and Nagasaki, so in practice the West did not have atomic bombs available to use in a war in Europe. The West did have a mighty Air Force, British Bomber Command and the United States Strategic Air Force. 'Tooey' Spaatz, who was the commander of the USAAF, strongly advocated, 'Let's leave the Air Force in being in England as a deterrent to the Russians.' All these ideas associated with the Cold War were very prominent in the minds of the American military, most especially the idea of deterrence.

ALGER HISS

None of us at any but the highest level knew of the atomic-bomb development; the first we knew was when it was dropped on Hiroshima, so I have to look back with hindsight.* I can only say, knowing something about Mr Baruch's cockiness and truculence as a person – and Mr Truman had some

---

* Hiss was fully aware of the development of the atom bomb – this is perhaps the clearest example of 'he who excuses himself accuses himself' in his long interview.

of these qualities – that if there was arrogance to American policy, possession of the atomic bomb did not minimise it. I consider myself a premature
revisionist. I was a revisionist before there were any other revisionists
because I saw things quite differently from the way many of my colleagues
did, and what happens in politics, as in art, is partly in the eye of the
beholder. They had been trained by different values than I – I was a New
Dealer, and there were not many New Dealists in the Department of State.

PROFESSOR GALBRAITH

It is true that in the late 1940s and 1950s American foreign policy passed
into the hands of the New York–Washington foreign-policy establishment.
Secretary of State Byrnes, whose knowledge of foreign policy depended on
position and not information, and it was the grandeur of the Dulles brothers [John Foster Dulles, Eisenhower's Secretary of State 1953–59; Allen
Dulles, Director of CIA 1953–61] as members of [the law firm] Sullivan &
Cromwell rather than their knowledge of the world which won them their
post, and in principle the only knowledge, the great fact of which they were
beholden was that their free enterprise was good and Communism was
wicked – and there was certainly a Cold War attitude, developed particularly
in the 1950s. As we now look back on it, it's dangerous and partly ludicrous.

LORD AVON

There've been many changes and formidable ones. The main difference I
suppose is that Europe's authority and power suffered very considerably.
Had the dictators not plunged us into that war, Europe today would be
the centre of authority over a wider part of the world. But as a result of
the war, Russia and the United States were left commanding the heights,
and European power by varying degrees was secondary and that position
has never really changed fundamentally, even the rise of China hasn't
changed that, so far.

DR FRANKLAND

The main effect was the nourishing of the spirit of nationalism in Asia. A
large part of Asia had been under British rule and most of that which had

not was under Dutch rule or some European rule. And the people were beginning to aspire to the creation of their own political institutions. The demonstration by Japan that the British could be beaten, and beaten very severely, naturally encouraged in the eyes of the people of South-East Asia the belief that they too might be able to secure a much stronger position against the British than they'd previously dreamed possible. This had a great effect on opinion on India and all over South-East Asia.

LORD LOUIS MOUNTBATTEN

Suddenly I found myself responsible as the Supreme Commander for an enormous area of the globe with a distance of six thousand miles across it, that's as far as from London to Bombay, with a hundred and twenty-eight million starving and rather rebellious people who had just been liberated, with a hundred and twenty-three thousand prisoners of war and internees, many of whom were dying and who we had to try and recover quickly. And at the very beginning I had some seven hundred thousand Japanese soldiers, sailors, and airmen to take in surrender, disarm and put into prison camps, awaiting transportation home. Even looking at that it sounded a big problem, but I had no idea what I really was in for. What I really was in for was trying to re-establish civilisation and the rule of law and order to this vast part of the world.

DR AMBROSE

Truman made the decision at Potsdam that no one would be allowed into Japan except for American troops. The United States had a major influence in western Germany, in France, in the United Kingdom and had its own industrial plant. What this meant was that of the six areas in the world that can support a modern war through industrial productivity – Japan, France, West Germany, Great Britain, USSR and the USA – the United States either controls or has a major influence in five of these. The Pacific has become an American lake: the US Navy has built bases throughout the Pacific during the war and it held on at the end of the war, and in addition extended itself into Japan and made Japan into a major military base. The one area of the world in which the United States did not have a predominant influence was the USSR but the Americans were in a very strong position in Asia because of their extremely strong position in the offshore islands, most of all in the Philippines, Japan, Okinawa and Formosa.

LORD LOUIS MOUNTBATTEN

It was of course an extraordinary stroke of fate that it all fell on the Supreme Commander, perhaps luckily because the Supreme Commander's not obliged to listen to anybody's advice, he is the dictator. I had very few advisers who were qualified to give me advice on this – very few people had studied this in military headquarters, after all – and I don't think that anybody particularly agreed with what I was going to do. But I must say they all followed it very loyally, they soon saw the point. I realised that I was setting the sign for all future developments of this sort, which is quite a heavy responsibility. I realised if I made the wrong decision there could be an absolute bloodbath throughout the world and indeed I believe any attempt at real suppression in my part of the world would have resulted in real civil war, in real fighting of a much worse nature than we had at any time.

DR AMBROSE

America wanted to have a very strong Japan, as a counter to the Soviets in the Far East and as a counter to what they feared was going to happen in China – already the handwriting was on the wall in China as to who was going to win the civil war there. The Americans wanted Japan rebuilt as quickly as possible and a highly industrialised Japan to emerge from the war within the American orbit. So they systematically excluded all of the Allies. The Aussies and the British had wanted reparations from Japan: they had suffered pretty badly at the hands of the Japanese and had a good claim for getting something back. The Americans absolutely refused and Japan had to pay no reparations at all. The Russians in the Far East, aside from gains of such places as Port Arthur, Manchuria and North Korea, get a Communist China. It's not clear that Stalin wanted a Communist China: he gave very little support to Mao to win the Chinese civil war. Both parties would soon enough have reason to wonder how good a deal they made, with the growth of Japan since the war and her economic position today, and obviously the Soviet Union has had enormous difficulties with China.

LORD LOUIS MOUNTBATTEN

I had two French colonels, one of them called Mitterrand, who at this precise moment is now Prime Minister of France. I had dropped him to the north of Vietnam and he was captured quite soon, and the very gallant fellow then escaped. In talking with General Philippe Leclerc, his aide reminded me quite recently that I said to him, 'When you go in with your troops I strongly advise you to make friends with the local insurgents to explain you've come back to help them, and not try and take vengeance on them. If you do that, then French Indochina will have the benefit of working with the French. If you go in, in a military way, in the long run you'll be defeated.' He said, 'I appreciate your advice, but I'm a soldier, my orders are to take over the military way and that's what I'll have to do.'

AMBASSADOR BOHLEN

For about twenty years, until the Vietnam business, the United States seemed to accept the world role that we had really thrust on us by history. Vietnam, to this country and to the effect of which is certainly not over, may take a number of years to really absorb and get over. What effect that has had on the American public's willingness to accept some responsibility abroad just has to be seen. I think there's certain areas where we still feel we have a duty, particularly in Israel. It is a certain open question as to whether the experience didn't give us a push in the direction of not so much isolationism as non-commitment.

PROFESSOR VANNEVAR BUSH

The lesson the Second World War taught us was to keep out of war. Fortunately I think the atomic bomb has done just that for the last generation and I hope and trust it will do it for another ten generations. By that time the world may become sane so that we won't need it. But you can be sure of this, no country, ruler or group of rulers is going to take its country into an atomic war for one reason – they know that no matter what else happens in that war, they themselves will not survive it. If they are not eliminated by the enemy they will be eliminated by their own people. As long as we have an atomic stand-off as we have today, I think we can rest and have bets with safety.

DR AMBROSE

Was a Russo-American conflict inevitable? Surely, no question – it mattered little if it was a Tsarist Russia or a Communist Russia. Of course all of these great world conflicts, of which the twentieth century had seen the worst, are always followed by a falling-out between the victors once they have lost everything that holds them together – the common enemy. Russian ambitions and American ambitions were bound to clash. Added to it is the ideological dispute between capitalism and Communism that heightened but did not create the tension. I think this is one of the few times in history when one can use the word 'inevitable'. I don't think there was a ghost of a chance of the Russians and Americans creating the kind of world they talked about during the war – an Atlantic Charter kind of world, or a United Nations kind of world, in which the victors continue to cooperate as they did during the war.

DR FRANKLAND

The principal effects of the war on people and political systems bore upon the countries in eastern Europe, Poland most of all, Czechoslovakia, Hungary, Romania and those countries. These people were hoping that the war would liberate them from the threat of Nazi tyranny and in fact at the end of it they found themselves in the Communist bloc, which was far less sinister than the Nazi bloc. This was a very solid achievement of the Second World War, a very much less sinister type of tyranny replaced a highly sinister tyranny. But this was not the freedom for which they'd hoped, and for which we had fought. But this was the product of Soviet power, which was necessary to the destruction of Germany. This was simply the price that has to be paid in order to gain the fighting alliance of the Soviet Union.

AMBASSADOR BOHLEN

The gains and losses from the war are a very big question and I don't know that I could answer because in the first place, if we hadn't won the war it would have meant that the Japanese and the Germans would've won it. And I just think you can imagine what kind of a world that would have been. It's true that the problem of Russia emerged shortly after the war, but I would say on the whole that was certainly the lesser of the two evils. Their society certainly didn't get much satisfaction out of the results of the war but I think this was inevitable within the Soviet system. On the other hand a large portion of the world is still able to exercise a certain degree of freedom, particularly in their internal affairs, and I think the world would have been quite intolerable under Nazi and Japanese rule.

GENERAL ALBERT WEDERMEYER

Well – did we win? The verdict of history will take account not only of the military victories won by the Allies but also of the tragic political results which flowed from those victories. We eliminated the tyranny of Nazism from Europe and of Japanese militarism from Asia, and we substituted the tyranny of Communism.

DR AMBROSE

There's a view around today that World War Two turned out disastrously for all concerned except possibly the Communists. I think one can be very positive about World War Two: the most important single result is that the Nazis were crushed, the militarists in Japan were crushed, the Fascists in Italy were crushed, and surely justice has never been better served.

MAJOR GENERAL OTTO-ERNST REMER

I am quite convinced that Hitler never wanted a world war because at the beginning of it we were not at all prepared for one. Our production was in no way up to it. One has to regard Hitler as a reformer and an innova-tor for Germany and for Europe. He wanted a new kind of society and he wanted Europe to be a counterweight to America's pure capitalism and

Russia's pure Communism. He wanted to create a form of living which suited us Europeans because we have to live in a very limited space compared to the two world giants. One has to look at Hitler in this light, as an innovator of a new form of life.

CHAPTER 35

REFLECTIONS

Remember, *the last episode of the series, began with an aerial shot of Oradour-sur-Glane, the French village where the Waffen-SS massacred the population as a reprisal for partisan activities. Hundreds of villages suffered the same fate on the Eastern Front. The programme did not mention that the officers responsible for the atrocity at Oradour died fighting with fanatical bravery in Normandy, perhaps because it would have pointed to the uncomfortable conclusion that men indifferent to their own survival are unlikely to be respectful of the lives of others. The tone was elegiac, dwelling on human loss but also, through the agency of J Glenn Gray whose important book* The Warriors: Reflections on Men in Battle *was published in 1970, seeking to say something profound about conflict. I think it worked well, and I have also used Dr Gray's eloquent words to give structure to what would otherwise be a grab-bag of quotable quotes.*

I am a baby-boomer, born ten months after VE day, and my life and career have been dominated by an acute awareness of what I owe to the sacrifices of the two generations before mine. They fought and killed and died in battle so that I should not have to, and for the freedoms we all take for granted. Perhaps they were not, intrinsically, better people than we are, but their times called for sacrifice and heroism and if afterwards they felt a sense of entitlement it is entirely forgivable. Hard cases notoriously make bad law and perhaps the same may be said about whatever conclusions may be drawn from the Second World War. We may not be called upon to find out whether we lack 'moral fibre', or to explore the ambivalence of lethal vengeance, but video footage of 'smart bombs' at work seems to have increased the fascination with destruction that worried Dr Gray so much. Humanity remains much the same and the world has been at war throughout history – it was simply convulsed by it, on an almost unimaginable scale, in 1939–45.

DR J GLENN GRAY
US Army Intelligence Officer and author
War is a study in extreme situations and one's mood does shift at an astonishing rate. You can be scared to death one minute and laughing the next, you can be filled with hatred one minute and filled with love the next. War is excruciatingly boring; I have never been so totally absolutely bored as I was in the Army. But I could also say that I have never been so intensely engaged and involved – a few minutes later, very often.

LEO GARIEPY
Canadian tank commander, D-Day
Sir, I was frightened when I left Canada in 1940 and I didn't stop being frightened until I got back home in 1945.

DR GRAY
I noticed different soldiers had different relations to death. One of the more common was that of a coward's relation, for him death is the greatest enemy. I had a friend called Mac who was convinced that every German was out to kill him personally and that every spot of earth where he was, was going to be the target for a shell or a bomb. He died a thousand deaths in my presence. He used to sleep beside me and he could tell even in his sleep when incoming shells landed within a mile or two. That kind of relation is negative. The opposite perhaps is the dare-devil soldier who almost courts death. In our southern France landing I was cowering under our Jeep because German shells were landing all around our boat, and I watched through the mass of harness and gear an American captain smoking a cigarette and flicking the ash off into the water, and I watched his hand, fascinated. It wasn't even quivering as much as mine is right now. I had the most irrational desire to creep through the gear and put my arms around him and embrace that fellow – although I've never wanted to embrace a man in my life.

SERGEANT BILL BECKETT

Sherwood Foresters group, Nottingham pub

We were in the front line at Anzio and there was somebody, one of his pals got sniped, got hit by a sniper, and he just grabbed his rifle and just went charging out of his position straight across into no man's land trying to find the bloke that had done it. I think Jerry stuffed about fifty bullets in him before he dropped. Everybody just stood there looking at him as he went crazy. A young chap. This is the kind of thing that people would never believe if you tell them. You know you've got to see these things happen to believe them.

DR GRAY

After a few weeks in the line I got away one afternoon and climbed up into the Apennines, and met the old hermit. I think he was significant for me, a perspective on the war. Here was an old man who was curiously uninvolved, remote from the war. I had been totally cut up by the war and couldn't imagine anybody who wasn't so. And the old hermit had a simplicity, a kind of naivety that enabled me to raise my consciousness. I happened to be reading *War and Peace* at the time and discovered that Tolstoy had found a few Russian peasants that never knew what Napoleon's army was doing in Russia or that it was even a foreign army. This doubled the perspective that I, a hundred years later, should meet somebody in Italy who didn't know that there was a war on, and what it was all about, gave me a kind of perspective and an insulation against the total involvement that hitherto had been my lot. He was sitting smoking dried Italian grass and I gave him a bowlful of my own good tobacco. I came from a farm and feel at home with farmers and country people. His donkey was near by and he had a little grass hut where he slept. We sat down and began to talk and of course the artillery in the valley below opened up and he began to ask me questions about the war and I gradually became aware that he didn't know what was going on. My attempts to explain faltered, not only because of my rather poor Italian but because I suddenly realised that I couldn't explain to him why Americans and Britishers were fighting in Italy against Germans, with Italians on both sides. It seemed an impossible task. Even had he been speaking my own language I wouldn't have been able to tell him what the war was about because I really didn't know myself in any deeper sense. It was one of those strange, curious experiences that enable one to step back, so I've never forgotten that old Italian.

BILL MAULDIN

American cartoonist with Stars and Stripes

The British 56th Division was still taking Salerno when we moved into it, that is our little group moved in to publish a newspaper. We took over this apartment, which I guess belonged to one of the local-government officials because he'd left, and it was a large and very elegant apartment. One room had a piano in it and I was sitting at the piano playing with one finger and sort of noodling around trying to think up a cartoon idea and this British soldier, I mean you couldn't have made a better cartoon of a typical British infantryman – he was grimy, he was dirty, he had his helmet on, he had his rifle, he had grenades all over him, and he had this young fifteen-year-old Italian chick with him, who was a very buxom lass who did not look inexperienced in spite of her age – and he nodded very politely and then ignored me totally and went to the cupboard in the corner and found some nice lace table napery, whatever it is. He found a doily which he placed on the floor – he was very delicate because the room was full of plaster dust – and proceeded to co-habit with this girl on the doily. And meanwhile I'm sitting there picking out a tune on the piano, watching the whole thing. They never gave me a chance to leave, really, and so then they left and the girl smiled over her shoulder at me and the soldier said, 'So long, Yank,' or something like that and went back out, back to battle. It was the weirdest and most sort of dreamlike thing I can remember out of the whole war, this little episode, which lasted all of five minutes.

DR GRAY

I experienced, all the way through in Italy and in France, the most amazing paradoxes, the contrast between the miseries of war and the insistencies of love. This kind of contrast made me think that love and war are indissolubly linked to each other in ways that haven't been dealt with sufficiently since the early Greeks – the very first documents of Western civilisation have dealt with the marriage of love and war, of Aphrodite and Aries. The women brought, specially in Italy and France but also in Germany, an element that was in striking contrast to the hideous experience of the day and I think many of the women themselves were tremendously moved by this experience. There was tenderness in these affairs that we found totally lacking in our ordinary military experience. The two complimented each other, often made possible soldiers day-to-day advances; I couldn't over-emphasise the importance of the element that women brought. Many of the affairs were casual, much of it simply the kind of sexual outlet, but I was impressed by a deeper element of tenderness, of seriousness, softness, kind-ness – one felt awfully grateful to the girls in those days for the experience of joy that they brought in an otherwise joyless existence.

DAME VERA LYNN
Popular singer and 'The Forces' Sweetheart'
I was trying to get over this togetherness bit, trying to bring the separated parties closer together. It was very difficult for a lot of the wives and sweethearts to actually write to their men folk what they really thought and what they felt, and by my singing the kind of songs that I did I was doing it for them, in a way that they could understand. The songs were simple, the lyrics were straight to the point and in a way interpreting their thoughts for them. I think that was what happened. In days of crisis there's always this feeling, this sentiment, which of course is nostalgia for the future. I had a set plan, and I hope it worked, and I think it did, just to bring separated beings together.

DR GRAY
I speak of the lust of the eye, a biblical phrase which I particularly like because much of the appeal of battle is simply this attraction of the outlandish. But there is an element of beauty in this. Soldiers learn to experience in warfare a kind of ecstasy which literally means getting outside oneself. I try to think of it in terms of an adjoining, one could be drawn into, absorbed by a spectacle, I think especially of southern

France, the terrific bombardment. Our planes coming over, I literally expected the coast to detach itself and go into the ocean. But to watch this was to forget you had to get into landing boats and make off the shore. It was just a terrific spectacle in which, I think everybody, including myself, was drawn into it, so we forget all about ourselves and it's not quite right to say we enjoyed it, we were totally absorbed, lost in the spectacle.

PROFESSOR ALICJA IWANSKA
Warsaw-uprising survivor, exile and sociologist
I have lost some dear friends but I still think that in comparison with other ways of dying, in particular with Poles of Jewish origin who were killed in the gas chambers, or in comparison with Poles executed by state execution, or death by accident, I think it's a great privilege to be killed for something. I think everybody would feel that way. There's nothing worse than impersonal death, it's not connected, you know. When you lose connection between merit and when you lose the idea of guilt then there is nothing left, you stop being human.

TOM FITZPATRICK
9th Australian Division, Eighth Army
The war was a turning point in my life in many ways. I think I was probably a self-centred man before the war, had a rather high idea of my own importance. But serving, in the junior ranks particularly, that may have helped. I was just one of millions of men whereas up to the war I felt that I was something more exclusive – that's hardly the word, but I do feel perhaps it gave me a sense of humility.

GUARDSMAN SHEARER
Scots Guards group, Glasgow pub
Although we were all as thick as thieves, we were so preoccupied with the business of eating, sleeping, fighting, surviving that we didn't really find time to have the sort of conversation that we might have now, sitting here. I certainly never remember discussing the outcome of the war or whether

the Germans were right or we were right or anything like that at all. I mean it was just day-to-day honest-to-goodness living together, and very pleasant it was.

WYNFORD VAUGHAN-THOMAS
BBC radio broadcaster

The strange thing about war, it was awful, miserable, burning cities, unbelievable squalor, a horror that no civilisation could go through, yet when you look back you don't remember the horror so much. The fact that there was somebody beside you who went through it all with you, and who occasionally took the burden on himself, was braver than you, who steadied your nerves, who was prepared to take risks that you weren't prepared to take, and a feeling of comradeship is the one thing that emerges out of any war. I know it's a cliché but it's there and it's what takes you through the war. That's really why I've become far more sympathetic to the British Legion. When I was young I couldn't understand why people would want to go to Cenotaph ceremonies. I go now, I am proud to go and I remember the people who don't come back. Perhaps the younger generation don't want to know about the war, but they darn well should know that there were people as young as themselves who died and sacrificed themselves, and out of it comes this terrible feeling in my mind of waste, and yet of proud comradeship.

PRIVATE WHITMORE
Sherwood Foresters group, Nottingham pub

We were all one big happy family, there was no doubt about that, and what was yours was mine and what was mine was yours sort of thing. It helped to broaden your outlook on life a bit, especially someone like myself who'd never seen the sea till I was in the Army. I didn't realise there was such things as Geordies and Scousers and all that sort of thing. I suppose it did us all good in one sense – it'd perhaps do some of them good today to go in the Army.

DR GRAY

It's something less than friendship, it's one of the basic kinds of community, people who have been together in danger – exposed, hardship – have a certain feeling for each other, a dependency on each other that is very strong, a very intense emotion, much of it unconscious, unreflective at least, but very real. This deserter has lost his comrade and felt that he lost a particular part of himself. I couldn't exaggerate the importance of comradeship, it's what we mean by morale. In the Army, soldiers train together who fight together, eat and sleep together, begin to feel their egos are social and communal, no longer are they contained within their own skins. They can re-create this experience and these experiences are something at least I avoid as I would the plague. There's something very artificial about it if you have ever been to a Legionnaire convention, these middle-aged balding pot-bellied men, trying to behave as they did in the war and don't succeed – it's very sad, very pathetic. Perhaps one should say this experience of comradeship is something very different from friendship, it's real, it's intense, but it's brief and it's related to the context of the experience. There's no such thing as re-creating it; you can't have a buddy after you have been long enough in civilian life.

JIMMY THOMAS

Merchant seaman

What I found when I came home, and I've been disgusted with myself ever since, was that the readjustment to their kind of life, the life that I'd led before myself, was virtually impossible because however much you hate being in a war the things you come back to seem very, very trivial. The local council talking about a new gents' lavatory and things like this don't seem to matter at all. And of course these things matter to the people around you so I shut up and shut myself in for about a year. I must have behaved extremely badly. I'm well aware of it and I've never forgotten it and never cease to feel sorry for it because I think it must have made life pretty intolerable for people around me. But it was just that I couldn't communicate. I had lost my sense of communication with people that I'd known all those years because I'd begun to understand an entirely new breed of people who were all sewn together – being in a common thing, I think that was it. A lot of people I know, when I've mentioned this have said exactly the same thing. I couldn't be bothered to talk to my family at table or anything and I just kept getting up and walking out of the house and not coming back for hours. I think they were very upset.

DR NOBLE FRANKLAND

Bomber Command navigator, historian and Director of the Imperial War Museum

It is extremely various: lots of people are maimed completely, either mentally or physically, but I suppose the majority of those who survive, survive apparently intact. But there must be marked effects and I think in some ways the effects are very good on people because they feel that, to a certain extent, they've been able to fulfil themselves and I think a lot of people go right through life without ever feeling a sense of fulfilment. But those who take part in hectic war operations usually get a sense of fulfilment, especially if they believe in what they're trying to do, which I think in war people tend to do very readily. On the other hand there are very bad effects, perhaps one of the less obvious ones is that people who undertake these operations have a tendency to feel afterwards that society owes them something very special. And when the war is over they tend to go home and expect people to look up to them and to look after them, which is not what people are going to do at all. And I think that's one of the very bad effects of war; this produces a frustrated feeling in the man, and he feels society's cheated him and his effort was in vain and not worth while, which is tragic.

HERMAN PHEFFER

Disabled US service veteran

We had this orthopaedic surgeon from Baltimore and he gave the definition that I've used all these years about sympathy for the disabled. He says, 'Son, you know where you find sympathy? You find it in the dictionary between shit and syphilis.' I was very fortunate that friends of mine who came to visit with me brought along a fellow who had both arms off in

World War One, plus his buddy who had both legs off, also in World War One, and he showed me his appliances and the way they were made in those days – he had a couple of nude bathing beauties stuck on this appliances. He said, 'You're not going to dance, you're not going to roller-skate but you're going to do anything you ever want just as much as you want to do it – but', he says, 'you're the one who's going to do it, no one else.'

GUARDSMAN SHEARER

There was one time during the advance, approaching Münster, we were driving through the woods and demolition experts had set the charges and the trees would drop down. And, lo and behold, coming cycling along as large as life was the fellow who had set them off, on a pedal cycle, and behind him the trees were just dropping and he cycled towards us. He couldn't care less. What happened after that I'd better draw a blank over. He didn't finish the war.

DR GRAY

It's human nature, you notice it with boys who love to break windows to hear the glass tinkle, but there are a great many soldiers who take a pleasure in destroying people, wasting things and would kill beyond any kind of necessity. They took a delight in shooting anything that moved. I find this aspect of human nature is not discussed enough but it is one of the causes of warfare. I don't know what the limits are but I did know certain soldiers, killers, who are very distinct from ordinary soldiers who kill only when they need to, and who never become killers. It isn't all that different I suppose from the delight hunters have in killing antelope or deer. I discussed it as one of the appeals of battle in addition to the lust of the eye and appeal of comradeship. It threatens our whole civilisation and we in America have this kind of thing now in civilian life. I think it is an extreme in human nature where you can't simply go back and regret a few minutes later, it grows on you. And if you get experienced killers such as some of the SS were, and I'm afraid some of our own paratroops, no, you can't revert very quickly to regret. I don't say that people are incurable or anything but they tend to be pretty joyless types. I noticed them in rest camp: they would sometimes simply attack the locals, they were notoriously restless and even their own officers were often afraid of them. I don't know about artillery men and pilots. Pilots are people who kill at a distance but have a great delight in implements and in precision bombing and so on. But the further you are from the target the less likely you are to have any kind of real understanding of what devilry your weapons are causing. We're all unable to imagine what people are feeling a few hundred yards away. Lack of imagination is one of the greatest human weaknesses, I think.

DR FRANKLAND

There are always unhealthy members of society, this is one of the perennial problems of life, but I take, in general, the opposite view that it's unhealthy not to study these events; it's much better to come to terms with these dreadful things that have happened rather than try and sweep them under the carpet and pretend they didn't happen. I think children who confront these situations in the right way, at the right stage in their life, are far more likely to grow up as healthy citizens than those who, for perhaps idealistic reasons on the part of their teachers or parents, are denied the opportunity. I think this leads to much more complex psychological results than simply studying the facts and bringing them out into the open.

HARRY MITCHELL
British 50th Division, Eighth Army

I was a stretcher-bearer, I had no rifle or anything like that and I was frightened, running about in a sweat, and we eventually got into these holes and tried to find out who was where. There was this Italian lying above the ground outside this hole with not a stitch on where the blast had caught him. I realised there was no good my going to him and I got in the hole with a friend of mine, another stretcher-bearer, and we decided to have a smoke, open our Players and have a cigarette and talk of the sort of thing we'd gone through, you know, how horrible it was. And there was this Italian laying on top of his trench and all he kept saying was,

'Mamma mia, mamma mia'. After an hour or so everything was so quiet and eerie that he got on people's nerves and along somewhere one of our fellows hollered out, 'I'll give you mamma mia in a minute, mate,' typical Cockney expression. And he still said 'Mamma mia' and the next thing we heard was a .303-rifle shot and the 'Mamma mia' stopped – that was his lot, you know.

DR KONRAD MORGEN
SS investigating magistrate

I can still remember a conversation I had with the Reichs Doctor SS, Professor Dr Grawitz, in Berlin just before I went to Auschwitz. Dr Grawitz had a good reputation in Germany and in the learned international circles, and in particular his father was a great humanist and his son had a classical education. This highly intelligent man said to me, in relation to the dental gold, whenever he slept he dreamt about it, and he could feel little men who were hammering on his teeth and then he had to think of the dental gold that was disappearing in Auschwitz. But the fact that millions of human beings, daily, hourly were losing their lives – he didn't think about that, that didn't cost him any sleepless nights. The only human feeling one can credit this man with is that he had considered how one could kill people painlessly. In fact his biggest problem was that not just the killing itself should be painless but also that the victims should have no mortal fear beforehand. Death must come unexpectedly and suddenly. And this man had thought it all out, from apparently humane motives, but it transpired in practice that the cunning way they camouflaged and hid the truth was the only reason that this whole system ran so smoothly without a hitch on this enormous scale.

WYNFORD VAUGHAN-THOMAS

Belsen made me a stupidly determined optimist because you cannot believe that humanity is like this. If you do that, there's nothing ahead of us. If this is what lies underneath all our minds, if you take the lid off and there's a Belsen underneath, what are we talking about? I can't believe it, I mustn't believe it, I will not believe it.

URSULA GRAY

Dresden resident, post-war wife of author J Glenn Gray

I will always remember a couple under the next tree were quarrelling and it seemed to us so unbelievable. You are fighting for your life, you don't know if the next minute you are still on this earth and here they are quarrelling. It impressed me so deeply, we talk often about it, how people even under circumstances of despair still are basically the same. I'll bet these people were quarrelling at home and it made no difference that they are here in an air raid and next minute they might be dead. I have a very strong feeling that this should never happen to people. If they do not get any better for something like that there's just nothing we can hope for.

DR GRAY

It was a silly sight, when I first saw it everything was destroyed, his house and all of his premises, the fence even. The only thing left was the gate that was only partially destroyed and as I went by he was repairing the gate. I laughed but later I began to feel that this urge for preservation was a great contrast to the love of destruction and I've learned to cherish this preservation love because it is one of the few dependable enemies of warfare. After the war in Germany I noticed the Germans were building houses that seemed destined to last for a hundred years when they couldn't be sure that actually the houses would last for five years and I ask myself why do they build so solidly. The only answer is a deep impulse in man to build for the future, it gives them a kind of assurance that peace will last.

DR FRANKLAND

One of the greatest effects of war on people who take part in it is the extent to which it tends to cut them off from both their elders and their own children. One's parents, when one is at war, really either don't want to know, or are unable to know because warfare developed so rapidly and they can't envisage the circumstances that their sons are in. And the same thing applies in a different way between father and son. In my own relationship with my parents at the time, and with my children today, they in a sense neither can nor wish to envisage the circumstances in which we lived in the war. And we have a rather arrogant sort of feeling that they ought to understand these dreadful things that happened to us, but they don't. Now I think people are cut off from these generations. There is a generation gap under any circumstances but I think war, as in so many aspects of life, tends to emphasise those sort of considerations, and very much so in creating and nourishing a generation gap.

ALBERT SPEER
Nuremberg defendant

I think the consequences of Hitler's life are still obvious to everybody, not only in Germany but in the whole world, and many things we are suffering from are the direct result of Hitler's activities. So when I am saying that I can't have any kind of feelings about him, that's because of what he did to the world. And I am thinking too what he did to my family and myself, because to lose twenty years of lifetime and for children to grow up without their fathers is something which is caused by Hitler.

PRIVATE ROBERT REED
2nd New Zealand Division, Eighth Army

I thought we were part of the British effort – one British effort. In my own case when the war broke out I realised that it had to be fought and in my own heart it was a privilege to serve your country in its time of need.

J B PRIESTLEY
English author and broadcaster

I don't think I'm sentimentalising if I say that, to me – and after all I've lived a good long time now – the British were absolutely at their best in the Second World War. They were never as good, certainly in my lifetime, before it and I'm sorry to say I think they have never been quite so good after it.

GENERAL MARK CLARK
Commander United Nations in Korea

I'm not trying to get sentimental but as I've reached a ripe old age and look back on my experiences in World War Two, where as a comparatively junior officer I was catapulted into High Command, which was hard because I passed over a lot of older, equally capable friends of mine. But I think my greatest feeling of satisfaction was being associated with the British troops. I found them to be fine soldiers, perfectly willing to die if need be to accomplish their mission. We had our differences at times, as you naturally would, but when I was given command of your Fifteenth Army Group, a British Army Group with a completely British headquarters – in the middle of the night notified by Mr Churchill – I think that was my crowning period of happiness and pride. And I did take over the Fifteenth Army Group and I led it until the end of the war and took the surrender, as commander of the Fifteenth Army Group, of the German forces in Italy. I'll always be proud of the privilege of having that opportunity.

MICHAEL FOOT
Left-wing Labour MP

It is impossible to minimise the extent of how the whole public mind seemed to awake people with a great sense of community spirit during the war. It was the nearest thing that I've seen in my lifetime to the operation of a kind of socialist state – a democratic, socialist state of citizens believing that they could influence by their actions, speedily, what was going to be done, and that the whole world could be changed by the way they operated. They saw the world was changed by their actions in the war and they thought that could be translated into political action as well. It was extremely exciting but some of the political leaders, maybe because they were so deeply involved in their own pursuits, they didn't appreciate what was happening.

NORMAN CORWIN
American 'Poet Laureate of the radio'

World War Two shook us up – it made literally a melting pot of us. Men who had shared antagonisms and hostilities and distrust found themselves together on the same transports, in the same units, in the same trenches and in the same operations. The beginnings of racial integration I think can be traced back to that war.

BRIGADIER GENERAL LEON JOHNSON

Awarded the Medal of Honor for leading the attack on the Ploesti Romanian oilfields in August 1943

One thing you have to bear in mind – we did win the war. Maybe we made mistakes: I think you could say, well, you could have put this division against that division, this division did a great job and that division didn't do as well, or you could say this force did well and that force did less well. I think there's enough glory to go around – and enough pain and enough effort. You know, war is a nasty business. I'm not even sure who wins the wars. I don't know how you lose a war but it's awfully hard to know when you've won one. But the main point is that put together, working together, the Allies – and I bring in too the Poles and the Czechs and all the other people that belonged to the RAF, the RAF itself, the Free French – all those people, working together with the United States and the Canadians, did a very successful operation with a lot less loss than we had in World War One. We did accomplish what was set out to be done.

DR GRAY

I don't believe in collective guilt exactly but one of the things that seemed to cause most guilt in World War Two was this failure to discriminate between combatants and non-combatants. I felt even then, as many other soldiers did, that we were guilty of indiscriminate, terroristic harming. Many soldiers had to (particularly artillery men and flyers) kill innocent women and children. In this sense there is such a thing as collective guilt in so far as this was the decision made at the highest levels and approved by many people. It seems to me there's been a great deterioration in modern warfare in moral sense, because in the old days there was a sharp distinction between soldiers and civilians. More and more you see this distinction disappearing.

GROUP CAPTAIN 'HAMISH' MAHADDIE

Bomber Command Pathfinder Force

I'm frequently asked what my attitude was at the end of the war. Well, quite apart from an enormous feeling of relief, my own viewpoint was that the war for me had been a complete failure, because of the sixty million square-headed bastards still living.

PRIVATE DENIS GUDGEON
British serviceman, Japanese prisoner of war
Oh, no, they weren't normal human beings, they were definitely bestial. I personally have no time for them, never will. I've always felt that when that B-29 dropped the first atomic bomb on Hiroshima, it has always been my regret that the bomb didn't have sufficient power to cause all four Japanese islands to disappear into the Pacific Ocean. That's been my view and it still is.

LORD SHAWCROSS
Chief British prosecutor at Nuremberg
I think the main lesson of the trial is that all men in public life should appreciate that those who are in a position to control the destinies of governments and states are themselves personally responsible for the actions into which they lead the states they control. Hitherto that was not the case, but now it must be realised by those who participate in government that they share a collective and individual responsibility for any wrongful acts, criminal actions, actions in breach of international law which their governments may take.

AIR CHIEF MARSHAL SIR ARTHUR HARRIS
Commander-in-Chief, RAF Bomber Command
People don't like the idea of getting bombs down the back of their neck, especially politicians. The only people who make war in this world, after all, are the politicians. The public doesn't make war, it's the politicians and for the first time those who make wars realise that they'll be the first to get hit in the neck – and a damned good thing.

PRIVATE NOEL GARDINER
2nd New Zealand Division, Eighth Army
We fought because we thought it was right to fight in the circumstances and we would fight again in the same circumstances, but we hope there

won't be any further wars. The way the world's being handled at the moment I have my doubts about it, but I still think you've got to be optimistic and positive about these things.

GRAND ADMIRAL KARL DÖNITZ

I think that I now have said enough about the war, which is past now for over twenty-five years. I bow in reverence before the memory of the men who lost their lives in this war on both sides, and I think that we all hope that we never shall have such a war again.

APPENDIX

ABOUT
THE WORLD AT WAR
TV SERIES

Narrated by Sir Laurence Olivier with a musical score by Carl Davis, Thames Television's acclaimed film history of the Second World War stands as one of the most massive undertakings in television-documentary history.

The World at War contains remarkable interviews with the statesmen and military leaders of the time and it uses film from national and private sources, much of it never screened before. In fact, film research in eighteen countries yielded over three million feet of archive film and nearly a million feet of interviews and location material. Above all, it brings to the screen the memories and experiences of ordinary men and women – American and Japanese, British and German, Russian and European, in uniform and out – who lived and fought throughout the most momentous conflict in world history.

The idea of producing a definitive televisual history of the Second World War came from Jeremy Isaacs, then a producer with Thames Television. He presented an initial plan for the programme to the board of Thames in the autumn of 1970. It was a daunting project for an independent-television company to take on – 26 episodes of one hour in length, shown once a week over a period of six months. Isaacs delivered a two-line description of each episode and, amazingly, 25 of these went on to be made. Having received board approval, Isaacs set about assembling his team, and they went to work in early 1971. It is a monument to their skills and the subsequent success of the programme that many members of this team went on to even bigger and better things.

Director David Elstein would become Director of Programmes at Thames before being appointed Chief Executive of Channel 5. Writer Charles Douglas-Home became editor of *The Times*, while another producer, Ted Childs, is one of the most influential makers of television drama in the UK, responsible for hits such as *The Sweeney*, *Inspector Morse* and *Kavanagh QC*. Jeremy Isaacs himself became the founding Chief Executive of Channel 4 Television from 1981 to 1988 and later General Director of the Royal Opera House. He was knighted in 1996 for services to broadcasting and the arts.

Back in 1971 writers were selected, together with the rest of the crew, and the gargantuan research project began. One of the most difficult tasks was identifying and tracking down subjects for interview, particularly as many of those involved in the war preferred that the world forget they existed. Months of painstaking research led to some spectacular results. Among those interviewed were Hitler's Armaments Minister, Albert Speer; Himmler's Adjutant, Karl Wolff; Hitler's secretary, Traudl Junge; Hollywood star and USAAF bomber pilot, James Stewart; then Foreign Secretary, later Prime Minister, Anthony Eden, and Head of RAF Bomber Command, Arthur 'Bomber' Harris.

Isaacs, however, was determined that the series should balance out the 'view from the top' with the 'view from the bottom' – that those on the front line and on the receiving end of bombing were equally as important as the strategists and the politicians. Thus *The World at War* features such fascinating characters as the torpedo-tanker crewman who drifted for weeks in the Atlantic without water but who somehow lived to tell the tale; the Leningrad housewife who endured a 1,000-day siege; the D-Day GI who was there when the ramp on the landing craft went down in front of a hail of bullets, and, of course those who survived the horrors of Auschwitz.

Meanwhile, researchers were going through a huge amount of archive film, much of it held at the Imperial War Museum in London. The Nazis were remarkably thorough in recording even their most abhorrent atrocities – much of it in colour – and *The World at War* would become one of the first television documentaries to exploit these resources completely.

At the same time, work was also being progressed on the script, the logo, the music and the titles. It was to be 18 months before the title sequence was perfected to Isaac's satisfaction – those sombre black-and-white images set over burning text that would become one of the most memorable in television history.

The first programme, *A New Germany*, went out on Wednesday, 31 October 1973, at 9pm, and the series went on to achieve excellent ratings for a documentary. One edition, *Morning*, the story of the D-Day landings, made it into the top 10 that week, unheard of for a programme of that nature. *The World at War* was deemed a great success, and as a result further 'specials' were produced, narrated this time by Eric Porter. Indeed, when shown on BBC2 over Christmas 2002, *The World at War* received a higher rating than *Friends*, which was shown at the same time on Channel 4.

The World at War has since been broadcast in nearly 100 countries around the world, and, given its length, it is certain that it is showing somewhere at any given moment in time. It has won many 'outstanding documentary' accolades including an International Emmy.

Since its first release on DVD in 2001, which contained the complete 26-episode series and six specials, the original production team including Sir Jeremy

Isaacs, Alan Afriat and Sue McConachy were brought back together in 2003 to film a *Making of The World at War Retrospective*. This was included in a thirtieth-anniversary special box set, which was packaged along with a facsimile of the original BAFTA *The World at War* booklet. The retrospective is now included in the standard box set.

The World at War endures as a monumental achievement. Most importantly, it still remains as fresh and awe-inspiring as it did when it was first broadcast. The interview and the archive footage will never change; the analysis remains correct.

AWARDS

The National Television Critics Award – for Best Documentary Series to producer Jeremy Isaacs

George Polk Memorial Award – for the Most Outstanding Documentary on American Television to Jeremy Isaacs

American National Academy of Television Arts and Sciences Emmy Award – for Outstanding Documentary Achievements in programmes dealing with artistic, historic or cultural subjects.

The Society of Film and Television Arts Technical Craft Award – for Alan Afriat, supervising film editor

World Jewish Film and Television Festival – a silver award to *Genocide*, episode 20 of *The World at War*

The World at War is available for purchase on DVD from www.freemantlehome entertainment.com.

EPISODE SUMMARY

Part One, disk one
The making of the series
Filmed shortly after the series was broadcast, this is the story behind the production process and the challenges involved in summarising years of history and millions of feet of archive footage.
Presented by Jeremy Isaacs, directed by Peter Tiffin

A New Germany: 1933–1939
Germany, a nation stricken by humiliating defeat and emerging from crippling economic depression, looks to one man for a resurgence of hope and dignity. That man is Adolf Hitler.
Written by Neal Ascherson, directed by Hugh Raggett

Distant War: September 1939–May 1940
In eastern Europe, the full force of the Nazi machine rolls on – but, in Britain, an uneasy calm settles on the nation. It is the 'phoney' war, with the sound of distant guns thundering ominously on the horizon.
Written by Laurence Thompson, produced and directed by David Elstein

France Falls: May–June 1940
France discovers it is woefully unprepared for modern warfare as the Nazi war machine easily skirts around the Maginot line. Britain retreats and prepares for invasion.
Written and produced by Peter Batty

Part One, disk two
Alone: May 1940–May 1941
After Dunkirk, Britain faces the German onslaught. Although the RAF wins the Battle of Britain, the cities are blitzed and on the Continent the last Allies are conquered. The outlook is grim.
Written by Laurence Thompson, produced and directed by David Elstein

Barbarossa: June–December 1941
Hitler at last turns his tanks towards Russia. After a succession of devastating victories, the Germans delay and the fierce Russian winter takes a grip.
Written and produced by Peter Batty

Banzai: Japan 1931–1942
At war since 1931 on the Chinese mainland, the Japanese hope for easy victories over the British and Dutch. And then on 7 December 1941, Japan makes their infamous attack on Pearl Harbor.
Written and produced by Peter Batty

On Our Way: USA 1939–1942
Americans are divided between fighting the Japanese and the Nazis. Hitler solves the problem by declaring war on the USA.
Written and produced by Peter Batty

Part Two, disk one
The Desert: North Africa 1940–1943
For two years the Eighth Army and Rommel's Afrika Corps fight in the wastes of North Africa. Finally the tide turns at El Alamein.
Written and produced by Peter Batty

Stalingrad: June 1942–February 1943
Hitler's early successes in Russia made him reckless and he resolves to capture Stalingrad. The battle lasts six months with the Russians emerging as victors. The Wehrmacht never recovers.
Written by Jerome Kuehl, directed by Hugh Raggett

Wolf-pack: U-boats in the Atlantic 1939–1944
In a war of high technology and animal courage: the German U-boats fight Allied merchantmen, hounding them in packs.
Written by J P W Mallalieu, produced and directed by Ted Childs

Red Star: the Soviet Union 1941–1943
For two years the Soviet Army fights the Germans almost alone. After one of the greatest land battles in history, the Soviet Union survives and triumphs – but with a loss of no less than twenty million of its people.
Written by Neal Ascherson, produced and directed by Martin Smith

Part Two, disk two
Whirlwind: Bombing Germany September 1939–April 1944
Bomber Command begin bombing German cities by night and the Americans reinforce the attacks by day: a whirlwind of terror and destruction that will win the war.
Written by Charles Douglas-Home, produced by Ted Childs

Tough Old Gut: Italy November 1942–June 1944
Churchill called Italy the 'soft underbelly of the crocodile' and thought the Allies could cut through it to the heart of Germany. But the soft underbelly turned out to be a 'tough old gut'.
Written by David Wheeler, produced by Ben Shepherd

It's A Lovely Day Tomorrow: Burma 1942–1943
Vera Lynn sang of a lovely day tomorrow, but the war in Burma was mud and monsoon. Britain's largest Army learned to master the jungle and fought the Japanese to a standstill.
Written by John Williams, produced and directed by John Pett

Home Fires: Britain 1940–1944
Finding strength in unity at home in Britain during the war, it was a time of gas masks, Winston Churchill, Dig for Victory, evacuation, George Formby, the Land Army, ITMA, the Squander Bug and the Beveridge Report.
Written by Angus Calder, produced by Phillip Whitehead

Part Three, disk one
Inside the Reich: Germany 1940–1944
Initial victory in Europe turns sour after the defeat at Stalingrad, yet Germany prepares to fight to the end – even after an assassination attempt on the Führer.
Written by Neal Ascherson, produced by Phillip Whitehead

Morning: June–August 1944
The Western Allies resolve to invade Europe. England becomes a floating supply dump and the British and Americans assemble the largest invasion fleet in history. It is 6 June 1944 – D-Day.
Written by John Williams, produced and directed by John Pett

Occupation: Holland 1940–1944
Though a neutral country, Holland is attacked by Germany without warning in 1940. During the next four years, life carries on seemingly without incident, but underneath Resistance never dies.
Written by Charles Bloomberg, produced and directed by Michael Darlow

Pincers: August 1944–March 1945
The end of the war appears close at hand with the liberation of Paris in 1944, but the British and Americans disagree on how to advance. Meanwhile, Poland suffers devastating losses to achieve victory.
Written and produced by Peter Batty

Part Three, disk two
Genocide: 1941–1945
The Nazis are racist; the Aryans are a master race, others, particularly the Jews, are sub-human. Himmler's SS sets about ridding Europe of millions of Jews.
Written by Charles Bloomberg, produced by Michael Darlow

Nemesis: Germany February–May 1945
Hitler retreats to the Führer bunker in Berlin as Germany crumbles around him and his lieutenants abandon him to a fate of suicide. Meanwhile, the Russians raise the Red Flag in Berlin.
Written by Stuart Hood, produced by Martin Smith

Japan: 1941–1945
Initially apprehensive about the outcome of declaring war, the Japanese quickly turn to celebration with early victory. In the end, their worst fears are unimaginably exceeded.
Written by Courtney Browne, produced by Hugh Raggett

Pacific: February 1942–July 1945
The Americans fight their way across the Pacific towards Japan and the Philippines. Perhaps the bloodiest campaign of all: each island has to be taken by storm – and the Japanese fight to the last man.
Written by David Wheeler, produced and directed by John Pett

Part Four, disk one
The Bomb: February–September 1945
Western scientists have developed a new, immensely powerful weapon – the atomic bomb. On 6 August 1945, the *Enola Gay* delivers the world's first atomic bomb to Hiroshima. The world would be altered for ever.
Written and produced by David Elstein

Reckoning: 1945 … And After
The war ends slowly and messily. Britain is victorious but exhausted and the superpowers confront each other as they decide the fate of Europe.
Written and produced by Jerome Kuehl

Remember

For many, the Second World War was the most significant experience of their lives. Heartbreaking first-hand remembrances from a vast array of survivors on both sides of the war.

Written and produced by Jeremy Isaacs

Part Four, disk two
Secretary to Hitler

Traudl Junge found herself in Berlin during the war because she wanted to be a ballet dancer. A friend told her about a job vacancy in Hitler's Chancellery; she applied for it and, looking like Hitler's mistress Eva Braun, she became one of his private secretaries. Traudl Junge saw Hitler at close quarters, shared his public life and was with him in the bunker at the end.

Produced by Susan McConachy

From War to Peace

Renowned historian Stephen Ambrose examines the aftermath of the Second World War. Was peace truly gained? Or did a new war with weapons of policy take its place? An interview with Professor Stephen Ambrose.

Produced by Jerome Kuehl

Warrior

Reflections of men at war, compiled from interviews and archive film obtained for *The World at War* series. A measured and decidedly unromantic look at the heat of battle, *Warrior* weaves together eyewitness accounts and rarely seen archive footage to reveal the deadly realities of combat.

Edited and produced by Alan Afriat, poems by R N Currey, Sean Jennet, Ruthven Tod. Executive producer, Jerome Kuehl. Production manager, Liz Sutherland

Part Five, disk one
Hitler's Germany: the People's Community 1933–1939

The harsh outcome of the First World War left Germany ripe for Adolf Hitler and his Nazi Party's swift rise to power, promising a devastated nation's return to international prominence. See how the Germans worked, played and organise themselves for war as the Third Reich set the stage for the Second World War.

Written by Jerome Kuehl. Produced by Raye Farr. Production manager, Liz Sutherland. Associate producer, Alan Afriat. Executive producer, Jerome Kuehl

Hitler's Germany: Total War 1939–1945
Continuing the in-depth look at Hitler's regime through the lives of ordinary citizens, this special presentation shows how they coped with mass bombing, invasion and ultimately, defeat.
Written by Jerome Kuehl. Produced by Raye Farr. Production manager, Liz Sutherland. Associate producer, Alan Afriat. Executive producer, Jerome Kuehl

Two Deaths of Adolf Hitler
Years after his death, mystery still surrounds the circumstances under which Adolf Hitler ended his life. Did he die from a self-inflicted gunshot? Or did he swallow cyanide with his recent bride Eva Braun?
Executive producer, Jerome Kuehl. Produced and directed by Martin Smith. Production manager, Liz Sutherland. Associate producer, Alan Afriat

Part Five, disk two
The Final Solution: part one
Examining the growth of the Nazi racial doctrines from their origins to 1939, we see the terrifying and unforgettable stories as told by death-camp survivors and also compelling interviews with German participants.
Written and directed by Michael Darlow. Associate producer, Jerome Kuehl. Production manager, Liz Sutherland

The Final Solution: part two
Archive photographs and shocking footage, filmed by the Nazis themselves, capture the full horror of Germany's systematic extermination of millions of Jews and other non-Aryan civilians. Unflinching and often disturbing, this is a profound and necessary examination into the darkest corners of humanity.
Written and directed by Michael Darlow. Associate producer, Jerome Kuehl. Production manager, Liz Sutherland

30th Anniversary Disk
Making of the series
In this two-hour thirtieth-anniversary retrospective, we commemorate the original 1973 broadcast with new interviews with the makers of the programme.

Experiences of war
Prominent scholars and military figures recount specifics of the war, from first-hand accounts of Okinawa to the D-Day landings and analyse key wartime actions

in these previously unseen and extended interviews taken from the archives at the Imperial War Museum, London.

Produced by Fremantle Home Entertainment, music by Carl Davis

DVD Extras: Imperial War Museum Photo Gallery, Biographies, Brief History of *The World at War*, Episode Summaries, Speeches/Songs & Newsreels and Maps

Series producer, Jeremy Isaacs. Narrated by Eric Porter. Chief historical adviser, Dr Noble Frankland DFC. Music, Carl Davis

PERMISSIONS

With thanks to the following organisations and companies for permission to reproduce their photographs:

Bildarchiv Preußischer Kulturbesitz: colour section 1, page 1 (bottom right), page 4 (top), page 7 (top), page 8 (both photos); colour section 2, page 1 (top), page 3 (bottom), page 5 (top), page 6 (both photos)

Corbis: colour section 2, page 2 (both photos), page 3 (top), page 8 (bottom)

Ethell Collection, ww2color.com: colour section 1, page 6 (both photos); colour section 2, page 4 (both photos)

FremantleMedia Stills Library: colour section 1, page 1 (top right, bottom left), page 2 (top right, bottom left)

Imperial War Museum: b/w section 1, page 1 (top right HU 004128, bottom left NA 007113, bottom right B 015727), page 2 (top HU 053442, middle CHN 000138, bottom NYP 068066), page 3 (top O 000227, middle NYP 068075, bottom H 001628), page 5 (top C 005422, bottom HU 001129), page 6 (top H 009155, middle H 014250, bottom NYP 068086), page 7 (top HUY 017222, bottom C 003575), page 8 (bottom OEM 006631); b/w section 2, page 2 (top A 028205, middle HU 005163, bottom misc 060748), page 3 (top C 003677, bottom CH 013020), page 5 (top left NA 000480, top right BU 001292, bottom 9496), page 6 (bottom left MH 007873, bottom right IND 003595), page 7 (bottom IWM FLM 002571); colour section 1, page 1 (top left E 026621), page 2 (top left CH 014129, bottom right E 016458), page 3 (top COL 000107, bottom TR 001342), page 4 (bottom COL 000142), page 5 (top TR 000210, bottom TR 002047); colour section 2, page 1 (bottom TR 001001-1), page 8 (top TR 002828)

Ullstein Bild: colour section 1, page 7 (bottom); colour section 2, page 5 (bottom)

United States Holocaust Memorial Museum: b/w section 1, page 1 (top left); b/w section 2, page 4 (all three photos), page 8 (all three photos). The views or opinions expressed in this book, and the context in which the images are used, do not necessarily reflect the views or policy of, nor imply approval or endorsement by, the United States Holocaust Memorial Museum

US National Archive: b/w section 1, page 4 (both photos), page 8 (top); b/w section 2, page 1 (both photos), page 3 (middle), page 6 (top, middle), page 7 (top); colour section 2, page 7 (both photos)

INDEX OF INTERVIEWEES

GENERAL INDEX